MCAT®
GENERAL
CHEMISTRY
REVIEW

WITHDRAWAL

MCAT®

GENERAL CHEMISTRY REVIEW

REVIEW

The Staff of Kaplan

KAPLAN PUBLISHING
New York

Published by Kaplan Publishing, a division of Kaplan, Inc.
1 Liberty Plaza, 24th Floor
New York, NY 10006

Printed in the United States of America

10 9 8 7 6 5 4 3 2 1

ISBN: 978-1-60714-639-1

Kaplan Publishing books are available at special quantity discounts to use for sales promotions, employee premiums, or educational purposes. For more information or to purchase books, please call the Simon & Schuster special sales department at 866-506-1949.

Planet Friendly Publishing
✔ Made in the United States
✔ Printed on Recycled Paper
GREEN EDITION   Learn more at www.greenedition.org

• Manufacturing books in the United States ensures compliance with strict environmental laws and eliminates the need for international freight shipping, a major contributor to global air pollution. Printing on recycled paper helps minimize our consumption of trees, water and fossil fuels.
• Trees Saved: 101 • Air Emissions Eliminated: 9,720 pounds
• Water Saved: 46,813 gallons • Solid Waste Eliminated: 2,842 pounds

Contents

KAPLAN'S EXPERT MCAT TEAM

Kaplan has been preparing premeds for the MCAT for more than 40 years. In the past 15 years alone, we've helped more than 400,000 students prepare for this important exam and improve their chances for medical school admission.

Marilyn Engle

MCAT Master Teacher; Teacher Trainer; Kaplan National Teacher of the Year, 2006; Westwood Teacher of the Year, 2007; Westwood Trainer of the Year, 2007; Encino Trainer of the Year, 2005

John Michael Linick

MCAT Teacher; Boulder Teacher of the Year, 2007; Summer Intensive Program Faculty Member

Dr. Glen Pearlstein

MCAT Master Teacher; Teacher Trainer; Westwood Teacher of the Year, 2006

Matthew B. Wilkinson

MCAT Teacher; Teacher Trainer; Lone Star Trainer of the Year, 2007

Thanks to Jason Baserman, Jessica Brookman, Da Chang, John Cummins, David Elson, Jeff Koetje, Alex Macnow, Andrew Molloy, Josh Rohrig and Amjed Saffarini.

ABOUT SCIENTIFIC AMERICAN

As the world's premier science and technology magazine, and the oldest continuously published magazine in the United States, *Scientific American* is committed to bringing the most important developments in modern science, medicine, and technology to 3.5 million readers worldwide in an understandable, credible, and provocative format.

Founded in 1845 and on the "cutting edge" ever since, *Scientific American* boasts over 140 Nobel laureate authors, including Albert Einstein, Francis Crick, Stanley Prusiner, and Richard Axel. *Scientific American* is a forum where scientific theories, and discoveries are explained to a broader audience.

Scientific American published its first foreign edition in 1890 and, in 1979, was the first Western magazine published in the People's Republic of China. Today, *Scientific American* is published in 17 foreign language editions with a total circulation of more than 1 million worldwide. *Scientific American* is also a leading online destination (www.ScientificAmerican.com), providing the latest science news and exclusive features to more than 2 million unique visitors monthly.

The knowledge that fills our pages has the power to inspire, to spark new ideas, paradigms, and visions for the future. As science races forward, *Scientific American* continues to cover the promising strides, inevitable setbacks and challenges, and new medical discoveries as they unfold.

How to Use this Book

Kaplan MCAT General Chemistry, along with the other four books in our MCAT Subject series, brings the Kaplan classroom experience to you—right in your home, at your convenience. This book offers the same Kaplan content review, strategies, and practice that make Kaplan the #1 choice for MCAT prep. All that's missing is the teacher.

To guide you through this complex content, we've consulted our best MCAT instructors to call out **Key Concept**, to offer **Bridge** to better understanding of the material, and **Mnemonic** devices to assist in learning retention. When you see these sidebars, you will know you're getting the same insight and knowledge that classroom students receive in person. Look for these as well as references to the **Real World** and **MCAT expertise** callouts throughout the book.

HIGH-YIELD MCAT REVIEW

Following the content section, you will find a **High-Yield Questions** section. These questions tackle the most frequently tested topics found on the MCAT. For each type of problem, you will be provided with a stepwise technique for solving the question, as well as important directional points on how to solve it—specifically for the MCAT.

Our experts have again called out the **Key Concepts**, which show you which terms to review. Next, the **Takeaways** box offers a concise summary of the problem-solving approach best used. **Things to Watch Out For** points out any caveats to the approach discussed, which can lead to wrong answer choices. Finally, **Similar Questions** allows you to practice the stepwise technique on analogous, open-ended questions.

STAR RATING

The star rating is a Kaplan-exclusive system to help you focus your studies, using a 6-star scale. Two factors are considered when determining the rating for each topic: the "learnability" of the topic—or how easy it is to master—and the frequency with which it appears on the MCAT exam. For example, a topic that presents relatively little difficulty to master and appears with relatively high frequency on the MCAT would receive a higher star rating (e.g., 5 or 6 stars) than a topic which is very difficult to master and appears less frequently on the test. The combination of these two factors represented by the star rating will help you prioritize and direct your MCAT studies.

We're confident that this guide and our award-winning instructors can help you achieve your goals of MCAT success and admission to med school. Good luck!

Introduction to the MCAT

The Medical College Admission Test (MCAT) is different from any other test you've encountered in your academic career. It's not like the knowledge-based exams from high school and college, where emphasis was on memorizing and regurgitating information. Medical schools can assess your academic prowess by looking at your transcript. The MCAT isn't even like other standardized tests you may have taken, where the focus was on proving your general skills.

Medical schools use MCAT scores to assess whether you possess the foundation upon which to build a successful medical career. Though you certainly need to know the content to do well, the stress is on thought process, because the MCAT is above all else a critical thinking test. That's why it emphasizes reasoning, analytical thinking, reading comprehension, data analysis, writing, and problem-solving skills.

Though the MCAT places more weight on your thought process, you must have a strong grasp of the required core knowledge. The MCAT may not be a perfect gauge of your abilities, but it is a relatively objective way to compare you with students from different backgrounds and undergraduate institutions.

The MCAT's power comes from its use as an indicator of your abilities. Good scores can open doors. Your power comes from preparation and mindset because the key to MCAT success is knowing what you're up against. That's where this section of this book comes in. We'll explain the philosophy behind the test, review the sections one by one, show you sample questions, share some of Kaplan's proven methods, and clue you in to what the test makers are really after. You'll get a handle on the process, find a confident new perspective, and achieve your highest possible scores.

ABOUT THE MCAT

Information about the MCAT CBT is included below. For the latest information about the MCAT, visit www.kaptest.com/mcat.

MCAT CBT

Format	U.S.—All administrations on computer
	International—Most on computer with limited paper and pencil in a few isolated areas
Essay Grading	One human and one computer grader
Breaks	Optional break between each section
Length of MCAT Day	Approximately 5.5 hours
Test Dates	Multiple dates in January, April, May, June, July, August, and September
	Total of 24 administrations each year.
Delivery of Results	Within 30 days. If scores are delayed notification will be posted online at www.aamc.org/mcat
	Electronic and paper
Security	Government-issued ID
	Electronic thumbprint
	Electronic signature verification
Testing Centers	Small computer testing sites

Go online and sign up for a local Kaplan Pre-Med Edge event to get the latest information on the test.

PLANNING FOR THE TEST

As you look toward your preparation for the MCAT consider the following advice:

Complete your core course requirements as soon as possible. Take a strategic eye to your schedule and get core requirements out of the way now.

Take the MCAT once. The MCAT is a notoriously grueling standardized exam that requires extensive preparation. It is longer than the graduate admissions exams for business school (GMAT, 3½ hours), law school (LSAT, 3¼ hours) and graduate school (GRE, 2½ hours). You do not want to take it twice. Plan and prepare accordingly.

KAPLAN

THE ROLE OF THE MCAT IN ADMISSIONS

More and more people are applying to medical school and more and more people are taking the MCAT. It's important for you to recognize that while a high MCAT score is a critical component in getting admitted to top med schools, it's not the only factor. Medical school admissions officers weigh grades, interviews, MCAT scores, level of involvement in extracurricular activities, as well as personal essays.

In a Kaplan survey of 130 pre-med advisors, 84 percent called the interview a "very important" part of the admissions process, followed closely by college grades (83%) and MCAT scores (76%). Kaplan's college admissions consulting practice works with students on all these issues so they can position themselves as strongly as possible. In addition, the AAMC has made it clear that scores will continue to be valid for three years, and that the scoring of the computer-based MCAT will not differ from that of the paper and pencil version.

REGISTRATION

The only way to register for the MCAT is online. The registration site is: www.aamc.org/mcat.

You will be able to access the site approximately six months before your test date. Payment must be made by MasterCard or Visa.

Go to www.aamc.org/mcat/registration.htm and download *MCAT Essentials* for information about registration, fees, test administration, and preparation. For other questions, contact:

> MCAT Care Team
> Association of American Medical Colleges
> Section for Applicant Assessment Services
> 2450 N. St., NW
> Washington, DC 20037
> www.aamc.org/mcat
> Email: mcat@aamc.org

Keep in mind that you will want to take the MCAT in the year prior to your planned med school start date. Don't drag your feet gathering information. You'll need time not only to prepare and practice for the test, but also to get all your registration work done.

The MCAT should be viewed just like any other part of your application: as an opportunity to show the medical schools who you are and what you can do. Take control of your MCAT experience.

ANATOMY OF THE MCAT

Before mastering strategies, you need to know exactly what you're dealing with on the MCAT. Let's start with the basics: The MCAT is, among other things, an endurance test.

If you can't approach it with confidence and stamina, you'll quickly lose your composure. That's why it's so important that you take control of the test.

The MCAT consists of four timed sections: Physical Sciences, Verbal Reasoning, Writing Sample, and Biological Sciences. Later in this section we'll take an in-depth look at each MCAT section, including sample question types and specific test-smart hints, but here's a general overview, reflecting the order of the test sections and number of questions in each.

Physical Sciences

Time	70 minutes
Format	• 52 multiple-choice questions: approximately 7–9 passages with 4–8 questions each • approximately 10 stand-alone questions (not passage-based)
What it tests	basic general chemistry concepts, basic physics concepts, analytical reasoning, data interpretation

Verbal Reasoning

Time	60 minutes
Format	• 40 multiple-choice questions: approximately 7 passages with 5–7 questions each
What it tests	critical reading

Writing Sample

Time	60 minutes
Format	• 2 essay questions (30 minutes per essay)
What it tests	critical thinking, intellectual organization, written communication skills

Biological Sciences

Time	70 minutes
Format	• 52 multiple-choice questions: approximately 7–9 passages with 4–8 questions each • approximately 10 stand-alone questions (not passage-based)
What it tests	basic biology concepts, basic organic chemistry concepts, analytical reasoning, data interpretation

The sections of the test always appear in the same order:

Physical Sciences

[optional 10-minute break]

Verbal Reasoning

[optional 10-minute break]

Writing Sample

[optional 10-minute break]

Biological Sciences

SCORING

Each MCAT section receives its own score. Physical Sciences, Verbal Reasoning, and Biological Sciences are each scored on a scale ranging from 1–15, with 15 as the highest. The Writing Sample essays are scored alphabetically on a scale ranging from J to T, with T as the highest. The two essays are each evaluated by two official readers, so four critiques combine to make the alphabetical score.

The number of multiple-choice questions that you answer correctly per section is your "raw score." Your raw score will then be converted to yield the "scaled score"—the one that will fall somewhere in that 1–15 range. These scaled scores are what are reported to medical schools as your MCAT scores. All multiple-choice questions are worth the same amount—one raw point— and *there's no penalty for guessing.* That means that *you should always select an answer for every question, whether you get to that question or not!* This is an important piece of advice, so pay it heed. Never let time run out on any section without selecting an answer for every question.

The raw score of each administration is converted to a scaled score. The conversion varies with administrations. Hence, the same raw score will not always give you the same scaled score.

Your score report will tell you—and your potential medical schools—not only your scaled scores, but also the national mean score for each section, standard deviation, national scoring profile for each section, and your percentile ranking.

WHAT'S A GOOD SCORE?

There's no such thing as a cut-and-dry "good score." Much depends on the strength of the rest of your application (if your transcript is first rate, the pressure to strut your stuff on the MCAT isn't as intense) and on where you want to go to school (different schools have different score expectations). Here are a few interesting statistics:

or each MCAT administration, the average scaled scores are approximately 8s for Physical Sciences, Verbal Reasoning, and Biological Sciences, and N for the Writing Sample. You need scores of at least 10–11s to be considered competitive by most medical schools, and if you're aiming for the top you've got to do even better, and score 12s and above.

You don't have to be perfect to do well. For instance, on the AAMC's Practice Test 5R, you could get as many as 10 questions wrong in Verbal Reasoning, 17 in Physical Sciences, and 16 in Biological Sciences and still score in the 80th percentile. To score in the 90th percentile, you could get as many as 7 wrong in Verbal Reasoning, 12 in Physical Sciences, and 12 in Biological Sciences. Even students who receive perfect scaled scores usually get a handful of questions wrong.

It's important to maximize your performance on every question. Just a few questions one way or the other can make a big difference in your scaled score. Here's a look at recent score profiles so you can get an idea of the shape of a typical score distribution.

Physical Sciences				Verbal Reasoning		
Scaled Score	Percent Achieving Score	Percentile Rank Range		Scaled Score	Percent Achieving Score	Percentile Rank Range
15	0.1	99.9–99.9		15	0.1	99.9–99.9
14	1.2	98.7–99.8		14	0.2	99.7–99.8
13	2.5	96.2–98.6		13	1.8	97.9–99.6
12	5.1	91.1–96.1		12	3.6	94.3–97.8
11	7.2	83.9–91.0		11	10.5	83.8–94.2
10	12.1	71.8–83.8		10	15.6	68.2–83.7
9	12.9	58.9–71.1		9	17.2	51.0–68.1
8	16.5	42.4–58.5		8	15.4	35.6–50.9
7	16.7	25.7–42.3		7	10.3	25.3–35.5
6	13.0	12.7–25.6		6	10.9	14.4–25.2
5	7.9	04.8–12.6		5	6.9	07.5–14.3
4	3.3	01.5–04.7		4	3.9	03.6–07.4
3	1.3	00.2–01.4		3	2.0	01.6–03.5
2	0.1	00.1–00.1		2	0.5	00.1–01.5
1	0.0	00.0–00.0		1	0.0	00.0–00.0
Scaled Score Mean = 8.1 Standard Deviation = 2.32				Scaled Score Mean = 8.0 Standard Deviation = 2.43		

Writing Sample				Biological Sciences		
Scaled Score	Percent Achieving Score	Percentile Rank Range		Scaled Score	Percent Achieving Score	Percentile Rank Range
T	0.5	99.9–99.9		15	0.1	99.9–99.9
S	2.8	94.7–99.8		14	1.2	98.7–99.8
R	7.2	96.0–99.3		13	2.5	96.2–98.6
Q	14.2	91.0–95.9		12	5.1	91.1–96.1
P	9.7	81.2–90.9		11	7.2	83.9–91.0
O	17.9	64.0–81.1		10	12.1	71.8–83.8
N	14.7	47.1–63.9		9	12.9	58.9–71.1
M	18.8	30.4–47.0		8	16.5	42.4–58.5
L	9.5	21.2–30.3		7	16.7	25.7–42.3
K	3.6	13.5–21.1		6	13.0	12.7–25.6
J	1.2	06.8–13.4		5	7.9	04.8–12.6
		02.9–06.7		4	3.3	01.5–04.7
		00.9–02.8		3	1.3	00.2–01.4
		00.2–00.8		2	0.1	00.1–00.1
		00.0–00.1		1	0.0	00.0–00.0
75th Percentile = Q 50th Percentile = O 25th Percentile = M				Scaled Score Mean = 8.2 Standard Deviation = 2.39		

WHAT THE MCAT REALLY TESTS

It's important to grasp not only the nuts and bolts of the MCAT, so you'll know *what* to do on Test Day, but also the underlying principles of the test so you'll know *why* you're doing what you're doing on Test Day. We'll cover the straightforward MCAT facts later. Now it's time to examine the heart and soul of the MCAT, to see what it's really about.

THE MYTH

Most people preparing for the MCAT fall prey to the myth that the MCAT is a straightforward science test. They think something like this:

> "*It covers the four years of science I had to take in school: biology, chemistry, physics, and organic chemistry. It even has equations. OK, so it has Verbal Reasoning and Writing, but those sections are just to see if we're literate, right? The important stuff is the science. After all, we're going to be doctors.*"

Well, here's the little secret no one seems to want you to know: The MCAT is not just a science test; it's also a thinking test. This means that the test is designed to let you demonstrate your thought process, not only your thought content.

The implications are vast. Once you shift your test-taking paradigm to match the MCAT modus operandi, you'll find a new level of confidence and control over the test. You'll begin to work with the nature of the MCAT rather than against it. You'll be more efficient and insightful as you prepare for the test, and you'll be more relaxed on Test Day. In fact, you'll be able to see the MCAT for what it is rather than for what it's dressed up to be. We want your Test Day to feel like a visit with a familiar friend instead of an awkward blind date.

THE ZEN OF MCAT

Medical schools do not need to rely on the MCAT to see what you already know. Admission committees can measure your subject-area proficiency using your undergraduate coursework and grades. Schools are most interested in the potential of your mind.

In recent years, many medical schools have shifted pedagogic focus away from an information-heavy curriculum to a concept-based curriculum. There is currently more emphasis placed on problem solving, holistic thinking, and cross-disciplinary study. Be careful not to dismiss this important point, figuring you'll wait to worry about academic trends until you're actually in medical school. This trend affects you right now, because it's reflected in the MCAT. Every good tool matches its task. In this case the tool is the test, used to measure you and other candidates, and the task is to quantify how likely it is that you'll succeed in medical school.

Your intellectual potential—how skillfully you annex new territory into your mental boundaries, how quickly you build "thought highways" between ideas, how confidently and creatively you solve problems—is far more important to admission committees than your ability to recite Young's modulus for every material known to man. The schools assume they can expand your knowledge base. They choose applicants carefully because expansive knowledge is not enough to succeed in medical school or in the profession. There's something more. It's this "something more" that the MCAT is trying to measure.

Every section on the MCAT tests essentially the same higher-order thinking skills: analytical reasoning, abstract thinking, and problem solving. Most test takers get trapped into thinking they are being tested strictly about biology, chemistry, and so on. Thus, they approach each section with a new outlook on what's expected. This constant mental gear-shifting can be exhausting, not to mention counterproductive. Instead of perceiving the test as parsed into radically different sections, you need to maintain your focus on the underlying nature of the test: It's designed to test your thinking skills, not your information-recall skills. Each test section presents a variation on the same theme.

WHAT ABOUT THE SCIENCE?

With this perspective, you may be left asking these questions: "What about the science? What about the content? Don't I need to know the basics?" The answer is a resounding "Yes!" You must be fluent in the different languages of the test. You cannot do well on the MCAT if you don't know the basics of physics, general chemistry, biology, and organic chemistry. We recommend that you take one year each of biology, general chemistry, organic chemistry, and physics before taking the MCAT, and that you review the content in this book thoroughly. Knowing these basics is just the beginning of doing well on the MCAT. That's a shock to most test takers. They presume that once they recall or relearn their undergraduate science, they are ready to do battle against the MCAT. Wrong! They merely have directions to the battlefield. They lack what they need to beat the test: a copy of the test maker's battle plan!

You won't be drilled on facts and formulas on the MCAT. You'll need to demonstrate ability to reason based on ideas and concepts. The science questions are painted with a broad brush, testing your general understanding.

TAKE CONTROL: THE MCAT MINDSET

In addition to being a thinking test, as we've stressed, the MCAT is a standardized test. As such, it has its own consistent patterns and idiosyncrasies that can actually work in your favor. This is the key to why test preparation works. You have the opportunity to familiarize yourself with those consistent peculiarities, to adopt the proper test-taking mindset.

The following are some overriding principles of the MCAT mindset that will be covered in depth in the chapters to come:

- Read actively and critically.
- Translate prose into your own words.
- Save the toughest questions for last.
- Know the test and its components inside and out.
- Do MCAT-style problems in each topic area after you've reviewed it.
- Allow your confidence to build on itself.
- Take full-length practice tests a week or two before the test to break down the mystique of the real experience.
- Learn from your mistakes—get the most out of your practice tests.
- Look at the MCAT as a challenge, the first step in your medical career, rather than as an arbitrary obstacle.

That's what the MCAT mindset boils down to: Taking control. Being proactive. Being on top of the testing experience so that you can get as many points as you can as quickly and as easily as possible. Keep this in mind as you read and work through the material in this book and, of course, as you face the challenge on Test Day.

Now that you have a better idea of what the MCAT is all about, let's take a tour of the individual test sections. Although the underlying skills being tested are similar, each MCAT section requires that you call into play a different domain of knowledge. So, though we encourage you to think of the MCAT as a holistic and unified test, we also recognize that the test is segmented by discipline and that there are characteristics unique to each section. In the overviews, we'll review sample questions and answers and discuss section-specific strategies. For each of the sections—Verbal Reasoning, Physical/Biological Sciences, and the Writing Sample—we'll present you with the following:

- **The Big Picture**
  You'll get a clear view of the section and familiarize yourself with what it's really evaluating.

- **A Closer Look**
  You'll explore the types of questions that will appear and master the strategies you'll need to deal with them successfully.

- **Highlights**
  The key approaches to each section are outlined, for reinforcement and quick review.

TEST EXPERTISE

The first year of medical school is a frenzied experience for most students. In order to meet the requirements of a rigorous work schedule, students either learn to prioritize and budget their time or else fall hopelessly behind. It's no surprise, then, that the MCAT, the test specifically designed to predict success in the first year of medical school, is a high-speed, time-intensive test. It demands excellent time-management skills as well as that sine qua non of the successful physician—grace under pressure.

It's one thing to answer a Verbal Reasoning question correctly; it's quite another to answer several correctly in a limited time frame. The same goes for Physical and Biological Sciences—it's a whole new ballgame once you move from doing an individual passage at your leisure to handling a full section under actual timed conditions. You also need to budget your time for the Writing Sample, but this section isn't as time sensitive. When it comes to the multiple-choice sections, time pressure is a factor that affects virtually every test taker.

So when you're comfortable with the content of the test, your next challenge will be to take it to the next level—test expertise—which will enable you to manage the all-important time element of the test.

THE FIVE BASIC PRINCIPLES OF TEST EXPERTISE

On some tests, if a question seems particularly difficult you'll spend significantly more time on it, as you'll probably be given more points for correctly answering a hard question. Not so on the MCAT. Remember, every MCAT question, no matter how hard, is worth a single point. There's no partial credit or "A" for effort, and because there are so many questions to do in so little time, you'd be a fool to spend 10 minutes getting a point for a hard question and then not have time to get a couple of quick points from three easy questions later in the section.

Given this combination—limited time, all questions equal in weight— you've got to develop a way of handling the test sections to make sure you get as many points as you can as quickly and easily as you can. Here are the principles that will help you do that:

1. FEEL FREE TO SKIP AROUND

One of the most valuable strategies to help you finish the sections in time is to learn to recognize and deal first with the questions that are easier and more familiar to you. That means you must temporarily skip those that promise to be difficult and time-consuming, if you feel comfortable doing so. You can always come back to these at the end, and if you run out of time, you're much better off not getting to questions you may have had difficulty with, rather than not getting to potentially feasible material. Of course, because there's no guessing penalty, always put an answer to every question on the test, whether you get to it or not. (It's not practical to skip passages, so do those in order.)

This strategy is difficult for most test takers; we're conditioned to do things in order, but give it a try when you practice. Remember, if you do the test in the exact order given, you're letting the test makers control you. You control how you take this test. On the other hand, if skipping around goes against your moral fiber and makes you a nervous wreck—don't do it. Just be mindful of the clock, and don't get bogged down with the tough questions.

2. LEARN TO RECOGNIZE AND SEEK OUT QUESTIONS YOU CAN DO

Another thing to remember about managing the test sections is that MCAT questions and passages, unlike items on the SAT and other standardized tests, are not presented in order of difficulty. There's no rule that says you have to work through the sections in any particular order; in fact, the test makers scatter the easy and difficult questions throughout the section, in effect rewarding those who actually get to the end. Don't lose sight of what you're being tested for along with your reading and thinking skills: efficiency and cleverness.

Don't waste time on questions you can't do. We know that skipping a possibly tough question is easier said than done; we all have the natural instinct to plow through test sections in their given order, but it just doesn't pay off on the MCAT. The computer won't be impressed if you get the toughest question right. If you dig in your heels on a tough question, refusing to move on until you've cracked it, well, you're letting your ego get in the way of your test score. A test section (not to mention life itself) is too short to waste on lost causes.

3. USE A PROCESS OF ANSWER ELIMINATION

Using a process of elimination is another way to answer questions both quickly and effectively. There are two ways to get all the answers right on the MCAT. You either know all the right answers, or you know all the wrong answers. Because there are three times as many wrong answers, you should be able to eliminate some if not all of them. By doing so you either get to the correct response or increase your chances of guessing the correct response. You start out with a 25 percent chance of picking the right answer, and with each eliminated answer your odds go up. Eliminate one, and you'll have a $33\frac{1}{3}$ percent chance of picking the right one, eliminate two, and you'll have a 50 percent chance, and, of course, eliminate three, and you'll have a 100 percent chance. Increase your efficiency by actually crossing out the wrong choices on the screen using the strike-through feature. Remember to look for wrong-answer traps when you're eliminating. Some answers are designed to seduce you by distorting the correct answer.

4. REMAIN CALM

It's imperative that you remain calm and composed while working through a section. You can't allow yourself to become so rattled by one hard reading passage that it throws off your performance on the rest of the section. Expect to find at least one killer passage in every section, but remember, you won't be the only one to have trouble with it. The test is curved to take the tough material into account. Having trouble with a difficult question isn't going to ruin your score—but getting upset about it and letting it throw you off track will. When you understand that part of the test maker's goal is to reward those who keep their composure, you'll recognize the importance of not panicking when you run into challenging material.

5. KEEP TRACK OF TIME

Of course, the last thing you want to happen is to have time called on a particular section before you've gotten to half the questions. Therefore, it's essential that you pace yourself, keeping in mind the general guidelines for how long to spend on any individual question or passage. Have a sense of how long you have to do each question, so you know when you're exceeding the limit and should start to move faster.

So, when working on a section, always remember to keep track of time. Don't spend a wildly disproportionate amount of time on any one question or group of questions. Also, give yourself 30 seconds or so at the end of each section to fill in answers for any questions you haven't gotten to.

SECTION-SPECIFIC PACING

Let's now look at the section-specific timing requirements and some tips for meeting them. Keep in mind that the times per question or passage are only averages; there are bound to be some that take less time and some that take more. Try to stay balanced. Remember, too, that every question is of equal worth, so don't get hung up on any one. Think about it: If a question is so hard that it takes you a long time to answer it, chances are you may get it wrong anyway. In that case, you'd have nothing to show for your extra time but a lower score.

VERBAL REASONING

Allow yourself approximately eight to ten minutes per passage and respective questions. It may sound like a lot of time, but it goes quickly. Keep in mind that some passages are longer than others. On average, give yourself about three or four minutes to read and then four to six minutes for the questions.

PHYSICAL AND BIOLOGICAL SCIENCES

Averaging over each section, you'll have about one minute and 20 seconds per question. Some questions, of course, will take more time, some less. A science passage plus accompanying questions should take about eight to nine minutes, depending on how many questions there are. Stand-alone questions can take anywhere from a few seconds to a minute or more. Again, the rule is to do your best work first. Also, don't feel that you have to understand everything in a passage before you go on to the questions. You may not need that deep an understanding to answer questions, because a lot of information may be extraneous. You should overcome your perfectionism and use your time wisely.

WRITING SAMPLE

You have exactly 30 minutes for each essay. As mentioned in discussion of the seven-step approach to this section, you should allow approximately five minutes to prewrite the essay, 23 minutes to write the essay, and two minutes to proofread. It's important that you budget your time, so you don't get cut off.

COMPUTER-BASED TESTING STRATEGIES

ARRIVE AT THE TESTING CENTER EARLY

Get to the testing center early to jump-start your brain. However, if they allow you to begin your test early, decline.

USE THE MOUSE TO YOUR ADVANTAGE

If you are right-handed, practice using the mouse with your left hand for Test Day. This way, you'll increase speed by keeping the pencil in your right hand to write on your scratch paper. If you are left-handed, use your right hand for the mouse.

KNOW THE TUTORIAL BEFORE TEST DAY

You will save time on Test Day by knowing exactly how the test will work. Click through any tutorial pages and save time.

PRACTICE WITH SCRATCH PAPER

Going forward, always practice using scratch paper when solving questions because this is how you will do it on Test Day. Never write directly on a written test.

GET NEW SCRATCH PAPER

Between sections, get a new piece of scratch paper even if you only used part of the old one. This will maximize the available space for each section and minimize the likelihood of you running out of paper to write on.

REMEMBER YOU CAN ALWAYS GO BACK

Just because you finish a passage or move on, remember you can come back to questions about which you are uncertain. You have the "marking" option to your advantage. However, as a general rule minimize the amount of questions you mark or skip.

MARK INCOMPLETE WORK

If you need to go back to a question, clearly mark the work you've done on the scratch paper with the question number. This way, you will be able to find your work easily when you come back to tackle the question.

LOOK AWAY AT TIMES

Taking the test on computer leads to faster eye-muscle fatigue. Use the Kaplan strategy of looking at a distant object at regular intervals. This will keep you fresher at the end of the test.

PRACTICE ON THE COMPUTER

This is the most critical aspect of adapting to computer-based testing. Like anything else, in order to perform well on computer-based tests you must practice. Spend time reading passages and answering questions on the computer. You often will have to scroll when reading passages.

Part I
Review

Atomic Structure

"Salting the water makes the pasta cook faster because the salt raises the boiling point. It's chemistry—it's a colligative property." My colleague stared me down, as if the intensity of his gaze gave further credence to his pronouncement. It was late on a Friday afternoon, about 5:00 P.M., and the science of cooking had become the topic of discussion that would carry us through the final hour of the workweek. However, here we were, arguing over the relative merits of culinary and scientific justifications for adding salt to pasta water. We were two opposing camps: one side arguing that adding salt to the water served no real purpose other than to flavor the pasta as it absorbed the water; the other side—the one of my colleague and his compatriots—fighting in the name of science. Finally, we agreed on a plan toward resolution and a lasting peace. We would calculate the actual chemical impact of the salt in the water and answer the question *Why add salt to pasta water?* once and for all.

Well, you can figure out the details of the calculation if you are so inclined, but suffice it to say that I wouldn't be telling you this story if I hadn't been proven correct. Our calculation showed that the amount of salt that most of us would probably consider a reasonably sufficient quantity for a large pot of boiling water had minimal impact on the boiling point temperature of the resulting solution. To be clear, the addition of the salt did raise the boiling point temperature—and even those of us arguing against the "scientific justification" never denied that it would. Nevertheless, the calculated rise in boiling point was exceedingly small, because the solution we imagined had such a low molality. The truth of the matter is this: Adding salt to cooking water in reasonable amounts does not measurably increase the boiling point temperature or decrease the cooking time. The salt merely flavors the food as it cooks in the dilute solution.

Why introduce a book of general chemistry for the MCAT review by telling you a story about food preparation? Am I telling you this simply to showcase an instance in which I won an argument? No, it's because chemistry is the study of the stuff of life or, to put it more properly, the nature and behavior of matter. Chemistry is the investigation of the atoms and molecules that make up our bodies, our possessions, the world around us, and of course, the food that we eat. There are different branches of chemistry, two of which are tested directly on the MCAT—general inorganic chemistry and organic chemistry—but ultimately all investigations in the realm of chemistry are seeking to answer the questions that confront us in the form (literally, "form": the shape, structure, mode, and essence) of the physical world that surrounds us.

At this point, you're probably saying the same thing you say when talking about physics: *But I'm premed. Why do I need to know any of this? What good will this do me as a doctor? Do I only need to know this for the MCAT?* Let me make it clearer for you: *How can you expect to be an effective doctor for your patients—who are made of the organic and inorganic stuff—unless you understand how this stuff makes up and affects the human body?*

So, let's get down to the business of learning and remembering the principles of the physical world that help us understand what all this stuff is, and how it works, and why it behaves the way it does, at both the molecular and macroscopic levels. In the process of reading through these chapters and applying your knowledge to practice questions, you'll prepare yourself for success not only on the Physical Science section of the MCAT but also in the medical care of your patients and the larger communities you will serve as a trained physician.

This first chapter starts our review of general chemistry with a consideration of the fundamental unit of matter, the atom, and the even smaller particles that constitute the atom: protons, neutrons, and electrons. We will also review the two models of the atom with a particular focus on how the two models are similar and different.

Subatomic Particles

Although you may have encountered in your university-level chemistry classes such subatomic particles as quarks, leptons, gluons, and other particles whose names sound as if they were picked up from a *Star Trek* episode, the MCAT's approach to atomic structure is much simpler. There are three subatomic particles that you must understand.

MCAT Expertise

The building blocks of the atom are also the building blocks of knowledge for the General Chemistry concepts tested on the MCAT. By understanding these interactions, we will be able to use that knowledge as the "nucleus" of understanding to all of General Chemistry.

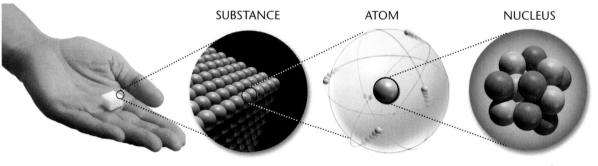

SUBSTANCE   ATOM   NUCLEUS

Figure 1.1

PROTONS

Protons are found, along with neutrons, in the nucleus of an atom. Each proton has an amount of charge equal to the fundamental unit of charge (1.6×10^{-19} C), and we

KAPLAN

denote this fundamental unit of charge as "+1" for the proton. Protons have a mass of approximately one **atomic mass unit,** or **amu**. The atomic number (Z) of an element is equal to the number of protons found in an atom of that element. The atomic number is like your Social Security number; it acts as a unique identifier for each element because no two elements have the same one. All atoms of a given element have the same atomic number, although, as we will see, they do not necessarily have the same atomic mass.

NEUTRONS

Neutrons are the Switzerland of an atom; they are neutral, which means that they have no charge. A neutron's mass is only slightly larger than that of the proton, and together, the protons and the neutrons of the nucleus make up almost the total mass of an atom. Every atom has a characteristic mass number, which is the sum of the protons and neutrons in the atom's nucleus. The number of neutrons in the nuclei of atoms of a given element may vary; thus, atoms of the same element will always have the same atomic number but will not necessarily have the same mass number. Atoms that share an atomic number but have different mass numbers are known as *isotopes* of the element. The convention $_Z^A X$ is used to show both the atomic number (Z) and the mass number (A) of atom X.

ELECTRONS

If you think of the nucleus as a game of checkers, the electrons would be children who express varying degrees of interest in playing or watching the game. Electrons move around in pathways in the space surrounding the nucleus and are associated with varying levels of energy. Each electron has a charge equal to that of a proton but with the opposite (negative) charge, denoted by "−1." The mass of an electron is approximately $\frac{1}{1,836}$ that of a proton. Because subatomic particle masses are so small, the electrostatic force of attraction between the unlike charges of the proton and electron is far greater than the gravitational force of attraction based on their respective masses.

Going back to our checkers analogy, consider how children form rough circles surrounding a game of checkers; the children sitting closer to the game are more interested in it than the children who are sitting on the periphery. Similarly, electrons are placed in pathways of movement that are progressively farther and farther from the nucleus. The electrons closer to the nucleus are at lower (electric potential) energy levels, while those that are in the outer regions (or shells) have higher energy. Furthermore, if you've ever seen children sitting around a game, you know that the "troublemakers" are more likely to sit on the periphery, which allows them to take advantage of an opportunity for mischief when it arises—and so it is also for electrons. Those in the outermost energy level, or shell, called the *valence electrons,* experience the least electrostatic draw to their nucleus and so are much more likely

Bridge

The valence, or outer, electrons will be very important to us in both General and Organic Chemistry. Knowing how tightly held those electrons are will allow us to understand many of an atom's properties and how it interacts with other atoms.

to become involved in bonds with other atoms (filling empty spaces in other atoms' valence shells). Generally speaking, the valence electrons determine the reactivity of an atom. In the neutral state, there are an equal number of protons and electrons; a gain of electron(s) results in the atom gaining a negative charge, while a loss of electron(s) results in the atom gaining a positive charge. A positively charged atom is a cation, and a negatively charged atom is an anion.

Some basic features of the three subparticles are shown in Table 1.1.

Table 1.1

Subatomic Particle	Symbol	Relative Mass	Charge	Location
Proton	$_1^1H$	1	+1	Nucleus
Neutron	$_0^1n$	1	0	Nucleus
Electron	e	0	−1	Electron Orbitals

Example: Determine the number of protons, neutrons, and electrons in a nickel-58 atom and in a nickel-60 2+ cation.

Solution: ^{58}Ni has an atomic number of 28 and a mass number of 58. Therefore, ^{58}Ni will have 28 protons, 28 electrons, and 58 − 28, or 30, neutrons.

In the $^{60}Ni^{2+}$ species, the number of protons is thet same as in the neutral ^{58}Ni atom. However, $^{60}Ni^{2+}$ has a positive charge because it has lost two electrons; thus, Ni^{2+} will have 26 electrons. Also the mass number is two units higher than for the ^{58}Ni atom, and this difference in mass must be due to two extra neutrons; thus, it has a total of 32 neutrons.

Atomic Weights and Isotopes ★★★☆☆

ATOMIC WEIGHT

As we've seen, the mass of one proton is defined as approximately one amu. The size of the atomic mass unit is defined as exactly $\frac{1}{12}$ the mass of the carbon-12 atom, approximately 1.66×10^{-24} grams (g). Because the carbon-12 nucleus has six protons and six neutrons, an amu is really the average of the mass of a proton and a neutron. Because the difference in mass between the proton and the neutron is so small, the mass of the proton and the neutron are each about equal to 1 amu. Thus,

Key Concept

- Atomic number (Z) = number of protons.
- Mass number (A) = number of protons + number of neutrons.
- Number of protons = number of electrons (in a neutral atom).

the **atomic mass** of any atom is simply equal to the mass number (sum of protons and neutrons) of the atom. A more common convention used to define the mass of an atom is the **atomic weight**. The atomic weight is the mass in grams of one mole of atoms of a given element and is expressed as a ratio of grams per mole (g/mol). A mole is the number of "things" equal to **Avogadro's number**: 6.022×10^{23}. For example, the atomic weight of carbon is 12 g/mol, which means that 6.022×10^{23} carbon atoms (1 mole of carbon atoms) have a combined mass of 12 grams (see Chapter 4, Compounds and Stoichiometry). One gram is then equal to one mole of amu.

ISOTOPES

The term *isotope* comes from the Greek, meaning "the same place." Isotopes are atoms of the same element (hence, occupying the same *place* on the periodic table of the elements) that have different numbers of neutrons (which means that these atoms of the same element have different mass numbers). Isotopes are referred to by the name of the element followed by the mass number (e.g., carbon-12 has six neutrons, carbon-13 has seven neutrons, etc.). Only the three isotopes of hydrogen are given unique names: protium (Greek *protos*; first) has one proton and an atomic mass of 1 amu; deuterium (Greek *deuteros*; second) has one proton and one neutron and an atomic mass of 2 amu; tritium (Greek *tritos*; third) has one proton and two neutrons and an atomic mass of 3 amu. Because isotopes have the same number of protons and electrons, they generally exhibit the same chemical properties.

In nature, almost all elements exist as two or more isotopes, and these isotopes are usually present in the same proportions in any sample of a naturally occurring element. The presence of these isotopes accounts for the fact that the accepted

Mnemonic

Mole Day is celebrated at 6:02 on October 23 (6:02 on 10/23) because of Avogadro's number (6.02×10^{23}). We will revisit this number in Chapter 4 when we discuss moles in more detail.

Key Concept

Bromine is listed in the periodic table as having a mass of 79.9 amu. This is an average of the two naturally occurring isotopes, bromine-79 and bromine-81, which occur in almost equal proportions. There are no bromine atoms with an actual mass of 79.9 amu.

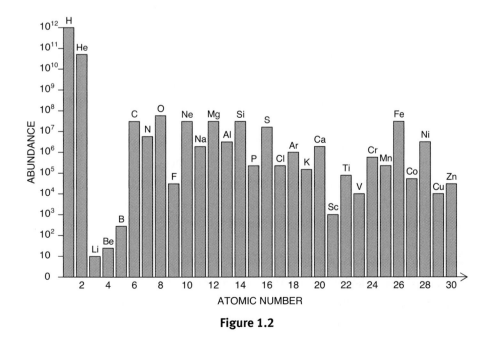

Figure 1.2

atomic weight for most elements is not a whole number. The masses listed in the periodic table are weighted averages that account for the relative abundance of various isotopes. See Figure 1.2 for the relative abundances in nature of the first several elements. Hydrogen, which is very abundant, has three isotopes.

> **Example:** Element Q consists of three different isotopes, A, B, and C. Isotope A has an atomic mass of 40 amu and accounts for 60 percent of naturally occurring Q. The atomic mass of isotope B is 44 amu and accounts for 25 percent of Q. Finally, isotope C has an atomic mass of 41 amu and a natural abundance of 15 percent. What is the atomic weight of element Q?
>
> **Solution:** $0.60(40 \text{ amu}) + 0.25(44 \text{ amu}) + 0.15(41 \text{ amu}) = 24.00 \text{ amu} + 11.00 \text{ amu} + 6.15 \text{ amu} = 41.15 \text{ amu}$
>
> The atomic weight of element Q is 41.15 g/mol.

Bohr's Model of the Hydrogen Atom ★★★☆☆

We've come a long way from J. J. Thomson's 1904 "plum pudding" model of the atom as negatively charged "corpuscles" (what we call electrons) surrounded by a density of positive charge that others (but not Thomson himself) likened to free-moving negatively charged "plums" suspended in a positively charged "pudding." We kid you not; we couldn't make this stuff up if we tried. In 1910, Ernest Rutherford provided experimental evidence that an atom has a dense, positively charged nucleus that accounts for only a small portion of the atom's volume. Eleven years earlier, Max Planck developed the first quantum theory, proposing that energy emitted as electromagnetic radiation from matter comes in discrete bundles called *quanta*. The **energy value** of a quantum, he determined, is given by this equation:

$$E = hf$$

where h is a proportionality constant known as **Planck's constant**, equal to 6.626×10^{-34} J • s, and f (sometimes designated as the Greek letter v, which looks a lot like the English letter v; sometimes you'll hear students say, "*Eee equals eich-vee*") is the frequency of the radiation.

BOHR MODEL OF THE HYDROGEN ATOM

Danish physicist Niels Bohr, in 1913, used the work of Rutherford and Planck to develop his model of the electronic structure of the hydrogen atom. Starting from Rutherford's findings, Bohr assumed that the hydrogen atom consisted of a central proton around which an electron traveled in a circular orbit and that the centripetal force acting on the electron as it revolved around the nucleus was the electrical force between the positively charged proton and the negatively charged electron.

Bohr used Planck's quantum theory to correct certain assumptions that classical physics made about the pathways of electrons. Classical mechanics postulates that an object revolving in a circle, such as an electron, may assume an infinite number of values for its radius and velocity. The angular momentum ($L = mvr$) and kinetic energy ($KE = \frac{1}{2}mv^2$) of the object, therefore, can take on any value. However, by incorporating Planck's quantum theory into his model, Bohr placed restrictions on the value of the angular momentum of the electron revolving around the hydrogen nucleus. Analogous to quantized energy, the **angular momentum of an electron**, Bohr predicted, is quantized according to the following equation:

$$L = \frac{n\text{h}}{2\pi}$$

where h is Planck's constant and n is the quantum number, which can be any positive integer. Because the only variable is the quantum number, n, the angular momentum of an electron changes only in discrete amounts with respect to the quantum number.

Bohr then related the permitted angular momentum values to the **energy of the electron** to obtain the following equation:

$$E = -\frac{R_{\text{H}}}{n^2}$$

where R_{H} is the experimentally determined **Rydberg constant**, equal to 2.18×10^{-18} J/electron. Therefore, like angular momentum, the energy of the electron changes in discrete amounts with respect to the quantum number. A value of zero energy was assigned to the state in which the proton and electron are separated completely, meaning that there is no attractive force between them. Therefore, the electron in any of its quantized states in the atom will have a negative energy as a result of the attractive forces between the electron and proton; hence the negative sign in the previous energy equation. Now, don't let this confuse you, because ultimately, the only thing the energy equation is saying is that the energy of an electron increases the further out from the nucleus that it is located. Remember that as the denominator (n^2, in this case) increases, the fraction gets smaller. However, here we are working with negative fractions that get smaller as n^2 increases. As negative numbers get smaller, they move to the right on the number line, toward zero. So, even though the absolute value is getting smaller (e.g., -8, -7, -6, etc.), its true value is increasing. Think of the concept of quantized energy as the change in gravitational potential energy that you experience when you ascend or descend a flight of stairs. Unlike a ramp, on which you could take an infinite number of steps associated with a continuum

MCAT Expertise

When we see a formula in our review or on Test Day, we need to focus on ratios and relationships rather than the equation as a whole. This simplifies our "calculations" to a conceptual understanding, which is usually enough to lead us to the right answer.

Key Concept

At first glance, it may not be clear that the energy (E) is directly proportional to the principle quantum number (n) in this equation. Take notice of the negative charge, which causes the values to approach zero from a greater negative value as n increases (thereby increasing the energy). The negative sign is as important as n's place in the fraction when it comes to determining proportionality.

of potential energy changes, a staircase only allows you certain changes in height and, as a result, allows only certain discrete (quantized) changes of potential energy.

Bohr came to describe the structure of the hydrogen atom as a nucleus with one proton forming a dense core around which a single electron revolved in a defined pathway of a discrete energy value. Transferring an amount of energy exactly equal to the difference in energy between one pathway, or **orbit**, and another, resulted in the electron "jumping" from one pathway to a higher energy one. These pathways or orbits had increasing radii, and the orbit with the smallest radius in which hydrogen's electron could be found was called the **ground state** and corresponded to $n = 1$. When the electron was promoted to a higher energy orbit (one with a larger radius), the atom was said to be in the **excited state**. Bohr likened his model of the hydrogen atom to the planets orbiting the sun, in which each planet traveled along a (roughly) circular pathway at set distances (and energy values) with respect to the sun. In spite of the fact that Bohr's model of the atom was overturned within the span of two decades, he was awarded the Nobel Prize in Physics in 1922 for his work on the structure of the atom and to this day is considered one of the greatest scientists of the 20th century.

APPLICATIONS OF THE BOHR MODEL

The Bohr model of the hydrogen atom (and other one-electron systems, such as He^+ and Li^{2+}) is useful for explaining the atomic emission spectrum and atomic absorption spectrum of hydrogen, and it is helpful in the interpretation of the spectra of other atoms.

Atomic Emission Spectra

At room temperature, the majority of atoms in a sample are in the ground state. However, electrons can be excited to higher energy levels by heat or other energy forms to yield the excited state of the atom. Because the lifetime of the excited state is brief, the electrons will return rapidly to the ground state, resulting in the emission of discrete amounts of energy in the form of photons. The **electromagnetic energy** of these photons can be determined using the following equation:

$$E = \frac{hc}{\lambda}$$

where h is Planck's constant, c is the speed of light in a vacuum (3.00×10^8 m/s), and λ is the wavelength of the radiation.

The different electrons in an atom can be excited to different energy levels. When these electrons return to their ground states, each will emit a photon with a wavelength characteristic of the specific energy transition it undergoes. The quantized energies of light emitted under these conditions do not produce a continuous spectrum (as expected from classical physics). Rather, the spectrum is composed of light at specified

MCAT Expertise

Note that all systems tend toward minimal energy; thus on the MCAT, atoms of any element will generally exist in the ground state unless subjected to extremely high temperatures or irradiation.

Bridge

$E = hf$ for photons in physics. This also holds true here because we know that $c = f\lambda$. This is based on the formula $v = f\lambda$ for photons.

frequencies and is thus known as a *line spectrum*, where each line on the emission spectrum corresponds to a specific electronic transition. Because each element can have its electrons excited to different distinct energy levels, each one possesses a unique atomic emission spectrum, which can be used as a fingerprint for the element. One particular application of atomic emission spectroscopy is in the analysis of stars and planets: While a physical sample may be impossible to procure, the light from a star can be resolved into its component wavelengths, which are then matched to the known line spectra of the elements.

The Bohr model of the hydrogen atom explained the atomic emission spectrum of hydrogen, which is the simplest emission spectrum among all the elements. The group of hydrogen emission lines corresponding to transitions from the upper energy levels $n > 2$ to $n = 2$ (that is to say, the pattern of photon emissions from the electron falling from the $n > 2$ energy level to the $n = 2$ energy level) is known as the *Balmer series* and includes four wavelengths in the visible region. The group corresponding to transitions from the upper levels $n > 1$ to $n = 1$ (that is to say, the emissions of photons from the electron falling from the higher energy levels to the ground state) is called the *Lyman series*, which includes larger energy transitions and therefore shorter photon wavelengths in the UV region of the electromagnetic spectrum.

When the energy of each frequency of light observed in the emission spectrum of hydrogen was calculated according to Planck's quantum theory, the values obtained closely matched those expected from energy level transitions in the Bohr model. That is, the energy associated with a change in the quantum number from an initial higher value n_i to a final lower value n_f is equal to the energy of the photon predicted by Planck's quantum theory. Combining Bohr's and Planck's calculations, we arrive at

$$E = \frac{hc}{\lambda} = -R_H \left[\frac{1}{n_i^2} - \frac{1}{n_f^2} \right]$$

The energy of the emitted photon corresponds to the precise difference in energy between the higher-energy initial state and the lower-energy final state.

Atomic Absorption Spectra

When an electron is excited to a higher energy level, it must absorb energy. The energy absorbed that enables an electron to jump from a lower-energy level to a higher one is characteristic of that transition. This means that the excitation of electrons in the atoms of a particular element results in energy absorption at specific wavelengths. Thus, in addition to a unique emission spectrum, every element possesses a characteristic absorption spectrum. Not surprisingly, the wavelengths of absorption correspond directly to the wavelengths of emission because the difference in energy between levels remains unchanged. Identification of elements present in a gas phase sample requires absorption spectra.

Real World

Emissions from electrons in molecules, or atoms dropping from an excited state to a ground state, give rise to fluorescence. We see the color of the emitted light.

You've just been put through a series of paragraphs crammed with technical language (mumbo jumbo is too strong a term; after all, you are sufficiently intelligent to grasp these concepts). That said, at least a few pairs of eyes reading this book will have gone glassy by this point. Therefore, let's bring this back to the realm of experience by way of analogy. We've already discussed equating the energy levels available to electrons to stairs on a staircase. Taking this analogy one step further, so to speak: Let's imagine that you and your friend are walking side-by-side up a set of stairs. You have very long legs, so it is your habit to take two, sometimes even three, steps at a time; your friend has short legs and so takes one, or at most two, steps at a time. The pattern by which you jump from a lower step to a higher one will be characteristic to you and you alone and will be quite different from the pattern by which your friend jumps from a lower step to a higher one, which will be unique to her. Furthermore, you have to invest energy into the process of ascending the staircase. This in a nutshell is the significance of the atomic absorption spectrum. The atomic emission spectrum is simply a record of the process in reverse.

Quantum Mechanical Model of Atoms ★★★☆☆

While Bohr's model marked a significant advancement in the understanding of the structure of atoms (at least we were no longer talking about plum pudding), his model ultimately proved inadequate to explain the structure and behavior of atoms containing more than one electron. The model's failure was a result of Bohr's not taking into account the repulsion between multiple electrons surrounding one nucleus. Modern quantum mechanics has led to a more rigorous and generalized study of the electronic structure of atoms. The most important difference between Bohr's model and the modern quantum mechanical model is that Bohr postulated that electrons follow a clearly defined circular pathway or orbit at a fixed distance from the nucleus, whereas modern quantum mechanics has shown that this is not the case. Rather, we now understand that electrons move rapidly in extraordinarily complex patterns within regions of space around the nucleus called **orbitals**. The confidence by which those in Bohr's time believed they could identify the location (or pathway) of the electron is now replaced by a more modest suggestion that the best we can do is describe the probability of finding an electron within a given region of space surrounding the nucleus. In the current quantum mechanical model, it is impossible to pinpoint exactly where an electron is at any given moment in time, and this is expressed best by the **Heisenberg uncertainty principle**: *It is impossible to simultaneously determine, with perfect accuracy, the momentum and the position of an electron.* If we want to assess the position of an electron, the electron has to stop (thereby changing its momentum); if we want to assess its momentum, the electron has to be moving (thereby changing its position).

QUANTUM NUMBERS

Modern atomic theory postulates that any electron in an atom can be completely described by four quantum numbers: n, l, m_l, m_s. Furthermore, according to the Pauli exclusion principle, no two electrons in a given atom can possess the same set of four quantum numbers. The position and energy of an electron described by its quantum numbers is known as its *energy state*. The value of n limits the value of l, which in turn limits the values of m_l. Think of this like a country: A country has a defined number of states, and each state has a defined number of cities or towns. The values of the quantum numbers qualitatively give information about the orientation of the orbital. As we examine the four quantum numbers more closely, pay attention especially to l and m_l, as these two tend to give students the greatest difficulty.

Principal Quantum Number

The first quantum number is commonly known as the **principal quantum number** and is denoted by the letter n. This is the quantum number used in Bohr's model that can theoretically take on any positive integer value. The larger the integer value of n, the higher the energy level and radius of the electron's orbit(al). Within each shell of some n value, there is a capacity to hold a certain number of electrons equal to $2n^2$, and the capacity to hold electrons increases as the n value increases. The difference in energy between two shells decreases as the distance from the nucleus increases because the energy difference is a function of $[1/n_i^2 - 1/n_f^2]$. For example, the energy difference between the $n = 3$ and the $n = 4$ shells is less than the energy difference between the $n = 1$ and the $n = 2$ shells. The term *shell* brings to mind the notion of eggshells, and you've probably heard the analogy between n values and eggshells of increasing size. This is fine as long as you don't extend the analogy to the point that you are thinking about electron pathways as precisely defined orbits. Nevertheless, if thinking about eggshells helps you to remember that the principal quantum number says something about the overall energy of the electron orbitals as a function of distance from the nucleus, then go with it.

Azimuthal Quantum Number

The second quantum number is called the **azimuthal (angular momentum) quantum number** and is designated by the letter l. The second quantum number refers to the shape and number of subshells within a given principal energy level (shell). The azimuthal quantum number is very important because it has important implications for chemical bonding and bond angles. The value of n limits the value of l in the following way: For any given value of n, the range of possible values for l is 0 to $(n - 1)$. For example, within the first principal energy level, $n = 1$, the only possible value for l is 0; within the second principal energy level, $n = 2$, the possible values for l are 0 and 1. A simpler way to remember this relationship is that the n-value also tells you the number of possible subshells.

Bridge

A larger integer value for the principal quantum number indicates a larger radius and higher energy. This is similar to gravitational potential energy, where the higher the object is above the earth, the higher its potential energy will be.

Therefore, there's only one subshell in the first principal energy level; there are two subshells within the second principal energy level; there are three subshells within the third principal energy level, and so on. The subshells also go by names other than the integer value of l: The $l = 0$ subshell is also known as the s subshell; the $l = 1$ subshell is also known as the p subshell; the $l = 2$ subshell is known as the d subshell; and finally, the $l = 3$ subshell is the f subshell. You're probably more used to working with these letter names than with the integer values.

The maximum number of electrons that can exist within a given subshell is equal to $4l + 2$. The energies of the subshells increase with increasing l value; however, the energies of subshells from different principal energy levels may overlap. For example, the $4s$ subshell will have a lower energy than the $3d$ subshell. This is why, ultimately, the image of increasingly larger eggshells falls short of adequately serving as an analogy.

Magnetic Quantum Number

The third quantum number is the **magnetic quantum number** and is designated m_l. The magnetic quantum number specifies the particular orbital within a subshell where an electron is highly likely to be found at a given moment in time. Each orbital can hold a maximum of two electrons. The possible values of m_l are the integers between $-l$ and $+l$, including 0. For example, the s subshell, with its l value $= 0$, limits the possible m_l value to 0, and since there is a single value of m_l for the s subshell, there is only one orbital in the s subshell. The p subshell, with its l value $= 1$, limits the possible m_l values to -1, 0, $+1$, and since there are three values for m_l for the p subshell, there are three orbitals in the p subshell. The d subshell has five orbitals, and the f subshell has seven orbitals. The shape of the orbitals, as the number of orbitals, is dependent upon the subshell in which they are found. The s subshell orbital is spherical, while the three p subshell orbitals are each dumbbell shaped along the x-, y-, and z-axes. In fact, the p orbitals are often referred to as p_x, p_y, and p_z. The shapes of the orbitals in the d and f subshells are much more complex, and the MCAT will not expect you to answer questions about their appearance. Of course, any discussion of orbital shape must not allow for a literal interpretation of the term, since we are using the term to describe "densities of probabilities" for finding electrons in regions of space surrounding the nucleus.

Spin Quantum Number

The fourth quantum number is called the **spin quantum number** and is denoted by m_s. In classical mechanics, an object spinning about its axis has an infinite number of possible values for its angular momentum. However, this does not apply to the electron, which has two spin orientations designated $+\frac{1}{2}$ and $-\frac{1}{2}$. Whenever two electrons are in the same orbital, they must have opposite spins.

Key Concept

For any principal quantum number n, there will be n possible values for l.

Key Concept

For any value of l, there will be $2l + 1$ possible values for m_l. For any n, this produces n^2 possible values of m_l (i.e., n^2 orbitals).

Key Concept

For any value of n, there will be a maximum of $2n^2$ electrons (i.e., two per orbital).

In this case, they are often referred to as paired. Electrons in different orbitals with the same m_s values are said to have **parallel spins**.

The quantum numbers for the orbitals in the second principal energy level, with their maximum number of electrons noted in parentheses, are shown in Table 1.2.

Table 1.2

n	2(8)			
ℓ	0(2)		1(6)	
m_ℓ	0(2)	+1(2)	0(2)	−1(2)
m_s	$+\dfrac{1}{2}, -\dfrac{1}{2}$	$+\dfrac{1}{2}, -\dfrac{1}{2}$	$+\dfrac{1}{2}, -\dfrac{1}{2}$	$+\dfrac{1}{2}, -\dfrac{1}{2}$

ELECTRON CONFIGURATION AND ORBITAL FILLING

For a given atom or ion, the pattern by which subshells are filled and the number of electrons within each principal energy level and subshell are designated by its **electron configuration**. In this notation, the first number denotes the principal energy level, the letter designates the subshell, and the superscript gives the number of electrons in that subshell. For example, $2p^4$ indicates that there are four electrons in the second (p) subshell of the second principal energy level. By definition, this also implies that the energy levels below $2p$ (that is, $1s$ and $2s$) have already been filled (see Figure 1.3).

To write out an atom's electron configuration, you need to know the order in which subshells are filled. They are filled from lower to higher energy, and each subshell will fill completely before electrons begin to enter the next one. You don't really need to memorize this ordering because there are two very helpful ways of recalling this. The $(n + l)$ rule can be used to rank subshells by increasing energy. This rule states that the lower the sum of the values of the first and second quantum numbers $(n + l)$, the lower the energy of the subshell. This is a very helpful rule to remember for Test Day. If two subshells possess the same $(n + l)$ value, the subshell with the lower n value has a lower energy and will fill with electrons first. The other helpful way to recall this ordering is the flow diagram in Figure 1.3, which also gives the order in which electrons will fill the shells and subshells. We recommend that you quickly write out this flow diagram on the scratch material provided at the testing center at the start of your Physical Science section for quick and easy reference throughout the section.

MCAT Expertise

Remember that the shorthand used to describe the electron configuration is derived directly from the quantum numbers.

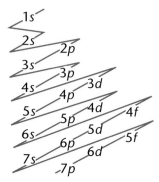

Figure 1.3

> **Example:** Which will fill first, the 3*d* subshell or the 4*s* subshell?
>
> **Solution:** For 3*d*, $n = 3$ and $\ell = 2$, so $(n + \ell) = 5$. For 4*s*, $n = 4$ and $\ell = 0$, so $(n + \ell) = 4$. Therefore, the 4*s* subshell has lower energy and will fill first. This can also be determined from the chart by examination.

MCAT Expertise

Remember this chart for Test Day—being able to re-create it quickly on your scratch paper may save you some time and get you that higher score!

If you are asked to determine which subshells are filled, you must know the number of electrons in the atom. In the case of a neutral (uncharged) atom, the number of electrons equals the number of protons, which can be found by the atomic number of the element. If the atom is charged, the number of electrons is

- equal to the atomic number *plus* the extra electrons if the ion is negatively charged; or
- equal to the atomic number *minus* the missing electrons if the ion is positively charged.

In subshells that contain more than one orbital, such as the 2*p* subshell with its three orbitals, the orbitals will fill according to **Hund's rule**, which states that within a given subshell, orbitals are filled such that there are a maximum number of half-filled orbitals with parallel spins. Electrons are somewhat curmudgeonly and misanthropic in that they don't like the company of other electrons. They prefer to spend as much time alone as possible. Therefore, an electron will be happier (at a lower energy level) if it is placed into an empty orbital rather than being forced to share its living quarters with another electron. (If you ever had to share a bedroom with a sibling, you know exactly what we're talking about.) Of course, the basis for this preference is the fact that all electrons have a negative charge and, as like charges, they exert repelling forces against each other; these forces must be overcome for two electrons to be in the same orbital.

Mnemonic

Hund's rule is like sitting down on a bus. Everyone wants an empty seat, but we have to start pairing up after all the seats are half filled.

Example: What are the written electron configurations for nitrogen (N) and iron (Fe) according to Hund's rule?

Solution: Nitrogen has an atomic number of 7. Thus, its electron configuration is $1s^2\,2s^2\,2p^3$. According to Hund's rule, the two s-orbitals will fill completely, while the three p-orbitals will each contain one electron, all with parallel spins.

$$\underset{1s^2}{\underline{\uparrow\downarrow}}\quad \underset{2s^2}{\underline{\uparrow\downarrow}}\quad \underset{2p^3}{\underline{\uparrow\ \uparrow\ \uparrow}}$$

Iron has an atomic number of 26, and its $4s$ subshell fills before the $3d$. Using Hund's rule, the electron configuration will be as follows:

$$\underset{1s^2}{\underline{\uparrow\downarrow}}\quad \underset{2s^2}{\underline{\uparrow\downarrow}}\quad \underset{2p^6}{\underline{\uparrow\downarrow\,\uparrow\downarrow\,\uparrow\downarrow}}\quad \underset{3s^2}{\underline{\uparrow\downarrow}}\quad \underset{3p^6}{\underline{\uparrow\downarrow\,\uparrow\downarrow\,\uparrow\downarrow}}\quad \underset{3d^6}{\underline{\uparrow\downarrow\,\uparrow\,\uparrow\,\uparrow\,\uparrow}}\quad \underset{4s^2}{\underline{\uparrow\downarrow}}$$

Iron's electron configuration is written as $1s^2\,2s^2\,2p^6\,3s^2\,3p^6\,3d^6\,4s^2$. Subshells may be listed either in the order in which they fill (e.g., $4s$ before $3d$) or with subshells of the same principal quantum number grouped together, as shown here. Both methods are correct.

Bridge

Half-filled and fully filled orbitals have lower energies than intermediate states. We will see this again with transition metals.

The presence of paired or unpaired electrons affects the chemical and magnetic properties of an atom or molecule. The magnetic field of materials made of atoms with unpaired electrons will cause the unpaired electrons to orient their spins in alignment with the magnetic field, and the material will be weakly attracted to the magnetic field. These materials are considered **paramagnetic**. Materials consisting of atoms that have all paired electrons will be slightly repelled by a magnetic field and are said to be **diamagnetic**.

VALENCE ELECTRONS

The valence electrons of an atom are those electrons that are in its outermost energy shell, most easily removed, and available for bonding. As with the unruly children sitting farthest from the checkers game who are most likely to get themselves into trouble, the valence electrons are the "active" electrons of an atom and to a large extent dominate the chemical behavior of the atom. For elements in Groups IA and IIA (Groups 1 and 2), only the outermost s subshell electrons are valence electrons. For elements in Groups IIIA through VIIIA (Groups 13 through 18), the outermost s and p subshell electrons in the highest principal energy level are valence electrons. For transition elements, the valence electrons are those in the outermost s subshell and in the d subshell of the next-to-outermost energy shell. For the inner transition elements (that is, those in the lanthanide and actinide series), the valence electrons include those in the s subshell of the outermost energy level, the d subshell of the next-to-outermost energy shell, and the f subshell of the energy shell two levels below the outermost shell. All elements in period 3 and below may accept electrons into their d subshell, which allows them to hold more than eight electrons in their

Mnemonic

Remember that *para*magnetic means that a magnetic field will cause *para*llel spins in unpaired electrons and therefore cause an attraction.

MCAT Expertise

The valence electron configuration of an atom helps us understand its properties and is ascertainable from the periodic table (the only "cheat sheet" available on the MCAT!). The "EXHIBIT" button on the bottom of the screen on Test Day will bring up a window with the periodic table. Use it often!

valence shell, in apparent "violation" of the octet rule (see Chapters 2 and 3). We'll learn that this is perfectly acceptable for these elements, however, and is occasionally preferred.

> **Example:** Which are the valence electrons of elemental iron, elemental selenium, and the sulfur atom in a sulfate ion?
>
> **Solution:** Iron has 8 valence electrons: 2 in its $4s$ subshell and 6 in its $3d$ subshell.
>
> Selenium has 6 valence electrons: 2 in its $4s$ subshell and 4 in its $4p$ subshell. Selenium's $3d$ electrons are not part of its valence shell.
>
> Sulfur in a sulfate ion has 12 valence electrons: its original 6 plus 6 more from the oxygens to which it is bonded. Sulfur's $3s$ and $3p$ subshells can contain only 8 of these 12 electrons; the other 4 electrons have entered the sulfur atom's $3d$ subshell, which in elemental sulfur is empty.

Conclusion

Congratulations! You've made it through the first chapter, and as far as we can tell, you're still alive and there seems to have been minimal shedding of tears and blood. Good! Now that we have covered topics related to the most fundamental unit of matter, the atom, you're set to advance your understanding of the physical world in more complex ways. This chapter described the characteristics and behavior of the three subatomic particles—the proton, the neutron, and the electron. In addition, it compared and contrasted the two most recent models of the atom. The Bohr model is adequate for describing the structure of one-electron systems, such as the hydrogen atom or the helium ion, but fails to describe adequately the structure of more complex atoms. The quantum mechanical model theorizes that electrons are found, not in discrete-pathway orbits, but in "clouds of probability," or orbitals, by which we can predict the likelihood of finding electrons within given regions of space surrounding the nucleus. Both theories tell us that the energy levels available to electrons are not infinite but discrete and that the energy between levels is a precise amount called a *quantum*. The four quantum numbers completely describe the position and energy of any electron within a given atom. Finally, we learned two simple recall methods for the order in which electrons fill the shells and subshells of an atom and that the valence electrons are the troublemakers in an atom—and the ones we need to keep our eyes on.

CONCEPTS TO REMEMBER

- ☐ The subatomic particles include the proton, which has a positive charge; the neutron, which has no charge; and the electron, which has a negative charge. The nucleus contains the protons and neutrons, while the electrons reside in regions of space. The element's atomic number is its number of protons, while the sum of an electron's protons and neutrons is its mass number.

- ☐ Isotopes are atoms of a given element that have different mass numbers because they have different numbers of neutrons in their nuclei. Because they have the same atomic number, they are all of the same elemental type. Most isotopes of elements are identified by the element followed by the mass number (e.g., carbon-12, carbon-13, carbon-14). The three isotopes of hydrogen go by different names: protium, deuterium, and tritium.

- ☐ Bohr proposed a model of the atom with a dense, positively charged nucleus surrounded by electrons revolving around the nucleus in defined pathways of distinct energy levels called *orbits*.

- ☐ The energy of an electron is quantized, which is to say that there is not an infinite range of energy levels available to an electron. Electrons can exist only at certain energy levels, and the energy of an electron increases the farther it is from the nucleus. The energy difference between energy levels is called a quantum.

- ☐ For an electron to jump from a lower energy level to a higher one, it must absorb an amount of energy precisely equal to the energy difference between the two levels. Every element has a characteristic atomic absorption spectrum. When electrons return from the excited state to the ground state, they emit an amount of energy that is exactly equal to the energy difference between the two levels. Every element has a characteristic atomic emission spectrum. Sometimes the electromagnetic energy emitted corresponds to a frequency in the visible light range.

- ☐ The quantum mechanical model posits that electrons do not travel in defined orbits but rather in complex patterns called orbitals. An orbital is a region of space around the nucleus defined by the probabilities of finding an electron in that region of space. The Heisenberg uncertainty principle states that it is impossible to know at the same time both an electron's position and its momentum.

- ☐ There are four quantum numbers. These numbers completely describe any electron in an atom. The principal quantum number, n, describes the average energy of an orbital. The azimuthal quantum number, l, describes the subshells within a given principal energy level. The magnetic quantum number, m_l, specifies the particular orbital within a subshell where an electron is likely to be found at a given moment in time. The spin quantum number, m_s, indicates the spin orientation of an electron in an orbital.

☐ The system of designating the placement of electrons into the principal energy levels, subshells, and orbitals is electron configuration. For example, $1s^2 2s^2 2p^6 3s^2$ is the electron configuration for magnesium. A neutral magnesium atom has 12 electrons: two in the s-orbital of the first energy level, two in the s-orbital of the second energy level, 6 in the p-orbitals of the second energy level, and 2 in the s-orbital of the third energy level. The two electrons in the s-orbital of the third energy level are the valence electrons for the magnesium atom.

☐ Electrons fill the principle energy levels and subshells according to increasing energy, which can be determined by the $(n + l)$ rule. Electrons fill orbitals according to Hund's rule, which states that electrons prefer to be unpaired with parallel spins.

☐ Valence electrons are those electrons in the outermost shell and/or those available for interaction (bonding) with other atoms. For the representative elements, the valence electrons are found in s- and/or p-orbitals. For the transition elements, the valence electrons are found in s-, d-, and f-orbitals. Many atoms interact with other atoms to form bonds so as to complete the octet in the valence shell.

EQUATIONS TO REMEMBER

☐ $E = hf$

☐ $E = \dfrac{-R_H}{n^2}$

☐ $E = \dfrac{hc}{\lambda}$

☐ $E = \dfrac{hc}{\lambda} = -R_H \left[\dfrac{1}{n_i^2} - \dfrac{1}{h_f^2} \right]$

Practice Questions

1. Which of the following is the correct electron configuration for Zn^{2+}?

   A. $1s^2 2s^2 2p^6 3s^2 3p^6 4s^0 3d^{10}$
   B. $1s^2 2s^2 2p^6 3s^2 3p^6 4s^2 3d^8$
   C. $1s^2 2s^2 2p^6 3s^2 3p^6 4s^2 3d^{10}$
   D. $1s^2 2s^2 2p^6 3s^2 3p^6 4s^0 3d^8$

2. Which of the following quantum number sets describes a possible element?

   A. $n = 2$; $l = 2$; $m_l = 1$; $m_s = +\frac{1}{2}$
   B. $n = 2$; $l = 1$; $m_l = -1$; $m_s = +\frac{1}{2}$
   C. $n = 2$; $l = 0$; $m_l = -1$; $m_s = -\frac{1}{2}$
   D. $n = 2$; $l = 0$; $m_l = 1$; $m_s = -\frac{1}{2}$

3. What is the maximum number of electrons allowed in a single atomic energy level in terms of the principal quantum number n?

   A. $2n$
   B. $2n + 2$
   C. $2n^2$
   D. $2n^2 + 2$

4. Which of the following equations describes the maximum number of electrons that can fill a sub-shell?

   A. $2l + 2$
   B. $4l + 2$
   C. $2l^2$
   D. $2l^2 + 2$

5. Which of the following substances is most likely to be diamagnetic?

   A. Hydrogen
   B. Iron
   C. Cobalt
   D. Sulfur

6. An electron returns from an excited state to its ground state, emitting a photon at $\lambda = 500$ nm. What would be the magnitude of the energy change if this process were repeated such that a mole of these photons were emitted?

   A. 3.98×10^{-19} J
   B. 3.98×10^{-21} J
   C. 2.39×10^5 J
   D. 2.39×10^3 J

7. Suppose an electron falls from $n = 4$ to its ground state, $n = 1$. Which of the following effects is most likely?

   A. A photon is absorbed.
   B. A photon is emitted.
   C. The electron gains velocity.
   D. The electron loses velocity.

8. Which of the following compounds is not a possible isotope of carbon?

   A. ^6C
   B. ^{12}C
   C. ^{13}C
   D. ^{14}C

9. According to the Heisenberg uncertainty principle, which of the following properties of a particle can an observer measure simultaneously?

   I. Position

   II. Momentum

   III. Velocity

   A. I and II
   B. I and III
   C. II and III
   D. I, II, and III

10. Which of the following electronic transitions would result in the greatest gain in energy for a single hydrogen electron, assuming that its ground state is $n = 1$?

   A. An electron moves from $n = 6$ to $n = 2$.
   B. An electron moves from $n = 2$ to $n = 6$.
   C. An electron moves from $n = 3$ to $n = 4$.
   D. An electron moves from $n = 4$ to $n = 3$.

11. Suppose that a chemical species fills its orbitals as shown.

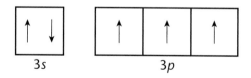

   3s   3p

   This compound could be said to obey which of the following laws of atomic physics?

   A. Hund's rule
   B. Heisenberg uncertainty principle
   C. Bohr's model
   D. Pauli exclusion principle

12. How many total electrons are in a ^{133}Cs cation?

   A. 54
   B. 55
   C. 78
   D. 133

13. The atomic mass of hydrogen is 1.008 amu. What is the percent composition of hydrogen by isotope, assuming that hydrogen's only isotopes are ^{1}H and ^{2}D?

   A. 92% H, 8% D
   B. 99.2% H, 0.8% D
   C. 99.92% H, 0.08% D
   D. 99.992% H, 0.008% D

14. Consider the two sets of quantum numbers shown in the table, which describe two different electrons in the same atom.

n	l	m_l	m_s
1	1	1	$+\frac{1}{2}$
2	1	-1	$+\frac{1}{2}$

   Which of the following terms best describes these two electrons?

   A. Parallel
   B. Opposite
   C. Antiparallel
   D. Paired

15. Which of the following species is represented by the electron configuration $1s^2 2s^2 2p^6 3s^2 3p^6 4s^1 3d^5$?

   A. Cr
   B. Mn$^+$
   C. Fe^{2+}
   D. both (A) and (B)

16. Which of the following statements is NOT true of an electron's ground state?

   A. The electron is at its lowest possible energy level.
   B. The electron is in a quantized energy level.
   C. The electron is traveling along its smallest possible orbital radius.
   D. The electron is static.

17. Which of the following experimental conditions would NOT excite an electron out of the ground state?

   A. Radiation
   B. High temperature
   C. High pressure
   D. None of the above

Small Group Questions

1. Which orbital fills first: $4s$ or $3d$? Which is first to give up electrons?

2. Why do atoms have neutrons? What purpose do they serve?

Explanations to Practice Questions

1. A

Because an electron was pulled off the neutral parent atom, consider how that parent atom was formed and which electron it would be willing to give up. Zn° has 30 electrons, so it would have an electron configuration of $1s^2 2s^2 2p^6 3s^2 3p^6 4s^2 3d^{10}$. Subshells strongly prefer to be completely empty, exactly half full, or completely full. Therefore, the best way to lose two electrons and form Zn^{2+} is to pull them both out of the $4s$-orbital. (B) implies that electrons are pulled out of the d-orbital, (C) presents the configuration of the uncharged zinc atom, and (D) shows the configuration that would exist if four electrons were removed.

2. B

The azimuthal quantum number l cannot be higher than $n - 1$, ruling out (A). The m_l number, which describes the chemical's magnetic properties, can only be an integer value between $-l$ and l, and it cannot be equal to 1 if $l = 0$, ruling out (C) and (D).

3. C

The correct answer is (C). For any value of n there will be a maximum of $2n^2$ electrons, i.e., two per orbital.

4. B

This formula describes the number of electrons in terms of the azimuthal quantum number l, which ranges from 0 to $n - 1$, n being the principal quantum number.

Subshell	Azimuthal Quantum Number (l)	Number of Electrons
s	0	2
p	1	6
d	2	10
f	3	14

Using the data in the table, the quickest way to solve this problem is to choose a subshell and plug in its l value to solve for the number of electrons. If more than one option works, discard the others and test the remaining possibilities using another subshell.

5. D

Sulfur is diamagnetic as opposed to ferromagnetic (iron, cobalt) or paramagnetic (hydrogen). Ferromagnetism refers, loosely, to the ability of a surface to attract an external magnetic field. It is characteristic of iron (Fe), from which it derives its name. More specifically, paramagnetism describes the tendency of valence electrons to align with the same spin in the presence of a strong magnetic field. Strongly paramagnetic materials, including transition metals, are usually called ferromagnetic. Transition metals like iron are characterized by a "sea" of electrons moving freely about the surface, which makes it easier for all these electrons to align in one direction. (This electron "sea" is an imprecise model, but it's good enough for the MCAT.) It is harder for more stable elements (e.g., oxygen, halogens, noble gases) to align their electrons in one orientation because their orbitals are nearly filled; these substances are known as diamagnetic. Sulfur has a similar atomic structure to oxygen, so it is also diamagnetic.

6. C

The problem requires the MCAT favorite equation $E = hf$, where h = 6.626×10^{-34} (Planck's constant) and f is the frequency of the photon. (Memorize Planck's constant!) One can calculate the frequency of the photon using the provided wavelength, 500 nm, with the equation $f = c/\lambda$, where c = 3×10^8 m/s, the speed of light. Here, $f = (3 \times 10^8$ m/s)/500 $\times$ 10^{-9} m, or 6×10^{14} s^{-1} (1 Hz = 1 s^{-1}). That leads to $E = hf$, or $E = (6.626 \times 10^{-34}) \times (6 \times 10^{14}$ Hz$) = 3.98 \times 10^{-19}$ J. (Don't worry about memorizing the units of Planck's constant—energy is always in joules!) However, the problem includes an additional trick, in that the answer must account for a mole of photons. The $E = hf$ equation works for a single photon only. Thus, the answer must account for this using Avogadro's number, 6.022×10^{23} photons. Multiply: (3.98 $\times 10^{-19}$ J/photon) $\times$ (6.022×10^{23} photons) = 2.39×10^5 J.

7. B

There is not enough information in the problem to determine how the velocity of the electron will change. There will be some energy change, however, as the electron must lose energy to return to the minimum energy ground state. That will require emitting radiation in the form of a photon, (B).

8. A

Recall that the superscript (i.e., the A in ^AC) refers to the mass number of an atom, which is equal to the number of protons plus the number of neutrons present in an element. (Sometimes a text will list the atomic number, Z, or total number of protons, under the mass number A.) According to the periodic table, carbon contains 6 protons; therefore, its atomic number $(Z) = 6$. An isotope contains the same number of protons and a different number of neutrons as the element. Carbon is most likely to have an atomic number of 12, for 6 protons and 6 neutrons. (C) and (D) are possible isotopes that would have more neutrons than does ^{12}C. The ^{6}C isotope is unlikely. It would mean that there were 6 protons and 0 neutrons, and it would probably collapse under the stress of the positive charge.

9. C

The Heisenberg uncertainty principle states that you cannot know the position and momentum of a particle simultaneously, which eliminates (A) and (D). Momentum depends on velocity (recall from Newtonian mechanics that $p = mv$), so in order to calculate momentum, velocity must be known. (C) explains this.

10. B

For the electron to *gain* energy, it must absorb photons to jump up to a higher energy level. This eliminates (A) and (D). Between (B) and (C), there is a bigger jump between $n = 2$ and $n = 6$ than there is between $n = 3$ and $n = 4$. Therefore, (B) represents the greatest energy gain.

11. A

The MCAT covers qualitative topics more often than quantitative topics in this unit. It is critical to be able to distinguish the fundamental principles that determine electron organization, which are usually known by the names of the scientists who discovered them. The Heisenberg uncertainty principle refers to the momentum and position of a single electron, and the Bohr model was an early attempt to describe the behavior of the single electron in a hydrogen atom. (D) is tempting, but (A) is more complete and therefore the correct answer. The element shown here, nitrogen, is often used to demonstrate Hund's rule because it is the smallest element with a half-filled p subshell. Hund's rule explains that electrons fill empty orbitals first, and in fact, the three p-electrons in this image each occupy a separate orbital. Hund's rule is really a corollary of the Pauli exclusion principle, in that the Pauli exclusion principle suggests that each orbital contains two electrons of opposite spin. Additional electrons must fill new orbitals so the compound remains stable in its ground state.

12. A

The quickest way to solve this problem is to use the periodic table and find out how many protons are in Cs atoms; there are 55. Neutral Cs atoms would also have 55 electrons. A Cs cation is most likely to have a single positive charge because it has one unpaired s-electron. This translates to one fewer electron than the number or protons, or 54 electrons.

13. B

The easiest way to approach this problem is to set up a system of two algebraic equations, where x and y are the percentages of H (mass = 1 amu) and D (mass = 2 amu), respectively. Your setup should look like the following system:

$x + y = 1$ (proportion H (x) + proportion D (y) in whole, $x\% + y\% = 100\%$).

$1x + 2y = 1.008$ (the total atomic mass).

Substitute one variable for the other so the atomic mass is in terms of one variable ($1 - y = x$), then solve for the other percentage ($[1 - y] + 2y = 1.008$ simplifies to $0.008 = y$, or 0.8% D). That plus 99.2 percent H makes 100 percent. Another way to examine this problem is if we had 50 percent of H and 50 percent of D, we could probably imagine an atomic mass of 1.5 amu. Therefore, if 50 percent D gave a mass of 1.5 amu, 80 percent D would yield an atomic mass of 1.8 amu. Eight percent would result in 1.08 amu, and 0.8 percent in 1.008 amu, which is the desired mass.

14. A

The terms in the answer choices refer to the magnetic spin of the two electrons. The quantum number m_s represents this property as a measure of the electrons' relative intrinsic angular momentum. These electrons' spins are parallel, in that their spins are aligned in the same direction ($m_s = +\frac{1}{2}$ for both species). (B), (C), and (D) suppose that $m_s = +\frac{1}{2}$ for one electron and $-\frac{1}{2}$ for the other. (D) implies that the two electrons have opposite spins but lie within the same orbital.

15. D

When dealing with ions, you cannot directly approach electronic configurations based on the number of electrons they currently hold. First examine the neutral atom's configuration, and then determine which electrons would have been removed.

Neutral Atom's Configuration	Ion's Configuration
Cr^0: [Ar] $4s^1 3d^5$	—
Mn^0: [Ar] $4s^2 3d^5$	Mn^+: [Ar] $4s^1 3d^5$
Fe^0: [Ar] $4s^2 3d^6$	Fe^{2+}: [Ar] $4s^0 3d^6$

Due to the stability of half-filled d-orbitals, neutral chromium assumes the electron configuration of [Ar] $4s^1 3d^5$. Mn must lose one electron from its initial configuration to become the Mn^+ cation. That electron would come from the $4s$-orbital, because the $3d$-orbital would strongly prefer to remain half-full. This d-orbital's desire to be half-full trumps the s-orbital's desire to be completely full, because it is at a higher energy. Fe must lose two electrons to become Fe^{2+}. They'll both be lost from the same orbital, because the scientist can't pick and choose which electrons to take! Moreover, the only way Fe^{2+} could hold the configuration in the question stem would be if one d-electron and one s-electron were lost together. Therefore, both answer choices (A) and (B) match the electron configuration in the question stem.

16. D

(D) is the only incorrect statement in the set. Electrons are assumed to be in motion in any energy level, even in the ground state. All of the other statements are true. An electron's ground state describes its position at the lowest and most stable energy level, i.e., lowest n value. It must be an integer value in the ground state and in the excited state. This number gives a relative indication of the electron's distance from the nucleus, so it must have the smallest radius of all the energy levels. The farther the electron moves from the nucleus, the greater energy it needs to overcome its attractive forces.

17. C

High pressure is unlikely to excite an electron out of the ground state unless it causes an extreme change in temperature, which would add enough energy to the system to promote the electron. There is not enough information in the problem to determine whether the stated high pressure would be high enough, as the answer is too generic. Irradiation has the same effect as temperature.

The Periodic Table

The pharmacological history of lithium is an interesting window into the scientific and medical communities' attempt to take advantage of the chemical and physical properties of an element for human benefit. By the mid-1800s, the medical community was showing great interest in theories that linked uric acid to a myriad of maladies. When it was discovered that solutions of lithium carbonate dissolved uric acid, therapeutic preparations containing the lithium carbonate salt became popular. Even nonmedical companies tried to profit from lithium's reputation as a cure-all by adding it to their soft drinks.

Eventually, fascination with theories of uric acid wore off, and lithium's time in the spotlight seemed to be coming to an end. Then, in the 1940s, doctors began to recommend salt-restricted diets for cardiac patients. Lithium chloride was made commercially available as a salt (sodium chloride) substitute. Unfortunately, lithium is quite toxic at fairly low concentrations, and when medical literature in the late 1940s reported several incidents of severe poisonings and multiple deaths—some associated with only minor lithium overdosing—U.S. companies voluntarily withdrew all lithium salts from the market. Right around this time, Australian psychiatrist John Cade proposed the use of lithium salts for the treatment of mania. Cade's clinical trials were quite successful. In fact, his use of lithium salts to control mania was the first instance of successful medical treatment of a mental illness—and lithium carbonate became commonly prescribed in Europe for manic behavior. Not until 1970 did the U.S. Food and Drug Administration finally approve the use of lithium carbonate for manic illnesses.

Lithium (Li) is a chemical element with atomic number 3. It is an alkali metal, very soft, and under standard conditions it is the least-dense solid element, with a specific gravity of 0.53. Lithium is so reactive that it does not naturally occur on earth in its elemental form, being found only in various salt compounds.

Why would medical scientists pay attention to this particular element? What would make medical scientists believe that lithium chloride would be a good substitute for sodium chloride for patients on salt-restricted diets? The answers lie in the periodic table.

The Periodic Table

In 1869, Russian chemist Dmitri Mendeleev published the first version of his **periodic table**, in which he showed that ordering the known elements according to atomic weight produced a pattern of periodically recurring physical and chemical properties. Since then, the periodic table of the elements has been revised, using the work of physicist Henry Moseley, to organize the elements on the basis of increasing atomic number rather than atomic weight. Using this revised table, the properties of certain elements that had not yet been discovered were predicted. Experimentation later confirmed a number of these predictions. The periodic table puts into visual representation the principle of the periodic law: The chemical and physical properties of the elements are dependent, in a periodic way, upon their atomic numbers.

The modern periodic table arranges the elements into **periods** (rows) and **groups** (columns), also known as **families**. There are seven periods, representing the principal quantum numbers $n = 1$ through $n = 7$. Each period is filled sequentially, and each element in a given period has one more proton and one more electron (in the neutral state) than the element to its left. Groups or families include elements that have the same electronic configuration in their **valence shell**, which is the outermost shell, and share similar chemical properties. The electrons in the valence shell, known as the valence electrons, are the farthest from the nucleus and have the greatest amount of potential energy of all the electrons in the atom. Their higher potential energy and the fact that they are held less tightly by the nucleus allows them to become involved in chemical bonds with other elements (by way of the valence shells of the other elements); the valence shell electrons largely determine the chemical reactivity and properties of the element.

The Roman numeral above each group represents the number of valence electrons. The Roman numeral is combined with the letter A or B to separate the elements into two larger classes. The A elements are known as the representative elements and include groups IA, IIA, IIIA, IVA, VA, VIA, VIIA, and VIIIA. The elements in these groups have their valence electrons in the orbitals of either s or p subshells. The B elements are known as the nonrepresentative elements and include the transition elements, which have valence electrons in the s and d subshells, and the lanthanide and actinide series, which have valence electrons in the s, d, and f subshells. For the representative elements, the Roman numeral and the letter designation determine the electron configuration. For example, an element in Group VA will have five valence electrons and a valence electron configuration of s^2p^3. The MCAT does not require you to know the corresponding association between Roman numerals and valence electron configuration for the nonrepresentative elements, however. The use of Roman numerals and letters to identify a particular family is confusing, because European and North American scientists traditionally have used the Roman numeral–letter system in different ways. In light of this, IUPAC developed and recommends a group identification system using Arabic numbers, 1–18, starting with the alkali metals on the left and ending with the noble gases on the right.

Periodic Properties of the Elements

★★★★☆☆

MCAT Expertise

Don't try to memorize the periodic table. You will have access to it on Test Day. *Do* understand its configuration and trends so that you can use it efficiently to get a higher score!

We hope that it goes without saying that the MCAT will *not* expect you to have memorized the entire periodic table. Those of you with biology backgrounds may need the services of a Sherpa to find any element beyond the fourth period. The even less adventurous among you may never have ventured past chlorine! Fortunately, the periodic table is a guide unto itself, sort of a self-referencing GPS for all the elements. Remember, the modern table is organized in such a way to represent visually the periodicity of chemical and physical properties of the elements. The periodic table, then, can provide you with a tremendous amount of information that otherwise would have to be memorized. While you do not need to "memorize" the periodic table for the MCAT (or ever), you absolutely need to understand the trends within the periodic table that will help you predict the chemical and physical behavior of any element you encounter on the MCAT (and in your medical career).

A few basic facts to keep in mind, before we examine the trends in detail: First, as we've already mentioned, as you move from element to element, left to right across a period, electrons and protons are added one at a time. As the "positivity" of the nucleus increases, the electrons surrounding the nucleus, including those in the valence shell, experience a stronger electrostatic pull toward it. This causes the electron cloud, the "outer boundary" of which is defined by the valence shell electrons, to move closer and bind more tightly to the nucleus. This electrostatic attraction between the valence shell electrons and the nucleus is known as the **effective nuclear charge (Z_{eff})**, which is a measure of the net positive charge experienced by the outermost electrons. For elements within the same period, then, Z_{eff} increases from left to right.

Second, as one moves down the elements of a given group, the principal quantum number increases by one each time. This means that the valence electrons are increasingly separated from the nucleus by a greater number of filled principal energy levels, which can also be called "inner shells." The result of this increased separation is a reduction in the electrostatic attraction between the valence electrons and the positively charged nucleus. These outermost electrons are held less tightly as the principal quantum number increases. As you go down a group, the increase in the shielding effect of the additional insulating layer of inner shell electrons negates the increase in the positivity of the nucleus (the nuclear charge). Thus, the Z_{eff} is more or less constant among the elements within a given group. In spite of this, the valence electrons are held less tightly to the nucleus due to the increased separation between them.

Third, and finally, we can generally say that elements behave in such a way to gain or lose electrons so as to achieve the stable octet formation possessed by the inert (noble) gases (Group VIII or Group 18). We will soon learn (Chapter 3) that this so-called "octet rule" is hardly a rule at all, as a far greater number of elements can be exceptions to this rule than elements that always follow it. Nevertheless, for now, let's just keep in mind that elements, especially the ones that have biological roles, tend to want to have eight electrons in their valence shell.

These three facts can be your guiding principles as you work toward an understanding of the more particular trends demonstrated among the elements organized as they are in the periodic table. In fact, all you really need to remember is the trend for effective nuclear charge across a period and the impact of increasing the number of inner shells down a group in order to correctly "derive" all the other trends.

ATOMIC RADIUS

If we imagine one atom of any element to essentially be a little cloud of electrons with a dense core of protons and neutrons, then the atomic radius of an element is equal to one-half the distance between the centers of two atoms of that element that are just touching each other. (We can't measure atomic radius by examining a single atom because the electrons are constantly moving around and it becomes impossible to mark the outer boundary of the electron cloud.) As we move across a period from left to right, protons and electrons are added one at a time to the atoms. Because the electrons are being added only to the outermost shell and the number of inner-shell electrons (which act as insulation between the nucleus and the valence electrons) remains constant, the increasing positive charge of the nucleus holds the outer electrons more closely and more tightly. The Z_{eff} increases left to right across a period, and as a result, *atomic radius decreases from left to right across a period.*

As we move down a group, the increasing principal quantum number implies that the valence electrons will be found farther away from the nucleus because the number of inner shells is increasing, separating the valence shell from the nucleus. Although the Z_{eff} remains essentially constant, *atomic radius increases in a group from top to bottom.* In summary, within each group, the largest atom will be at the bottom, and within each period, the largest atom will be within Group IA (Group 1).

IONIZATION ENERGY

Ionization energy (*IE*), also known as **ionization potential**, is the energy required to remove an electron completely from a gaseous atom or ion. Removing an electron from an atom always requires an input of energy (it's always **endothermic**; see Chapter 6). Anybody who has ever volunteered to make fundraising calls for a nonprofit organization knows that considerable energy must be invested in convincing a person to give a charitable donation, no matter how charitable the potential donor may be. Some are easier to convince than others are, but in the end, every donation is secured by a lot of hard work, effective communication, and skillful playing of the guilt and pity

MCAT Expertise

As an electron and a proton get farther away from one another, it becomes easier to pull them apart. This will help us understand all the trends with respect to the radius.

cards. The higher the atom's Z_{eff} or the closer the valence electrons are to the nucleus, the more tightly they are bound to the atom. This makes it more difficult to remove one or more electrons, so the ionization energy increases. *Thus, ionization energy increases from left to right across a period and decreases in a group from top to bottom.* Furthermore, the subsequent removal of a second or third electron requires increasing amounts of energy, because the removal of more than one electron necessarily means that the electrons are being removed from an increasingly cationic species. The energy necessary to remove the first electron is called the **first ionization energy**; the energy necessary to remove the second electron from the univalent cation to form the divalent cation is called the **second ionization energy**, and so on. For example:

$$Mg(g) \longrightarrow Mg^+(g) + e^- \quad \text{First Ionization Energy} = 7.646 \text{ eV}$$
$$Mg^+(g) \longrightarrow Mg^{2+}(g) + e^- \quad \text{Second Ionization Energy} = 15.035 \text{ eV}$$

Elements in Groups I and II (Groups 1 and 2) have such relatively low ionization energies that they are called the active metals. The active metals never exist naturally in their neutral elemental (native) forms; they are always found in ionic compounds, minerals, or ores. The loss of one electron (from the alkali metals) or the loss of two electrons (from the alkaline earth metals) results in the formation of a stable, filled valence shell. As you might imagine from the trend, the Group VIIA (Group 17) elements, the halogens, are a miserly group of penny pinchers and aren't willing to give up their electrons to anybody. In fact, in their monatomic ion form, they are found only as anions, having greedily taken one electron from another atom to complete their octets. As you might guess, the halogens have very large ionization energies and the smaller the halogen atom, the higher the ionization energy.

The only group less willing to give up their valence electrons is the inert elements (noble gases). They already have a very stable electron configuration and are unwilling to disrupt that stability by losing an electron. Inert gases are among the elements with the highest ionization energies.

ELECTRON AFFINITY

The greedy halogens are among the worst of the bunch of elements that tend to hoard their electrons toward themselves. These elements also tend to be very anxious to gain the number of electrons necessary to complete their octets. Like nervous little squirrels frantically running around in search of nuts to pack into their accommodating cheek pouches, these elements go in search of other atoms that are willing to give up their electrons. When a gaseous atom of a particular elemental identity gains one or more electrons to complete its octet, it relaxes and breathes a sigh of relief. This "sigh of relief" is a release of a quantity of energy called the electron affinity. Because energy is released when an atom gains an electron, we can describe this process as **exothermic**. By convention, the electron affinity is reported as a positive energy value, even though by the conventions of thermodynamics, exothermic processes

> **Mnemonic**
>
> To recall the various trends, remember this: Cesium, Cs, is the largest, most metallic, and least electronegative of all naturally occurring elements. It also has the smallest ionization energy and the least exothermic electron affinity.

have negative energy changes. Regardless of the sign, just remember that electron affinity is *released* energy. The stronger the electrostatic pull (that is, the Z_{eff}) between the nucleus and the valence shell electrons, the greater the energy release will be when the atom gains the electron. *Thus, electron affinity increases across a period from left to right.* Because the valence shell is farther away from the nucleus as the principal quantum number increases, *electron affinity decreases in a period from top to bottom.* Groups IA and IIA (Group 1 and 2) have very low electron affinities, preferring rather to give up one or two electrons, respectively, to achieve the octet configuration of the prior noble gas. Group VIIA (Group 17) elements have very high electron affinities because they need to gain only one electron to achieve the octet configuration of the immediately following noble gases in Group VIIIA (Group 18). Although the noble gases are the group of elements farthest to the right and would be predicted to have the highest electron affinities according to the trend, they actually have electron affinities on the order of zero, since they already possess a stable octet and cannot readily accept an electron. Elements of other groups generally have low electron affinity values.

ELECTRONEGATIVITY

No, we are not referring to pessimistic electrons. Electronegativity is a measure of the attractive force that an atom will exert on an electron in a chemical bond. The greater the electronegativity of an atom, the greater is its attraction for bonding electrons. Electronegativity values are related to ionization energies: The lower the ionization energy, the lower the electronegativity; the higher the ionization energy, the higher the electronegativity. The electronegativity value for any element is not measured directly and there are different scales used to express it. The most common scale is the Pauling electronegativity scale, which ranges from 0.7 for cesium, the least electronegative (most electropositive) element, to 4 for fluorine, the most electronegative element. *Electronegativity increases across a period from left to right and decreases in a period from top to bottom.* Figure 2.1 Summarizes the behavior of atoms in terms of the periodic table.

Mnemonic

In contrast to cesium, fluorine (F) is the smallest, most electronegative element. It also has the largest ionization energy and most exothermic electron affinity.

MCAT Expertise

Electronegativity might better be called "nuclear positivity." It is a result of the nucleus' attraction for electrons; that is, the Z_{eff} perceived by the electrons in a bond.

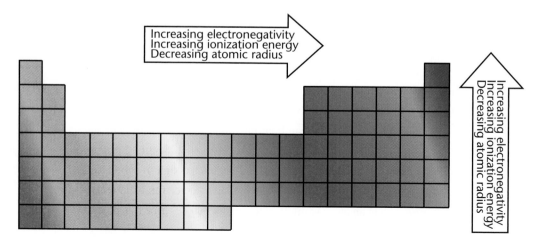

Figure 2.1

Types of Elements ★★☆☆☆

It's often been said that birds of a feather flock together, and this is no less true for the elements. When we consider the trends of chemical reactivity and physical properties taken together, we begin to identify whole clans, if you will, of elements that share sets of similarities. These larger collections of elements, which span groups and periods, are divided into three categories: metals, nonmetals, and metalloids (semimetals).

METALS

Metals, found both on the left side and in the middle of the periodic table, include the active metals, the transition metals, and the lanthanide and actinide series of elements. Metals are shiny solids, except for mercury, which is a liquid under standard state conditions. They generally have high melting points and densities, but there are exceptions, such as lithium, which has a density that is about half that of water. Metals have the ability to be deformed without breaking; the ability of metal to be hammered into shapes is called **malleability**, and its ability to be drawn into wires is called **ductility**. At the atomic level, low Z_{eff}, low electronegativity (high electropositivity), large atomic radius, and low ionization energy define metals. These characteristics make it fairly easy for metals to give up one or more electrons. Many of the transition metals, for example, are known to have two oxidation states, and some have more than that. Because the valence electrons of all metals are only loosely held to their atoms, they are essentially free to move, which makes metals generally good conductors of heat and electricity (some are better than others). The valence electrons of the active metals are found in the s subshell, those of the transition metals are found in the d subshell, and those of the lanthanide and actinide series elements are found in the f subshell. Some transition metals—such as copper, nickel, silver, gold, palladium, and platinum—are relatively nonreactive, a property that makes them ideal substances for the production of coins and jewelry.

NONMETALS

Nonmetals are found on the upper right side of the periodic table. The metals claim that the nonmetals are jealous of them for their shiny hair and sparkly personalities. The nonmetals scoff back, yet quietly steal electrons from them. Nonmetals are generally brittle in the solid state and show little or no metallic luster. They have high ionization energies, electron affinities, and electronegativities; have small atomic radii; and are usually poor conductors of heat and electricity. Nonmetals are less unified in their chemical and physical properties than are the metals. They are separated from the metals by a diagonal band of elements called the metalloids.

METALLOIDS

The metalloids are also called the semimetals because they possess characteristics that are between those of metals and nonmetals. The electronegativities and ionization energies of the metalloids lie between those of metals and nonmetals. Their physical properties, such as densities, melting points, and boiling points, vary widely and can be combinations of metallic and nonmetallic characteristics. For example, silicon has a metallic luster but is brittle and a poor conductor. The particular reactivity of the metalloids is dependent upon the elements with which they are reacting. Boron (B), for example, behaves as a nonmetal when reacting with sodium (Na) and as a metal when reacting with fluorine (F). The elements classified as metalloids form a "staircase" on the periodic table and include boron, silicon, germanium, arsenic, antimony, tellurium, and polonium.

The Chemistry of Groups   ★★☆☆☆

ALKALI METALS

The **alkali metals**, Group IA (Group 1), possess most of the classic physical properties of metals, except that their densities are lower than those of other metals (as is true of lithium). The alkali metals have only one loosely bound electron in their outermost shells, and their Z_{eff} values are very low, giving them the largest atomic radii of all the elements in their respective periods. The very low Z_{eff} values also result in low ionization energies, low electron affinities, and low electronegativities, and these atoms easily lose one electron to form univalent cations. They react very readily with nonmetals, especially halogens.

ALKALINE EARTH METALS

The **alkaline earth metals**, Group IIA (Group 2), also possess many properties characteristic of metals. They share most of the characteristics of the alkali metals, except that they have slightly higher effective nuclear charges and so have slightly smaller atomic radii. They have two electrons in their valence shell, both of which are easily removed to form divalent cations. Together, the alkali and alkaline earth metals are called the active metals because they are so reactive that they are not naturally found in their elemental (neutral) state.

HALOGENS

The **halogens**, Group VIIA (Group 17), are highly reactive nonmetals with seven valence electrons. They are rather "desperate" to complete their octets by each gaining an additional electron. The halogens are highly variable in their physical properties. For instance, the halogens range from gaseous (F_2 and Cl_2) to liquid (Br_2) to solid (I_2) at room temperature. Their chemical reactivity is more uniform, and due to their very high electronegativities and electron affinities, they are especially reactive toward the alkali and alkaline earth metals. Fluorine has the highest electronegativity of all the elements. The halogens are so reactive that they are not naturally found in their elemental state but rather as ions (called *halides*).

Real World

Metalloids share some properties with metals, and others with nonmetals. For instance, metalloids make good semiconductors due to their electrical conductivity.

Key Concept

Alkali and alkaline earth metals are both metallic in nature because they both lose electrons easily from the *s*-orbital of their valence shells.

MCAT Expertise

Halogens are seen often on the MCAT. Remember that they only need one more electron to become "noble" (have that full valence shell).

NOBLE GASES

The **noble gases**, Group VIIIA (Group 18), are also known as the inert gases because they have very low chemical reactivities as a result of their filled valence shells. They have high ionization energies, little or no tendency to gain or lose electrons, and no real electronegativities. They are essentially snobby elements, as they refuse to mingle with the hoi polloi. After all, they already have everything they need. The noble gases have low boiling points, and all exist as gases at room temperature.

TRANSITION METALS

The **transition elements**, Groups IB to VIIIB (Groups 3 to 12), are all considered metals and as such have low electron affinities, low ionization energies, and low electronegativities. These metals are very hard and have high melting and boiling points. They tend to be quite malleable and are good conductors due to the loosely held electrons that are progressively filling the *d* subshell orbitals in the valence shell. One of the unique properties of the transition metals is that many of them can have different possible charged forms, or **oxidation states**, because they are capable of losing various numbers of electrons from the *s*- and *d*-orbitals of the valence shell. For instance, copper (Cu), in Group 1B (Group 11), can exist in either the +1 or the +2 oxidation state, and manganese (Mn), in Group VIIB (Group 7), can have the +2, +3, +4, +6, or +7 oxidation state. Because of this ability to attain different positive oxidation states, transition metals form many different ionic and partially ionic compounds. The dissolved ions can form complex ions either with molecules of water (hydration complexes) or with nonmetals, forming highly colored solutions and compounds (e.g., $CuSO_4 \cdot 5H_2O$), and this complexation may enhance the relatively low solubility of certain compounds. For example, AgCl is insoluble in water but quite soluble in aqueous ammonia due to the formation of the complex ion $[Ag(NH_3)_2]^+$. The formation of complexes causes the *d*-orbitals to split into two energy sublevels. This enables many of the complexes to absorb certain frequencies of light—those containing the precise amount of energy required to raise electrons from the lower to the higher *d* sublevel. The frequencies not absorbed (known as the subtraction frequencies) give the complexes their characteristic colors.

> **MCAT Expertise**
>
> Transition metals are present in biological systems and are therefore often seen on the MCAT (think iron in hemoglobin). You don't need to memorize them, but be able to use your knowledge from these first two chapters to understand how the transition metals ionize and act.

Conclusion

Now that we have completed our review of the periodic table of the elements, commit to understanding (not just to memorizing) the trends of physical and chemical properties that will allow you to answer quickly the questions on the MCAT. You will find, as you progress through the chapters of this book, that your foundational understanding of the elements will help you develop a richer, more nuanced understanding of their general and particular behaviors. Topics in general chemistry that may have given you trouble in the past will be understandable from the perspective of the behaviors and characteristics that you have reviewed here.

CONCEPTS TO REMEMBER

☐ The periodic table of the elements organizes the elements according to their atomic numbers and reveals a repeating pattern of similar chemical and physical properties. Elements in the same row are in a period, while those elements in a column are in a group. Elements in the same period have the same principal energy level, n. Elements in the same group have the same valence shell electron configuration.

☐ The valence electrons are those located in the outer shell and/or are available for interaction (bonding) with other atoms. The representative elements have their valence electrons in either s- or s- and p-orbitals. The nonrepresentative elements (the transition elements) have their valence electrons either in s- and d- or in s-, d-, and f-orbitals.

☐ Effective nuclear charge (Z_{eff}) is the net positive charge experienced by electrons in the valence shell. Z_{eff} increases from left to right across a period, with little change in value from top to bottom in a group. Valence electrons become increasingly separated from the nucleus as the principal energy level, n, increases from top to bottom in a group. These two trends are the basis for all the other trends exhibited by the elements in the periodic table.

☐ Atomic radius decreases from left to right across a period and increases from top to bottom in a group.

☐ Ionization energy (*IE*) is the amount of energy necessary to remove an electron from the valence shell. It increases from left to right across a period and decreases from top to bottom in a group.

☐ Electron affinity is the amount of energy released when an atom gains an electron in its valence shell. It increases from left to right across a period and decreases from top to bottom in a group.

☐ Electronegativity is a measure of the attractive force that an atom in a chemical bond will exert on the electron pair of the bond. It increases from left to right across a period and decreases from top to bottom in a group.

☐ There are three general classes of elements:

— The metals, located on the left and middle of the periodic table, including the active metals and the transition metals

— The nonmetals, located in the upper right side of the periodic table, including hydrogen, carbon, oxygen, nitrogen, and phosphorus, among others

— The metalloids or semimetals, located in a staircase formation between the metals and nonmetals, with qualities and behaviors that are combinations of those of the metals and nonmetals

☐ The alkali and alkaline earth metals are the most reactive of all metals; they exist only in their ionic forms, having given up one or two electrons, respectively, in order to achieve the electronic configuration of the prior noble gas. The transition metals are less reactive, and many can have two or more oxidation states.

☐ The halogens are very reactive nonmetals and are highly electronegative. They need only one electron to complete their octets and are naturally found only in the anionic state. The noble gases are the least reactive of all the elements because they have the stable octet in their valence shell. They have very high ionization energies and virtually nonexistent electronegativities.

Practice Questions

1. Lithium and sodium have similar chemical properties. For example, both can form ionic bonds with chloride. Which of the following best explains this similarity?

   A. Both lithium and sodium ions are positively charged.
   B. Lithium and sodium are in the same group of the periodic table.
   C. Lithium and sodium are in the same period of the periodic table.
   D. Both lithium and sodium have low atomic weights.

2. Carbon and silicon, elements used as the basis of biological life and synthetic computing, respectively, have some similar chemical properties. Which of the following describes a difference between the two elements?

   A. Carbon has a smaller atomic radius than silicon.
   B. Silicon has a smaller atomic radius than carbon.
   C. Carbon has fewer valence electrons than silicon.
   D. Silicon has fewer valence electrons than carbon.

3. What determines the length of an element's atomic radius?

   I. The number of valence electrons
   II. The number of electron shells
   III. The number of neutrons in the nucleus

   A. I only
   B. II only
   C. I and II only
   D. I, II, and III

4. Ionization energy contributes to an atom's chemical reactivity. An accurate ordering of ionization energies, from lowest ionization energy to highest ionization energy, would be

   A. Be, first ionization energy < Be, second ionization energy < Li, first ionization energy.
   B. Be, second ionization energy < Be, first ionization energy < Li, first ionization energy.
   C. Li, first ionization energy < Be, first ionization energy < Be, second ionization energy.
   D. Li, first ionization energy < Be, second ionization energy < Be, first ionization energy.

5. Selenium is often an active component of treatments for scalp dermatitis. What type of element is selenium?

   A. Metal
   B. Metalloid
   C. Halogen
   D. Nonmetal

6. The properties of atoms can be predicted, to some extent, by their location within the periodic table. Which property or properties increase in the direction of the arrows shown?

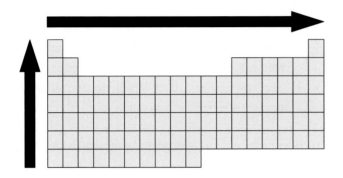

I. Electronegativity

II. Atomic radius

III. First ionization energy

A. I only

B. II only

C. I and III only

D. II and III only

7. Metals are often used for making wires that conduct electricity. Which of the following properties of metals explains why?

A. Metals are malleable.

B. Metals have high electronegativities.

C. Metals have valence electrons that can move freely.

D. Metals have high melting points.

8. Which of the following is an important property of the set of elements shaded in the periodic table shown?

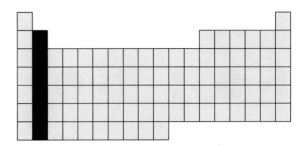

A. These elements are the best electrical conductors in the periodic table.

B. These elements form divalent cations.

C. The second ionization energy for these elements is lower than the first ionization energy.

D. The atomic radii of these elements decrease as one moves down the column.

9. When dissolved in water, which of the following ions is most likely to form a complex ion with H_2O?

A. Na^+

B. Fe^{2+}

C. Cl^-

D. S^{2-}

10. How many valence electrons are present in elements in the third period?

A. 2

B. 3

C. The number decreases as the atomic number increases.

D. The number increases as the atomic number increases.

11. Which of the following elements has the highest electronegativity?

A. Mg

B. Cl

C. Zn

D. I

12. Of the four atoms depicted here, which has the highest electron affinity?

A.   B.

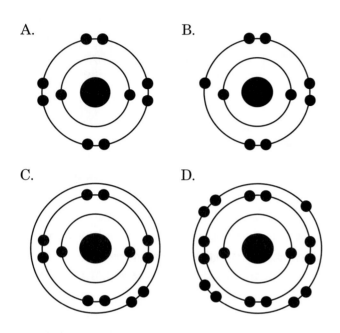

C.   D.

13. Which of the following is true of an atom with a large atomic radius?

  A. The atom is most likely to be on the right side of the periodic table.

  B. The atom is likely to have a high second ionization energy.

  C. The atom is likely to have low electronegativity.

  D. The atom is likely to form ionic bonds.

14. Which of the following atoms/ions has the largest effective nuclear charge?

  A. Cl

  B. Cl⁻

  C. K

  D. K⁺

15. Why do halogens often form ionic bonds with alkaline earth metals?

  A. The alkaline earth metals have much higher electron affinities than the halogens.

  B. By sharing electrons equally, the alkaline earth metals and halogens both form full octets.

  C. Within the same row, the halogens have smaller atomic radii than the alkaline earth metals.

  D. The halogens have much higher electron affinities than the alkaline earth metals.

16. What is the outermost orbital of elements in the third period?

  A. *s*-orbital

  B. *p*-orbital

  C. *d*-orbital

  D. *f*-orbital

Small Group Questions

1. Mercury (Hg) exists as a liquid at room temperature. Why, then, is it classified as a metal? What metallic properties might it possess?

2. The transition metals in group VIIIB could theoretically have eight different oxidation states. In reality, that does not hold true. Why not?

Explanations to Practice Questions

1. B

To answer this question, one must first recall that the periodic table is organized with periods (rows) and groups (columns). This method of organization allows elements to be organized such that some chemical properties can be predicted based on an element's position in the table. Groups (columns) are particularly significant because they represent sets of elements with the same outer electron configuration. In other words, all elements within the same group will have the same configuration of *valence electrons,* which in turn will dictate many of the chemical properties of those similar elements. Although (A) is true, the fact that both ions are positively charged does not explain the similarity in chemical properties as effectively as does answer (B); most other metals, whether or not they are similar to lithium and sodium, produce positively charged ions. (C) is not true, because periods are rows and lithium and sodium are in the same column. Finally, although lithium and sodium do have relatively low atomic weights, so do several other elements that do not share those same properties.

2. A

This question assesses understanding of a key periodic trend: atomic radii. As one moves from left to right across a period (row), atomic radii decrease. This occurs because as more protons are added to the nucleus and more electrons are added within the same shell, there is no increased shielding between the protons and electrons, but there is increased attractive electrostatic force. This effect decreases the atomic radius. In contrast, as one moves from top to bottom down a group (column), extra electron shells accumulate, despite the fact that the valence configurations remain identical. These extra electron shells provide shielding between the positive nucleus and the outermost electrons, decreasing the electrostatic forces and increasing the atomic radius. Because carbon and silicon are in the same group, and silicon is farther down the periodic table, it will have a larger atomic radius because of its extra electron shell. (C) and (D) are incorrect because all elements in the same group have the same number of valence electrons.

3. C

Atomic radius is determined by multiple factors. Of the choices given, the number of valence electrons does have an impact on the atomic radius. As one moves across a period (row), protons and valence electrons are added, and the electrons are more strongly attracted to the central protons. This attraction tightens the atom, shrinking the atomic radius. The number of electron shells is also significant, as demonstrated by the trend when moving down a group (column). As more electron shells are added that separate the positively charged nucleus from the outermost electrons, the electrostatic forces are weakened, and the atomic radius increases. The number of neutrons, III, is irrelevant, because it does not impact these attractive forces. Statements I and II are correct, and III is incorrect.

4. C

Ionization energy is related to the same set of forces that explains atomic radius, as well as the rules governing maintenance of a full valence shell octet. The first set of rules dictates that the stronger the attractive forces between the outer electron (the electron to be ionized) and the positively charged nucleus, the more energy will be required to ionize. As a result, strong attractive forces, which make the atomic radius smaller toward the right of a period or the top of a group, will also increase the first ionization energy. With this information alone, one could guess that ionization energies for beryllium (Be) should be higher than those for Li (lithium), eliminating (A) and (B). How should we choose between the two ionization energies for beryllium? The first ionization energy is usually dramatically lower than the second. This property holds true for the same reasons previously discussed. For example, upon removing one electron from beryllium, the ion is Be^{1+}, which has one more proton in its nucleus than it has electrons surrounding it. Thus, there is a heightened electrostatic force between the positive nucleus and the now less-negative electron cloud, meaning that all remaining electrons will be held more tightly than before. Removing a second electron will be even more difficult than the initial electron removal, making the second ionization energy higher than the first. Furthermore, the first ionization energy for Li is 520.2 kJ/mol, the first ionization energy for Be is 899.5 kJ/mol, and the second ionization energy for Be is 1,757.1 kJ/mol.

5. D

Selenium is on the right side of the periodic table (atomic number 34), too far right to be a metal or metalloid. However, it does not lie far enough to the right to fall under column 7A, which would classify it as a halogen. It is a nonmetal.

6. C

The trend in the periodic table demonstrated by the figure is correct for increasing electronegativity and first ionization energy. Electronegativity describes how strong an attraction an element will have for electrons in a bond. A nucleus with a stronger electrostatic pull due to its positive charge will have a higher electronegativity. An arrow pointing toward the right represents this because effective nuclear charge increases toward the right side of a period. This mirrors the trend for ionization energies, because a stronger nuclear pull will also lead to increased first ionization energy, as the forces make it more difficult to remove an electron. The vertical arrow can be explained by the size of the atoms. As size decreases, the proximity of the outermost electrons to the positive inner nucleus increases, making the positive charge more effective at attracting new electrons in a chemical bond (which leads to higher electronegativity). Similarly, the more effective the positive nuclear charge, the higher the first ionization energy. Because I and III are both correct, we can choose answer choice (C).

7. C

All four descriptions of metals are true, but the most significant property that contributes to their ability to conduct electricity is the fact that they have valence electrons that can move freely (C). Large atomic radii, low ionization energies, and low electronegativities all contribute to the ability of metals' outermost electrons to be easily removed, but it's the free movement of electrons that actually conducts the electricity.

8. B

This block represents the alkaline earth metals, which form divalent cations, or ions with a +2 charge. All of the elements in Group IIA have two electrons in their outermost *s*-orbital. Because loss of these two electrons would then leave a full octet as the outermost shell, becoming a divalent cation is a stable configuration for all of the alkaline earth metals. Although some of these elements might be great conductors, it's an exaggeration to say that they are the best ones on the periodic table, so (A) is incorrect. (C) is also incorrect because although forming a divalent cation is a stable configuration for the alkaline earths, the second ionization energy is still always higher than the first due to the increased positive nuclear charge when compared with the outer negative charge from the electrons. Finally, (D) is incorrect because atomic radii increase when moving down a group of elements because the number of electron shells increases.

9. B

Iron, Fe^{2+}, is a transition metal. Transition metals can often form more than one ion. Iron, for example, can be Fe^{2+} or Fe^{3+}. The transition metals, in these various oxidation states, can often form hydration complexes (complexes with water). Part of the significance of these complexes is that when a transition metal can form a complex, its solubility within the complex solvent will increase. The other ions given might dissolve readily in water, but because none of them are transition metals, they won't form complexes.

10. D

This question is simple if you recall that "periods" name the horizontal rows of the periodic table, while "families" refer to its columns. Within the same period, an additional valence electron is added with each step towards the right side of the table.

11. B

This question requires knowledge of the trends of electronegativity within the periodic table. Electronegativity increases as one moves from left to right across periods for the same reasons that effective nuclear force increases. Electronegativity *decreases* as one moves down the periodic table, because there are more electron shells separating the nucleus from the outermost electrons. The noble gases, however, also have extremely low electronegativities because they already have full valence shells and do not desire additional electrons. The most electronegative atom in the periodic table is fluorine. The answer choice closest to fluorine is (B), chlorine. Although iodine (D) will be fairly electronegative, its higher atomic radius and position farther down on the periodic table make it less electronegative than Cl. The remaining answer choices, Mg and Li, are elements with very low electronegativities. Because they have only two and one valence electrons, respectively, they are more likely to lose these electrons in a bond than to gain electrons; the loss of electrons would leave them with a full octet. Metals like these are often called electropositive.

12. B

Electron affinity is related to several factors, including atomic size (radius) and filling of the valence shell. As atomic radius increases, the distance between the inner protons in the nucleus and the outermost electrons increases, thereby decreasing the attractive forces between protons and electrons. Additionally, as more electron shells are added from period to period, these shells shield the outermost electrons increasingly from inner protons. As a result, increased atomic radius will lead to lower electron affinity. Because atoms are in a low-energy state when their outermost valence electron shell is filled, atoms needing only one or two electrons to complete this shell will have high electron affinities. In contrast, atoms with already full valence shells (a full octet of electrons) will have very low electron affinities, because adding an extra electron would

require a new shell. With this information, it is clear that (C) and (D) will likely have lower electron affinities than (A) and (B) because there is an extra electron shell "shielding" the nucleus from the outer electrons. Answer (A) is incorrect because its valence electron shell is already full with a complete octet, granting it extremely low electron affinity. Finally, (B) has one electron missing from its outermost shell, as does (D). This valence electron configuration is conducive to wanting to accept electrons readily—or to having a high electron affinity. (B) is the configuration of chlorine, while (D) is bromine. (B) is a better answer than (D), however, because the additional shell of electrons shielding the nucleus in (D) will decrease its electron affinity when compared with (B).

13. C

Electronegativity is the only property listed that has a consistent inverse correlation with atomic radius. Highly electronegative atoms hold bonding electrons tightly, while atoms with low electronegativity hold bonding electrons loosely. In atoms with large atomic radii, the distance between the outermost electrons used for bonding and the central positively charged nucleus is large. This increased distance means that the positively charged nucleus has little ability to attract new, bonding electrons toward it. In comparison, if the atomic radius is small, the force from the positively charged protons will have a stronger effect, because the distance through which they have to act is decreased. (A) is incorrect because atomic radius decreases when moving from left to right across periods in the periodic table. (B) is incorrect because atomic radius alone does not give enough information for one to ascertain the second ionization energy; it is also significant to consider the valence electron configuration. Additionally, all atoms have high second ionization energies. Finally, there is insufficient information supporting (D).

14. D

The effective nuclear charge refers to the strength with which the protons in the nucleus can "pull" additional electrons. This phenomenon helps to explain electron affinity, electronegativity, and ionization energy. In Cl, the nonionized chlorine atom, the nuclear charge is balanced by the surrounding electrons: 17+/17−. The chloride ion, in contrast, has a lower effective nuclear charge, because there are more electrons than protons: 17+/18−. Next, elemental potassium also has a "balanced" effective nuclear charge: 19+/19−. K^+, ionic potassium, has a higher effective nuclear charge than any of the other options do, because it has more protons than electrons: 19+/18−. Thus, the potassium ion, (D), is the correct answer.

15.   D

Ionic bonds are bonds formed through unequal sharing of electrons. These bonds typically occur because the electron affinities of the two bonded atoms differ greatly. For example, the halogens have high electron affinities because adding a single electron to their valence shells would create full outer octets. In contrast, the alkaline earth metals have very low electron affinities and are more likely to be electron donors because the loss of two electrons would leave them with full outer octets. This marked difference in electron affinity is the best explanation for the formation of ionic bonds between these two groups. (A) states the opposite and is incorrect, because the halogens have high electron affinity and the alkaline earth metals have low affinity. (B) is incorrect because equal sharing of electrons is a classic description of covalent bonding, not ionic. (C) is a true statement but is not relevant to why ionic bonds form.

16.   C

In the first period, all elements have only an s-orbital. In the second period onwards, a $2p$-orbital is present. In the third period, we find $3s$-, $3p$-, and $3d$-orbitals. Though $3d$ appears to be part of the fourth period, it still shares the same principal quantum number as $3s$ and $3p$ ($n = 3$) and is therefore still applicable.

Bonding and Chemical Interactions

The Maillard reaction is one of the more important chemical processes that occur in the process of cooking and baking. (Yes, here we go with food preparation, again. This is, in fact, relevant to your MCAT preparation.) The reaction mechanism itself is one with which you are (or will be) closely familiar from your studies of organic chemistry: a nucleophilic reaction between the amino terminus of the peptide chain of a protein and the carbonyl functionality of a sugar to form an N-substituted glycosylamine. This compound then undergoes a complex series of rearrangements and other reactions to produce a set of compounds that gives cooked food its pleasing brown color and delectable flavor. For no food preparation is this reaction more important than for meat (or meat substitute for all you vegetarians out there).

When the surface of the meat (or meat substitute) comes into contact with the hot surface of a pan or grill, the proteins and sugars on the meat exterior begin interacting through the Maillard reaction. The pan must be sufficiently hot to bring the exterior of the meat to a temperature of around 155°C (310°F), which is the optimal temperature for the reaction to occur. Of course, those willing to shell out $50 or more for a steak at a fine steakhouse are expecting perfection and good taste through and through, not just on the surface. So how does a grill master achieve the impossible: generating very high heat for the exterior but not overcooking the interior? The answer, or at least part of it, is this: drying the meat. When meat that has a lot of water on its exterior surface hits the hot pan, the first process that takes place is the boiling of the water. Boiling is a phase change from liquid to gas and occurs at a constant temperature; water's boiling point is 100°C (212°F). Because this temperature is considerably lower than that necessary for the Maillard reaction, no browning will occur and the flavor compounds so sought after will not form. Rather, the meat will essentially steam, and the end product will be a lifeless, overcooked hunk of toughened proteins unworthy of its hefty price tag. The lesson here is, if you want a tasty steak, always dry your meat!

Of course, the real lesson is the topic of discussion for this chapter: bonding and chemical interactions. We will not actually address complex chemical bonding, such as that which takes place in the Maillard reaction, in this chapter. (We cannot stress enough, however, that the nucleophilic mechanism by which many reactions, like the Maillard reaction, proceed will be tested in the MCAT's Biological Sciences section.) Rather, this chapter will address the basics of chemical bonding and interactions. Here, we will investigate the nature and behavior of covalent and ionic bonds. We will also review a system by which bonding electrons are accounted for, Lewis structures, and go over the main principles of valence shell electron pair repulsion (VSEPR) theory. Finally, we will recount the various modes of interaction between molecules, the intermolecular forces.

Bonding ★★★★☆

The atoms of most elements, except for a few noble gases, can combine to form **molecules**. The atoms in most molecules are held together by strong attractive forces called **chemical bonds**, which are formed via the interaction of the valence electrons of the combining atoms. The chemical and physical properties of the resulting compound are usually very different from those of the constituent elements. For example, elemental sodium, an alkali metal, is so reactive that it can actually produce fire when reacting with water (the reaction is highly exothermic), and elemental chlorine gas is so toxic that it was used for chemical warfare during World War I. However, when an atom of sodium and an atom of chlorine react, the produced ionic compound, sodium chloride, is safe for us to eat. You may know it better as common table salt!

Why do atoms join together to form compounds? Why do the sodium atom and the chlorine atom form sodium chloride? For many molecules, the constituent atoms have bonded according to the octet rule, which states that an atom tends to bond with other atoms until it has eight electrons in its outermost shell, thereby forming a stable electron configuration similar to that of the noble gases. However, this is not a hard and fast rule, more a "rule of thumb," and as we suggested in the first chapter, there are more elements that can be exceptions to the rule than there are elements that follow the rule without exception. These "exceptional" elements include hydrogen, which can only have two valence electrons (achieving the configuration of helium); lithium and beryllium, which bond to attain two and four valence electrons, respectively; boron, which bonds to attain six valence electrons; and all elements in period 3 and below, which can expand the valence shell to include more than eight electrons by incorporating d-subshell orbitals. For example, in certain compounds, chlorine can form seven covalent bonds, thereby holding 14 electrons in its valence shell.

A simple way to remember all the exceptions is as follows:

- Hydrogen is excused from the octet rule because it doesn't have enough "space" for eight electrons, it only has the one s-subshell (which can hold a maximum of two electrons).
- Lithium, beryllium, and boron are just lazy—they have enough room because they have both s- and p-orbitals to hold a total of eight electrons, but they'd rather not put in all the hard work to get all eight.
- All the elements in period 3 and below have extra storage space in their attics, so they can hold more than eight electrons if they want to.

Another way to remember the exceptions (and one that's even easier) is to remember the common elements that almost always abide by the octet rule: carbon, nitrogen, oxygen, fluorine, sodium, and magnesium. (We include the last two even though they lose—rather than gain—sufficient electrons to end up with a completed octet.)

We classify chemical bonds into two distinct types: ionic and covalent. In **ionic bonding**, one or more electrons from an atom with lower ionization energy, typically a metal, are transferred to an atom with greater electron affinity, typically a nonmetal, and the electrostatic force of attraction between opposite charges holds the resulting ions together. This is the nature of the bond in sodium chloride, where the positively charged sodium **cation** is electrostatically attracted to the negatively charged chloride **anion**. In **covalent bonding**, an electron pair is shared between the two atoms, typically two nonmetals, which have relatively similar values of electronegativity. The degree to which the pair of electrons is shared equally or unequally between the two atoms determines the degree of polarity in the covalent bond. If the electron pair is shared equally, the covalent bond is **nonpolar**; if the pair is shared unequally, the bond is **polar**. If both electrons being shared were contributed by only one of the two atoms, the bond is called **coordinate covalent**.

Ionic Bonds   ★★☆☆☆

Ionic bonds form between atoms that have significantly different electronegativities. The atom that loses the electron(s) becomes a cation, and the atom that gains the electron(s) becomes an anion. The resulting ionic bond is the electrostatic force of attraction between the opposite charges of the ions. There is no sharing of electrons in an ionic bond. For this electron transfer to occur, the difference in electronegativity must be greater than 1.7 on the 4.0-Pauling scale. In general, you will recognize ionic bonds forming between the alkali metals and the alkaline earth metals of Groups IA and IIA (Groups 1 and 2) and the halogens of Group VIIA (Group 17). The atoms of the active metals have one or two electrons, which they hold onto only loosely. The atoms of the halogens are strongly "interested in" gaining one more electron to complete their valence shells. These tendencies explain the formation of the ionic bond in, say, sodium chloride, which we've already discussed.

Mnemonic

The *t* in cation looks like a plus sign: ca + ion.

Ionic compounds have characteristic physical properties, which you should recognize for Test Day. Because of the strength of the electrostatic force between the ionic constituents of the compound, ionic compounds have very high melting and boiling points. The melting point of sodium chloride is greater than 800°C. Many ionic compounds dissolve readily in aqueous and other polar solvent solutions and, in the molten or aqueous state, are good conductors of electricity. In the solid state, the ionic constituents of the compound form a crystalline lattice consisting of repeating positive and negative ions in which the attractive forces between oppositely charged ions maximize, while the repulsive forces between ions of like charge minimize.

For example, if you were to analyze the atomic structure of the salt you just spread over the meat that you're going to grill up for dinner, you would see that each sodium ion is surrounded by six chloride ions and each chloride is surrounded by six sodium ions. This is a lattice formation known as 6:6 coordinated. (The optimal time to salt meat is about 30 minutes prior to cooking so that the salt has sufficient time to draw fluid to the surface by osmosis, creating a salt solution, which then gets drawn back into the muscle fiber once again. This results in well-seasoned meat through the entire thickness, not just at the surface.)

Covalent Bonds

When two or more atoms with similar electronegativities interact, the energy required to form ions through the complete transfer of one or more electrons is greater than the energy that would be released upon the formation of an ionic bond. That is to say, when two atoms of similar tendency form a compound to attract electrons in a bond, it is energetically unfavorable to form ions. So, rather than struggling to form ions, the atoms simply opt to share the electrons as a compromise, which allows them both to fill their valence shells. The binding force between the atoms is not ionic; rather, it is the attraction that each electron in the shared pair has for the two positive nuclei of the bonded atoms.

Covalent compounds contain discrete molecular units with relatively weak intermolecular interactions. Consequently, these compounds tend to have lower melting and boiling points, and because they do not break down into constituent ions, they are poor conductors of electricity in the liquid state or in aqueous solutions.

PROPERTIES OF COVALENT BONDS

The formation of one covalent bond may not be sufficient to fill the valence shell for a given atom. Thus, many atoms can form bonds with more than one other atom, and each atom can form multiple bonds between itself and another atom, with few exceptions. Two atoms sharing one, two, or three pairs of electrons are said to be joined by a single, double, or triple covalent bond, respectively. The number of shared electron pairs between two atoms is called the bond order; hence, a single bond has a bond order of one, a double bond has a bond order of two, and a triple bond has a bond order of three. Three features characterize a covalent bond: bond length, bond energy, and polarity.

Bond Length

If the arrangement of atoms in covalent bonds can be likened to two wooden spools connected by a dowel in a very sophisticated children's construction set, then the length of the dowel is analogous to the length of the bond between the atoms sharing the electron pair(s). Bond length is the average distance between the two nuclei of the atoms involved in the bond. As the number of shared electron pairs increases, the two atoms are pulled closer together, leading to a decrease in bond lengths. Thus, for a given pair of atoms, a triple bond is shorter than a double bond, which is shorter than a single bond.

Bond Energy

Bond energy is the energy required to break a bond by separating its components into their isolated, gaseous atomic states. Just as it becomes increasingly difficult to snap a tree branch of increasing thickness, the greater the number of pairs of electrons shared between the atomic nuclei, the more energy is required to "break" the bond(s) holding the atoms together. Thus, triple bonds have the greatest bond energy, and single bonds have the lowest bond energy. We will discuss bond energy and calculations involving actual bond energy values (called bond enthalpy) in Chapter 6, Thermochemistry. By convention, the greater the bond energy is, the "stronger" the bond.

Polarity

As in the case of two people who decide to share some commodity for the purpose of achieving a larger goal and who must then decide the degree to which the common commodity will be shared equally or unequally between them (that commodity might be money, land, pizza, or an apartment), atoms that come together in covalent bonds also "negotiate" the degree to which their sharing of electron pair(s) will be equal or unequal. The nature and degree of sharing between the nuclei of two atoms in a covalent bond is determined by the relative difference in their respective electronegativities, with the atom of higher electronegativity getting the larger "share" of the electron pair(s). A polar bond is a dipole, with the positive end of the dipole at the less electronegative atom and the negative end at the more electronegative atom.

Nonpolar Covalent Bond

When atoms that have identical or nearly identical electronegativities share electron pair(s), they do so with equal distribution of the electrons. This is called a **nonpolar covalent bond**, and there is no separation of charge across the bond. Of course, only bonds between atoms of the same element will have exactly the same electronegativity and, therefore, share with perfectly equal distribution the pair(s) of electrons in the covalent bond. Examples of diatomic molecules include H_2, Cl_2, O_2, and N_2. At the same time, many bonds can be said to be approximately nonpolar. For example, the electronegativity difference between carbon and hydrogen is so sufficiently small that we can usually consider the C–H bond to be effectively nonpolar.

Polar Covalent Bond

Of course nobody really likes to share anything. We only say we do because we know that's what expected of us. When nobody's looking, a child will grab a

---

Bridge

We will see a great example of covalent bonds in organic chemistry, and we can see here the inverse proportionality between bond length and strength.

	Bond Length	Bond Strength
C–C	longest	weakest
C=C	medium	medium
C≡C	shortest	strongest

few extra candies for herself, and even adults are known to fight over property lines, the last slice of pizza, or whether someone paid his fair share of the dinner tab. Atoms of elements that differ moderately in their electronegativities will share their electrons unevenly, resulting in **polar covalent bonds**. While the difference in their electronegativities (typically between 0.4 and 1.7 Pauling units) is not enough to result in the formation of an ionic bond, it is sufficient to cause a separation of charge across the bond, with the more electronegative element acquiring a greater portion of the electron pair(s) and taking on a partial negative charge, δ^-, and the less electronegative element acquiring a smaller portion of the electron pair(s) and taking on a partial positive charge, δ^+. For instance, the covalent bond in HCl is polar because the two atoms have a moderate difference in electronegativity (approximately 0.9). The chlorine atom gains a partial negative charge, and the hydrogen atom gains a partial positive charge. The difference in charge between the atoms is indicated by an arrow crossed at its tail end (giving the appearance of a "plus" sign) pointing toward the negative end, as shown in Figure 3.1.

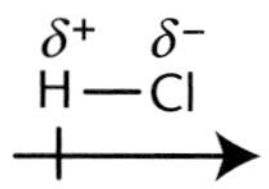

Figure 3.1

A molecule that has such a separation of positive and negative charges is called a polar molecule. The **dipole moment** of the polar bond or polar molecule is a vector quantity, μ, defined as the product of the charge magnitude (q) and the distance between the two partial charges (r):

$$\mu = qr$$

The dipole moment vector, represented by an arrow pointing from the positive to the negative charge, is measured in Debye units (coulomb-meter). Please note that the convention used by chemists for designating the direction of the dipole moment from positive to negative is the opposite of the convention used by physicists, who designate the direction of a dipole moment from negative to positive.

COORDINATE COVALENT BOND

In a coordinate covalent bond, the shared electron pair comes from the lone pair of one of the atoms in the molecule, while the other atom involved in the bond contributes nothing to the relationship. (This works great for atoms but might not be the best way to form a lasting marriage!) Once such a bond forms, however, it is indistinguishable from any other covalent bond. The distinction is only helpful for keeping track of the valence electrons and formal charges (see Figure 3.2). Coordinate covalent bonds are typically found in Lewis acid-base compounds (see Chapter 10, Acids and Bases). A Lewis acid is any compound that will accept a lone pair of electrons, while a Lewis base is any compound that will donate a pair of electrons to form a covalent bond; for example, as in the reaction between borontrifluoride (BF_3) and ammonia (NH_3) shown in Figure 3.2.

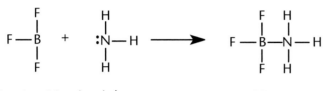

Lewis acid   Lewis base   Lewis acid-base compound

Figure 3.2

NH_3 donates a pair of electrons to form a coordinate covalent bond; thus, it acts as a Lewis base. BF_3 accepts this pair of electrons to form the coordinate covalent bond; thus, it acts as a Lewis acid. Lewis acids, incidentally, are commonly encountered in some often-tested organic chemistry reactions, such as *anti* addition across double bonds, and as catalysts in electrophilic aromatic substitutions (EAS).

COVALENT BOND NOTATION

The electrons that are involved in a covalent bond are in the valence shell and are called bonding electrons, while those electrons in the valence shell that are not involved in the covalent bond are called nonbonding electrons. The unshared electron pairs can also be called lone electron pairs, because they are associated only with one atomic nucleus. Because atoms can bond with other atoms in many different possible combinations, the **Lewis structure** system of notation has been developed to keep track of the bonded and nonbonded electron pairs. You may think of Lewis structures as a kind of bookkeeping. The number of valence electrons attributed to a particular atom in the Lewis structure of a molecule is not necessarily the same as the number of valence electrons the atom would have as an isolated atom, and the difference accounts for what is referred to as the **formal charge** of that atom in a particular Lewis structure. Often, more than one Lewis structure can be drawn for a molecule. If the possible Lewis structures differ in the way the atoms are connected (that is to say, they differ in their bond connectivity or arrangement), then the Lewis structures represent different possible compounds. If the Lewis structures show the same bond connectivity and differ only in the arrangement of the electron pairs, then these structures represent different **resonance** forms for a single compound. Lewis structures do *not* represent the actual or even theoretical geometry of a real compound. Their usefulness lies in showing you the different possible ways in which atoms may be combined to form different compounds or resonances of a single compound. When more than one arrangement can be made, you can assess the likelihood of each arrangement by checking the formal charges on the atoms in

Key Concept

When dealing with Lewis dot structures, we only deal with the eight valence electrons (*s*- and *p*-orbitals of the outer shell) on each atom. Remember that some atoms can expand their octets by utilizing the *d*-orbitals in this outer shell, but this will only take place with atoms in period 3 or greater.

each arrangement. The arrangement that minimizes the number of formal charges, or minimizes the value of formal charges, is the arrangement that most likely represents the actual compound.

Lewis Structures

A Lewis structure, or **Lewis dot symbol**, is the chemical symbol of an element surrounded by dots, each representing one of the *s* and/or *p* valence electrons of the atom. The Lewis symbols of the elements in the second period of the periodic table are shown in Table 3.1.

Table 3.1

·Li	Lithium	·N̈·	Nitrogen
·Be·	Beryllium	·Ö:	Oxygen
·Ḃ·	Boron	·F̈:	Fluorine
·C̈·	Carbon	:N̈e:	Neon

Just as a Lewis symbol is used to represent the distribution of valence electrons in an atom, it can also be used to represent the distribution of valence electrons in a molecule. For example, the Lewis symbol of a fluoride ion, F^-, is $:\ddot{F}:^-$; the Lewis structure of the diatomic molecule F_2 is . Certain steps must be followed in assigning a Lewis structure to a molecule. The steps are outlined here, using HCN as an example. (Hydrogen cyanide, an extremely poisonous compound, is found in small amounts in the pits of fruits such as cherries and apples.)

MCAT Expertise

All of the Kaplan strategies are based on methodical approaches to problems and concepts, which save you time on Test Day.

- Write the skeletal structure of the compound (i.e., the arrangement of atoms). In general, the least electronegative atom is the central atom. Hydrogen (always) and the halogens F, Cl, Br, and I (usually) occupy the end position.

  In HCN, H must occupy an end position. Of the remaining two atoms, C is the least electronegative and, therefore, occupies the central position. The skeletal structure is as follows:

  $$H–C–N$$

- Count all the valence electrons of the atoms. The number of valence electrons of the molecule is the sum of the valence electrons of all atoms present:

  H has 1 valence electron;

  C has 4 valence electrons;

  N has 5 valence electrons; therefore,

  HCN has a total of 10 valence electrons.

- Draw single bonds between the central atom and the atoms surrounding it. Place an electron pair in each bond (bonding electron pair).

$$H : C : N$$

Each bond has two electrons, so $10 - 4 = 6$ valence electrons remain.

- Complete the octets (eight valence electrons) of all atoms bonded to the central atom, using the remaining valence electrons still to be assigned. (Recall that H is an exception to the octet rule because it can have only two valence electrons.) In this example, H already has two valence electrons in its bond with C.

$$H : C : \ddot{\underset{..}{N}} :$$

- Place any extra electrons on the central atom. If the central atom has less than an octet, try to write double or triple bonds between the central and surrounding atoms using the nonbonding, unshared lone electron pairs.

The HCN structure above does not satisfy the octet rule for C because C possesses only four valence electrons. Therefore, two lone electron pairs from the N atom must be moved to form two more bonds with C, creating a triple bond between C and N. Finally, bonds are drawn as lines rather than pairs of dots.

$$H{-}C{\equiv}N :$$

Now, the octet rule is satisfied for all three atoms, because C and N have eight valence electrons and H has two valence electrons.

Formal Charge

In evaluating a Lewis structure to determine whether or not it may likely represent the actual arrangement of atoms in a compound, you will calculate the formal charge on each atom in the proposed Lewis structure. In doing so, you must be aware that you are assuming a perfectly equal sharing of all bonded electron pairs, regardless of actual differences in electronegativity, such that each electron pair is split evenly between the two atomic nuclei that share it. When you compare the number of electrons assigned to an atom in a Lewis structure (assigning one electron of each bonded pair to each of the atoms involved in the bond) to the number of electrons normally found in that atom's valence shell, the difference between the two numbers is the formal charge. A fairly simple equation you can use to calculate formal charge is

$$\text{Formal Charge} = V - N_{nonbonding} - \tfrac{1}{2}N_{bonding}$$

where V is the normal number of electrons in the atom's valence shell, $N_{nonbonding}$ is the number of nonbonding electrons, and $N_{bonding}$ is the number of bonding

MCAT Expertise

Practice with many molecules and remembering the number of bonds that common central atoms usually form will make this formula easier to use on Test Day. For example, the nitrogen atom below normally has three bonds and one lone pair. Here, it is feeling generous and sharing more than usual; therefore, it will have a positive charge. If a molecule is selfish and shares less than usual, it will be negative (as we often see with oxygen atoms).

electrons. The charge of an ion or compound is equal to the sum of the formal charges of the individual atoms comprising the ion or compound.

Example: Calculate the formal charge on the central N atom of $[NH_4]^+$.

Solution: The Lewis structure of $[NH_4]^+$ is

$$\left[\begin{array}{c} H \\ | \\ H-N-H \\ | \\ H \end{array} \right]^+$$

Nitrogen is in group VA; thus it has five valence electrons. In $[NH_4]^+$,

N has 4 bonds (i.e., eight bonding electrons and no nonbonding electrons).

So $V = 5$; $N_{bonding} = 8$; $N_{nonbonding} = 0$.

Formal charge $= 5 - \dfrac{1}{2}(8) - 0 = +1$

Thus, the formal charge on the N atom in $[NH_4]^+$ is +1.

Let us offer a brief note of explanation on the difference between formal charge and oxidation number, as we are sure that you lay awake at night pondering such questions. It's quite simple, really: Formal charge underestimates (ignores, actually) the effect of electronegativity differences, while oxidation numbers overestimate the effect of electronegativity, assuming that the more electronegative atom will in fact have a 100 percent share of the bonding electron pair. For example, in a molecule of CO_2 (carbon dioxide), the formal charge on each of the atoms would be 0, but the oxidation number of each of the oxygen atoms would be −2 and the carbon would have an oxidation number of +4. In reality, the distribution of electron density between the carbon and oxygen atoms lies somewhere between the extremes predicted by the formal charges and the oxidation states.

Resonance

As we've suggested, you may be able to draw two or more nearly identical Lewis structures that demonstrate the same arrangement between the atoms but differ in the specific placement of some pairs of electrons. These are called **resonance structures**. The actual electronic distribution in the real compound is a hybrid, or composite, of all the possible resonances. For example, SO_2 has three resonance structures, two of which are minor: O=S–O and O–S=O. The third is the major

Bridge

Resonance will be important when we discuss aromatic compounds and carboxylic acids in Organic Chemistry. It allows for great stability by spreading electrons and negative charges over a larger area.

structure: O=S=O. The nature of the bonds within the actual compound is a hybrid of these three structures; indeed, spectral data indicate that the two S–O bonds are identical and equivalent. This phenomenon is known as resonance, and the actual structure of the compound is called the **resonance hybrid**. Resonance structures are expressed with a double-headed arrow between them.

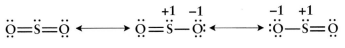

Figure 3.3

The last two resonance structures of sulfur dioxide shown in Figure 3.3 have equivalent energy or stability. Often, nonequivalent resonance structures may be written for a compound. In these cases, the more stable the structure, the more it contributes to the character of the resonance hybrid. Conversely, the less stable the resonance structure is, the less that structure contributes to the resonance hybrid. It should be apparent by now that the minor resonances for SO_2 are so because they induce a separation of charge such that the oxygen with the single bond and the extra lone-pair electron has a formal charge of -1 and the sulfur with the three bonds has a formal charge of $+1$. The major resonance structure is so because each atom has a formal charge of 0. Use formal charge to assess the stability of particular resonance structures qualitatively according to the following guidelines:

- A Lewis structure with small or no formal charges is preferred over a Lewis structure with large formal charges.
- A Lewis structure with less separation between opposite charges is preferred over a Lewis structure with a large separation of opposite charges.
- A Lewis structure in which negative formal charges are placed on more electronegative atoms is more stable than one in which the negative formal charges are placed on less electronegative atoms.

Key Concept

As noted before about atoms striving for nobility, here we see that molecules do the same. Charges that are spread over multiple atoms are more stable because they are essentially diluted.

Example: Write the resonance structures for [NCO]⁻.

Solution: 1. C is the least electronegative of the three given atoms, N, C, and O. Therefore the C atom occupies the central position in the skeletal structure of [NCO]⁻.

NCO

2. N has 5 valence electrons;
C has 4 valence electrons;
O has 6 valence electrons;
and the species itself has one negative charge.
Total valence electrons = $5 + 4 + 6 + 1 = 16$.

3. Draw single bonds between the central C atom and the surrounding atoms, N and O. Place a pair of electrons in each bond.

$$N : C : O$$

4. Complete the octets of N and O with the remaining $16 - 4 = 12$ electrons.

$$:\ddot{N} : C : \ddot{O}:$$

5. The C octet is incomplete. There are three ways in which double and triple bonds can be formed to complete the C octet: Two lone pairs from the O atom can be used to form a triple bond between the C and O atoms:

$$\overset{-2}{:\ddot{N}} - \overset{0}{C} \equiv \overset{+1}{O}:$$

Or one lone electron pair can be taken from both the O and the N atoms to form two double bonds, one between N and C, the other between O and C:

$$\overset{-1}{:\ddot{N}} = \overset{0}{C} = \overset{0}{\ddot{O}}:$$

Or two lone electron pairs can be taken from the N atom to form a triple bond between the C and N atoms:

$$\overset{0}{:N} \equiv \overset{0}{C} - \overset{-1}{\ddot{O}}:$$

These three are all resonance structures of [NCO]$^-$.

6. Assign formal charges to each atom of each resonance structure.

The most stable structure is this:

$$\overset{0}{:N} \equiv \overset{0}{C} - \overset{-1}{\ddot{O}}:$$

because the negative formal charge is on the most electronegative atom, O.

Exceptions to the Octet Rule

We have stated repeatedly throughout this and earlier chapters: The octet rule has many exceptions. In addition to hydrogen, helium, lithium, beryllium, and boron, which are exceptions because they cannot or do not reach the octet, all elements in or beyond the third period may be exceptions because they can have more than eight electrons in their valence shells. These electrons can be placed into orbitals of the d-subshell, and as a result, atoms of these elements can form more than four bonds. On Test Day, don't automatically discount a Lewis structure that shows an atom with more than four bonds—the test makers may be testing your ability to recognize the capability of many atoms to expand their valence shells beyond the octet. Always think critically about the information provided in the passage or question stem and synthesize it with the understanding that you are gaining here today and in your ongoing preparation.

Consider the sulfate ion, SO_4^{2-}. When drawing the Lewis structure of the sulfate ion, giving the sulfur 12 valence electrons permits three of the five atoms to be assigned a formal charge of zero. The sulfate ion can be drawn in six resonance forms, each with the two double bonds attached to a different combination of oxygen atoms (see Figure 3.4).

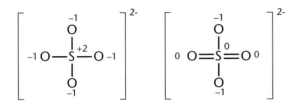

Figure 3.4

GEOMETRY AND POLARITY OF COVALENT MOLECULES

Because Lewis structures do not in any way suggest or reflect the actual geometric arrangement of atoms in a compound, we need another system that provides that information. One such system is known as **valence shell electron pair repulsion theory** (VSEPR theory). This theory is actually dependent upon Lewis structure, so they go hand in hand.

Valence Shell Electron Pair Repulsion (VSEPR) Theory

VSEPR theory uses Lewis structure to predict the molecular geometry of covalently bonded molecules. It states that the three-dimensional arrangement of atoms surrounding a central atom is determined by the repulsions between the bonding and the nonbonding electron pairs in the valence shell of the central atom. These electron pairs arrange themselves as far apart as possible, thereby minimizing the repulsive forces (see Table 3.2). The following steps are used to predict the geometrical structure of a molecule using the VSEPR theory:

- Draw the Lewis structure of the molecule.
- Count the total number of bonding and nonbonding electron pairs in the valence shell of the central atom.
- Arrange the electron pairs around the central atom so that they are as far apart from each other as possible. For example, the compound AX_2 has the Lewis structure X : A : X. The A atom has two bonding electron pairs in its valence shell. To position these electron pairs as far apart as possible, their geometric structure should be linear:

X–A–X

Table 3.2

Regions of Electron Density	Example	Geometric Arrangement of Electron Pairs Around the Central Atom	Shape	Angle between Electron Pairs
2	$BeCl_2$	X – A – X	linear	180°
3	BH_3	(trigonal arrangement)	trigonal planar	120°
4	CH_4	(tetrahedral arrangement)	tetrahedral	109.5°
5	PCl_5	(trigonal bipyramidal arrangement)	trigonal bipyramidal	90°, 120°, 180°
6	SF_6	(octahedral arrangement)	octahedral	90°, 180°

MCAT Expertise

Knowing the tetrahedral shape will be particularly useful because it is often present in carbon, nitrogen, and oxygen.

Example: Predict the geometry of NH_3.

Solution: 1. The Lewis structure of NH_3 is

2. The central atom, N, has three bonding electron pairs and one nonbonding electron pair, for a total of four electron pairs.
3. The four electron pairs will be farthest apart when they occupy the corners of a tetrahedron. As one of the four electron pairs is a lone pair, the observed geometry is trigonal pyramidal, shown in Figure 3.5.

Figure 3.5

In describing the shape of a molecule, only the arrangement of atoms (not electrons) is considered. Even though the electron pairs are arranged tetrahedrally, the shape of NH_3 is pyramidal. It is not trigonal planar because the lone pair repels the three bonding electron pairs, causing them to move as far away as possible.

Example: Predict the geometry of CO_2.

Solution: The Lewis structure of CO_2 is $\ddot{O}::C::\ddot{O}$.

The double bond behaves just like a single bond for purposes of predicting molecular shape. This compound has two groups of electrons around the carbon. According to the VSEPR theory, the two sets of electrons will orient themselves 180° apart, on opposite sides of the carbon atom, minimizing electron repulsion. Therefore, the molecular structure of CO_2 is linear: $\ddot{O}=C=\ddot{O}$.

One subtlety that students sometimes miss is the difference between electronic geometry and molecular geometry. Electronic geometry describes the spatial arrangement of all pairs of electrons around the central atom, including the bonding and the lone pairs. Molecular geometry describes the spatial arrangement of only the bonding pairs of electrons, in much the same way that the geometry of an object made from our sophisticated construction set would be determined by the position of the wooden spools attached to the dowels. For example, consider the fact that CH_4 (methane), NH_3 (ammonia), and H_2O all have the same electronic geometry: In each compound, four pairs of electrons surround the central atom. This is tetrahedral electronic geometry. However, because each has a different number of lone pairs, each has a different molecular geometry. Methane has tetrahedral geometry, ammonia has trigonal pyramidal, and water has angular or bent geometry. The distinction is important, and the MCAT will primarily focus on molecular geometry, but there is one important implication of electronic geometry: the determination of the ideal bond angle. Tetrahedral electronic geometry,

Key Concept

The shapes from Table 3.2 refer to *electronic geometry,* which is different from *molecular geometry*. In Figure 3.5, we see an ammonia molecule that has a tetrahedral *electronic* structure but is considered to have a *molecular* structure that is trigonal pyramidal.

for example, is associated with an ideal bond angle of 109.5°. Thus, molecular geometries that deviate from tetrahedral electronic geometry, such as those of ammonia and water, have bond angles that are deviations from 109.5°. You may have been tempted to say, for example, that water's bond angle is a deviation from linear geometry with its ideal bond angle of 180°, but this is not the case. The actual bond angle in water is around 104.5°, a deviation from 109.5°.

Polarity of Molecules

When two atoms of different electronegativities bond covalently by sharing one or more pairs of electrons, the resulting bond is polar, with the more electronegative atom possessing the greater share of the electron density. However, the mere presence of bond dipoles does not necessarily result in a molecular dipole; that is, an overall separation of charge across the molecule. We must first consider the molecular geometry and the vector addition of the bond dipoles based upon that molecular geometry. A compound with nonpolar bonds is always nonpolar; a compound with polar bonds may be polar or nonpolar, depending upon the spatial orientation of the polar bonds within the given molecular geometry.

A compound composed of two atoms bound by a polar bond must have a net dipole moment and is therefore polar. The two equal and opposite partial charges are localized on the two atoms at the ends of the compound. HCl (hydrogen chloride) is a good example of this, because the bond between the hydrogen and chlorine atom is polar (with the hydrogen atom assuming a partial positive charge and the chlorine atom assuming a partial negative charge); the compound must also be polar, with a molecular dipole moment in the same direction and same magnitude as the bond dipole moment. A compound consisting of more than two atoms bound with polar bonds may be either polar or nonpolar, because the overall dipole moment of a molecule is the vector sum of the individual bond dipole moments. If the compound has a particular molecular geometry such that the bond dipole moments cancel each other (i.e., if the vector sum is zero), then the result is a nonpolar compound. For instance, CCl_4 has four polar C–Cl bonds, but because the molecular geometry of carbon tetrachloride is tetrahedral, the four bond dipoles point to the vertices of the tetrahedron and, therefore, cancel each other out, resulting in a nonpolar compound (see Figure 3.6).

MCAT Expertise

Back to that tug-of-war from earlier, sometimes we can see the winner before the final flag. A polar covalent bond will have one atom that carries more electron density than the other does (and therefore a partial negative charge) but hasn't won the match yet.

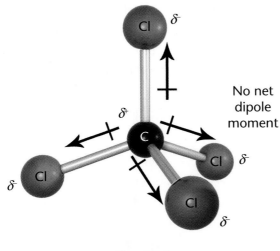

Figure 3.6

However, when the molecular geometry is such that the bond dipoles do not cancel each other, the molecule will have a net dipole moment and, therefore, will be polar. For instance, the O–H bonds in H_2O are polar, with each hydrogen molecule assuming a partial positive charge and the oxygen assuming a partial negative charge. Because water's molecular geometry is angular (bent), the vector summation of the bond dipoles results in a molecular dipole moment from the partially positive hydrogen end to the partially negative oxygen end, as illustrated in Figure 3.7.

Key Concept

A molecule with polar bonds need not be polar: The bond dipole moments may cancel each other out, resulting in a nonpolar molecule. Although a molecule with polar bonds need not be polar overall, a polar molecule must have polar bonds.

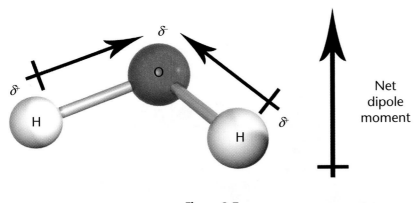

Figure 3.7

ATOMIC AND MOLECULAR ORBITALS

To finish our discussion of covalent bonds, we need to address the issue of atomic and molecular orbitals. If you remember back to the first chapter, we described the modern understanding of the atom as a dense, positively charged nucleus surrounded by clouds of electrons organized into orbitals (regions in space surrounding the nucleus within which there are certain probabilities of finding an electron). The four quantum numbers completely describe the energy and position of any electron of an atom. While the principal quantum number indicates the average energy level of the orbitals, the azimuthal quantum number, *l*, describes the subshells within each principal energy level, *n*. When $l = 0$, this indicates the *s*-subshell, which has one orbital that is spherical in shape. The 1*s*-orbital $(n = 1, l = 0)$ is plotted in Figure 3.8.

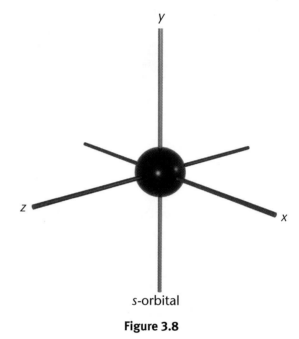

s-orbital

Figure 3.8

When $l = 1$, this indicates the *p*-subshell, which has three orbitals shaped like barbells along the *x, y,* and *z* axes at right angles to each other. The *p*-orbitals are plotted in Figure 3.9.

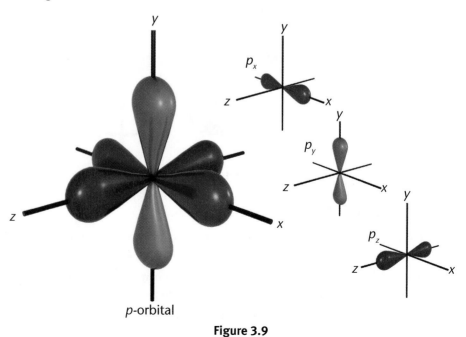

p-orbital

Figure 3.9

Although well beyond the scope of the MCAT, mathematical analyses of the wave function of the orbitals are used to determine and assign plus and minus signs to each lobe of the p-orbitals. The shapes of the five d-orbitals and the seven f-orbitals are more complex and need not be memorized for the MCAT. When two atoms bond to form a compound, the atomic orbitals interact to form a molecular orbital that describes the probability of finding the bonding electrons. Molecular orbitals are obtained by combining the wave functions of the atomic orbitals. Qualitatively, the overlap of two atomic orbitals describes this. If the signs of the two atomic orbitals are the same, a bonding orbital forms. If the signs are different, an antibonding orbital forms.

Two different patterns of overlap are observed in the formation of molecular bonds. When orbitals overlap head-to-head, the resulting bond is called a sigma (σ) bond. Sigma bonds allow for relatively free rotation, because the electron density of the bonding orbital is a single linear accumulation between the atomic nuclei. When the orbitals overlap in such a way that there are two parallel electron cloud densities, a pi (π) bond is formed. Pi bonds do not allow for free rotation because the electron densities of the orbital are parallel. To picture this difference, imagine pushing your fists together and rotating them as they touch—this is a sigma bond. Now imagine putting your arms out in front of you, holding them parallel to each other with your elbows bent at about right angles while another person slips two rubber bands around your forearms, one near the elbows and the second closer to the wrists. With the rubber bands on, try bringing one forearm up toward you while you extend your other forearm out away from you. The parallel tension provided by the rubber bands makes it quite difficult to rotate your forearms in opposite directions. This is a pi bond.

The Intermolecular Forces ★★★★★☆

Like guests at a cocktail party who mingle but ultimately have little to say to each other, atoms and compounds participate in weak electrostatic interactions. The strength of these intermolecular interactions can impact certain physical properties of the compounds, such as melting and boiling point. The weakest of the intermolecular interactions are the dispersion forces, also known as London forces. Next, are the dipole–dipole interactions, which are of intermediate strength. Finally, we have the strongest type of interaction, the hydrogen bond, which is a misnomer because there is no sharing or transfer of electrons, and consequently, it is not a true bond. We must keep in mind, however, that even hydrogen bonds, the strongest of these interactions, have only about 10 percent the strength of a covalent bond, so these electrostatic interactions can be overcome with additions of small or moderate amounts of energy.

Bridge

The pi bonds of alkenes, alkynes, aromatic compounds, and carboxylic acid derivates are what lend the ever-important functionalities in organic chemistry.

Bridge

These intermolecular forces are the binding forces that keep a substance together in its solid or liquid state (see Chapter 8). These same forces determine whether two substances are miscible or immiscible in the solution phase (see Chapter 9).

LONDON FORCES

The bonding electrons in nonpolar covalent bonds may appear, on paper, to be shared equally between two atoms, but at any point in time, they will be located randomly throughout the orbital. For these instantaneous moments, then, the electron density may be unequally distributed between the two atoms. This results in rapid polarization and counterpolarization of the electron cloud and the formation of short-lived dipole moments. These dipoles interact with the electron clouds of neighboring compounds, inducing the formation of more dipoles. The momentarily negative end of one molecule will cause the closest region in any neighboring molecule to become temporarily positive itself, thus causing the other end of this neighboring molecule to become temporarily negative, which in turn induces other molecules to become temporarily polarized, and the entire process begins all over again. The attractive interactions of these short-lived and rapidly shifting dipoles are called **dispersion forces** or **London forces**.

Dispersion forces are the weakest of all the intermolecular interactions because they are the result of induced dipoles that change and shift moment by moment. They do not extend over long distances and are, therefore, significant only when molecules are close together. The strength of the London force also depends on the degree to which and the ease by which the molecules can be polarized (that is to say, how easily the electrons can be shifted around). Large molecules in which the electrons are far from the nucleus are relatively easy to polarize and, thus, possess greater dispersion forces. Think about two plates—a big dinner plate and a small teacup saucer—with nearly equal numbers of marbles on each. The marbles will roll around more, and may be distributed more unequally, on the bigger plate than on the smaller saucer. Nevertheless, don't underestimate the importance of the dispersion forces. If it weren't for them, the noble gases would not liquefy at any temperature because no other intermolecular forces exist between the noble gas atoms. The low temperatures at which the noble gases liquefy is to some extent indicative of the magnitude of the dispersion forces between the atoms.

DIPOLE–DIPOLE INTERACTIONS

Polar molecules tend to orient themselves in such a way that the opposite ends of the respective molecular dipoles are closest to each other: The positive region of one molecule is close to the negative region of another molecule. This arrangement is energetically favorable because an attractive electrostatic force is formed between the two molecules.

Dipole–dipole interactions are present in the solid and liquid phases but become negligible in the gas phase because of the significantly increased distance between gas particles. Polar species tend to have higher melting and boiling points than

Real World

While London forces (a type of van der Waals force) are the weakest of the intermolecular attractions, when there are millions of these interactions, as there are on the bottom of a gecko's foot, there is an amazing power of adhesion, which is demonstrated by the animal's ability to climb smooth vertical, even inverted, surfaces.

those of nonpolar species of comparable molecular weight. You should realize that London forces and dipole–dipole interactions are different not in kind but in degree. Both are electrostatic forces between opposite partial charges; the difference is only in the strength and in the permanence of the molecular dipole.

HYDROGEN BONDS

Hydrogen bonds are a favorite of the MCAT! So understand them well, and you will be able to answer every question pertaining to their nature, behavior, and effects. A hydrogen bond is actually only a specific, unusually strong form of dipole–dipole interaction, which may be intra- or intermolecular. Please understand that hydrogen bonds are not actually bonds—there is no sharing or transfer of electrons between two atoms. When hydrogen is bound to a highly electronegative atom, such as fluorine, oxygen, or nitrogen, the hydrogen atom carries little of the electron density of the covalent bond. The hydrogen atom acts essentially as a naked proton (it is a *little* scandalous!). The positively charged hydrogen atom interacts with the partial negative charge of oxygen, nitrogen, or fluorine on nearby molecules. Substances that display hydrogen bonding tend to have unusually high boiling points compared with compounds of similar molecular formula that do not hydrogen bond. The difference derives from the energy required to break the hydrogen bonds. A very good example of this difference, which you absolutely need to understand for the MCAT, is the difference between a carboxylic acid, which can form hydrogen bonds between molecules of itself, and the acyl halide, a derivative of the carboxylic acid, which has substituted a halogen for the hydroxyl group and which cannot form hydrogen bonds with molecules of itself. The boiling point of propanoic acid (MW = 74 g/mol) is 141°C, but the boiling point of propanoyl chloride (MW = 92.5 g/mol) is 80°C. Hydrogen bonding is particularly important in the behavior of water, alcohols, amines, and carboxylic acids. It is no overstatement to say that if it weren't for water's ability to form hydrogen bonds and exist in the liquid state at room temperature, we would not exist (at least not in the form we recognize as "human").

Conclusion

This chapter built upon our knowledge of the atom and the trends demonstrated by the elements in the periodic table to understand the different ways by which atoms partner together to form compounds, either (a) exchanging electrons to form ions, which are then held together by the electrostatic force of attraction that exists between opposite charges, or (b) sharing electrons to form covalent bonds. We discussed the nature and characteristics of covalent bonds, noting their relative lengths and energies as well as polarities. The review of Lewis structures and VSEPR theory will prepare you for predicting likely bond arrangements, resonance structures, and molecular geometry. Finally, we compared the relative strengths of the most important intermolecular electrostatic interactions, noting that even the strongest of these, the hydrogen bond, is still much weaker than an actual covalent bond. The next time you're searing meat in a skillet or browning toast in a toaster, take a moment to consider what's actually going on at the atomic and molecular level. It's not just cooking; it's science!

CONCEPTS TO REMEMBER

☐ Atoms come together to form compounds through bonds. Many atoms interact with other atoms in order to achieve the octet electron configuration in their valence shell. There are two types of bonds: ionic and covalent.

☐ Ionic bonds form when a very electronegative atom gains one or more electrons from a much less electronegative atom; the strong electrostatic force of attraction between opposite charges holds the resulting anion and cation together. Covalent bonds form when two atoms share one or more pairs of electrons. The force of the bond is due to the electrostatic attraction between the electrons in the bond and each of the positively charged nuclei of the bonding atoms.

☐ Covalent bonds are characterized by their length, energy, and polarity. A single covalent bond exists when two atoms share one pair of electrons, a double bond exists when two atoms share two pairs of electrons, and a triple bond exists when two atoms share three pairs of electrons. Triple bonds are the shortest and have the highest bond energy. Single bonds are the longest and have the lowest bond energy.

☐ Although all covalent bonds involve a sharing of one or more electron pairs, the electron density of the bonding electrons may not be distributed equally between the bonding atoms. This gives rise to a polar bond, with the more electronegative atom receiving the larger share of the bonding electron density.

☐ Lewis structures are bookkeeping devices used to keep track of the valence electrons of atoms and their various possible arrangements in a compound. Evaluation of formal charge on each atom in the arrangement can help determine which arrangement is most likely to be representative of the actual bond connectivity. Lewis structures that demonstrate the same atomic arrangement but differ in the distribution of electron pairs are called resonance structures. The actual molecular positioning of electrons is a "weighted" hybrid of all the possible resonance structures called a resonance hybrid.

☐ VSEPR theory helps us predict the actual three-dimensional arrangement of bonded and nonbonded electron pairs around the central atom in a compound. The theory states that nonbonded electrons (lone pairs) exert strong electrostatic repulsive forces against the bonded pairs of electrons and, as a result, the electron pairs arrange themselves as far apart as possible in order to minimize the repulsive forces.

☐ A molecular dipole is the resultant of all the bond dipole vectors in the molecule. A compound consisting of only nonpolar bonds will by definition be nonpolar. A compound consisting of one polar bond will by definition be polar (although perhaps insignificantly). A compound consisting of two or more polar bonds may be polar or nonpolar, depending on the molecular geometry and the vector addition of the bond dipoles.

☐ Atomic orbitals overlap their + and − lobes to result in bonding or antibonding molecular orbitals. When the signs of the overlapping atomic orbitals are the same, the result is a bonding molecular orbital. When the signs are opposite, the result is an antibonding orbital.

☐ Sigma bonds involve head-to-head (or end-to-end) overlap of electron cloud density and thus allow for relatively low-energy rotation. Pi bonds involve parallel overlap of electron cloud density and thus do not allow for low-energy rotation.

☐ The intermolecular interactions are electrostatic interactions that weakly hold molecules together. They generally are significant only over short distances and in the solid or liquid state. The weakest intermolecular interaction is the dispersion force (London force), which results from the moment-by-moment changing unequal distribution of the electron cloud density across molecules. A more moderate-strength intermolecular interaction is the dipole–dipole interaction, which exists between the opposite ends of permanent molecular dipoles. The strongest of these intermolecular interactions is the hydrogen bond, which is a special case of the dipole–dipole interaction between the hydrogen atom attached to either oxygen, nitrogen, or fluorine and another oxygen, nitrogen, or fluorine on another molecule—or sometimes, if the molecule is large enough, even the same molecule. One of the most important occurrences of hydrogen bonding is that between water molecules.

EQUATIONS TO REMEMBER

☐ $\mu = qr$

☐ Formal charge $= V - N_{nonbonding} - \frac{1}{2}N_{bonding}$

Practice Questions

1. What is the character of the bond in carbon monoxide?

   A. Ionic
   B. Polar covalent
   C. Nonpolar covalent
   D. Coordinate covalent

2. Which of the following molecules has the oxygen atom with the most negative formal charge?

   A. H_2O
   B. CO_3^{2-}
   C. O_3
   D. CH_2O

3. Which of the following structure(s) contribute most to NO_2's resonance hybrid?

I.

$$-\overset{\cdot\cdot}{\underset{\cdot\cdot}{O}} - \overset{\cdot}{\overset{+}{N}} = \overset{\cdot\cdot}{O}$$

II.

$$\overset{\cdot\cdot}{\underset{\cdot\cdot}{O}} = \overset{\cdot}{\overset{+}{N}} - \overset{\cdot\cdot}{\underset{\cdot\cdot}{O}}{:}^-$$

III.

$$-\overset{\cdot\cdot}{\underset{\cdot\cdot}{O}} - \overset{\cdot\cdot}{\overset{2+}{N}} - \overset{\cdot\cdot}{\underset{\cdot\cdot}{O}}{:}^-$$

   A. I only
   B. III only
   C. I and II
   D. I, II, and III

4. Order the following compounds shown from lowest to highest boiling point:

   I.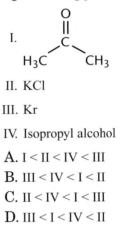

   II. KCl

   III. Kr

   IV. Isopropyl alcohol

   A. I < II < IV < III
   B. III < IV < I < II
   C. II < IV < I < III
   D. III < I < IV < II

5. Both CO_3^{2-} and ClF_3 have three atoms bonded to a central atom. What is the best explanation for why CO_3 has trigonal planar geometry, while ClF_3 is trigonal bipyramidal?

   A. CO_3 has multiple resonance structures, while ClF_3 does not.
   B. CO_3 has a charge of –2, while ClF_3 has no charge.
   C. ClF_3 has lone pairs on its central atom, while CO_3 has none.
   D. CO_3 has lone pairs on its central atom, while ClF_3 has none.

6. Which of the following has the largest dipole moment?

   A. HCN
   B. H_2O
   C. CCl_4
   D. SO_2

7. Despite the fact that both C_2H_2 and NCH contain triple bonds, the lengths of these triple bonds are not equal. Which of the following is the best explanation for this finding?

   A. In C_2H_2, since the triple bond is between similar atoms, it is shorter in length.
   B. The two molecules have different resonance structures.
   C. Carbon is more electronegative than hydrogen.
   D. Nitrogen is more electronegative than carbon.

8. Which of the following is the best explanation of the phenomenon of hydrogen bonding?

   A. Hydrogen has a strong affinity for holding onto valence electrons.
   B. Hydrogen can only hold two valence electrons.
   C. Electronegative atoms disproportionately carry shared pairs when bonded to hydrogen.
   D. Hydrogen bonds have ionic character.

9. Which of the following best describes the character of the bonds in a molecule of ammonium?

   A. Three polar covalent bonds
   B. Four polar covalent bonds
   C. Two polar covalent bonds, two coordinate covalent bonds
   D. Three polar covalent bonds, one coordinate covalent bond

10. Although the octet rule dictates much of molecular structure, some atoms can exceed the octet rule and be surrounded by more than eight electrons. Which of the following is the best explanation for why some atoms can exceed the octet rule?

    A. Atoms that exceed the octet rule already have eight electrons in their outermost electron shell.
    B. Atoms that exceed the octet rule only do so when bonding with transition metals.
    C. Atoms that exceed the octet rule can do so because they have d-orbitals in which extra electrons can reside.
    D. Some atoms can exceed the octet rule because they are highly electronegative.

11. Which of the following types of intermolecular forces is the most accurate explanation for why noble gases can liquefy?

    A. Van der Waals forces
    B. Ion-dipole interactions
    C. Dispersion forces
    D. Dipole-dipole interactions

12. What is correct electron configuration for elemental chromium?

    A. [Ar] $3p^6$
    B. [Ar] $3d^5 4s^1$
    C. [Ar] $3d^6$
    D. [Ar] $3d^4 4s^2$

13. In the structure shown, which atom(s) has/have the most positive charge?

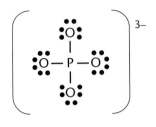

A. The phosphorus atom has the most positive charge.
B. All atoms share the charge equally.
C. The four oxygens share the highest charge.
D. The oxygen at the peak of the trigonal pyramidal geometry has the most positive charge.

14. Which of the following is the best name for the new bond formed in the reaction shown?

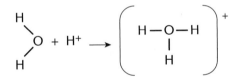

A. Polar covalent bond
B. Ionic bond
C. Coordinate covalent bond
D. Hydrogen bond

15. Both BF_3 and NH_3 have three atoms bonded to the central atom. Which of the following is the best explanation of why the geometry of these two molecules is different?

A. BF_3 has three bonded atoms and no lone pairs, which makes its geometry trigonal pyramidal.
B. NH_3 is sp^3 hybridized, while BF_3 is sp^2 hybridized.
C. NH_3 has one lone pair.
D. BF_3 is nonpolar, while NH_3 is polar.

16. Which of the following is a proper Lewis structure for $BeCl_2$?

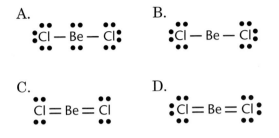

17. Which of the following best describes an important property of bond energy?

A. Bond energy increases with increasing bond length.
B. The more shared electron pairs comprising a bond, the higher the energy of that bond.
C. Single bonds are more difficult to break than double bonds.
D. Bond energy and bond length are unrelated.

18. Which of the following is true about the polarity of molecules?

A. Polarity is dependent on the vector sum of dipole moments.
B. Polarity does not depend upon molecular geometry.
C. If a molecule is comprised of one or more polar bonds, the molecule is polar.
D. If a molecule is comprised of one or more nonpolar bonds, the molecule is nonpolar.

Small Group Questions

1. Why does bond length decrease with increasing bond strength?

2. Predict two elements whose hydrides (H^-) would contain incomplete octets.

Explanations to Practice Questions

1. B

Carbon monoxide, CO, has a double bond between carbon and oxygen, with the carbon retaining one lone pair and oxygen retaining two lone pairs. In polar covalent bonds, the difference in electronegativity between the bonded atoms is great enough to cause electrons to move disproportionately toward the more electronegative atom but not great enough to transfer electrons completely (i.e., to form an ionic bond). This is the case for CO. Oxygen is more electro-negative than carbon, so electrons will be disproportionately carried on the oxygen, leaving the carbon atom with a slight positive charge. Nonpolar covalent bonds occur between atoms that have the same electronegativity, for example, the carbon–carbon bond in $CH_3–CH_3$. Coordinate covalent bonding occurs through donation of a lone pair from a Lewis base to a Lewis acid.

2. B

To answer this question, you must understand the contribution of resonance structures to average formal charge. In CO_3^{2-}, there are three possible resonance structures. Each of the three oxygen atoms carries a formal charge of -1 in two out of the three structures. This averages to approximately $-\frac{2}{3}$ charge on each oxygen atom, which is more than the other answer choices. To prove this, estimate the formal charges on each oxygen atom in the other answer choices. There are no formal charges in H_2O, which has no resonance structures. In ozone, O_3, there are two possible resonance structures. The central oxygen carries a positive charge in both structures, and each outer oxygen carries a negative charge in one of the two possible resonance structures. This leaves an average charge of $-\frac{1}{2}$ on the two outer oxygens, which is less than the $-\frac{2}{3}$ in CO_3^{2-}. Finally, CH_2O has no resonance structures and, therefore, no formal charge on oxygen.

3. C

The two greatest contributors are structures I and II. Resonance structures are representations of how charges are shared across a molecule. In reality, the charge distribution is a weighted average of contributing resonance structures. The most stable resonance structures are those that minimize charge on the atoms in the molecule; the more stable the structure, the more that it will contribute to the overall charge distribution in the molecule. Structure I has a -1 charge on one oxygen and a single positive charge on the central nitrogen atom. Structure II has the exact same distribution, except the negative charge is on the other oxygen. It is equally as stable as structure I, so they both contribute equally to the hybrid. Structure III involves two negative charges (one on each oxygen) and a $+2$ charge on the central nitrogen. With so many charges, it's less stable than structures I and II and, thus, is not an important resonance structure for NO_2.

4. D

The key to answering this question is to understand the types of intermolecular forces that exist in each of these molecules. Kr (III) is a noble gas with a full octet, so the only intermolecular forces present are dispersion forces (also called London forces), the weakest type of intermolecular forces. This means that these molecules are held together extremely loosely and will be the easiest to transition from the organized liquid phase to the disorganized gaseous phase. In fact, because Kr is a noble *gas*, assume that it's usually in the gaseous state and therefore has a low boiling point. Next, decide between two polar molecules: acetone (I) and isopropyl alcohol (IV). Both have the benefit of dipole–dipole forces, which are stronger than dispersion forces. Dipole–dipole forces arrange polar molecules such that the positive ends associate with their neighbors' negative ends, which keeps these molecules in close proximity to one another. So which boils at a higher temperature? Alcohols are known for their ability to hydrogen bond, which significantly raises boiling point. Hydrogen bonding occurs when an electronegative atom (fluorine, oxygen, or nitrogen) binds to hydrogen, stripping it of electron density and leaving it with a partial positive charge. That partial positive charge can then associate with nearby partial negative charges. These forces are even stronger than dipole–dipole interactions, so isopropyl alcohol will boil at a higher temperature than acetone. Finally, the strongest interactions are ionic, and these exist in compounds such as potassium chloride (II).

5.   C

The central atom in CO_3, carbon, has no lone pairs. It has three resonance structures, each of which involves a double bond between carbon and one of the three oxygens. Having made four bonds, carbon has no further orbitals for bonding or to carry lone pairs. This makes CO_3's geometry trigonal planar. Alternatively, ClF_3 also has three bonds, one to each of three fluoride atoms. However, chloride still maintains two extra lone pairs (without which the formal charge on the central chloride atom is +4; with the two lone pairs it is zero, a more stable configuration). These lone pairs each inhabit one orbital, meaning that the central chloride must organize five items about itself: three bonds to fluorides and two lone pairs. The best configuration for maximizing the distance between all of these groups is trigonal bipyramidal. (A) is true but does not account for the difference in geometry. Similarly, although (B) is true, the charge does not explain a difference in geometry. (D) is incorrect; CO_3 has no lone pairs on its central atom, while ClF_3 has two lone pairs.

6.   A

The best way to approach this problem is to draw the structure of each of these molecules, then consider the electronegativity of each bond as it might contribute to an overall dipole moment. HCN is the correct answer because of large differences in electronegativity, aligned in a linear fashion. There is a strong dipole moment in the direction of nitrogen, without any other moments canceling it out. H_2O has two dipole moments, one from each hydrogen pointing

in the direction of oxygen. The molecule is bent, and the dipole moments partially cancel out. There *is* a molecular dipole, but it is not as strong as HCN's. Sulfur dioxide has a similar bent configuration, so its dipole will be smaller than that of HCN. Another consideration for sulfur dioxide is that oxygen and sulfur do not have a large difference in electronegativity, so even the individual bond dipoles are smaller than those we have seen so far. CCl_4 has a tetrahedral geometry. Although each of the individual C–Cl bonds is highly polar, the orientation of these bonds causes the dipoles to cancel each other out fully, yielding no overall dipole moment.

7.   D

Bond lengths decrease as the bond order increases, and they also decrease in a trend moving up the periodic table's columns or to the right across to the periodic table's rows. In this case, because both C_2H_2 and NCH have triple bonds, we cannot compare the bond lengths based upon bond order. We must then rely on other periodic trends. The bond length decreases when moving to the right along the periodic table's rows because more electronegative atoms have shorter atomic radii. The nitrogen in NCH is likely to hold its electrons closer, or in a shorter radius, than the carbon in C_2H_2. (B) is incorrect because there are no significant resonance structures contributing to the character of either triple bond. (C) expresses a true statement but one that is irrelevant to the length of the carbon–carbon triple bond.

8.   C

(C) correctly describes the underlying forces of hydrogen bonding. Electronegative atoms bound to hydrogen disproportionately pull covalently bonded electrons toward themselves, which leaves hydrogen with a partial positive character. That partial positive charge is attracted to nearby negative or partial-negative charges, such as those on other electronegative atoms. (A) is not true; hydrogen has little electronegativity and does not hold its valence electrons closely. (B) is a true statement but not descriptive enough to explain hydrogen bonding. (D) is not correct; although these bonds are highly polarized, they are not ionic.

9. D

First recall that ammonium is NH_4^+, while ammonia (commonly confused) is NH_3. It helps to associate the suffix *-ium* with a charged form of the molecule. Once you remember that ammonium is NH_4^+, eliminate any answer choice that only accounts for three bonds [answer choice (A)]v. Next, it helps to recall that ammonium is formed by the association of NH_3 (uncharged, with a lone pair on the nitrogen) with a positively charge hydrogen cation (no lone pairs). In other words, NH_3 is a Lewis base, while H^+ is a Lewis acid. This type of bonding, between Lewis acid and base, is a coordinate covalent bond. Thus, you know that there is one coordinate covalent bond in this molecule, making (D) the correct answer.

10. C

This question addresses the issue of when the octet rule can be violated. All atoms that are in the third or higher period have *d*-orbitals, each of which can hold 10 electrons. The typical eight "octet" electrons reside in *s*- and *p*-orbitals. (A) and (B) do not explain why more than eight electrons can be held. Electronegativity is irrelevant to whether or not an atom can exceed the octet rule, making (D) incorrect.

11. C

All of the listed types of forces dictate interactions among different types of molecules. However, noble gases are entirely uncharged and do not have polar covalent bonds, ionic bonds, or dipole moments. Recognize that the only types of forces listed that could relate to noble gases could be van der Waals forces (A) or dispersion forces (C). Of these two, *van der Waals forces* is an umbrella term that includes both dispersion and dipole–dipole interactions (which you've already eliminated). Because not all van der Waals forces apply, rule that out as the correct answer and stick with dispersion forces. Dispersion forces are a specific type of interaction that occurs among all bonded atoms due to the unequal sharing of electrons at any given moment in the electron's orbit. This unequal sharing allows for instantaneous partial positive and partial negative charges within the molecule. Though these interactions are small, they are necessary for liquefaction.

12. B

The key to this question is understanding the pattern of filling for *s*- and *d*-orbitals among the transition metals. There are 24 electrons in chromium, 6 more than are present in argon. Where will these six electrons lie? It is advantageous for *d*-orbitals to be half filled. Therefore, one electron will fill each of the five 3*d*-orbitals. It will take less energy to put the sixth electron into an *s*-orbital than it would to add it to one of the *d*-orbitals that already has an electron (and force it to be no longer half filled).

13. A

In this Lewis diagram, the PO_4^{3-} molecule has an overall formal charge of -3. The four oxygens each would be assigned a formal change of -1, based on the following formula: Formal charge = V (valence electrons in the free atom) $-\frac{1}{2} N_{bonding}$ (electrons shared in bonds) $-N_{nonbonding}$ (lone pairs/free electrons). For each oxygen, we calculate: FC = $6 - \frac{1}{2}(2) - 6 = -1$. For the central phosphorus, assume then that with a total formal charge of -3 and four oxygens with a change of -1 each, the phosphorus must have a formal charge of $+1$. Alternatively, calculate its formal charge as FC = $5 - \frac{1}{2}(8) - 0 = +1$. Considering this molecule's other resonance structures, you'd come to the same conclusion— that phosphorus is the most positive atom.

14. C

The reaction in this question shows a water molecule, which has two lone pairs of electrons on the central oxygen, combining with a free hydrogen ion. The resulting molecule, H_3O^+, has formed a new bond between H^+ and H_2O. This bond is created through the sharing one of oxygen's lone pairs with the free H^+ ion. This is essentially a donation of a shared pair of electrons from a Lewis base (H_2O) to a Lewis acid (H^+, electron acceptor). The charge in the resulting molecule is $+1$, and it is mostly present on the central oxygen, which now only has one lone pair. This type of bond, formed from a Lewis acid and Lewis base, is called a coordinate covalent bond.

15. B

NH_3 has three hydrogen atoms bonded to the central nitrogen and one lone pair on the central nitrogen. These four groups—three atoms, one lone pair—lead NH_3 to be sp^3 hybridized. By hybridizing all three *p*-orbitals and the one *s*-orbital, four groups are arranged about the central atom, maximizing the distances between the groups to minimize the energy of the configuration. NH_3's hybridization leads to its tetrahedral electronic geometry yet trigonal pyramidal molecular geometry. In contrast, BF_3 has three atoms but no lone pairs, resulting in sp^2 hybridization. Its shape is called trigonal planar. (A) is incorrect; although BF_3 does has three bonded atoms and no lone pairs, its geometry is not trigonal pyramidal. (C) is tempting because NH_3 has a lone pair, but this answer choice is not complete enough to explain the differences in molecular geometry. Finally, although (D) is also true, the polarity of the molecules does not explain their geometry; rather, the molecules' different geometries contribute to the overall polarity of the molecules.

16. B

Most atoms require eight valence electrons to follow the octet rule. However, some atoms, like beryllium, can have fewer than eight valence electrons (suboctet). As a result, when bonding with chloride, beryllium is likely to form only two bonds, using its own two outer valence electrons and one from each chloride to form $BeCl_2$, as drawn in (B). (A) is incorrect because Be cannot both bond to chloride *and* have lone pairs. (C) assumes that all three atoms need their octets filled, and (D) places 10 electrons on each chlorine.

17. B

This answer requires an understanding of the trends that cause higher or lower bond energies. Bonds of high energy are those that are difficult to break. These bonds tend to have more shared pairs of electrons and, thus, cause a stronger attraction between the two atoms in the bonds. This stronger attraction also means that the bond length of a high-energy, high-order bond (i.e., a triple bond) is shorter than that of its lower-energy counterparts (i.e., single or double bonds). Thus, (A) is incorrect; bond energy increases with *decreasing* bond length. Single bonds are longer than double bonds. Thus, (C) is incorrect; single bonds are *easier* to break than double bonds. Finally, as previously discussed, bond energy *is* inversely related to bond length, making (D) incorrect.

18. A

Polarity is precisely described by the first answer choice. Dipole moments describe the relationship of shared electrons between two bonded atoms. If there is a dipole moment between two atoms, then the electrons in their shared bond are preferentially centered on one atom, typically the more electronegative of the two. The polarity of a molecule is then defined as the vector sum of these dipole moments in the molecule's three-dimensional configuration. For example, although individual carbon–chloride bonds have dipole moments with a partial negative charge on chloride, the molecule CCl_4 has a tetrahedral configuration. Thus, the four polarized bonds cancel each other out for no net dipole moment, creating a nonpolar molecule. Based on this description, it is clear that (B) is incorrect, because molecular geometry is an essential component of determining molecular polarity. For the same reasons described previously, it is possible for a nonpolar molecule to contain one or more polar bonds, making (C) incorrect. Finally, it is possible for a molecule to contain at least one nonpolar bond and yet be a polar molecule. For example, CH_3CH_2Cl has a nonpolar bond (C–C), yet a molecular dipole exists. In its tetrahedral arrangement, the one polar bond between C–Cl will have a dipole moment, creating a net polarity of the molecule in the direction of the chloride atom.

Compounds and Stoichiometry

Oh—what is that smell? You and your mother are taking an afternoon walk through the public rose garden, a pleasant activity for a pleasant summer day, and everything was so pleasant until you smelled . . . *it*, whatever *it* is. Your mother doesn't have to wonder long until her own olfactory system is screeching the alarm, too. *Oh, it's just horrible. It smells like rancid almonds.* Although your better instincts tell you to walk quickly away, you pause and, holding your breath, crouch down to get a better look. You are a premed, after all, and you did just synthesize cinnamaldehyde in your orgo lab, so your curiosity is understandable.

Scanning the leaves of some plants at the base of the rosebush, you notice a few green bugs whose backs give the impression of a shield. A small stick lies temptingly close to your foot. You can't resist and so you grab the stick and position it for optimal poking, but just as the pointy end gets within a few inches of the insect, which now senses that its own pleasant afternoon is about to be ruined, it raises its hind quarters in the direction of the stick—that is to say, in your direction—exposing its sophisticated defense weaponry. *Stink bugs!* you exclaim, as you drop the stick and take what you believe are a sufficient number of steps to remove yourself from the bug's bombing range.

Our world is filled with aromas and odors, some pleasant and some not so much. What is it that we are smelling when we "smell something"? Well, every odor that we perceive is the result of an interaction between the chemical receptors of our olfactory systems and some chemical compound. A stink bug "stinks" because it produces a highly concentrated solution of volatile compounds that we (and anything else that would dare to disturb it) perceive as malodorous, noxious, and irritating. It's a pretty ingenious defense system: Make yourself so disgusting, so distasteful, that everyone will leave you alone, or at least think twice before bothering or eating you. Interestingly enough, the primary compounds in the stink bug's stink bomb are hydrogen cyanide (a highly toxic compound that inhibits cytochrome c oxidase, thereby blocking aerobic respiration) and benzaldehyde.

Wait, benzaldehyde? Yes, benzaldehyde—that relatively simple compound consisting of a benzene ring substituted with an aldehyde functional group. You need to recognize it for the Biological Sciences section of the MCAT. Remember that we classify benzene ring compounds as part of the larger class of molecules called aromatic compounds. Therefore, you can smell benzaldehyde because it is aromatic and, like some other aromatic compounds, it vaporizes at room temperature and reaches your olfactory system as gas particles. Now, you might be surprised to learn that benzaldehyde is the key ingredient in artificial almond extract. At low concentrations, it gives a pleasant aroma of toasted almonds. However, at high concentrations, its odor is that of rotten, stinking almonds, and it is a noxious irritant to skin, eyes, and the respiratory tract. We do not recommend stink bug juice as a suitable cooking substitute for almond extract.

Benzaldehyde is a compound composed of seven carbon atoms, six hydrogen atoms, and one oxygen atom. One mole of benzaldehyde has a mass of 106.12 grams. It can react with other atoms or compounds to form new compounds (pure substances composed of two or more elements in a fixed proportion). They can be broken down by chemical means to produce their constituent elements or other compounds. They are characterized according to the same systems of traits: physical properties and chemical reactivities.

This chapter focuses on compounds and their reactions. It reviews the various ways in which compounds are represented: Empirical and molecular formulas and percent composition will be defined and explained. There is a brief overview of the major classes of chemical reactions, which we will examine more closely in subsequent chapters, and finally, there is a recap of the steps involved in balancing chemical equations with a particular focus on identifying limiting reagents and calculating reaction yields.

Molecules and Moles ★★★★☆☆

A molecule is a combination of two or more atoms held together by covalent bonds. It is the smallest unit of a compound that displays the identifying properties of that compound. Molecules can be composed of two atoms of the same element (e.g., N_2 and O_2) or may be composed of two or more atoms of different elements, as in CO_2, $SOCl_2$, and C_6H_5CHO (benzaldehyde). Because reactions usually involve a very large number of molecules, far too many to count individually, we usually measure amounts of compounds in terms of moles or grams, using molecular weight to interconvert between these units.

Ionic compounds do not form true molecules because of the way in which the oppositely charged ions arrange themselves in the solid state. As solids, they can be considered as nearly infinite, three-dimensional arrays of the charged particles that comprise the compound. Remember, in Chapter 3 we mentioned that NaCl in the solid state is a 6:6 coordinated lattice in which each of the Na^+ ions is surrounded by six Cl^- ions and each of the Cl^- ions is surrounded by six Na^+ ions. As you might imagine, this makes it rather difficult to clearly define a sodium chloride molecular unit. Because no molecule actually exists, molecular weight becomes meaningless, and the term *formula weight* is used instead. (However, this is a technical distinction over which you ought not to sacrifice too much sleep.)

MOLECULAR WEIGHT

We've mentioned already that the term *atomic weight* is a misnomer, because it is a measurement of mass, not weight (another distinction not worth any sacrifice of sleep), and the same applies here to our discussion of **molecular weight**: It's really

Bridge

Ionic compounds form from combinations of elements with large electronegativity differences (that sit far apart on the periodic table), such as sodium and chlorine. Molecular compounds form from the combination of elements of similar electronegativity (that sit close to each other on the periodic table), such as carbon with oxygen.

a measurement of mass. Molecular weight, then, is simply the sum of the atomic weights of all the atoms in a molecule, and its units are atomic mass units (amu). Similarly, the **formula weight** of an ionic compound is found by adding up the atomic weights of the constituent ions according to its empirical formula (see the following example), and its units are grams.

> **Example:** What is the molecular weight of $SOCl_2$?
>
> **Solution:** To find the molecular weight of $SOCl_2$, add together the atomic weights of each of the atoms.
>
> $$
> \begin{aligned}
> 1S &= 1 \times 32 \text{ amu} &= \ \ 32 \text{ amu} \\
> 1O &= 1 \times 16 \text{ amu} &= \ \ 16 \text{ amu} \\
> 2Cl &= 2 \times 35.5 \text{ amu} &= \underline{\ \ 71 \text{ amu}} \\
> \text{molecular weight} & &= 119 \text{ amu}
> \end{aligned}
> $$

MOLE

We defined the term *mole* in Chapter 1, Atomic Structure, but let's briefly review it. A **mole** is a quantity of any thing (molecules, atoms, dollar bills, chairs, etc.) equal to the number of particles that are found in 12 grams of carbon-12. That seems like an awfully strange point of comparison, so all you really need to remember is that "mole" is a quick way of indicating that we have an amount of particles equal to **Avogadro's number**, 6.022×10^{23}. One mole of a compound has a mass in grams equal to the molecular weight of the compound expressed in amu and contains 6.022×10^{23} molecules of that compound. For example, 62 grams of H_2CO_3 (carbonic acid) represents one mole of the acid compound and contains 6.022×10^{23} molecules of H_2CO_3. The mass of one mole of a compound, called its molar weight or molar mass, is usually expressed as g/mol. Therefore, the molar mass of H_2CO_3 is 62 g/mol. You may be accustomed to using the term *molecular weight* to imply molar mass. Technically this is not correct, but nobody is going to rap your knuckles with a ruler for this minor infraction.

Real World

Here we mention Avogadro's number again and can see that the mole is just a unit of convenience, like the dozen is a convenient unit for eggs.

The formula for determining the number of moles of a substance present is

$$\text{mol} = \text{Weight of sample (g)}/\text{Molar weight (g/mol)}$$

> **Example:** How many moles are in 9.52 g of $MgCl_2$?
>
> **Solution:** First, find the molar mass of $MgCl_2$.
>
> $$1(24.31 \text{ g/mol}) + 2(35.45 \text{ g/mol}) = 95.21 \text{ g/mol}$$
>
> Now, solve for the number of moles.
>
> $$\frac{9.52}{95.21 \text{ g/mol}} = 0.10 \text{ mol of } MgCl_2$$

EQUIVALENT WEIGHT

Equivalent weight and the related concept of equivalents are a source of confusion for many students. Part of the problem may be the context in which equivalents and equivalent weights are discussed: acid-base reactions, redox reactions, and precipitation reactions, all three of which themselves can be sources of much student confusion and anxiety. So let's start with some very basic discussion, and then, in later chapters, we will see how these concepts and calculations apply to these three types of reactions.

Generally, some compounds or elements have different capacities to act in certain ways, not in terms of their characteristics or behaviors, like electronegativity or ionization energy, but rather the ability of certain elements or compounds to act more potently than others in performing certain reactions. For example, one mole of HCl has the ability to donate one mole of hydrogen ions (H^+) in solution, but one mole of H_2SO_4 has the ability to donate two moles of hydrogen ions, and one mole of H_3PO_4 has the ability to donate three moles of hydrogen ions. Another example to consider is the difference between Na and Mg: One mole of sodium has the ability to donate one mole of electrons, while one mole of magnesium has the ability to donate two moles of electrons. To find one mole of hydrogen ions for a particular acid-base reaction, we could "source" those protons from one mole of HCl, or we could instead use a half-mole of H_2SO_4. If we're using H_3PO_4, we'd only need one-third of a mole. This is what we mean by "different capacities to act in certain ways." If we need only one mole of hydrogen ions, it would be a waste to use an entire mole of H_3PO_4, which could donate three times what we need. We are defining the concept of **equivalents**: How many moles of the "thing we are interested in" (i.e., protons, hydroxide ions, electrons, or ions) will the number of moles of the compound present produce? One mole of hydrogen ions (one equivalent) will be donated by one mole of HCl, but two moles of hydrogen ions (two equivalents) will be donated by one mole of H_2SO_4, and three moles of hydrogen ions (three equivalents) will be donated by one mole of H_3PO_4. Simply put, an equivalent is a mole of charge.

Having discussed the concept of equivalents, we can now introduce a calculation that will be helpful on the MCAT, especially for problems of acid-base chemistry. So far, this discussion has been focused on the mole-to-mole relationship between, say, an acid compound and the hydrogen ions it donates. However, sometimes we need to work in units of mass rather than moles. Just as one mole of HCl will donate one mole (one equivalent) of hydrogen ions, a certain mass amount of HCl will donate one equivalent of hydrogen ions. This amount of compound, measured in grams, that produces one equivalent of the monovalent particle of interest (protons, hydroxide ions, electrons, or ions) is called the **gram equivalent weight,** and the equation is

$$\text{Gram equivalent weight} = \text{Molar mass}/n$$

where n is the number of protons, hydroxide ions, electrons, or monovalent ions "produced" or "consumed" per molecule of the compound in the reaction. For example, you would need 46 grams of H_2SO_4 (molar mass = 98 g/mol) to produce one equivalent of hydrogen ions, because each molecule of H_2SO_4 can donate two hydrogen ions ($n = 2$). Simply put, an equivalent weight of a compound is the mass that provides one mole of charge.

If the amount of a compound in a reaction is known and you need to determine how many equivalents are present, use the following equation:

$$\text{Equivalents} = \text{Mass of compound (g)/Gram equivalent weight (g)}$$

Finally, we can now introduce the measurement of normality without too much fear of causing the almost-always-fatal head explosion. *Normality*, as the term suggests, is a measure of concentration. The units for normality are equivalents/liter. A 1 N solution of acid contains a concentration of hydrogen ions equal to 1 mole/liter; a 2 N solution of acid contains a concentration of hydrogen ions equal to 2 moles/liter. The actual concentration of the acidic compound may be the same or different from the normality, because different compounds have different capacities to donate hydrogen ions. In a 1 N acid solution consisting of dissolved HCl, the molarity of HCl is 1 M, because HCl is a monoprotic acid, but if the dissolved acid is H_2SO_4, then the molarity of H_2SO_4 in a 1 N acid solution is 0.5 M, because H_2SO_4 is a diprotic acid. The conversion from normality of acid solution to molarity of acidic compound is

$$\text{Molarity} = \text{Normality}/n$$

where n is the number of protons, hydroxide ions, electrons, or monovalent ions "produced" or "consumed" per molecule of the compound in the reaction.

There is a real benefit to working with equivalents and normality because it allows a direct comparison of quantities of the "thing" you are most interested in. Face it, in an acid-base reaction, you really only care about the hydrogen ion and/or the hydroxide ion. Where they come from is not really your primary concern. So it is very convenient to be able to say that one equivalent of acid (hydrogen ion) will neutralize one equivalent of base (hydroxide ion). The same could not necessarily be said to be true if we were dealing with moles of acidic compound and moles of basic compound. For example, one mole of HCl will not completely neutralize one mole of $Ca(OH)_2$, because one mole of HCl will donate one equivalent of acid but $Ca(OH)_2$ will donate two equivalents of base.

Conceptually, that was the most challenging discussion in this chapter. Let's move on to review ways in which compounds are represented.

Representation of Compounds ★★★☆☆

There are different ways of representing compounds and their constituent atoms. We've already reviewed a couple of these systems (Lewis dot structures and VSEPR theory) in Chapter 3. In organic chemistry, it is common to encounter "skeletal" representations of compounds, called structural formulas, to show the various bonds between the constituent atoms of a compound. Inorganic chemistry typically represents compounds by showing the constituent atoms without representing the actual bond connectivity or atomic arrangement. For example, $C_6H_{12}O_6$ (which you ought to recognize is the molecular formula for glucose) tells us that this particular compound consists of 6 atoms of carbon, 12 atoms of hydrogen, and 6 atoms of oxygen, but there is no indication in the molecular formula of how the different atoms are arranged or how many bonds exist between each of the atoms.

LAW OF CONSTANT COMPOSITION

The **law of constant composition** states that any pure sample of a given compound will contain the same elements in the identical mass ratio. For example, every sample of H_2O will contain two hydrogen atoms for every one oxygen atom, or in terms of mass, for every one gram of hydrogen, there will be eight grams of oxygen. We're sorry to say that it doesn't matter whether the water you drink is sourced from deep springs in the Fiji Islands or flows out of a tap connected to a shallow well. The law of constant composition says that water is water.

EMPIRICAL AND MOLECULAR FORMULAS

There are two ways to express a formula—the elemental composition—for a compound. The **empirical formula** gives the simplest whole number ratio of the elements in the compound. The **molecular formula** gives the exact number of atoms of each element in the compound and is usually a multiple of the empirical formula. For example, the empirical formula for benzene is CH, while the molecular formula is C_6H_6. For some compounds, the empirical and molecular formulas are the same, as in the case of H_2O. For the reasons previously discussed, ionic compounds, such as NaCl or $CaCO_3$, will only have empirical formulas.

PERCENT COMPOSITION

The **percent composition by mass** of an element is the weight percent of a given element in a specific compound. To determine the percent composition of an element X in a compound, the following formula is used:

% Composition = (Mass of X in formula/Formula weight of compound) × 100%

You can calculate the percent composition of an element by using either the empirical or the molecular formula; just be sure to use to the appropriate mass measurement:

formula weight for empirical formula or molar mass for molecular formula. Formula weight is simply the mass of the atoms in the empirical formula of a compound.

You can determine the molecular formula if both the percent compositions and molar mass of the compound are known. The following examples demonstrate such calculations.

Example: What is the percent composition of chromium in $K_2Cr_2O_7$?

Solution: The formula weight of $K_2Cr_2O_7$ is

$$2(39 \text{ g/mol}) + 2(52 \text{ g/mol}) + 7(16 \text{ g/mol}) = 294 \text{ g/mol}$$

$$\% \text{ composition of Cr} = \frac{2(52 \text{ g/mol})}{294 \text{ g/mol}} \times 100$$

$$= 0.354 \times 100$$

$$= 35.4 \text{ percent}$$

Example: What are the empirical and molecular formulas of a compound that contains 40.9 percent carbon, 4.58 percent hydrogen, and 54.52 percent oxygen and has a molar mass of 264 g/mol?

Method One: First, determine the number of moles of each element in the compound by assuming a 100-gram sample; this converts the percentage of each element present directly into grams of that element. Then convert grams to moles:

$$\# \text{mol of C} = \frac{40.9 \text{ g}}{12 \text{ g/mol}} = 3.41 \text{ mol}$$

$$\# \text{mol of H} = \frac{4.58 \text{ g}}{1 \text{ g/mol}} = 4.58 \text{ mol}$$

$$\# \text{mol of O} = \frac{54.52 \text{ g}}{16 \text{ g/mol}} = 3.41 \text{ mol}$$

Next, find the simplest whole number ratio of the elements by dividing the number of moles by the smallest number obtained in the previous step.

$$C : \frac{3.41}{3.41} = 1.00 \qquad H : \frac{4.58}{3.41} \approx 1.33 \qquad O : \frac{3.41}{3.41} = 1.00$$

Finally, the empirical formula is obtained by converting the numbers obtained into whole numbers (multiplying them by an integer value).

$$C_1H_{1.33}O_1 \times 3 = C_3H_4O_3$$

$C_3H_4O_3$ is the empirical formula. To determine the molecular formula, divide the molar mass by the formula weight. The resultant value is the number of empirical formula units in the molecular formula.

The empirical formula weight of $C_3H_4O_3$ is

$$3(12 \text{ g/mol}) + 4(1 \text{ g/mol}) + 3(16 \text{ g/mol}) = 88 \text{ g/mol}$$

$$\frac{264 \text{ g/mol}}{88 \text{ g/mol}} = 3$$

$C_3H_4O_3 \times 3 = C_9H_{12}O_9$ is the molecular formula.

Method Two: When the molar mass is given, it is generally easier to find the molecular formula first. This is accomplished by multiplying the molar mass by the given percentages to find the grams of each element present in one mole of compound, then dividing by the respective atomic weights to find the mole ratio of the elements:

$$\# \text{ mol of C} = \frac{(0.409)(264) \text{ g}}{12 \text{ g/mol}} = 9 \text{ mol}$$

$$\# \text{ mol of H} = \frac{(0.0458)(264) \text{ g}}{1 \text{ g/mol}} = 12 \text{ mo}$$

$$\# \text{ mol of O} = \frac{(0.5452)(264) \text{ g}}{16 \text{ g/mol}} = 9 \text{ mol}$$

Thus, the molecular formula, $C_9H_{12}O_9$, is the direct result.

The empirical formula can now be found by reducing the subscript ratio to the simplest integral values.

Key Concept

The molecular formula is either the same as the empirical formula or a multiple of it. To calculate the molecular formula, you need to know the mole ratio (this will give you the empirical formula) and the molecular weight (molecular weight ÷ empirical formula weight will give you the multiplier for the empirical formula to molecular formula conversion).

Types of Chemical Reactions ★★★☆☆

This section reviews the major classes of chemical reactions. As it has probably already become apparent to you in your inorganic and organic chemistry classes, it would be quite impossible to memorize every single individual reaction that could occur. Fortunately, there is no need to memorize any reaction, as long as you take the time now and throughout your preparation for the MCAT to learn and understand the recognizable patterns of reactivities between compounds. Some classes of compounds react in very "stereotyped" ways, or at least appear to react in stereotyped ways, because of the MCAT's focus on a particular subset of a chemical's reactivities. The MCAT has a tendency to typecast certain compounds, in spite of repeated protests made by the compounds' talent agents.

COMBINATION REACTIONS

A **combination reaction** has two or more reactants forming one product. The formation of sulfur dioxide by burning sulfur in air is an example of a combination reaction.

$$S \ (s) + O_2 \ (g) \rightarrow SO_2 \ (g)$$

Key Concept

Combination reactions generally have more reactants than products.

$A + B \rightarrow C$

DECOMPOSITION REACTIONS

A **decomposition reaction** is the opposite of a combination reaction: A single compound reactant breaks down into two or more products, usually as a result of heating or electrolysis. An example of decomposition is the breakdown of mercury (II) oxide. (The Δ [delta] sign over a reaction arrow represents the addition of heat.)

$$2 \, HgO \,(s) \xrightarrow{\Delta} 2 \, Hg \,(l) + O_2 \,(g)$$

SINGLE-DISPLACEMENT REACTIONS

Sometimes one atom in a molecule gets tired of the other ("I love you, but I'm not *in love* with you…"), and divorce becomes inevitable when something better comes along. This is a **single-displacement** reaction: an atom (or ion) of one compound is replaced by an atom of another element. For example, zinc metal will displace copper ions in a copper sulfate solution to form zinc sulfate.

$$Zn \,(s) + CuSO_4 \,(aq) \rightarrow Cu \,(s) + ZnSO_4$$

Single-displacement reactions are often further classified as redox reactions, which will be discussed in great detail in Chapter 11, Redox Reactions and Electrochemistry. Not to carry the analogy to the point of ridiculousness, but just to make the point: Cu in $CuSO_4$ has an oxidation state of +2, but when it leaves the compound, it gains two electrons (the Cu^{+2} is reduced to Cu)—you may think of this as Cu^{+2} getting an alimony settlement or gaining back its dignity for leaving that no-good cheater, SO_4^{2-}. On the other side, Zn loses its dignity (in the form of two electrons) when it desperately throws itself into the arms of SO_4^{2-}.

DOUBLE-DISPLACEMENT REACTIONS

Well, if you think atoms are acting scandalously in single-displacement reactions, just wait until you get a load of the atomic depravity in double-displacement reactions. In double-displacement reactions, also called metathesis, elements from two different compounds swap places with each other (hence, the name *double-displacement*) to form two new compounds. This type of reaction occurs when one of the products is removed from the solution as a precipitate or gas or when two of the original species combine to form a weak electrolyte that remains undissociated in solution. For example, when solutions of calcium chloride and silver nitrate are combined, insoluble silver chloride forms in a solution of calcium nitrate.

$$CaCl_2 \,(aq) + 2AgNO_3 \,(aq) \rightarrow Ca(NO_3)_2 \,(aq) + 2AgCl \,(s)$$

NEUTRALIZATION REACTIONS

Neutralization reactions are a specific type of double displacement in which an acid reacts with a base to produce a salt. For example, hydrochloric acid and sodium, hydroxide will react to form sodium chloride and water.

$$HCl \,(aq) + NaOH \rightarrow NaCl \,(aq) + H_2O$$

Key Concept

Decomposition reactions generally have more products than reactants.

$C \rightarrow A + B$

Bridge

Acids and bases (which we will see in Chapter 10) combine in neutralization reactions to produce salts and water.

Net Ionic Equations ★★☆☆☆

Just as in our discussion of equivalents and normality, in which we admitted that we really care about the acid and the base functionalities themselves rather than the compounds that are donating the hydrogen protons and hydroxide ions, here we have another opportunity to confess our little secrets. Come on, say it with us—you'll feel better getting this off your chest: When it comes to many reactions, there are certain species that we find boring and want to ignore. For example, in many reactions, such as displacements, the ionic constituents of the compounds are in solution, so we can write the chemical reaction in ionic form. In the previous example involving the reaction between zinc and copper (II) sulfate, the ionic equation would be

$$Zn\,(s) + Cu^{2+}\,(aq) + SO_4^{2-}\,(aq) \rightarrow Cu\,(s) + Zn^{2+}\,(aq) + SO_4^{2-}\,(aq)$$

You'll notice that the $SO_4^{2-}\,(aq)$ is just hanging, not really doing anything. It's not taking part in the overall reaction but simply remains in the solution unchanged. We call such species **spectator ions**. They're like boring people who go to parties and just stand around, taking up space. Because the SO_4^{2-} ion isn't doing anything of interest, we can ignore it and write a net ionic reaction showing only the species that actually participate in the reaction:

$$Zn\,(s) + Cu^{2+}\,(aq) \rightarrow Cu\,(s) + Zn^{2+}\,(aq)$$

Net ionic equations list only the cool people at the party who are actually doing fun stuff. They are important for demonstrating the actual reaction that occurs during a displacement reaction.

Balancing Equations ★★★★☆☆

> **MCAT Expertise**
>
> It is unlikely that you will come across a question that explicitly asks you to balance an equation. However, you will need to recognize unbalanced reactions and quickly add the necessary coefficients. Look at the
>
> 1) charge on each side; and
>
> 2) number of atoms of each element.

Balancing a checkbook is a dying art. In this age of automated and computer banking, it's easy enough to monitor the account balance without taking the time to record by hand each and every transaction. Nevertheless, the art of balancing chemical equations is one in which you must be skilled, and you ought to expect the MCAT to test your understanding of the steps involved. Because chemical equations express how much and what type of reactants must be used to obtain a given quantity of product, it is of utmost importance that the reaction be balanced so as to reflect the laws of conservation of mass and charge. The mass of the reactants consumed must equal the mass of products generated. More specifically, you must ensure that the number of atoms on the reactant side equals the number of atoms on the product side. **Stoichiometric coefficients**, which are placed in front of the compound, are used to indicate the number of moles of a given species involved in the reaction. For example, the balanced equation expressing the formation of water is

$$2\,H_2\,(g) + O_2\,(g) \rightarrow 2\,H_2O\,(l)$$

The coefficients indicate that two moles of H_2 gas must be reacted with one mole of O_2 gas to produce two moles of water. In general, stoichiometric coefficients are given as whole numbers.

The steps you take to balance a chemical reaction are necessary to ensure you have the correct recipe. You wouldn't want to bake a cake using a recipe that didn't properly balance the amounts of flour, eggs, sugar, and butter, and you wouldn't want to conduct an experiment or chemical process without the balanced equation.

Let's review the steps involved in balancing a chemical equation, using an example.

> **Example:** Balance the following reaction.
>
> $$C_4H_{10}(\ell) + O_2(g) \rightarrow CO_2(g) + H_2O(\ell)$$
>
> **Solution:** First, balance the carbons in the reactants and products.
>
> $$C_4H_{10} + O_2 \rightarrow 4\,CO_2 + H_2O$$
>
> Second, balance the hydrogens in the reactants and products.
> $$C_4H_{10} + O_2 \rightarrow 4\,CO_2 + 5\,H_2O$$
>
> Third, balance the oxygens in the reactants and products.
> $$2\,C_4H_{10} + 13\,O_2 \rightarrow 8\,CO_2 + 10\,H_2O$$
>
> Finally, check that all of the elements, and the total charges, are balanced correctly. If there is a difference in total charge between the reactants and products, then the charge will also have to be balanced. (Instructions for balancing charge are found in Chapter 11.)

Applications of Stoichiometry ★★★★★☆

Once you've balanced the chemical equation, you then have a very valuable tool for solving many chemical reaction problems on the MCAT. Perhaps the most useful bit of information to glean from a balanced reaction is the mole ratios of reactants consumed to products generated. Furthermore, you can also generate the mole ratio of one reactant to another or one product to another. All these ratios can be generated by a comparison of the stoichiometric coefficients. In the example involving the formation of water, we now understand that for every one mole of hydrogen gas consumed, one mole of water can be produced, but that for every one mole of oxygen gas consumed, two moles of water can be produced. Furthermore, we see that, mole-to-mole, hydrogen gas is being consumed at a rate twice that of oxygen gas.

Stoichiometry problems usually involve at least a few unit conversions, so you must be careful when working through these types of problems to ensure that units cancel out appropriately, leaving you with the desired unit(s) of the answer choices. Pay close

Key Concept

When balancing equations, focus on the least represented elements first and work your way to the most represented element of the reaction (usually oxygen or hydrogen).

MCAT Expertise

Because the MCAT is a critical-thinking test, we might see application and analysis questions related to limiting reactants or percent yields.

attention to the following problem, which demonstrates a clear and easy-to-follow method for keeping track of the numbers, the calculations, and the unit conversions.

> **Example:** How many grams of calcium chloride are needed to prepare 72 g of silver chloride according to the following equation?
>
> $$CaCl_2\,(aq) + 2\,AgNO_3\,(aq) \rightarrow Ca(NO_3)_2\,(aq) + 2\,AgCl\,(s)$$
>
> **Solution:** Noting first that the equation is balanced, 1 mole of $CaCl_2$ yields 2 moles of AgCl when it is reacted with 2 moles of $AgNO_3$. The molar mass of $CaCl_2$ is 110 g, and the molar mass of AgCl is 144 g.
>
> $$72\,g\,AgCl \times \frac{1\,mol\,AgCl}{144\,g\,AgCl} \times \frac{1\,mol\,CaCl_2}{2\,mol\,AgCl} \times \frac{110\,g\,CaCl_2}{1\,mol\,CaCl_2}$$
>
> Thus, 27.5 g of $CaCl_2$ are needed to produce 72 g of AgCl.

Limiting Reactant

If you recall some of the experiments that you ran in your general chemistry lab, you know that rarely did you ever use stoichiometric quantities of compounds. Remember that stoichiometric coefficients are usually whole numbers and refer to the number of moles of the particular reactants and products. Some common compounds, like $CaCO_3$, have molar masses in excess of 100 g/mol, and using such quantities per student would make for a very, very expensive lab. Rarely, then, are reactants added in the exact stoichiometric proportions as shown in the balanced equation. As a result, in most reactions, one reactant will be used up (consumed) first. This reactant is known as the **limiting reactant** because it limits the amount of product that can be formed in the reaction. The reactant that remains after all the limiting reactant is used up is called the **excess reactant**.

For problems involving the determination of the limiting reactant, you must keep in mind two principles:

1. All comparisons of reactants must be done in units of moles. Gram-to-gram comparisons will be useless and maybe even misleading.
2. It is not the absolute mole quantities of the reactants that determine which reactant is the limiting reactant. Rather, the rate at which the reactants are consumed (the stoichiometric ratios of the reactants) combined with the absolute mole quantities determines which reactant is the limiting reactant.

> **Example:** If 28 g of Fe react with 24 g of S to produce FeS, what would be the limiting reagent? How many grams of excess reagent would be present in the vessel at the end of the reaction?
>
> The balanced equation is $Fe + S \xrightarrow{\Delta} FeS$.

Solution: First, determine the number of moles for each reactant.

$$28\,g\,Fe \times \frac{1\,mol\,Fe}{56\,g} = 0.5\,mol\,Fe$$

$$24\,g\,S \times \frac{1\,mol\,S}{32\,g} = 0.75\,mol\,S$$

Since 1 mole of Fe is needed to react with 1 mole of S, and there are 0.5 moles Fe for every 0.75 moles S, the limiting reagent is Fe. Thus, 0.5 moles of Fe will react with 0.5 moles of S, leaving an excess of 0.25 moles of S in the vessel. The mass of the excess reagent will be

$$Mass\,of\,S = 0.25\,mol\,S \times \frac{32\,g}{1\,mol\,S}$$

$$= 8\,g\,of\,S$$

Yields

Sometimes chemistry lab professors like to torture students by grading them on the purity of their products and the yields of their experiments. The enjoyment for the professor comes from watching crazed premed students desperately scraping their glassware in the forlorn hope that they might be able to capture just enough errant product to increase yield by a few measly percentage points. The "yield" of a reaction is either the amount of product predicted (theoretical yield) or obtained (raw or actual yield) when the reaction is carried out. **Theoretical yield** is the maximum amount of product that can be generated, predicted from the balanced equation, assuming that all of the limiting reactant is consumed, no side reactions have occurred, and the entire product has been collected. Theoretical yield, as your experience has most certainly taught you by now, is rarely ever attained through the actual chemical reaction. **Actual yield** is the amount of product that you are actually able to obtain. The ratio of the actual yield to the theoretical yield, multiplied by 100 percent, gives you the **percent yield**, and this number is the fragile thread by which so many premeds fear their future careers hang.

Percent yield = (Actual yield/Theoretical yield) × 100%

MCAT Expertise

An experimental-type passage that involves a chemical reaction may include a pseudo-discrete question that involves finding the percent yield.

Example: What is the percent yield for a reaction in which 27 g of Cu is produced by reacting 32.5 g of Zn in excess CuSO4 solution?

Solution: The balanced equation is as follows:

$$Zn\,(s) + CuSO_4\,(aq) \rightarrow Cu\,(s) + ZnSO_4\,(aq)$$

Calculate the theoretical yield for Cu.

$$32.5\,g\,Zn \times \frac{1\,mol\,Zn}{65\,g} = 0.5\,mol\,Zn$$

$$0.5\,mol\,Zn \times \frac{1\,mol\,Cu}{1\,mol\,Zn} = 0.5\,mol\,Cu$$

$$0.5\,mol\,Cu \times \frac{64\,g}{1\,mol\,Cu} = 32\,g\,Cu = theoretical\,yield$$

Finally, determine the percent yield.

$$\frac{27\,g}{32\,g} \times 100\% = 84\%$$

MCAT Expertise

When we are given an excess of one reagent on the MCAT, we know that the other reactant is the limiting reagent. Be sure to take advantage of these easy cues when they appear on Test Day!

Conclusion

We began our consideration of compounds with a particularly odoriferous one: benzaldehyde. As a compound, it is made from constituent atoms of different elements in a set ratio defined by its empirical or molecular formula. Each molecule of a compound has a defined mass that is measured as its molecular weight. The mass of one mole of any compound is determined from its molar mass in the units of grams/mole. We reviewed the basic classifications of reactions commonly tested on the MCAT: combination, decomposition, single-displacement, and double-displacement reactions. Furthermore, we are now confident in our understanding of the steps necessary to balance any chemical reaction; we are ready to tackle more stoichiometric problems in preparation for Test Day.

Before moving to the next chapters discussing chemical kinetics and thermodynamics, let us offer our heartiest congratulations to you. If you have been reading these chapters in order, you have now completed one-third of this general chemistry review! Take note of this, in part, because it is an important milestone in your progress toward success on Test Day and you should be proud of your accomplishments, but mostly because these first four chapters have introduced you to the fundamental concepts of chemistry—everything from the structure of the atom and trends of the elements to bonding and the formation of compounds. The understanding you have gained so far will be the foundation for your comprehension of even the most difficult general chemistry concept tested on the MCAT. Keep moving forward with your review of general chemistry; don't get stuck in the details. Those will come to you best through the application of the basic principles to MCAT practice passages and questions.

And remember, now that you've read this chapter, the next time somebody says, "Oh, what stinks?" your response can be more than just, "Oh, sorry."

CONCEPTS TO REMEMBER

☐ A compound is a pure substance composed of two or more elements in a fixed proportion. Compounds can react with other elements or compounds to form new compounds and be broken down by chemical means to produce their constituent elements or other compounds, which can themselves go on to become involved in other reactions.

☐ Molecular weight is the mass in amu of the constituent atoms in a compound, given by the molecular formula, which gives the exact number of atoms of each element in a compound. Empirical formula weight is the mass of the constituent atoms in a compound's empirical formula, which is the smallest whole number ratio of the elements in a compound. Molar mass is the mass in grams of one mole (6.022×10^{23} molecules) of a compound.

☐ An equivalent is a measure of capacity to react in a certain way. One equivalent is an amount of a chemical compound equal to one mole of hydrogen ions or hydroxide ions in acid-base reactions or one mole of electrons in redox chemistry. Gram equivalent weight is the mass in grams of a compound that will yield one equivalent of hydrogen ions, hydroxide ions, or electrons. Normality is the ratio of equivalents per liter.

☐ Combination reactions occur when two or more reactants combine to form one product.

☐ Decomposition reactions occur when one reactant is chemically broken down into two or more products, usually by heat or electrolysis.

☐ Single-displacement reactions occur when an atom or ion of one compound is replaced by an atom or ion of another element.

☐ Double-displacement reactions occur when elements from two different compounds trade places with each other to form two new compounds. Neutralization reactions are a specific type of double displacement in which an acid reacts with a base to produce a solution of salt and water.

☐ Net ionic equations ignore spectator ions to focus only on the species that actually participate in the reaction.

☐ The steps for balancing chemical equations are as follows:

— Balance the nonhydrogen and nonoxygen atoms.

— Balance the oxygens.

— Balance the hydrogens.

— Balance charge if necessary.

☐ Balanced reactions are essential for calculating limiting reactant (the reactant that will be consumed first in a chemical reaction) and yields. Theoretical yield is the maximum amount of product that can be formed, assuming all limiting reactant is consumed. Actual yield is the amount of product collected from a chemical reaction. Percent yield is the ratio of actual yield divided by theoretical yield, multiplied by 100 percent.

EQUATIONS TO REMEMBER

☐ Number of moles $= \dfrac{\text{Weight of sample (g)}}{\text{Molar weight (g/mol)}}$

☐ Gram equivalent weight $= \dfrac{\text{Molar mass}}{n}$

☐ Equivalents $= \dfrac{\text{Mass of compound (g)}}{\text{Gram equivalent weight (g/equivalent)}}$

☐ Molarity $= \dfrac{\text{Normality}}{n}$

☐ % Composition $= \dfrac{\text{Mass of X in formula}}{\text{Formula weight of compound}} \times 100\%$

☐ Percent yield $= \dfrac{\text{Actual yield}}{\text{Theoretical yield}} \times 100\%$

Practice Questions

1. Which of the following best describes ionic compounds?

   A. Ionic compounds are formed from molecules containing two or more atoms.
   B. Ionic compounds are formed of charged particles and are measured by molecular weight.
   C. Ionic compounds are formed of charged particles that share electrons equally.
   D. Ionic compounds are three-dimensional arrays of charged particles.

2. Which of the following has a formula weight between 74 and 75 grams per mole?

   A. KCl
   B. $C_4H_{10}O$
   C. $[LiCl]_2$
   D. BF_3

3. Which of the following is the gram equivalent weight of H_2SO_4?

   A. 98.08 g/mol
   B. 49.04 g/mol
   C. 196.2 g/mol
   D. 147.1 g/mol

4. Which of the following molecules CANNOT be expressed by the empirical formula CH?

   A. Benzene
   B. Ethyne

   C.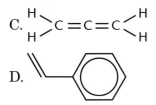

   D.

5. In which of the following compounds is the percent composition of carbon closest to 63 percent?

   A. Acetone
   B. Ethanol
   C. C_3H_8
   D. Methanol

6. What is the most accurate characterization of the reaction shown?

   $$Ca(OH)_2\ (aq) + H_2SO_4\ (aq) \longrightarrow$$
   $$CaSO_4\ (aq) + H_2O\ (\ell)$$

   A. Single-displacement
   B. Neutralization
   C. Double-displacement
   D. Redox

7. In the reaction shown, if 39.03 g of Na_2S are reacted with 113.3 g of $AgNO_3$, how much, if any, of either reagent will be left over once the reaction has gone to completion?

   $$Na_2S + 2\ AgNO_3 \longrightarrow Ag_2S + 2\ NaNO_3$$

   A. 41.37 g $AgNO_3$
   B. 13.00 g Na_2S
   C. 26.00 g Na_2S
   D. 74.27 g $AgNO_3$

8. Using a given mass of $KClO_3$, how would one calculate the mass of oxygen produced in the following reaction, assuming it goes to completion?

$$2\ KClO_3 \longrightarrow 2\ KCl + 3\ O_2$$

A. $\dfrac{(\text{grams } KClO_3 \text{ consumed})(3 \text{ moles } O_2)(\text{molar mass } O_2)}{(\text{molar mass } KClO_3)(2 \text{ moles } KClO_3)}$

B. $\dfrac{(\text{grams } KClO_3 \text{ consumed})(\text{molar mass } O_2)}{(\text{molar mass } KClO_3)(2 \text{ moles } KClO_3)}$

C. $\dfrac{(\text{molar mass } KClO_3)(2 \text{ moles } KClO_3)}{(\text{grams } KClO_3 \text{ consumed})(\text{molar mass } O_2)}$

D. $\dfrac{(\text{grams } KClO_3 \text{ consumed})(3 \text{ moles } O_2)}{(\text{molar mass } KClO_3)(2 \text{ moles } KClO_3)(\text{molar mass } O_2)}$

9. Aluminum metal can be used to remove tarnish from silver when the two solid metals are placed in water, according to the following reaction.

$$3\ AgO + 2\ Al \longrightarrow 3\ Ag + Al_2O_3$$

This reaction is a

  I. double-displacement reaction.

  II. single-displacement reaction.

  III. redox reaction.

  IV. combination reaction.

A. II only

B. I and III

C. II and III

D. IV only

10. Which of the following type(s) of reaction(s) generally has/have the same number of reactants and products?

  I. Single-displacement reaction

  II. Double-displacement reaction

  III. Combination reaction

A. I only

B. II only

C. II and III

D. I and II

11. Which of the following is the correct net ionic reaction for the reaction of copper with silver nitrate?

A. $Cu + AgNO_3 \longrightarrow Cu(NO_3)_2 + Ag$

B. $Cu + 2\ Ag^+ + NO_3^- \longrightarrow Cu^{2+} + 2\ NO_3^- + 2\ Ag^+$

C. $2\ Ag^+ + 2\ NO_3^- \longrightarrow 2\ NO_3^- + 2\ Ag^+$

D. $Cu + 2\ Ag^+ \longrightarrow Cu^{2+} + 2\ Ag$

12. In the process of photosynthesis, carbon dioxide and water combine with energy to form glucose and oxygen, according to the following equation.

$$CO_2 + H_2O + \text{Energy} \longrightarrow C_6H_{12}O_6 + O_2$$

What is the theoretical yield, in grams, of glucose if 30.00 grams of water are reacted with excess carbon dioxide and energy, in the balanced equation?

A. 50.02 grams glucose

B. 300.1 grams glucose

C. 30.03 grams glucose

D. 1,801 grams glucose

13. One way to test for the presence of iron in solution is by adding potassium thiocyanate to the solution. The product when this reagent reacts with iron is $FeSCN^{2+}$, which creates a dark red color in solution via the following net ionic equation.

$$Fe^{3+} (aq) + SCN^- \longrightarrow FeSCN^{2+}$$

How many grams of iron sulfate would be needed to produce 2 moles of $FeSCN^{2+}$?

A. 400 grams
B. 800 grams
C. 200 grams
D. 500 grams

Small Group Questions

1. Can the Law of Constant Composition be applied to solutions?

2. What is the purpose of calculating a reactant's gram equivalent weight?

Explanations to Practice Questions

1. D

Ionic compounds are composed of atoms held together by ionic bonds. Ionic bonds associate charged particles with disparate electronegativities; for example, sodium (Na^+) with chloride (Cl^-). In ionic bonds, electrons are not really "shared" but are rather donated from the less electronegative atom to the more electronegative atom. As a result, ionic compounds are not formed from true molecules, as are covalent compounds. (A) and (B) both describe covalent compounds; their smallest unit is a molecule, which is typically described in terms of molecular weight and moles. In contrast, ionic compounds are measured using "formula weights" and are made of three-dimensional arrays of their charged particles, as indicated in (D). (C) is incorrect because ionic compounds do not share electrons equally; equal sharing occurs in covalent bonds.

2. A

Of the compounds listed, only (A) and (C) are ionic compounds, which are measured in "formula weights." The other options, (B) and (D), are covalent compounds and thus are measured in "molecular weight." This clues us in to the fact that we don't really even need to examine choices (B) and (D). (A) consists of potassium (39.0983 g) plus chloride (35.453 g), which has a total weight of 74.551 grams. (C) is made up of 2 lithiums (2×6.941 g) and 2 chlorides (2×35.4527 g), whose sum exceeds 75 grams.

3. B

First, it is helpful to know the molecular weight of one mole of H_2SO_4, which is found by adding the molecular weight of the atoms that constitute the molecule: $2 \times$ (molecular weight of hydrogen) + $1 \times$ (molecular weight of sulfur) + $4 \times$ (molecular weight of oxygen) = 2×1.00794 g + 32.065 g + 4×15.9994 g = 98.078 g. Next, you must understand what

the term *gram equivalent weight* means. Gram equivalent weight is the weight (in grams) that would release one acid equivalent. Because H_2SO_4 has two hydrogens per molecule, the gram equivalent weight is 98.078 g/mole divided by 2, or 49.039 g/mole. All of the other answer choices are multiples of this number.

4. C

The definition of an empirical formula is a formula that represents a molecule with the simplest ratio, in whole numbers, of the atoms/elements comprising the compounds. In this case, given the empirical formula CH, any molecule with carbon and hydrogen atoms in a 1:1 ratio would be accurately represented by this empirical formula. Benzene, C_6H_6 (A), is thus correct, as is ethyne, C_2H_2 (B). (D) has eight carbon atoms and eight hydrogen atoms, making it correct as well. (C) is incorrect, and thus the right answer, because it has three carbon atoms while having four hydrogens. Both its molecular and empirical formulas would be C_3H_4, because this formula represents the smallest whole number ratio of its constituent elements.

5. A

The percent composition of any given element within a molecule is equal to the molecular mass of that element in the molecule, divided by the formula or molecular weight of the compound, times 100%. In this case, acetone, C_3H_6O, has a total molecular weight of (12.0107 g $\times 3 + 1.00794$ g $\times 6 + 15.994$ g $\times 1$) = 58.074 g/mol, of which 12.0107 g $\times 3 = 36.0321$ g/mol is from carbon. Thus, the percent composition of carbon is 63.132%. With this calculation serving as an example, you can calculate the percent composition for ethanol (C_2H_6O; MW = 41.023 g/mol) to be 58.556%; for C_3H_8 (MW = 44.096 g/mol) to be 81.713%; and for methanol (CH_4O; MW = 32.036 g/mol) to be 37.491%. These calculations make it clear that although both acetone (A) and ethanol (B) have percent compositions of carbon close to 63%, acetone is closer (within 1%).

6. B

This reaction is a classic example of a neutralization reaction, in which an acid and a base react to form water and a new aqueous compound. Although this reaction may also appear to fit the criteria for a double-displacement reaction, in which two molecules essentially "exchange" with each other, neutralization is a more specific description of the process. A single-displacement reaction is typically a redox (reduction/oxidation) reaction in which one element is replaced in the molecules; thus (A) and (D) are incorrect.

7. B

In this question, you are first given the masses of both reactants used to start the reaction. To figure out what will be left over, we must first determine which species is the limiting reagent. First, determine the molecular weight of each of the reactants: $Na_2S = 78.05$ g/mol; $AgNO_3 = 169.9$ g/mol. We find that we are given 0.5 mol Na_2S for the reaction and 0.6669 mol $AgNO_3$. Because we need two molar equivalents of $AgNO_3$ for every mole of Na_2S, $AgNO_3$ is the limiting reagent, and the correct answer choice will be in grams of Na_2S. Next, determine how much of the Na_2S will be left over by figuring out how much will be used if it reacts with all of the $AgNO_3$.

Use half as much Na_2S as $AgNO_3$:

$[(1.000$ mol $Na_2S)/(2.000$ mol $AgNO_3)] \times 0.6669$ mol $AgNO_3 = 0.3334$ mol Na_2S

Then subtract this amount of reagent used from the total available:

0.5000 mol $Na_2S - 0.3334$ mol $Na_2S = 0.1666$ mol excess Na_2S

Finally, determine the mass that this represents:

0.1666 mol excess $Na_2S \times 78.05$ g/mol $Na_2S = 13.00$ g Na_2S

(A) and (D) are incorrect because there will be no remaining $AgNO_3$. (C) is the mass in 0.33 mol of Na_2S, and you would have gotten this if we mixed it up with 0.166 mol.

8. A

You're told that you must begin with some given mass of $KClO_3$, x grams. To use it to determine a mass of another product, we must convert it to moles. Thus far, you would have

$$(\text{grams } KClO_3 \text{ consumed}) \times \frac{\text{mol } KClO_3}{\text{g } KClO_3} = \frac{(\text{grams } KClO_3 \text{ consumed})}{(\text{molar mass } KClO_3, \text{ grams/mol})}$$

which is equal to the number of moles of $KClO_3$.

This first step eliminates (C).

Next, convert the number of moles of $KClO_3$ to the number of moles of oxygen, according to the balanced equation presented in the question stem:

$$\text{mol } KClO_3 \times \frac{(3 \text{ moles } O_2)}{(2 \text{ moles } KClO_3)}$$

Putting both steps together, the equation thus far is

$$\frac{(\text{grams } KClO_3 \text{ consumed})(3 \text{ moles } O_2)}{(\text{molar mass } KClO_3)(2 \text{ moles } KClO_3)}$$

This second step eliminates (B) because it does not use the correct molar ratio between $KClO_3$ and O_2. The final step is to convert the number of moles of oxygen to a mass, in grams of O_2. At this point in your equation, the number of moles is in the numerator, and you want the number of grams of oxygen in the numerator, so multiply your ratio by the molar mass of oxygen, as shown in (A).

9. C

In the reaction, there is a single displacement (II), with the silver in silver oxide being replaced by the aluminum to form aluminum oxide. This single-displacement reaction also necessitates a transfer of electrons in a reduction/oxidation reaction or "redox" reaction (III). Therefore, the correct answer is both II and III, (C). A double-displacement reaction (I) typically takes two compounds and causes two displacements, whereas only one occurs in this question. Combination reactions (IV) generally take two atoms or molecules and combine them to form one product, usually with more reactants than products, which also is not the case in this question.

10. D

Typically, single-displacement (or oxidation/reduction) reactions and double-displacement reactions both have the same number of reactants and products. For example, single-displacement reactions are often of the following form (M = metal 1; M' = metal 2; A = anion):

$$M + M'A \rightarrow M' + MA$$

In this type of reaction, M takes the place of M' in combining with an anion. Typically, a process of oxidation and reduction of the involved metals enables this. Double-displacement reactions also tend to have the same number of reactants and products, represented by this type of reaction (C = cation 1; C' = cation 2; A = anion 1; A' = anion 2):

$$CA + C'A' \rightarrow C'A + CA'$$

In this reaction, the two compounds essentially "swap" anions/cations, beginning and ending with two compounds.

Combination reactions typically have more reactants than products, represented by the following reaction:

$$A + B \rightarrow C$$

11. D

A net ionic equation represents each of the ions comprising the compounds in the reactants and products as individual ions, instead of combining them as molecules. Thus, (A) is not a net ionic reaction. The term *net* means that the correct answer does not include any spectator ions (ions that do not participate in the reaction). In this reaction, nitrate (NO_3^-) remains unchanged. You can eliminate any answer choice that includes it, which leaves only (D).

12. A

This is a popular equation that you've probably seen before. What's missing from it are the coefficients! This is an unbalanced equation. To get anywhere with this problem, you have to balance it first.

$$6CO_2 + 6H_2O + energy \rightarrow C_6H_{12}O_6 + 6O_2$$

The theoretical yield is the amount of product synthesized if the limiting reagent is completely used up. This question therefore asks how much glucose is produced if the limiting reagent is 30 grams of water. First, calculate the number of moles of water represented by 30 grams by dividing by its molecular weight (18.01 g/mol). You'll have a lot of conversion factors, so wait until the end to multiply it all out.

$$30 \text{ g water} \frac{(1 \text{ mol water})}{(18 \text{ g water})}$$

Next, add conversion factors to find the equivalent number of moles of glucose.

$$30 \text{ g water} \frac{(1 \text{ mol water})(1 \text{ mol glucose})}{(18 \text{ g water})(6 \text{ mol water})}$$

Finally, convert moles of glucose into grams of glucose by multiplying by its molecular weight (180.2 grams / mol glucose).

$$30 \text{ g water} \frac{(1 \text{ mol water})(1 \text{ mol glucose})(180 \text{ grams glucose})}{(18 \text{ g water})(6 \text{ mol water})(1 \text{ mol glucose})}$$

After crossing out equal terms from the numerator and denominator, you are left with this:

$$30 \cancel{\text{ g water}} \frac{(1 \cancel{\text{ mol water}})(1 \cancel{\text{ mol glucose}})(180 \text{ grams glucose})}{(18 \cancel{\text{ g water}})(6 \cancel{\text{ mol water}})(1 \cancel{\text{ mol glucose}})}$$

$$= \frac{(30)(180 \text{ grams glucose})}{(18)(6)}$$

Dividing 18 and 6 into our numerators will yield 50 grams of glucose.

13. A

What you are shown is a net ionic equation. To answer this question, work backward from the amount of product to the reactant with its spectator ions (in this case, sulfate).

First, for every two moles of FeSCN we create, we must react two moles of Fe^{3+}. Therefore, you're looking for the mass of iron sulfate that can provide two moles of iron.

Next, determine the charge on sulfate, which is –2 and iron, which in this case is +3. Therefore, iron sulfate must be present as follows:

$$Fe_2(SO_4)_3$$

The molecular formula tells you that each mole of iron sulfate releases two moles of atomic iron. Therefore, you only need one mole of iron sulfate for this reaction, which means the molar mass of iron sulfate is the answer.

$$2 \text{ Fe: } (2)(55.8 \text{ g})$$
$$3 \text{ S: } (3)(32.1 \text{ g})$$
$$\underline{12 \text{ O: } (12)(16.0 \text{ g})}$$
$$399.9 \text{ g}$$

Chemical Kinetics and Equilibrium

It's Friday night, and you're on the first call of your pediatrics rotation. You're a third-year medical student now, and you're anxious to see some action. Hanging out in the call room near the ED of the children's hospital, you get a page from the resident: *Come to the emergency room, now*, she says. *They just brought in a kid with DKA.* DKA, you know, stands for diabetic ketoacidosis and is a fairly common way for undiagnosed Type I diabetes to present. Entering the child's room, the examination is already under way; he's young—about 10 years old—conscious but agitated, and the most obvious sign—what you notice immediately—is his rapid, shallow breathing. You see he's already receiving IV fluids and an insulin drip.

Later that evening, after the boy has stabilized, you and the resident are talking about diabetes and DKA. You remembered from your second-year lessons about endocrine pathophysiology that ketoacidosis can arise as a result of the body's metabolism of fatty acids when insulin production finally shuts down in Type I diabetes. Because most of the cells of the human body can't import glucose without the aid of insulin, the glucose accumulates in the plasma of the blood, producing hyperglycemia even as the cells of the body are in a state of glucose starvation. Fatty acids are metabolized into ketone bodies as an alternative energy source. Some of the ketones produced are ketoacids, and as the diabetic crisis continues and worsens, the concentration of these ketoacids increases, resulting in a plasma pH below 7.35 (metabolic acidosis). The combination of the acidosis, progressively severe dehydration due to the osmotic effect of glucose "spilling into" the urine, and other negative effects of the severe insulin depletion result in the host of signs and symptoms of diabetic ketoacidosis. You ask the resident why the boy was hyperventilating, and she takes a piece of paper and writes out the following:

$$H^+ (aq) + HCO_3^- (aq) \rightarrow H_2CO_3 (aq) \rightarrow CO_2 (g) + H_2O (l)$$

It's Le Châtelier's principle, she deadpans, disappointed that you didn't remember that. *The respiratory system is trying to compensate for the metabolic acidosis; the increased breathing rate allows the patient to blow off more CO₂, which causes the equilibrium to shift to the right. Hydrogen ions combine with bicarbonate ions to produce carbonic acid, which dissociates into CO₂ gas to replace the gas that's being expelled from the lungs. Of course, the desired result is a decrease in the hydrogen ion concentration, which stabilizes the pH and keeps it from getting crazy low. It's not perfect, but if you catch them soon enough, the pH hasn't gone so low that they've essentially become a scrambled egg. You should know all of this by now.*

You recognize the equation. In fact, you even remember studying it for your MCAT. *What was that all about? Oh yeah, chemical equilibrium. Wow, chemistry really is essential for medical school!*

This chapter focuses on two primary topics: chemical kinetics and chemical equilibrium. As the term suggests, chemical kinetics is the study of reaction rates, the effects of reaction conditions on these rates, and the mechanisms implied by such observations. Chemical equilibrium is a dynamic state of a chemical reaction at which the concentrations of reactants and products stabilize over time in a low-energy configuration. Pay particular attention to the concepts of chemical equilibrium, as we will return to them in our review of solutions, acid-base, and redox chemistry.

Chemical Kinetics ★★★★☆☆

Reactions can be spontaneous or nonspontaneous; the change in Gibbs free energy determines whether or not a reaction will occur, by itself, without outside assistance (see Chapter 6, Thermochemistry). However, even if a reaction is spontaneous, this does not necessarily mean that it will run quickly. In fact, nearly every reaction that our very lives depend upon, while perhaps spontaneous, proceeds so slowly that without the aid of enzymes and other catalysts, we might not ever actually "see" the reaction occur over the course of an average human lifetime. In biology, we discuss the function of enzymes, which selectively enhance the rate of certain reactions (by a factor of 10^6 to 10^{14}) over other thermodynamically feasible reaction pathways, thereby determining the course of cellular metabolism, the collection of all chemical reactions in a living cell. For now, however, let us review the topics of reaction mechanisms, rates, rate laws, and the factors that affect them.

REACTION MECHANISMS

Very rarely is the balanced reaction equation, with which we work to calculate limiting reactants and yields, an accurate representation of the actual steps involved in the chemical process from reactants to products. Many reactions proceed by more than one step, the series of which is known as the **mechanism** of a reaction and the sum of which gives the **overall reaction** (the one that you, typically, are asked to balance). When you know the accepted mechanism of a reaction, this helps you explain the reaction's rate, position of equilibrium, and thermodynamic characteristics (see Chapter 6). Consider this generic reaction:

$$\text{Overall reaction: } A_2 + 2B \rightarrow 2AB$$

On its own, this equation seems to imply a mechanism in which two molecules of B collide with one molecule of A_2 to form two molecules of AB. Suppose instead, however, that the reaction actually takes place in two steps:

$$\text{Step 1: } A_2 + B \rightarrow A_2B \quad \text{(slow)}$$
$$\text{Step 2: } A_2B + B \rightarrow 2AB \quad \text{(fast)}$$

You'll note that the two steps, taken together, give the overall (net) reaction. The molecule A_2B, which does not appear in the overall reaction, is called an **intermediate**. Reaction intermediates are often difficult to detect, because they may be consumed almost immediately after they are formed, but a proposed mechanism that includes

Bridge

Mechanisms are proposed pathways for a reaction that must coincide with rate data information from experimental observation. We will be studying mechanisms more in Organic Chemistry.

intermediates can be supported through kinetic experiments. One of the most important points for you to remember is that the slowest step in any proposed mechanism is called the rate-determining step, because it acts like a kinetic "bottleneck," preventing the overall reaction from proceeding any faster than the slowest step. It holds up the entire process in much the same way that the overall rate of an assembly line production can only be as fast as the slowest step or slowest person (who will probably soon find himself out of a job).

Reaction Rates   ★★★★★☆

Reactions, unfortunately, do not come with handy built-in speedometers. We can't just look at a dial or gauge and read the reaction rate. It takes a little more effort than that. To determine the rate at which a reaction proceeds, we must take measurements of concentrations of reactants and products and note their change over time.

DEFINITION OF RATE

If we consider a generic reaction, $2A + B \rightarrow C$, in which one mole of C is produced from every two moles of A and one mole of B, we can describe the rate of this reaction in terms of either the disappearance of reactants over time or the appearance of products over time. Because the reactants, by definition, are being consumed in the process of formation of the products, we place a minus sign in front of the rate expression in terms of reactants. For the previous reaction, the rate of the reaction with respect to A is $-\Delta[A]/\Delta t$, with respect to B is $-\Delta[B]/\Delta t$, and with respect to C is $\Delta[C]/\Delta t$. You'll notice that the stoichiometric coefficients for the reaction are not equal, and this tells you that the rates of change of concentrations are not equal. Because two moles of A are consumed for every mole of B consumed, $\text{rate}_{-\Delta[A]} = 2\,\text{rate}_{-\Delta[B]}$. Furthermore, for every two moles of A consumed, only one mole of C is produced; thus, we can say that the $\text{rate}_{-\Delta[A]} = 2\,\text{rate}_{\Delta[C]}$. Based on the stoichoimetry, you can see that the rate of consumption of B is equal to the rate of production of C. To show a standard rate of reaction in which the rates with respect to all reaction species are equal, the rate of concentration change of each species should be divided by the species' stoichiometric coefficient:

$$\text{rate} = \frac{-1\Delta[A]}{2\Delta t} = -\frac{\Delta[B]}{\Delta t} = \frac{\Delta[C]}{\Delta t},$$

And for the general reaction $aA + bB \rightarrow cC + dD$:

$$\frac{-1\Delta[A]}{a\Delta t} = -\frac{1\Delta[B]}{b\Delta t} = \frac{-1\Delta[C]}{c\Delta t} = \frac{-1\Delta[D]}{d\Delta t}$$

Rate is expressed in the units of moles per liter per second (mol/L/s) or molarity per second (M/s).

DETERMINATION OF RATE LAW

Here's something you can take to the bank (that is, to the MCAT testing center): In the Physical Sciences section of the MCAT, it is extremely unlikely that the test

MCAT Expertise

Remember that the stoichiometric coefficients for the overall reaction will most likely be different from those for the rate-determining step and will, therefore, not be the same as the order of the reaction.

maker will give you a reaction equation that you can merely look at and write the correct rate law. Therefore, on the MCAT, whenever you are asked to determine the rate law for a reaction in which you are given the net equation, the first thing you will do is look for experimental data.

However, we're getting ahead of ourselves, so let's start with the basics. For nearly all forward, irreversible reactions, the rate is proportional to the product of the concentrations of the reactants, each raised to some power. For the general reaction

$$a\text{A} + b\text{B} \rightarrow c\text{C} + d\text{D}$$

the rate is proportional to $[\text{A}]^x[\text{B}]^y$. By including a proportionality constant, k, we can say that rate is determined according to the following equation:

$$\text{rate} = \text{k}[\text{A}]^x[\text{B}]^y$$

This expression is called the **rate law** for the general reaction shown here, where k is the reaction rate coefficient or rate constant. Rate is always measured in units of concentration over time; that is, molarity/second. The exponents x and y (or x, y, and z, if there are three reactants, etc.) are called the orders of the reaction: x is the order with respect to reactant A, and y is order with respect to reactant B. The overall order of the reaction is the sum of $x + y$ ($+ z \ldots$). These exponents may be integers, fractions, or zero and must be determined experimentally. The MCAT will focus almost entirely on zero-, first-, second-, and third-order reactions only. Furthermore, in most cases, the exponents will be integers.

MCAT Expertise

Note that the exponents in the rate law are not equal to the stoichiometric coefficients, unless the reaction actually occurs via a single-step mechanism. Also, note that product concentrations never appear in a rate law. Don't fall into the common trap of confusing the rate law with an equilibrium expression!

Before we go any further in our consideration of rate laws, we must offer a few warnings about common traps that students often fall into. The first—and most common—is the mistaken assumption that the orders of a reaction are the same as the stoichiometric coefficients in the balanced overall equation. Pay close attention to this: *The values of* x *and* y *usually aren't the same as the stoichiometric coefficients.* The orders of a reaction are usually must be determined experimentally. There are only two cases in which you can take stoichiometric coefficients as the orders of reaction. The first is when the reaction mechanism is a single step and the balanced "overall" reaction is reflective of the entire chemical process. The second is when the complete reaction mechanism is given and the rate-determining step is indicated. The stoichiometric coefficients on the reactant side of the rate-determining step are the orders of the reaction. Occasionally, even this can get a little complicated when the rate-determining step involves an intermediate as a reactant, in which case you must derive the intermediate molecule's concentration by the law of mass action (that is, the equilibrium constant expression) for the step that produced it.

The second trap to be wary of is mistaking the equilibrium aspect of the law of mass action for the kinetic aspect. The equations for the two aspects do look similar, and if you're not alert, you may mistake one for the other or use one when you should be using the other. The expression for equilibrium includes the concentrations of all the species in the reaction, both reactants and products. The expression for chemical kinetics, the rate law expression, includes only the reactants. K_{eq} tells you where the reaction's equilibrium position lies. The rate tells you how quickly the reaction will get there (that is, reach equilibrium).

The third trap we need to warn you about is regarding the rate constant, k. Technically speaking, it's not a constant, because its particular value for any specific chemical reaction will depend on the activation energy for that reaction and the temperature at which the reaction takes place. However, for a specific reaction at a specific temperature, the rate coefficient is constant. For a reversible reaction, the K_{eq} is equal to the ratio of the rate constant, k, for the forward reaction, divided by the rate constant, k_{-1}, for the reverse reaction (see Chapter 6, Thermochemistry).

The fourth and final trap we need to warn you about is that the notion and principles of equilibrium apply to the system only at the end of the reaction; that is, the system has reached equilibrium. The reaction rate, while it theoretically can be measured at any time, is usually measured at or near the beginning of the reaction to minimize the effects of the reverse reaction.

Experimental Determination of Rate Law

We've stated this a few times now, but it bears repeating: The values of k, *x*, and *y* in the rate law equation (rate = $k[A]^x[B]^y$) must usually be determined experimentally for a given reaction at a given temperature. Although rate laws can be quite complex and the orders of the reaction difficult to discern, the MCAT limits its coverage of this topic to fairly straightforward reaction mechanisms, experimental data, and rate laws.

The first step in determining a rate law for a specific reaction is to write out the generic rate law on the scratch material provided for you at the testing center. Then look for the necessary data. Typically, you'll recognize a chart that includes initial concentrations of the reactants and the initial rates of product formation as a function of the reactant concentrations. Usually, the data for three or four trials are included in the chart.

Once you've located the data, the next step is to identify a pair of trials in which the concentration of one of the reactants is changed while the concentration of all other reactants remains constant. Under these conditions, any change in rate of product formation (if there is any) from the one trial to the other is due solely to the change in concentration of one reactant. Let's imagine that compound A's concentration is constant, while the concentration of B has been doubled. If the rate of the formation of product C has subsequently quadrupled, then you can say to yourself (using your in-the-head-voice, because nobody wants to hear you

MCAT Expertise

Traditionally, the MCAT has loved rate problems. With practice, you'll be able to do these quickly in your head with minimal paper-and-pencil calculations. Remember to look for pairs of reaction trials in which the concentration of only one species changes while the other(s) remain constant.

talk to yourself on Test Day!), "Doubling the concentration of B has resulted in a quadrupling of the production rate of C, so to determine the order of the reaction, y, with respect to reactant B, I need to calculate the power by which the number 2 must be raised to equal 4. Because $2^y = 4$, $y = 2$." (Kaplan wants you to think exactly this way. When you read this sentence, exactly as we've written it, you will be analyzing the data in the correct manner and working through the correct process for generating the correct rate law.)

The next step is to repeat this process for the other reactant, using different data from a different pair of trials, always making sure that the concentration of only the reactant whose order you are trying to determine is changed from one trial to the other while the concentration of any other reactant remains the same. Once you've determined the orders of the reaction with respect to each reactant, you then can write the complete rate law, replacing the x and the y (and sometimes z) with actual numbers. To determine the value of the rate constant k, you will need to plug in actual values—you can use the data from any one of the trials; pick whichever trial has the most arithmetically convenient numbers—for the reactant concentrations and the product formation rate, once you know the values for the exponent for each reactant.

Example: Given the data below, find the rate law for the following reaction at 300 K.

$$A + B \rightarrow C + D$$

Trial	$[A]_{initial}(M)$	$[B]_{initial}(M)$	$r_{initial}(M/sec)$
1	1.00	1.00	2.0
2	1.00	2.00	8.1
3	2.00	2.00	15.9

Solution: First, look for two trials in which the concentrations of all but one of the substances are held constant.

a) In Trials 1 and 2, the concentration of A is kept constant, while the concentration of B is doubled. The rate increases by a factor of 8.1/2.0, approximately 4. Write down the rate expression of the two trials.

Trial 1: $r_1 = k[A]^x[B]^y = k(1.00)^x(1.00)^y$

Trial 2: $r_2 = k[A]^x[B]^y = k(1.00)^x(2.00)^y$

Divide the second equation by the first:

$$\frac{r_2}{r_1} = \frac{8.1}{2.0} = \frac{k(1.00)^x(2.00)^y}{k(1.00)^x(1.00)^y} = (2.00)^y$$

$$4 = (2.00)^y$$

$$y = 2$$

b) In Trials 2 and 3, the concentration of B is kept constant, while the concentration of A is doubled; the rate is increased by a factor of 15.9/8.1, approximately 2. The rate expressions of the two trials are as follows:

$$\text{Trial 2: } r_2 = k(1.00)^x (2.00)^y$$
$$\text{Trial 3: } r_3 = k(2.00)^x (2.00)^y$$

Divide the second equation by the first,

$$\frac{r_3}{r_2} = \frac{15.9}{8.1} = \frac{k(2.00)^x (2.00)^y}{k(1.00)^x (2.00)^y} = (2.00)^x$$

$$2 = (2.00)^x$$

$$x = 1$$

So $r = k[A][B]^2$

The order of the reaction with respect to A is 1 and with respect to B is 2; the overall reaction order is $1 + 2 = 3$.

To calculate k, substitute the values from any one of the above trials into the rate law; e.g.,

$$2.0 \text{ M/sec} = k \times 1.00 \text{ M} \times (1.00 \text{ M})^2$$
$$k = 2.0 \text{ M}^{-2} \text{ sec}^{-1}$$

Therefore, the rate law is $r = 2.0 \text{ M}^{-2} \text{ sec}^{-1} [A][B]^2$.

REACTION ORDERS

We classify chemical reactions on the basis of kinetics into classes of reactions called zero-order, first-order, second-order, mixed-order, or higher-order reactions. We will continue to consider the generic reaction $aA + bB \rightarrow cC + dD$ for this discussion.

Zero-Order Reactions

A zero-order reaction is one whose rate of formation of product C is independent of changes in concentrations of any of the reactants, A and B. These reactions have a constant reaction rate equal to the rate coefficient (rate constant) k. The rate law for a zero-order reaction is

$$\text{rate} = k[A]^0[B]^0 = k$$

where k has units of M·s⁻¹. (Remember that any number raised to the zero power equals 1.) We will remind you that the rate constant itself is dependent upon temperature; thus, it is possible to change the rate for a zero-order reaction by changing the temperature. The only other way to change the rate of a zero-order reaction is by the addition of a catalyst, which lowers the energy of activation, thereby increasing the value of k.

First-Order Reactions

A first-order reaction (order = 1) has a rate that is directly proportional to only one reactant, such that doubling the concentration of, say, reactant A results in a doubling of the rate of formation of product C. The rate law for a first-order reaction is

$$rate = k[A]^1 \text{ or } rate = k[B]^1$$

where k has units of s^{-1}. A classic example of a first-order reaction is the process of radioactive decay. From the rate law, in which the rate of decrease of the amount of a radioactive isotope A is proportional to the amount of A,

$$rate = \frac{-\Delta[A]}{\Delta t} = k[A],$$

The concentration of radioactive substance A at any time t can expressed mathematically as

$$[A_t] = [A_o]e^{-kt}$$

where $[A_o]$ is the initial concentration of A, $[A_t]$ is the concentration of A at time t, k is the rate constant, and t is time. It is important to recognize that a first-order rate law with a single reactant suggests that the reaction begins when the molecule undergoes a chemical change all by itself, without a chemical interaction and, usually, without a physical interaction with any other molecule.

Second-Order Reactions

A second-order reaction (order = 2) has a rate that is proportional either to the product of the concentrations of two reactants or to the square of the concentration of a single reactant (and zero-order with respect to any other reactant). The following rate laws all reflect second-order reactions:

$$rate = k[A]^1[B]^1 \text{ or } rate = k[A]^0[B]^2 = k[B]^2 \text{ or } rate = k[A]^2[B]^0 = k[A]^2$$

where k has units of $M^{-1}sec^{-1}$. It is important to recognize that a second-order rate law often suggests a physical collision between two reactant molecules, especially if the rate law is first-order with respect to each of the two reactants.

Higher-Order Reactions

Fortunately there are very few—almost zero—reactions in which a single-reaction step involves a termolecular process; in other words, there are almost no elementary processes whose rate is third-order with respect to a single reactant. This is because it is almost impossible to get three particles to collide simultaneously. Any order higher than 3 is virtually unknown.

Mixed-Order Reactions

Mixed-order reactions sometimes refer to noninteger orders (fractions) and in other cases to reactions whose order varies over the course of the reaction. Fractions are more specifically described as broken-order, and in recent times, the term *mixed-order* has come to refer solely to reactions whose order changes over time. Knowing those two definitions will probably be enough for you on Test Day.

An example of a mixed-order reaction is a catalyzed reaction whose rate law is given by

$$\text{Rate} = \frac{k_1[E][A]^2}{k_2 + k_3[A]},$$

where A is the single reactant and E the catalyst. (The overall reaction and its mechanism are beyond the relevance and scope of the MCAT, and the derivation of this rate law is even more unnecessary!) The result of the large value for [A] at the beginning of the reaction is that $k_3[A] \gg k_2$, and the reaction will appear to be first-order; at the end of the reaction, $k_2 \gg k_3[A]$ because [A] will have a low value, making the reaction appear to be second-order. While the MCAT will not ask you to derive a rate expression for a mixed-order reaction, you are responsible for being able to recognize how the rate order changes as the specific reactant concentration changes.

THEORIES OF THE MOLECULAR BASIS OF CHEMICAL REACTIONS

It's one thing to say "A_2 reacts with B_2 to form 2AB"; it's quite another to be able to describe, as precisely as possible, the actual interactions that occur between A_2 and B_2 to produce AB at some rate. Various theories have been proposed to explain the events that are taking place at the atomic level through the process of a reaction.

Collision Theory of Chemical Kinetics

For a reaction to occur, molecules must collide with each other in much the same way that for children to enjoy themselves, there usually must be some rough physical contact involved; that is, of course, until someone's eye gets poked out. The **collision theory of chemical kinetics** states that the rate of a reaction is proportional to the number of collisions per second between the reacting molecules.

The theory suggests, however, that not all collisions result in a chemical reaction. An effective collision (that is, one that leads to the formation of products) occurs only if the molecules collide with each other in correct orientation and sufficient energy to break the existing bonds and form new ones. Not every punch that a professional boxer throws is going to result in a knockout, only the ones that have the right angle and energy. The minimum energy of collision necessary for a reaction to take place is called the **activation energy**, E_a or the **energy barrier**. Only a fraction of colliding particles have enough kinetic energy to exceed the activation energy. This means that only a fraction of all collisions are effective. The rate of a reaction can therefore be expressed as follows:

$$\text{rate} = fZ$$

where Z is the total number of collisions occurring per second and f is the fraction of collisions that are effective.

Transition State Theory

The discussion of this theory introduces us to some terms that will be more fully defined and explored in the next chapter, Thermochemistry, so if some of these concepts are not clear to you, be patient, because you'll have another opportunity to consider them more carefully soon enough.

When molecules collide with sufficient energy at least equal to the activation energy, they form a **transition state** in which the old bonds are weakened and the new bonds begin to form. The transition state then dissociates into products, and the new bonds are fully formed. For the reaction $A_2 + B_2 = 2AB$, the change along the reaction coordinate, which is a measure of the extent to which the reaction has progressed from reactants to products, can be represented as shown in Figure 5.1.

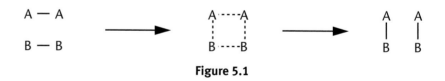

Figure 5.1

> **Key Concept**
>
> Relative to reactants and products, transition states have the highest energy. So they are only theoretical structures and cannot be isolated. Nevertheless, we can still use the proposed structures to understand better the reactions in which they are involved.

The **transition state**, also called the **activated complex**, has greater energy than either the reactants or the products and is denoted by the symbol ‡. An amount of energy at least equal to the activation energy is required to bring the reactants to this energy level. Once an activated complex is formed, it can either dissociate into the products or revert to reactants without any additional energy input. Transition states are distinguished from reaction intermediates in that, existing as they do at energy maxima, transition states exist on a continuum rather than having distinct identities and finite lifetimes.

A potential energy diagram illustrates the relationship between the activation energy, the heats of reaction, and the potential energy of the system. The most important features to recognize in such diagrams are the relative energies of all of the products and reactants. The **enthalpy change of the reaction (ΔH)** is the difference between the potential energy of the products and the potential energy of the reactants (see Chapter 6). A negative enthalpy change indicates an **exothermic reaction** (one in which heat is given off), and a positive enthalpy indicates an **endothermic reaction** (one in which heat is absorbed). The activated complex, the transition state, exists at the top of the energy barrier. The difference in potential energies between the activated complex and the reactants is the activation energy of the forward reaction; the difference potential in energies between the activated complex and the products is the activation energy of the reverse reaction.

For example, consider the formation of HCl from H_2 and Cl_2. The overall reaction is

$$H_2\,(g) + Cl_2\,(g) \leftrightarrow 2\,HCl\,(g)$$

Figure 5.2 shows that the reaction is exothermic. The potential energy of the products is less than the potential energy of the reactants; heat is evolved, and the enthalpy change of the reaction is negative.

Key Concept

$-\Delta H$ = exothermic = heat given off

$+\Delta H$ = endothermic = heat absorbed

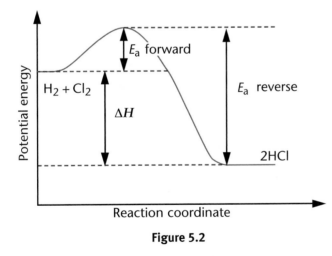

Figure 5.2

MCAT Expertise

Kinetics and thermodynamics should be considered separately. Note that the potential energy of the product can be raised or lowered, thereby changing the value of ΔH without affecting the value of forward E_a.

FACTORS AFFECTING REACTION RATE

If you imagine a group of children playing together in a rough-and-tumble game of tag, we can identify certain conditions that would result in a more vigorous, more fun, more effective game. We can use this analogy to remember the factors that can affect chemical reaction rates.

Reactant Concentrations

A group of children playing tag will probably have more fun the greater the number of children playing: The participation of more children equals more opportunities to chase, trip, and tag each other. The greater the concentrations of the reactants,

MCAT Expertise

We saw earlier in this chapter that increasing reactant concentrations might increase the reaction rate, but be aware of each reactant's order before making this assumption.

the greater the number of effective collisions per unit time. Therefore, the reaction rate will increase for all but zero-order reactions. For reactions occurring in the gaseous state, the partial pressures of the gas reactants serve as a measure of concentration (see Chapter 7, The Gas Phase).

Temperature

You can imagine that children's enthusiasm for playing tag outside increases as the temperature warms from the bone-chilling snowstorms of winter to the pleasant sun of June. For nearly all reactions, the reaction rate will increase as the temperature increases. Because the temperature of a substance is a measure of the particles' average kinetic energy, increasing the temperature increases the average kinetic energy of the molecules. Consequently, the proportion of molecules having energies greater than E_a (thus capable of undergoing reaction) increases with higher temperature. You'll often hear that raising the temperature of a system by 10°C will result in an approximate doubling of the reaction rate. You have to be careful with this approximation, as it is *generally* true for biological systems but not so for many other systems. (Don't forget also: If the temperature gets too high, a catalyst may denature—and then the reaction rate plummets!)

Medium

The rate at which a reaction takes place may also be affected by the medium in which it takes place. Just as children playing tag would prefer to play on a grassy field, but another group of children wanting to get a game of ice hockey going would be looking for an ice rink, some molecules are more likely to react with each other in aqueous environments, while others are more likely to react in a nonaqueous solvent, such as DMSO (dimethylsulfoxide) or ethanol. Furthermore, the physical state of the medium (liquid, solid, or gas) can also have a significant effect. Generally, polar solvents are preferred because their molecular dipole tends to polarize the bonds of the reactants, thereby lengthening and weakening them, which permits the reaction to occur faster.

Catalysts

Catalysts are substances that increase reaction rate without themselves being consumed in the reaction. Catalysts interact with the reactants, either by adsorption or through the formation of intermediates, and stabilize them so as to reduce the energy of activation necessary for the reaction to proceed. While many catalysts, including all enzymes, chemically interact with the reactants, upon formation of the products, they return to their original chemical state. They may increase the frequency of collisions between the reactants; change the relative orientation of the reactants, making a higher percentage of the collisions effective; donate electron density to the reactants; or reduce intramolecular bonding within reactant molecules. In **homogeneous catalysis**, the catalyst is in the same phase (solid, liquid, gas) as the reactants. In **heterogeneous catalysis**, the catalyst is in a distinct phase. Figure 5.3 compares the energy profiles of catalyzed and uncatalyzed reactions.

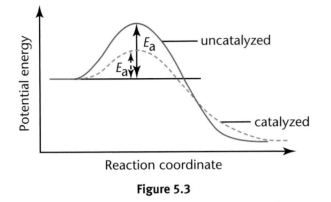

Figure 5.3

If you look closely at the energy profiles in the figure, you'll notice that the only effect of the catalyst is the decrease in the energies of activation, E_a, for both the forward and reverse reactions. The presence of the catalyst has no impact on the potential energies of the reactants or the products or the difference between them. This means that catalysts change only the rate of reactions, and in fact, they change the forward rate and the reverse rate by the same factor. Consequently, they have no impact whatsoever on the equilibrium position or the measure of K_{eq}. Of course, you have to remember that as useful as catalysts are in biological and nonbiological systems, catalysts are not miracle workers: They will not transform a nonspontaneous reaction into a spontaneous one; they only make spontaneous reactions go more quickly toward equilibrium.

Equilibrium

We've been dancing around this term for the past couple of pages now. We warned you not to confuse the chemical equilibrium expression for the rate expression. We stressed that catalysts make reactions go faster toward their equilibrium position but that they can't actually change the equilibrium position or alter the value of K_{eq}. Well, now we're really going to get into it—and you'd better start paying attention, because the principles and concepts that are the focus of the rest of this chapter will direct our discussion in the upcoming chapters about some of the most important general chemistry topics for the MCAT: solutions, acids and bases, and redox reactions.

DYNAMIC EQUILIBRIUM OF REVERSIBLE CHEMICAL REACTIONS

So far, in our discussion of reaction rates, we have been assuming that the reactions were **irreversible**; that is, the reaction proceeds in one direction only, the reaction goes to completion, and the amount of product formed is the maximum as

> **Bridge**
>
> Enzymes are essential to most biological processes.

> **Bridge**
>
> Equilibrium, like biological homeostasis, is a dynamic process that seeks to find balance in all systems. We can use this concept to our advantage on the MCAT in all four of the basic sciences. Equilibria are dynamic, meaning that they *do* undergo change but their *net* change will be zero.

determined by the amount of limiting reactant present. **Reversible reactions** are those in which the reaction can proceed in one of two ways: forward and reverse. (From the perspective of the direction in which the overall reaction is written, the forward reaction is the one that goes from "reactants" on the left to "products" on the right.) Reversible reactions usually do not proceed to completion because (by definition) the products can react together to re-form the reactants. When the reaction system is closed and no products or reactants are removed or added, the system will eventually "settle" into a state in which the rate of the forward reaction equals the rate of the reverse reaction and the concentrations of the products and reactants are constant. In this **dynamic equilibrium** state, the forward and reverse reactions are occurring—they haven't stopped, as would be the case in a static equilibrium—but they are going at the same rate; thus, there is no net change in the concentrations of the products or reactants. Consider the following generic reversible reaction:

$$A \leftrightarrow B$$

At equilibrium, the concentrations of A and B are constant (though not necessarily equal), and the reactions $A \rightarrow B$ and $B \rightarrow A$ continue to occur at equal rates.

Equilibrium can be thought of as a balance between the two reactions (forward and reverse). Better still, equilibrium should be understood on the basis of entropy, which is the measure of the distribution of energy throughout a system or between a system and its environment. For a reversible reaction at a given temperature, the reaction will reach equilibrium when the system's entropy—or energy distribution—is at a maximum and the Gibbs free energy of the system is at a minimum.

LAW OF MASS ACTION

For a generic reversible reaction $aA + bB \rightarrow cC + dD$, the **law of mass action** states that if the system is at equilibrium at a given temperature, then the following ratio is constant:

$$K_{eq} = \frac{[C]^c [D]^d}{[A]^a [B]^b}$$

The law of mass action is actually related to the expressions for the rates of the forward and reverse reactions. Consider the following one-step reversible reaction:

$$2A \leftrightarrow B + C$$

Because the reaction occurs in one step, the rates of the forward and reverse reactions are given by

$$rate_f = k_f[A]^2, \text{ and } rate_r = k_r[B][C]$$

When $rate_f = rate_r$, the system is in equilibrium. Because the rates are equal, we can set the rate expressions for the forward and reverse reactions equal to each other:

$$k_f[A]^2 = k_r[B][C] \text{ and } \frac{k_f}{k_r} = \frac{[B][C]}{[A]^2}$$

Because k_f and k_r are both constants, we can define a new constant K_c, where K_c is called the equilibrium constant and the subscript c indicates that it is in terms of concentration. (When dealing with gases, the equilibrium constant is referred to a K_p, and the subscript p indicates that it is in terms of pressure.) For dilute solutions, K_c and K_{eq} are used interchangeably. The new equation can thus be written

$$K_c = K_{eq} = \frac{[B][C]}{[A]^2}$$

While the forward and the reverse reaction rates are equal at equilibrium, the concentrations of the reactants and products are not usually equal. This means that the forward and reverse reaction rate constants, k_f and k_r, are not usually equal. The ratio of k_f to k_r is K_c (K_{eq}).

$$\frac{k_f}{k_r} = K_c = K_{eq}$$

When a reaction occurs by more than one step, the equilibrium constant for the overall reaction is found by multiplying together the equilibrium constants for each step of the reaction. When you do this, the equilibrium constant for the overall reaction is equal to the concentrations of the products divided by the concentrations of the reactants in the overall reaction, each concentration term raised to the stoichiometric coefficient for the respective species. The forward and reverse rate constants for the nth step are designated k_n and k_{-n}, respectively. For example, if the reaction

$$a\text{A} + b\text{B} \rightarrow c\text{C} + d\text{D} \ldots$$

occurs in three steps, then

$$K_c = \frac{k_1 k_2 k_3}{k_{-1} k_{-2} k_{-3}} = \frac{[C]^c [D]^d}{[A]^a [B]^b}$$

Example: What is the expression for the equilibrium constant for the following reaction?

$$3 \text{ H}_2 \, (g) + \text{N}_2 \, (g) \rightleftarrows 2 \text{ NH}_3 \, (g)$$

Solution: $K_c = \dfrac{[\text{NH}_3]^2}{[\text{H}_2]^3 [\text{N}_2]}$

REACTION QUOTIENT

The law of mass action defines the position of equilibrium by stating that the ratio of the product of the concentrations of the products, each raised to their respective stoichiometric coefficients, to the product of the concentrations of the reactants, each raised to their respective stoichiometric coefficients, is constant. However, equilibrium is a state that is achieved only through time. Depending on the actual rates of the forward and reverse reactions, equilibrium might be achieved in minutes or years. What can we use as a kind of "timer" that tells us how far along in the process toward equilibrium the reaction has reached? We can take another measurement of concentrations called the reaction quotient, Q_c. At any point in time of a reaction, we can measure the concentrations of all the reactants and products and calculate the reaction quotient according to the following equation:

$$Q_c = \frac{[C]^c[D]^d}{[A]^a[B]^b}$$

You should be struck by how similar this looks to the equation for K_{eq}. It's the same form, but the information it provides is quite different. While the concentrations used for the law of mass action are equilibrium (constant) concentrations, when calculating a value of Q_c for a reaction, the concentrations of the reactants and products may not be constant. In fact, if Q_c changes over time because the concentrations of reaction species are changing, the reaction by definition is not at the equilibrium state. Thus, the utility of Q_c is not the value itself but rather the comparison that can be made of the calculated Q_c at any given moment in time of the reaction to the known K_{eq} for the reaction at a given temperature. For any reaction, if

- $Q_c < K_{eq}$, then the reaction has not yet reached equilibrium.
- $Q_c > K_{eq}$, then the reaction has exceeded equilibrium.
- $Q_c = K_{eq}$, then the reaction is in dynamic equilibrium.

Any reaction that has not yet reached the equilibrium state, as indicated by $Q_c < K_{eq}$, will continue spontaneously in the forward direction (that is, consuming reactants to form products) until the equilibrium ratio of reactants and products is reached. Any reaction in the equilibrium state will continue to react in the forward and reverse direction, but the reaction rates for the forward and reverse reactions will be equal and the concentrations of the reactants and products will be constant, such that $Q_c = K_{eq}$. Once a reaction is at equilibrium, any further "movement" either in the forward direction (resulting in an increase in products) or in the reverse direction (resulting in the re-formation of reactants) will be nonspontaneous. In Chapter 6, Thermochemistry, we'll review methods of introducing changes in systems at equilibrium and discuss how those systems respond in terms of enthalpy, spontaneity, and entropy.

PROPERTIES OF THE LAW OF MASS ACTION

Remember the following characteristics of the law of mass action and the equilibrium constant expression:

- The concentrations of pure solids and pure liquids (the solvent, really) do not appear in the equilibrium constant expression, because for the purposes of the MCAT, their concentrations do not change in the course of the reaction. (Actually, the concentrations of any pure solids and/or pure liquids are included in the expression, but we assign them a value of 1 and "hide" the actual concentrations by incorporating them into the equilibrium constant.

- K_{eq} is characteristic of a particular reaction at a given temperature: The equilibrium constant is temperature dependent.
- Generally, the larger the value of K_{eq}, the farther to the right we'll find the equilibrium and the more complete the reaction.
- If the equilibrium constant for a reaction written in one direction is K_{eq}, the equilibrium constant for the reaction written in reverse is $1/K_{eq}$.

Le Châtelier's Principle ★★★★★☆

We can think of few other examples of a scientist's legacy being so tarnished by such rampant mispronunciation of her or his name. While we can all be thankful that the MCAT is not an oral examination with penalties for mispronunciation, let's just clear it up once and for all: Henry Louis's surname is pronounced lə'shäd·əl'ya. The principle that bears his name, and for which he is most famous, states that a system to which a "stress" is applied tends to shift so as to relieve the applied stress. No matter what the particular form the stress takes (e.g., change in concentration of one component or another, change in pressure, or change in temperature), the effect of the stress is to cause the reaction to move temporarily out of its equilibrium state, either because the concentrations or partial pressures of the system are no longer in the equilibrium ratio or because the equilibrium ratio has actually changed as a result of a change in the temperature of the system. The reaction then responds by reacting in whichever direction (that is, either forward or reverse) that results in a re-establishment of the equilibrium state.

CHANGES IN CONCENTRATION OF A REACTANT SPECIES

When you add or remove reactants or products from a reaction in equilibrium, you are causing the reaction to be no longer at its energy minimum state. Metaphorically, you have pushed the reaction, like a ball, up a little ways along the slope of the energy hills on either side of the energy valley. The actual effect is that with the change in concentration of one or another of the chemical species, you have caused the system to have a ratio of products to reactants that is not equal to the equilibrium ratio. In other words, changing the concentration of either a reactant or a product results in $Q_c \neq K_{eq}$. By adding reactant or removing product, you have created a situation in which $Q_c < K_{eq}$, and the reaction will spontaneously move in the forward direction, increasing the value of Q_c until $Q_c = K_{eq}$. By removing reactant or adding product, you have created a situation in which $Q_c > K_{eq}$, and the reaction will spontaneously react in the reverse direction, thereby decreasing the value of Q_c until once again $Q_c = K_{eq}$. A simple way to remember this is: The system will always react in the direction away from the added species or toward the removed species.

MCAT Expertise

Le Châtelier's principle applies to a wide variety of systems and, as such, appears as a fundamental concept in both MCAT science sections.

Bridge

Remember this equation:

$$CO_2 + H_2O \rightarrow HCO_3^- + H^+$$

In the tissues, there is a lot of CO_2, and the reaction shifts to the right. In the lungs, CO_2 is lost, and the reaction shifts to the left. Note that blowing off CO_2 (hyperventilation) is used as a mechanism of dealing with acidosis (excess H^+).

We often take advantage of this particular tendency of chemical reactions in order to improve the yield of chemical reactions. For example, where possible in the industrial production of chemicals, products of reversible reactions are removed as they are formed so as to prevent the reactions from ever reaching their equilibrium states. The reaction will continue to go in the forward direction, producing more and more product (assuming continual replenishment of reactants as they are consumed in the reaction). You could also drive a reaction forward by starting with higher concentrations of reactants. This will lead to an increase in the absolute quantities of products formed, but the reaction would still eventually reach its equilibrium state, unless product was removed as it formed.

CHANGES IN PRESSURE (BY CHANGING VOLUME)

Because liquids and solids are essentially incompressible, only chemical reactions that involve at least one gas species will be affected by changes to the system's volume and pressure. When you compress a system, its volume decreases, and the total pressure increases. The increase in the total pressure is associated with an increase in the partial pressures of all the gases in the system, and this results in the system no longer being in the equilibrium state, such that $Q_p \neq K_{eq}$. The system will move either forward or in reverse but always toward whichever side has the lower total number of moles of gas. This result is a consequence of the ideal gas law, which tells us that there is a direct relationship between the number of moles of gas and the pressure of the gas. If you increase the pressure on a system, it will respond by decreasing the pressure by means of decreasing the number of gas moles present. (In this case, the volume of the system was decreased *and then held constant* while the system returned to its equilibrium state.) When you expand a system, its volume increases, and the total pressure and partial pressures decrease. The system is no longer in its equilibrium state and will react in the direction of the side with the greater number of moles of gas.

Consider the following reaction:

$$N_2\,(g) + 3H_2 \leftrightarrow 2NH_3\,(g)$$

The left side of the reaction has a total of four moles of gas molecules, whereas the right side has only two moles. When the pressure of this system is increased, the system will react in the direction that produces fewer moles of gas. In this case, that direction is to the right: More ammonia will form. However, if the pressure is decreased, the system will react in the direction that produces more moles of gas; the favored reaction will be the reverse, and more reactants will re-form.

CHANGE IN TEMPERATURE

Le Châtelier's principle tells us that changing the temperature of a system will also cause the system to react in a particular way so as to "return" to its equilibrium state, but we have to be careful here, because unlike the effect of changing concentrations or pressures, the result of changing temperature is not simply a change in the reaction quotient, Q_c or Q_p, but a change in K_{eq}. The change in temperature doesn't cause the concentrations or partial pressures of the reactants and products to change immediately, so the Q immediately after the temperature change is the same before the temperature change. Before the temperature change, the system was at equilibrium, and Q was equal to K_{eq}; now after the temperature change, K_{eq} is a different value (because it depends on temperature), so $Q \neq K_{eq}$. The system has to move in whichever direction allows it to reach its new equilibrium state at the new temperature. That direction is determined by the enthalpy of the reaction (see Chapter 6, Thermochemistry). You can think of heat as a reactant if the reaction is endothermic ($+\Delta H$) and as a product if the reaction is exothermic ($-\Delta H$). Thinking about heat as a reactant or product allows you to apply the principle that we discussed in regards to concentration changes to temperature changes. For example, consider the following exothermic reaction:

$$A \leftrightarrow B + heat \ (-\Delta H)$$

If we placed this system in an ice bath, its temperature would decrease, driving the reaction to the right to replace the heat lost. Conversely, if the system were placed in a boiling water bath, the reaction would shift to the left due to the increased "concentration" of heat. All of this is to say that on Test Day, when you are asked to predict the direction a reaction would go in response to a change in temperature, you must look for the enthalpy change for the reaction, which will be given somewhere in the passage, figure, or question stem.

Conclusion

We've discussed some very important concepts and principles in this chapter related to the studies of reaction rates and chemical equilibria. We began with a consideration of chemical reactions and the mechanisms that illustrate the possible individual steps necessary to transform reactants into products. We demonstrated the way to derive a reaction's rate law through the analysis of experimental data, and we looked at the factors that can affect the rates of chemical reactions. The second part of this chapter focused on the law of mass action and the significance of the equilibrium state of a chemical reaction. With our understanding of the significance of K_{eq} and Q, we are able to predict the direction that a reaction will go in response to various stresses—concentration, pressure, or temperature changes—that might be applied to a system.

You've worked through another chapter and reviewed some very important topics for Test Day. We cannot stress enough how much all of your hard work and dedication will pay off in points on the MCAT. There's more to learn and review, but you have already made great progress and will continue to do so. Take pride in the work you are doing, and have confidence in yourself and in your preparation with Kaplan.

> **Key Concept**
>
> The reaction
> **A (aq) + 2 B (g) $\leftrightarrow$ C (g) + heat**
>
> | Will shift to the right if... | Will shift to the left if... |
> | --- | --- |
> | • A or B added | • C added |
> | • C removed | • A or B removed |
> | • pressure increased or volume reduced | • volume increased or pressure reduced |
> | • temperature reduced | • temperature increased |

CONCEPTS TO REMEMBER

☐ Reaction mechanisms propose a series of steps, the sum of which gives the overall reaction that explains the chemical processes in the transformation of reactants into products. The slowest step in a reaction mechanism is the rate-determining step, and it limits the maximum rate at which the reaction can proceed.

☐ Reaction rates can be measured in terms of the rate of disappearance of reactant or the appearance of product, as measured by changes in their respective concentrations.

☐ The generic rate law is rate = $k[A]^x[B]^y$, and a particular reaction's actual rate law usually must be determined by analyzing experimental rate data that relate concentrations of reactants to rates of product formation.

☐ For a reaction to occur, molecules of reactants must collide with each other at the proper angle and with an amount of kinetic energy at least as great as the energy maximum of the transition state, known as the energy of activation, E_a.

☐ Reaction rates can be increased by increasing reactant concentrations (except for zero-order reactions), increasing the temperature, changing the medium, or adding a catalyst.

☐ Reversible chemical reactions will eventually "settle" into an energy minimum state (for which there is maximum entropy) called equilibrium. This is a dynamic equilibrium in which the concentrations of reactants and products are constant because the rates of the forward and reverse reactions are equal.

☐ The law of mass action gives the equilibrium constant (K_{eq}) expression. It states that at equilibrium, the ratio of products to reactants will be constant. At equilibrium, the ratio of the forward rate to the reverse rate will be equal to one; however, the ratio of the equilibrium concentrations of products to reactants will usually not be equal to one.

☐ The reaction quotient, Q_c, is a calculated value involving reactant and product concentrations at any time within a reaction. Comparison of the calculated Q_c value to the known K_{eq} value will tell you "where" the reaction is with respect to its equilibrium state.

☐ Pure solids and pure liquids are not included in the law of mass action, and K_{eq} is temperature dependent.

☐ Le Châtelier's principle states that a chemical system that experiences a stress (changes to concentration, pressure, or temperature) will react in whichever direction results in the re-establishment of the equilibrium state.

EQUATIONS TO REMEMBER

☐ rate = $k[A]^x[B]^y$

☐ $K_{eq} = \dfrac{[C]^c[D]^d}{[A]^a[B]^b}$ at equilibrium

☐ $\dfrac{k_f}{k_r} = K_c = K_{eq}$

☐ $Q_c = \dfrac{[C]^c[D]^d}{[A]^a[B]^b}$

Practice Questions

1. In a third-order reaction involving two reactants and two products, doubling the concentration of the first reactant causes the rate to increase by a factor of 2. What will happen to the rate of this reaction if the concentration of the second reactant is cut in half?

    A. It will increase by a factor of 2.
    B. It will increase by a factor of 4.
    C. It will decrease by a factor of 2.
    D. It will decrease by a factor of 4.

2. In a certain equilibrium process, the activation energy of the forward reaction is greater than the activation energy of the reverse reaction. This reaction is

    A. endothermic.
    B. exothermic.
    C. spontaneous.
    D. nonspontaneous.

3. Carbonated beverages are produced by dissolving carbon dioxide in water to produce carbonic acid

    $$CO_2\ (g) + H_2O\ (l) \rightleftharpoons H_2CO_3\ (aq)$$

    When a bottle containing carbonated water is opened, the taste of the beverage gradually changes until all of the carbonation is lost. Which of the following statements best explains this phenomenon?

    A. The change in pressure and volume causes the reaction to shift to the left, thereby decreasing the amount of aqueous carbonic acid.
    B. The change in pressure and volume causes the reaction to shift to the right, thereby decreasing the amount of gaseous carbon dioxide.
    C. Carbonic acid reacts with environmental oxygen and nitrogen.
    D. Carbon dioxide reacts with environmental oxygen and nitrogen.

4. A certain chemical reaction is endothermic. It occurs spontaneously. Which of the following must be true for this reaction?

    I. $\Delta H > 0$

    II. $\Delta G < 0$

    III. $\Delta S > 0$

    A. I only
    B. I and II only
    C. II and III only
    D. I, II, and III

5. A certain ionic salt, A_3B, has a molar solubility of 10 M at a certain temperature. What is the K_{sp} of this salt at the same temperature?

A. 10^4
B. 3×10^4
C. 2.7×10^5
D. 8.1×10^5

6. Acetic acid dissociates in solution according to the following equation:

$$CH_3COOH \rightleftharpoons CH_3COO^- + H^+$$

If sodium acetate is added to a solution of acetic acid in excess water, which of the following effects would be observed in the solution?

A. Decreased pH
B. Increased pH
C. Decreased pK_a
D. Increased pK_a

7. A certain chemical reaction follows the following rate law:

$$Rate = k [NO_2] [Br_2]$$

Which of the following statements describe(s) the kinetics of this reaction?

I. The reaction is a second-order reaction.
II. The amount of NO_2 consumed is equal to the amount of Br_2 consumed.
III. The rate will not be affected by the addition of a compound other than NO_2 and Br_2.

A. I only
B. I and II only
C. I and III only
D. III only

8. The following data shown in the table were collected for the combustion of the theoretical compound XH_4:

$$XH_4 + 2 O_2 \rightarrow XO_2 + 2 H_2O$$

Trial	$[XH_4]_{initial}$ (M)	$[O_2]_{initial}$ (M)	Rate (M/min)
1	0.6	0.6	12.4
2	0.6	2.4	49.9
3	1.2	2.4	198.3

What is the rate law for the reaction described here?

A. $Rate = k [XH_4] [O_2]$
B. $Rate = k [XH_4] [O_2]^2$
C. $Rate = k [XH_4]^2 [O_2]$
D. $Rate = k [XH_4]^2 [O_2]^2$

9. Which of the following actions does NOT affect the equilibrium of a reaction?

A. Adding/subtracting heat
B. Adding/removing a catalyst
C. Increasing/decreasing concentration of reactants
D. Increasing/decreasing volume of reactants

10. In a sealed 1 L container, 1 mol of nitrogen gas reacts with 3 mol of hydrogen gas to form 0.05 mol of NH_3. Which of the following is closest to the K_{eq} of the reaction?

A. 0.0001
B. 0.001
C. 0.01
D. 0.1

FOR QUESTIONS 11–13, CONSIDER THE FOLLOWING ENERGY DIAGRAM SHOWN IN FIGURE 1:

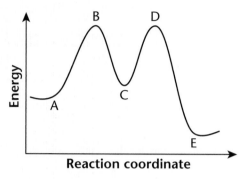

11. The overall reaction depicted by this energy diagram is

A. endothermic, because point B is higher than point A.

B. endothermic, because point C is higher than point A.

C. exothermic, because point D is higher than point E.

D. exothermic, because point A is higher than point E.

12. Which process has the highest activation energy?

A. The first step of the forward reaction

B. The first step of the reverse reaction

C. The second step of the forward reaction

D. The second step of the reverse reaction

13. Which of the following components of the reaction mechanism will NEVER be present in the reaction vessel when the reaction coordinate is at point B?

A. Reactants

B. Products

C. Intermediates

D. Catalysts

14. Consider the following two reactions:

$$3A + 2B \rightleftharpoons 3C + 4D \quad \text{(Reaction 1)}$$

$$4D + 3C \rightleftharpoons 3A + 2B \quad \text{(Reaction 2)}$$

If K_{eq} for reaction 1 is equal to 0.1, what is K_{eq} for reaction 2?

A. 0.1

B. 1

C. 10

D. 100

15. Which of the following statements would best describe the experimental result if the temperature of the following theoretical reaction were decreased?

$$A + B \rightleftharpoons C + D \quad \Delta H = -1.12 \text{ kJ/mol}$$

A. [C] + [D] would increase.

B. [A] + [B] would increase.

C. ΔH would increase.

D. ΔH would decrease.

16. Compound A has a K_a of approximately 10^{-4}. Which of the following compounds is most likely to react with a solution of compound A?

A. HNO_2

B. NO_2

C. NH_3

D. N_2O_5

17. The following system obeys second-order kinetics.

$$2NO_2 \rightarrow NO_3 + NO \qquad \text{(slow)}$$

$$NO_3 + CO \rightarrow NO_2 + CO_2 \qquad \text{(fast)}$$

What is the rate law for this reaction?

A. Rate = k $[NO_2]$ $[CO]$.

B. Rate = k $[NO_2]^2$ $[CO]$.

C. Rate = k $[NO_2]$ $[NO_3]$.

D. Rate = k $[NO_2]^2$.

18. The potential energy diagram shown represents four different reactions.

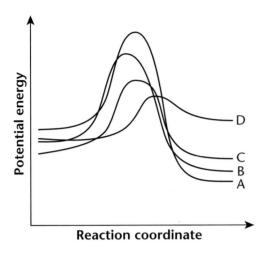

Assuming identical conditions, which of the reactions displayed on the energy diagram proceeds the fastest?

A. A
B. B
C. C
D. D

Small Group Questions

1. Because catalysts affect reaction rate, why don't we include their concentrations in reaction rate laws?

2. Do zero-order reactions contradict the collision theory of chemical kinetics?

3. How can Le Châtelier's principle be used to manipulate reactions?

Explanations to Practice Questions

1. D

Based on the information given in the question, the rate is first-order with respect to the concentration of the first reactant; when the concentration of that reactant doubles, the rate also doubles. Because the reaction is third-order, the sum of the exponents in the rate law must be equal to 3. Therefore, the rate law is defined as follows:

$$\text{Rate} = k\,[\text{reactant 1}]^1\,[\text{reactant 2}]^2$$

So the concentration of reactant 2 must be squared in order to write a rate law that represents a third-order reaction. When the concentration of reactant 2 is multiplied by ½, the rate will be multiplied by $(½)^2 = ¼$.

2. A

Before you try to answer this question, you should draw a potential energy diagram for the system.

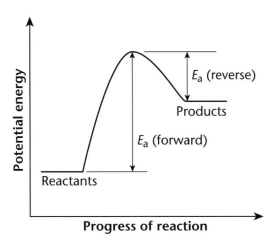

If the activation energy of the forward reaction is greater than the activation energy of the reverse reaction, then the products must have a higher enthalpy than the reactants. The overall energy of the system is higher at the end than it was in the beginning. The net enthalpy change is positive, indicating an endothermic reaction. Spontaneity is correlated with Gibbs free energy (ΔG).

3. A

Carbon dioxide gas evolves and leaves the bottle, which decreases the total pressure of the reactants. Le Châtelier's principle explains that a decrease in pressure shifts the equilibrium so as to increase the number of moles of gas present. This particular reaction will shift to the left, thereby decreasing the amount of carbonic acid and increasing the amount of carbon dioxide and water. Oxygen and nitrogen are not highly reactive and are unlikely to combine spontaneously with CO_2 or H_2CO_3.

4. D

ΔH is always positive for an endothermic reaction (meaning that option I is correct), and ΔG is always negative for a spontaneous reaction (meaning that option II is correct). Based on these two facts, ΔS can be determined by the free energy equation: $\Delta G = \Delta H - T\Delta S$, which can be rewritten as: $T\Delta S = \Delta H - \Delta G$. If ΔH is positive and ΔG is negative, $\Delta H - \Delta G$ must be positive. This means that $T\Delta S$ is positive. T (the temperature of the system in Kelvin) is always positive, so ΔS must also be positive. Therefore, option III is also correct. (A), (B), and (C) all include true but incomplete statements.

5. C

Recall that the K_{sp} of a salt is equal to the product of the concentrations of each of the salt's ions in saturated solution. Each molecule of this salt dissociates into three A^+ ions and one B^{3-} ion, so K_{sp} is equal to $[A^+][A^+][A^+][B^{3-}] = [A^+]^3[B^{3-}]$. The molar solubility of the salt is equal to the total number of moles of the salt in solution. The molar solubility of the salt is 10 M. Thus, the A^+ ion is present in a concentration of 30 M (3 A^+ ions per molecule), and the B^{3-} ion is present in a concentration of 10 M (one B^{3-} ion per molecule). These values can be substituted into the K_{sp} expression to yield $K_{sp} = [30\ M]^3[10\ M] = (27 \times 10^3)(10^1) = 27 \times 10^4 = 2.7 \times 10^5$.

6. B

Adding sodium acetate increases the number of acetate ions present. According to Le Châtelier's principle, this change will push this reaction to the left, resulting in a decrease in the number of free H^+ ions. Because pH is determined by the hydrogen ion concentration, a decrease in the number of free protons will increase the pH. This problem can also be solved with the K_a equation: $K_a = [CH_3COO^-][H^+]/[CH_3COOH]$. An acid's K_a will remain constant under a given temperature and pressure, eliminating (C) and (D). For K_a to remain unchanged while $[CH_3COO^-]$ increases, $[H^+]$ must decrease or $[CH_3COOH]$ must increase. A decrease in products would require an increase in reactants, and vice versa, so the final effect would be both an increase in $[CH_3COOH]$ and a decrease in $[H^+]$. Again, removing hydrogen ions will increase the pH of the solution.

7. A

If the sum of the exponents (orders) on the concentration of each species in the rate law is equal to 2, then the reaction is second-order. That's the case in this situation, so option I is correct. Option II is incorrect because the exponents in the rate law are unrelated to stoichiometric coefficients, so NO_2 and Br_2 could be present in any ratio in the original reaction and still be first-order. Option III is incorrect because the rate can be affected by a wide variety of compounds. A catalyst, for example, could increase the rate, but it wouldn't be included in the rate law. Any compound that would preferentially react with NO_2 or Br_2 (including strong acids/bases and strong oxidizing/reducing agents) would decrease the concentration of reactants and decrease the rate. Only I is valid; therefore, (A) is the correct answer.

8. C

In the first two trials, the concentration of XH_4 is held constant, while the concentration of O_2 is multiplied by 4. Because the rate of the reaction is also increased by a factor of approximately 4, oxygen must be a first-order reactant. Analyze the other reactant in the last two trials, XH_4. When you double its concentration, the rate of the reaction quadruples. That means XH_4 is a second-order reactant.

Until it becomes intuitive, use math to get to the right answer.

Write the following equations:

Trial 1: $rate_1 = 12.4 = k[XH_4]^x [O_2]^y = k(1.00)^x (0.6)^y$

Trial 2: $rate_2 = 49.9 = k[XH_4]^x [O_2]^y = k(1.00)^x (2.4)^y$

Plug in the values given in the question stem. When you divide Trial 2 by Trial 1, it simplifies to $4.02 = 4^y$, so y is approximately equal to 1. Next, a similar procedure allows you to calculate the order of $[XH_4]$ using trials 2 and 3.

Trial 2: $rate_2 = 49.9 = k[XH_4]^x [O_2]^y = k(0.6)^x (2.4)^1$

Trial 3: $rate_3 = 198.3 = k[XH_4]^x [O_2]^y = k(1.2)^x (2.4)^1$

Inserting the values you know, you find that the x exponent must be 2. Based on this, conclude that the experimental rate law is $= k [XF_4]^2 [O_2]$.

9. B

The equilibrium of a reaction can be changed by several factors. If you recall Le Châtelier's principle, you can rule out any answer choice that would shift the direction of an equilibrium. Adding or subtracting heat would shift the equilibrium based on the enthalpy change of the reaction. Adding reactant concentration would shift the equilibrium in the direction of the product, and the opposite would occur if concentrations were decreased. Changing the volume of a reactant would change its concentration, so that would have the same effect. Only (B), adding or removing a catalyst, would change the reaction rate without changing where the equilibrium lies.

10. A

The first step to answering this question is to write out the balanced equation for the reaction of H_2 and N_2 to produce NH_3 [$N_2 + 3H_2 \rightarrow 2NH_3$]. This means that K_{eq} is equal to $[NH_3]^2/([H_2]^3[N_2])$. Because the volume is 1 L, the amount of each gas (in moles) is equal to the value of the concentration of each gas (in M). We can plug these concentrations back into the K_{eq} expression to get $K_{eq} = (0.05)^2/([3]^3[1])$, which is equal to $(0.0025)/(27)$. This is approximately equal to 0.0001, and approximations are appropriate for the MCAT.

11. D

A system is exothermic if energy is released by the reaction. For exothermic reactions, the net energy change is negative, and the potential energy stored in the final products is lower than the potential energy stored in the initial reactants. Point E, which represents the energy of the final products, is lower on the energy diagram than point A, which represents the energy of initial reactants. Thus, energy must have been given off. While point A is useful for determining the energy of the overall reaction, point B represents the activation energy of the first transition state, and point C suggests an intermediate. (C) references the difference between points D and E, which only indicates the change in energy from the transition state of the second reaction step to the final products.

12. B

The activation energy of a reaction is equal to the distance on the y-axis from the energy of the reactants to the peak energy prior to formation of products. The activation energy of the first step of the forward reaction, for example, is equal to the distance along the y-axis from point A to point B. The largest energy increase on this graph occurs during the progress between point E and point D, which represents the first step of the reverse reaction.

13. B

This energy diagram presents a two-step system. The first reaction proceeds from point A to point C, and the second reaction proceeds from point C to point E. This means that the reactants predominate at point A, the intermediates predominate at point C, and the products predominate at point E. Point B, which is between points A and C, is the energy threshold at which most of the reactant starts to be converted into intermediate, so the reactant and the intermediate will both be present at this point. No product is produced until after point C, so it will not be present in the reaction mixture. Catalysts may be present in the mixture at any point, depending on the nature and the quantity of the catalyst.

14. C

Reaction 2 is simply the reverse of reaction 1. Because K_{eq} of reaction 1 is equal to [products]/[reactants], K_{eq} of reaction 2 must be equal to [reactants]/[products]. This means that K_{eq} for reaction 2 is the inverse of K_{eq} of reaction 1, so the answer is $1/0.1 = 10$.

15. A

A negative ΔH value always indicates an exothermic reaction, meaning that the forward reaction produces heat. Visualize that as follows:

$$A + B \rightleftharpoons C + D + heat$$

This means that removing heat by decreasing the temperature is similar to removing any other product of the reaction. To compensate for this loss, the reaction will shift to the right, causing an increase in the concentrations of C and D as well as a decrease in the concentrations of A and B.

16. C

K_a is equal to the ratio of products to reactants in a dissociated acid. A compound with a K_a greater than 10^{-7} contains more H^+ cations than HA^- anions, which makes it a weak acid (unless K_a is several orders of magnitude higher than 1, which would indicate a strong acid). This means that the compound in question is acidic and that it is likely to react with a compound that is basic. Of the four answer choices, NH_3 is the only base. Also remember that a K_a of 10^{-4} leads to a pKa of 4, which is a good approximation for the pKa of several organic acids.

17. D

To answer this question, you will need to recall that the slow step of a reaction is the rate-determining step. The rate is always related to the concentrations of the reactants in the slow step, so NO_2 is the only compound that should be included in the correct answer. The concentration of NO_2 is squared in the rate law because, according to the question, the reaction obeys second-order kinetics.

18. D

The faster a reaction can reach its activation energy, the faster it will proceed to completion. Because this question states that all conditions are equal, the reaction with the lowest activation energy will have the fastest rate. (D) illustrates the smallest difference between the initial and peak potential energies, so that reaction can overcome its activation energy more easily than the other proposed scenarios on the energy diagram. (A), (B), and (C) have higher activation energies.

Thermochemistry

Back in the "bad old days," before people became aware of the environmental havoc wreaked by Styrofoam, we used to drink our coffee from Styrofoam cups. Now, of course, coffee is usually served in paper cups consisting of some percentage of post-consumer recycled material, enveloped in a thin cardboard sleeve (also typically made from recycled material) for added insulation against the hot contents. In those rare instances when coffee is served in Styrofoam, the bearer of the cup may receive a few withering glances from those especially passionate about environmentalism and at the very least will probably feel a little guilty for using it.

While Styrofoam might be bad for the environment, it is certainly a good insulator. That's why it was the material of choice for disposable coffee cups for so long. It keeps hot things (like coffee) hot and cool things (like your hands—relative to the coffee) cool. The layer of Styrofoam protects your hands from too quickly absorbing the energy from the hot coffee and getting burned. Paper coffee cups just aren't as effective at insulation as Styrofoam cups are; hence, the need for the cardboard sleeve as an extra layer of protection.

Styrofoam cups are such good insulators that they can be used as holding containers for certain calorimetry experiments. "Coffee-cup calorimetry," which uses Styrofoam cups to measure heats of solution and specific heats of metals and other materials, is low-tech, yet it can produce remarkably accurate results, as long as care has been taken to calibrate the calorimeter and to minimize heat loss through the top. The next time you are at your favorite overpriced coffee chain, standing at the milk and sugar station, think about what you are doing when you mix the cold milk into the hot coffee. What you have there in your hand is really a little science experiment. If you took the time to measure the masses and temperatures of the hot coffee and the cold milk before mixing them, measured the drink's temperature after you had stirred them up, and then looked up the specific heats for water and milk, you would have enough information to calculate the amount of heat exchanged between the hot coffee and the cold milk. (And if you *really* wanted to be accurate, you would include in your calculation the mass of the little wooden stirrer and its specific heat as well!) Of course, if you actually used the milk and coffee station as your lab bench, you may be putting your life at risk in the hands of the angry, under- and overcaffeinated mob standing behind you impatiently waiting their turn.

This chapter will review the basic principles of thermochemistry, which is the study of the energy changes that accompany chemical and physical processes. Starting from the first law of thermodynamics, which states that energy is never created or destroyed but at most simply changed from one form to another, we will analyze the calculations that are done to quantify the various changes or exchanges in energy as a system moves from some initial state to a final state. As we go along, we will define what is meant by system and surroundings, state functions, heat, enthalpy, entropy, and Gibbs free energy.

Systems and Processes   ★★☆☆☆

For whatever reason, students seem to have some anxiety over what, exactly, constitutes a system and what, by exclusion from the system, constitute the surroundings or environment. Perhaps the problem isn't so much with the definitions, which are fairly straightforward, but the way in which the boundary between the two can be "moved" to suit the interests of the experimenter or observer. Simply put, the system is the matter that is being observed. It's the total amount of reactants and products, say, in a chemical reaction. It's the amount of solute and solvent used to create a solution. It could even be the gas inside a balloon. Then the surroundings, or environment, are everything outside of what you're looking at. However, the boundary between system and surroundings is not permanently fixed, and it can be moved. For example, you might consider the mass of coffee in your coffee cup to be the system and the cup containing it to be the environment. If this is the way you set your boundary, then you're probably interested in determining, say, the amount of heat transferred from the hot coffee to the cooler coffee cup. Alternatively, you might define the system as the hot coffee and the cup and the environment as the air surrounding the coffee cup. If this is the way you've defined your boundary, then you're probably interested in the heat exchange between the hot coffee/cup system and the cooler surrounding air. The boundary can be extended out farther and farther, until ultimately the entire mass of the universe is included in the system, at which point there are no surroundings. Where you place the boundary is really a decision based on what matter you're interested in studying.

Systems can be further characterized by whether or not they can exchange heat and/or matter with the surroundings. A system may be characterized as follows:

- **Isolated**—The system cannot exchange energy (heat and work) or matter with the surroundings; for example, an insulated bomb calorimeter.
- **Closed**—The system can exchange energy (heat and work) but not matter with the surroundings; for example, a steam radiator.
- **Open**—The system can exchange both energy (again, heat and work) and matter with the surroundings; for example, a pot of boiling water.

When a system experiences a change in one or more of its properties (such as concentration of reactant or product, temperature, or pressure), we say that it undergoes a **process**. While processes, by definition, are associated with changes of state of systems, some processes are uniquely identified by some property that is constant throughout the process. For example, **isothermal** processes occur when the system's temperature is constant. Constant temperature implies that the total internal energy of the system is constant throughout the process. **Adiabatic** processes occur when no heat is exchanged between the system and the environment; thus, the heat content of the system is constant throughout the process. Finally, **isobaric** processes occur when the pressure of the system is constant. Isothermal and isobaric processes are common, because it is usually easy to control temperature and pressure.

Processes themselves can be also classified as spontaneous or nonspontaneous. A spontaneous process is one that can occur by itself without having to be driven by energy from an outside source. Calculating the change in the Gibbs free energy (ΔG) for a process, such as a chemical reaction, allows us to predict whether the process will be spontaneous or nonspontaneous. The same quantities that are used to calculate the change in the Gibbs free energy, ΔH and ΔS, can also tell us whether or not the process will be temperature-dependent; that is, spontaneous at some temperatures and nonspontaneous at others (see the section on Gibbs free energy).

Spontaneous reactions, as you'll recall from our discussion of chemical kinetics and equilibrium in Chapter 5, will not necessarily happen quickly and may not go to completion. Many spontaneous reactions have very high activation energies and, therefore, rarely actually take place. For example, when was the last time you saw a match ignite itself spontaneously? Or for that matter, when was the last time you or a loved one spontaneously combusted? However, provide an amount of thermal energy (generated by the friction associated with "striking the match") that equals or exceeds the energy of activation, and the match will light and burn spontaneously. Combustion, the combination of the chemical components of the match with molecular oxygen in the air, will not need any additional external energy input in order to proceed once the energy of activation has been supplied. Some spontaneous reactions proceed very slowly. The role of enzymes, biological catalysts, is to selectively enhance the rate of certain spontaneous but slow chemical reactions so that the biologically necessary products can be formed at a rate sufficient for sustaining life. As we learned in Chapter 5, some reactions do not go to completion but settle into a low-energy state called equilibrium. Spontaneous reactions may go to completion, but many simply reach equilibrium with dynamically stable concentrations of reactants and products.

States and State Functions   ★★★☆☆

Every year in January, the president of the United States speaks to the nation in a State of the Union address. In the speech, the president gives an assessment of the parameters by which we can measure the relative well-being of the nation and its citizens. There is usually discussion of war or peace; economic indicators; domestic programs; and other measurements of the social, political, and economic status of the country. These indicators help the people understand where they "are" as a nation in comparison to where they were the year prior, but less so how they got to where they are now.

Similarly, the state of a system is described by certain macroscopic properties of the system. These properties, or state functions, describe the system in an equilibrium state. They cannot describe the process of the system; that is, how the system got to its current equilibrium. They are useful only for comparing one equilibrium state to another. The pathway taken from one equilibrium state to another is described quantitatively by the process functions, the most important of which are mechanical work (W) and heat (Q).

The state functions include temperature (T), pressure (P), volume (V), density (ρ), internal energy (E or U), enthalpy (H), entropy (S), and Gibbs free energy (G). When the state of a system changes from one equilibrium to another, one or more of these state functions will change. In addition, while state functions are independent of the path (process) taken, they are not necessarily independent of one another. For example, Gibbs free energy is related to enthalpy, entropy, and temperature, as you will see.

Because systems can be in different equilibrium states at different temperatures and pressures, a set of **standard conditions** has been defined for measuring the enthalpy, entropy, and Gibbs free energy changes of a reaction. The standard conditions are defined as 25°C (298 K) and 1 atm. Don't confuse standard conditions with **standard temperature and pressure (STP)**, for which the temperature is 0°C (273 K) and 1 atm. This common MCAT Test Day mistake is easily made but also easily avoided. You'll use standard conditions for thermodynamic problems of enthalpy or free energy, but you'll use STP for ideal gas calculations.

Under standard conditions, the most stable form of a substance is called the **standard state** of that substance. You should recognize the standard states for some elements and compounds commonly encountered on the test. For example, H_2 (g), H_2O (l), NaCl (s), O_2 (g), and C (s) (graphite) are the most stable forms of these substances under standard conditions. Recognizing whether or not a substance is in its standard state is important for thermochemical calculations, such as heats of reactions and, in particular, the heat of formation. The changes in enthalpy, entropy, and free energy that occur when a reaction takes place under standard conditions are called the **standard enthalpy**, **standard entropy**, and **standard free energy** changes, respectively, and are symbolized by $\Delta H°$, $\Delta S°$, and $\Delta G°$.

The rest of this chapter will focus on the following state functions: enthalpy, entropy (energy dispersal), and free energy, with some concluding remarks on spontaneity.

Heat

★★★★☆☆

Before we can examine the first of the four state functions that are the focus of this chapter, we must address the topic of heat, which is a source of some confusion for students. Perhaps the greatest barrier to a proper understanding of heat is the semantic conflation of the terms *heat* and *temperature*. Many people use these terms interchangeably in everyday conversation. We might say, for example, that a midsummer afternoon was unbearably hot or that the temperature exceeded 100°F. Both convey the sense that the day was very, very warm, but what makes sense in everyday conversation needs to be clarified for a proper understanding of thermochemical principles. **Temperature (*T*)** is related to the average kinetic energy of the particles of the substance whose temperature is being measured. Temperature is the way that we scale how hot or cold something is (but not necessarily how hot or cold something feels to us: For reasons that will become clear in our discussion of specific heat, blacktop will feel hotter to our bare feet than a wooden boardwalk would, even if they are at the same temperature). We are familiar with a few temperature scales: Fahrenheit, Celsius, and Kelvin. The average kinetic energy of the particles in a substance is related to the thermal energy of the substance, but because we must also include consideration of how much substance is present to calculate total thermal energy content, the most we can say about temperature is that when a substance's thermal energy increases, its temperature increases also. Nevertheless, we cannot say that something that is hot necessarily has greater thermal energy (in absolute terms) than a substance that is cold. For example, we might determine that a large amount of cool water has greater *total* heat content than a very small amount of very hot water.

Heat (*Q*) is the transfer of energy from one substance to another as a result of their difference in temperature. In fact, the zeroth law of thermodynamics implies that objects are in thermal equilibrium only when their temperatures are equal. Heat is therefore a process function, not a state function: We can quantify how much thermal energy is transferred between two or more objects as a result of their difference in temperatures by measuring the heat transferred.

The first law of thermodynamics states that the change in the total internal energy (ΔU) of a system is equal to the amount of heat (thermal energy) transferred (Q) to the system minus the amount of work (W) (another form of energy transfer by the application of force through displacement) done by the system. This can be expressed mathematically as follows:

$$\Delta U = Q - W$$

> ## Key Concept
> Remember that heat and temperature are different. Heat is a specific form of energy that can enter or leave a system, while temperature is a measure of the average kinetic energy of the particles in a system.

Because heat and work are measured independently, we can assess the transfer of energy in the form of heat through any process regardless of the work done (or not done). Processes in which the system absorbs heat are called endothermic $(+\Delta Q)$, while those processes in which the system releases heat are called exothermic $(-\Delta Q)$. The unit of heat is the unit of energy: joule (J) or calorie (c) for which 1 c = 4.184 J.

You know how people who live in really hot desert climates, when asked, "How can you stand the heat?" often respond by pointing out, "But it's a dry heat!" Well, there's some truth to that. One of the most important ways that the body works to prevent overheating is through the production of sweat—that exocrine secretion of water, electrolytes, and urea. However, it's not the production of sweat, per se, that is the cooling mechanism. It's the evaporation of the sweat that helps cool the body. Evaporation (vaporization) from the liquid to gas phase is an endothermic process: Energy must be absorbed for the particles of the liquid to gain enough kinetic energy to escape into the gas phase. So the sweat that is excreted onto the skin must absorb energy in order to evaporate. Where does that necessary energy come from? It comes from the body itself. Hot, arid desert air has lower partial pressure of water vapor than humid tropical air, so sweat vaporizes more readily in the dry air than it does in the humid air. Although it might be hard to believe that any temperature in excess of 100°F could ever be considered comfortable, it probably is true that most people will feel more comfortable in "dry heat" than in "tropical heat."

When substances of different temperatures are brought into thermal contact with each other (that is, some physical arrangement that allows for the transfer of heat energy), energy—in the form of heat—will transfer from the warmer substance to the cooler substance. When a substance undergoes a chemical reaction that is exothermic or endothermic, heat energy will be exchanged between the system and the environment. The process of measuring transferred heat is called calorimetry. Two basic types of calorimetry that you should know and understand for Test Day include constant-pressure calorimetry and constant-volume calorimetry. The coffee-cup calorimeter, introduced at the beginning of this lesson, is a low-tech example of a constant-pressure calorimeter, while the bomb calorimeter is an example of a constant-volume calorimeter. *Constant-pressure* and *constant-volume* are terms used to describe the conditions under which the heat changes are measured.

The heat (q) absorbed or released in a given process is calculated from this equation:

$$q = mc\Delta T$$

where m is the mass, c is the **specific heat** of the substance, and ΔT is the change in temperature (in either Celsius or Kelvin). Specific heat is the amount of energy required to raise the temperature of one gram or kilogram of a substance by one

Key Concept

Endothermic: positive ΔH

Exothermic: negative ΔH

degree Celsius or one unit Kelvin. Specific heat values will be provided for you on Test Day, but one value that you need to remember is the specific heat of H_2O (*l*): one calorie per gram per Celsius degree (1 c/g°C). Speaking of easy to remember, you ought not have any problem remembering this equation, given that $q = mc\Delta T$ looks like "*q* equals MCAT."

Constant-Volume Calorimetry

To picture the setup of a constant-pressure calorimeter, just think of the coffee-cup calorimeter: an insulated container covered with a lid and filled with a solution in which a reaction or some physical process, such as dissolution, is occurring. The pressure, which is just the atmospheric pressure, remains constant throughout the process. The setup of a constant-volume calorimeter is perhaps a little less familiar to you or harder to picture. Furthermore, the term *bomb calorimeter* sounds rather ominous. Well, don't worry—this isn't some relic from the Cold War. Perhaps "bomb" is a bit misleading: A more accurately descriptive term is "decomposition vessel." This better reflects what is actually taking place. A sample of matter, typically a hydrocarbon, is placed in the steel decomposition vessel, which is then filled with almost pure O_2 gas. The decomposition vessel is then placed in an insulated container holding a known mass of water. The contents of the decomposition vessel are ignited by an electric ignition mechanism. The material combusts (burns) in the presence of the oxygen, and the heat that is evolved in the combustion is the heat of the reaction. Because $W = P\Delta V$, no work is done in an isovolumic ($\Delta V = 0$) process, so $W_{calorimeter} = 0$. Furthermore, because of the insulation, the whole calorimeter can be considered isolated from the rest of the universe, so we can identify the "system" as the sample plus oxygen and steel and the surroundings as the water. Because no heat is exchanged between the calorimeter and the rest of the universe, $Q_{calorimeter}$ is 0. So $\Delta U_{system} + \Delta U_{surroundings} = \Delta U_{calorimeter} = Q_{calorimeter} - W_{calorimeter} = 0$. Therefore, $\Delta U_{system} = -\Delta U_{surroundings}$. Because no work is done, $q_{system} = -q_{surroundings}$, and $m_{steel}c_{steel}\Delta T + m_{oxygen}c_{oxygen}\Delta T = -m_{water}c_{water}\Delta T$.

Note that by using the layer of insulation to isolate the entire calorimeter from the rest of the universe, we've created an adiabatic process. This means that no heat is exchanged between the calorimeter and the rest of the universe, but it *is* exchanged between the steel decomposition vessel and the surrounding water. As the previous derivation shows, heat exchange between the system and its surroundings makes it possible for us to calculate the heat of the combustion.

Enthalpy

Most reactions in the lab occur under constant pressure (at 1 atm) in closed thermodynamic systems. To express heat changes at constant pressure, chemists use the

term **enthalpy (H)**. Enthalpy is a state function, so we can calculate the change in enthalpy (ΔH) for a system that has undergone a process—for example, a chemical reaction—by comparing the enthalpy of the final state to the enthalpy of the initial state, irrespective of the path taken. The change in enthalpy is equal to the heat transferred into or out of the system at constant pressure. To find the enthalpy change of a reaction, ΔH_{rxn}, you must subtract the enthalpy of the reactants from the enthalpy of the products:

$$\Delta H_{rxn} = H_{products} - H_{reactants}$$

A positive ΔH_{rxn} corresponds to an endothermic process, and a negative ΔH_{rxn} corresponds to an exothermic process. It is not possible to measure enthalpy directly; only ΔH can be measured, and only for certain fast and spontaneous processes. Several standard methods have been developed to calculate ΔH for any process.

Standard Heat of Formation

The **standard enthalpy of formation** of a compound, ΔH°_f, is the enthalpy change that would occur if one mole of a compound in its standard state were formed directly from its elements in their respective standard states. Remember that standard state is the most stable physical state of an element or compound at 298 K and 1 atm. Note that ΔH°_f of an element in its standard state, by definition, is zero. The ΔH°_f's of most known substances are tabulated. You do not need to memorize these values, as they will be provided for you as necessary.

Standard Heat of Reaction

The **standard heat of a reaction**, ΔH°_{rxn}, is the hypothetical enthalpy change that would occur if the reaction were carried out under standard conditions. What this means is that all reactants must be in their standard states and all products must be in their standard states. This can be calculated by taking the difference between the sum of the standard heats of formation for the products and the sum of the standard heats of formation of the reactants:

$$\Delta H^\circ_{rxn} = \Sigma(\Delta H^\circ_f \text{ of products}) - \Sigma(\Delta H^\circ_f \text{ of reactants})$$

Hess's Law

Enthalpy is a state function and is a property of the equilibrium state, so the pathway taken for a process is irrelevant to the change in enthalpy from one equilibrium state to another. As a consequence of this, **Hess's law** states that enthalpy changes of reactions are additive. When thermochemical equations (chemical equations for which energy changes are known) are added to give the net equation for a reaction, the corresponding heats of reaction are also added to give the net heat of reaction. You can think of Hess's law as being embodied in the enthalpy

Key Concept

State functions are path-independent. Always.

equations we've already introduced. For example, we can describe any reaction as the result of breaking down the reactants into their component elements, then forming the products from these elements. The enthalpy change for the reverse of any reaction has the same magnitude, but the opposite sign, as the enthalpy change for the forward reaction. Therefore,

$$\Delta H \text{ (reactants} \to \text{elements)} = -\Delta H \text{ (elements} \to \text{reactants)}$$

The ΔH_{rxn} written as

$$\Delta H_{rxn} = \Delta H \text{ (reactants} \to \text{elements)} + \Delta H \text{ (elements} \to \text{products)}$$

becomes

$$\Delta H_{rxn} = -\Delta H \text{ (elements} \to \text{reactants)} + \Delta H \text{ (elements} \to \text{products)}$$
$$= \Delta H \text{ (elements} \to \text{products)} - \Delta H \text{ (elements} \to \text{reactants)}$$

Thus,

$$\Delta H^{\circ}_{rxn} = \Sigma (\Delta H^{\circ}_{f} \text{ of products)} - \Sigma (\Delta H^{\circ}_{f} \text{ of reactants)}$$

Consider the following phase change:

$$Br_2 (l) \to Br_2 (g) \qquad \Delta H^{\circ}_{rxn} = 31 \text{ kJ/mol}$$

The enthalpy change for the phase change is called the heat of vaporization (ΔH°_{vap}). As long as the initial and final states exist at standard conditions, the ΔH°_{rxn} will always equal the ΔH°_{vap}, irrespective of the particular pathway that the process takes in vaporization. For example, it's possible that $Br_2 (l)$ could first decompose to Br atoms, which then recombine to form $Br_2 (g)$, giving the following reaction mechanism. However, because the net reaction is the same as the one shown previously, the change in enthalpy will be the same.

$$Br_2 (l) \to Br_2 (g) \qquad \Delta H = (31 \text{ kJ/mol})(1 \text{ mol}) = 31 \text{ kJ}$$

Example: Given the following thermochemical equations:

a) $C_3H_8 (g) + 5 O_2 (g) \to 3 CO_2 (g) + 4 H_2O (l)$ $\Delta H_a = -2{,}220.1 \text{ kJ}$
b) $C (graphite) + O_2 (g) \to CO_2 (g)$ $\Delta H_b = -393.5 \text{ kJ}$
c) $H_2 (g) + 1/2 O_2 (g) \to H_2O (l)$ $\Delta H_c = -285.8 \text{ kJ}$

Calculate ΔH for this reaction:

d) $3 C (graphite) + 4 H_2 (g) \to C_3H_8 (g)$

MCAT Expertise

When doing a problem like this on the MCAT, make sure to switch signs when you reverse the equation. Also, make sure to multiply by the correct stoichiometric coefficients when performing your calculations.

Solution: Equations a, b, and c must be combined to obtain equation d. Since equation d contains only C, H_2, and C_3H_8, we must eliminate O_2, CO_2, and H_2O from the first three equations. Equation a is reversed to get C_3H_8 on the product side (this gives equation e). Next, equation b is multiplied by 3 (this gives equation f) and c by 4 (this gives equation g). The following addition is done to obtain the required equation d: $3b + 4c + e$.

e) $\quad 3\, CO_2\,(g) + 4\, H_2O\,(l) \rightarrow C_3H_8\,(g) + 5\, O_2\,(g)\quad \Delta H_e = 2{,}220.1\ kJ$

f) $\quad 3 \times [C\,(graphite) + O_2\,(g) \rightarrow CO_2\,(g)]\qquad \Delta H_f = 3 \times -393.5\ kJ$

g) $\quad 4 \times [H_2\,(g) + \dfrac{1}{2}\, O_2\,(g) \rightarrow H_2O\,(l)]\quad \Delta H_g = 4 \times -285.8\ kJ$

$3\, C\,(graphite) + 4\, H_2\,(g) \rightarrow C_3H_8\,(g)\qquad \Delta H_d = -103.6\ kJ$
$\quad$ where $\Delta H_d = \Delta H_e + \Delta H_f + \Delta H_g$.

It is important to realize that Hess's law applies to *any* state function, including entropy and Gibbs free energy.

Bond Dissociation Energy

Hess's law can also be expressed in terms of bond enthalpies, also called **bond dissociation energies**, when these are given. Bond dissociation energy is the average energy that is required to break a particular type of bond between atoms in the gas phase (remember, bond dissociation is an endothermic process). Bond dissociation energy is given as kJ/mol of bonds broken. For example, the bond enthalpy of the double bond in the diatomic oxygen molecule O_2 is 498 kJ/mol (of double bonds broken). The tabulated bond enthalpies for bonds found in compounds other than diatomic molecules are the average of the bond energies for the bonds in many different compounds. For example, the C–H bond enthalpy (415 kJ/mol) that you will find listed in a table of bond enthalpies is averaged from measurements of the individual C–H bond enthalpies of thousands of different organic compounds. Please note that bond formation, the opposite of bond breaking, has the same magnitude of energy but is negative rather than positive; that is, energy is released when bonds are formed. The enthalpy change associated with a reaction is given by

Key Concept

Because it takes energy to pull two atoms apart, bond breakage is always endothermic. The reverse process, bond formation, must always be exothermic.

$$\Delta H_{rxn} = \Sigma \Delta H_{bonds\ broken} + \Sigma \Delta H_{bonds\ formed}$$
$$= \text{total energy absorbed} - \text{total energy released}$$

For example,

$$H_2\,(g) \rightarrow 2H\,(g) \qquad \Delta H = 436\ kJ/mol$$

In this decomposition reaction, diatomic hydrogen gas is cleaved to produce mono-atomic hydrogen gas. For each mole of H_2 cleaved, 436 kJ of energy is absorbed by the system in order to overcome the bonding force. Since energy is absorbed, the bond-breaking reaction is endothermic.

If you have a hard time remembering whether bond formation or dissociation is endothermic, think about bonds as if they were two bar magnets stuck together. You have to exert pulling forces (invest energy) to pull apart two bar magnets (endothermic). On the other hand, the two bar magnets, once separated, "want" to come back together because they exert an attractive force between their opposite poles. Allowing them to stick together reduces their potential energy (exothermic).

Example: Calculate the enthalpy change for the following reaction:
$$C(s) + 2\ H_2(g) \rightarrow CH_4(g) \quad \Delta H = ?$$

Bond dissociation energies of H–H and C–H bonds are 436 kJ/mol and 415 kJ/mol, respectively.

$$\Delta H_f \text{ of } C(g) = 715 \text{ kJ/mol}$$

Solution: CH_4 is formed from free elements in their standard states (C in solid and H_2 in gaseous state).

Thus here, $\Delta H_{rxn} = \Delta H_f$.

The reaction can be written in three steps:
  a) $C\ (s) \rightarrow C\ (g)$ $\quad\quad\quad\quad\quad\quad \Delta H_1$
  b) $2\ [H_2\ (g) \rightarrow 2\ H\ (g)]$ $\quad\quad\quad 2\Delta H_2$
  c) $C\ (g) + 4\ H\ (g) \rightarrow CH_4\ (g)$ $\quad \Delta H_3$

and $\Delta H_f = [\Delta H_1 + 2\ \Delta H_2] + [\Delta H_3]$.

$$\Delta H_1 = \Delta H_f C\ (g) = 715 \text{ kJ/mol}$$

ΔH_2 is the energy required to break the H–H bond of one mole of H_2. So,

$$\Delta H_2 = \text{bond energy of } H_2$$
$$= 436 \text{ kJ/mol}$$

ΔH_3 is the energy released when 4 C–H bonds are formed. So,

$$\Delta H_3 = -(4 \times \text{bond energy of C–H})$$
$$= -(4 \times 415 \text{ kJ/mol})$$
$$= -1{,}660 \text{ kJ/mol}$$

(**Note:** Because energy is released when bonds are formed, ΔH_3 is negative.)

Therefore,

$$\Delta H_{rxn} = \Delta H_f = [715 + 2(436)] - (1{,}660) \text{ kJ/mol}$$
$$= -73 \text{ kJ/mol}$$

MCAT Expertise

With practice, you'll become accustomed to the patterns and shortcuts that will make things easier on Test Day.

Key Concept

The larger the alkane reactant, the more numerous the combustion products.

Heats of Combustion

One more type of standard enthalpy change that you should be aware of for the MCAT is the **standard heat of combustion**, ΔH°_{comb}. Because measurements of enthalpy change require a reaction to be spontaneous and fast, combustion reactions are the ideal process for such measurements. Most combustion reactions presented on the MCAT occur in the presence of O_2 in the atmosphere, but keep in mind that there are other combustion reactions in which oxygen is not the oxidant. Diatomic fluorine, for example, can be used as an oxidant, and hydrogen gas will combust with chlorine gas to form gaseous hydrochloric acid and, in the process, will evolve a large amount of heat and light characteristic of combustion reactions. The reactions listed in the C_3H_8 (g) example shown earlier are combustion reactions with O_2 (g) as the oxidant. Therefore, the enthalpy change listed for each of the three reactions is the ΔH_{comb} for each of the reactions.

Entropy ★★★☆☆

Many, many students are genuinely perplexed by the concept of entropy. Enthalpy makes, perhaps, intuitive sense, especially when the energy change from reactants to products is large, fast, and dramatic (as in combustion reactions involving explosions). Entropy seems to be less intuitive. Except that it isn't. In fact, our understanding of what constitutes normal life experience and even the passage of time is based, fundamentally, upon the property of entropy. Consider, for example, how "normal" each of the following seems to you: hot tea cools down, frozen drinks melt, iron rusts, buildings crumble, balloons deflate, living things die, and so on.

These examples have a common denominator: In all of them, energy of some form or another is going from being localized or concentrated to being spread out or dispersed. The thermal energy in the hot tea is spreading out to the cooler air that surrounds it. The thermal energy in the warmer air is spreading out to the cooler frozen drink. The chemical energy in the bonds of elemental iron and oxygen is released and dispersed as a result of the formation of the more stable (lower-energy) bonds of iron oxide (rust). The potential energy of the building is released and dispersed in the form of light, sound, and heat (motional energy) of the ground and air as the building crumbles and falls. The motional energy of the pressurized air is released to the surrounding atmosphere as the balloon deflates. The chemical energy of all the molecules and atoms in living flesh is released into the environment during the process of death and decay.

This is the **second law of thermodynamics**: Energy spontaneously disperses from being localized to becoming spread out if it is not hindered from doing so. Pay attention to this: *The usual way of thinking about entropy as "disorder" must not be taken too literally, a trap that many students fall into. Be very careful in thinking*

Key Concept

Entropy changes that accompany phase changes (see Chapter 8) can be easily estimated, at least qualitatively. For example, freezing is accompanied by a decrease in entropy, as the relatively disordered liquid becomes a well-ordered solid. Meanwhile, boiling is accompanied by a large increase in entropy, as the liquid becomes a much more disordered gas. For any substance, sublimation will be the phase transition with the greatest entropy change.

about entropy as disorder. The old analogy between a messy (disordered) room and entropy is arguably deficient and may not only hinder understanding but actually increase confusion.

Entropy, then, according to statistical mechanics, is the measure of the spontaneous dispersal of energy at a specific temperature: *how much* energy is spread out, or *how widely* spread out energy becomes, in a process. The equation for calculating the change in entropy is

$$\Delta S = \frac{Q_{rev}}{T}$$

where ΔS is the change in entropy, Q_{rev} is the heat that is gained or lost in a reversible process (a process that proceeds with infinitesimal changes in the system), and T is the temperature in Kelvin. The units of entropy are usually kJ/mol • K. When energy is distributed into a system at a given temperature, its entropy increases. When energy is distributed out of a system at a given temperature, its entropy decreases.

Notice that the second law states that energy will spontaneously disperse; it does not say that energy can never be localized or concentrated. However, the concentration of energy will rarely, if ever, happen spontaneously in a closed system (there is an exceedingly small but measurable chance that it could, but this is beyond the scope of the MCAT). Work usually must be done to concentrate energy. For example, refrigerators move thermal energy against a temperature gradient (that is, they cause heat to be transferred from "cool" to "warm"), thereby "concentrating" energy outside of the system in the surroundings. Nevertheless, refrigerators consume a lot of energy (they do a lot of work) to accomplish this movement of energy against the temperature gradient.

[FROM ORDER TO DISORDER]

ENTROPY IN THE KITCHEN

A raw egg exemplifies the asymmetry of time: A fresh one breaks easily, but a broken one does not spontaneously put itself together again, for the simple reason that there are more ways to be broken than not. In physics jargon, the broken egg has a higher entropy.

One way to be pristine

Several ways to be slightly cracked

Myriad ways to be fully smashed

Figure 6.1

The second law has been described as "time's arrow," because there is a unidirectional limitation on the movement of energy by which we recognize "before and after" or "new and old." For example, you would instantly recognize whether a video recording of an explosion was running forward or backward. This is what is meant by the phrase "time's arrow." Another way of understanding this is to say that energy in a closed system will spontaneously spread out and entropy will increase if it is not hindered from doing so. Remember that a system can be variably defined to include ultimately the entire universe; in fact, the second law ultimately claims that the entropy of the universe is increasing. That is to say, energy concentrations at any and all locations in the universe are in the process of becoming distributed and spread out.

$$\Delta S_{universe} = \Delta S_{system} + \Delta S_{surroundings} > 0$$

Entropy is a state function, so a change in entropy from one equilibrium state to another is pathway-independent and only depends upon the difference in entropies of the final and initial states:

$$\Delta S = S_{final} - S_{initial}$$

The standard entropy change for a reaction, ΔS°_{rxn}, is calculated using the standard entropies of reactants and products:

$$\Delta S^{\circ}_{rxn} = \Sigma \Delta S^{\circ}_{products} - \Sigma \Delta S^{\circ}_{reactants}$$

Gibbs Free Energy ★★★★☆

The final state function that we will examine in this chapter is Gibbs free energy, G. Now, you can be sure that Josiah Gibbs isn't giving it away for free. Actually, given that the man died way back in 1903, it's unlikely that he's got much more energy to give away, anyway. This state function is a combination of the two that we've just examined: enthalpy and entropy. The change in Gibbs free energy, ΔG, is a measure of the change in the enthalpy and the change in entropy as a system undergoes a process, and it indicates whether a reaction is spontaneous or nonspontaneous. The change in the free energy is the maximum amount of energy released by a process, occurring at constant temperature and pressure, that is available to perform useful work. The change in Gibbs free energy is defined as follows:

$$\Delta G = \Delta H - T\Delta S$$

where T is the temperature in Kelvin and $T\Delta S$ represents the total amount of energy that is absorbed by a system when its entropy increases reversibly.

Mnemonic

$\Delta G = \Delta H - T\Delta S$. Get High Test Scores!

A helpful visual aid for conceptualizing Gibbs free energy is to think of it as a valley between two hills. Just as a ball would tend to roll down the hill into the valley and eventually come to rest at the lowest point in the valley (as long as nothing prevents it from doing so), any system, including chemical reactions, will move in whatever direction results in a reduction of the free energy of the system. The bottom of the valley, the lowest point, represents equilibrium, and the sides of the hill represent the various points in the pathway toward or away from equilibrium. Movement toward the equilibrium position is associated with a decrease in Gibbs free energy ($-\Delta G$) and is spontaneous, while movement away from the equilibrium position is associated with an increase in Gibbs free energy ($+\Delta G$) and is nonspontaneous. You wouldn't quite believe your eyes if, all of a sudden, the ball at the bottom of the valley began to roll up the hill with no assistance. Once at the energy minimum state, the position of equilibrium (the bottom of the valley), the system will resist any changes to its state, and the change in free energy is zero for all systems at equilibrium. To summarize:

1. If ΔG is negative, the reaction is spontaneous.
2. If ΔG is positive, the reaction is nonspontaneous.
3. If ΔG is zero, the system is in a state of equilibrium; thus $\Delta H = T\Delta S$.

Key Concept

Recall that thermodynamics and kinetics are separate topics. When a reaction is thermodynamically spontaneous, it has no bearing on how fast it goes. It only means that it will proceed *eventually* without external energy input.

Because the temperature in Gibbs free energy is in units of Kelvin, it is always positive. Therefore, the effects of the signs on ΔH and ΔS and the effect of temperature on the spontaneity of a process can be summarized as follows:

ΔH	ΔS	Outcome
−	+	spontaneous at all temperatures
+	−	nonspontaneous at all temperatures
+	+	spontaneous only at high temperatures
−	−	spontaneous only at low temperatures

Key Concept

ΔG is temperature-dependent when ΔH and ΔS have the same sign.

Phase changes are examples of temperature-dependent processes. The phase changes of water should be familiar to you. Have you ever wondered why water doesn't boil at, say, 20°C instead of 100°C? Well, first of all, be thankful that it doesn't because 20°C is room temperature. It'd be hard to keep a glass of water, not to mention you, around for very long. (Water makes up almost 99 percent of the total number of molecules in the human body. Excluding adipose tissue, the human body is about 75 percent water by mass!) So we all know that water boils at 100°C, but why? The answer lies in phase transformation:

$$H_2O\ (l) \rightarrow H_2O\ (g) \qquad \Delta H_{vap} = 40.65\ \text{kJ/mol}$$

When water boils, hydrogen bonds (H-bonds) are broken, and the water molecules gain sufficient potential energy to escape into the gas phase. Thus, boiling (vaporization) is an endothermic process, and ΔH is positive. As thermal energy is transferred to the water molecules, energy is distributed through the molecules entering the gas phase, and entropy is positive and $T\Delta S$ is positive. Both ΔH and $T\Delta S$ are positive, so the reaction will be spontaneous only if $T\Delta S$ is greater than ΔH, giving a negative ΔG. These conditions are met only when the temperature of the system is greater than 373 K (100°C). Below 100°C, the free energy change is positive, and boiling is nonspontaneous; the water remains a liquid. At 100°C, $\Delta H = T\Delta S$ and $\Delta G = 0$; equilibrium between the liquid and gas phases is established in such a way that the water's vapor pressure equals the ambient pressure. This is the definition of the boiling point: the temperature at which the vapor pressure equals the ambient pressure.

It is very important to remember that the rate of a reaction depends on the activation energy E_a, not the ΔG. Spontaneous reactions may be fast or slow. Sometimes a reversible reaction may produce two products that differ both in their stability, as measured by the change in the Gibbs free energy associated with their production, and in their kinetics, as measured by their respective energies of activation. Sometimes the thermodynamically more stable product will have the slower kinetics due to higher activation energy. In this situation, we talk about kinetic versus thermodynamic reaction control. For a period of time after the reaction begins, the "dominant" product—that is, the major product—will be the one that is produced more quickly as a result of its lower energy of activation. The reaction can be said to be under kinetic control at this time. Given enough time, however, and assuming a reversible process, the dominant product will be the thermodynamically more stable product as a result of its lower free energy value. The reaction can then be said to be under thermodynamic control. Eventually, the reaction will reach its equilibrium, as defined by its K_{eq} expression.

A quick illustration may help to make this distinction clearer. Cats are famous for their ability to find the warmest spot in a house to take a nap. (Frankly, we find the word *nap* a bit lacking in its descriptive power as a reference to the 16+ hours per day that the typical house cat sleeps!) Imagine a cat wandering through a house on a sunny but cold winter day. She scurries up the staircase from the basement to the first floor and discovers a luscious patch of sunlight and basks in the warmth. She knows that there's something even better up the next flight of stairs on the second floor: a roaring fire in the big brick fireplace. But she's so tired and the sunlight is warm enough for now. So she lies down and sleeps for a little while. Eventually, though, the thought of all that crackling heat is too much to resist. So, she gets up, stretches, scurries up the second flight of stairs (*Oh—so much energy to get up these stairs!* she complains.) and nestles down in front of the fireplace. Sighing the sigh of pure contentment, she resolves never to leave this spot.

Standard Gibbs Free Energy

By now, it shouldn't surprise you to learn that the free energy change of reactions can be measured under standard state conditions to yield the **standard free energy**, ΔG°_{rxn}. For standard free energy determinations, the concentrations of any solutions in the reaction are 1 M. The standard free energy of formation of a compound, ΔG°_{f}, is the free energy change that occurs when 1 mole of a compound in its standard state is produced from its respective elements in their standard states under standard state conditions. The standard free energy of formation for any element in its most stable form under standard state conditions (and therefore already in its standard state) is, by definition, zero. The standard free energy of a reaction, ΔG°_{rxn}, is the free energy change that occurs when that reaction is carried out under standard state conditions; that is, when the reactants in their standard states are converted to the products in their standard states, at standard conditions of temperature (298 K) and pressure (1 atm). For example, under standard state conditions, conversion of carbon in the form of diamond to carbon in the form of graphite is spontaneous (because graphite is the standard state for carbon). However, the reaction rate is so slow that the conversion is never actually observed. You can imagine the distress caused to brides around the world if suddenly all those very expensive diamonds turned into the form of carbon used in pencils.

$$\Delta G^{\circ}_{rxn} = \Sigma(\Delta G^{\circ}_{f} \text{ of products}) - \Sigma(\Delta G^{\circ}_{f} \text{ of reactants})$$

Free Energy, K_{eq} and Q

We can derive the standard free energy change for a reaction from the equilibrium constant K_{eq} for this reaction:

$$\Delta G^{\circ}_{rxn} = -RT\, ln\, K_{eq}$$

where K_{eq} is the equilibrium constant, R is the gas constant, and T is the temperature in K. This is a very valuable equation to know and understand for the MCAT, as it allows you to make not only quantitative evaluations of the free energy change of a reaction that goes from standard state concentrations of reactants to equilibrium concentrations of reactants and products, but also qualitative assessment of the spontaneity of the reaction. The greater the value of K_{eq} is, the more positive the value of its natural log. The more positive the natural log, the more negative the standard free energy change. The more negative the standard free energy change, the more spontaneous the reaction.

Once a reaction begins, however, the standard state conditions (i.e., 1 M solutions) no longer hold. The value of the equilibrium constant must be replaced with another number that is reflective of where the reaction is in its path toward equilibrium. To determine the free energy change for a reaction that is in

> **MCAT Expertise**
>
> To make things easy for Test Day: Note the similarity of this equation to Hess's law. Almost any state function could be substituted for ΔG here.

progress, we relate ΔG_{rxn} (not $\Delta G°_{rxn}$) to the reaction quotient Q. We reviewed Q in Chapter 5, Chemical Kinetics and Equilibrium. As a reminder,

$$Q = \frac{[C]^c[D]^d}{[A]^a[B]^b}$$

And the relation between ΔG_{rxn} and Q is given as follows:

$$\Delta G_{rxn} = \Delta G°_{rxn} + RT \ln Q$$

where R is the gas constant and T is the temperature in Kelvin. This can be simplified to

$$\Delta G_{rxn} = RT \ln\left(\frac{Q}{K_{eq}}\right)$$

This reaction is very useful for quick qualitative assessments of Test Day problems in which you are asked to determine the spontaneity of a reaction at some point in the reaction process. By calculating the value of the reaction quotient and then comparing that value to the known equilibrium constant for the reaction, you will be able to predict whether the free energy change for the reaction is positive (giving a nonspontaneous reaction) or negative (giving a spontaneous reaction). That is, if the ratio of Q/K_{eq} is less than one ($Q < K_{eq}$), then the natural log will be negative and the free energy change will be negative, so the reaction will spontaneously proceed forward until equilibrium is reached. If the ratio of Q/K_{eq} is greater than one ($Q > K_{eq}$), then the natural log will be positive, and the free energy change will be positive. In that case, the reaction will spontaneously move in the reverse direction until equilibrium is reached. Of course, if the ratio is equal to one, then that means that the reaction quotient is equal to the equilibrium constant; the reaction is at equilibrium, and by definition, the free energy change is zero (the natural log of 1 is 0).

Conclusion

We began our discussion of thermochemistry with a review of different ways in which we characterize systems (isolated, closed, etc.) and processes (adiabatic, isothermal, etc.). We then further classified systems according to their state functions: system properties such as volume, pressure, temperature, enthalpy, entropy, and Gibbs free energy that describe the equilibrium state. We defined enthalpy as the heat content of the system and the change in enthalpy as the change in heat content of the system from one equilibrium state to another. Enthalpy is characterized as the energy found in the intermolecular interactions and in the bonds of the compounds in the system. We explored the various ways Hess's law can be applied to calculate the total enthalpy change for a series of reactions. Moving on to entropy, we described this property as a measure of the degree to which energy in a system becomes spread out through a process. There is danger in thinking too literally about entropy as "disorder," as a system's entropy may be increasing even if there is no observable change in the system's macroscopic disorder (e.g., ice warming from $-10°C$ to $-5°C$). Gibbs free energy combines enthalpy and entropy considerations, and the change in Gibbs function determines whether a process will be spontaneous or nonspontaneous. When the change in Gibbs function is negative, the process is spontaneous, but when the change in Gibbs function is positive, the process is nonspontaneous.

Great job! This is a difficult material, but your focus and attention to these topics will pay off in points on Test Day. The changes in energy that accompany chemical processes are tested heavily on the MCAT.

CONCEPTS TO REMEMBER

☐ Systems can be characterized as isolated (no heat or matter exchange), closed (no matter exchange), or open (both heat and matter exchange possible).

☐ Some processes are identified by some constant property of the system: isothermal (constant internal energy/temperature), adiabatic (no heat exchange), and isobaric (constant pressure).

☐ State functions are physical properties of a system that describe the equilibrium state; as such, changes in state functions are pathway-independent. Some examples of state functions are temperature, volume, pressure, internal energy, enthalpy, entropy, and Gibbs free energy.

☐ Standard state of a substance is the most stable form (phase) of the substance under standard state conditions (298 K and 1 atm). Standard enthalpy, standard entropy, and standard free energy changes are measured under standard state conditions.

☐ Heat and temperature are not the same thing. Temperature is a scale related to the average kinetic energy of the molecules in a substance. Heat is the transfer of energy that results from two objects at different temperatures being put in thermal contact with each other. Heat energy transferred from one substance to another is measured by the methods of calorimetry.

☐ Enthalpy is a measure of the potential energy of a system found in the intermolecular interactions and bonds of molecules. Hess's law states that the total change in the potential energy of a system is equal to the changes in potential energies of the individual steps (reactions) of the process.

☐ Entropy is a measure of the degree to which energy has been spread out through a system or between a system and its surroundings. It is a ratio of heat transferred per unit Kelvin. Systems reach maximum possible entropy (maximum possible energy dispersal) only at equilibrium.

☐ Gibbs free energy is a calculation involving both enthalpy and entropy values for a system. The change in Gibbs function determines whether a process is spontaneous or nonspontaneous. When the change in Gibbs function is negative, the process is spontaneous, but when the change in Gibbs function is positive, the process is nonspontaneous.

☐ Temperature-dependent processes are those that change between spontaneous and nonspontaneous at a certain temperature. For example, water freezes spontaneously only at temperatures below 273 K and boils spontaneously only at temperatures above 373 K.

☐ The larger and more positive the value of the equilibrium constant is, the more spontaneous a reaction will be (that is, the more negative the change in Gibbs function for the system as it moves from its initial position to its equilibrium).

EQUATIONS TO REMEMBER

- [ ] $U = Q - W$

- [ ] $q = mc\Delta T$

- [ ] $\Delta H^\circ_{rxn} = \Sigma(\Delta H^\circ_f \text{ of products}) - \Sigma(\Delta H^\circ_f \text{ of reactants})$

- [ ] $\Delta H_{rxn} = \Sigma\Delta H_{\text{bonds broken}} + \Sigma\Delta H_{\text{bonds formed}}$

- [ ] $\Delta S = \dfrac{Q_{rev}}{T}$

- [ ] $\Delta S^\circ_{rxn} = \Sigma\Delta S^\circ_{\text{products}} - \Sigma\Delta S^\circ_{\text{reactants}}$

- [ ] $\Delta G^\circ_{rxn} = \Sigma(\Delta G^\circ_f \text{ of products}) - \Sigma(\Delta G^\circ_f \text{ of reactants})$

- [ ] $\Delta G^\circ_{rxn} = -RT \ln K_{eq}$

- [ ] $\Delta G_{rxn} = RT \ln\left(\dfrac{Q}{K_{eq}}\right)$

Practice Questions

1. Consider the cooling of an ideal gas in a closed system. This process is illustrated in the pressure-volume graph shown in Figure 1.

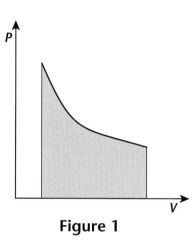

Figure 1

Based on the information in Figure 1, the process is

A. adiabatic.
B. isobaric.
C. isothermal.
D. Two of the above

2. A reaction has a positive entropy and enthalpy. What can be inferred about the progress of this reaction from this information?

A. The reaction is spontaneous.
B. The reaction is nonspontaneous.
C. The reaction is at equilibrium.
D. There is not enough information to determine if the reaction is spontaneous.

3. Pure sodium metal spontaneously combusts upon contact with room temperature water. What is true about the equilibrium constant of this combustion reaction at 25°C?

A. $K_{eq} < 1$.
B. $K_{eq} > 1$.
C. $K_{eq} = 1$.
D. There is not enough information to determine the equilibrium constant.

4. Which of the following processes has the most exothermic heat of reaction?

A. Combustion of ethane
B. Combustion of propane
C. Combustion of n-butane
D. Combustion of isobutane

5. Methanol reacts with acetic acid to form methyl acetate and water, as shown in the following table in the presence of an acid catalyst.

$$CH_3OH \ (\ell) + CH_3COOH \ (aq) \longrightarrow CH_3COOCH_3 \ (aq) + H_2O \ (\ell)$$

Type of Bond	Bond Disassociation Energy (kJ/mol)
C−C	348
C−H	413
C=O	805
O−H	464
C−O	360

What is the heat of formation of methyl acetate in kJ/mol?

A. 0 kJ/mol
B. 464 kJ/mol
C. 824 kJ/mol
D. 1,288 kJ/mol

6. At standard temperature and pressure, a chemical process is at equilibrium. What is the free energy of reaction (ΔG) for this process?

A. $\Delta G > 0$.
B. $\Delta G < 0$.
C. $\Delta G = 0$.
D. There is not enough information to determine the free energy of reaction.

7. For a certain chemical process, $\Delta G° = -4.955$ kJ/mol. What is the equilibrium constant K_{eq} for this reaction?

A. $K_{eq} = 0.13$
B. $K_{eq} = 7.4$
C. $K_{eq} = 8.9$
D. $K_{eq} = 100$

8. Consider the chemical reaction in the vessel depicted in the following diagram.

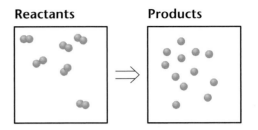

Reactants   **Products**

A. The reaction is spontaneous.
B. The reaction is nonspontaneous.
C. The reaction is at equilibrium.
D. There is not enough information to determine if the reaction is spontaneous.

Suppose $\Delta G_{rxn}° = -2{,}000$ kJ/mol for a chemical reaction. At 300 K, what is the change in Gibb's free energy, ΔG?

A. $\Delta G = -2{,}000$ kJ/mol $+ (300 \text{ K})$ $(8.314 \text{ Jmol}^{-1}\text{K}^{-1})\ln(Q)$.
B. $\Delta G = -2{,}000$ kJ/mol $- (300 \text{ K})$ $(8.314 \text{ Jmol}^{-1}\text{K}^{-1})\ln(Q)$.
C. $\Delta G = -2{,}000$ kJ/mol $+ (300 \text{ K})$ $(8.314 \text{ Jmol}^{-1}\text{K}^{-1})\log(Q)$.
D. $\Delta G = -2{,}000$ kJ/mol $- (300 \text{ K})$ $(8.314 \text{ Jmol}^{-1}\text{K}^{-1})\log(Q)$.

10. An ideal gas undergoes a reversible expansion at constant pressure. Which of the following terms could describe this expansion?

I. Adiabatic
II. Isothermal
III. Isobaric

A. I only
B. I and II only
C. I and III only
D. I, II, and III

11. A chemical reaction has a negative enthalpy and a negative entropy. Which of the following terms describes the energy of this reaction?

A. Exothermic

B. Endothermic

C. Endergonic

D. Exergonic

12. Consider the chemical reaction in the vessel pictured in the following figure.

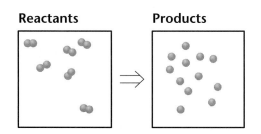

Reactants   **Products**

What can we say about the entropy of this reaction?

A. $\Delta S > 0$

B. $\Delta S < 0$

C. $\Delta S = 0$

D. There is not enough information in the picture to determine ΔS.

13. Which of the following statements is true of a spontaneous process?

A. $\Delta G > 0$ and $K_{eq} > Q$

B. $\Delta G > 0$ and $K_{eq} < Q$

C. $\Delta G < 0$ and $K_{eq} > Q$

D. $\Delta G < 0$ and $K_{eq} < Q$

14. Which of the following devices would be the most appropriate to use to measure the heat capacity of a liquid?

A. Thermometer

B. Calorimeter

C. Barometer

D. Volumetric flask

15. Which of the following equations does not state a law of thermodynamics?

A. $\Delta E_{system} + \Delta E_{surroundings} = \Delta E_{universe}$.

B. $\Delta S_{system} + \Delta S_{surroundings} = \Delta S_{universe}$.

C. $\Delta H_{system} + \Delta H_{surroundings} = \Delta H_{universe}$.

D. $S_{universe} = 0$ at $T = 0$ K.

16. A reaction coordinate for a chemical reaction is displayed in the graph below.

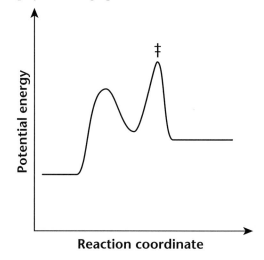

Which of the following terms describes the energy of this reaction?

A. Endothermic

B. Exothermic

C. Endergonic

D. Exergonic

Small Group Questions

1. Why is energy required to break bonds? Why is it released when bonds are formed?

2. Why is ΔH so much easier to determine than instantaneous H (enthalpy)? What standard methods have been developed to help scientists find H through calculations?

3. What is the difference between exergonic and exothermic? What is the difference between endergonic and endothermic?

Explanations to Practice Questions

1. A

The process is adiabatic. *Adiabatic* describes any thermodynamic transformation that does not involve a heat transfer (Q). An adiabatic process can be either reversible or irreversible, though for MCAT purposes, adiabatic expansions or contractions refer to volume changes in a closed system without experimentally significant losses or gains of heat. The internal energy of the system changes ($U = -P\Delta V$, where $U = Q - W$, $W = P\Delta V$, and $Q = 0$). (B) is incorrect because isobaric processes occur at constant pressures. (C) is incorrect because an isothermal process requires a heat transfer at constant temperature, and there is no heat transfer along an adiabatic curve. Once it becomes clear that the process is adiabatic, that rules out (D).

2. D

There is not enough information in the problem to determine whether or not the reaction is nonspontaneous. Start with $\Delta G = \Delta H - T\Delta S$. If the signs of enthalpy and entropy are the same, the reaction is temperature-dependent. If the signs of these terms are different, we can find the sign of ΔG without using temperature. The most common thermochemistry questions on the MCAT test your ability to manipulate and interpret the $\Delta G = \Delta H - T\Delta S$ equation. Memorize it.

3. B

Sodium oxidizes easily at standard conditions. No calculation is necessary here. There is enough information in the problem to predict the equilibrium constant, eliminating (D). If $K_{eq} < 1$, the reverse reaction is favored, indicating that the forward reaction is nonspontaneous. If $K_{eq} = 1$, the reaction is at equilibrium. If $K_{eq} > 1$, the forward reaction proceeds spontaneously. The question states that the sample spontaneously combusts at room temperature (i.e., 25°C). The answer is (B), $K_{eq} > 1$.

4. C

Combustion involves the reaction of a hydrocarbon with oxygen to produce carbon dioxide and water. Longer hydrocarbon chains yield greater amounts of combustion products and release more heat in the process (i.e., the reaction is more exothermic). Isobutane combusts less easily than *n*-butane because of its branched structure.

5. A

At first glance, this might seem like a math-heavy problem, but it really doesn't require any calculations at all. We just have to keep track of which bonds are broken and which bonds are formed. Remember, breaking bonds requires energy, while forming bonds releases energy.

Nucleophile: methanol's oxygen CH_3O-H
Electrophile: acetic acid's carbonyl carbon CH_3COOH

Through nucleophilic attack and leaving group separation, substitution occurs so that CH_3O takes the place of acetic acid's OH to create methyl acetate. A proton transfer occurs between methanol and acetic acid's leaving group, OH.

Bonds broken:
1 O–H (−464 kJ/mol): Proton leaves methanol.
1 C–O (−360 kJ/mol): Between the carbonyl carbon and the hydroxyl oxygen in acetic acid

Bonds formed:
1 C–O (+360 kJ/mol): Between the carbonyl carbon and the attacking oxygen
1 O–H (+464 kJ/mol): Between the leaving group oxygen and the transferred proton

The sum of all our bonding events is 0 kJ. We can reason through this intuitively. If one O–H bond is broken and another is made, the two values will cancel each other out, and the net energy change must be 0 kJ. Similarly, if one C–O bond is broken and another is made, the net energy change will also be 0 kJ.

6. C

Standard temperature and pressure indicates 0°C and 1 atm. Gibbs free energy is temperature-dependent. If a reaction is at equilibrium, $\Delta G = 0$. (C) is the correct answer.

7. B

The correct answer is (B), using $K_{eq} = e^{-\Delta G^\circ / RT}$ from $\Delta G^\circ = -RT\ln(K_{eq})$. Use $e = 2.7$. R is the gas constant, 8.314 $Jmol^{-1}K^{-1}$, and $T = 298$ K, because of the standard-state sign.

Convert −4.955 kJ to −4,955 J and then round −4,955 to −5,000. Let's also round 298 K to 300 K. The exponent's denominator will be 8.314 × 300, which we can estimate as 2,500.

$$\frac{-G^\circ}{RT} = \frac{-(-4,955.14 \text{ J/mol})}{(8.314 \text{ J mol}^{-1}\text{K}^{-1})(298 \text{ K})} = \frac{5,000 \text{ J}}{2,500} = 2$$

So we're left with $e^{(-5,000/-2,500)} = K_{eq}$, or $e^2 = K_{eq}$.

Plugging in 2.7 for e, we can calculate $2.7^{(2)} = K_{eq}$. Because 2^2 is 4 and 3^2 is 9, we can assume that we want an answer choice somewhere in between, which eliminates (A) and (D). Let's use some logic to choose between (B) and (C). Obviously, 8.9 is very close to 9, so we can assume that its square root is very, very close to 3 (it's actually around 2.984). The answer choice should be a bit smaller, so (B), 7.4, is correct.

8. D

There is not enough information available to determine the energy of this reaction. Only its entropy is obvious.

9. A

This problem asks you to calculate the free energy of reaction at nonstandard conditions, which you can do using the equation $\Delta G = \Delta G^\circ + RT\ln(Q)$. (R is the gas constant, 8.314 $Jmol^{-1}K^{-1}$).

10. C

There is not enough information to deduce anything about reaction temperature, which eliminates (B) and (D). Adiabatic and isothermal processes are necessarily opposite because adiabatic processes do not involve heat transfers. A reaction at constant pressure can be either adiabatic (no heat transfer to change volume) or isobaric (constant pressure, as the word roots imply).

11. A

This question requires interpreting the equation $\Delta G = \Delta H - T\Delta S$. Endergonic (C) indicates a nonspontaneous reaction, and an exergonic reaction (D) indicates a spontaneous reaction. In contrast, endothermic and exothermic reactions suggest the sign of the enthalpy of the reaction. The problem does not provide enough information to determine the free energy of this temperature-dependent reaction. (A) is the correct answer.

12. A

Disorder in the vessel increases over the course of the reaction, so (A) is correct. While we cannot make a quantitative determination of entropy from the picture, we can estimate the relative amount of disorder from the beginning to the end of the reaction in the vessel.

13. C

For a process to occur spontaneously, Q must be less than K_{eq} and will therefore have a tendency to move in the direction toward equilibrium. A spontaneous reaction's free energy is negative by convention. (C) is the correct answer. (A), (B), and (D) are opposites.

14. B

A calorimeter measures specific heat or heat capacity. Though calorimeters often incorporate thermometers, the thermometer itself only tracks heat transfers, not the specific heat value itself, so (A) is incorrect. (C) is irrelevant; barometers measure changes in pressure. (D) is also incorrect, as volumetric flasks measure liquid quantities, not the heat capacity of the liquid.

15. C

Memorize the laws of thermodynamics prior to Test Day; they may be stated in several different forms. You should know the equation and how to rephrase it into a sentence or two. The first law often confuses students—keep in mind that it refers to the overall energy of the universe, not to the enthalpy of the universe, even though *enthalpy* is usually substituted for this term in introductory college chemistry experiments. The third law (absolute zero) is not an equation, so keep that in mind as you work.

16. A

Eliminate (C) and (D), which describe the free energy of reaction and cannot be determined from this graph. If the heat of formation of the products is greater than that of the reactants, the reaction is endothermic. We can determine this information by their relative magnitude on the graph. An exothermic graph would reflect products with a lower enthalpy than that of the reactants.

The Gas Phase

We are literally surrounded by gas. We walk through it, run through it, breathe it in, breathe it out, burp it, pass it, and if it weren't for the fact that we are denser than air, we'd be swimming in it. Gases behave in ways that we find useful, interesting, and entertaining. How else to explain the almost universal human delight in balloons: helium balloons, hot air balloons, circus balloon animals, *99 Luftballons*? The topic of discussion for this chapter is not, alas, the art of fashioning balloon animals or the deeper meaning of the Cold War–era German protest song. We will discuss the MCAT favorites—the gas phase and the ideal gas laws. We will begin our discussion of ideal gases and the kinetic molecular theory that describes them. We will then examine each of the laws that govern the behavior of ideal gases and conclude with an evaluation of the ways in which the behavior of real gases deviate from that predicted by the ideal gas law.

Before we get started with our discussion of gases, here's a fun little experiment that you can try on your own, not only to get you thinking about the characteristics of gases but also to help you connect gas behaviors to some of the principles of Newtonian physics that you must know and understand for Test Day. (The MCAT will be making these kinds of connections, so you should be preparing for that now.)

The next time you're leaving a birthday party, holiday celebration, bar or bat mitzvah, christening, wedding, or funeral, snag a helium balloon on your way out. (Balloons at funerals? Hey—some people like to go out smiling!) Tie the helium balloon to the gearshift lever between the front seats, making sure that the balloon is floating freely. Once you're on an open road, accelerate the car abruptly, and as you do, watch the balloon. What do you predict will happen to the balloon as the car accelerates? What do you observe? You might think, based on how you feel when you are sitting in a car accelerating forward, that the balloon will be pushed toward the back of the car due to its inertia. After all, isn't this what happens to you? You feel pushed back into your seat as a result of your inertia, which is resisting the car's forward force and acceleration. However, the balloon's movement isn't what we might predict. In fact, it's the opposite: The balloon shifts forward as the car accelerates forward because the balloon is filled with helium, one of the noble gases. The molecular weight of helium is 4 grams/mole, while that of air, which is mostly nitrogen and oxygen, is about 29 grams/mole. This means that air is about seven times denser than helium. Because the denser air in which the balloon is floating has more mass than the helium-filled balloon, the air will have greater inertia. In fact, we can approximate the balloon's inertia as practically nonexistent. Therefore, as the car accelerates forward, everything that has significant mass, including the air in the car, resists the forward motion (has inertia) and shifts toward the back of the car (even though, of course, everything in the car is accelerating forward, just not as quickly as the car itself). As the air shifts toward the back, a pressure gradient builds up such that there is greater air pressure in the back of the car than in the front, and this pressure difference results in a pushing force against the balloon that is directed from the back toward the front. Responding to this force, the balloon shifts forward in the direction of the car's acceleration. Who would think that general chemistry and physics could be so much fun? Well, if you've been paying attention: We do!

The Gas Phase   ★★☆☆☆

Matter can exist in three different physical forms, called **phases** or **states**: gas, liquid, and solid. We will discuss liquids and solids in Chapter 8, Phases and Phase Changes. The **gaseous phase** is the simplest to understand, since all gases display similar behavior and follow similar laws regardless of their particular chemical identities. Like liquids, gases are classified as fluids because they can flow. The atoms or molecules in a gaseous sample move rapidly and are far apart from each other. In addition, only very weak intermolecular forces exist between gas particles; this results in certain characteristic physical properties, such as the ability to expand to fill any volume and to take on the shape of a container. (This last characteristic defines fluids—liquids and gases—generally.) Gases are also easily, although not infinitely, compressible, which distinguishes them from liquids.

We can define the state of a gaseous sample generally by four variables: pressure (P), volume (V), temperature (T), and number of moles (n). Gas pressures are usually expressed in units of atmospheres (atm) or in units of millimeters of mercury (mm Hg), which are equivalent to torr. The SI unit for pressure, however, is the pascal (Pa). The mathematical relationships among all of these units are

$$1 \text{ atm} = 760 \text{ mm Hg} = 760 \text{ torr} = 101.325 \text{ kPa}$$

On the MCAT, you'll encounter any or all of these units, so become familiar with them through your practice problems. The volume of a gas is generally expressed in liters (L) or milliliters (mL). Temperature is usually given in Kelvin (K). Many processes involving gases take place under certain conditions, called **standard temperature and pressure**, or **STP**, which refers to conditions of 273.13 K (0°C) and 1 atm.

Please carefully note that **STP conditions** are not identical to **standard state conditions.** The two standards involve different temperatures and are used for different purposes. STP (273 K and 1 atm) is generally used for gas law calculations; standard state conditions (298 K and 1 atm) are used when measuring standard enthalpy, entropy, free energy changes, and voltage.

MCAT Expertise

On the MCAT, remember that STP is different from standard state. Temperature at STP is 0°C (273.15 K). Temperature at standard state is 25°C (298.15 K).

Ideal Gases ★★★★☆

When we examine the behavior of gases under varying conditions of temperature and pressure, we assume that the gases are ideal. An ideal gas represents a hypothetical gas whose molecules have no intermolecular forces and occupy no volume. Although real gases deviate from this ideal behavior at high pressures and low temperatures, many real gases demonstrate behavior that is close to ideal.

Kinetic Molecular Theory of Gases ★★★★☆

This mouthful of a theory was developed in the second half of the 19th century, well after the laws describing gas behavior had been developed. In fact, the **kinetic molecular theory** was developed to explain the behavior of gases, which the laws merely described. The gas laws demonstrate that all gases show similar physical characteristics and behavior irrespective of their particular chemical identity. The behavior of real gases deviates from the ideal behavior predicted under the assumptions of this theory, but these deviations may be corrected for in calculations. The combined efforts of Boltzmann, Maxwell, and others led to a simple explanation of gaseous molecular behavior based on the motion of individual molecules. Like the gas laws, which we will examine shortly, the kinetic molecular theory was developed in reference to ideal gases, although it can be applied with reasonable accuracy to real gases as well.

ASSUMPTIONS OF THE KINETIC MOLECULAR THEORY

1. Gases are made up of particles whose volumes are negligible compared to the container volume.
2. Gas atoms or molecules exhibit no intermolecular attractions or repulsions.
3. Gas particles are in continuous, random motion, undergoing collisions with other particles and the container walls.
4. Collisions between any two gas particles are elastic, meaning that there is conservation of both momentum and kinetic energy.
5. The average kinetic energy of gas particles is proportional to the absolute temperature (in Kelvin) of the gas, and it is the same for all gases at a given temperature, irrespective of chemical identity or atomic mass.

APPLICATIONS OF THE KINETIC MOLECULAR THEORY OF GASES

It's fairly straightforward to imagine, based on the assumptions just listed, gas particles as lots of little rubber balls bouncing into and off each other and off the walls of their container. Of course, rubber balls, like real gas particles, have measurable mass and volume, and not even the bounciest rubber balls will collide in a completely elastic manner.

Average Molecular Speeds

According to the kinetic molecular theory of gases, the average kinetic energy of a gas particle is proportional to the absolute temperature of the gas:

$$KE = \frac{1}{2}mv^2 = \frac{3}{2}kT$$

where k is the Boltzmann constant, which serves as a bridge between macroscopic and microscopic behavior (that is, as a bridge between the behavior of the gas as a whole and the individual gas molecules). This equation shows that the speed of a gas particle is related to its absolute temperature. However, because of the large number of rapidly and randomly moving gas particles, which may travel distances as short as 6×10^{-6} cm before colliding with another particle or the container wall, the speed of an individual gas molecule is nearly impossible to define. Therefore, the speeds of gases are defined in terms of their average molecular speed. One way to define an average speed is to determine the average kinetic energy per particle and then calculate the speed to which this corresponds. The resultant quantity, known as the root-mean-square speed (u_{rms}), is given by the following equation:

$$u_{rms} = \left(\frac{3\,RT}{MM}\right)^{\frac{1}{2}}$$

where R is ideal gas constant and MM is the molecular mass.

A Maxwell-Boltzmann distribution curve shows the distribution of speeds of gas particles at a given temperature. Figure 7.1 shows a distribution curve of molecular speeds at two temperatures, T_1 and T_2, where T_2 is greater than T_1. Notice that the bell-shaped curve flattens and shifts to the right as the temperature increases, indicating that at higher temperatures, more molecules are moving at higher speeds.

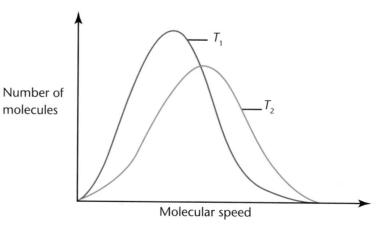

Figure 7.1

MCAT Expertise

Again, understanding concepts will be much more fruitful on Test Day than memorizing all of the facts. The higher the temperature, the faster the molecules move. The larger the molecules, they slower they move.

Example: What is the average speed of sulfur dioxide molecules at 37°C?

Solution: The gas constant R = 8.314 J/(K • mol) should be used, and *MM* must be expressed in kg/mol.

$$u_{rms} = \left(\frac{3RT}{MM}\right)^{1/2}$$

$$u_{rms} = \left[\frac{3(8.314 \text{ J}/\text{K mol})(310.15\text{K})}{0.064 \text{ kg}/\text{mol}}\right]^{1/2}$$

$$u_{rms} = [120871.3 \text{ J}/\text{kg}]^{1/2}$$

Use the conversion factor 1 J = 1 kg • m²/s²:

$$u_{rms} = \sqrt{120871.3 \text{ kg} \bullet \text{m}^2/\text{s}^2 \bullet \text{kg}}$$

$$u_{rms} = 347.7 \text{ m}/\text{s}$$

Graham's Law of Diffusion and Effusion

Ours is a highly aromatic world. The smells and aromas of food, flowers, exhaust, rot, wet dog, and skunk are instantly recognizable and elicit in us reactions of delight or disgust. In our introduction to Chapter 4, Compounds and Stoichiometry, we explained that our sense of smell depends upon the interactions between vaporized compounds and the chemical receptors of the olfactory epithelium located inside our nasal cavities. The rate at which those gaseous compounds travel will determine what we'd smell first: a flower or a skunk.

The movement of gas molecules through a mixture (such as air) is called **diffusion**. The kinetic molecular theory of gases predicts that heavier gases diffuse more slowly than lighter ones do because of their differing average speeds. (Because all gas particles have the same average kinetic energy at the same temperature, it must be that particles with greater mass travel at a slower average velocity.) In 1832, Thomas Graham showed mathematically that under isothermal and isobaric conditions, the rates at which two gases diffuse are inversely proportional to the square root of their molar masses. Thus,

$$\frac{r_1}{r_2} = \left(\frac{MM_2}{MM_1}\right)^{1/2} = \sqrt{\left(\frac{MM_2}{MM_1}\right)}$$

where r_1 and r_2 are the diffusion rates of gas 1 and gas 2, respectively, and MM_1 and MM_2 are the molar masses of gas 1 and gas 2, respectively. You know by now that the MCAT commonly tests students' understanding of ratios. From this equation, you can see that a gas that has a molar mass four times that of another gas will travel half as fast as the lighter gas.

Effusion is the flow of gas particles under pressure from one compartment to another through a small opening. Graham used the kinetic molecular theory of gases to show that for two gases at the same temperature, the rates of effusion are proportional to the average speeds. He then expressed the rates of effusion in terms of molar mass and found that the relationship is the same as that for diffusion:

$$\frac{r_1}{r_2} = \left(\frac{MM_2}{MM_1}\right)^{1/2} = \sqrt{\left(\frac{MM_2}{MM_1}\right)}$$

> **Key Concept**
>
> Diffusion: When gases mix with one another. Effusion: When a gas moves through a small hole under pressure. Both will be slower for larger molecules.

Latex balloons are often filled with a 60/40 mixture of helium and air. Latex is a fairly porous material that allows for the effusion of the gas mixture contained inside. Since the weighted average molar mass of air (consisting of about 78% N_2 and 21% O_2) is about 29 grams/mole and the molar mass of helium is 4 grams/mole, the helium gas will effuse almost three times faster than the air. This is why helium balloons have such a fleeting life span and perhaps explains in part their ability to enchant us.

Ideal Gas Behavior ★★★★☆

The ideal gas law was first stated in 1834 by Benoît Paul Émile Clapeyron, more than 170 years after Sir Robert Boyle has pesrformed his experimental studies on the relationship between pressure and volume in the gas state. In fact, by the time the ideal gas law found its expression, Boyle's law, Charles' law, and even Dalton's law had already been well established. Historical considerations aside, it will benefit us to examine the ideal gas law first so that we can then understand the other laws, which had been "discovered" first, to be only special cases of the ideal gas law.

One more important discovery that preceded Clapeyron's formulation of the ideal gas law was Amedeo Avogadro's formulation in 1811, known as Avogadro's principle, that all gases at a constant temperature and pressure occupy volumes that are directly proportional to the number of moles of gas present. Equal amounts of all gases at the same temperature and pressure will occupy equal volumes. For example, one mole of any gas, irrespective of its chemical identity, will occupy 22.4 liters at STP.

$$\frac{n}{V} = k \text{ or } \frac{n_1}{V_1} = \frac{n_2}{V_2}$$

where n_1 and n_2 are the number of moles of gas 1 and gas 2, respectively, and V_1 and V_2 are the volumes of the gases, respectively.

IDEAL GAS LAW

The ideal gas law shows the relationships among four variables that define a sample of gas: pressure (P), volume (V), temperature (T), and number of moles (n). The law combines the mathematical relationships earlier determined by the work of Boyle, Charles, and Gay-Lussac with Avogadro's principle and is represented by this equation:

$$PV = nRT$$

where R is a constant known as the gas constant, which has a value of 8.21×10^{-2} (L • atm)/(mol • K). Be aware that the gas constant can be expressed in other units. On the MCAT, you may also encounter R given as 8.314 J/(K • mol), which is derived when SI units of pascal (for pressure) and cubic meters (for volume) are substituted into the ideal gas law. Although the value(s) for R will be given to you on Test Day (as will the values for almost all constants), it is important that you learn to recognize the appropriate value for R based on the units of the variables as they are given to you in the passage or question stem. The variables in the law itself become easy to remember if you "sound out" the law: "piv-nert"

MCAT Expertise

$PV = nRT$. Knowing this equation means we can derive others based on the answer we are looking to find.

Example: What volume would 12 g of helium occupy at 20°C and a pressure of 380 mm Hg?

Solution: The ideal gas law can be used, but first, all of the variables must be converted to yield units that will correspond to the expression of the gas constant as 0.0821 L • atm/(mol • K).

$$P = 380 \text{ mm Hg} \times \frac{1 \text{ atm}}{760 \text{ mm Hg}} = 0.5 \text{ atm}$$

$$T = 20°C + 273.15 = 293.15 \text{ K}$$

$$n = 12 \text{ g He} \times \frac{1 \text{ mol He}}{4.0 \text{ g}} = 3 \text{ mol He}$$

$$PV = nRT$$

$$(0.5 \text{ atm})(V) = (3 \text{ mol He})\left(0.0821 \frac{\text{L} \cdot \text{atm}}{\text{mol} \cdot \text{K}}\right)(293.15 \text{ K})$$

$$V = 144.4 \text{ L}$$

The ideal gas law is useful to you not only for standard calculations of pressure, volume, or temperature of a gas under a set of given conditions but also for determinations of gas density and molar mass.

Density

We define density as the ratio of the mass per unit volume of a substance and, for gases, express it in units of grams per liter (g/L). The ideal gas law contains variables for volume and number of moles, so we can rearrange the law to calculate the density of any gas:

$$PV = nRT$$

where
$$n = \frac{m}{MM} \left(\frac{\text{mass in grams}}{\text{molar mass}} \right)$$

Therefore,
$$PV = \left(\frac{m}{MM} \right) RT$$

and
$$d = \frac{m}{V} = \frac{P(MM)}{RT}$$

Because success on the MCAT depends on your ability to think critically, analyze the information provided to you, and discern which of it is necessary and useful and what's merely a "red herring," you should work to become comfortable in approaching problems from different angles, thereby ensuring that you will have many "tools" in your Test Day "tool belt." As an example, let's consider a second approach to determining the density of a gas that could prove useful to you on the MCAT.

For this approach, we need to start with the volume of a mole of gas at STP, which is 22.4 L. We will then calculate the effect of pressure and temperature on the volume (to the degree that they differ from STP conditions). Finally, we'll calculate the density by dividing the mass by the new volume. The following equation can be used to relate changes in temperature, volume, and pressure of a gas:

$$\frac{P_1 V_1}{T_1} = \frac{P_2 V_2}{T_2}$$

where the subscripts 1 and 2 refer to the two states of the gas (at STP and at the conditions of actual temperature and pressure). If you look carefully at this equation, you'll notice that this assumes that the number of moles of gas is held constant, and in fact, we could write the equation as follows:

$$\frac{PV}{T} = nR = \text{constant}$$

To calculate a change in volume, the equation is rearranged as follows:

$$V_2 = V_1 \left(\frac{P_1}{P_2} \right) \left(\frac{T_2}{T_1} \right)$$

V_2 is then used to find the density of the gas under nonstandard conditions:

$$d = \frac{m}{V_2}$$

On Test Day, you may find it helpful to visualize how the changes in pressure and temperature affect the volume of the gas, and this can serve as a check to make sure that you have not accidentally switched the values of pressure and temperature in the numerator and denominator of the respective pressure and temperature ratios. For example, you would be able to predict (without even doing the math) that doubling the temperature would result in doubling the volume, and doubling the pressure would result in halving the volume, so doubling both at the same time results in a final volume that is equal to the original volume.

Example: What is the density of HCl gas at 2 atm and 45°C?

Solution: At STP, a mole of gas occupies 22.4 liters. Because the increase in pressure to 2 atm decreases volume, 22.4 L must be multiplied by $\left(\dfrac{1 \text{ atm}}{2 \text{ atm}}\right)$. Because the increase in temperature increases volume, the temperature factor will be $\left(\dfrac{318 \text{ K}}{273 \text{ K}}\right)$.

$$V_2 = \left(\frac{22.4 \text{ L}}{\text{mol}}\right)\left(\frac{1 \text{ atm}}{2 \text{ atm}}\right)\left(\frac{318 \text{ K}}{273 \text{ K}}\right) = \frac{13.0 \text{ L}}{\text{mol}}$$

$$d = \left(\frac{36 \text{ g/mol}}{13.0 \text{/mol}}\right) = 2.77 \text{ g/L}$$

Molar Mass

Sometimes the identity of a gas is unknown, and the molar mass (see Chapter 4, Compounds and Stoichiometry) must be determined in order to identify it. Using the equation for density derived from the ideal gas law, we can calculate the molar mass of a gas in the following way. The pressure and temperature of a gas contained in a bulb of a given volume are measured, and the mass of the bulb plus sample is measured. Then, the bulb is evacuated (the gas is removed), and the mass of the empty bulb is determined. The mass of the bulb plus sample minus the mass of the evacuated bulb yields the mass of the sample. Finally, the density of the sample is determined by dividing the mass of the sample by the volume of the bulb. This gives the density at the particular conditions of the given temperature and pressure. Using $V_2 = V_1 (P_1/P_2)(T_2/T_1)$, we then calculate the volume of the gas at STP (substituting 273 K for T_2 and 1 atm for P_2). The ratio of the sample mass divided by V_2 gives the density of the gas at STP. The molar mass can then be calculated as the product of the gas's density at STP and the STP volume of any gas, 22.4 L/mol.

Example: What is the molar mass of a 2 L sample of gas that weighs 8 g at a temperature of 15°C and a pressure of 1.5 atm?

$$d = \frac{8\,g}{2\,L} \text{ at } 15°C \text{ and } 1.5 \text{ atm}$$

$$V_{STP} = (2\,L)\left(\frac{273\,K}{288\,K}\right)\left(\frac{1.5\,\text{atm}}{1\,\text{atm}}\right) = 2.84\,L$$

$$\frac{8\,g}{2.84\,L} = 2.82\,g/L \text{ at STP}$$

$$\left(\frac{2.82\,g}{L}\right)\left(\frac{22.4\,L}{\text{mol}}\right) = 63.2\,g/\text{mol}$$

SPECIAL CASES OF THE IDEAL GAS LAW

Now that we have considered the ideal gas law as the mathematical relationship between four variables that define the state of a gas (pressure, volume, temperature, and moles of gas), we can examine two special cases of the ideal gas law in which some of the variables are held constant as the gas system undergoes a process. Even though the following two laws were developed before the ideal gas law, it is conceptually helpful to understand them as simple special cases of the more general ideal gas law.

Boyle's Law

Robert Boyle conducted a series of experimental studies in 1660 that led to his formulation of a law that now bears his name: Boyle's law. His work showed that for a given gaseous sample held at constant temperature (isothermal conditions) the volume of the gas is inversely proportional to its pressure:

$$PV = k, \text{ or } P_1V_1 = P_2V_2$$

where k is a proportionality constant and the subscripts 1 and 2 represent two different sets of pressure and volume conditions. Careful examination of Boyle's law shows that it is, indeed, simply the special case of the ideal gas law in which n, R, and T are constant:

$$PV = nRT = \text{constant}$$

A plot of volume versus pressure for a gas is shown in Figure 7.2.

Key Concept

Boyle's law is a derivation of the ideal gas law and states that pressure and volume are inversely related: When one increases, the other decreases.

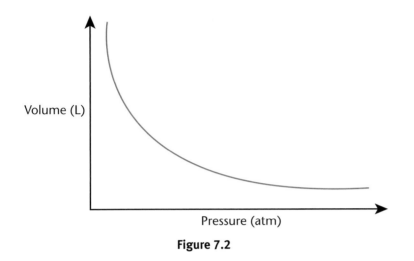

Figure 7.2

MCAT Expertise

Sometimes it is easier to remember the shape of the graph to help you recall the variables' relationship on Test Day. Here we can see that as pressure increases, the volume decreases, and vice versa. These ratios and relationships will often answer questions on the MCAT without your having to do any math.

Example: Under isothermal conditions, what would be the volume of a 1 L sample of helium if its pressure is changed from 12 atm to 4 atm?

Solution: $P_1 = 12$ atm $\quad P_2 = 4$ atm
$V_1 = 1$ L $\quad V_2 = X$
$P_1 V_1 = P_2 V_2$
12 atm (1 L) = 4 atm (X)
$\dfrac{12}{4}$ L $= X$
$X = 3$ L

Law of Charles and Gay-Lussac

In the early 19th century Gay-Lussac published findings based, in part, on earlier unpublished work by Charles; hence, the law of Charles and Gay-Lussac is more commonly known simply as Charles' law. The law states that at constant pressure, the volume of a gas is proportional to its absolute temperature, expressed in degrees Kelvin. (Remember the conversion from Celsius to Kelvin is $T_K = T_{°C} + 273.15$.) Expressed mathematically, Charles' law is

$$\frac{V}{T} = k \text{ or } \frac{V_1}{T_1} = \frac{V_2}{T_2}$$

where, again, k is a proportionality constant and the subscripts 1 and 2 represent two different sets of temperature and volume conditions. Careful examination of Charles' law shows that it is another special case of the ideal gas law in which n, R, and P are constant:

$$\frac{V}{T} = \frac{n\text{R}}{P} = \text{constant}$$

Key Concept

Charles' law is also a derivation of the ideal gas law and states that volume and temperature are directly proportional: When one increases, the other does too.

A plot of temperature versus volume is shown in Figure 7.3. It is interesting to note that if one extrapolates the V versus T plot for a gas back to where $V = 0$ (as it should for an ideal gas), we find that $T \to 0$ K!

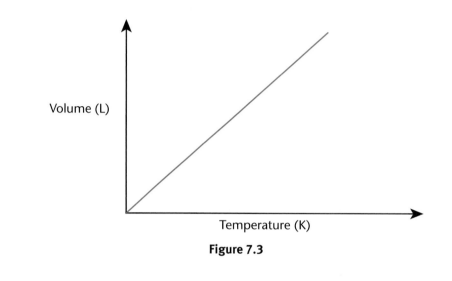

Figure 7.3

Example: If the absolute temperature of 2 L of gas at constant pressure is changed from 283.15 K to 566.30 K, what would be the final volume?

Solution:

$$T_1 = 283.15 \text{ K} \qquad V_1 = 2 \text{ L}$$
$$T_2 = 566.30 \text{ K} \qquad V_2 = X$$

$$\frac{V_1}{T_1} = \frac{V_2}{T_2}$$

$$\frac{2 \text{ L}}{283.15 \text{ K}} = \frac{X}{566.30 \text{ K}}$$

$$X = \frac{2 \text{ L} (566.30 \text{ K})}{283.15 \text{ K}}$$

$$X = 4 \text{ L}$$

DALTON'S LAW OF PARTIAL PRESSURES

When two or more gases are found in one vessel without chemical interaction, each gas will behave independently of the other(s). That is to say that each gas will behave as if it were the only gas in the container. Therefore, the pressure exerted by each gas in the mixture will be equal to the pressure that gas would exert if it were the only one in the container. The pressure exerted by each individual gas is called the partial pressure of that gas. In 1801, John Dalton derived an expression, now known as Dalton's law of partial pressures, which states that the total pressure of a gaseous mixture is equal to the sum of the partial pressure of the individual components. The equation for Dalton's law is

$$P_T = P_A + P_B + P_C + \cdots$$

The partial pressure of a gas is related to its mole fraction and can be determined using the following equations:

$$P_A = P_T X_A$$

where $\qquad X_A = \dfrac{n_A}{n_T}$ (moles of A / total moles of all gases)

Example: A vessel contains 0.75 mol of nitrogen, 0.20 mol of hydrogen, and 0.05 mol of fluorine at a total pressure of 2.5 atm. What is the partial pressure of each gas?

First calculate the mole fraction of each gas.

$$X_{N_2} = \frac{0.75 \text{ mol}}{1.00 \text{ mol}} = 0.75 \qquad X_{H_2} = \frac{0.20 \text{ mol}}{1.00 \text{ mol}} = 0.20 \qquad X_{F_2} = \frac{0.05 \text{ mol}}{1.00 \text{ mol}} = 0.05$$

Then calculate the partial pressure.

$$P_A = X_A P_T$$
$$P_{N_2} = (2.5 \text{ atm})(0.75) \qquad P_{H_2} = (2.5 \text{ atm})(0.20) \qquad P_{F_2} = (2.5 \text{ atm})(0.05)$$
$$= 1.875 \text{ atm} \qquad\qquad = 0.5 \text{ atm} \qquad\qquad = 0.125 \text{ atm}$$

Real Gases ★★★☆☆

Throughout our discussion of the laws and theory that describe and explain the behavior of gases, we have stressed that the fundamental assumption is a gas that behaves ideally. However, our world is not one of ideal gases but rather real ones, and real gases have volumes and interact with each other in measurable ways. In general, the ideal gas law is a good approximation of the behavior of real gases, but all real gases deviate from ideal gas behavior to some extent, particularly when the gas atoms or molecules are forced into close proximity under high pressure and at low temperature. Under these "nonideal" conditions, the molecular volume and intermolecular forces become significant.

You can think of these nonideal conditions as the degree to which human populations are "forced" to interact with each other in high-population density regions. In 2007, for example, the population density of Washington, D.C., was 9,581 people per square mile, whereas that of Alaska (the least densely populated state in the Union at that time) was 1.2 people per square mile. Quite literally, the personal space of

an individual living in the nation's capital cannot be ignored, whereas the vast physical separation between people living in Alaska (on average) makes the notion of "personal space" so insignificant as to be almost laughable. Continuing the human-as-real-gas analogy, how often do people say to each other on a hot and humid day, "Ugghh, don't come near me. It's too hot!"? And how many romantic songs include imagery of lovers snuggling together on a cold evening trying to keep warm?

DEVIATIONS DUE TO PRESSURE

As the pressure of a gas increases, the particles are pushed closer and closer together. As the condensation pressure for a given temperature is approached, intermolecular attraction forces become more and more significant, until the gas condenses into the liquid state (see "Gas-Liquid Equilibrium" in Chapter 8).

At moderately high pressure (a few hundred atmospheres), a gas's volume is less than would be predicted by the ideal gas law due to intermolecular attraction. At extremely high pressure, however, the size of the particles becomes relatively large compared to the distance between them, and this causes the gas to take up a larger volume than would be predicted by the ideal gas law.

DEVIATIONS DUE TO TEMPERATURE

As the temperature of a gas is decreased, the average velocity of the gas molecules decreases, and the attractive intermolecular forces become increasingly significant. As the condensation temperature is approached for a given pressure, intermolecular attractions eventually cause the gas to condense to a liquid state (see "Gas-Liquid Equilibrium" in Chapter 8).

As the temperature of a gas is reduced toward its condensation point (which is the same as its boiling point), intermolecular attraction causes the gas to have a smaller volume than that which would be predicted by the ideal gas law. The closer the temperature of a gas is to its boiling point, the less ideal is its behavior.

VAN DER WAALS EQUATION OF STATE

There are several gas equations, or gas laws, that attempt to correct for the deviations from ideality that occur when a gas does not closely follow the ideal gas law. The van der Waals equation of state is one such equation:

$$\left(P + \frac{n^2 a}{V^2}\right)(V - nb) = nRT$$

where a and b are physical constants experimentally determined for each gas. The a term corrects for the attractive forces between molecules (*a* for *attractive*) and as

---

MCAT Expertise

On the MCAT, an understanding of nonideal conditions will help with determining how gases' behavior may deviate.

Key Concept

Note that if a and b are both zero, the van der Waals equation reduces to the ideal gas law.

such will be smaller for gases that are small and less polarizable (such as helium), larger for gases that are larger and more polarizable (such as Xe or N_2), and largest for polar molecules such as HCl and NH_3. The b term corrects for the volume of the molecules themselves. Larger values of b are thus found for larger molecules. Numerical values for a are generally much larger than those for b.

Example: Find the correction in pressure necessary for the deviation from ideality for 1 mole of ammonia in a 1 liter flask at 0°C. (For NH_3, a = 4.2, b = 0.037)

Solution: According to the ideal gas law,

$P = nRT/V = (1)(0.0821)(273)/(1) = 22.4$ atm, while according to the van der Waals equation,

$$P = \frac{nRT}{(V - nb)} - \frac{n^2a}{V^2} = \frac{(1)(0.821)(273)}{(1 - 0.037)} - \frac{1^2(4.2)}{1}$$

$$= 23.3 - 4.2 = 19.1 \text{ atm}$$

The pressure is thus 3.3 atm less than would be predicted from the ideal gas law, or an error of 15 percent.

MCAT Expertise

Be familiar with the concepts embodied by this equation but do not spend too much time working with it or memorizing it, as it is not likely to be tested directly on the MCAT.

Note that including the correction term (a) has the effect of increasing the observed pressure (*P*) to that predicted by the ideal gas law.

Conclusion

In this chapter, we reviewed the basic characteristics and behaviors of gases. The kinetic molecular theory of gases lays out the explanation for the behavior of ideal gases as described by the ideal gas law. The ideal gas law shows the mathematical relationship among four variables associated with gases: pressure, volume, temperature, and number of moles. We examined special cases of the ideal gas law in which temperature (Boyle's law) or pressure (Charles' law) is held constant. Boyle's law shows that when temperature is held constant, there is an inverse relationship between pressure and volume. Charles' law shows that when pressure is held constant, there is a direct relationship between temperature and volume. We also examined Dalton's law, which relates the partial pressure of a gas to its mole fraction and the sum of the partial pressures of all the gases in a system to the total pressure of the system. Finally, we examined the ways in which real gases deviate from the predicted behaviors of ideal gases. The van der Waals equation of state is a useful equation for correcting deviations based on molecular interactions and volumes.

From helium-filled balloons to the bubbles of carbon dioxide in a glass of soda, from the pressurized gases used for scuba diving to the air we breathe on land, gases are all around us. And yet, for all the different gases that bubble, flow, and settle in and through our daily living experiences, they behave in remarkably similar ways. Expect that the MCAT will treat gases with the level of attention that is appropriate to their importance in our physical lives.

CONCEPTS TO REMEMBER

☐ Gases are the least dense phase of matter. They are classified, along with liquids, as fluids because they flow in response to shearing forces and conform to the shape of their containers. Unlike liquids, however, gases are compressible.

☐ The state of a gas system can be characterized by four properties: pressure, volume, temperature, and number of moles. Standard temperature and pressure (STP) is a set of conditions common in the study of gases; standard temperature is 273 K (0°C), and standard pressure is 1 atm.

☐ Ideal gases are described by the kinetic molecular theory of gases, which characterizes gases as composed of particles with negligible volume, with no intermolecular forces, in continuous and random motion, undergoing elastic collisions with each other and the walls of their container, and having an average kinetic energy that is proportional to the temperature.

☐ Graham's law of diffusion and effusion states that for two or more gases at the same temperature, a gas with lower molar mass will diffuse or effuse more rapidly than a gas with higher molar mass.

☐ Regardless of chemical identity, equal amounts of gases occupy the same volume if they are at the same temperature and pressure. For example, one mole of any gas occupies 22.4 liters at STP.

☐ The ideal gas law, $PV = nRT$, describes the mathematical relationship among the four variables of the gas state for an ideal gas.

☐ Boyle's law is a special case of the ideal gas law for which temperature is held constant; it shows an inverse relationship between pressure and volume.

☐ Charles' law is a special case of the ideal gas law for which pressure is held constant; it shows a direct relationship between temperature and volume.

☐ Dalton's law of partial pressure states that the individual gas components of a mixture of gases will exert individual pressures, called partial pressures, in proportion to their mole fractions. The total pressure of a mixture of gases is equal to the sum of the individual partial pressures of the individual gas components.

☐ The behavior of real gases deviates from that predicted by the ideal gas law, especially under conditions of very high pressure or very low temperature. The van der Waals equation of state is used to correct for deviations due to intermolecular attractions and molecular volumes.

EQUATIONS TO REMEMBER

☐ $KE = \dfrac{1}{2}mv^2 = \dfrac{3}{2}kT$

☐ $u_{rms} = \left(\dfrac{3RT}{MM}\right)^{1/2}$

☐ $\dfrac{r_1}{r_2} = \left(\dfrac{MM_2}{MM_1}\right)^{1/2} = \sqrt{\left(\dfrac{MM_2}{MM_1}\right)}$

☐ $PV = nRT$

☐ $d = \dfrac{m}{V} = \dfrac{P(MM)}{RT}$

☐ $PV = k$ or $P_1V_1 = P_2V_2$

☐ $\dfrac{V}{T} = k$ or $\dfrac{V_1}{T_1} = \dfrac{V_2}{T_2}$

☐ $P_A = P_T X_A$

☐ $\left(P + \dfrac{n^2 a}{V^2}\right)(V - nb) = nRT$

Practice Questions

1. Based on your knowledge of gases, what conditions would be least likely to result in ideal gas behavior?

   A. High pressure and low temperature
   B. Low temperature and large volume
   C. High pressure and large volume
   D. Low pressure and high temperature

2. Calculate the density of neon gas at STP in g L^{-1}. The molar mass of neon can be approximated to 20.18 g mol^{-1}.

   A. 452.3 g L^{-1}
   B. 226.0 g L^{-1}
   C. 1.802 g L^{-1}
   D. 0.9009 g L^{-1}

3. A leak of helium gas through a small hole occurs at a rate of 3.22×10^{-5} mol s^{-1}. Compare the leakage rates of neon and oxygen gases to helium at the same temperature and pressure.

   A. Neon will leak faster than helium; oxygen will leak slower than helium.
   B. Neon will leak faster than helium; oxygen will leak slower than helium.
   C. Neon will leak slower than helium; oxygen will leak slower than helium.
   D. Neon will leak slower than helium; oxygen will leak faster than helium.

4. A 0.040 gram piece of magnesium is placed in a beaker of hydrochloric acid. Hydrogen gas is generated according to the following equation:

   $$Mg\,(s) + 2\,HCl\,(aq) \rightarrow MgCl_2\,(aq) + H_2\,(g)$$

   The gas is collected over water at 25°C, and the pressure during the experiment reads 784 mm Hg. The gas displaces a volume of 100 mL. The vapor pressure of water at 25°C is approximately 24.0 mm Hg. From this data, calculate how many moles of hydrogen are produced.

   A. 4.22×10^{-3} moles hydrogen
   B. 4.09×10^{-3} moles hydrogen
   C. 3.11 moles hydrogen
   D. 3.20 moles hydrogen

5. The properties of ideal gases state that ideal gases

   I. have no volume.
   II. have no attractive forces between them.
   III. have no mass.

   A. I, II, and III
   B. I only
   C. I and II only
   D. I and III only

6. An 8.01 g sample of NH_4NO_3 (s) is placed into an evacuated 10.00 L flask and heated to 227°C. After the NH_4NO_3 totally decomposes, what is the approximate pressure in the flask?

$$NH_4NO_3\ (s) \rightarrow N_2O\ (g) + H_2O\ (g)$$

A. 0.600 atm
B. 0.410 atm
C. 1.23 atm
D. 0.672 atm

7. The kinetic molecular theory states that

A. the average kinetic energy of a molecule of gas is directly proportional to the temperature of the gas in Kelvin.
B. collisions between gas molecules are inelastic.
C. elastic collisions result in a loss of energy.
D. all gas molecules have the same kinetic energy.

8. The plots of two gases at STP are shown below. One of the gases is 1.0 L of helium, and the other is 1.0 L of bromine. Which plot corresponds to each gas and why?

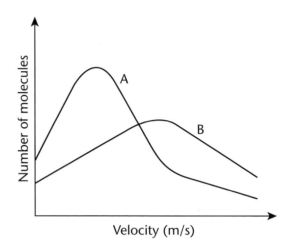

A. Curve A is helium and curve B is bromine, because helium has a smaller molar mass than bromine.
B. Curve A is helium and curve B is bromine, because the average kinetic energy of bromine is greater than the average kinetic energy of helium.
C. Curve A is bromine and curve B is helium, because helium has a smaller molar mass than bromine.
D. Curve A is bromine and curve B is helium, because the average kinetic energy of bromine is greater than the average kinetic energy of helium.

9. A balloon at standard temperature and pressure contains 0.20 moles of oxygen and 0.60 moles of nitrogen. What is the partial pressure of oxygen in the balloon?

A. 0.20 atm
B. 0.30 atm
C. 0.60 atm
D. 0.25 atm

10. The temperature at the center of the sun can be estimated based on the approximation that the gases at the center of the sun have an average molar mass equal to 2.00 g/mole. Approximate the temperature at the center of the sun using these additional values: The pressure equals 1.30×10^9 atm, and the density at the center equals 1.20 g/cm³.

A. 2.6×10^7 K
B. 2.6×10^{10} K
C. 2.6×10^4 K
D. 2.6×10^6 K

11. The gaseous state of matter is characterized by the following properties:

I. Gases are compressible.

II. Gases assume the volume of their container.

III. Gas particles exist as diatomic molecules.

A. I and II only
B. I and III only
C. III only
D. I, II, and III

12. A gas at a temperature of 27°C has a volume of 60.0 mL. What temperature change is needed to increase this gas to a volume of 90.0 mL?

A. A reduction of 150°C
B. An increase of 150°C
C. A reduction of 40.5°C
D. An increase of 40.5°C

13. A gaseous mixture contains nitrogen and helium and has a total pressure of 150 torr. The nitrogen particles comprise 80 percent of the gas, and the helium particles make up the other 20 percent of the gas. What is the pressure exerted by each individual gas?

A. 100 torr nitrogen, 50.0 torr helium
B. 120 torr nitrogen, 30.0 torr helium
C. 30.0 torr nitrogen, 150 torr helium
D. 50.0 torr nitrogen, 100 torr helium

14. In which of the following situations is it impossible to predict how the pressure will change for a gas sample?

A. The gas is cooled at a constant volume.
B. The gas is heated at a constant volume.
C. The gas is heated, and the volume is simultaneously increased.
D. The gas is cooled, and the volume is simultaneously increased.

Small Group Questions

1. How does the addition or removal of gas B from a vessel affect the partial pressure of gas A?

2. Is hydrogen bonding present in steam?

Explanations to Practice Questions

1. A

Gases deviate from ideal behavior at higher pressures, which forces molecules closer together. The closer they are, the more they can participate in intermolecular forces, which violate the definition of an ideal gas. As the temperature of a gas is reduced, the average velocity of the gas molecules decreases, and the attractive intermolecular forces become more significant. This results in the loss of another characteristic of an ideal gas, and thus less ideal behavior. Answer choices that include the opposite, high temperature and low pressure, are incorrect because gases behave most ideally under these conditions. At high temperatures, molecules will move quickly and exhibit random motion and elastic collisions, which is a property of ideal gases. In an ideal gas it is assumed that there are no intermolecular attractions between gas molecules, which is valid at low pressures when there is ample space between them.

2. D

Density equals mass divided by volume. The mass of 1 mole of neon gas equals 20.18 grams. At STP, 1 mole of neon occupies 22.4 L. Dividing the mass, 20.18 grams, by the volume, 22.4 L, gives an approximate density of 0.9009 g L^{-1}.

3. C

Graham's law of effusion states that the relative rates of effusion of two gases at the same temperature and pressure are given by the inverse ratio of the square roots of the masses of the gas particles. In equation form, Graham's law can be represented by: $Rate_1/Rate_2 = \sqrt{(MM_2/MM_1)}$. If a molecule has a higher molecular weight, then it will leak at a slower rate than a gas with a lower molecular weight. Both neon and oxygen gases will leak at slower rates than helium because they both weigh more than helium.

4. B

The pressure of the gas is calculated by subtracting the vapor pressure of water from the measured pressure during the experiment: 784 mm Hg – 24 mm Hg = 760 mm Hg, or 1 atm. The ideal gas law can be used to calculate the moles of hydrogen gas. The volume of the gas equals 0.100 L, the temperatures equals 298 K, and R = 0.0821 (L atm / mol K). Solving the equation $PV = nRT$ for n gives 4.09×10^{-3} moles of hydrogen. (A) is incorrect and would result from mistakenly using 784 mm Hg of the pressure instead of the pressure adjusted for water vapor. (C) and (D) would both result from incorrectly using a pressure in mm Hg instead of converting to atm while using the gas constant R = 0.0821 (L atm / mol K).

5. C

Ideal gases are said to have no attractive forces between molecules. They are considered to have point masses, which theoretically take up no volume.

6. C

The first thing to do is balance the given chemical equation. The coefficients, from left to right, are 1, 1, and 2. The mass of solid, 8.01 grams, can be converted to moles of gas product by dividing by the molar mass of $NH_4NO_3(s)$ (80.06 g) and multiplying by the molar ratio of 3 moles of gas product to one mole of $NH_4NO_3(s)$. This gives approximately 0.300 moles of gas product. The ideal gas equation can be used to obtain the pressure in the flask. The values are as follows: R equals 0.0821 (L atm / mole K), the temperature in Kelvin is 500 K, and the volume is 10.00 L. Solving for P in the equation $PV = nRT$ gives a pressure of about 1.23 atm.

7. A

The average kinetic energy is directly proportional to the temperature of a gas in Kelvin. The kinetic molecular theory states that collisions between molecules are elastic and thus do not result in a loss of energy. The kinetic energy of each gas molecule is not the same.

8. C

At STP, the difference between the distribution of velocities for helium and bromine gas is due to the difference in molar mass $(Rate_1/Rate_2) = \sqrt{\left(\dfrac{MM_2}{MM_1}\right)}$. Helium has a smaller molar mass than bromine. Particles with small

masses travel faster than those with large masses, so the helium gas corresponds to curve B with higher velocities. (A) and (B) are incorrect because they inaccurately identify each curve on the graph. Given that the gases are at the same temperature (STP), we can recall that temperature relates to kinetic energy (KE). $KE = \dfrac{3}{2}kT$. The gases average KE, therefore should be the same. Therefore, answer (D) is also incorrect.

9. D

At STP, the pressure inside the balloon equals 1 atm. The total number of moles in the balloon equals 0.20 moles plus 0.60 moles, or 0.80 moles. P_{O_2} equals the mole fraction of oxygen (0.20/0.80) times the total pressure, 1 atm. The partial pressure of oxygen is 0.25 atm.

10. A

The ideal gas law can be modified to include density and determine the temperature of the sun.

n = mass/molecular weight

density (denoted D for this problem) = $mass/V$

The density is given in g/cm³ and must be converted to g/L so the units cancel in the above equation. Because 1 cm³ equals 1 mL and there are 1,000 mL in 1 L, the density can be multiplied by 1,000 to be converted to g/L.

$$PV = nRT$$

$$PV = \frac{(mass)RT}{MW}$$

$$T = \frac{PV(MW)}{R(mass)}$$

$$T = \frac{(P)(MW)}{(R)(D)}$$

$$= \frac{(1.3 \times 10^9 \text{ atm})(2 \text{ g/mol})}{(0.0821 \text{ atm L/mol K})(1.20 \text{ g/cm}^3)(1{,}000 \text{ cm}^3/\text{L})}$$

$$= 2.6 \times 10^7 \text{ K}$$

11. A

Gases are compressible, because they travel freely with large amounts of space between molecules. Because gas particles are far apart from each other and in rapid motion, they tend to take up the volume of their container. Many gases that exist as diatomic molecules (i.e., O_2, H_2, N_2), but this is not a property that characterizes all gases.

12. B

We will use $V_1/T_1 = V_2/T_2$. First, we must convert the temperature to Kelvin by adding 273 to get 300 K as the initial temperature. Plugging into the equation and solving for T_2 gives 450 K. Subtracting the initial temperature, 300 K, gives an increase of 150 K. They are measured by the same increments, so an increase of 150 K corresponds to an increase of 150°C.

13. B

The partial pressure of each gas is found by multiplying the total pressure by the mole fraction of the gas. Because 80 percent of the molecules are nitrogen, the mole fraction of nitrogen gas is equal to 0.80. Similarly, for helium, the mole fraction is 0.20, because helium comprises 20 percent of the gas molecules. To find the pressure exerted by nitrogen, multiply the total pressure (150 torr) by 0.80 to obtain 120 torr of nitrogen. To find the pressure exerted by helium, multiply the total pressure by 0.20 to get 30 torr of helium.

14. C

Both a change in temperature and a change in volume can affect the gas's pressure. So if one of those two variables is kept constant (i.e., (A) and (B)), we'll definitely be able to predict which way the pressure will change. At a constant volume, heating the gas will increase its pressure, and cooling the gas will decrease it. What about when both temperature and volume are changing? If they have the same effect on pressure, then we can still predict which way it will change. This is the case in (D). Cooling the gas and increasing its volume both decrease pressure. (C), on the other hand, presents us with too vague a scenario for us to predict definitively the change in pressure. Heating the gas would amplify the pressure, while increasing the volume would decrease it. Without knowing the magnitude of each influence, it's impossible to say whether the pressure would increase, decrease, or stay the same.

8

Phases and Phase Changes

Thwak! Thwak! "Stupid ketchup bottle! Why . . . won't you . . . come . . . out?!" Few things are more frustrating than ketchup that just refuses to budge. It usually happens with newly opened bottles, and the "stuck ketchup" phenomenon is so common that there's almost a ritualized nature to the process of getting it "unstuck": Unscrew the top, turn the bottle on its side, and give it a few gentle shakes. If it doesn't come out right away, the next step is the administration of a few sturdy whacks with the palm of the hand against the bottom of the bottle. This is usually accompanied by some mild epithet suggestive of ketchup's alleged lack of intelligence (see quote above). More often than not, the physical abuse imposed upon the bottle only results in soft-tissue bruising and perhaps an alarming increase in the violent nature of the anti-ketchup epithets. Finally the ritual ends in an act of stabbing, and the evidence to convict is the spilled pool of red and the seemingly blood-coated butter knife that rests along the edge of the plate next to the pile of crispy french fries.

You can't really blame the ketchup, though. It doesn't know any better. In fact, it's only acting according to its nature as a member of a unique class of liquids called Bingham fluids. Bingham fluids do not begin to flow immediately upon application of shear stress. Unlike Newtonian fluids, such as water or vegetable oil, which begin to flow as soon as a finite amount of shear stress is applied, Bingham fluids will only begin to flow when a minimum force value called the yield value is exceeded. Essentially, Bingham fluids behave like solids under static conditions and flow, as fluids, only when a shear stress at least equal to the yield value is applied. The sharp blows that you apply to the bottle of ketchup are usually strong enough to exceed ketchup's yield value. Unfortunately for the diner who ends up with a plate (and probably lap) flooded with ketchup, ketchup also belongs to a class of liquids known as pseudo-plastic fluids, which demonstrate the property of shear thinning. Shear-thinning liquids display reducing viscosity with increasing shear rate (related to fluid velocity). That ketchup is stuck, like a solid, in that bottle, until it isn't (because the yield value has been exceeded), at which point it begins to flow and the faster it flows, the more it "thins" and becomes less viscous. The result is the mess on your plate and lap.

Our discussion in this chapter will focus on the three phases of matter, with particular emphasis on liquids and solids. (The gaseous phase has been discussed extensively in the previous chapter.) When the attractive forces between molecules (i.e., van der Waals forces, etc.) overcome the kinetic energy that keeps them apart in the gas phase, the molecules move closer together, entering the liquid or solid phase. The liquid and solid phases are often referred to as the condensed phases because of their higher densities compared to that of the gaseous phase. Molecules in the liquid and solid phases have lower degrees of freedom of movement than those in the gaseous phase as a result of the stronger intermolecular forces that dominate in the liquid and solid phases. After characterizing fluids and solids, we will review phase equilibria and phase diagrams. We will conclude our consideration of the phases of matter by reviewing the colligative properties of solutions.

Solids ★★☆☆☆

We recognize **solids** by their rigidity and resistance to flow. The intermolecular attractive forces among the atoms, ions, or molecules of the solid matter hold them in a rigid arrangement. Although particles in the solid phase do not demonstrate linear motion, this does not mean that they do not possess any kinetic energy. The motion of particles in the solid phase, however, is mostly limited to vibration. As a result, solids have definite shapes (usually independent of the shape of a container) and volumes. Note that on the MCAT, solids (and liquids, for that matter) are considered to be incompressible; that is, a given mass of any solid or liquid will have a constant volume regardless of changes in pressure.

For most substances, the solid phase is the densest phase. A notable, and tested, exception to this generalization is water. Water in its solid phase (ice) is less dense than it is in its liquid phase due to the grater spacing between the molecules in the crystalline structure of ice. The spacious lattice of ice crystals is stabilized by the hydrogen bonds between water molecules. Water molecules in the liquid phase also interact through hydrogen bonds, but because the water molecules are moving around, the lattice arrangement is absent, and the molecules are able to move closer to each other. In fact, water's density reaches a maximum around 4°C. The density decreases at temperatures above 4°C because the increasing kinetic energy of the water molecules causes the molecules to move further apart. Between 4°C and 0°C, the density decreases because the lattice organization of hydrogen bonds is beginning to form.

The molecular arrangement of particles in the solid phase can be either **crystalline** or **amorphous**. Crystalline solids, such as the ionic compounds (e.g., NaCl), possess an ordered structure; their atoms exist in a specific three-dimensional geometric arrangement or lattice with repeating patterns of atoms, ions, or molecules. Amorphous solids, such as glass, plastic, and candle wax, lack an ordered three-dimensional arrangement. The particles of amorphous solids are fixed in place but not in the lattice arrangement that characterizes crystalline solids. Most solids are crystalline in structure. The two most common forms of crystals are metallic and ionic crystals.

Key Concept

Because the molecules in liquids and solids are much closer together than those in a gas, intermolecular forces must be considered as though there is no such thing as "ideal" behavior. These forces do allow us to predict behavior, although differently so.

Key Concept

Crystalline structures allow for a balance of both attractive and repulsive forces to minimize energy.

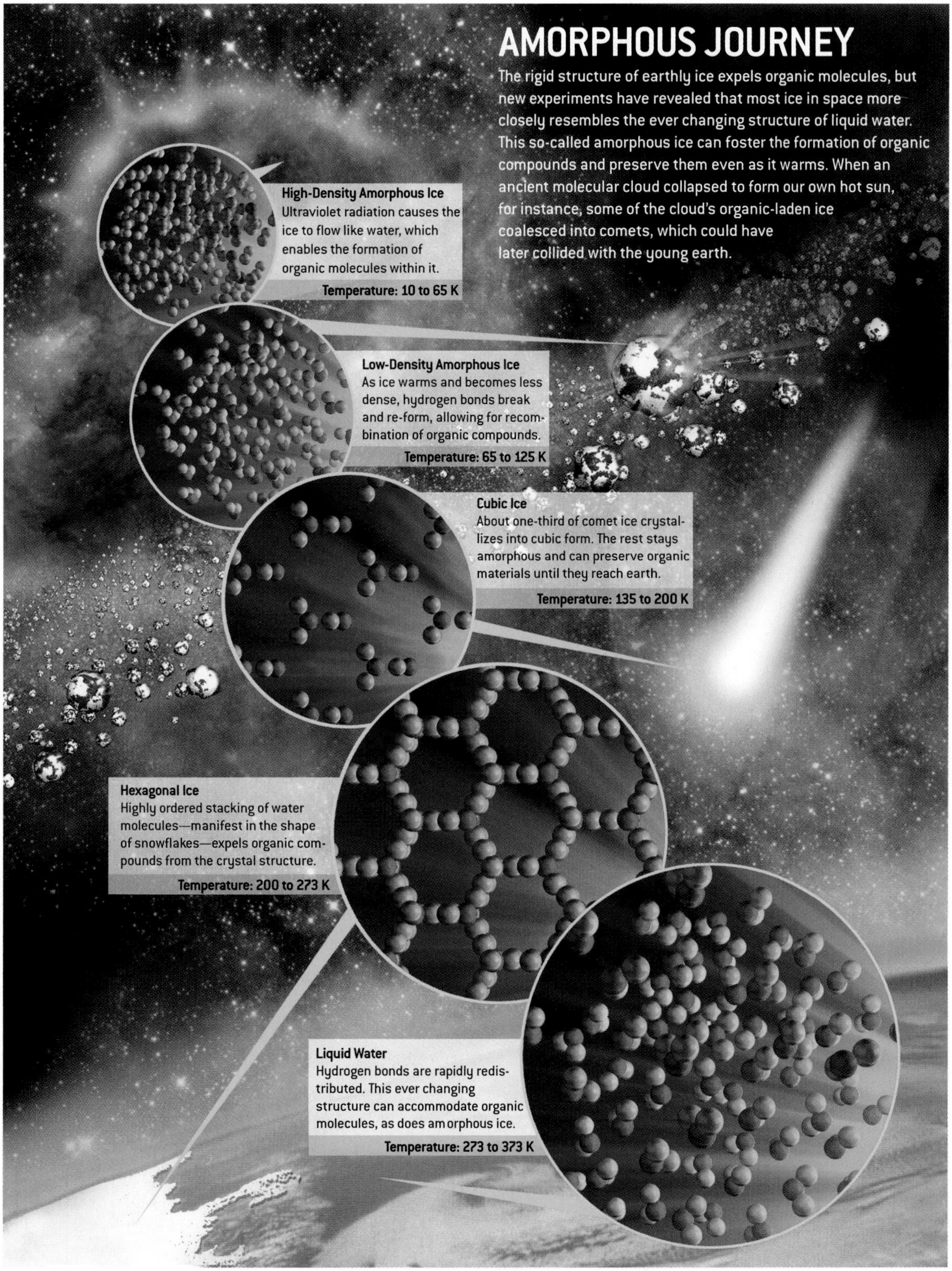

AMORPHOUS JOURNEY

The rigid structure of earthly ice expels organic molecules, but new experiments have revealed that most ice in space more closely resembles the ever changing structure of liquid water. This so-called amorphous ice can foster the formation of organic compounds and preserve them even as it warms. When an ancient molecular cloud collapsed to form our own hot sun, for instance, some of the cloud's organic-laden ice coalesced into comets, which could have later collided with the young earth.

High-Density Amorphous Ice
Ultraviolet radiation causes the ice to flow like water, which enables the formation of organic molecules within it.
Temperature: 10 to 65 K

Low-Density Amorphous Ice
As ice warms and becomes less dense, hydrogen bonds break and re-form, allowing for recombination of organic compounds.
Temperature: 65 to 125 K

Cubic Ice
About one-third of comet ice crystallizes into cubic form. The rest stays amorphous and can preserve organic materials until they reach earth.
Temperature: 135 to 200 K

Hexagonal Ice
Highly ordered stacking of water molecules—manifest in the shape of snowflakes—expels organic compounds from the crystal structure.
Temperature: 200 to 273 K

Liquid Water
Hydrogen bonds are rapidly redistributed. This ever changing structure can accommodate organic molecules, as does amorphous ice.
Temperature: 273 to 373 K

Figure 8.1

Ionic solids are aggregates of positively and negatively charged ions that repeat according to defined patterns of alternating cations and anions. As a result, the solid mass of a compound, such as NaCl, does not contain discrete molecules (see Chapter 4, Compounds and Stoichiometry). The physical properties of ionic solids include high melting points, high boiling points, and poor electrical conductivity in the solid state but high conductivity in the molten state or in aqueous solution. These properties are due to the compounds' strong electrostatic interactions, which also cause the ions to be relatively immobile in the solid phase. Ionic structures are given by empirical formulas that describe the ratio of atoms in the lowest possible whole numbers. For example, the empirical formula $BaCl_2$ gives the ratio of barium to chloride atoms within the crystal.

Metallic solids consist of metal atoms packed together as closely as possible. Metallic solids have high melting and boiling points as a result of their strong covalent attractions. Pure metallic masses (consisting of a single metal element) are usually described as layers of spheres of roughly similar radii, stacked layer upon layer in a "staggered" arrangement such that one sphere in one layer fits into the indented space between the spheres that sit above and below it. These staggered arrangements (body-centered cubic and face-centered cubic, see below) are more common than layers of spheres stacked to form perfectly aligned columns of spheres (see simple cubic, below), because the staggered arrangement minimizes the separation between the atoms.

The repeating units of crystals (both ionic and metallic) are represented by **unit cells**. There are many types of unit cells. Chapter 4, Compounds and Stoichiometry, referred to the geometric arrangement of Na^+ and Cl^- ions in table salt as 6:6 coordinated, meaning that each sodium ion is surrounded by (coordinated by) six chloride ions, and each chloride ion is surrounded by (coordinated by) six sodium ions. This particular arrangement is also known as face-centered cubic. There are three **cubic unit cells**, and you should recognize these for the MCAT: **simple cubic, body-centered cubic**, and **face-centered cubic**. Figure 8.2 illustrates these unit cells as ball-and-stick models.

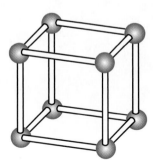
simple cubic

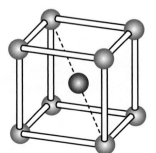
body-centered cubic

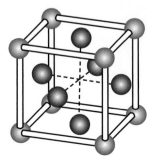
face-centered cubic

Figure 8.2

In the ball-and-stick models illustrated, the anions are represented as small spheres separated by a lot of space, but more accurately, the spheres are packed quite closely. Figure 8.3 illustrates this. In the ionic unit cell, the spheres represent the anions; the spaces between the anions are occupied by the smaller cations. In most ionic compounds, the anion, which has gained one or more electrons, is much larger than the cation, which has lost one or more electrons. (The cations are *not* shown in Figures 8.2 and 8.3.)

simple cubic   body-centered cubic   face-centered cubic

Figure 8.3

Liquids ★★☆☆☆

The **liquid phase**, along with the solid phase, is considered a condensed phase because the spacing between the particles is reduced in comparison to that between gas particles. Furthermore, we assume that liquids, like solids, are incompressible, meaning that their volumes do not change in any significant way as a result of moderate pressure changes. But don't let all this talk of liquid as a "condensed phase" mislead you: There is still a lot of space separating liquid particles. You can "observe" this space for yourself through a very simple experiment. Fill a glass with very hot tap water all the way to the top of the glass, making sure that the water surface is actually "bulging" up above the level of the rim of the glass. Carefully add powdered sugar, by the teaspoon, to the water. Do not allow the spoon to touch the surface of the water, and do not stir the solution. The hot water will dissolve the sugar on its own. Repeat the process. You will be able to add several teaspoons of sugar to the water before it spills out of the cup. The sugar dissolved into the empty spaces that separate the water molecules!

Liquids are categorized as **fluids** (along with gases) because they do not resist shearing forces and flow when subjected to them. They also conform to the shapes of their containers. These behaviors are a result of the high degree of freedom of movement liquids possess. Like gas molecules, liquid molecules can move about in random motion and are disordered in their arrangement. Both liquids and gases are able to diffuse. Liquid molecules near the surface of the liquid can gain enough kinetic energy to escape into the gas phase; this is called evaporation.

One of the most important properties of liquids is their ability to mix—both with each other and with other phases—to form solutions (see Chapter 9, Solutions). The degree to which two liquids can mix is called their **miscibility**. While ethanol and water are completely **miscible**, oil and water are almost completely **immiscible**; that is, their molecules tend to repel each other due to their polarity differences. You're certainly familiar with the expression "Like dissolves like." Oil and water normally form separate layers when mixed, with the oil layer above the water because it is less dense. Organic chemistry takes advantage of the solubility differences of immiscible liquids to separate compounds through the method of liquid-liquid extraction. Agitation of two immiscible liquids can result in the formation of a fairly homogenous mixture called an **emulsion**. Although they look like solutions, emulsions are actually mixtures of discrete particles too small to be seen distinctly. Shaking a cruet of extra virgin olive oil and balsamic vinegar, seasoned with sea salt and fresh ground pepper, makes for a simple but delicious emulsion for your mixed baby greens salad.

Phase Equilibria ★★☆☆☆

In an isolated system, **phase changes** (solid $\leftrightarrow$ liquid $\leftrightarrow$ gas) are reversible, and equilibrium of phases will eventually be reached. For example, at 1 atm and 0°C in an isolated system, an ice cube and the water in which it is floats are in equilibrium. In other words, some of the ice may absorb heat (from the liquid water) and melt, but since that heat is being removed from the liquid water, an equal amount of the liquid water will freeze and form ice. Thus, the relative amounts of ice and water remain constant. Equilibrium between the liquid and gas states of water will be established in a closed container, such as a plastic water bottle with the cap screwed on tightly. At room temperature and atmospheric pressure, most of the water in the bottle will be in the liquid phase, but a small number of molecules at the surface will gain enough kinetic energy to escape into the gas phase; likewise, a small number of gas molecules will lose sufficient kinetic energy to re-enter the liquid phase. After a while, equilibrium is established, and the relative amounts of water in the liquid and gas phases become constant—at room temperature and atmospheric pressure, equilibrium occurs when the air above the water has about 3 percent humidity. Phase equilibria are analogous to the dynamic equilibria of reversible chemical reactions for which the concentrations of reactants and products are constant because the rates of the forward and reverse reactions are equal.

GAS-LIQUID EQUILIBRIUM

The temperature of any substance in any phase is related to the average kinetic energy of the molecules that make up the substance. However, as we saw in Chapter 7, not all the molecules have exactly the same instantaneous speeds. Therefore, the

Key Concept

As with all equilibria, the rates of the forward and reverse processes will be the same.

molecules possess a range of instantaneous kinetic energy values. In the liquid phase, the molecules have relatively large degrees of freedom of movement. Some of the molecules near the surface of the liquid may have enough kinetic energy to leave the liquid phase and escape into the gaseous phase. This process is known as **evaporation** (or **vaporization**). Each time the liquid loses a high-energy particle, the temperature of the remaining liquid decreases. Evaporation is an endothermic process for which the heat source is the liquid water. Of course, the liquid water itself may be receiving thermal energy from some other source, as in the case of a puddle of water drying up under the hot summer sun or a pot of water on the stovetop. Given enough energy, the liquid will completely evaporate.

In covered or closed container, the escaping molecules are trapped above the solution. These molecules exert a countering pressure, which forces some of the gas back into the liquid phase; this process is called **condensation**. Condensation is facilitated by lower temperature or higher pressure. Atmospheric pressure acts on a liquid in a manner similar to that of an actual physical lid. As evaporation and condensation proceed, the respective rates of the two processes become equal, and equilibrium is reached. The pressure that the gas exerts over the liquid at equilibrium is the vapor pressure of the liquid. Vapor pressure increases as temperature increases, since more molecules have sufficient kinetic energy to escape into the gas phase. The temperature at which the vapor pressure of the liquid equals the ambient (also known as external, applied, or atmospheric) pressure is called the **boiling point**: At boiling, vaporization happens throughout the entire volume of the liquid, not just near its surface. The bubbles of gas that rise from your pot of boiling pasta water are gaseous water molecules, plus the small amounts of atmospheric gases (mostly nitrogen and oxygen gas) that had been dissolved in the water.

LIQUID-SOLID EQUILIBRIUM

We've already illustrated the equilibrium that can exist between the liquid and the solid phases of water at 0°C. Even though the atoms or molecules of a solid are confined to definite locations, each atom or molecule can undergo motions about some equilibrium position. These vibrational motions increase when heat is applied. From our understanding of entropy, we can say that the availability of energy microstates increases as the temperature of the solid increases. In basic terms, this means that the molecules have greater freedom of movement, and energy disperses. If atoms or molecules in the solid phase absorb enough energy, the three-dimensional structure of the solid will break down, and the atoms or molecules will escape into the liquid phase. The transition from solid to liquid is called **fusion** or **melting**. The reverse process, from liquid to solid, is called **solidification**, **crystallization**, or **freezing**. The temperature at which these processes occur is called the melting point or freezing point, depending on the direction of the transition. Whereas pure crystalline solids have distinct, very sharp melting points, amorphous solids, such as glass, plastic, and candle wax, tend to melt (or solidify) over a larger range of temperatures due to their less-ordered molecular distribution. One of the surest signs that a dinner party has come to its natural and necessary conclusion is when the dinner guests start playing with the liquid wax dripping down the side of the candlesticks, allowing it to cool and solidify on their fingertips.

GAS-SOLID EQUILIBRIUM

The final phase equilibrium is that which exists between the gas and solid phase. When a solid goes directly into the gas phase, the process is called **sublimation**. Dry ice (solid CO_2) sublimes at room temperature and atmospheric pressure; the absence of the liquid phase makes it a convenient refrigerant and a fun addition to punch bowls at parties. The reverse transition, from the gaseous to the solid phase, is called **deposition**. In organic chemistry, a device known as the cold finger (the name sounds more malicious than it actually is) is used to purify a product that is heated under reduced pressure to cause it to sublimate. The desired product is usually more volatile than the impurities, so the gas is purer than the original product and the impurities are left in the solid state. The gas then deposits onto the cold finger, which has cold water flowing through it, yielding a purified solid product that can be collected. Another common instance of sublimation is "freezer burn" on meats and vegetables that are stored for long periods in the freezer. The frozen water in the meat or vegetables will slowly sublimate over time, and what is left is fit only for the garbage. On the other hand, sublimation is used to produce freeze-dried foods, such as coffee, "emergency survival meals," and perhaps most (in)famously, astronaut ice cream. The crackly frost of late autumn mornings in colder climates is formed by deposition of water vapor in the air.

THE GIBBS FUNCTION

As with all equilibria, the thermodynamic criterion for each of the phase equilibria is that the change in Gibbs free energy must be equal to zero ($\Delta G = 0$). For an equilibrium between a gas and a solid,

$$\Delta G = G(g) - G(s) = 0$$

Therefore, $G(g) = G(s)$

The same is true of the Gibbs functions for any other phase equilibria.

HEATING CURVES

When a compound is heated, the temperature rises until the melting or boiling points are reached. Then the temperature remains constant as the compound is converted to the next phase (i.e., liquid or gas, respectively). Once the entire sample is converted, then the temperature begins to rise again. See the heating curves depicted in Figure 8.4.

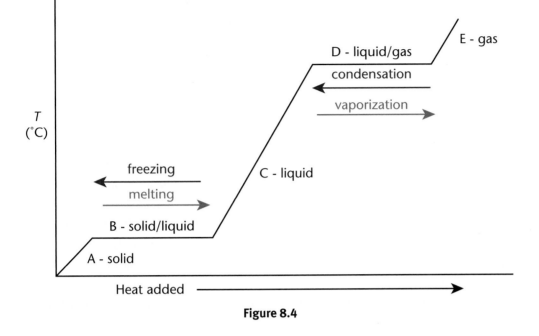

Figure 8.4

Phase Diagrams

★★☆☆☆

Phase diagrams are graphs that show the temperatures and pressures at which a substance will be thermodynamically stable in a particular phase. They also show the temperatures and pressures at which phases will be in equilibrium.

SINGLE COMPONENT

The phase diagram for a single compound is shown in Figure 8.5.

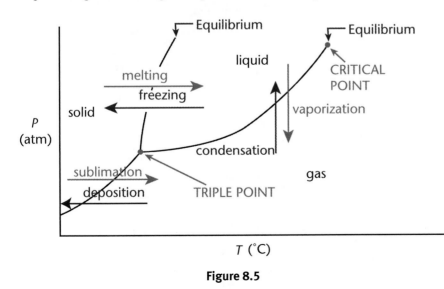

Figure 8.5

> **Key Concept**
>
> Every pure substance has a characteristic phase diagram.

Real World

Because of H_2O's unique properties, ice floats and ice skates flow smoothly over ice. This all "boils" down to the negative slope of the solid-liquid equilibrium line in its phase diagram. Because the density of ice is less than that of liquid H_2O, an increase in pressure (at a constant temperature) will actually melt ice (the opposite of the substance seen in Figure 8.5).

The lines on a phase diagram are called the **lines of equilibrium** or the **phase boundaries** and indicate the temperature and pressure values for the equilibria between phases. The lines of equilibrium divide the diagram into three regions corresponding to the three phases—solid, liquid, and gas—and they themselves represent the phase transformations. Line A represents crystallization/fusion, line B vaporization/condensation, and line C sublimation/deposition. In general, the gas phase is found at high temperatures and low pressures, the solid phase is found at low temperatures and high pressures, and the liquid phase is found at moderate temperatures and moderate pressures. The point at which the three phase boundaries meet is called the **triple point**. This is the temperature and pressure at which the three phases exist in equilibrium. The phase boundary that separates the solid and the liquid phases extends indefinitely from the triple point. The phase boundary between the liquid and gas phases, however, terminates at a point called the critical point. This is the temperature and pressure above which there is no distinction between the phases. Although this may seem to be an impossibility—after all, it's possible always to distinguish between the liquid and the solid phase—such "supercritical fluids" are perfectly logical. As a liquid is heated in a closed system its density decreases and the density of the vapor sitting above it increases. The critical point is the temperature and pressure at which the two densities become equal and there is no distinction between the two phases. The heat of vaporization at this point and for all temperatures and pressures above the critical point values is zero. So it's certainly possible to create a supercritical fluid, but definitely not common (in everyday life). Rest assured that you have never come close to approaching, say, the critical point temperature and pressure for water, no matter how much "industrial strength" your high-pressure home espresso machine possesses: 647 K (374°C or 705°F) and 22.064 MPa (218 atm).

A triple-point cell is a vacuum-tight flask containing water vapor, liquid water, and an ice mantle that has formed around an inner test tube.

Figure 8.6

MULTIPLE COMPONENTS

The phase diagram for a mixture of two or more components is complicated by the requirement that the composition of the mixture, as well as the temperature and pressure, must be specified. For example, consider a solution of two liquids, A and B, shown in Figure 8.7. The vapor above the solution is a mixture of the vapors of A and B. The pressures exerted by vapor A and vapor B on the solution are the vapor pressures that each exerts above its individual liquid phase. Raoult's law enables one to determine the relationship between the vapor pressure of gaseous A and the concentration of liquid A in the solution.

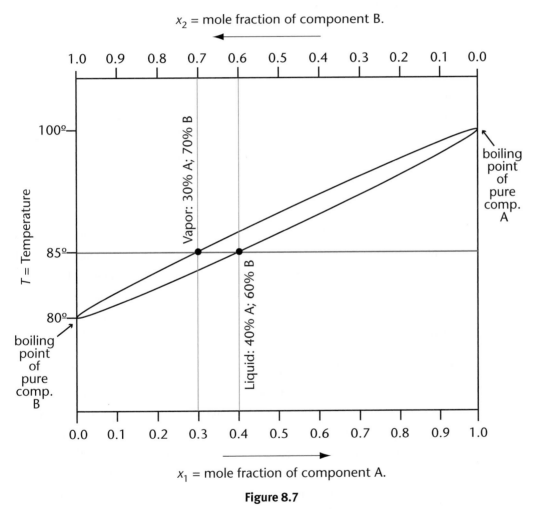

Figure 8.7

Curves such as this show the different compositions of the liquid phase and the vapor phase above a solution for different temperatures. The upper curve is the composition of the vapor, while the lower curve is that of the liquid. It is this difference in composition that forms the basis of distillation, an important separation technique in organic chemistry. For example, if we were to start with a mixture of A and B at a proportion of 40 percent A and 60 percent B and heat it to that solution's boiling

MCAT Expertise

On the MCAT, you should be able to identify and understand each area and every line of a phase diagram.

point (85°C), the resulting vapor would not have the same composition as the liquid solution because the two compounds have different volatilities. Compound B is more volatile because it has the lower boiling point. Therefore, vapor B should be in larger proportion to vapor A, compared to the proportion of B to A in the liquid phase. Because the boiling point temperature for this 60–40 mixture is 85°C, the vapor will also be at 85°C. At this temperature, we can tell from the graph that the vapor composition will be 30 percent A and 70 percent B. Indeed, the proportion of the more volatile compound, in this case compound B, has been enhanced. Repeated rounds of boiling (vaporization) and condensation will ultimately yield a pure sample of compound B.

Colligative Properties ★★☆☆☆

All the way back at the start of this book, we suggested that adding salt to water will yield a solution whose boiling point is higher than that of the pure water. While this is a true statement, we also suggested that the quantity of salt that is normally added to a pot of cooking water is not sufficient to cause a significant rise in the boiling point or a significant decrease in the cooking time. In culinary practice, adding salt to your cooking water merely (but importantly) contributes to the flavor of the food. The measurable change in boiling point of a solution compared to that of the pure solvent is one of the **colligative properties** of solutions. The colligative properties are physical properties of solutions that are dependent upon the concentration of dissolved particles but not upon the chemical identity of the dissolved particles. These properties—vapor pressure depression, boiling point elevation, freezing point depression, and osmotic pressure—are usually associated with dilute solutions (see Chapter 9, Solutions).

VAPOR PRESSURE DEPRESSION

When you add solute to a solvent and the solute dissolves, the solvent in solution has a vapor pressure that is lower than the vapor pressure of the pure solvent for all temperatures. For example, consider compound A in Figure 8.7. Compound A in its pure form (mole fraction = 1.0) has a boiling point of 100°C. Based on this information alone, we can assume that compound A is water. Compound B, which is more volatile than water and boils in pure form (mole fraction = 1.0) at around 80°C could be ethanol, which has a boiling point of 78.3°C. When a small amount of ethanol is added to water to create a dilute solution, say 90 percent water and 10 percent alcohol, the boiling point is around 95°C, and the vapor composition above the solution will be about 80 percent water and 20 percent ethanol. The relative decrease in the proportion of water in the vapor above the dilute water-alcohol solution is related to the decrease in the vapor pressure of water above the solution.

Key Concept

This goes hand in hand with boiling point elevation. The lowering of a solution's vapor pressure would mean that a higher temperature is required to overcome atmospheric pressure, thereby raising the boiling point.

If the vapor pressure of A above pure solvent A is designated by P°_A and the vapor pressure of A above the solution containing B is P_A, the vapor pressure decreases as follows:

$$\Delta P = P^{\circ}_A - P_A$$

In the late 1800s, the French chemist François Marie Raoult determined that this vapor pressure decrease is also equivalent to

$$\Delta P = X_B P^{\circ}_A$$

where X_B is the mole fraction of the solute B in solution with solvent A. Because $X_B = 1 - X_A$ and $\Delta P = P^{\circ}_A - P_A$, substitution into the previous equation leads to the common form of **Raoult's law**:

$$P_A = X_A P^{\circ}_A$$

where X_A is the mole fraction of the solvent A in the solution. Similarly, the expression for the vapor pressure of the solute in solution (assuming it is volatile) is given by:

$$P_B = X_B P^{\circ}_B$$

Raoult's law holds only when the attraction between the molecules of the different components of the mixture is equal to the attraction between the molecules of any one component in its pure state. When this condition does not hold, the relationship between mole fraction and vapor pressure will deviate from Raoult's law. Solutions that obey Raoult's law are called **ideal solutions**.

BOILING POINT ELEVATION

When a nonvolatile solute is dissolved into a solvent to create a solution, the boiling point of the solution will be greater than that of the pure solvent. Earlier, we defined the boiling point as the temperature at which the vapor pressure of the liquid equals the ambient (external) pressure. We've just seen that adding solute to a solvent results in a decrease in the vapor pressure of the solvent in the solution at all temperatures. If the vapor pressure of a solution is lower than that of the pure solvent, then more energy (and consequently a higher temperature) will be required before its vapor pressure equals the ambient pressure. The extent to which the boiling point of a solution is raised relative to that of the pure solvent is given by the following formula:

$$\Delta T_b = i K_b m$$

where ΔT_b is the boiling point elevation, K_b is a proportionality constant characteristic of a particular solvent (and will be given to you on Test Day), m is the molality of the solution [molality = moles of solute per kilogram of solvent (mol/kg); see Chapter 9, Solutions] and i is the van't Hoff factor, which is the moles of particles dissolved into a solution per mole of solute molecules. For example, $i = 2$ for NaCl because each molecule of sodium chloride dissociates into two particles, a sodium ion and a chloride ion, when it dissolves.

FREEZING POINT DEPRESSION

The presence of solute particles in a solution interferes with the formation of the lattice arrangement of solvent molecules associated with the solid state. Thus, a greater amount of energy must be removed from the solution (resulting in a lower temperature) in order for the solution to solidify. For example, pure water freezes at 0°C, but for every mole of solute dissolved in 1 kg (1 liter) of water, the freezing point is lowered by 1.86°C. Therefore, the K_f for water is −1.86°C/m. As is the case for K_b, the values for K_f are unique to each solvent and will be given to you on Test Day. The formula for calculating the freezing point depression for a solution is

$$\Delta T_f = iK_f m$$

where ΔT_f is the freezing point depression, K_f is the proportionality constant characteristic of a particular solvent, m is the molality of the solution, and i is the van't Hoff factor.

If you've ever wondered why we salt roads in the winter, this is why: The salt mixes with the snow and ice and initially dissolves into the small amount of liquid water that is in equilibrium with the solid phase (the snow and ice). The solute in solution causes a disturbance to the equilibrium such that the rate of melting is unchanged (because the salt can't interact with the solid water that is stabilized in a rigid lattice arrangement), but the rate of freezing is decreased (the solute displaces some of the water molecules from the solid-liquid interface and prevents liquid water from entering into the solid phase).

This imbalance causes more ice to melt than water to freeze. Melting is an endothermic process, so heat is initially absorbed from the liquid solution, causing the solution temperature to fall below the ambient temperature. Now, there is a temperature gradient and heat flows from the "warmer" air to the "cooler" aqueous solution; this additional heat facilitates more melting—even though the temperature of the solution is actually colder than it was before the solute was added! The more the ice melts into liquid water, the more the solute is dispersed through the liquid. The resulting salt solution, by virtue of the presence of the solute particles, has a lower freezing point than the pure water and remains in the liquid state even at temperatures that would normally cause pure water to freeze.

Could we use table sugar instead of salt? Absolutely—but sugar is more expensive. Could we use LiCl instead of NaCl? Absolutely—but NaCl is a lot easier and more economical. Besides, we've heard of manic drivers in need of a mood stabilizer, but manic roads? Could we use magical fairy dust? Absolutely—as long as magical fairy dust is soluble in water. In other words, it doesn't matter what the solute is. Freezing point depression is a colligative property that depends only upon the concentration of particles, not upon their identity.

OSMOTIC PRESSURE

One of the most important roles of the cell membrane is to maintain the unique differences between the intracellular and extracellular compartments. Both of these compartments are aqueous solutions separated by the cell membrane, which functions as a semipermeable barrier. Channels and pumps in the membrane serve to create and maintain concentration gradients of various solutes on either side of the membrane. A delicate balance of water influx and efflux must be established in order to prevent the cell from becoming dehydrated and shrinking or waterlogged and possibly bursting. The extracellular compartment itself is in continuity with the plasma compartment of the blood. A balance between these two compartments is dependent upon two pressures: the hydrostatic pressure of the blood generated by the contraction of the heart and the osmotic pressure of the plasma compartment, primarily established by the concentration of plasma proteins such as albumin. (Since the osmotic pressure of the plasma compartment is based on the concentration of plasma protein, it is also called oncotic pressure.) The hydrostatic pressure tends to push fluid volume out of the vascular compartment into the extracellular compartment, while the osmotic pressure tends to pull fluid volume back into the vascular compartment from the extracellular compartment.

Consider a container separated into two compartments by a semipermeable membrane (which, by definition, selectively permits the passage of certain molecules). One compartment contains pure water, while the other contains water with dissolved solute. The membrane allows water but not solute to pass through. Because substances tend to flow, or diffuse, from higher to lower concentration (which results in an increase in entropy), water will diffuse from the compartment containing pure water into the compartment containing the water-solute mixture. This net flow will cause the water level in the compartment containing the solution to rise above the level in the compartment containing pure water.

Because the solute cannot pass through the membrane, the concentrations of solute in the two compartments can never be equal. However, the hydrostatic pressure exerted by the water level in the solute-containing compartment will eventually oppose the influx of water; thus, the water level will rise only to the point at which it exerts a sufficient pressure to counterbalance the tendency of water to flow across the membrane. This pressure, defined as the **osmotic pressure (Π)** of the solution, is given by this formula:

$$\Pi = iMRT$$

Bridge

Osmosis explains how many biological systems regulate their fluid levels.

where M is the molarity of the solution, R is the ideal gas constant, T is the absolute temperature (in Kelvin), and i is the van't Hoff factor. The equation clearly shows that osmotic pressure is directly proportional to the molarity of the solution. Thus, osmotic pressure, like all colligative properties, depends only upon the presence of the solute, not its chemical identity.

One application of osmotic pressure is a particular method of water purification called reverse osmosis (RO). In reverse osmosis, impure water is placed into one container separated from another container by a semipermeable membrane. High pressure is applied to the impure water, which forces it to diffuse across the membrane, filling the compartment on the other side of the membrane with purified water. Because the water is being forced across the membrane in the direction opposite its concentration gradient (that is, the water is being forced from the compartment with the lower concentration of water to the compartment with the higher concentration of water), large pressures (higher than the solution's osmotic pressure) are needed to accomplish the purification.

Conclusion

In this chapter, we have reviewed the important concepts and calculations related to the condensed phases of the solid and liquid states of matter. For solids, we learned that the organization of the particles is either in a three-dimensional lattice formation, producing a crystalline structure, or in a less-ordered arrangement described as amorphous. Ionic and metallic solids have crystalline structure, while glass, plastic, and candle wax have amorphous structure. The particles that make up a crystalline structure can be organized in many ways; the basic repeating unit of that organization is called the unit cell. We reviewed the three cubic unit cells. Liquids, like gases, are defined by their ability to flow in response to shearing forces. Liquids that can mix together are called miscible, while those that repel each other and separate into different layers, like oil and water, are called immiscible. We examined the equilibria that exist between the different phases and noted that the change in Gibbs function for each phase change in equilibrium is zero, as is the case for all equilibria. Finally, we examined the colligative properties of solutions and the mathematics that govern them. The colligative properties—vapor pressure depression, boiling point elevation, freezing point depression, and osmotic pressure—are physical properties of solutions that depend upon the concentration of dissolved particles but not upon their chemical identity.

We concluded this chapter with an overview of the colligative properties of solutions; the next chapter will continue the review of the behaviors and characteristics of solutions and the mathematics of solution chemistry that will earn you points on Test Day.

CONCEPTS TO REMEMBER

☐ In the solid and liquid phases, the atoms, ions, or molecules are sufficiently condensed to allow the intermolecular forces, such as van der Waals, dipole–dipole, and hydrogen bonds, to hold the particles together and restrict their degrees of freedom of movement.

☐ Solids are defined by their rigidity (ability to maintain a shape independent of a container) and resistance to flow.

☐ The molecular arrangement in solids can be either crystalline or amorphous. Crystalline structure is a three-dimensional lattice arrangement of repeating units called the unit cell. Amorphous solids lack this lattice arrangement.

☐ Liquids are defined as fluids because they flow in response to shearing forces and assume the shape of their container.

☐ Liquids like water and alcohol will mix together and are called miscible; liquids like water and oil will not mix together and are called immiscible. Agitation of immiscible liquids will result in an emulsion.

☐ Phase equilibria will exist at certain temperatures and pressures for each of the different phase changes: fusion (crystallization), vaporization (condensation), and sublimation (deposition).

☐ The change in Gibbs free energy for phase equilibria is zero.

☐ The phase diagram of a given system graphs the phases and phase equilibria as a function of temperature and pressure.

☐ The phase diagram for a solution consisting of multiple components indicates the composition of the liquid and the vapor at different temperatures and pressures.

☐ The colligative properties—vapor pressure depression, boiling point elevation, freezing point depression, and osmotic pressure—are physical properties of solutions that depend upon the concentration of dissolved particles but not upon their chemical identity.

EQUATIONS TO REMEMBER

☐ $P_A = X_A P^o_A$

☐ $\Delta T_b = iK_b m$

☐ $\Delta T_f = iK_f m$

☐ $\Pi = iMRT$

Practice Questions

1. Which of the following substances is illustrated by the phase diagram in the figure below?

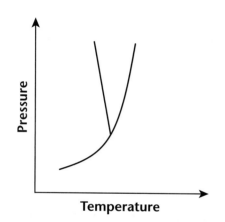

A. CO_2
B. NaCl
C. Ne
D. H_2O

2. Which of the following proportionalities best describes the relationship between the number of intermolecular forces and heat of vaporization for a given substance?

A. They are proportional.
B. They are inversely proportional.
C. Their relationship cannot be generalized.
D. There is no relationship between them.

3. Which of the following molecules is likely to have the highest melting point?

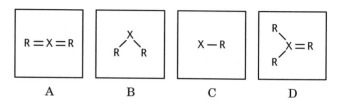

4. Which of the following physical conditions favors a gaseous state for most substances?

A. High pressure and high temperature
B. Low pressure and low temperature
C. High pressure and low temperature
D. Low pressure and high temperature

5. Which of the following explanations best describes the mechanism by which solute particles affect the melting point of ice?

A. Melting point elevates because the kinetic energy of the substance increases.
B. Melting point elevates because the kinetic energy of the substance decreases.
C. Melting point depresses because solute particles interfere with lattice formation.
D. Melting point depresses because solute particles enhance lattice formation.

6. In the figure below, which phase change is represented by the arrow?

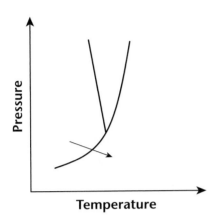

A. Condensation
B. Deposition
C. Sublimation
D. Vaporization

7. Which of the following situations would most favor the change of water from a liquid to a solid?

I. Decreased solute concentration of a substance

II. Decreased temperature of a substance

III. Decreased pressure on a substance

A. I only
B. II only
C. I and II only
D. II and III only

8. The heats of vaporization of four substances are given in the table below. Which of these substances has the lowest boiling point?

Comparative Heats of Vaporization

Liquid	Heat Required (cal/g)
Chlorine	67.4
Ether	9.4
Carbon dioxide	72.2
Ammonia	295

A. Chlorine
B. Ether
C. Carbon dioxide
D. Ammonia

9. What factor(s) determine whether or not two liquids are miscible?

A. Molecular size
B. Molecular polarity
C. Density
D. Both B and C

10. Alloys are mixtures of new metals in either the liquid or solid phase. Which of the following is usually true of alloys?

 A. The melting/freezing point of an alloy will be lower than that of either of the component metals because the new bonds are stronger.

 B. The melting/freezing point of an alloy will be lower than that of either of the component metals because the new bonds are weaker.

 C. The melting/freezing point of an alloy will be greater than that of either of the component metals because the new bonds are weaker.

 D. The melting/freezing point of an alloy will be greater than that of either of the component metals because the new bonds are stronger.

11. The osmotic pressure at STP of a solution made from 1 L of NaCl (*aq*) containing 117 g of NaCl is

 A. 44.77 atm.
 B. 48.87 atm.
 C. 89.54 atm.
 D. 117 atm.

Small Group Questions

1. On water's pressure-temperature phase diagram, the boundary between liquid and solid has a negative slope. Explain this phenomenon, focusing on how density affects pressure and temperature.

2. Which would have a greater effect on the boiling point of one liter of water: 2 moles of sodium nitrate or 1 mole of carbonic acid? What pieces of information do we need to calculate this answer?

Explanations to Practice Questions

1. D

For the scope of the MCAT, water is the only substance that has a solid/liquid equilibrium line with a negative slope. We are not expected to know specific phase diagrams for other compounds.

2. A

Intermolecular forces hold molecules closer to one another, which relates to the compound's phase. As there are more intermolecular forces, the amount of heat needed to change phase (such as in vaporization) increases as well, thus showing a proportional, positive relationship.

3. B

This molecule is likely to have unequal sharing of electrons, which means it will be polar. Polarity often leads to increased bonding because of the positive-negative attractive forces between molecules. Greater bonding or stronger intermolecular forces both lead to higher melting points, because more heat is needed to break these interactions and cause liquefaction. (A) is nonpolar, making its intermolecular forces weaker than (B) or (C). (D) is only weakly polar, because the geometry of this molecule will make some of the polarized bonds cancel each other out. (C) will have some polarity but less than (B), because only one bond is polarized.

4. D

We can imagine a high-pressure situation as one in which molecules are in close proximity (low-volume container) and forced to interact with one another. Intermolecular attractions are necessary in the solid and liquid phases but assumed to be negligible in the gas phase. So we can assume that high pressure is not conducive to the gaseous state. What about temperature? Because temperature is a measure of average kinetic energy of the molecules, an increase in the average kinetic energy increases molecules' ability to move apart from one other, ultimately entering a gaseous state. Decreasing the temperature (or kinetic energy) or increasing pressure both favor the more organized liquid and solid phases.

5. C

Melting point depresses upon solute addition, making (A) and (B) incorrect. Solute particles interfere with lattice formation, the highly organized state in which solid molecules align themselves. Colder than normal conditions are necessary to create the solid structure.

6. C

This answer choice shows movement from the solid to gas phase, which is, by definition, sublimation.

7. C

Both I and II are correct. Dissolved solutes interfere with the crystalline lattice bonds of a solid and, therefore, favor the liquid side of the equilibrium. Conversely, a decreased amount of solute would favor a solid state (I). Additionally, decreased temperature (II) is a decrease in the average kinetic energy of the molecules, making lower-energy phases (i.e. solid) more likely to exist. Finally, decreasing pressure (III) would actually favor higher-energy phases (i.e., liquid or gas) over solids. The only answer choice that includes both I and II is (C).

8. B

(B) has the lowest heat required for vaporization, which by definition determines the boiling point or the lowest temperature required for phase change from liquid to gas. All of the other answer choices have higher heats of vaporization, as seen in the table associated with the question.

9. B

The miscibility of two liquids strongly depends on their polarities. A polar liquid can mix with another polar liquid, and a nonpolar liquid can mix with another nonpolar liquid. In general, however, polar and nonpolar liquids are not miscible with each other. (A), molecular size, and (C), the density of a liquid, do not directly affect the miscibility (although (C) should remind you that two immiscible liquids will form separate layers, with the denser liquid on the bottom). Thus, (B) is the only correct choice.

10. B

The bonds between different metal atoms in an alloy are much weaker than those between the atoms in pure metals. Therefore, breaking these bonds requires less energy than does breaking the bonds in pure metals. The more stable the bonds are in a compound, the higher the melting and freezing points. They tend to be lower for alloys than for pure metals. Alternately, an alloy can be looked at as a solid solution; impurities lower the melting point.

11. C

The osmotic pressure (Π) of a solution is given by $\Pi = iMRT$. At STP, $T = 273$ K. R, the ideal gas constant, equals 8.2×10^{-2} L $\bullet$ atm/K $\bullet$ mol. To determine the molarity, find the formula weight of NaCl from the periodic table; FW = 58.5 g/mol. The number of moles in the solution described is

$$\frac{117 \text{ g/L}}{58.5 \text{ g/mol}} = 2 \text{ mol undissociated NaCl/L}$$

However, because NaCl is a strong electrolyte, it will completely dissociate in aqueous solution, yielding 4 moles of particles per liter of solution (i.e., 2 moles of Na^+ and 2 moles of Cl^-). Thus,

$$\Pi = (4 \text{ mol/L})(8.2 \times 10^{-2} \text{ L} \bullet \text{atm/K} \bullet \text{mol})(273 \text{ K})$$
$$= 89.54 \text{ atm}$$

Remember that colligative properties depend on the number of particles, not their identity.

9

Solutions

What do first aid instant cold packs and sweet tea have in common? Not much, you might think, but both, in fact, demonstrate the same principles of solution chemistry. Instant cold packs contain two compartments, one holding water and the other ammonium nitrate. When you bend the pack, the two compartments break open, allowing the ammonium nitrate to dissolve into the water. Sweet tea is made by dissolving a large amount of sugar into strongly brewed tea—the sweetest of the sweet teas may approach 22 brix, which means that in every 100 grams of tea, there are 22 grams of sugar. (As a point of reference, this is about twice the sweetness of regular cola.) When the ammonium nitrate or the sugar dissolves in the water to produce the respective solutions, three events must take place. First, the intermolecular interactions between the molecules of ammonium nitrate (or between the sugar molecules) must be broken. Second, the intermolecular interactions between the molecules of water must be broken. Third, new intermolecular interactions between the ammonium nitrate and the water molecules (or between the sugar and the water) must be formed.

We know from our discussion in Chapter 3, Bonding and Chemical Interactions, that energy is required to break these intermolecular interactions and that energy is released when new ones are formed. For the creation of both the ammonium nitrate and sugar solutions, more energy is needed to break the original intermolecular interactions than is released when new intermolecular interactions are formed. Thus, the creation of both of these solutions is an endothermic process. Now, the formation of the ammonium nitrate solution is much more endothermic than the formation of the sugar solution. And this is why ammonium nitrate is useful in instant cold packs. When it dissolves in water, the system must absorb an amount of energy equal to 6.14 kcal/mol of ammonium nitrate. The heat is absorbed from the surrounding environment, and the pack feels cool to the touch.

Although the dissolution of sugar into water is not as strongly endothermic, we nevertheless have an intuitive understanding of the process's endothermicity because we all know that the easiest way to dissolve lots of sugar into water (such as tea or coffee) is to heat up the water and then add the sugar. Because heating the water increases the solubility of sugar, it must be that the dissolution of sugar into water is an endothermic process (think application of Le Châtelier's principle and changes in temperature from Chapter 5, Chemical Kinetics and Equilibrium).

In this chapter, our focus will be on the characteristics and behaviors of solutions. We have already begun our consideration of solutions in the previous chapter with our review of the colligative properties. We will now continue that review by examining the nature of solutions, the formation of aqueous solutions, measurements of solution concentration, and finally, the qualitative and quantitative evaluation of solution equilibria.

Nature of Solutions ★★★☆☆

Many important chemical reactions, both in the laboratory and in nature, take place in solution, including almost all reactions in living organisms. **Solutions** are homogenous (the same throughout) mixtures of two or more substances that combine to form a single phase, usually the liquid phase. The MCAT will focus generally on solids dissolved into liquid aqueous solutions, but it's important to remember that solutions can be formed from different combinations of the three phases of matter. For example, gases can be dissolved in liquids (e.g., the carbonation of soda); liquids can be dissolved in other liquids (e.g., ethanol in water); solids can even be dissolved in other solids (e.g., metal alloys). Incidentally, gases "dissolved" into other gases can be thought of as solutions but are more properly defined as **mixtures**, because gas molecules don't really interact all that much (one of the postulates of the kinetic molecular theory of gases). Just a point of minor clarification: All solutions are considered mixtures, but not all mixtures are considered solutions.

A solution consists of a **solute** (e.g., NaCl, NH_3, $C_6H_{12}O_6$, CO_2, etc.) dissolved (dispersed) in a **solvent** (e.g., H_2O, benzene, ethanol, etc.). The solvent is the component of the solution whose phase remains the same after mixing. If the two substances are already in the same phase (for example, a solution of two liquids), the solvent is the component present in greater quantity. And if the two same-phase components are in equal proportions in the solution, the component considered the solvent is the one that is more commonly identified as a solvent. Solute molecules move about freely in the solvent and interact with the solvent by way of interparticle forces such as ion–dipole, dipole–dipole, or hydrogen bonding. Dissolved solute molecules are also relatively free to interact with other dissolved molecules of different chemical identity; consequently, chemical reactions occur easily in solution.

SOLVATION

Not to be confused with the path to eternal life, **solvation** is the electrostatic interaction between solute and solvent molecules. This is also known as **dissolution**, and when water is the solvent, it is called **hydration**, and the resulting solution is an aqueous solution. Solvation involves breaking intermolecular interactions between solute molecules and between solvent molecules and forming new intermolecular interactions between solute and solvent molecules.

When the new interactions (attractions) are stronger than the original ones, solvation is exothermic, and the process is favored at low temperatures. The dissolution of gases into liquids, such as CO_2 into water, is an exothermic process because the only significant interactions that must be broken are those between water molecules. CO_2, as a gas, demonstrates minimal intermolecular interaction, and thus the dissolution of CO_2 gas into water is overall exothermic (and Le Châtelier's principle tells us this is the reason that lowering the temperature of a liquid favors solubility of a gas in the liquid.) This is also why opening a two-liter container of warm soda is risky: The warm soda has very low solubility for the CO_2 gas, and when the pressure is released upon twisting the cap open, a lot of the CO_2 gas escapes (precipitates, comes out of the solution) with some amount of violence, carrying with it a lot of the liquid itself. We've all seen—or suffered—the aftermath of a warm soda too hastily opened.

When the new interactions (attractions) are weaker than the original ones, solvation is endothermic, and the process is favored at high temperatures. Most dissolutions are of this type. Two such examples have already been given: dissolving sugar or ammonium nitrate into water. Since the new interactions between the solute and solvent are weaker than the original interactions between the solute molecules and between the solvent molecules, energy (heat) must be supplied to facilitate the formation of these weaker, less stable interactions. Sometimes the overall strength of the new interactions is approximately equal to the overall strength of the original interactions. In this case, the overall enthalpy change for the dissolution is close to zero. These types of solutions approximate the formation of an **ideal solution**, for which the enthalpy of dissolution is equal to zero.

The spontaneity of dissolution is not dependent only upon the enthalpy change; solutions may form spontaneously for both endothermic and exothermic dissolutions. The second property that contributes to the spontaneity or nonspontaneity of a solution is the entropy change that occurs in the process. At constant temperature and pressure, entropy always increases upon dissolution. As with any process, the spontaneity or nonspontaneity of dissolution depends upon the change in Gibbs function: Spontaneous processes result in a decrease of free energy, while nonspontaneous processes result in an increase of free energy. Thus, whether dissolution will happen spontaneously or not depends upon both the change in enthalpy and change in entropy for the solute and solvent of the system.

Consider, for example, the formation of another common solution, one that we've mentioned a number of times in this book: sodium chloride, table salt, dissolved in water. When NaCl dissolves in water, its component ions dissociate from each other and become surrounded by water molecules. For this new interaction to occur, ion–ion interactions between the Na^+ and Cl^- must be broken, and hydrogen bonds between water molecules must also be broken. This step requires energy and is therefore endothermic. Because water is polar, it can interact with each of the component ions through ion–dipole interactions: The partially positive hydrogen end of the water molecules will surround the Cl^- ions, and the partially negative oxygen end of the water molecules will surround the Na^+ ions. The formation of these ion–dipole bonds is exothermic, but not as much so as the endothermicity of breaking the old ones (although it is quite close). As a result, the overall dissolution of table salt into water is endothermic (+0.93 J/mol) and favored at high temperatures.

We've considered the enthalpy change for the formation of a sodium chloride solution, and now we need to examine the entropy change. Remember that entropy can be thought of as the measure of the degree to which energy is disbursed throughout a system or the measure of the amount of energy distributed from the system to the surroundings at a given temperature. Another way to understand entropy is the measure of molecular disorder, or the number of energy microstates available to a system at a given temperature. When solid sodium chloride dissolves into water, the rigidly ordered arrangement of the sodium and chloride ions is broken up, as the ion–ion interactions are disrupted and new ion–dipole interactions with the water molecules are formed. The ions, freed from their lattice arrangement, have a greater number of energy microstates available to them (in simpler terms, they are freer to move around in different ways), and consequently, their energy is more distributed and their entropy increases. The water, however, becomes more restricted in its movement because it is now interacting with the ions. The number of energy microstates available to it (that is, the water molecules' ability to move around in different ways) is reduced, so the entropy of the water decreases. But the increase in the entropy experienced by the dissolved sodium chloride is greater than the decrease in the entropy experienced by the water, so the overall entropy change is positive—energy is overall disbursed by the dissolution of sodium chloride in water. Because of the relatively low endothermicity and relatively large positive change in entropy, sodium chloride will spontaneously dissolve in liquid water.

SOLUBILITY

We need to know more than just whether or not dissolution of a solute into a solvent will be spontaneous or nonspontaneous. We also want to know how much solute will dissolve into a given solvent. The **solubility** of a substance is the maximum amount of that substance that can be dissolved in a particular solvent at a particular temperature. When this maximum amount of solute has been added, the dissolved solute is in equilibrium with its undissolved state, and we say that the solution is **saturated**. If more solute is added, it will not dissolve. For example, at 18°C, a maximum of 83 g of glucose ($C_6H_{12}O_6$) will dissolve in 100 mL of H_2O. Thus, the solubility of glucose is 83 g/100 mL. If more glucose is added to an already saturated glucose solution, it will not dissolve but rather will remain in solid form, **precipitating** to the bottom of the container. A solution in which the proportion of solute to solvent is small is said to be **dilute**, and one in which the proportion is large is said to be **concentrated**. Note that both dilute and concentrated solutions are still considered unsaturated if the maximum equilibrium concentration (saturation) has not been reached.

The solubility of substances into different solvents is ultimately a function of thermodynamics. When the change in Gibbs function is negative at a given temperature for the dissolution of a given solute into a given solvent, the process will be spontaneous, and the solute is said to be soluble. When the change in Gibbs function is positive at a given temperature for the dissolution of a given solute into a given solvent, the process will be nonspontaneous, and the solute is said to be insoluble. Some solute/solvent systems have very large negative ΔGs, so dissolution is very spontaneous and a lot of solute can be dissolved into the solvent. Others have very small negative ΔGs, so dissolution is only slightly spontaneous and as a result only a little solute can be dissolved into the solvent. Those solutes that dissolve minimally in the solvent (usually water) are called the **sparingly soluble salts**.

AQUEOUS SOLUTIONS

The most common type of solution is the aqueous solution, in which the solvent is water. The aqueous state is denoted by the symbol (*aq*). Because aqueous solutions are so common and so important to biological systems (e.g., you), the MCAT focuses on them above all others. We wish we could tell you otherwise, but for Test Day, you are expected to remember the general solubility rules for aqueous solutions. We know, we know—they are not the easiest or most fun to remember, but no one ever promised you that this would always be fun. (We promised you that we would help you have *some* fun in this preparation process.) There are seven general solubility rules:

1. All salts of alkali metals are water soluble.
2. All salts of the ammonium ion (NH_4^+) are water soluble.
3. All chlorides, bromides, and iodides are water soluble, with the exceptions of Ag^+, Pb^{2+}, and Hg_2^{2+}.
4. All salts of the sulfate ion (SO_4^{2-}) are water soluble, with the exceptions of Ca^{2+}, Sr^{2+}, Ba^{2+}, and Pb^{2+}.
5. All metal oxides are insoluble, with the exception of the alkali metals and CaO, SrO, and BaO, all of which hydrolyze to form solutions of the corresponding metal hydroxides.
6. All hydroxides are insoluble, with the exception of the alkali metals and Ca^{2+}, Sr^{2+}, and Ba^{2+}.
7. All carbonates (CO_3^{2-}), phosphates (PO_4^{3-}), sulfides (S^{2-}), and sulfites (SO_3^{2-}) are insoluble, with the exception of the alkali metals and ammonium.

On the MCAT, there is one infallible solubility rule: *All sodium salts are completely soluble, and all nitrate salts are completely soluble.* Thus, if a problem gives you a concentration of sodium fluoride, you know that the compound is completely soluble in water. Sodium and nitrate ions are generally used as counterions to what is really chemically important; for example, if a pH problem gives you a sodium formate

MCAT Expertise

Because most solutions involve water as the solvent in the real world, it is not a surprise that they are common on the MCAT. These solubility rules are not bad to know, but memorizing them all may be a little excessive. It is never a bad thing to know facts, but being able to apply them is more important. Know rules 1 and 2 for sure and be aware of some of the more common insoluble exceptions, like Pb^{2+} and Ag^+.

concentration of 0.10 M, it is really telling you that the concentration of the formate ion is 0.10 M, because the sodium ion concentration does not affect pH. The only time you need to worry about the nitrate ion concentration is in a redox reaction, for the nitrate ion can function—though only weakly—as an oxidizing agent; otherwise, merely focus on the cation as the chemically reacting species.

Ions ★★★★☆☆

Ionic solutions are of particular interest to chemists because certain important types of chemical reactions—acid-base and oxidation-reduction reactions, for instance—take place in ionic solutions. It shouldn't come as a surprise to you by now that if chemists take particular interest in this area of chemistry, so will the MCAT. In fact, acid-base and oxidation-reduction reactions are themselves important topics for the MCAT, so you can begin your review of those topics (Chapters 10 and 11) by reviewing with us now the characteristics and behaviors of ions.

CATIONS AND ANIONS

Ionic compounds are made up of positively charged cations and negatively charged anions. Ionic compounds are held together by the ionic bond, which is the force of electrostatic attraction between oppositely charged particles. The word *cation* (and especially the organic chemistry variant, *carbocation*) has tripped up unsuspecting students for years, who, having never heard the word spoken aloud before, almost invariably pronounce it as the last two syllables of "vacation" (as if a carbocation were some fun carbon-based holiday…we humbly admit to having made the mistake ourselves at a point in the less glorious distant past.)

The nomenclature of ionic compounds is based on the names of the component ions.

1. For elements (usually metals) that can form more than one positive ion, the charge is indicated by a Roman numeral in parentheses following the name of the element.

$$Fe^{2+} \text{ Iron (II)} \qquad Cu^{+} \text{ Copper (I)}$$
$$Fe^{3+} \text{ Iron (III)} \qquad Cu^{2+} \text{ Copper (II)}$$

2. An older but still commonly used method is to add the endings **-ous** or **-ic** to the root of the Latin name of the element to represent the ions with lesser or greater charge, respectively.

$$Fe^{2+} \text{ Ferrous} \qquad Cu^{+} \text{ Cuprous}$$
$$Fe^{3+} \text{ Ferric} \qquad Cu^{2+} \text{ Cupric}$$

3. Monatomic anions are named by dropping the ending of the name of the element and adding **-ide**.

H^- Hydride	S^{2-} Sulfide
F^- Fluoride	N^{3-} Nitride
O^{2-} Oxide	P^{3-} Phosphide

4. Many polyatomic anions contain oxygen and are therefore called **oxyanions**. When an element forms two oxyanions, the name of the one with less oxygen ends in **-ite** and the one with more oxygen ends in **-ate**.

NO_2^- Nitrite	SO_3^{2-} Sulfite
NO_3^- Nitrate	SO_4^{2-} Sulfate

5. When the series of oxyanions contains four oxyanions, prefixes are also used. **Hypo-** and **per-** are used to indicate less oxygen and more oxygen, respectively.

ClO^- Hypochlorite

ClO_2^- Chlorite

ClO_3^- Chlorate

ClO_4^- Perchlorate

6. Polyatomic anions often gain one or more H^+ ions to form anions of lower charge. The resulting ions are named by adding the word **hydrogen** or **dihydrogen** to the front of the anion's name. An older method uses the prefix **bi-** to indicate the addition of a single hydrogen ion.

HCO_3^- Hydrogen carbonate or bicarbonate

HSO_4^- Hydrogen sulfate or bisulfate

$H_2PO_4^-$ Dihydrogen phosphate

ION CHARGES

Ionic species, by definition, have charge. Cations have positive charge, and anions have negative charge. Some elements are found naturally only in their charged forms, while others may exist naturally in the charged or uncharged state. Furthermore, some elements can have several different charges or oxidation states. Some of the charged atoms or molecules that you might commonly encounter on the MCAT include the active metals, the alkali metals (group IA) and the alkaline earth metals (group IIA), which have charge of +1 and +2, respectively, in the natural state. Many of the transition metals, such as copper, iron, and chromium, can exist in different positively charged states. Nonmetals, which are found on the right side of the periodic table, generally form anions. For example, all the halogens (Group VIIA) form monatomic anions with a charge of -1. All elements in a given group tend to form monatomic ions with the same charge (e.g., Group IA elements have charge of $+1$). Note that there are anionic species that contain metallic elements (e.g., MnO_4^- [permanganate] and CrO_4^{2-} [chromate]); even so, the metals have positively charged oxidation states. (Also note that in the oxyanions of the halogens, such as ClO^- and ClO_2^-, the halogen is assigned a positive oxidation state.) The trends of ionicity as we've described them here are helpful but are complicated by the fact that many elements have intermediate electronegativity and are consequently less likely to form ionic compounds and by the left-to-right transition from metallic to nonmetallic character.

ELECTROLYTES

In spite of the fact that ionic compounds are made of ions, solid ionic compounds tend to be poor conductors of electricity, because the charged particles are rigidly set in place by the lattice arrangement that serves as the basic framework for crystalline solids. In aqueous solutions, however, the lattice arrangement is disrupted by the ion–dipole interactions between the ionic constituents and the water molecules. The freed-up ions are now able to move around, and as a result, the solution of ions is able to conduct electricity. Solutes that enable their solution to carry currents are called electrolytes. The electrical conductivity of aqueous solutions is governed, then, by the presence and concentration of ions in the solution. Pure water, which has no ions other than the very few hydrogen ions and hydroxide ions that result from water's low-level autodissociation, is a very poor conductor.

The tendency of an ionic solute to dissociate into its constituent ions in water may be high or low. A solute is considered a strong electrolyte if it dissociates completely into its constituent ions. Examples of strong electrolytes include certain ionic compounds, such as NaCl and KI, and molecular compounds with highly polar covalent bonds that dissociate into ions when dissolved, such as HCl in water. A weak electrolyte, on the other hand, ionizes or hydrolyzes incompletely in aqueous solution, and only some of the solute is dissolved into its ion constituents. Examples include Hg_2I_2 ($K_{sp} = 4.5 \times 10^{-29}$), acetic acid and other weak acids, ammonia, and other weak bases (see Chapter 10, Acids and Bases). Many compounds do not ionize at all in aqueous solution, retaining their molecular structure in solution, which usually limits their solubility. These compounds are called nonelectrolytes and include many nonpolar gases and organic compounds, such as O_2 (g), CO_2 (g), and glucose.

Key Concept

Oxyanions of transition metals like the MnO_4^- and CrO_4^{2-} ions shown here have an inordinately high oxidation number on the metal. As such, they tend to gain electrons in order to reduce this oxidation number and thus make good oxidizing agents. (See Chapter 11.)

Bridge

Because electrolytes ionize in solution, they will produce a larger effect on colligative properties (see Chapter 8) than one would expect from the given concentration.

Concentration ★★★★☆

Concentration denotes the amount of solute dissolved in a solvent. There are many different ways of expressing concentration, and different units have been standardized that you may encounter in everyday situations. For example, alcohol content in liquors like vodka, gin, or rum is expressed in volume percent (volume of solute divided by volume of solution times 100 percent). Alcoholic proof is twice the volume percent. The sugar content of orange juice and other fruit juices is measured in units of degrees Brix (°Bx), which is a weight (actually mass) percent: mass of glucose divided by mass of solution times 100 percent.

UNITS OF CONCENTRATION

On the MCAT test, you will work with concentrations of solutions commonly expressed as percent composition by mass, mole fraction, molarity, molality, and normality.

Percent Composition by Mass

The percent composition by mass ($w/w\%$) of a solution is the mass of the solute divided by the mass of the solution (solute plus solvent), multiplied by 100 percent.

> **Example:** What is the percent composition by mass of a salt water solution if 100 g of the solution contains 20 g of NaCl?
>
> **Solution:** $\dfrac{20\,g\ NaCl}{100\ g} \times 100 + 20\%$ NaCl solution

Mole Fraction

The mole fraction (X) of a compound is equal to the number of moles of the compound divided by the total number of moles of all species with the system. The sum of the mole fractions in a system will always equal 1. Mole fraction is used to calculate the vapor pressure depression of a solution, as well as the partial pressures of gases in a system.

> **MCAT Expertise**
>
> It is important to have a good idea of how to work with all of these ways of expressing concentration because more than one may show up on Test Day.

Example: If 92 g of glycerol is mixed with 90 g of water, what will be the mole fractions of the two components? (MW of $H_2O = 18$; MW of $C_3H_8O_3 = 92$.)

Solution:

$$90 \text{ g water} = 90 \text{ g} \times \frac{1 \text{ mol}}{18 \text{ g}} = 5 \text{ mol}$$

$$92 \text{ g glycerol} = 92 \text{ g} \times \frac{1 \text{ mol}}{92 \text{ g}} = 1 \text{ mol}$$

$$\text{Total mol} = 5 + 1 = 6 \text{ mol}$$

$$X_{water} = \frac{5 \text{ mol}}{6 \text{ mol}} = 0.833$$

$$X_{glycerol} = \frac{1 \text{ mol}}{6 \text{ mol}} = 0.167$$

$$X_{water} + X_{glycerol} = 0.833 + 0.167 = 1$$

Molarity

The molarity (M) of a solution is the number of moles of a solute per liter of solution. Solution concentrations are usually expressed in terms of molarity, and you will be working mostly with molarity on the MCAT. The molarity of a solution is written using brackets. Please note that the volume term in the denominator of molarity refers to the solution volume, *not* the solvent volume used to prepare the solution—although often the two values are close enough that we can approximate the solution volume by the solvent volume. We use molarity for the law of mass action, rate laws, osmotic pressure, pH and pOH, and the Nernst equation.

MCAT Expertise

Note that for dilute solutions, the volume of the solution is approximately equal to the volume of solvent used, which simplifies our need for calculation on Test Day.

Example: If enough water is added to 11 g of $CaCl_2$ to make 100 mL of solution, what is the molarity of the solution?

Solution:

$$\frac{11 \text{ g CaCl}_2}{110 \text{ g CaCl}_2 / \text{mol CaCl}_2} = 0.1 \text{ mol CaCl}_2$$

$$100 \text{ mL} \times \frac{1 \text{ L}}{1,000 \text{ mL}} = 0.1 \text{ L}$$

$$\text{molarity} = \frac{0.1 \text{ mol}}{0.1 \text{ L}} = 1 \text{ M}$$

Molality

The molality (m) of a solution is the number of moles of solute per kilogram of solvent. For dilute aqueous solutions at 25°C, the molality is approximately equal to molarity, because the density of water at this temperature is 1 kilogram per liter (1 kg/L). However, note that this is an approximation and true only for dilute aqueous solutions. (As aqueous solutions become more concentrated with solute, their densities become significantly different from that of pure water; most water-soluble solutes have molecular weights significantly greater than that of water, so the density of the solution increases as the concentration increases.) You won't use molality very often, so be mindful of the special situations when it is required: boiling point elevation and freezing point depression.

Example: If 10 g of NaOH are dissolved in 500 g of water, what is the molality of the solution?

Solution:

$$\frac{10 \text{ g NaOH}}{40 \text{ g NaOH / mol NaOH}} = 0.25 \text{ mol NaOH}$$

$$500 \text{ g} \times \frac{1 \text{ kg}}{1,000 \text{ g}} = 0.5 \text{ kg}$$

$$\text{molality} = \frac{0.25 \text{ mol}}{0.5 \text{ kg}} = 0.5 \text{ mol / kg} = 0.50 \text{ m}$$

Normality

We discussed the related concepts of gram equivalent weight, equivalents, and normality (N) in Chapter 4. We would urge you to review those relevant sections. The normality of a solution is equal to the number of equivalents of solute per liter of solution. An equivalent, or gram equivalent weight, is a measure of the reactive capacity of a molecule. Most simply, an equivalent is equal to a mole of charge.

To calculate the normality of a solution, you need to know for what purpose the solution is being used, because it is the concentration of the reactive species with which we are concerned. For example, in acid-base reactions, we are most concerned with the concentration of hydrogen ions; in oxidation-reduction reactions, we are most concerned with the concentration of electrons. Normality is unique among concentration units in that it is reaction-dependent. For example, in acidic solution, 1 mole of the permanganate ion (MnO_4^-) will readily accept 5 moles of electrons, so a 1 M solution would be 5 N. However, in alkaline solution, 1 mole of permanganate will accept only 3 moles of electrons, so in alkaline solution, a 1 M permanganate solution would be 3 N.

MCAT Expertise

Simple ideas on Test Day will make things easier. So, when you come across normality you can think of it as "molarity of the stuff of interest" in the reaction.

DILUTION

A solution is diluted when solvent is added to a solution of high concentration to produce a solution of lower concentration. The concentration of a solution after dilution can be conveniently determined using the equation:

$$M_i V_i = M_f V_f$$

where M is molarity, V is volume, and the subscripts i and f refer to the initial and final values, respectively.

> **Example:** How many mL of a 5.5 M NaOH solution must be used to prepare 300 mL of a 1.2 M NaOH solution?
>
> **Solution:**
> $$5.5 \, M \times V_i = 1.2 \, M \times 0.3 \, L$$
> $$V_i = \frac{1.2 \, M \times 0.3 \, L}{5.5 \, M}$$
> $$V_i = 0.065 \, L = 65 \, mL$$

Solution Equilibria ★★★★☆

Our last topic for this chapter on solutions picks up on a theme that we began discussing in Chapter 5, Chemical Kinetics and Equilibrium. The process of solvation, like other reversible chemical and physical processes, tends toward an equilibrium position defined as the lowest energy state of a system under given conditions of temperature and pressure. Related to determinations of equilibrium is the characterization of processes as spontaneous or nonspontaneous: Systems tend to move spontaneously toward the equilibrium position, but any movement away from equilibrium is nonspontaneous. In the process of creating a solution, the equilibrium is defined as the saturation point and the solute concentration is at its maximum value for the given temperature and pressure. Immediately after solute has been introduced into a solvent, most of the change taking place is dissociation, because no dissolved solute is initially present. However, once solute is dissolved, the reverse process, precipitation of the solute, will begin to occur. When the solution is dilute (unsaturated), the thermodynamically favored process is dissolution, and initially, the rate of dissolution will be greater than the rate of precipitation. As the solution becomes more concentrated and approaches saturation, the rate of dissolution lessens while the rate of precipitation increases. Eventually, the saturation point of the solution is reached, and the solution exists in a state of dynamic equilibrium for which the rates of dissolution and precipitation are equal and the concentration of dissolved solute reaches a steady state (that is, constant) value. Neither dissolution nor precipitation is more thermodynamically favored at equilibrium than the other (because favoring either one of them would necessarily result in the solution no longer being in a state of equilibrium), so the change in free energy is zero, as is the case for all systems at equilibrium.

An ionic solid introduced into a polar solvent dissociates into its component ions, and the dissociation of such a solute in solution may be represented by

$$A_mB_n \ (s) \leftrightarrow mA^{n+} \ (aq) + nB^{m-} \ (aq)$$

On Test Day, when you are working through any problem of solution chemistry, the first step you must take is to write out the balanced dissolution equation for the ionic compound in question. This first step is essential for correctly calculating solubility product constant, ion product, molar solubility, or common ion effect. In other words, it is the essential first step for nearly every solution chemistry problem you will see on the MCAT.

THE SOLUBILITY PRODUCT CONSTANT

Most solubility problems on the MCAT deal with solutions of sparingly soluble salts, which are ionic compounds that have very low solubility in aqueous solutions. You may wonder why any ionic compound would not be highly soluble in water. The determination for the degree of solubility is the relative changes in enthalpy and entropy associated with the dissolution of the ionic solute at a given temperature and pressure. One common sparingly soluble salt is silver chloride, AgCl, which dissolves according to the following equation:

$$AgCl \ (s) \leftrightarrow Ag^+ \ (aq) + Cl^- \ (aq)$$

The law of mass action can be applied to a solution at equilibrium; that is to say, when the solution is saturated and the solute concentration is maximum and dynamically stable. For a saturated solution of the ionic compound with the formula A_mB_n, the equilibrium constant for its solubility in aqueous solution, called the solubility product constant K_{sp}, can be expressed by

$$K_{sp} = [A^{n+}]^m[B^{m-}]^n$$

where the concentrations of the ionic constituents are equilibrium (saturation) concentrations. For example, we can express the K_{sp} of silver chloride as follows:

$$K_{sp} = [Ag^+][Cl^-]$$

You'll notice that for the law of mass action of solutions, the denominator seems to be missing. Well, if you think back to our discussion of the properties of the equilibrium constant in Chapter 5, you'll remember that we don't include the concentration of the pure solids or pure liquids. Since the silver chloride solution was formed by adding pure solid silver chloride to pure water, neither the solid silver chloride nor the water is included.

Solubility product constants, like all other equilibrium constants (K_{eq}, K_a, and K_b) are temperature-dependent. When the solution consists of a gas dissolved into a liquid, the value of the equilibrium constant, and hence the "position" of equilibrium (saturation), will also depend on pressure. Generally speaking, the solubility product constant increases with increasing temperature for nongas solutes and decreases for gas solutes. Higher pressures favor dissolution of gas solutes and therefore the K_{sp} will be larger for gases at higher pressures than at lower ones. This last point is especially relevant to deep-sea divers. Because gases become more soluble in solution as pressure increases, a diver who has spent time at significant depths under water will have more nitrogen gas dissolved in her blood. (Nitrogen gas is the main inert gas in the air we breathe.) If she rises to the surface too quickly, the abrupt decompression will lead to an abrupt decrease in gas solubility in the plasma, resulting in the formation of nitrogen gas bubbles in her bloodstream. The gas bubbles can get lodged in the small vasculature of the peripheral tissue, mostly around the large joints of the body, causing pain and tissue damage (hence the name of the condition is the "bends"). The condition is painful and dangerous, and can be fatal if not properly prevented or treated.

As solute dissolves into solvent the system approaches saturation, at which point no more solute can be dissolved and any excess will precipitate to the bottom of the container. You may not know whether the solution has reached saturation, and so to determine "where" the system is with respect to the equilibrium position, you will calculate a value called the ion product (I.P.), which is analogous to the reaction quotient Q for chemical reactions. The ion product equation has the same form as the equation for the solubility product constant. The difference is that the concentrations that you use are the concentrations of the ionic constituents at that given moment in time.

$$\text{I.P.} = [A^{n+}]^m[B^{m-}]^n$$

where the concentrations are not necessarily equilibrium (saturation) concentrations. As with the reaction quotient Q, the utility of the I.P. lies in comparing its value to that attained at equilibrium, in this case, the known K_{sp}. Each salt has its own distinct K_{sp} at a given temperature and pressure. If, at a given set of temperature and pressure conditions, a salt's I.P. is less than the salt's K_{sp}, then the solution is not yet at equilibrium and we say that it is unsaturated. For unsaturated solutions, dissolution is thermodynamically favored over precipitation. If the I.P is greater than the K_{sp}, then the solution is beyond equilibrium and we say that it is supersaturated. It's possible to create a supersaturated solution by dissolving solute into a hot solvent and then slowly cooling the solution. A supersaturated solution is thermodynamically unstable, and any disturbance to the solution, like the addition of more solid solute or other solid particles or further cooling of the solution, will cause spontaneous precipitation of the excess dissolved solute. If the calculated I.P. is equal to the known K_{sp}, then the solution is at equilibrium, the rates of dissolution and precipitation are equal, and the concentration of solute is at the maximum (saturation) value.

Example: The molar solubility of $Fe(OH)_3$ in an aqueous solution was determined to be 4.5×10^{-10} mol/L. What is the value of the K_{sp} for $Fe(OH)_3$?

Solution: The molar solubility (the solubility of the compound in mol/L) is given as 4.5×10^{-10} M. The equilibrium concentration of each ion can be determined from the molar solubility and the balanced dissociation reaction of $Fe(OH)_3$. The dissociation reaction is:

$$Fe(OH)_3(s) \rightleftarrows Fe^{3+}(aq) + 3OH^-(aq)$$
$$K_{sp} = [Fe^{3+}][OH^-]^3$$
$$[OH^-] = 3\,[Fe^{3+}]; \qquad [Fe^{3+}] = 4.5 \times 10^{-10} \text{ M}$$
$$K_{sp} = [Fe^{3+}](3[Fe^{3+}])^3$$
$$K_{sp} = 27\,[Fe^{3+}]^4$$
$$K_{sp} = (4.5 \times 10^{-10})[3(4.5 \times 10^{-10})]^3$$
$$K_{sp} = 27(4.5 \times 10^{-10})^4$$
$$K_{sp} = 1.1 \times 10^{-36}$$

Example: What are the concentrations of each of the ions in a saturated solution of $PbBr_2$, given that the K_{sp} of $PbBr_2$ is 2.1×10^{-6}? If 5 g of $PbBr_2$ are dissolved in water to make 1 L of solution at 25°C, would the solution be saturated, unsaturated, or supersaturated?

Solution: The first step is to write out the dissociation reaction:

$$PbBr_2(s) \rightleftarrows Pb^{2+}(aq) + 2Br^-(aq)$$
$$K_{sp} = [Pb^{2+}][Br^-]^2$$

Let x equal the concentration of Pb^{2+}. Then $2x$ equals the concentration of Br^- in the saturated solution at equilibrium (as $[Br^-]$ is 2 times $[Pb^{2+}]$).

$$(x)(2x)^2 = 4x^3$$
$$2.1 \times 10^{-6} = 4x^3$$

Solving for x, the concentration of Pb^{2+} in a saturated solution is 8.07×10^{-3} M and the concentration of Br^- ($2x$) is 1.61×10^{-2} M. Next, we convert 5 g of $PbBr_2$ into moles:

$$5\text{ g} \times \frac{1 \text{ mol } PbBr_2}{367 \text{ g}} = 1.36 \times 10^{-2} \text{ mol}$$

1.36×10^{-2} mol of $PbBr_2$ is dissolved in 1 L of solution, so the concentration of the solution 1.36×10^{-2} M. Because this is higher than the concentration of a saturated solution, this solution would be supersaturated.

Key Concept

Every slightly soluble salt of general formula MX_3 will have $K_{sp} = 27x^4$, where x is the molar solubility.

Key Concept

Every slightly soluble salt of general formula MX_2 will have $K_{sp} = 4x^3$, where x is the molar solubility.

Key Concept

Every slightly soluble salt of general formula MX will have $K_{sp} = x^2$, where x is the molar solubility.

THE COMMON ION EFFECT

The solubility of a substance varies depending on the temperature of the solution, the solvent, and, in the case of a gas-phase solute, the pressure. Solubility is also affected by the addition of other substances to the solution.

One of the more common solution chemistry problems on the MCAT is calculation of the concentration of a salt in a solution that already contains a common ionic constituent. The solubility of a salt is considerably reduced when it is dissolved in a solution that already contains one of its constituent ions compared to its solubility in the pure solvent. This reduction in molar solubility is called the common ion effect. Molar solubility (M) is the concentration, in moles per liter (mol/L), of the solute in the solution at equilibrium at a given temperature. If X moles of A_mB_n (s) can be dissolved in Y liters of solution to reach saturation, then the molar solubility of A_mB_n (s) is X mol/Y L. Let us repeat the important effect of the common ion: Its presence results in a reduction in the molar solubility of the salt. *Note well that the presence of the common ion has no effect on the value of the solubility product constant for the salt.* For example, if a salt such as CaF_2 is dissolved into a solvent already containing Ca^{2+} ions (from some other salt, perhaps $CaCl_2$), the solution will dissolve less CaF_2 compared to the amount that would be dissolved in the pure solvent before the I.P. equals K_{sp}. The common ion effect is really nothing other than Le Châtelier's principle in action. Because the solution already contains one of the constituent ions from the right side of the dissociation equilibrium, we can see that the system will shift away from that side toward the left side, where we find the solid salt. A solution system shifting toward the left (solid salt reactant) is not going to favor dissolution. As a result, molar solubility for the solid is reduced, and less of the solid dissolves in the solution (for the same K_{sp}).

Example: The K_{sp} of AgI in aqueous solution is 1×10^{-16} mol/L. If a 1×10^{-5} M solution of $AgNO_3$ is saturated with AgI, what will be the final concentration of the iodide ion?

Solution: The concentration of Ag^+ in the original $AgNO_3$ solution will be 1×10^{-5} mol/L. After AgI is added to saturation, the iodide concentration can be found by this formula:

$$1 \times 10^{-16} = [Ag^+][I^-]$$
$$= (1 \times 10^{-5})[I^-]$$
$$[I^-] = 1 \times 10^{-11} \text{ mol/L}$$

If the AgI had been dissolved in pure water, the concentration of both Ag^+ and I^- would have been 1×10^{-8} mol/L. The presence of the common ion, silver, at a concentration 1,000 times higher than what it would normally be in a silver iodide solution has reduced the iodide concentration to 1,000 of what it would have been otherwise. An additional 1×10^{-11} mol/L of silver will, of course, dissolve in solution along with the iodide ion, but this will not significantly affect the final silver concentration, which is much higher.

Conclusion

Our review of solution chemistry has provided an opportunity for us to consider the nature of solutions, solutes, and solvents and the manner of interaction between solutes and solvents in the formation of solutions. We reviewed solubility and the rules that reflect the solubility of common compounds in water. The different ways of expressing the amount of solute in solution were identified, and examples were given for each unit of concentration, including percent composition, mole fraction, molarity, molality, and normality. Finally, we reviewed the thermodynamic principles of solution equilibria and defined unsaturated, saturated, and supersaturated solutions with reference to ion product (I.P.) and solubility product constant (K_{sp}), as well as the common ion effect from the perspective of Le Châtelier's principle for a solution at equilibrium.

CONCEPTS TO REMEMBER

☐ Solutions are homogenous mixtures of two or more substances that combine to form a single phase, generally the liquid phase. The most important kind of solution for the MCAT is the aqueous solution. Solvents dissolve solutes by a process of surrounding the solute particles and interacting with them by way of electrostatic forces; this is called solvation.

☐ Most dissolutions are endothermic. However, the dissolution of gas into liquid is exothermic.

☐ Solubility is the maximum amount of substance that can be dissolved in a particular solvent at a particular temperature. Molar solubility is the molar concentration of solute in a saturated solution.

☐ Units of solution concentration include percent composition by mass (mass of solute divided by mass of solution times 100%), mole fraction (moles of solute divided by total number of moles of substances in solution), molarity (moles of solute divided by liters of solution), molality (moles of solute divided by kilograms of solvent), and normality (number of equivalents divided by liters of solution).

☐ A saturated solution is in equilibrium for that particular temperature. K_{sp} is the solubility product constant for a given solute in a given solvent at a given temperature.

☐ Calculation of the ion product (I.P.), followed by comparison to the known K_{sp}, helps to determine if a solution is unsaturated (I.P < K_{sp}), saturated (I.P = K_{sp}), or supersaturated (I.P. > K_{sp}).

☐ When an ionic compound is dissolved into a solution that already contains one of the constituent ions, the molar solubility for that ionic compound will be significantly decreased from the value normally demonstrated by the same ionic compound in the pure solvent at the same temperature. This is the common ion effect. It is an application of Le Châtelier's principle to solutions.

EQUATIONS TO REMEMBER

☐ $M_i V_i = M_f V_f$ (the dilution law)

☐ $K_{sp} = [A^{n+}]^m[B^{m-}]^n$ for $A_m B_n$ $(s) \leftrightarrow mA^{n+}$ $(aq) + nB^{m-}$ (aq)

☐ I.P. $= [A^{n+}]^m[B^{m-}]^n$

Practice Questions

1. An aqueous solution was prepared by mixing 70 grams of sugar ($C_{12}H_{12}O_{11}$) into 100 grams of water. The solution has a boiling point of 101.11°C. What is the molar mass of the solute? ($K_b = 0.512$°C.)

   A. 322.58 g/mol
   B. 32.26 g/mol
   C. 123.24 g/mol
   D. 233.59 g/mol

2. Which phase of solvent and solute, respectively, can form a solution?

   I. Solid solvent, gaseous solute

   II. Solid solvent, solid solute

   III. Gaseous solvent, gaseous solute

   A. I and II only
   B. II and III only
   C. I and III only
   D. I, II, and III

3. Two organic liquids, pictured in the figure below, are combined to form a solution. Based on the structures, will the solution closely obey Raoult's law?

   benzene   toluene

   A. Yes, the liquids differ due to the additional methyl group on toluene and, therefore, will not deviate from Raoult's law.
   B. Yes, the liquids are very similar and, therefore, will not deviate from Raoult's law.
   C. No, the liquids differ due to the additional methyl group on toluene and, therefore, will deviate from Raoult's law.
   D. No, the liquids both contain benzene rings, which will interact with each other and cause deviation from Raoult's law.

4. The diagram in Figure 1 shows two arms separated by an impermeable membrane. What would happen to the level of liquid in the two branches if the membrane were replaced with a semipermeable membrane that allowed water molecules to move across the membrane?

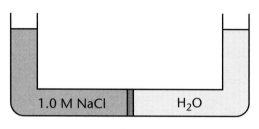

Figure 1

A. The level on the right would decrease, and the level on the left would increase.

B. The level would remain the same on both sides.

C. The level on the right would increase, and the level on the left would decrease.

D. The level on the right would stay the same, and the level on the left would increase.

5. The process of formation of a liquid solution can be better understood by breaking the process into three steps:

1. Breaking the solution into individual components

2. Making room for the solute in the solvent by overcoming intermolecular forces in the solvent

3. Allowing solute–solvent interactions to occur to form the solution

The overall energy change to form a solution can be estimated by taking the sum of each of the three steps. For steps 1 through 3, will each step most likely be endothermic or exothermic? The order for each answer choice is step 1, step 2, followed by step 3.

A. Endothermic, exothermic, endothermic

B. Exothermic, endothermic, endothermic

C. Exothermic, exothermic, endothermic

D. Endothermic, endothermic, exothermic

6. The entropy change when a solution forms can be expressed by the term ΔS°_{soln}. When an ion dissolves and water molecules are ordered around it, the ordering would be expected to make a negative contribution to ΔS°_{soln}. An ion that has more charge density will have a greater hydration effect, or ordering of water molecules. Based on this information, which of the following compounds will have the most negative ΔS°_{soln}?

A. KCl

B. LiF

C. CaS

D. NaCl

7. A 0.01 M solution of a nonelectrolyte has an osmotic pressure of 15.0 mm Hg. What is the osmotic pressure of a 0.02 M solution of $Mg(NO_3)_2$? The temperature of both solutions is the same.

A. 7.5 mm Hg

B. 30 mm Hg

C. 45 mm Hg

D. 90 mm Hg

8. One hundred grams of sugar are dissolved in a cup of hot water at 80°C. The cup of water contains 300.00 mL of water. What is the mass percentage of sugar in the resulting solution? (Sugar = $C_{12}H_{22}O_{11}$, density of water at 80°C = 0.975 g/mL.)

A. 25.0%

B. 25.5%

C. 33.3%

D. 34.2%

9. Which of the following combinations of liquids would be expected to have a vapor pressure higher than the vapor pressure that would be predicted by Raoult's law?

A. Ethanol and hexane

B. Acetone and water

C. Isopropanol and methanol

D. Nitric acid and water

10. The salt KCl is dissolved in a beaker of water that you are holding. You can feel the solution cool as the KCl dissolves. From this observation you conclude that

A. $\Delta S°_{soln}$ is large enough to overcome the unfavorable $\Delta H°_{soln}$.

B. KCl is mostly insoluble in water.

C. $\Delta S°_{soln}$ must be negative when KCl dissolves.

D. Boiling point elevation will occur in this solution.

11. Which of the following will give the greatest increase in the boiling point of water when it is dissolved in 1.00 kg H_2O?

A. 0.46 mol calcium sulfate

B. 0.54 mol iron (III) nitrate

C. 1.09 mol acetic acid

D. 1.11 mol sucrose

12. At sea level and 25°C, the solubility of oxygen gas in water is 1.25×10^{-3} M. In a city in the United States that lies high above sea level, the atmospheric pressure is 0.800 atm. What is the solubility of oxygen in water in this city?

A. 1.05×10^{-3} M

B. 1.56×10^{-3} M

C. 1.00×10^{-3} M

D. 1.25×10^{-3} M

13. Lead is a dangerous element that exists in the environment in large quantities due to man-made pollution. Lead poisoning has many symptoms, including mental retardation in children. If a body of water is polluted with lead ions at 30 ppb (parts per billion), what is the concentration of lead in molarity? (Density of water is 1 g/mL, ppb equals grams per 10^9 grams of solution.)

A. 6.2×10^{-7} M Pb^{2+}

B. 1.4×10^{-10} M Pb^{2+}

C. 1.4×10^{-7} M Pb^{2+}

D. 6.2×10^{-6} M Pb^{2+}

14. Which of the following is/are correct?

I. NaF is an electrolyte.

II. Glucose is a nonelectrolyte.

III. CH_3OH is a weak electrolyte.

IV. CH_3CH_2COOH is a weak electrolyte.

A. I, III, and IV only

B. I and II only

C. II, and IV only

D. I, II, and IV only

15. Which one of the following is not a colligative property?

A. Boiling point elevation

B. Vapor pressure of a mixture

C. Osmotic pressure

D. Entropy of dissolution

16. The following equilibrium exists when AgBr is in solution:

$$AgBr_{(s)} \longleftrightarrow Ag^+_{(aq)} + Br^-_{(aq)}$$
$$K_{sp} = 7.7 \times 10^{-13}$$

Calculate the solubility of AgBr in g/L in a solution of 0.0010 M NaBr.

A. 7.7×10^{-13} g/L

B. 8.3×10^{-12} g/L

C. 7.7×10^{-10} g/L

D. 8.3×10^{-8} g/L

17. When ammonia, NH_3, is a solvent, complex ions can form. For example, dissolving AgCl in NH_3 will result in the complex ion $Ag(NH_3)^{2+}$. What effect would you expect the formation of complex ions to have on the solubility of a compound like AgCl in NH_3?

   A. The solubility of AgCl will increase, because complex ion formation will cause more ions to exist in solution, which interact with AgCl to cause it to dissociate.
   B. The solubility of AgCl will increase, because complex ion formation will consume Ag^+ molecules and cause the equilibrium to shift away from solid AgCl.
   C. The solubility of AgCl will decrease, because Ag^+ ions are in complexes and the Ag^+ ions that are not complexed will want to associate with Cl^- to form solid AgCl.
   D. The solubility of AgCl will decrease, because complex ion formation will consume Ag^+ molecules and cause the equilibrium to shift toward the solid AgCl.

18. Detergents are compounds that are dissolved in water. However, they are also able to dissolve hydrophobic stains, such as oil and grease in clothing and other fabrics. How are these compounds able to fulfill both hydrophilic and hydrophobic functions?

   A. They contain a hydrophobic core molecule encased in a hydrophilic shell.
   B. They can ionize into two parts; one part is ionic, and the other part is hydrophobic.
   C. They have two states; in water they are ionic, and in hydrophobic solvents they form nonpolar ring structures.
   D. They have two functionally distinct parts; one side is a hydrophobic chain, and the other end is polar and ionic.

Small Group Questions

1. How does the presence of common ions in solution affect K_{sp}? I.P. (Q_{sp})?

2. Discuss the circumstances that permit solvation. What forces are involved?

Explanations to Practice Questions

1. A

The equation $\Delta T_b = iK_b m$ can be used to solve this problem. The change in boiling point is found by subtracting the boiling point of water (the solvent), 100°C, from the elevated boiling point, 101.11°C. Using the given value for K_b, we solve for the molality of the solution and get 2.17 moles/kg. Convert to grams by dividing by 1,000 and then multiply by the mass of the solution, 100 g, to get the moles of solute. To obtain the molar mass, divide the mass of the solute, 70 g, by the number of moles, 0.217 moles, to get a molar mass of 322.58 g/mole. (B) would indicate a problem in unit conversions because the answer is off by an order of magnitude. (C) and (D) are wrong and would result from multiplying 1.11 by the K_b instead of dividing. (Note: Sugar does not dissociate in water, thus the van't Hoff factor (i) is equal to one.)

2. D

All three choices can make a solution as long as the two components create a mixture that is of uniform appearance (homogenous). Hydrogen in platinum is an example of a gas in a solid. The air we breathe is an example of a homogenous mixture of a gas in a gas. Brass and steel are examples of homogenous mixtures of solids.

3. B

Benzene and toluene are both organic liquids and have very similar properties. They are both nonpolar and are almost exactly the same size. Raoult's law states that ideal solution behavior is observed when solute–solute, solvent–solvent, and solute–solvent interactions are very similar. Therefore, benzene and toluene in solution will be predicted to behave as a nearly ideal solution. (A) states that the liquids would follow Raoult's law because they are different. It is true that the compounds are slightly different, but the difference is

negligible in terms of Raoult's law. (C) and (D) are incorrect because they state that the solution would not obey Raoult's law.

4. A

If the membrane became permeable to water, then water molecules would move to the side with the higher solute concentration, according to the principles of osmosis. The left side has a higher concentration of solute (NaCl), so water will move toward the left in an attempt to balance the concentrations of each side. The level on the left will rise because of the excess water molecules, and the level on the right will fall due to a loss of water molecules.

5. D

The first step will most likely be endothermic, because energy is required to break molecules apart. The second step is also endothermic, because the intermolecular forces in the solvent must be overcome to allow incorporation of solute particles. The third step will most likely be exothermic, because polar water molecules will interact with the dissolved ions and release energy.

6. C

CaS will cause the most negative ΔS°_{soln} because the Ca^{2+} and S^{2-} ions have the highest charge density compared to the other ions. All of the other ions have charges of +1 or −1, whereas Ca^{2+} and S^{2-} each have charges with an absolute value of 2. To arrange all four species in order of highest to lowest charge density, we'd have to take ion size into account. Smaller ions have higher charge densities. For example, LiF will have a higher charge density than KCl. It follows that the ΔS°_{soln} is more negative for LiF than for KCl.

7. D

A nonelectrolyte solution will not dissociate into ions in solution. Its effective molarity in solution will be the same as the number of moles that were dissolved. On the other hand, an electrolyte like $Mg(NO_3)_2$ will dissociate into three ions (Mg and $2NO_3^-$). The effective molarity, which is important for colligative properties, will be three times the number of moles that were dissolved. Osmotic pressure is a colligative property and will, therefore, be three times larger for $Mg(NO_3)_2$ compared to a nonelectrolyte. The molarity of $Mg(NO_3)_2$, 0.02 M, is two times larger than the nonelectrolyte solution (0.01 M). The nonelectrolyte's osmotic pressure will have to be multiplied by three and then by two for $Mg(NO_3)_2$: 15 mm Hg $\times 3 \times 2$ equals 90 mm Hg. We can use the osmotic pressure formula to check our work.

Osmotic pressure: $\Pi = MRT$

$$T_1 = T_2, \text{ so } \frac{\Pi_1}{M_1 R} = \frac{\Pi_2}{M_2 R}.$$

R terms cancel, and we're solving for Π_2, so we're left with

$$\Pi_2 = \frac{M_2 \Pi_1}{M_1} = \frac{(0.02 \text{ M}) (3 \text{ particles per mol}) (15 \text{ mm Hg})}{(0.01 \text{ M})}$$

$$= 90 \text{ mm Hg}$$

8. B

The mass percent of a solute equals the mass of the solute divided by the mass of the total solution. To find the mass of the solution, first find the mass of the solvent, water. Multiplying the volume of the solution by the density gives a mass of 292.5 grams of water. Adding 100 grams of sugar yields a solution with a mass of 392.5 grams. Next, divide 100 grams of sugar by 392.5 grams and multiply by 100 to get a percentage. (A) can be arrived at if water's density at 80°C is assumed to be 1 g/mL. If we had forgotten to add the solute's mass to the solvent's, we'd have calculated 34.2 (100/292.5) percent, which is (D). (C) neglects both the addition step and the correct density value (100/300 = 33.3%).

9. A

Mixtures that have a higher vapor pressure than predicted by Raoult's law have stronger solvent–solvent and solute–solute interactions than solvent–solute interactions. Therefore, particles do not want to stay in solution and more readily evaporate, creating a higher vapor pressure than an ideal solution. Two liquids that have different properties, like hexane (hydrophobic) and ethanol (hydrophilic, small), would not have many interactions with each other to cause positive deviation. (B) and (C) are composed of liquids that are similar to one another and that would not show significant deviation from Raoult's law because they neither attract nor repel one another. (D) contains two liquids that would interact well with each other, causing a negative deviation from Raoult's law. When attracted to one other, liquids prefer to stay in liquid form and have a lower vapor pressure than predicted by Raoult's law.

10. A

Dissolution is governed by enthalpy and entropy, which are related by the equation $\Delta G^\circ_{soln} = \Delta H^\circ_{soln} - T\Delta S^\circ_{soln}$. The cooling of the solution indicates that heat is used up in this bond-breaking reaction. In other words, dissolution is endothermic, and ΔH is positive. The reaction is occurring spontaneously, so ΔG must be negative. The only way that a positive ΔH can result in a negative ΔG is if entropy, ΔS, is a large, positive value. If $T\Delta S$ has a larger absolute value than ΔH, ΔG will be negative. Conceptually, that means that the only way the solid can dissolve is if the increase in entropy is great enough to overcome the decrease in enthalpy. (B) is incorrect because it is clearly stated in the question stem that KCl dissolves. (C) is incorrect because ΔS°_{soln} must be positive in order for KCl to dissolve. Finally, (D) is incorrect because solute dissolution would cause boiling point to elevate, not depress. Additionally, it is not a piece of evidence that could be found simply by observing the beaker's temperature change.

11. B

The equation to determine the change in boiling point of a solution is as follows: $\Delta T_b = m_b(K_b)$. m_b is the molality of the solution, and K_b is the boiling point elevation constant. In this case, the solvent is always water, so K_b will be the same for each solution and we don't need it to find our answer. What we do need to know is how many particles dissociate from each original species. This is referred to as the van't Hoff factor (i) and is multiplied by our molality to demonstrate an effective molality. We'll use effective molality values to determine which will cause the greatest change in boiling point.

Species	Number of Moles	Number of Dissolved Particles	$i \times m$ (Effective Molality)
$CaSO_4$	0.46	2	0.92
$Fe(NO_3)_3$	0.54	4	2.16
CH_3COOH	1.09	Some 2, most 1	$1.09 < x < 2.18$
$C_{12}H_{22}O_{11}$	1.11	1	1.11

It looks like we need to decide between iron (III) nitrate and acetic acid. No more calculations are necessary because the fact that acetic acid is a weak acid tells us that only a few particles will dissociate into H^+ and acetate$^-$. So the x that we are curious about is most likely closer to 1.09 than 2.18. We can certainly conclude that it will be less than 2.16. Iron (III) nitrate will have the largest effect on boiling point.

12. C

The solubility of gases in liquids is directly proportional to the atmospheric pressure. Therefore, we should expect a decrease in solubility upon experiencing the decreased atmospheric pressure in Denver. Because 0.800 atm is 80% of the pressure at sea level (1 atm), oxygen's solubility will be 80% of 1.25×10^{-3}, which yields 1.00×10^{-3} M. (A) is a miscalculation, (B) suggests that pressure and solubility are inversely related, and (D) implies that atmospheric temperature will not affect solubility.

13. C

30 ppb of Pb^{2+} is equivalent to 30 grams of Pb^{2+} in 10^9 grams of solution. Water's density will help us convert from mass to volume. Dividing by the molar mass of Pb^{2+}, 207 g/mole, will result in Pb^{2+}'s molarity, 1.4×10^{-7} M.

$$\frac{(30\,\text{g Pb}^{2+})\,(1\,\text{g H}_2\text{O})\,(1{,}000\,\text{mL})\,(1\,\text{mol Pb}^{2+})}{(10^9\text{g H}_2\text{O})\,(1\,\text{mL H}_2\text{O})\,(1\,\text{L})\,(207\,\text{g Pb}^{2+})} = 1.44 \times 10^{-7}\text{M}$$

14. D

An electrolyte is a molecule that dissociates into free ions and behaves as an electrically conductive medium. Number I, NaF, is an electrolyte because it dissociates to form the ions Na^+ and F^-. Number II, glucose, is a nonelectrolyte because it has a ring structure that dissolves but does not dissociate. Number III, CH_3OH, has a pKa of approximately 15 and is not likely to ionize in solution. Therefore, it is not an electrolyte. Number IV, acetic acid, is a weak acid (pKa = 4.7) and also a weak electrolyte because it will partially ionize in solution.

15. D

A colligative property depends solely upon the number of molecules and disregards the identity of the molecules. (A), (B), and (C) are all properties based on the composition of a solution, determined by the number of molecules that are dissolved in the solution. (D), the entropy of dissolution, will depend on the chemical properties of the substance, such as charge density and electron affinity. Therefore, the entropy of dissolution is not a colligative property.

16. D

The solubility of AgBr can be solved by using the K_{sp} value given in the equation.

$$AgBr \leftrightarrow Ag^+ + Br^-$$
$$K_{sp} = [Ag^+][Br^-] = 7.7 \times 10^{-13}$$

Assuming that the same amount of cations and anions dissolve, we can refer to Ag^+ and Br^- both as x.

$$K_{sp} = [x][x] = 7.7 \times 10^{-13}$$

However, there is already 0.001 M Br^- in solution. To account for that, we'll add it in to the K_{sp} equation.

$$K_{sp} = [x][x + 0.001\,\text{M}] = 7.7 \times 10^{-13}$$

We know 0.001 is much bigger than the square root of 10^{-13}. In other words, it's much bigger than x, and x is insignificant in comparison. So we'll approximate Br^-'s concentration as 0.001 M and solve for silver. The solubility of Ag^+ is the same as AgBr's because one molecule of Ag^+ dissociates per molecule of AgBr.

$$K_{sp} = [x][\cancel{x} + 0.001 \text{ M}] = 7.7 \times 10^{-13}$$
$$K_{sp} = [x][0.001 \text{ M}] = 7.7 \times 10^{-13}$$
$$x = \frac{7.7 \times 10^{-13}}{1 \times 10^{-3}} = 7.7 \times 10^{-10} \text{ M}$$

We find that $[Ag^+]$ is 7.7×10^{-10} M Ag^+. This value can be converted to g/L by multiplying by the molar mass of silver, 107.9 grams/mole.

$$(7.7 \times 10^{-10} \text{ mol/L})(107.9 \text{ g/mol}) = 8.3 \times 10^{-8} \text{ g/L}$$

17. B

Formation of complex ions between silver ions and ammonia will cause more molecules of solid AgCl to dissociate. The equilibrium is driven toward dissociation, because the Ag^+ ions are essentially being removed from solution when they complex with ammonia. This rationale is based upon Le Châtelier's principle, stating that when a chemical equilibrium experiences a change in concentration, the system will shift to counteract that change. (A) is incorrect because the complex ions may interact with AgCl but this is not the major reason for the increased solubility. (C) and (D) are incorrect because the solubility of AgCl will increase, not decrease.

18. D

Detergents are compounds that contain a long hydrophobic chain with a polar functional group on one end. The long hydrophobic chains can surround grease and oil droplets, while the polar heads face outward and carry the particles in a solution of water. (A) describes micelles, which are very different in configuration. (B) is internally inconsistent because ionization creates two ionic particles. (C) is incorrect because although multiple detergent molecules form a spherelike shape with oil or grease droplets enclosed, the individual molecules themselves do not form ring structures.

Acids and Bases

What would **YOU** do with **$5,000.00?**

Go to **kaptest.com/future**

to enter Kaplan's $5,000.00 Brighter Future Sweepstakes!

Kaplan $5,000 Brighter Future Sweepstakes 2010 Complete and Official Rules

1. NO PURCHASE IS NECESSARY TO ENTER OR WIN. A PURCHASE WILL NOT INCREASE YOUR CHANCES OF WINNING.

2. PROMOTION PERIOD. The "Kaplan $5,000 Brighter Future Sweepstakes" ("Sweepstakes") commences at 6:59 A.M. EST on April 1, 2010 and ends at 11:59 P.M. EST on March 31, 2011. Entry forms can be found online at kaptest.com/future. All online entries must be received by March 31, 2011 at 11:59 P.M. EST.

3. ELIGIBILITY. This Sweepstakes is open to legal residents of the 50 United States and the District of Columbia and Canada (excluding the Province of Quebec) who are sixteen (16) years of age or older as of April 1, 2010. Officers, directors, representatives and employees of Kaplan (from here on called "Sponsor"), its parent, affiliates or subsidiaries, or their respective advertising, promotion, publicity, production, and judging agencies and their immediate families and household members are not eligible to enter.

4. TO ENTER. To enter simply go to kaptest.com/future and fill-out the online entry form between April 1, 2010 and March 31, 2011.
As part of your entry, you will be asked to provide your first and last name, email address, permanent address and phone number, parent or legal guardian name if under eighteen (18), and the name of your undergraduate school.

LIMIT ONE ENTRY PER PERSON AND EMAIL ADDRESS. Multiple entries will be disqualified. Entries are void if they contain typographical, printing or other errors. Entries generated by a script, macro or other automated means are void. Entries that are mutilated, altered, incomplete, mechanically reproduced, tampered with, illegible, inaccurate, forged, irregular in any way, or otherwise not in compliance with these Official Rules are also void. All entries become the property of the Sponsor and will not be returned to the entrant. Sponsor and those working on its behalf will not be responsible for lost, late, misdirected or damaged mail or email or for Internet, network, computer hardware and software, phone or other technical errors, malfunctions and delays that may occur. Entries will be deemed to have been submitted by the authorized account holder of the email account from which the entry is made. The authorized account holder is the natural person to whom an email address is assigned by an Internet access provider, online service provider or other organization (e.g. business, educational institution, etc.) responsible for assigning email addresses for the domain associated with the submitted email address. By entering or accepting a prize in this Sweepstakes, entrants agree to be bound by the decisions of the judges, the Sponsor and these Official Rules and to comply with all applicable federal, state and local laws and regulations. Odds of winning depend on the number of eligible entries received.

5. WINNER SELECTION. One (1) winner will be selected for $5,000 USD from all eligible entries received in a random drawing to be held on or about May 11, 2011. The drawing will be conducted by an independent judge whose decisions shall be final and binding in all regards. Participants need not be present to win. Please note that if the entrant selected as the winner resides in Canada, he/she will have to correctly answer a timed, test-prep question in order to be confirmed as the winner and claim the prize.

6. WINNER NOTIFICATION AND VALIDATION. Winner of the drawing will be notified by mail within 10 days after the drawing. An Affidavit of Eligibility and Compliance with these Official Rules and a Liability and (unless prohibited) Publicity Release must be executed and returned by the potential winner within twenty-one (21) days after prize notification is sent. If the winner is under eighteen (18) years of age, the prize will be awarded to the winner's parent or legal guardian who will be required to execute an affidavit. Failure of the potential winner to complete, sign and return any requested documents within such period or the return of any prize notification or prize as undeliverable may result in disqualification and selection of an alternate winner in Sponsor's sole discretion. You are not a winner unless your submissions are validated.

In the event that a winner chooses not to accept his or her prize, does not respond to winner notification within the time period noted on the notification or does not return a completed Affidavit of Eligibility and Compliance with these Official Rules and a Liability and (unless prohibited) Publicity Release within twenty-one (21) days after prize notification is sent, the prize may be forfeited and an alternate winner selected in Sponsor's sole discretion.

7. PRIZES.

One (1) winner will be selected to win $5,000.00 USD.

Prize is not transferable. Any applicable taxes or fees are the winner's sole responsibility. All prizes must be redeemed within 21 days of notice of award.

8. GENERAL CONDITIONS. By entering the Sweepstakes or accepting the Sweepstakes prize, winner accepts all the conditions, restrictions, requirements and/or regulations required by the Sponsor in connection with the Sweepstakes. Unless otherwise prohibited by law, acceptance of a prize constitutes permission to use winner's name, picture, likeness, address (city and state) and biographical information for advertising and publicity purposes for this and/or similar promotions, without prior approval or compensation. Acceptance of a prize constitutes a waiver of any claim to royalties, rights or remuneration for said use. Winner agrees to release and hold harmless the Sponsor, its parent, affiliates and subsidiaries, and each of their respective directors, officers, employees, agents, and successors from any and all claims, damages, injury, death, loss or other liability that may arise from winner's participation in the Sweepstakes or the awarding, acceptance, possession, use or misuse of the prize. Sponsor reserves the right in its sole discretion to modify or cancel all or any portions of the Sweepstakes because of technical errors or malfunctions, viruses, hackers, or for other reasons beyond Sponsor's control that impair or corrupt the Sweepstakes in any manner. In such event, Sponsor shall award prizes at random from among the eligible entries received up to the time of the impairment or corruption. Sponsor also reserves the right in its sole discretion to disqualify any entrant who fails to comply with these Official Rules, who attempts to enter the Sweepstakes in any manner or through any means other than as described in these Official Rules, or who attempts to disrupt the Sweepstakes or the kaptest.com website or to circumvent any of these Official Rules.

9. WINNERS' LIST. Starting August 15, 2011, a winners' list may be obtained by sending a self-addressed, stamped envelope to: "$5,000 Kaplan Brighter Future Sweepstakes" Winners' List, Kaplan Test Prep and Admissions Marketing Department, 1440 Broadway, 8th Floor New York, NY 10018. All winners' list requests must be received by December 1, 2011.

10. USE OF ENTRANT AND WINNER INFORMATION. The information that you provide in connection with the Sweepstakes may be used for Sponsor's and select Corporate Partners' purposes to send you information about Sponsor's and its Corporate Partners' products and services. If you would like your name removed from Sponsor's mailing list or if you do not wish to receive information from Sponsor or its Corporate Partners, write to:

Direct Marketing Department
Attn: Kaplan Brighter Future Sweepstakes Opt Out
1440 Broadway
8th Floor
New York NY 10018

11. SPONSOR. The Sponsor of this Sweepstakes is: Kaplan Test Prep and Admissions and Kaplan Publishing, 1440 Broadway, 8th Floor New York, NY 10018.

12. THIS SWEEPSTAKES IS VOID WHERE PROHIBITED, TAXED OR OTHERWISE RESTRICTED BY LAW.

All trademarks are the property of their respective owner. PUB03812

There are many ways that drugs can enter the human body. The route of administration of a drug is the path by which that drug comes into contact with the body. According to the U.S. Food and Drug Administration's Data Standards Manual, there are no fewer than 110 distinct ways in which a drug can come in contact with and/or enter the human body in a local or systemic manner, including the catch-all route of "other." Some drugs can be applied as drops, salves, or creams to mucus membranes. Others are injected. Some employ a transdermal patch, while others are eaten, drunk, or inhaled. You will be challenged in medical school to learn and recall the routes of administration for many commonly prescribed medications and treatments. This is one of the more daunting memorization tasks that will be demanded of you during medical school and residency.

The route of administration of a drug compound is related to both the location of its target tissue (local or systemic), as well as the chemical and physical properties of the compound. For example, compounds that are water-soluble can be administered intravenously (an aqueous solution dripped directly into the bloodstream), while those that are lipid-soluble can be administered transcutaneously (from, say, a patch or a cream) or orally (in a pill or liquid suspension). The polarity, size, and charge of the drug compound will determine its solubility in polar or nonpolar environments and will be major contributing factors to the most effective and efficient route of administration.

Whether a drug compound has an ionic charge is usually a function of the acidic or basic nature of the compound. For example, a basic organic compound that is water-insoluble when neutral can be reacted with an acid to form a salt that, because it is ionic, will be water-soluble. Correspondingly, an acidic organic compound that is water-insoluble when neutral can be reacted with a base to form a water-soluble salt. On the other hand, the protonated (acidic) form of an organic compound can be reacted with a base to neutralize the compound and release it from its salt, changing (and usually reversing) its solubility in water.

Medical professionals aren't the only ones concerned about drug solubilities and routes of administration. There's a science to illegal drugs, too. People in the general population who use illegal drugs (and those who produce them) are knowledgeable about their available forms, as well as the most effective and efficient modes of delivery. One of the clearest examples of this is the difference in the ways that people use the two forms of cocaine. $C_{17}H_{21}NO_4$ (cocaine) is a large alkaloid compound derived from the coca plant. It is a central nervous stimulant that has been used medicinally, ceremonially, and recreationally since at least the pre-Columbian era. About 125 years ago, Pope Leo XIII purportedly carried around a hipflask filled with cocaine-laced wine called Vin Mariani. The 1886 original recipe for what is now the world's most famous cola included coca leaves (from which this famous cola derives its name). Cocaine was once used to treat heroin addiction. Sigmund Freud wrote rhapsodically about its ability to cause "exhilaration and lasting euphoria." By 1903, however, the *American Journal of Pharmacy* was warning that most cocaine abusers were "bohemians, gamblers, high- and low-class prostitutes, night porters, bell boys, burglars, racketeers, pimps, and casual laborers."

Today, cocaine is used primarily in two different forms. Most commonly, the alkaloid compound is reacted with hydrochloric acid (which protonates its tertiary amine functional group), extracted with water, and dried to an aqueous soluble powder (cocaine hydrochloride); this powder either is snorted (insufflated) into the nasal cavity, where it is absorbed into the capillary beds, or is injected directly into the venous circulation. The salt form, however, because it has a very high boiling point close to the temperature at which it burns, cannot be smoked. To produce a form of cocaine that can be vaporized and inhaled from a pipe, the cocaine hydrochloride must be reacted with a base, typically either ammonia (to produce pure "freebase cocaine") or sodium bicarbonate (to produce the less-pure "crack" cocaine). The base reacts with the protonated tertiary amine, removing the hydrogen ion to re-form the neutral alkaloid compound. The freebase cocaine is water-insoluble and usually extracted with ether, or it is left in the aqueous solution, which is heated and evaporated. The freebase or crack form of cocaine has a much lower boiling point; consequently, it can be smoked without risk of burning (combusting).

What a difference a little hydrogen ion can make! The complexities of drug delivery can in part be related to the presence or absence of the hydrogen ion—a mere proton! In this chapter, our focus will be those two classes of compounds—acids and bases—that are involved in so many important reactions. Acid-base reactions are an important focus for the MCAT; in fact, the neutralization reaction is one of the most commonly tested reaction types on Test Day. We will begin with a review of the different definitions of acids and bases and their properties, including the characterization of acids and bases as either strong or weak. Focusing on weak acids and bases, we will discuss the significance of the equilibrium constants, K_a and K_b, for acids and bases, respectively. Finally, we will review acid-base titrations and buffer systems.

Definitions ★★☆☆☆

Over the last century, chemists have used different definitions to identify compounds as acids or bases. Three definitions have been proposed, and each is progressively more inclusive: Every Arrhenius acid (or base) can also be classified as a Brønsted-Lowry acid (or base), and every Brønsted-Lowry acid (or base) can also be classified as a Lewis acid (or base).

ARRHENIUS

The first definitions of acids and bases were formulated by Svante Arrhenius toward the end of the 19th century. **Arrhenius** defined an **acid** as a species that dissociates in water to produce a hydrogen ion, H^+, and a **base** as a species that dissociates in water to produce a hydroxide ion, OH^-. These definitions, though useful for many reactions, fail to describe acidic and basic behavior in nonaqueous media.

BRØNSTED-LOWRY

A more general definition of acids and bases was proposed independently by Johannes Brønsted and Thomas Lowry in 1923. A **Brønsted-Lowry acid** is a species that donates hydrogen ions, while a **Brønsted-Lowry base** is a species that accepts hydrogen ions. The advantage of this definition over Arrhenius's is that it is not limited to aqueous solutions. For example, OH^-, NH_3, and F^- are all Brønsted-Lowry bases because each has the ability to accept hydrogen protons. However, neither NH_3 nor F^- can be classified as Arrhenius bases because they do not dissociate to produce OH^- ions in aqueous solutions. You'll notice, however, being the perceptive student that you are, that according to both of these definitions, there's only one way for a species to be an acid, and that is to produce a hydrogen ion. The only difference between the two definitions for acidic compounds is the requirement (or lack thereof) of an aqueous medium in the Arrhenius definition. Most acid-base chemistry on the Physical Sciences section of the MCAT will involve the transfer of hydrogen ions in accordance with the Brønsted-Lowry definitions.

Brønsted-Lowry acids and bases always occur in pairs because the definitions require the transfer of a proton from the acid to the base. These are **conjugate acid-base pairs** (see below). For example, H_3O^+ is the conjugate acid of the base H_2O, and NO_2^- is the conjugate base of HNO_2.

$$H_3O^+ \, (aq) \;\rightleftarrows\; H_2O \, (aq) + H^+ \, (aq)$$
$$HNO_2 \, (aq) \;\rightleftarrows\; NO_2^- \, (aq) + H^+ \, (aq)$$

LEWIS

At approximately the same time as Brønsted and Lowry, Gilbert Lewis also proposed definitions for acids and bases. **Lewis** defined an **acid** as an electron-pair acceptor (<u>a</u>cid = <u>a</u>cceptor) and a **base** as an electron-pair donor. Lewis's are the most inclusive definitions: Every Arrhenius acid is also a Brønsted-Lowry acid, and every Brønsted-Lowry acid is also a Lewis acid (and likewise for the bases). However, the converse is not true: The Lewis definition encompasses some species not included within the Brønsted-Lowry definition. For example, BCl_3 and $AlCl_3$ are species that can each accept an electron pair, which qualifies them as Lewis acids, but they will not donate a hydrogen ion, which disqualifies them as Brønsted-Lowry acids

MCAT Expertise

This is the most specific definition of acids and bases and is the least useful on the MCAT.

MCAT Expertise

The Brønsted-Lowry definition is a more general description and much more useful and common on the MCAT than the other two. It is all about the proton (H^+).

(or Arrhenius acids, for that matter). On the MCAT, you may encounter Lewis acids more often in the Biological Sciences section, specifically in the organic chemistry reactions for which Lewis acids act as catalysts, such as in the anti-addition of diatomic halogens to alkenes.

NOMENCLATURE OF ARRHENIUS ACIDS

The name of an Arrhenius acid is related to the name of the parent anion (the anion that combines with H^+ to form the acid). Acids formed from anions whose names end in *–ide* have the prefix **hydro-** and the ending *–ic*.

F^-	Fluoride	HF	Hydrofluoric acid
Br^-	Bromide	HBr	Hydrobromic acid

Acids formed from oxanions are called oxyacids. If the anion ends in *–ite* (less oxygen), then the acid will end with *–ous acid*. If the anion ends in *–ate* (more oxygen), then the acid will end with *–ic acid*. Prefixes in the names of the anions are retained. Some examples include the following:

ClO^-	Hypochlorite	HClO	Hypochlorous acid
ClO_2^-	Chlorite	$HClO_2$	Chlorous acid
ClO_3^-	Chlorate	$HClO_3$	Chloric acid
ClO_4^-	Perchlorate	$HClO_4$	Perchloric acid
NO_2^-	Nitrite	HNO_2	Nitrous acid
NO_3^-	Nitrate	HNO_3	Nitric acid

Properties of Acids and Bases ★★★★★★

Acids and bases are usually characterized according to their relative tendencies either to donate or to accept hydrogen ions. Furthermore, aqueous acid and base solutions can be characterized according to their concentrations of hydrogen and hydroxide ions.

AUTO-IONIZATION OF WATER AND HYDROGEN ION EQUILIBRIA

Since many acid-base reactions take place in water—and on the MCAT this is almost exclusively the case—it is very important that you understand the behavior of acidic and basic compounds vis-à-vis the acid-base behavior of water. Only then can you fully appreciate the meaning and significance of such terms as *strong acid* or *weak base* or measurements of pH or pOH.

The Acid-Base Behavior of Water

Water is a member of a unique class of compounds in the world of acids and bases. The H_2O molecule can act as either an acid or a base, depending on the acid-base nature of the species with which it is reacting. Water acts as an acid by donating one of its hydrogen ions, and it acts as a base by accepting a hydrogen ion. This leads us to the definition of an **amphoteric** species: one that in the presence of a base reacts like an acid and, in the presence of an acid, reacts like a base. As an amphoteric compound, water can react with itself, in a process called **auto-ionization**, in the following manner:

$$H_2O\ (l) + H_2O\ (l) \leftrightarrow H_3O^+\ (aq) + OH^-\ (aq)$$

One water molecule donates a hydrogen ion to another water molecule to produce the **hydronium ion** (H_3O^+) and the hydroxide ion (OH^+). By the way, some of you may be used to seeing the hydrogen ion represented simply as H^+, rather than as H_3O^+. This is fine, but it's important to remember that the proton is never just "free floating" in the solution; it's always attached to water or some other species that has the ability to accept it. Auto-ionization of water is a reversible reaction; therefore, the above equation is an equilibrium expression for this reversible reaction. For pure water at 298 K, the **water dissociation constant, K_w,** has been experimentally determined and is

$$K_w = [H_3O^+][OH^-] = 10^{-14} \text{ at } 25°C\ (298\text{ K})$$

Because each mole of water that auto-ionizes produces one mole each of hydrogen (or hydronium) ions and hydroxide ions, the concentrations of the hydrogen ions and hydroxide ions are always equal in pure water at equilibrium. Thus, the concentration of each of the ions in pure water at equilibrium at 298 K is 10^{-7} mol/L.

The concentrations of the two ions will not always be equal. In fact, they will only be equal when the solution is neutral. Nevertheless, the product of their respective concentrations must always equal 10^{-14} when the temperature of the solution is 298 K. For example, if a species is added to pure water and that species donates hydrogen ions to the water (i.e., the species is an acid), then the hydrogen ion concentration will increase, causing the water system to shift to reverse the auto-ionization process. The result is a decrease in the hydroxide ion concentration and a return to the equilibrium state. This is nothing other than Le Châtelier's principle in action as we've seen time and time again: The addition of product to a system at equilibrium (in this case, the addition of H^+ to the water system at equilibrium) causes the system to shift in direction away from the products, toward the reactants. The shift away from the product side necessarily leads to a decrease in the concentration of the hydroxide ion such that the product of the concentrations of the dissolved ions equals the K_w. The addition of a species that accepts hydrogen ions (i.e., a base), resulting in a decrease in the hydrogen ion concentration, will cause the water system to shift forward to replace the hydrogen ions. The increase in auto-ionization will necessarily lead to an increase in the hydroxide ion concentration and a return to the equilibrium state.

Before we introduce the scales used to measure the concentrations of hydrogen ions and hydroxide ions in different acid-base solutions, we want to emphasize the important thermodynamic principle, often unnoticed by students, contained in the water dissociation constant (K_w) expression. The K_w is an equilibrium constant; unless the temperature of the water is changed, the value for K_w cannot be changed. Thus, the product of the concentrations of the hydrogen ions and the hydroxide ions in the aqueous solution at 298 K must always equal 10^{-14}. At different temperatures, however, the value for K_w changes. At temperatures above 298 K, the value for K_w will increase, a direct result of the endothermic nature of the auto-ionization reaction.

pH and pOH Scales

The concentrations of hydrogen ions and hydroxide ions in aqueous solutions can vary significantly, and the vastness of the range makes measurements on a linear scale unmanageable. The scales of concentrations for acidic and basic solutions are condensed into something more manageable by being expressed in logarithmic terms, just like the decibel scale for sound intensity. These logarithmic scales are the **pH** and the **pOH** scales for the concentrations of the hydrogen and hydroxide ions, respectively.

We find that in many cases, the reactivity of a reaction involving an acid is not a function of hydrogen ion concentration but instead the logarithm of the hydrogen ion concentration (just as loudness of sound is a function of the logarithm of sound intensity). As a result, we often use the logarithmic pH and pOH scales to express the concentrations of the hydrogen and hydroxide ions, respectively.

pH and pOH are specific calculations of the more generic "p-scale." A p-scale is defined as the negative logarithm of the number of items. There's no reason why this logarithmic calculation cannot be applied to the population values of all the world's countries [pPop = $-\log(\text{population})$] or to the number of hairs on the head of every living human [pHair = $-\log(\text{hairs})$]. The log scale system could be applied to anything, but let's be real: pPop and pHair aren't going to earn us any Test Day points. It's much more valuable for us to understand the significance of the p-scale expression for the concentrations of hydrogen ions and hydroxide ions in acid and base aqueous solutions.

The pH of a solution is given by

$$pH = -\log[H^+] = \log(1/[H^+])$$

Likewise, the pOH of a solution is given by

$$pOH = -\log[OH^-] = \log(1/[OH^-])$$

For pure water at equilibrium at 298 K, the concentration of the hydrogen ion equals the concentration of the hydroxide ion and is 10^{-7} mol/L. Therefore, pure water at 298 K has a pH of 7 and a pOH of 7. (Note: $-\log 10^{-7} = 7$.)

From the water dissociation constant expression ($K_w = [H_3O^+][OH^-] = 10^{-14}$), we find that

$$pH + pOH = 14 \quad \text{(for aqueous solutions at 298 K)}$$

For any aqueous solution at 298 K, a pH less than 7 (or pOH greater than 7) indicates a relative excess of hydrogen ions, and the solution is acidic; a pH greater than 7 (or pOH less than 7) indicates a relative excess of hydroxide ions, and the solution is basic. A pH (or pOH) equal to 7 indicates equal concentrations of hydrogen and hydroxide ions, resulting in a neutral solution.

Estimating p-Scale Values

An essential skill that you must hone for Test Day, applicable to many problems involving acids and bases, is the ability to convert pH, pOH, pK_a, and pK_b values quickly into nonlogarithmic form and vice versa.

When the original value is a power of 10, the operation is relatively straightforward: Changing the sign on the exponent gives the corresponding p-scale value directly. For example,

> If $[H+] = 0.001$ or 10^{-3}, then the pH = 3 and pOH = 11.
> If $K_b = 1.0 \times 10^{-7}$, then $pK_b = 7$.

More difficulty arises (in the absence of a calculator or a superhuman ability to calculate logarithms in your head) when the original value is not an exact power of 10. The MCAT is not a math test, and it is not primarily interested in determining your ability to perform mathematical calculations. Exact calculation of the logarithmic value of a number that is not an integer power of 10 will be excessively onerous, if not outright impossible. The test writers are interested, however, in testing your ability to apply mathematical concepts appropriately in solving certain problems. Fortunately, there is a simple method of approximation that will be foolproof for Test Day.

Key Concept

This equation demonstrates a fundamental property of logarithms: The log of a product is equal to the sum of the logs; that is, $\log(xy) = \log x + \log y$.

MCAT Expertise

Other important properties of logarithms include these:

$\log x^n = n \log x$ and $\log 10^x = x$. From these two properties, one can derive the particularly useful relationship that will be seen on Test Day (and we can see in the example): $-\log 10^{-x} = x$.

If the nonlogarithmic value is written in proper scientific notation, it will look like $n \times 10^{-m}$, where n is a number between 1 and 10. Using the basic log rule that the $\log (xy) = \log x + \log y$, we can express the negative log of this product, $-\log (n \times 10^{-m})$, as $-\log (n) - \log (10^{-m})$. Since log refers to the common log with base of 10, we can simplify $-\log (n) - \log (10^{-m})$ to $-\log (n) - (-m)$, or $m - \log (n)$. Now, since n is a number between 1 and 10, its logarithm will be a fraction between 0 and 1 (note: $\log 1 = 0$ and $\log 10 = 1$). Thus, $m - \log (n)$ will be between $(m - 1)$ and $(m - 0)$. Furthermore, the larger n is (that is, the closer to 10), the larger the fraction, $\log (n)$ will be; consequently, the closer to $(m - 1)$ our answer will be. If this is too much to remember—and given the amount of information you need to remember for Test Day, it might be—all you need to remember is this: When the nonlogarithmic value is $n \times 10^{-m}$, the logarithmic value will be between $(m - 1)$ and m. It's that simple!

> **Example:** If $K_a = 1.8 \times 10^{-5}$, then $pK_a = 5 - \log 1.8$. Because 1.8 is small, its log will be small, and the answer will be closer to 5 than to 4. (The actual answer is 4.74.)

STRONG ACIDS AND BASES

Strong acids and bases are those that completely dissociate (or nearly so) into their component ions in aqueous solution. For example, when sodium hydroxide, NaOH, is added to water, the ionic compound dissociates, for all intents and purposes, completely according to the net ionic equation:

$$NaOH \ (s) = Na^+ \ (aq) + OH^- \ (aq)$$

Hence, in a 1 M solution of NaOH, complete dissociation gives 1 M OH^-. The pH and pOH for this solution can be calculated as follows:

$$pH = 14 - pOH = 14 - (-\log[OH^-]) = 14 + \log (1) = 14 + 0 = 14$$

Virtually no undissociated strong acid or base, such as NaOH, remains in solution, and we can consider the dissociation of strong acids and bases essentially as going to completion. In the NaOH example given above, you should note that in calculating the pH, we assumed that the concentration of OH^- associated with the auto-ionization of water is negligible compared to the concentration of OH^- due to the addition of the strong base. The contribution of OH^- and H^+ ions to an aqueous solution from the auto-ionization of water can be neglected only if the concentration of the acid or base is significantly greater than 10^{-7} M. Keeping this in mind as you solve acid-base problems on Test Day will help you avoid "silly" mistakes. For example, with your brain on "autopilot," you might calculate the pH of a 1×10^{-8} M solution of HCl (a strong acid) as 8, because $-\log (10^{-8}) = 8$. But a pH of 8 can't possibly describe an acidic solution (at least not at 298 K), because the presence of the acid will cause the hydrogen ion concentration to increase above 10^{-7} and the pH must be below 7.

So what went wrong in this case? The error was in not recognizing that the acid compound concentration is actually ten times less than the equilibrium concentration of hydrogen ions in pure water generated by water's autodissociation. Consequently, the hydrogen ion concentration from the water itself is significant and can't be ignored. Now, the addition of the acid results in the common ion effect (Le Châtelier's principle in action in ionic solutions) and causes the water system to shift away from the side of the ions, thereby reducing the concentration of hydrogen ions and hydroxide ions. The reversal of auto-ionization is thermodynamically favored to return the water system to equilibrium, and we can express this mathematically as

$$K_w = [H_3O^+][OH^-] = [x + (1.0 \times 10^{-8})](x) = 10^{-14}$$

where $x = [H_3O^+] = [OH^-]$ from the auto-ionization of water. Solving for x (using a calculator!) gives $x = 9.5 \times 10^{-8}$ M. The total concentration of hydrogen ions is $[H^+]_{total} = 9.5 \times 10^{-8} + 1.0 \times 10^{-8} = 1.05 \times 10^{-7}$ M. Notice that this indeed is slightly less than what the value would be if the common ion effect were not acting here $[(1.0 \times 10^{-7}) + (1.0 \times 10^{-8}) = 1.1 \times 10^{-7}]$. The pH of this acid solution can now be calculated as pH $= -\log(1.05 \times 10^{-7}) = 6.98$. This value is slightly less than 7, as it should be expected for a very dilute acidic solution. The point of all of this is: *Don't put your brain on autopilot on Test Day. Be alert and keep thinking critically, no matter how familiar the problem setups might seem to you!*

Strong acids commonly encountered in the laboratory and on the MCAT include HCl (hydrochloric acid), HBr (hydrobromic acid), HI (hydroiodic acid), H_2SO_4 (sulfuric acid), HNO_3 (nitric acid), and $HClO_4$ (perchloric acid). Strong bases commonly encountered include NaOH (sodium hydroxide), KOH (potassium hydroxide), and other soluble hydroxides of group IA and IIA metals. Calculation of the pH and pOH of strong acids and bases assumes complete dissociation of the acid or base in solution: $[H^+]$ = normality of strong acid and $[OH^-]$ = normality of strong base.

WEAK ACIDS AND BASES

Before we go any further in our discussion of acids and bases as "strong" or "weak," we want to ensure that you are making the mental distinction between the chemical behavior of an acid or base with respect to its tendency to dissociate (e.g., strong bases completely dissociate in aqueous solutions) and the concentration of acid and base solutions. Although we may casually describe a solution's concentration as "strong" or "weak," it is preferable to use the terms *concentrated* and *dilute*, respectively, because they are unambiguously associated with concentrations, not chemical behavior.

MCAT Expertise

Always be sure to think about the answer and whether it makes sense on Test Day. As seen in this paragraph, a basic pH for an acidic solution should make you think about what might be wrong with your answer.

MCAT Expertise

The K_w (like all equilibrium constants) will change if the temperature changes and, in turn, will change the pH scale. So be careful on the MCAT because our pH scale of 1–14 is only valid at 25°C.

Continuing our focus on the chemical behavior of acids and bases, we now must consider those acids and bases that only partially dissociate in aqueous solutions. These are called weak acids and bases. For example, a weak monoprotic acid, HA, will dissociate partially in water to achieve an equilibrium state:

$$HA\ (aq) + H_2O\ (l) \leftrightarrow H_3O^+\ (aq) + A^-\ (aq)$$

Since the system exists in an equilibrium state, we can write the dissociation equation to determine the **acid dissociation constant K_a** as

$$K_a = \frac{[H_3O^+][A^-]}{[HA]}$$

The smaller the K_a, the weaker the acid, and consequently, the less it will dissociate. Note that the concentration of water, while not seemingly included in the dissociation constant expression, is actually incorporated into the value of K_a ($K_{eq}\ [H_2O] = K_a$).

A weak monovalent base, BOH, undergoes dissociation to yield B^+ and OH^- in solution:

$$BOH\ (aq) \leftrightarrow B^+\ (aq) + OH^-\ (aq)$$

And the **base dissociation constant K_b** can be calculated according to

$$K_b = \frac{[B^+][OH^-]}{[BOH]}$$

The smaller the K_b, the weaker the base, and consequently, the less it will dissociate. As with the acid dissociation expression, the base dissociation expression incorporates the concentration of the water in the value of the K_b itself.

Generally speaking, we can characterize a species as a weak acid if its K_a is less than 1.0 and as a weak base if its K_b is less than 1.0. On the MCAT, molecular (that is, nonionic) weak bases are almost exclusively amines.

CONJUGATE ACID/BASE PAIRS

Since Brønsted and Lowry define an acid-base reaction as one in which a hydrogen ion (proton) is transferred from the acid to the base, the acid and base always occur in pairs called conjugates. A **conjugate acid** is the acid formed when a base gains a proton, and a **conjugate base** is the base that is formed when an acid loses a proton. For example,

$$HCO_3^-\ (aq) + H_2O \leftrightarrow CO_3^{2-}\ (aq) + H_3O^+\ (aq)$$

Bridge

Weak acids and bases are often seen on the MCAT in the Biological Sciences section.

Key Concept

Be aware of the relationship between conjugate acids and bases because you will need to recognize these on the MCAT. Taking a proton from a molecule will give you the conjugate base, and putting a proton on will give you the conjugate acid!

The CO_3^{2-} is the conjugate base of the HCO_3^- acid, and the H_3O^+ is the conjugate acid of the H_2O base. To find the K_a, we consider the equilibrium concentrations of the dissolved species:

$$K_a = \frac{[CO_3^{2-}][H_3O^+]}{[HCO_3^-]}$$

The reaction between bicarbonate (HCO_3^-) and water is reversible, so we can write it as follows:

$$CO_3^{2-}(aq) + H_2O(aq) \leftrightarrow HCO_3^-(aq) + OH^-(aq)$$

And write the K_b for CO_3^{2-} as follows:

$$K_b = \frac{[HCO_3^-][OH^-]}{[CO_3^{2-}]}$$

In a conjugate acid-base pair formed from a weak acid, the conjugate base is generally stronger than the conjugate acid. Note that this does not necessarily mean that a weak acid will produce a strong conjugate base or that a weak base will produce a strong conjugate acid, although it is always the case that a strong acid will produce a weak conjugate base (e.g., HCl/Cl^-) and a strong base will produce a weak conjugate acid (e.g., $NaOH/H_2O$). As it turns out, for HCO_3^- and CO_3^{2-}, the reaction of CO_3^{2-} with water to produce HCO_3^- and OH^- occurs to a greater extent (that is, is thermodynamically more favorable) than the reaction of HCO_3^- and water to produce CO_3^{2-} and H_3O^+.

When you add the previous two reversible reactions, you see that the net is simply the dissociation of water:

$$H_2O(l) + H_2O(l) \leftrightarrow H_3O^+(aq) + OH^-(aq)$$

Since the net reaction is the auto-ionization of water, the equilibrium constant for the reaction is $K_w = [H_3O^+][OH^-] = 10^{-14}$, which is the product of K_a and K_b. Remember: The product of the concentrations of the hydrogen ion and the hydroxide ion must always equal 10^{-14} for acid or base aqueous solutions. Because water itself is an amphoteric species (both a weak acid and a weak base), all acid-base reactivity in water ultimately reduces to the acid-base behavior of water, and all acid or base aqueous solutions are governed by the dissociation constant for water. Thus, if the dissociation constant for either the acid or its conjugate base is known, then the dissociation constant for the other can be determined using this equation:

$$K_a \text{ (conjugate acid)} \times K_b \text{(conjugate base)} = K_w = 10^{-14}$$

As you can now see, K_a and K_b are inversely related. In other words, if K_a is large, then K_b is small, and vice versa.

APPLICATIONS OF K_a AND K_b

The most common use of the acid and base dissociation constants is for the determination of the concentration of one of the species in the solution at equilibrium. On Test Day, you may be challenged to calculate the concentration of the hydrogen ion (or pH), the concentration of the hydroxide ion (or pOH), or the concentration of either the original acid or base. One such example is provided below to show you the important steps in solving quickly and correctly these types of problems.

To calculate the concentration of H^+ in a 2.0 M aqueous solution of acetic acid, CH_3COOH ($K_a = 1.8 \times 10^{-5}$), first write the equilibrium reaction:

$$CH_3COOH\ (aq) \leftrightarrow H^+\ (aq) + CH_3COO^-\ (aq)$$

Next, write the expression for the acid dissociation constant:

$$K_a = \frac{[H+][CH_3COO^-]}{[CH_3COOH]} = 1.8 \times 10^{-5}$$

Acetic acid is a weak acid, so the concentration of CH_3COOH at equilibrium is equal to its initial concentration, 2.0 M, less the amount dissociated, x. Likewise $[H^+] = [CH_3COO^-] = x$, because each molecule of CH_3COOH dissociates into one H^+ ion and one CH_3COO^- ion. Thus, the equation can be rewritten as follows:

$$K_a = \frac{[x][x]}{[2.0-x]} = 1.8 \times 10^{-5}$$

We can approximate that $2.0 - x \approx 2.0$ because acetic acid is a weak acid and only slightly dissociates in water. This simplifies the calculation of x:

$$K_a = \frac{[x][x]}{[2.0]} = 1.8 \times 10^{-5}$$
$$x = 6.0 \times 10^{-3}\ M$$

The fact that $[x]$ is so much less than the initial concentration of acetic acid (2.0 M) validates the approximation; otherwise, it would have been necessary to solve for x using the quadratic formula. That sounds rather unpleasant, doesn't it? Fortunately for you, the MCAT test writers select examples of weak acids and bases that allow you to make this approximation. (A rule of thumb is that the approximation is valid as long as x is less than 5 percent of the initial concentration.)

Key Concept

Once again, we are dealing with an equilibrium process here and can apply those principles to the problems dealing with weak acids and bases on the exam.

MCAT Expertise

This estimation makes life easy and will get you the correct answer on Test Day.

Salt Formation ★★★★☆☆

Acids and bases may react with each other, forming a salt (and often, but not always, water), in what is termed a **neutralization reaction** (see Chapter 4, Compounds and Stoichiometry). For example,

$$HA + BOH \leftrightarrow BA + H_2O$$

The salt may precipitate out or remain ionized in solution, depending on its solubility and the amount produced. Neutralization reactions generally go to completion. The reverse reaction, in which the salt ions react with water to give back the acid or base, is known as **hydrolysis**.

Four combinations of strong and weak acids and bases are possible:

1. Strong acid + strong base: e.g., $HCl + NaOH \leftrightarrow NaCl + H_2O$
2. Strong acid + weak base: e.g., $HCl + NH_3 \leftrightarrow NH_4Cl$
3. Weak acid + strong base: e.g., $HClO + NaOH \leftrightarrow NaClO + H_2O$
4. Weak acid + weak base: e.g., $HClO + NH_3 \leftrightarrow NH_4ClO$

The products of a reaction between equal concentrations of a strong acid and a strong base are a salt and water. The acid and base neutralize each other, so the resulting solution is neutral ($pH = 7$), and the ions formed in the reaction do not react with water.

The product of a reaction between a strong acid and a weak base is also a salt, but often no water is formed because weak bases are usually not hydroxides. However, in this case, the cation of the salt will react with the water solvent, re-forming the weak base in hydrolysis. For example,

$$HCl\ (aq) + NH_3\ (aq) \leftrightarrow NH_4^+\ (aq) + Cl^-\ (aq) \quad \text{Reaction I}$$
$$NH_4^+\ (aq) + H_2O\ (l) \leftrightarrow NH_3\ (aq) + H_3O^+\ (aq) \quad \text{Reaction II}$$

NH_4^+ is the conjugate acid of a weak base (NH_3), which is stronger than the conjugate base (Cl^-) of the strong acid HCl. NH_4^+ will then transfer a proton to H_2O to form the hydronium ion. The increase in the concentration of the hydronium ion will cause the water system to shift away from auto-ionization, thereby reducing the concentration of hydroxide ion. Consequently, the concentration of the hydrogen ion will be greater than that of the hydroxide ion at equilibrium, and as a result, the pH of the solution will fall below 7.

On the other hand, when a weak acid reacts with a strong base, the pH of the solution at equilibrium is in the basic range because the salt hydrolyzes to re-form the acid,

Bridge

Remember the reaction types discussed in Chapter 4? Well, here is our neutralization reaction.

with the concurrent formation of hydroxide ion from the hydrolyzed water molecules. The increase in the concentration of the hydroxide ion will cause the water system to shift away from auto-ionization, thereby reducing the concentration of the hydrogen ion. Consequently, the concentration of the hydroxide ion will be greater than that of the hydrogen ion at equilibrium, and as a result, the pH of the solution will rise above 7. Consider the reaction of acetic acid CH_3COOH (weak acid) with sodium hydroxide NaOH (strong base):

$$CH_3COOH \ (aq) + NaOH \ (aq) \leftrightarrow Na^+ \ (aq) + CH_3COO^- \ (aq) + H_2O \ (l) \ \text{Reaction I}$$
$$CH_3COO^- \ (aq) + H_2O \ (l) \leftrightarrow CH_3COOH \ (aq) + OH^- (aq) \ \text{Reaction II}$$

The pH of a solution containing a weak acid and a weak base depends on the relative strengths of the reactants. For example, the acid HClO has a $K_a = 3.2 \times 10^{-8}$, and the base NH_3 has a $K_b = 1.8 \times 10^{-5}$. Thus, an aqueous solution of HClO and NH_3 is basic because the K_a for HClO is less than the K_b for NH_3 (that is to say, HClO is weaker as an acid than NH_3 is as a base, and consequently, at equilibrium, the concentration of hydroxide ions will be greater than the concentration of hydrogen ions in the aqueous solution).

Polyvalence and Normality ★★★★☆

The relative acidity or basicity of an aqueous solution is determined by the relative concentrations of **acid** and **base equivalents**. An acid equivalent is equal to one mole of H^+ (or H_3O^+) ions; a base equivalent is equal to one mole of OH^- ions. Some acids and bases are **polyvalent**; that is, each mole of the acid or base liberates more than one acid or base equivalent. For example, the divalent acid H_2SO_4 undergoes the following dissociation in water:

$$H_2SO_4 \ (aq) + H_2O \ (l) \leftrightarrow H_3O^+ \ (aq) + HSO_4^- \ (aq)$$
$$HSO_4^- \ (aq) + H_2O \ (l) \leftrightarrow H_3O^+ \ (aq) + SO_4^{2-} \ (aq)$$

One mole of H_2SO_4 can produce two acid equivalents (2 moles of H_3O^+). You'll notice, if you look closely at the dissociation reaction for sulfuric acid, the first dissociation goes to completion but the second dissociation goes to an equilibrium state. The acidity or basicity of a solution depends upon the concentration of acidic or basic equivalents that can be liberated. The quantity of acidic or basic capacity is directly indicated by the solution's normality (see Chapter 9, Solutions). For example, since each mole of H_3PO_4 can yield three moles (equivalents) of H_3O^+, a 2 M H_3PO_4 solution would be 6 N (6 normal).

Another measurement useful for acid-base chemistry is **equivalent weight**. Chapter 4 defined and discussed this term extensively, and Chapter 9 reviewed it briefly. The gram equivalent weight is the mass of a compound that produces one equivalent (one mole of charge). For example, H_2SO_4 (molar mass: 98 g/mol) is a divalent acid, so each mole of the acid compound yields two acid equivalents. The gram equivalent weight is $98/2 = 49$ grams. That is, the complete dissociation of 49 grams of H_2SO_4 will yield one acid equivalent (one mole of H_3O^+). Common polyvalent acids include H_2SO_4, H_3PO_4, and H_2CO_3. Common polyvalent bases include $CaCO_3$, $Ca(OH)_2$, and $Mg(OH)_2$. Magnesium hydroxide is the active ingredient in the thick, "milky" over-the-counter preparation that is used as an antidote for occasional acid indigestion and diarrhea. Calcium carbonate ($CaCO_3$) is the active ingredient in the over-the-counter tablet preparation also used to treat an upset tummy.

Bridge

Recall that we spoke about gram equivalent weights in Chapter 4 and about normality and all units of concentration in Chapter 9.

Amphoteric Species ★★★★☆☆

An **amphoteric**, or **amphiprotic**, species is one that reacts like an acid in a basic environment and like a base in an acidic environment. In the Brønsted-Lowry sense, an amphoteric species can either gain or lose a proton. Water is the most common example. When water reacts with a base, it behaves as an acid:

$$H_2O + B^- \leftrightarrow HB + OH^-$$

When water reacts with an acid, it behaves as a base:

$$HA + H_2O \leftrightarrow H_3O^+ + A^-$$

The partially dissociated conjugate base of a polyvalent acid is usually amphoteric (e.g., HSO_4^- can either gain an H^+ to form H_2SO_4 or lose an H^+ to form SO_4^{2-}). The hydroxides of certain metals (e.g., Al, Zn, Pb, and Cr) are also amphoteric. Furthermore, species that can act as either oxidizing or reducing agents (see Chapter 11, Redox Reactions and Electrochemistry) are considered to be amphoteric as well, because by accepting or donating electron pairs, they act as Lewis acids or bases, respectively. A simple way of remembering the meaning of the term is to think of amphibian animals, such as frogs. Amphibians live both on land and in water. Water is the most common amphoteric species, being able to act as both an acid and a base, and *amph*ibians (both land and water living) = *amph*oteric compounds (both acid and base). As you might suspect, this is no mere linguistic coincidence; *amphi* comes from the Greek prefix meaning "on both sides" or "of both kinds."

Titration and Buffers ★★★★☆

Titration is a procedure used to determine the molarity of a known reactant in a solution. There are different types of titrations, including redox, acid-base, and complexometric (metal ion). The MCAT will likely test your understanding of titration procedures and calculations in the context of acid-base solutions. (Metal ion titration may appear on Test Day, but it is less commonly tested and will likely have an informative passage attached.) Titration is a common laboratory procedure, and almost certainly you have performed at least one titration (probably acid-base) in your academic career.

Titrations are accomplished by reacting a known volume of a solution of unknown concentration (called the titrand) with a known volume of a solution of known concentration (called the titrant). In acid-base titration, the **equivalence point** is reached when the number of acid equivalents present in the original solution equals the number of base equivalents added, or vice versa. It is important to emphasize that, while a strong acid/strong base titration will have an equivalence point at pH 7, the equivalence point *need not* always occur at pH 7. Also, when titrating polyprotic acids or bases (discussed later in this chapter), there are several equivalence points, as each different acidic or basic conjugate species is titrated separately. In problems involving titration or neutralization of acids and bases, the equation to remember is

$$N_a V_a = N_b V_b$$

where N_a and N_b are the acid and base normalities, respectively, and V_a and V_b are the volumes of acid and base solutions, respectively. (Note that as long as both volumes use the same units, the units used do not have to be liters.)

The equivalence point in an acid-base titration is determined in two common ways: either evaluated by using a graphical method, plotting the pH of the titrand solution as a function of added titrant by using a **pH meter** (see Figure 10.1), or estimated by watching for a color change of an added **indicator**. Indicators are weak organic acids or bases that have different colors in their protonated and deprotonated states. Because they are highly colored, indicators can be used in low concentrations and therefore do not significantly alter the equivalence point. The indicator must always be a weaker acid or base than the acid or base being titrated; otherwise, the indicator would be titrated first! The point at which the indicator actually changes color is not the equivalence point but rather the **end point**. If the indicator is chosen correctly and the titration is performed well, the volume difference (and therefore the error) between the end point and the equivalence point is usually small and may be corrected for or simply ignored.

Bridge

This formula should remind you of Chapter 9 . . . If not, turn back and take a look!

Bridge

A useful set of compounds (indicators) will change color as it goes between its conjugate acid and base forms:

H–Indicator ↔ H⁺ + Indicator⁻
(color 1)   (color 2)

This allows us to use it to follow a titration, and we can see that since it is an equilibrium process that we can apply Le Châtelier's principle. Adding H⁺ shifts equilibrium to the left. Adding OH⁻ removes H⁺ and therefore shifts equilibrium to the right.

Acid-base titrations can be performed for different combinations of strong and weak acids and bases. The most useful combinations are strong acid/strong base, weak acid/strong base, and weak base/strong acid. Weak acid/weak base titrations can be done but are not usually accurate (and therefore almost never performed), because the pH curve for the titration of a weak acid and weak base lacks the sharp change that normally indicates the equivalence point. Furthermore, indicators are less useful because the pH change is more gradual.

STRONG ACID AND STRONG BASE

Let's consider the titration of 10 mL of a 0.1 N solution of HCl with a 0.1 N solution of NaOH. Plotting the pH of the reaction solution versus the quantity of NaOH added gives the curve shown in Figure 10.1.

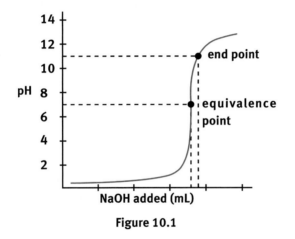

Figure 10.1

> **Key Concept**
>
> Our tug-of-war analogy for a bond between two atoms can be recycled in a different way with titrations. Whichever is stronger (our acid or our base) will determine the equivalence point for the titration. Here they are equal, so the equivalence point is at a neutral pH.

Because HCl is a strong acid and NaOH is a strong base, the equivalence point of the titration will be at pH 7, and the solution will be neutral. Note that the end point shown is close to, but not exactly equal to, the equivalence point; selection of a better indicator, one that changes colors at, say, pH 8, would have given a better approximation. Still, the amount of error introduced by the use of an indicator that changes color around pH 11 rather than, say, pH 8 is not especially significant: a mere fraction of a milliliter of excess NaOH solution.

In the early part of the curve (when little base has been added), the acidic species predominates, so the addition of small amounts of base will not appreciably change either the [OH⁻] or the pH. Similarly, in the last part of the titration curve (when an excess of base has been added), the addition of small amounts of base will not change the [OH⁻] significantly, and the pH remains relatively constant. The addition of base most alters the concentrations of H⁺ and OH⁻ near the equivalence point, and thus the pH changes most drastically in that region. *The equivalence point for strong acid/strong base titration is always at pH 7 (for monovalent species).*

If you are using a pH meter so that you can chart the change in pH as a function of volume of titrant added, you can make a good approximation of the equivalence point by locating the midpoint of the region of the curve with the steepest slope.

WEAK ACID AND STRONG BASE

Titration of a weak acid, HA (e.g., CH_3COOH), with a strong base, such as NaOH, produces the titration curve shown in Figure 10.2.

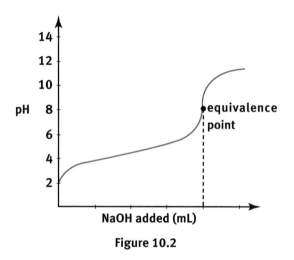

Figure 10.2

Key Concept

Note that any monoprotic weak acid titrated with a strong base will give a similar curve. The exact pH of the equivalence point depends on the identity of the weak acid, but the "tug-of-war" rule tells us it will be above 7.

Let's compare Figure 10.2 with Figure 10.1. The first difference we should notice is that the initial pH of the weak acid solution is greater than the initial pH of the strong acid solution. This makes sense because we know that weak acids don't dissociate to the same degree that strong acids do; therefore, the concentration of H_3O^+ will generally be lower (and pH will be higher) in a solution of weak acid. The second difference we should catch is the shapes of the curves. The pH curve for the weak acid/strong base titration shows a faster rise in pH for given additions of base. The pH changes most significantly early on in the titration, and the equivalence point is in the basic range. The third difference we should notice is the position of the equivalence point. While the equivalence point for strong acid/strong base titration is pH 7, the equivalence point for weak acid/strong base is above 7 (in the basic range). This is because the reaction between the weak acid (HA) and strong base (OH^-) produces a stronger conjugate base (A^-) and a weaker conjugate acid (H_2O). This produces a greater concentration of hydroxide ions than that of hydrogen ions at equilibrium (due to the common ion effect on the auto-ionization of water). *The equivalence point for weak acid/strong base titration is always in the basic range of the pH scale.*

WEAK BASE AND STRONG ACID

The appearance of the titration curve for a weak base titrand and strong acid titrant will look like the "inversion" of the curve for a weak acid titrand and strong base titrant. The initial pH will be in the basic range (typical range: pH 10–12) and will demonstrate a fairly quick drop in pH for additions of the strong acid. The equivalence point will be in the acidic pH range, because the reaction between the weak base and strong acid will produce a stronger conjugate acid and weaker conjugate base. The stronger conjugate acid will result in an equilibrium state with a concentration of hydrogen ions greater than that of the hydroxide ions. *The equivalence point for weak base/strong acid titration is always in the acidic range of the pH scale.*

POLYVALENT ACIDS AND BASES

The titration curve for a polyvalent acid or base looks different from that for a monovalent acid or base. Figure 10.3 shows the titration of Na_2CO_3 with HCl in which the divalent (the term diprotic is equivalent) acid H_2CO_3 is the ultimate product.

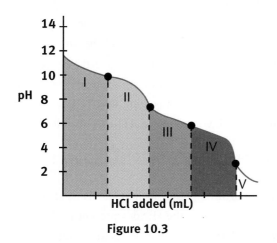

Figure 10.3

In region I, little acid has been added, and the predominant species is CO_3^{2-}. In region II, more acid has been added, and the predominant species are CO_3^{2-} and HCO_3^-, in relatively equal concentrations. The flat part of the curve is the first buffer region (see next section), corresponding to the pK_a of HCO_3^- ($K_a = 5.6 \times 10^{-11}$ implies $pK_a = 10.25$).

Region III contains the equivalence point, at which all of the CO_3^{2-} is finally titrated to HCO_3^-. As the curve illustrates, a rapid change in pH occurs at the equivalence point; in the latter part of region III, the predominant species is HCO_3^-.

In region IV, the acid has neutralized approximately half of the HCO_3^-, and now H_2CO_3 and HCO_3^- are in roughly equal concentrations. This flat region is the second buffer region of the titration curve, corresponding to the pK_a of H_2CO_3 ($K_a = 4.3 \times 10^{-7}$

implies $pK_a = 6.37$). In region V, the equivalence point for the entire titration is reached, as all of the HCO_3^- is finally converted to H_2CO_3. Again, a rapid change in pH is observed near the equivalence point as acid is added.

The titrations of the acidic and basic amino acids (which have acidic or basic side chains, respectively) will show curves similar to the one shown in Figure 10.3. But rather than two equivalence points, there will in fact be three: one corresponding to the titration of the carboxylic acid and a second corresponding to the titration of the amino acid, both of which are attached to the central carbon, and a third corresponding either to the acidic or basic side chain.

BUFFERS

A **buffer solution** consists of a mixture of a weak acid and its salt (which consists of its conjugate base and a cation) or a mixture of a weak base and its salt (which consists of its conjugate acid and an anion). Two examples of buffers that are common in the laboratory and commonly tested on the MCAT are a solution of acetic acid (CH_3COOH) and its salt, sodium acetate ($CH_3COO^-Na^+$), and a solution of ammonia (NH_3) and its salt, ammonium chloride ($NH_4^+Cl^-$). The acetic acid/sodium acetate solution is an acid buffer, and the ammonium chloride/ammonia solution is a base buffer. Buffer solutions have the useful property of resisting changes in pH when small amounts of strong acid or base are added. Consider a buffer solution of acetic acid and sodium acetate (the sodium ion has not been included because it is not involved in the acid-base reaction):

$$CH_3COOH\ (aq) + H_2O\ (l) \leftrightarrow H_3O^+\ (aq) + CH_3COO^-\ (aq)$$

When a small amount of strong base, such as NaOH, is added to the buffer, the OH^- ions from the NaOH react with the H^+ ions present in the solution; subsequently, more acetic acid dissociates (the system shifts to the right), restoring the $[H^+]$. The weak acid component of the buffer acts to neutralize the strong base that has been added. The resulting increase in the concentration of the acetate ion (the conjugate base) does not yield as large an increase in hydroxide ions as the unbuffered strong base would. Thus, the addition of the strong base does not result in a significant increase in $[OH^-]$ and does not appreciably change pH. Likewise, when a small amount of HCl is added to the buffer, H^+ ions from the HCl react with the acetate ions to form acetic acid. Acetic acid is weaker than the added hydrochloric acid (which has been neutralized by the acetate ions), so the increased concentration of acetic acid does not significantly contribute to the hydrogen ion concentration in the solution. Because the buffer maintains $[H^+]$ at relatively constant values, the pH of the solution is relatively unchanged.

In the human body, one of the most important buffers is the H_2CO_3/HCO_3^- conjugate pair in the plasma component of the blood. $CO_2\ (g)$, one of the waste products of cellular respiration, has low solubility in aqueous solutions. The majority of the CO_2 transported from the peripheral tissue to the lungs (where it will be exhaled out) is dissolved in the plasma in a "disguised" form. CO_2 (g) and water react in the following manner:

$$CO_2\ (g) + H_2O\ (l) \leftrightarrow H_2CO_3\ (aq) \leftrightarrow H^+\ (aq) + HCO_3^-\ (aq)$$

Carbonic acid (H_2CO_3) and its conjugate base, bicarbonate (HCO_3^-), form a weak acid buffer for maintaining the pH of the blood within a fairly narrow physiological range. The most important point to notice about this system for pH homeostasis is its direct connection to the respiratory system. In conditions of metabolic acidosis (excess of plasma H^+), for example, the respiratory rate (breathing rate) will increase in order to "blow off" a greater amount of carbon dioxide gas; this causes the system to shift from the right to the left, thereby restoring the normal physiological pCO_2 and in doing so, reducing the $[H^+]$ and buffering against dramatic and dangerous changes to the blood pH. One of the more interesting topics to ponder about the blood buffer system is why a weak acid buffer system was selected (evolutionarily speaking) as a primary mechanism for human blood pH homeostasis at around pH 7.4 (weakly basic). Buffers have a definite and narrow range of optimal buffering capability ($pK_a \pm 1$), and pH 7.4 is actually slightly above the outer limit of buffering capability for the carbonic acid/bicarbonate system ($pK_a = 6.1$). It's an interesting question—and one to which there is an answer—but we don't want to ruin all the surprises of medical school, so we will leave it unanswered for the time being.

You can think of buffer systems as kitchen sponges that soak up strong acids and strong bases to minimize changes in pH for a solution.

The **Henderson-Hasselbalch equation** is used to estimate the pH or pOH of a solution in the buffer region where the concentrations of the species and its conjugate are present in approximately equal concentrations. For a weak acid buffer solution,

$$pH = pK_a + \log \frac{[\text{conjugate base}]}{[\text{weak acid}]}$$

Note that when [conjugate base] = [weak acid] (in a titration, halfway to the equivalent point), the $pH = pK_a$ because $\log 1 = 0$. Buffering capacity is optimal at this pH.

Likewise, for a weak base buffer solution,

$$pOH = pK_b + \log \frac{[\text{conjugate acid}]}{[\text{weak base}]}$$

and $pOH = pK_b$ when [conjugate acid] = [weak base]. Buffering capacity is optimal at this pOH.

Key Concept

The Henderson-Hasselbalch equation is also useful in the creation of buffer solutions other than those formed during the course of a titration. By careful selection of the weak acid (or base) and its salt, a buffer at almost any pH can be produced.

One of the subtleties of buffer systems and Henderson-Hasselbalch calculations that usually goes unnoticed or misunderstood by students is the effect of changing the concentrations of the conjugate pair but not changing the ratio of their concentrations. Clearly, changing the concentrations of the buffer components in such a way that results in a change in their ratio will lead to a change in the pH of the buffer solution. But what about changing the concentrations while maintaining the ratio of the buffer components? For example, what is the effect on the system of doubling the concentrations of the acid and the base (thereby maintaining a constant ratio of the two)? Because we are taking the log of the ratio of the components, the logarithmic value will not change as long as the ratio doesn't change. If the ratio of the buffer components doesn't change, the pH of the buffer solution doesn't change. Nevertheless, something has changed, to be sure. The **buffering capacity**—the size of that kitchen sponge—has changed. Doubling the concentrations of the buffer components produces a buffer solution with twice the buffering capacity. The kitchen sponge is twice as big and can soak up twice as much acid or base.

Real World

Blood pH is maintained in a relatively small range (slightly above 7) by a bicarbonate buffer system. Too great a change in either direction would lead to acidosis or alkalosis.

Conclusion

In this chapter, we have reviewed the important principles of acid-base chemistry. We clarified the differences among the three definitions of acids and bases, including the nomenclature of some common Arrhenius acids. We investigated important properties of acids and bases, including the important acid-base behavior of water (auto-ionization) and hydrogen ion equilibria. We explained the mathematics of the pH and pOH logarithmic scales and demonstrated a useful Test Day shortcut for approximating the logarithmic value of hydrogen ion or hydroxide ion concentrations. Strong acids and bases are defined as compounds that completely dissociate in aqueous solutions, and weak acids and bases are compounds that dissociate only partially (to an equilibrium state). We discussed neutralization and salt formation upon reaction of acids and bases, and finally, we applied our fundamental understanding of acid-base reactivity to titrations, useful for determining the concentration of a known acid or base solution, and to weak acid and weak base buffers, useful for minimizing changes in pH upon addition of strong acid or base.

Wow! This was a long chapter, packed with a lot of concepts and information. You've certainly earned a break after this. You've just accomplished a major task in the overall effort to earn points on Test Day. You may not understand everything that you've just read, and you probably don't remember everything—and that's okay. Now that you've read through these concepts, take some time to work through some of your MCAT practice passages and questions related to these topics so that the concepts settle and solidify. If you find that you need to review for a second or third time some of the discussion points related to acid-base chemistry, we're always here for you in these pages.

If you've been paying attention (and we're sure you have been), you've probably noticed that you're now one chapter away from completing this review of general chemistry. While we don't want to offer our congratulations prematurely, we want to acknowledge all the hard work you've invested in this process. Keep it up: Success on Test Day is within your grasp!

CONCEPTS TO REMEMBER

☐ There are three definitions of acids and bases: Arrhenius—acids produce hydrogen ions, and bases produce hydroxide ions in aqueous solutions; Brønsted-Lowry—acids donate hydrogen ions, and bases accept hydrogen ions; and Lewis—acids accept electron pairs, and bases donate electron pairs.

☐ Water is an amphoteric species (both acid and base) and auto-ionizes to produce equilibrium concentrations of hydrogen ions and hydroxide ions equal to 10^{-7} M at 298 K. The K_w for water at 298 K is 10^{-14}. All aqueous acid or base solutions are defined by the equilibrium constant for water.

☐ pH and pOH scales are logarithmic and express the negative log of the molar concentration of the hydrogen ions or hydroxide ions, respectively. For aqueous solutions at 298 K, a pH less than 7 is acidic, and a pH greater than 7 is basic; a pH 7 is neutral.

☐ Strong acids and bases dissociate completely in aqueous solutions. Examples of strong acids include HCl, H_2SO_4, and HNO_3. Examples of strong bases include $NaOH$ and KOH.

☐ Weak acids and bases dissociate incompletely in aqueous solutions. They have K_a's or K_b's less than 1. Examples of weak acids include CH_3COOH, H_2CO_3, and H_2O. Examples of weak bases include NH_3 and H_2O.

☐ Brønsted-Lowry acid-base reactions always involve chemical pairs called conjugates: Strong acid produces weak conjugate base; strong base produces weak conjugate acid; a weaker acid produces a stronger conjugate base; a weaker base produces a stronger conjugate acid.

☐ An equivalent is equal to one mole of charge (hydrogen ions or hydroxide ions). Equivalent weight is the mass in grams of an acid or base compound that yields one acid or base equivalent (i.e., one mole of charge). Normality is the number of acid or base equivalents per liter of solution.

☐ Acid-base titration is used to determine the molar concentration of a known acid or base solution. The equivalence point is the point in the titration at which the equivalents of acid equal the equivalents of base.

☐ Strong acid/strong base titration has an equivalence point at pH 7. Strong acid/weak base titration has an equivalence point at pH less than 7. Strong base/weak acid titration has an equivalence point at pH greater than 7. Indicators approximate the equivalence point by a steady color change at end point.

☐ Buffers are weak acid/conjugate base or weak base/conjugate acid systems that act to absorb strong acids or bases from solutions, thereby minimizing pH changes within the buffered region. Buffers are most effective within ±1 of pK_a or pK_b.

EQUATIONS TO REMEMBER

☐ $K_w = [H_3O^+][OH^-] = 10^{-14}$ at 298 K

☐ $pH = -\log[H^+] = \log\left(\dfrac{1}{[H^+]}\right)$ and $pOH = -\log[OH^-] = \log\left(\dfrac{1}{[OH^-]}\right)$

☐ $pH + pOH = 14$ (for aqueous solutions at 298 K)

☐ $K_a = \dfrac{[H_3O^+][A^-]}{[HA]}$ and $K_b = \dfrac{[B^+][OH^-]}{[BOH]}$

☐ $K_a \times K_b = K_w = 10^{-14}$

☐ $N_a V_a = N_b V_b$

☐ $pH = pK_a + \log \dfrac{[\text{conjugate base}]}{[\text{weak acid}]}$

☐ $pOH = pK_b + \log \dfrac{[\text{conjugate acid}]}{[\text{weak base}]}$

Practice Questions

1. Which of the following is not a Brønsted-Lowry base?

A.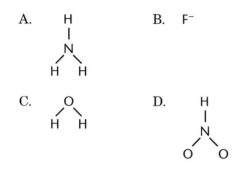
B. F⁻

C.
D.

2. What is the pH of a solution containing 5 mM H_2SO_4?

A. 1
B. 1.5
C. 2
D. 4

3. Which of the following is chloric acid?

A. $HClO_3$
B. ClO_3^-
C. $HClO_2$
D. $HClO$

4. Which of the following bases is the weakest?

A. KOH
B. NH_3
C. CH_3NH_2
D. $Ca(OH)_2$

5. The function of a buffer is to

A. speed up reactions between acids and bases.
B. resist changes in pH when small amounts of acid or base are added.
C. slow down reactions between acids and bases.
D. maintain a neutral pH.

6. What is the pH of the following solution shown below?

$pK_b = 3.45$	$[NH_4^+] = 70$ mM	$[NH_3] = 712$ mM

A. 4.45
B. 7.55
C. 11.56
D. 10.65

Answer questions 7–9 based on the titration curve of acid X shown below:

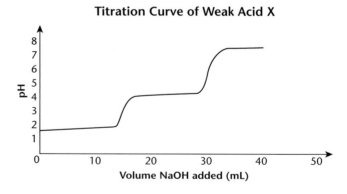

7. What is the approximate value of the first pK_a?

A. 1.9
B. 2.9
C. 3.8
D. 4.1

8. Where is the second equivalence point?

A. pH = 3.0

B. pH = 4.1

C. pH = 5.9

D. pH = 7.2

9. What is the approximate value of the second pK_a?

A. 3.6

B. 4.1

C. 5.5

D. 7.2

10. What is the approximate gram equivalent weight of phosphoric acid?

A. 25 g

B. 33 g

C. 49 g

D. 98 g

11. What is the $[H^+]$ of a 2 M aqueous solution of a weak acid "HXO_2" with $K_a = 3.2 \times 10^{-5}$?

A. 8.0×10^{-3} M

B. 6.4×10^{-5} M

C. 1.3×10^{-4} M

D. 4.0×10^{-3} M

12. A solution is prepared with an unknown concentration of a theoretical compound whose K_a is exactly 1.0. What is the pH of this solution?

A. Higher than 7

B. Exactly 7

C. Lower than 7

D. Impossible to determine

13. Which of the following is NOT a characteristic of an amphoteric species?

A. Can act as a base or an acid, depending on its environment.

B. Can act as an oxidizing or reducing agent, depending on its environment.

C. Is always protic.

D. Is always a nonpolar species.

14. What is the approximate pH of a 1.2×10^{-5} M aqueous solution of NaOH?

A. 4.85

B. 7.50

C. 9.15

D. 12.45

Small Group Questions

1. The Henderson-Hasselbach equation cannot be applied to all acids and bases. Explain why not.

2. Phosphoric acid is a polyprotic acid with K_a's of 7.1×10^{-3}, 6.3×10^{-8}, and 4.5×10^{-13}. Estimate its pK_b values.

Explanations to Practice Questions

1. D

A Brønsted-Lowry base is defined as a proton acceptor. (A), (B), and (C) can each accept a proton. (D), HNO_2, cannot.

2. C

First, we'll convert the concentration to 5×10^{-3} M. Next, since sulfuric acid is a strong acid, we can assume that both protons will dissociate. So the concentration of hydrogen ions is really $2 \times 5 \times 10^{-3}$, which simplifies to 1×10^{-2}. The equation for pH is $pH = -\log[H^+]$. If $[H^+] = 1 \times 10^{-2}$ M, then $pH = 2$.

3. A

Answering this question is simply a matter of knowing nomenclature. Acids ending in *–ic* are derivatives of anions ending in *–ate,* while acids ending in *–ous* are derivatives of anions ending in *–ite*. ClO_3^- is named chlorate because it has more oxygen than the other occuring ion, ClO_2^-, which is named chlorite. Therefore, $HClO_3$ is chloric acid.

4. B

Members of the IA and IIA columns on the periodic table combined with OH^- are always strong bases. This means (A) and (D) can be eliminated. (B) and (C) are both weak bases, but (B) is weaker than (C) because a positive charge would sit solely on ammonia's nitrogen. Methylamine, on the other hand, has a neighboring carbon (remember, alkyl groups are electron donating), which will help reduce the positive charge's stress on nitrogen.

5. B

The purpose of a buffer is to resist changes in the pH of a reaction. Buffers will not affect the kinetics of a reaction, so (A) and (C) are wrong. (D) is correct only in specific circumstances that require a pH of 7. Many natural buffer systems maintain pHs in the acidic or basic ranges.

6. C

The question is asking for pH, but because of the information given, we must first find the pOH and then subtract it from 14 to get the pH. The equation for pOH is:

$pOH = pK_b + \log\dfrac{[\text{conjugate acid}]}{[\text{weak base}]}$. When the given values are substituted into this equation ([conjugate acid] = 70mM; [weak base] = 712mM), we find that pOH = 2.44, so the pH = $14 - 2.44 = 11.56$

7. A

The first pK_a in this curve can be estimated by eye. It is located between the starting point (when no base had been added yet) and the first equivalence point. This point is approximately at 7–8 mL added, which corresponds to a pH of approximately 1.9. Notice that this region experiences very little change in pH. This is the defining characteristic of a buffer zone!

8. C

The second equivalence point is the midpoint of the second quick increase in slope. This corresponds approximately to pH = 5.9.

9. B

The value of the second pK_a is found at the midpoint between the first and second equivalence points. In this curve, that corresponds to pH = 4.1. Just like the first pKa, it is in the center of a flat buffering region.

10. B

Gram equivalent weight is the weight (in grams) that would release 1 acid equivalent. Because H_3PO_4 contains 3 acid equivalents, we find the gram equivalent weight by dividing the mass of one mole of the species by 3. Therefore, (B) is the correct answer.

11. A

This question requires the application of the acid dissociation formula:

$$K_a = \frac{[H^+][x^-]}{Hx}$$

Weak acids do not dissociate completely; therefore, all three species that appear in the formula will be present in solution. Hydrogen ions and conjugate base anions dissociate in equal amounts, so $[H^+] = [X^-]$. We don't know exactly how much they'll dissociate though, so we'll just stick in an x for both of those species. How much HX do we have? The original concentration minus x.

$$K_a = \frac{[x][x]}{[2M - x]}$$

Each of these x terms is quite small. The numerator becomes more significant because we'll end up with x^2, but we can simply ignore the x in the denominator. Let's also plug in our K_a value:

$$3.2 \times 10^{-5}\,M = \frac{x^2}{2M}$$

Now all we have to do is isolate x, which leads us to find that the $[H^+]$ is 8.0×10^{-3} M.

12. C

A higher K_a implies a stronger acid. Consider the following theoretical reaction, which defines the K_a of acid HA, $HA \leftrightharpoons H^+ + A^-$. In such a reaction, $K_a = [H^+][A^-] / [HA]$. A K_a near 1 therefore implies that there are enough hydrogen ions present to affect the pH significantly. Weak acids usually have a K_a that is several orders of magnitude below 1. Yet a detailed understanding of K_a is not necessary to answer this question. According to the pH scale, which sets the K_a of water at 10^{-7}, a compound with a K_a above 10^{-7} is acidic; even if the acid is very weak, it will still cause the pH to drop below 7.

13. D

An amphoteric species is one that can act either as an acid or a base, depending on its environment. Proton transfers are classic redox reactions, so (A) and (B) are true. (C) must be true because, by definition, an amphoteric molecule needs to have a proton to give up in order to act like an acid. (D) is false, and thus the correct answer, because amphoteric species can be either polar or nonpolar in nature. Some examples: HSO_4^-, NH_3, H_2O.

14. C

$$NaOH \leftrightharpoons Na^+ + OH^-$$

The balanced equation shows the same coefficients in front of each of the three species. So if the initial concentration of NaOH is 1.2×10^{-5}, then the concentration of Na^+ and OH^- must be also, because NaOH will completely dissociate.

Next, we'll find the pOH from $[OH^-]$. The pOH lies between 4 and 5. How did we find that? Well, 1.2×10^{-5} is between 10^{-5} and 10^{-4}. So its logarithm is between 4 and 5. Let's estimate 4.8.

We're ready to calculate pH from pOH.

$$pH = 14 - pOH = 14 - 4.8 = 9.2.$$

(C) is very close to 9.2, so it must be the right answer.

Redox Reactions and Electrochemistry

The mitochondria are the power company of your body. No, this doesn't mean that they send vaguely hostile letters threatening to cut off your electricity if you don't pay your overdue bill (although cells certainly do send loud and clear messages when there is an oxygen debt). Rather, like actual power companies, the primary purpose of the mitochondria is to manufacture a deliverable and usable form of energy. Certainly by now you are generally well aware of the complex processes by which the potential energy of chemical bonds, which is really just electric potential energy, in food molecules (carbohydrates, amino acids, and lipids) is converted into the potential energy of the phosphate bond in adenosine triphosphate (ATP). ATP is then delivered to different regions of the cell, where it is used to energize all of the processes essential to the maintenance of life.

The mitochondria generate tremendous amounts of ATP. (In humans, the average daily turnover of ATP is more than 50 kilograms!) Without a continuous supply and replenishment of ATP, we couldn't live for even a second in its absence: It powers the contraction of our heart muscle and maintains the membrane potential essential for neurological function (just to name a couple of life-essential roles of ATP). How do the mitochondria manufacture these packets of life-sustaining energy? You have read of the double-membrane structure of the mitochondria and their electron transport chain and F_1F_o ATP synthase. You have learned about oxidative phosphorylation and the role of O_2. But has it ever occurred to you that the mitochondria in more or less literal ways act as the batteries of the cell? Have you ever wondered at the similarity of the phrase *proton motive force* to another term that you have learned and used in the context of electrochemistry and circuits? Are proton motive force (pmf) and electromotive force (emf) the same thing or, at the very least, similar in nature?

In fact, the mitochondria do function in ways similar to batteries: There is separation and buildup of a charge gradient; there is potential difference (voltage) between separated compartments; there is movement of charge and dissipation of energy. We could say that mitochondria function in ways most similar to a particular type of electrochemical cell called the concentration cell. In both concentration cells and mitochondria, a concentration gradient of ions between two separated compartments connected to each other by some means of charge conduction establishes an electrical potential difference (a voltage). This voltage, called electromotive force in a concentration cell and proton motive force in the mitochondria, provides the "pressure to move" charge (that is, creates current) from one compartment to the other. In the concentration cell, a redox reaction takes place, and electrons move in the direction that causes the concentration gradient to be dissipated. In the mitochondria, the charge buildup is in the form of a hydrogen ion (proton) gradient between the intermembrane space and the matrix. Embedded in the inner membrane is the F_1F_o ATP synthase protein, which serves the dual role of proton channel (the conductive pathway) and catalyst (the electric motor) for the formation of the high-energy phosphate bond of ATP. As the hydrogen ions flow down their chemical-electrical gradient, energy is dissipated (remember, the positively charged ions are moving from high potential to low potential), and this energy is harnessed by the ATP synthase for the formation of ATP.

In this, the final chapter of our review of general chemistry for the MCAT, we will focus our attention on the study of the movement of electrons in chemical reactions. Such reactions are called oxidations and reductions, and because they always occur in pairs, they are usually referred to, in shorthand, as redox reactions. Electrochemistry is the study of the relationships between chemical reactions and electrical energy. We will learn of the ways in which the principles of electrochemistry can be applied to create different types of electrochemical cells, including galvanic (voltaic), electrolytic, and concentration cells. Regarding the thermodynamics of electrochemistry, we will focus on the significance of reduction potentials and examine the relationship among electromotive force, the equilibrium constant, and Gibbs function.

Oxidation-Reduction Reactions ★★★★★★

Reactions that involve the transfer of electrons from one chemical species to another can be classified as oxidation-reduction reactions. Now, that's quite a mouthful to say, so these reactions are commonly called "redox" reactions as a shorthand way of noting that oxidation and reduction are always coupled.

OXIDATION AND REDUCTION

The law of conservation of charge states that an electrical charge can be neither created nor destroyed. Thus, an isolated loss or gain of electrons cannot occur; **oxidation** (loss of electrons) and **reduction** (gain of electrons) must occur simultaneously, resulting in an electron transfer called a **redox reaction**. An **oxidizing agent** causes another atom in a redox reaction to undergo oxidation and is itself reduced. A **reducing agent** causes the other atom to be reduced and is itself oxidized. There are various memory devices designed to help you remember these terms. One that is especially well known is OIL RIG, which stands for "Oxidation Is Loss; Reduction Is Gain."

ASSIGNING OXIDATION NUMBERS

It is important, of course, to know which atom is oxidized and which is reduced. **Oxidation numbers** are assigned to atoms in order to keep track of the redistribution of electrons during chemical reactions. From the oxidation numbers of the reactants and products, it is possible to determine how many electrons are gained or lost by each atom. The oxidation number of an atom in a compound is assigned according to the following rules:

Mnemonic

OIL RIG stands for "Oxidation Is Loss, Reduction Is Gain," because, as we do often, we are talking about those all-important electrons. Alternatively, reduction is just what it sounds like: reduction of *charge*.

1. **The oxidation number of free elements is zero.** For example, the atoms in N_2, P_4, S_8, and He all have oxidation numbers of zero.

2. **The oxidation number for a monatomic ion is equal to the charge of the ion.** For example, the oxidation numbers for Na^+, Cu^{2+}, Fe^{3+}, Cl^-, and N^{3-} are +1, +2, +3, −1, and −3, respectively.

3. **The oxidation number of each Group IA element in a compound is +1. The oxidation number of each Group IIA element in a compound is +2.**

4. **The oxidation number of each Group VIIA element in a compound is −1, except when combined with an element of higher electronegativity.** For example, in HCl, the oxidation number of Cl is −1; in HOCl, however, the oxidation number of Cl is +1.

5. **The oxidation number of hydrogen is −1 in compounds with less electronegative elements than hydrogen (Groups IA and IIA).** Examples include NaH and CaH_2. The more common oxidation number of hydrogen is +1.

6. **In most compounds, the oxidation number of oxygen is −2.** This is not the case, however, in molecules such as OF_2. Here, because F is more electronegative than O, the oxidation number of oxygen is +2. Also, in peroxides, such as BaO_2, the oxidation number of O is −1 instead of −2 because of the structure of the peroxide ion, $[O-O]^{2-}$. (Note that Ba, a Group IIA element, cannot be a +4 cation.)

7. **The sum of the oxidation numbers of all the atoms present in a neutral compound is zero. The sum of the oxidation numbers of the atoms present in a polyatomic ion is equal to the charge of the ion.** Thus, for SO_4^{2-}, the sum of the oxidation numbers must be −2.

Example: Assign oxidation numbers to the atoms in the following reaction in order to determine the oxidized and reduced species and the oxidizing and reducing agents.

$$SnCl_2 + PbCl_4 \rightarrow SnCl_4 + PbCl_2$$

Solution: All these species are neutral, so the oxidation numbers of each compound must add up to zero. In $SnCl_2$, because there are two chlorines present and chlorine has an oxidation number of −1, Sn must have an oxidation number of +2. Similarly, the oxidation number of Sn in $SnCl_4$ is +4; the oxidation number of Pb is +4 in $PbCl_4$ and +2 in $PbCl_2$. Notice that the oxidation number of Sn goes from +2 to +4; it loses electrons and thus is oxidized, making it the reducing agent. Because the oxidation number of Pb has decreased from +4 to +2, it has gained electrons and been reduced. Pb is the oxidizing agent. The sum of the charges on both sides of the reaction is equal to zero, so charge has been conserved.

MCAT Expertise

Don't forget that you have the periodic table available to you on Test Day, so use it to organize your thoughts with regard to these rules rather than memorizing these on their own. Beware of transition metals but realize we can often figure their oxidation by default.

Key Concept

The conventions of formula writing put cation first and anion second. Thus NaH implies H^- while HCl implies H^+. So use the way the compound is written on the MCAT along with the periodic table to help you determine oxidation states.

BALANCING REDOX REACTIONS

Okay, okay. We know you don't like balancing redox reactions. We know that there are many steps involved and that it can sometimes be difficult to remember how to balance not only mass but charge as well. And we recognize the unfortunate fact that we've just presented you with seven rules of assigning oxidation numbers to understand and remember. And now we're giving you five steps to remember. And— hey, don't think we didn't just catch you rolling your eyes! Sigh all you want, but the truth of the matter is, the process of balancing redox reactions is tested on the MCAT. We might suggest that balancing redox reactions is sort of like balancing a checkbook, but we are hesitant to do so for at least two reasons: (1) balancing a checkbook isn't exactly "fun," and (2) aside from accountants (for whom it is simply part of their nature), we don't know anyone who actually balances his checkbook.

By assigning oxidation numbers to the reactants and products, you can determine how many moles of each species are required for conservation of charge and mass, which is necessary to balance the equation. To balance a redox reaction, both the net charge and the number of atoms must be equal on both sides of the equation. The most common method for balancing redox equations is the **half-reaction method**, also known as the **ion-electron method**, in which the equation is separated into two half-reactions—the oxidation part and the reduction part. Each half-reaction is balanced separately, and they are then added to give a balanced overall reaction. As we review the steps involved, let's consider a redox reaction between $KMnO_4$ and HI in an acidic solution.

$$MnO_4^- + I^- \rightarrow I_2 + Mn^{2+}$$

Step 1: Separate the two half-reactions.

$$I^- \rightarrow I_2$$
$$MnO_4^- \rightarrow Mn^{2+}$$

Step 2: Balance the atoms of each half-reaction. First, balance all atoms except H and O. Next, in an acidic solution, add H_2O to balance the O atoms and then add H^+ to balance the H atoms. (In a basic solution, use OH^- and H_2O to balance the O's and H's.)

To balance the iodine atoms, place a coefficient of 2 before the I^- ion.

$$2\,I^- \rightarrow I_2$$

For the permanganate half-reaction, Mn is already balanced. Next, balance the oxygens by adding 4 H_2O to the right side.

$$MnO_4^- \rightarrow Mn^{2+} + 4\,H_2O$$

MCAT Expertise

Methodical, step-by-step approaches like this one are great for the MCAT. Most often, you will not have to get through all of these steps before you can narrow down your answer choices. Often you will be able to find the correct answer halfway through the steps.

Finally, add H^+ to the left side to balance the 4 H_2Os. These two half-reactions are now balanced.

$$MnO_4^- + 8\ H^+ \rightarrow Mn^{2+} + 4\ H_2O$$

Step 3: Balance the charges of each half-reaction. The reduction half-reaction must consume the same number of electrons as are supplied by the oxidation half. For the oxidation reaction, add 2 electrons to the right side of the reaction:

$$2\ I^- \rightarrow I_2 + 2\ e^-$$

For the reduction reaction, a charge of +2 must exist on both sides. Add 5 electrons to the left side of the reaction to accomplish this:

$$5\ e^- + 8\ H^+ + MnO_4^- \rightarrow Mn^{2+} + 4\ H_2O$$

Next, both half-reactions must have the same number of electrons so that they will cancel. Multiply the oxidation half by 5 and the reduction half by 2.

$$5(2I^- \rightarrow I_2 + 2e^-)$$
$$2(5e^- + 8H^+ + MnO_4^- \rightarrow Mn^{2+} + 4\ H_2O)$$

Step 4: Add the half-reactions:

$$10\ I^- \rightarrow 5\ I_2 + 10\ e^-$$
$$16\ H^+ + 2\ MnO_4^- + 10\ e^- \rightarrow 2\ Mn^{2+} + 8\ H_2O$$

The final equation is this:

$$10\ I^- + 10\ e^- + 16\ H^+ + 2\ MnO_4^- \rightarrow 5\ I_2 + 2\ Mn^{2+} + 10\ e^- + 8\ H_2O$$

To get the overall equation, cancel out the electrons and any H_2Os, H^+s, or OH^-s that appear on both sides of the equation.

$$10\ I^- + 16\ H^+ + 2\ MnO_4^- \rightarrow 5\ I_2 + 2\ Mn^{2+} + 8\ H_2O$$

Step 5: Finally, confirm that mass and charge are balanced. There is a +4 net charge on each side of the reaction equation, and the atoms are stoichiometrically balanced.

Electrochemical Cells ★★★☆☆

Now we get to the fun part of electrochemistry! Here, we will review the way in which redox reactions can be used to supply energy that can be used to do work. We'll also cover the way in which energy can be used to drive certain useful redox reactions. You don't have to look too hard to find a battery in your immediate surroundings: a flashlight, your watch, the smoke detector, a cell phone, your cordless toothbrush—all these devices contain and run on batteries. You've even got lots of little chemiosmotic "batteries," as we discussed in the introduction, inside your cells.

Electrochemical cells are contained systems in which redox reactions occur. There are three types of electrochemical cells, **galvanic cells** (also known as **voltaic cells**), **electrolytic cells**, and **concentration cells**. Spontaneous reactions occur in galvanic cells and concentration cells, and nonspontaneous reactions in electrolytic cells. All three types contain **electrodes** at which oxidation and reduction occur. For all electrochemical cells, the electrode at which oxidation occurs is called the **anode**, and the electrode where reduction occurs is called the **cathode**. Furthermore, we can also generally state that for all electrochemical cells, the movement of electrons is from anode to cathode and current i runs from cathode to anode.

GALVANIC (VOLTAIC) CELLS

All of the nonrechargeable batteries that you have lying around your house or apartment, in battery-operated devices or stored away in their packaging along with the butter and cream cheese in your refrigerator (yes, many people do keep their batteries in the refrigerator, and there is some thermodynamic justification for the practice—although we can't prove that there is any particular benefit to keeping them with the butter and cream cheese—but we digress) are **galvanic cells**, also called **voltaic cells**. Realizing this, you will have no problem remembering the key principles of the operation of galvanic cells. Don't remember whether galvanic cells house a spontaneous or nonspontaneous redox reaction? Just think about the fact that you use household batteries to supply energy to do something useful, like power a flashlight. If energy is being supplied by the battery, then it must be the case that the redox reaction taking place is giving off energy, which means the reaction's free energy must be decreasing ($-\Delta G$) and the reaction must, therefore, be spontaneous. Don't remember whether galvanic cells have positive or negative electromotive forces? Again, just think about the battery in the flashlight. You know (from the thought sequence just described) that the change in Gibbs function is negative; emf always has the sign opposite to the change in free energy.

Let's examine the "inner workings" of a galvanic (voltaic) cell. Two **electrodes** of distinct chemical identity are placed in separate compartments, which we call

half-cells. The two electrodes are connected to each other by a conductive material, such as a copper wire. Along the wire, you may find various other components of a circuit, such as resistors or capacitors, but for now, let's keep our focus on the battery itself. Surrounding each of the electrodes is an electrolyte solution (aqueous), composed of cations and anions. As in Figure 11.1, the illustration of a **Daniell cell**, the cations in each of the two half-cell solutions may be of the same element as the respective metal electrode. Connecting the two solutions is a structure called the salt bridge, which consists of an inert salt.

When the electrodes are connected to each other by a conductive material, charge will begin to flow as the result of a redox reaction that is taking place between the two half-cells. The redox reaction in a galvanic cell is spontaneous, and therefore the change in Gibbs function for the reaction is negative ($-\Delta G$). As the spontaneous redox reaction proceeds (toward equilibrium, which we'll discuss next), the movement of charge (electrons) results in a conversion of electric potential energy into kinetic energy (the electrons are moving, after all, and small as they are, electrons do have mass). By separating the reduction and oxidation half-reactions into two compartments, we are able to harness this energy and use it to do work by connecting various electrical machines or devices into the circuit between the two electrodes. If you've ever stuck a 9-volt battery (the rectangular type with the + and − ends on the same side) to your tongue, you know full well the reality of energy transfer by redox reaction. If you've never stuck a 9-volt battery to your tongue, we recommend that you consider this an experience you can live without. Seriously, don't try it.

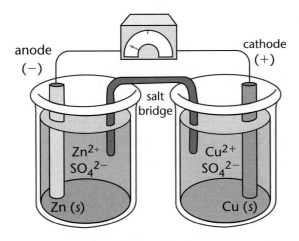

Figure 11.1

In the Daniell cell, a zinc bar is placed in an aqueous $ZnSO_4$ solution, and a copper bar is placed in an aqueous $CuSO_4$ solution. The anode of this cell is the zinc bar where Zn (s) is oxidized to Zn^{2+} (aq). The cathode is the copper bar, and it is the site of the reduction of Cu^{2+} (aq) to Cu (s). The half-cell reactions are written as follows:

$$Zn\ (s) \rightarrow Zn^{2+}\ (aq) + 2\ e^- \qquad (anode)$$
$$Cu^{2+}\ (aq) + 2\ e^- \rightarrow Cu\ (s) \qquad (cathode)$$

If the two half-cells were not separated, the Cu^{2+} ions would react directly with the zinc bar, and no useful electrical work would be obtained. Since the solutions (and electrodes) are physically separated, they must be connected to complete the circuit. Without connection, the electrons from the zinc oxidation half-reaction would not be able to get to the copper ions; thus, a wire (or other conductor) is necessary. However, if only a wire were provided for this electron flow, the reaction would soon cease, because an excess negative charge would build up in the solution surrounding the cathode and an excess positive charge would build up in the solution surrounding the anode. Eventually, the excessive charge accumulation would provide a counter voltage large enough to prevent the redox reaction from taking place, and the current would cease. This charge gradient is dissipated by the presence of a **salt bridge**, which permits the exchange of cations and anions. The salt bridge contains an inert electrolyte, usually KCl or NH_4NO_3, whose ions will not react with the electrodes or with the ions in solution. At the same time that the anions from the salt bridge (e.g., Cl^-) diffuse into the $ZnSO_4$ solution to balance out the charge of the newly created Zn^{2+} ions, the cations of the salt bridge (e.g., K^+) flow into the $CuSO_4$ solution to balance out the charge of the SO_4^{2-} ions left in solution when the Cu^{2+} ions are reduced to Cu and precipitate out of solution ("plate out") onto the copper cathode.

During the course of the reaction, electrons flow from the zinc bar (anode) through the wire and the voltmeter (if one is connected) toward the copper bar (cathode). The anions (Cl^-) flow externally (via the salt bridge) into the $ZnSO_4$, and the cations (K^+) flow into the $CuSO_4$. This flow depletes the salt bridge and, along with the finite quantity of Cu^{2+} in the solution, accounts for the relatively short lifetime of the cell.

A **cell diagram** is a shorthand notation representing the reactions in an electrochemical cell. A cell diagram for the Daniell cell is as follows:

$$Zn\ (s)\ |\ Zn^{2+}\ (x M\ SO_4^{2-})\ ||\ Cu^{2+}\ (y M\ SO_4^{2-})\ |\ Cu\ (s)$$

The following rules are used in constructing a cell diagram:

1. The reactants and products are always listed from left to right in this form:

    anode | anode solution || cathode solution | cathode

2. A single vertical line indicates a phase boundary.

3. A double vertical line indicates the presence of a salt bridge or some other type of barrier.

Key Concept

The purpose of the salt bridge is to exchange anions and cations to balance, or dissipate, newly generated charges.

MCAT Expertise

Know the shorthand notation for cells because it is possible that on Test Day they will not spell it all out for us.

ELECTROLYTIC CELLS

Electrolytic cells, in almost all of their characteristics and behavior, are the opposite of galvanic cells. Whereas galvanic cells house spontaneous redox reactions, which when allowed to proceed, generate current and deliver electrical energy, electrolytic cells house nonspontaneous reactions, which require the input of energy to proceed. Galvanic cells supply energy; electrolytic cells consume it. The change in Gibbs function for the redox reaction of an electrolytic cell is positive. The particular type of redox reaction that is driven by the external voltage source is called electrolysis, in which chemical compounds are decomposed. For example, electrolytic cells can be used to drive the nonspontaneous decomposition of water into oxygen and hydrogen gas. Another example, the electrolysis of molten NaCl, is illustrated in Figure 11.2.

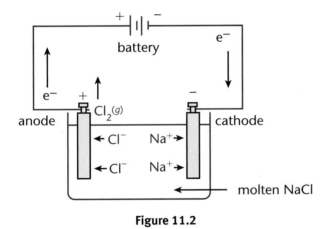

Figure 11.2

> **Mnemonic**
>
> *An*ions are negatively charged and travel to the *an*ode. *Cat*ions are positively charged and travel to the *cat*hode. The same principles apply to electrophoresis, a laboratory technique used to purify, separate, or identify compounds.

In this electrolytic cell, molten NaCl is decomposed into Cl_2 (*g*) and Na (*l*). The external voltage source ("battery" in Figure 11.2) supplies energy sufficient to drive a redox reaction in the direction that is thermodynamically unfavorable (i.e., nonspontaneous). In this example, Na^+ ions migrate toward the cathode, where they are reduced to Na (*l*). At the same time, Cl^- ions migrate toward the anode, where they are oxidized to Cl_2 (*g*). You'll notice that the half-reactions do not need to be separated into different compartments because the desired reaction is nonspontaneous. Furthermore, irrespective of the fact that a nonspontaneous reaction is being driven by an external voltage, it is still the case—as it always is for every type of electrochemical cell—that oxidation occurs at the anode and reduction occurs at the cathode. (Note that sodium is a liquid at the temperature of molten NaCl; it is also less dense than the molten salt and, thus, is easily removed as it floats to the top of the reaction vessel.) This cell is used in industry as the major means of sodium and chlorine production. You may be wondering why industry goes to all this trouble to produce these compounds and why these compounds just can't be dug up or pumped up from somewhere, rather than manufactured. Well, think about the thermodynamics of electrolysis. Energy is supplied to drive a nonspontaneous process. This means that the products of the reaction are not naturally favored. In fact—and we've mentioned this before (see Chapter 2, The Periodic Table)—sodium and chlorine are never found naturally in their elemental form because they are so reactive. So before we can use elemental sodium or chlorine gas, we have to make it ourselves first.

Michael Faraday was the first to define certain quantitative principles governing the behavior of electrolytic cells. He theorized that the amount of chemical change induced in an electrolytic cell is directly proportional to the number of moles of electrons that are exchanged during a redox reaction. The number of moles exchanged can be determined from the balanced half-reaction. In general, for a reaction that involves the transfer of n electrons per atom, M,

$$M^{n+} + ne^- \rightarrow M\ (s)$$

According to this equation, one mole of M(s) will be produced if n moles of electrons are supplied. Additionally, the number of moles of electrons needed to produce a certain amount of M(s) can now be related to the measurable electrical property of charge. One electron carries a charge of 1.6×10^{-19} coulombs (C). The charge carried by one mole of electrons can be calculated by multiplying this number by Avogadro's number, as follows:

$$(1.6 \times 10^{-19}\ C/e^-)(6.022 \times 10^{23}\ e^-/mol\ e^-) = 96,487\ C/mol\ e^-$$

This number is called **Faraday's constant,** and one **faraday (F)** is equivalent to the amount of charge contained in one mole of electrons (1 F = 96,487 coulombs, or J/V) or one equivalent. On the MCAT, you should round up this number to 100,000 C/mol e⁻ to make calculations more manageable.

CONCENTRATION CELLS

A **concentration cell** is a special type of voltaic cell: two half-cells connected by a conductive material, allowing a spontaneous redox reaction to proceed, generating a current and delivering energy. Just like a galvanic cell, the concentration cell houses a redox reaction that has a negative ΔG. The distinguishing characteristic of a concentration cell is in its design: The electrodes are chemically identical. For example, if both electrodes are copper metal (they are chemically identical), they have the same reduction potential so current is generated as a function of a concentration gradient established between the two solutions surrounding the electrodes. The concentration gradient results in a potential difference between the two compartments and drives the movement of electrons in the direction that results in equilibration of the ion gradient. Current will cease when the concentrations of ion species in the

Key Concept

$(1.6 \times 10^{-19})(6.022 \times 10^{23}) = 96,487$ C/mol e⁻ (~10^5 C/mol e⁻)

This number is called **Faraday's constant,** and one **faraday (F)** is equivalent to the amount of charge contained in one mole of electrons (1 F = 96,487 coulombs, or J/V).

half-cells are equal. This implies that the voltage (V) or emf of a concentration cell is zero when the concentrations are equal; the voltage as a function of concentrations can be calculated using the Nernst equation.

ELECTRODE CHARGE DESIGNATION

In a galvanic cell, current is spontaneously generated as electrons are released by the oxidized species at the anode and travel through the conductive material to the cathode, where the reduction occurs. Because the anode of a galvanic cell is the source of electrons, it is considered the negative electrode; the cathode is considered the positive electrode. Electrons, therefore, move from negative (low electric potential) to positive (high electric potential), while the current (by convention, the movement of positive charge) is from positive (high electric potential) to negative (low electric potential).

Conversely, the anode of an electrolytic cell is considered positive, because it is attached to the positive pole (the cathode) of the external voltage source (external battery) and so attracts anions from the solution. The cathode of an electrolytic cell is considered negative, because it is attached to the negative pole (the anode) of the external voltage source and so attracts cations from the solution.

In spite of this difference in designating charge (sign), oxidation takes place at the anode and reduction takes place at the cathode in both types of cells, and electrons always flow through the wire from the anode to the cathode. A simple mnemonic is that the CAThode attracts the CATions and the ANode attracts the ANions. In the Daniell cell, for example, the electrons created at the anode by the oxidation of the elemental zinc travel through the wire to the copper half-cell. There they attract copper(II) cations to the cathode, resulting in the reduction of the copper ions to elemental copper, and cations out of the salt bridge into the compartment. The anode, having lost electrons, attracts anions from the salt bridge into the compartment at the same time the Zn^{2+} ions formed by the oxidation process move away from the anode and toward the cathode.

Realize that this is an important distinction to understand not just for electrochemistry in the Physical Sciences section of Test Day but also for applications of electrochemistry in the Biological Sciences section. This distinction arises, for example, in a variant of electrophoresis, called isoelectric focusing, a technique often used to separate amino acids based on the unique isoelectric point (pI) of each amino acid. The positively charged amino acids (those that are protonated at the pH of the solution) will migrate toward the cathode; negatively charged amino acids (those that are deprotonated at the solution pH) will migrate instead toward the anode.

> **Key Concept**
>
> In an electrolytic cell, the anode is positive and the cathode is negative. In a galvanic cell, the anode is negative and the cathode is positive. However, in **both** types of cells, **reduction occurs at the cathode, and oxidation occurs at the anode.**

Reduction Potentials and the Electromotive Force

★★★☆☆

For galvanic cells, the direction of spontaneous movement of charge is from anode, the site of oxidation, to cathode, the site of reduction. This is simple enough to remember, but it begs the question; How do we determine which electrode species will be oxidized and which will be reduced? The relative tendencies of different chemical species to be reduced have been determined experimentally, using the tendency of the hydrogen ion (H^+) to be reduced as an arbitrary zero reference point.

REDUCTION POTENTIALS

A reduction potential is measured in volts (V) and defined relative to the **standard hydrogen electrode (SHE)**, which is arbitrarily given a potential of 0.00 volts. The species in a reaction that will be oxidized or reduced can be determined from the **reduction potential** of each species, defined as the tendency of a species to acquire electrons and be reduced. Each species has its own intrinsic reduction potential; the more positive the potential, the greater the species' tendency to be reduced. **Standard reduction potential, (E_{red}°)**, is measured under **standard conditions**: 25°C, 1 M concentration for each ion participating in the reaction, a partial pressure of 1 atm for each gas that is part of the reaction, and metals in their pure state. The relative reactivities of different half-cells can be compared to predict the direction of electron flow. *A higher E_{red}° means a greater relative tendency for reduction to occur, while a lower E_{red}° means a greater relative tendency for oxidation to occur.*

In galvanic cells, the electrode species with the higher reduction potential is the cathode, and the electrode species with the lower reduction potential is the anode. Since the species that has a stronger tendency to gain electrons is actually gaining electrons, the redox reaction is spontaneous, and the ΔG is negative, as we've seen. In electrolytic cells, the electrode species with the higher reduction potential is "forced" (by the external voltage source) to be oxidized and is, therefore, the anode. The electrode species with the lower reduction potential is "forced" to be reduced and is, therefore, the cathode. Since the movement of electrons is in the direction against the "tendency" of the respective electrochemical species, the redox reaction is nonspontaneous, and the ΔG is positive.

Key Concept

A reduction potential is exactly what it sounds like. It tells us how likely a compound is to be reduced. The higher the value, the more likely it is to be reduced.

> **Example:** Given the following half-reactions and E° values, determine which species would be oxidized and which would be reduced.
>
> $$Ag^+ + e^- \rightarrow Ag\ (s) \quad E^\circ = +0.8\ V$$
> $$Tl^+ + e- \rightarrow Tl\ (s) \quad E^\circ = -0.34\ V$$

Solution: Ag^+ would be reduced to $Ag(s)$ and $Tl(s)$ would be oxidized to Tl^+, because Ag^+ has the higher $E°$. Therefore, the reaction equation would be

$$Ag^+ + Tl\ (s) \rightarrow Tl^+ + Ag\ (s)$$

which is the sum of the two spontaneous half-reactions.

It should be noted that reduction and oxidation are opposite processes. Therefore, to obtain the oxidation potential of a given half-reaction, the reduction half-reaction and the sign of the reduction potential are both reversed. For instance, from the example above, the oxidation half-reaction and oxidation potential of $Tl(s)$ are

$$Tl\ (s) \rightarrow Tl^+ + e^- \qquad E° = +0.34\ V$$

THE ELECTROMOTIVE FORCE

Standard reduction potentials are also used to calculate the **standard electromotive force (emf or $E°_{cell}$)** of a reaction, the difference in potential between two half-cells at standard conditions. The emf of a reaction is determined by adding the standard reduction potential of the reduced species and the standard oxidation potential of the oxidized species. When adding standard potentials, *do not* multiply them by the number of moles oxidized or reduced.

$$\text{emf}° = E°_{cath} - E°_{anode} = E°_{red} + E°_{ox}$$

where $E°_{ox}$ is the oxidation potential of the anode, which is the negative of the reduction potential. *The standard emf of a galvanic cell is positive, while the standard emf of an electrolytic cell is negative.*

Example: Given that the standard reduction potentials for Sm^{3+} and $[RhCl_6]^{3-}$ are -2.41 V and $+0.44$ V, respectively, calculate the emf of the following reaction:

$$Sm^{3+} + Rh + 6\ Cl^- \rightarrow [RhCl_6]^{3-} + Sm$$

Solution: First, determine the oxidation and reduction half-reactions. As written, the Rh is oxidized, and the Sm^{3+} is reduced. Thus, the Sm^{3+} reduction potential is used as is, while the reverse reaction for Rh, $[RhCl_6]^{3-} \rightarrow Rh + 6\ Cl^-$, applies and the oxidation potential of $[RhCl_6]^{3-}$ must be used. Then, using the equation given, the emf can be calculated to be $(-2.41$ V$) + (-0.44$ V$) = -2.85$ V. The cell is thus electrolytic as written. From this result, it is evident that the reaction would proceed spontaneously to the left, in which case the Sm would be oxidized while $[RhCl_6]^{3-}$ would be reduced.

MCAT Expertise

Note that there are two ways to express emf. The first allows us to use only reduction potentials. The second asks us to change the sign of the "E_{red}" value in order to use an *oxidation potential*, which is the exact opposite of a reduction potential. Be careful on the MCAT to pay close attention to the value and sign of the numbers you are using . . . and DON'T multiply by the coefficients!

Thermodynamics of Redox Reactions ★★★★☆☆

Throughout our discussion of electrochemistry and the different types of electro-chemical cells, we have been making references to the spontaneity or nonspontane-ity of the redox reactions housed in each of the different cell types. Let's now look more formally at this topic by relating the state function of free energy to emf and the concentrations of the redox reactants and products to the voltage of a cell at a given point in time.

emf AND GIBBS FREE ENERGY

As you know well by now, the thermodynamic criterion for determining the sponta-neity of a reaction is the change in Gibbs free energy, ΔG, which is the change in the chemical potential of a reaction or the change in the amount of energy of a chemical system available to do work. In an electrochemical cell, the work done is dependent on the number of coulombs and the energy available. Thus, ΔG and emf are related as follows:

$$\Delta G = -n\mathrm{F}E_{cell}$$

where n is the number of moles of electrons exchanged, F is Faraday's constant, and E_{cell} is the emf of the cell. Keep in mind that if Faraday's constant is expressed in coulombs (J/V), then ΔG must be expressed in J, not kJ. (The astute student will notice the similarity of this relationship to that expressed by the physics formula $W = q\,\Delta V$ for the amount of work available or needed in the transport of a charge q across a potential difference ΔV! And if you didn't notice it before, you do now, so that means you are now astute!)

If the reaction takes place under standard conditions (298 K, 1 atm pressure, and all solutions at 1 M concentration), then the ΔG is the standard Gibbs free energy, and E_{cell} is the standard cell potential. The above equation then becomes

$$\Delta G° = -n\mathrm{F}E°_{cell}$$

You should notice the significance of the negative sign on the right side of the equa-tion. Being mindful of it will help you eliminate wrong answer choices that have the wrong sign for either the $\Delta G°$ or the $E°_{cell}$. For example, if you are asked to calculate the change in Gibbs function for a galvanic cell, you will immediately be able to eliminate the answer choices that have positive values, because you know that vol-taic cells have positive emfs and the equation tells you the change in Gibbs will have the opposite sign.

Bridge

Recall that if ΔG is positive, the reaction is not spontaneous; if ΔG is negative, the reaction is spontaneous. Go back to Chapter 6 if you need a review.

THE EFFECT OF CONCENTRATION ON emf

So far, we have considered the calculation of cell emf only under standard conditions (all the ionic species are 1 M, and all gases are at a pressure of 1 atm). However, electrochemical cells may have ionic concentrations that are greater or lesser than 1 M. In fact, for the concentration cell, the concentrations of the ion in the two compartments must be different, even if one of them is 1 M, for there to be a voltage and current. Concentration does have an effect on the emf of a cell: emf varies with the changing concentrations of the species involved. It can be determined by the use of the **Nernst equation**:

$$E_{cell} = E^{\circ}_{cell} - \left(\frac{RT}{nF}\right)(\ln Q)$$

where Q is the reaction quotient for the reaction at a given point in time. For example, for the following reaction,

$$a\text{A} + b\text{B} \rightarrow c\text{C} + d\text{D}$$

the reaction quotient can be calculated as follows:

$$Q = \frac{[\text{C}]^c[\text{D}]^d}{[\text{A}]^a[\text{B}]^b}$$

Although the expression for the reaction quotient Q has two terms for the concentrations of reactants and two terms for the concentrations of products, you need to remember that only the species in solution are included. When considering the case of the Daniell cell, for example, we need to think about which species of the redox reaction are in solution. Upon oxidation, the resulting cation will enter into solution, so the product concentration is the concentration of the oxidized species. Because the electrons are captured by the cations that surround the cathode in the reduction half-reaction, these cations are the reactants of the redox reaction, so the reactant concentration is the concentration of the species that gets reduced.

The emf of a cell can be measured by a **voltmeter**. A **potentiometer** is a kind of voltmeter that draws no current, and it gives a more accurate reading of the difference in potential between two electrodes.

emf AND THE EQUILIBRIUM CONSTANT (K$_{eq}$)

For reactions in solution, ΔG° can determined in another manner, as follows:

$$\Delta G^{\circ} = -RT \ln K_{eq}$$

where R is the gas constant 8.314 J/(K • mol), T is the absolute temperature in K, and K_{eq} is the equilibrium constant for the reaction.

Combining the two equations for standard free energy change (above), we see that

$$\Delta G^\circ = -nFE^\circ cell = -RT \ln K_{eq}$$

or simply

$$nFE^\circ_{cell} = RT \ln K_{eq}$$

If the values for n, T, and K_{eq} are known, then the E° cell for the redox reaction can be readily calculated. On the MCAT, you will not be expected to calculate (or even approximate) natural log values in your head. That being said, these equations will still be tested but in a more conceptual way. Analysis of the equations shows us that for redox reactions that have equilibrium constants less than 1 (which tells us that the equilibrium state favors the reactants), the E°_{cell} will be negative, because the natural log of any number less than 1 is negative. These properties are characteristic of electrolytic cells, which house nonspontaneous redox reactions. If the K_{eq} for the redox reaction is greater than 1 (which tells us that the equilibrium state favors the products), the E°_{cell} will be positive, because the natural log of any number greater than 1 is positive. These properties are characteristic of galvanic cells, which house spontaneous redox reactions. If the K_{eq} is equal to 1 (which tells us that the concentrations of the reactants and products are equal at equilibrium), the E°_{cell} will be equal to zero, because by definition of standard conditions (all ionic species at the same concentration, 1 M), the reaction is already at equilibrium. An easy way to remember this is $E^\circ_{cell} = 0$ V for any concentration cell, because, by definition, the equilibrium state of a concentration cell is when the concentrations of the ion in the two half-cells are equal ($K_{eq} = 1$ for concentration cell).

Conclusion

In this chapter, we covered the essential MCAT topics of redox reactions and electrochemistry. We reviewed the rules for assigning oxidation numbers to help us keep track of the movement of electrons from the species that are oxidized (reducing agents) to the species that are reduced (oxidizing agents). We also covered the sequence of steps involved in balancing redox reactions through the half-reaction method and the properties and behavior of the different types of electrochemical cells. Galvanic cells rely on spontaneous redox reactions to produce current and supply energy. The concentration cell is a special type of galvanic cell for which the current is dependent upon an ion concentration gradient rather than a difference in reduction potential between two chemically distinct electrodes. Electrolytic cells rely on external voltage sources to drive a nonspontaneous redox reaction called electrolysis. Finally, we considered the thermodynamics of the different cell types. Galvanic and concentration cells have positive emf and negative free energy changes. Electrolytic cells have negative emf and positive free changes.

Without further delay, we want to offer you our heartiest congratulations for completing this review of general chemistry for the MCAT. The hard work, time, and energy you have invested in a careful, thorough, and thoughtful review of the topics covered within the pages of this book will pay off in points on Test Day—you can be sure of that. We hope that we have been successful in meeting our goals in writing these review notes: to assess the general concepts and principles essential to answering correctly the general chemistry questions on the MCAT; to guide you in the development of critical thinking skills necessary for analyzing passages, question stems, and answer choices; and to provide holistic preparation for your Test Day experience. In addition to all of these, we had in mind the particular goals of helping you relate the science to your everyday life experiences and future experiences as a physician, demystify it, and have some fun in the process. We are grateful for the opportunity to partner with you in your journey to success on the MCAT and, beyond that, success in your medical education and future practice as a great physician!

CONCEPTS TO REMEMBER

☐ Oxidation is loss of electrons; reduction is gain of electrons (OIL RIG). Oxidation and reduction always occur as paired of reactions, in accordance with the law of conservation of charge.

☐ The oxidizing agent is the chemical species that causes another species to be oxidized and is itself reduced. The reducing agent is the chemical species that causes another species to be reduced and is itself oxidized. Assign oxidation numbers to identify the oxidizing and reducing agents.

☐ Redox reactions can be balanced by the half-reaction method:

— Separate the half-reactions.
— Balance the atoms in each half-reaction.
— Balance the charges in each half-reaction.
— Add the half-reactions.
— Confirm balance of mass and charge in redox reaction.

☐ There are two basic types of electrochemical cells: galvanic (voltaic) cells and electrolytic cells. Concentration cells are a special type of galvanic cell.

☐ Galvanic cells have spontaneous redox reactions, generate current, and supply energy. The ΔG is negative, and the E_{cell} is positive.

☐ Concentration cells have spontaneous redox reactions, generate current, and supply energy. Current is dependent upon ion concentration gradient, not the difference in reduction potential between two different electrodes. The $\Delta G°$ and the $E°_{cell}$ are both 0, because the current ceases when the concentrations of the ion are equal in both compartments.

☐ Electrolytic cells have nonspontaneous redox reactions, require external voltage to generate current, and consume energy. The ΔG is positive, and the E_{cell} is negative.

☐ Reduction potential, measured in volts (V), is a measure of a chemical species' tendency to be reduced (gain electrons) relative to the standard hydrogen electrode (SHE). The higher the reduction potential, the greater the tendency to gain electrons and be reduced.

☐ The standard emf of a cell is the difference between the standard reduction potential of the cathode minus the standard reduction potential of the anode.

☐ The Nernst equation is useful for calculating E_{cell} for all ion concentrations.

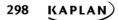

EQUATIONS TO REMEMBER

☐ $\text{emf}^\circ = E^\circ_{\text{cath}} - E^\circ_{\text{anode}} = E^\circ_{\text{red}} + E^\circ_{\text{ox}}$

☐ $\Delta G = -nFE_{\text{cell}}$ and $\Delta G^\circ = -nFE^\circ_{\text{cell}}$

☐ $E_{\text{cell}} = E^\circ_{\text{cell}} - \left(\dfrac{RT}{nF} \right) (\ln Q)$

☐ $\Delta G^\circ = -RT \ln K_{\text{eq}}$

☐ $\Delta G^\circ = -nFE^\circ\text{cell} = -RT \ln K_{\text{eq}}$ or $nFE^\circ_{\text{cell}} = RT \ln K_{\text{eq}}$

Practice Questions

1. An electrolytic cell is filled with water. Which of the following will move toward the cathode of such a cell?

   I. H^+ ions

   II. O^{2-} ions

   III. Electrons

   A. I only

   B. II only

   C. I and III

   D. II and III

2. Consider the following data:

Reaction	Reduction Potential
$Hg^{2+} + 2\ e^- \longrightarrow Hg$	+0.85 V
$Cu^+ + e^- \longrightarrow Cu$	+0.52 V
$Zn^{2+} + 2\ e^- \longrightarrow Zn$	−0.76 V
$Al^{3+} + 3\ e^- \longrightarrow Al$	−1.66 V

   The anode of a certain galvanic cell is composed of copper. Which of the metals from the data table can be used at the cathode?

   A. Hg

   B. Al

   C. Zn

   D. None of the above

3. Consider the following equation:

$$3\ Na\ (s) + H_3N\ (aq) \rightarrow Na_3N\ (s) + H_2\ (g)$$

   Which species acts as an oxidizing agent?

   A. H^+

   B. H_2N

   C. Na

   D. Na^+

4. How many electrons are involved in the following unbalanced reaction?

$$Cr_2O_7^{2-} + H^+ + e^- \rightarrow Cr^{2+} + H_2O$$

   A. 2

   B. 8

   C. 12

   D. 16

Questions 5 and 6 refer to the following two half-reactions:

$$O_2 + 4\ H^+ + 4\ e^- \rightarrow 2\ H_2O \qquad +1.23\ V\ (Reaction\ 1)$$
$$PbO_2 + 4\ H^+ + 2\ e^- \rightarrow Pb^{2+} + 2\ H_2O \quad +1.46\ V\ (Reaction\ 2)$$

5. If the two half-reactions combine to form a spontaneous system, what is the net balanced equation of the full reaction?

   A. $2\ PbO_2 + 4\ H^+ \rightarrow 2\ Pb^{2+} + O_2 + 2\ H_2O$

   B. $PbO_2 \rightarrow Pb^{2+} + O_2 + 2\ e^-$

   C. $Pb^{2+} + O_2 + 2\ H_2O \rightarrow 2\ PbO_2 + 4\ H^+$

   D. $Pb^{2+} + O_2 + 2\ e^- \rightarrow PbO_2$

6. Find the standard potential of the following reaction:

$$Pb^{2+} + O_2 + 2 H_2O \rightarrow 2 PbO_2 + 4 H^+$$

A. +0.23 V
B. −0.23 V
C. −1.69 V
D. +2.69 V

7. Rusting occurs due to the oxidation-reduction reaction of iron with environmental oxygen:

$$4 Fe\ (s) + 3 O_2\ (g) \rightarrow 2 Fe_2O_3\ (s)$$

Some metals, such as copper, are unlikely to react with oxygen. Which of the following best explains this observation?

A. Iron has a more positive reduction potential, making it more likely to donate electrons to oxygen.
B. Iron has a more positive reduction potential, making it more likely to accept electrons from oxygen.
C. Iron has a less positive reduction potential, making it more likely to donate electrons to oxygen.
D. Iron has a less positive reduction potential, making it more likely to accept electrons from oxygen.

8. Lithium aluminum hydride ($LiAlH_4$) is often used in laboratories because of its tendency to donate a hydride ion. Which of the following properties does $LiAlH_4$ exhibit?

A. Strong reducing agent
B. Strong oxidizing agent
C. Strong acid
D. Strong base

9. If the value of E°_{cell} is known, what other data is needed to calculate ΔG?

A. Equilibrium constant
B. Reaction quotient
C. Temperature of the system
D. Number of moles of electrons transferred

10. Which of the following compounds is least likely to be found in the salt bridge of a galvanic cell?

A. NaCl
B. SO_3
C. $MgSO_3$
D. NH_4NO_3

11. What is the oxidation number of chlorine in NaClO?

A. −1
B. 0
C. +1
D. +2

12. Which of the following is most likely to increase the rate of an electrolytic reaction?

A. Increasing the resistance in the circuit
B. Increasing the volume of electrolyte
C. Increasing the current
D. Increasing the pH

13. The following electronic configurations represent elements in their neutral form. Which element is the strongest oxidizing agent?

A. $1s^22s^2p^63s^2p^64s^2$
B. $1s^22s^2p^63s^2p^64s^23d^5$
C. $1s^22s^2p^63s^2p^64s^23d^{10}4p^1$
D. $1s^22s^2p^63s^2p^64s^23d^{10}4p^5$

Small Group Questions

1. How can a halogen have a positive oxidation number?

2. When adding standard potentials, why are we instructed not to multiply them by molar coefficients?

Explanations to Practice Questions

1. C

In an electrolytic cell, ionic compounds are broken up into their constituents; the cations (positively charged ions) migrate toward the cathode, and the anions (negatively charged ions) migrate toward the anode. In this case, the cations are H^+ ions (protons), so option I is correct. To balance charge, electrons are transported from the anode to the cathode, meaning that option III is also correct. Option II is incorrect for two reasons. First, it's unlikely that the anions would be O^{2-} rather than OH^-. Second, these anions would flow to the anode, not the cathode.

2. A

Oxidation occurs at the anode, and reduction occurs at the cathode. Since Cu is at the anode, it must be oxidized. Its standard reduction potential is +0.52 V, so its standard oxidation potential is –0.52 V. The half-reaction potentials in a feasible galvanic cell must add up to a value greater than 0, so we can answer this question by adding the oxidation potential of copper to the reduction potentials of the other metals and finding a reasonable match.

Mercury has a reduction potential of 0.85 V, which is enough to outweigh the potential contributed by copper (–0.52 V). The cell's emf would be +0.33 V. Zinc and aluminum both have negative reduction potentials, so the overall potential of the cell will be even lower than that of copper (–1.28 V and –2.18 V, respectively). Zinc and aluminum would only be viable options if we were dealing with an electrolytic cell.

3. A

The oxidizing agent is the species that is reduced in any given equation. In this problem, two H^+ ions from H_3N are reduced to one neutral H_2 atom. H_3N is not the reducing agent because the H^+ ions and the N^{3-} ions are independent of one another in solution.

4. B

First, let's balance the equation, first making sure all the atoms are present in equal quantities on both sides.

$$Cr_2O_7^{2-} + \underline{14}\ H^+ + e^- \rightarrow \underline{2}\ Cr^{2+} + \underline{7}\ H_2O$$

Now, let's adjust the number of electrons to balance the charge. Currently, the left side has a charge of +12 (–2 from dichromate and +14 from protons). The right side has a charge of +4 (+2 from each chromium cation). To decrease the charge on the left side from +12 to +4, we should add 8 electrons.

$$Cr_2O_7^{2-} + 14\ H^+ + \underline{8}\ e^- \rightarrow 2\ Cr^{2+} + 7\ H_2O$$

5. A

Both half-reactions are written as reductions, so one of the two must be reversed to perform oxidation. If a reaction represents a spontaneous process, then the overall potential must be positive. The only way to create a spontaneous oxidation-reduction system is by reversing Reaction 1 to produce a positive net potential.

$$2\ H_2O \rightarrow O_2 + 4\ H^+ + 4\ e^- \qquad -1.23\ V\ (\text{oxidation})$$

The half-reactions are each already balanced for mass and charge. Before we add them together, we must make sure each of them transfers the same number of electrons. Multiply all of Reaction 2's coefficients by 2 so that both reactions transfer 4 moles of electrons.

$$2\ H_2O \rightarrow O_2 + 4\ H^+ + 4\ e^- \qquad -1.23\ V\ (\text{oxidation})$$
$$2\ PbO_2 + 8\ H^+ + 4\ e^- \rightarrow 2\ Pb^{2+} + 4\ H_2O \quad +1.46\ V\ (\text{reduction})$$

Now, add the two reactions together.

$$2\ H_2O + 2\ PbO_2 + 8\ H^+ + 4\ e^- \rightarrow$$
$$O_2 + 4\ H^+ + 4\ e^- + 2\ Pb^{2+} + 4\ H_2O$$

Finally, let's erase duplicate instances of H^+, e^-, and H_2O.

$$2\ PbO_2 + 4\ H^+ \rightarrow O_2 + 2\ Pb^{2+} + 2\ H_2O$$

This yields the reaction in (A).

6. B

This reaction is simply the reverse of the net balanced equation we found in question 5. Since that equation referred to a spontaneous system, this equation must refer to a nonspontaneous system. Nonspontaneous systems have negative E_{cell} values, so we can eliminate (A) and (D). Here, Reaction 1 represents reduction, so its given reduction potential should remain the same (+1.23 V). Reaction 2 represents oxidation, so its given reduction potential needs to be multiplied by −1 (to yield −1.46 V). The sum of those two values is −0.23 V.

7. C

In the oxidation-reduction reaction of a metal with oxygen, the metal will be oxidized (donate electrons), and oxygen will be reduced (accept electrons). This fact allows us to immediately eliminate (B) and (D). You should also know that a species with a higher reduction potential is more likely to be reduced and a species with a lower reduction potential is more likely to be oxidized. Based on the information in the question, iron is oxidized more readily than copper; this means that iron has a lower reduction potential.

8. A

To answer this question, you must know that a hydride ion is composed of a hydrogen nucleus with two electrons, thereby giving it a negative charge and a considerable tendency to donate its extra electron. This means that $LiAlH_4$ is a strong reducing agent.

9. D

This answer comes directly from the equation relating Gibbs free energy and $E°_{cell}$. $\Delta G = -nFE°_{cell}$, where n is the number of moles of electrons transferred and F is the Faraday constant, 96,487 J•$V^{-1}mol^{-1}$.

10. B

Salt bridges contain inert electrolytes. Ionic compounds, such as (A), (C), and (D), are known to be strong electrolytes because they completely dissociate in solution. (B) cannot be considered an electrolyte because its atoms are covalently bound and will not dissociate in aqueous solution. (B) and (C) may appear similar, but there is an important distinction to be made. (C) implies that Mg^{2+} and SO_3^{2-} are the final, dissociated ionic constituents, while (B) implies that SO_3^{2-} might want to dissociate into smaller elements.

11. C

In NaClO (sodium hypochlorite), sodium carries its typical +1 charge, and oxygen carries its typical −2 charge. This means that the chlorine atom must carry a +1 charge in order to balance the overall −1 charge. Although this may seem atypical, it is not uncommon (NaClO, for instance, is the active ingredient in household bleach).

12. C

Current is defined in amperes, a unit that breaks down to coulombs per second. An increased current will mean that more electrons (coulombs) will be transported per second. (A) is incorrect because an increase in resistance will decrease the current, thereby producing the opposite of the desired effect. (B) is incorrect because the amount of electrolyte will only affect the amount of final product produced; it does not limit the rate. (D) is not always relevant because the pH only affects electrolytic reactions that involve acids and bases.

13. D

A strong oxidizing agent will be easily reduced, meaning that it will have a tendency to gain electrons. Atoms usually gain electrons if they are one or two electrons away from filling up their valence shell. (A) has a full 4s-orbital, meaning that it can only gain an electron if it gains an entire p subshell. (B) has a stable, half-full d-orbital, so it is unlikely to pick up electrons unless it can gain five. (C) has only a single electron in the outer shell, which can easily be lost upon ionization. (D) would fill up its p-orbital by gaining one electron, but the five electrons currently present would not be easily lost through ionization. (D) is the correct answer.

High-Yield Problem Solving Guide for General Chemistry

High-Yield MCAT Review

This is a **High-Yield Questions section**. These questions tackle the most frequently tested topics found on the MCAT. For each type of problem, you will be provided with a stepwise technique for solving the question and key directional points on how to solve for the MCAT specifically.

For each topic, you will find a "Takeaways" box, which gives a concise summary of the problem-solving approach, and a "Things to Watch Out For" box, which points out any caveats to the approach discussed above that usually lead to wrong answer choices. Finally, there is a "Similar Questions" box at the end so you can test your ability to apply the stepwise technique to analogous questions.

We're confident that this guide, and our award-wining Kaplan teachers, can help you achieve your goals of MCAT success and admission into medical school!

Good luck!

Key Concepts

Chapter 3

Polarity

Molecular symmetry

Melting points

Takeaways

Forces that stabilize a molecule more in the solid state than in the liquid state will cause a molecule to have a higher melting point.

Things to Watch Out For

Be careful not to confuse melting points with boiling points. Remember that in general, symmetry raises melting points, whereas branching lowers them.

Similar Questions

1) For straight-chain alkanes, which do you suppose have higher melting points: alkanes with an odd number of carbons, or those with an even number of carbons?

2) Which molecule would you expect to melt at a higher temperature, *n*-pentane or neopentane (2,2-dimethylpropane)? Why?

3) Between phenol (hydroxybenzene) and aniline (aminobenzene), which would melt at a higher temperature and why?

Melting Points

Arrange the following compounds in order of *increasing* melting point:

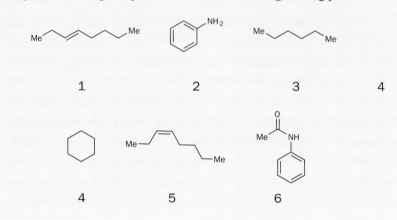

1) Separate the compounds by general polarity.

In this series, we can separate the compounds into three groups of two. The alkanes (**3** and **4**) will be the least polar and, therefore, will melt at the lowest temperature; the alkenes (**1** and **5**) will be in the middle, and the aromatic compounds (**2** and **6**) will melt at the highest temperature.

---

2) Examine each grouping for trends in polarity and/or molecular symmetry.

For the lowest-melting-point compounds, notice that cyclohexane has a higher degree of molecular symmetry than does *n*-hexane; this will cause it to melt at a significantly higher temperature.

With the alkenes, the *trans* alkene has more symmetry than the *cis* alkene, because the *cis* alkene has a rather large "kink" in the middle of the chain that prevents it from packing together as well in the crystal, thus lowering its melting point.

Finally, acetanilide (**6**) is significantly more polar than aniline (**2**), because the amide carbonyl bond is highly polar, causing these molecules to stick together better and consequently raising their melting point.

Therefore, the ordering of the compounds' melting points is as follows:

3 < 4 < 5 < 1 < 2 < 6

Polarity affects melting point just as it does boiling point: More polar molecules melt at a higher temperature because they tend to stick together better. Molecular symmetry also plays a more prominent role than with boiling point, because another consideration is how well molecules pack or "fit together" in the crystal. The more symmetrical a molecule is, the better it packs in the crystal, just as symmetrical puzzle pieces in a jigsaw puzzle fit together better than asymmetrical pieces.

High-Yield Problems continue on the next page

Key Concepts

Chapter 3

Boiling points

Intermolecular forces

Molecular symmetry

Boiling Points

Given the following five molecules, place them in order of increasing boiling point:

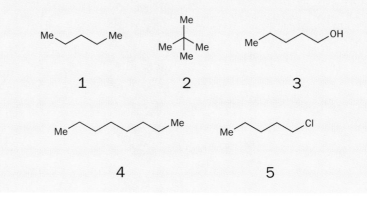

1   2   3   4

4   5

1) Look for unusually heavy molecules.

Remember that molecular weight is one of the key determinants of boiling point. Something that is extraordinarily heavy is going to be harder to boil than something that is lighter. In this case, all the molecules are in the same general range of molecular weight, so this factor won't help us place the molecules in order.

2) Look for highly polar functional groups.

Compounds **3** and **5** are going to have higher-than-usual boiling points. Between compounds **3** and **5**, compound **3** will boil at a higher temperature because it has a more polar functional group; also, the alcohol is capable of hydrogen bonding. Compound **3** will have hydrogen bonds that are a stronger version of dipole–dipole interactions.

The other factor that affects boiling point is the presence of polar functional groups. These groups help *increase* boiling point because they increase the attractions of molecules for each other.

Remember: *Hydrogen bonding is the strongest type of intermolecular attraction.*

Takeaways

Remember that only two factors affect relative boiling points between substances: *molecular weight* and *intermolecular forces*.

3) Look for the effect of dispersion forces.

Compound **4** will boil at a higher temperature than **1**, **2**, and **5** because it is longer (eight carbons versus five, which increases its London forces); therefore, there are more opportunities for it to attract other molecules of **4**.

Although **1**, **2**, and **5** all have the same surface area, the polar group on **5** gives it a higher boiling point than **1** and **2**.

*Remember: Dispersion forces are the only kind of intermolecular attractions that cause **nonpolar** molecules to stick together.*

4) Look for trends in the symmetry of molecules.

In this case, pentane, **1**, will boil higher than neopentane, **2**. This is because neopentane is more symmetrical and, therefore, a more compact molecule; thus, it has a less effective surface area. You can determine this by imagining a "bubble" around each molecule. Neopentane could very easily fit into a spherically shaped bubble, whereas pentane would require an elongated, elliptical bubble with a greater surface area.

If neopentane has a smaller surface area, then there are fewer opportunities for it to engage in dispersion-type attractions with other molecules of neopentane, making it a lower-boiling-point compound (the actual boiling points are 36.1°C for pentane and 9.4°C for neopentane).

At this point, we're really splitting hairs. Notice that compounds **1** and **2** are merely constitutional isomers of one another. If two molecules have the same weight and are relatively nonpolar, *symmetry* is the factor that decides which one will boil at a higher temperature.

5) Put it all together. Order the compounds as specified by the question.

The ordering of the boiling points will therefore be as follows:

2 < 1 < 5 < 4 < 3

Things to Watch Out For

Be sure to consider the factors in the order presented here. For example, polarity is more important than size.

Similar Questions

1) How could you easily alter the structure of compound **3** to lower its boiling point?

2) How could you easily alter the structure of compound **5** to raise its boiling point?

Rate Law from Experimental Results

Consider the nitration reaction of benzene, an example of electrophilic aromatic substitution:

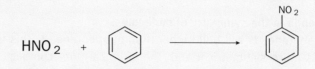

The rate data below were collected with the nitration of benzene carried out at 298 K. From this information, determine the rate law for this reaction.

Trial	$[C_6H_6]$ (M)	$[HNO_2]$ (M)	Initial Rate (M · s⁻¹)
1	1.01×10^{-3}	2.00×10^{-2}	5.96×10^{-6}
2	4.05×10^{-3}	2.00×10^{-2}	5.96×10^{-6}
3	3.02×10^{-3}	6.01×10^{-2}	5.4×10^{-5}

1) Write down the general form of the rate law.

Rate $= k[C_6H_6]^x[HNO_2]^y$

Remember: The general form of the rate law must include a constant, k, that is multiplied by the concentrations of each of the reactants raised to a certain power.

2) Determine the order of the reaction with respect to each reactant.

Choose two trials in which the concentration of one reagent is changing but the other is not. Take the *ratio* of these two trials and set up an equation.

$$\frac{\text{Rate of trial 2}}{\text{Rate of trial 1}} = \frac{k[C_6H_6]_2^x[HNO_2]_2^y}{k[C_6H_6]_1^x[HNO_2]_1^y}$$

Cancel the rate constants because they are equal to each other. Collect terms raised to the same exponent together.

$$\frac{\text{Rate of trial 2}}{\text{Rate of trial 1}} = \left(\frac{k[C_6H_6]_2}{k[C_6H_6]_1}\right)^x \left(\frac{[HNO_2]_2}{[HNO_2]_1}\right)^y$$

Plug and chug. Substitute numbers from the rate data table into the equation.

$$\frac{5.96 \times 10^{-6}}{5.96 \times 10^{-6}} = \left(\frac{4.05 \times 10^{-3}}{1.01 \times 10^{-3}}\right)^x \left(\frac{2.00 \times 10^{-2}}{2.00 \times 10^{-2}}\right)^y$$

$$1 = 4^x$$

The term raised to the *y* power disappears because 1 raised to any power equals 1. The only way that 4^x can equal 1 is if $x = 0$.

To determine the order with respect to HNO_2, note that there are no two trials in which the concentration of benzene stays the same. However, this does not matter, because the reaction is zero order with respect to benzene.

$$\frac{\text{Rate of trial 3}}{\text{Rate of trial 1}} = \left(\frac{[HNO_2]_3}{[HNO_2]_1}\right)^y$$

Plug in numbers from the table as before.

$$\left(\frac{5.40 \times 10^{-5}}{5.96 \times 10^{-6}}\right) = \left(\frac{6.01 \times 10^{-2}}{2.00 \times 10^{-2}}\right)^y$$

Simplify the numbers to make them easy to handle. Note that 5.40×10^{-5} is the same thing as 54.0×10^{-6}.

$$\left(\frac{54 \times 10^{-6}}{6 \times 10^{-6}}\right) = \left(\frac{6 \times 10^{-2}}{2 \times 10^{-2}}\right)^y$$

$$9 = 3^y$$

The only way this equation can be true is if $y = 2$.

---

3) Write down the rate law with the correct orders.

Rate $= k[C_6H_6]^0[HNO_2]^2 = k[HNO_2]^2$

> **Things to Watch Out For**
>
> Make sure that initially you select two trials where one reagent's concentration changes but all other concentrations are constant. Otherwise, you won't come out with the correct rate law!

Similar Questions

1) What is the value of the rate constant k for the original reaction above? What are its units?

2) Given the data below, determine the rate law for the reaction of pyridine with methyl iodide. Find the rate constant k for this reaction and its units. Use the rate law to determine what type of reaction this is.

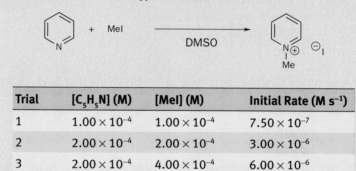

Trial	$[C_5H_5N]$ (M)	$[MeI]$ (M)	Initial Rate (M s^{-1})
1	1.00×10^{-4}	1.00×10^{-4}	7.50×10^{-7}
2	2.00×10^{-4}	2.00×10^{-4}	3.00×10^{-6}
3	2.00×10^{-4}	4.00×10^{-4}	6.00×10^{-6}

3) Cerium(IV) is a common inorganic oxidant. Determine the rate law for the following reaction and compute the value of the rate constant k along with its units.

$$Ce^{4+} + Fe^{2+} \rightarrow Ce^{3+} + Fe^{3+}$$

Trial	$[Ce4^+]$ (M)	$[Fe^{2+}]$ (M)	Initial Rate (M s^{-1})
1	1.10×10^{-5}	1.80×10^{-5}	2.00×10^{-7}
2	1.10×10^{-5}	2.80×10^{-5}	3.10×10^{-7}
3	3.40×10^{-5}	2.80×10^{-5}	9.50×10^{-7}

High-Yield Problems continue on the next page

Rate Law from Reaction Mechanisms

Key Concepts

Chapter 5

Equilibrium

Rate laws

Reaction mechanisms

Often, changing the medium of a reaction can have a dramatic effect on its mechanism. In the gas phase, HCl reacts with propene according to the following reaction mechanism:

Step 1: $HCl + HCl \rightleftharpoons H_2Cl_2$ (fast, equilibrium)

Step 2: $HCl + CH_3CHCH_2 \rightleftharpoons CH_3CHClCH_3^*$ (fast, equilibrium)

Step 3: $CH_3CHClCH_3^* + H_2Cl_2 \rightarrow CH_3CHClCH_3 + 2\ HCl$ (slow)

where CH_3CHCH_2 is propene and $CH_3CHClCH_3^*$ represents an excited state of 2–chloropropane.

Based on these reaction steps, derive the rate law for this reaction.

Takeaways

With reaction mechanisms, the goal is to eliminate the concentrations of intermediates, because they are usually high-energy species that exist only briefly.

1) Identify the slow step in the reaction and write down the rate law expression for that step.

$$Rate = k_3[CH_3CHClCH_3*][H_2Cl_2]$$

2) If intermediates exist in the rate law from step 1, use prior steps to solve for their concentration and eliminate them from the rate law.

$$k_1[HCl]^2 = k_{-1}[H_2Cl_2]$$

Here, we are taking advantage of the fact that step 1 of the mechanism is in equilibrium; therefore, the rates of the forward and reverse reactions are equal.

Solve for the concentration of H_2Cl_2, one of the intermediates from above.

$$[H_2Cl_2] = \frac{k_1}{k_{-1}}[HCl]^2$$

$$k_2[HCl][CH_3CHCH_2] = k_{-2}[CH_3CHClCH_3{}^*]$$

Step 2 from the mechanism is also in equilibrium, so the rates of the forward and reverse reactions are equal.

Solve for the intermediate, as above.

$$[CH_3CHClCH_3{}^*] = \frac{k_2}{k_{-2}}[HCl][CH_3CHCH_2]$$

Plug the concentrations into the rate law for the slow step.

$$rate = \left[k_3[\frac{k_2}{k_{-2}}[HCl][CH_3CHCH_2][\frac{k_1}{k_{-1}}HCl]^2 \right]$$

Similar Questions

1) What are the units of the rate in the original question? Based on this, what must the units of k_{obs} be for this reaction?

2) How does this rate law differ from the one that you might expect if this reaction were to be carried out in solution, instead of in the gas phase?

3) How would the key intermediates differ between this reaction in the gas phase and in solution?

Remember: *Intermediates are assumed to exist for only a brief period of time because they are produced in one step and consumed in another. Therefore, their concentration cannot be measured, and they* ***must*** *be eliminated from the rate law.*

Things to
Watch Out For

In this case, you may assume that the stoichiometric coefficients of each reactant are equal to the order. When you are presented with rate data, you *may not* make this assumption but must use the rate data to determine order.

3) Combine constants and simplify the rate law.

Combine all of the constants and concentrations.

$$\text{rate} = \left[\frac{k_1 k_2 k_3}{k_{-1} k_{-2}}\right] [HCl][CH_3CHCH_2][HCl]^2$$

$$\text{rate} = k_{obs} [HCl]^3 [CH_3CHCH_2],$$

$$\text{where } k_{obs} = \frac{k_1 k_2 k_3}{k_{-1} k_{-2}}$$

Remember: *A constant times a constant times a constant, and so on, is just another constant.*

Key Concepts

Chapter 5

Le Châtelier's principle

System stress

Le Châtelier's Principle

A chemistry student adds solid copper sulfate to water at room temperature. The resulting solution has an emerald blue color reminiscent of azulene. The student then adds a piece of aluminum foil to the solution and watches as a small hole develops in the foil. What could the student do to increase the rate at which the hole forms?

$$CuSO_4 \ (s) + 5 \ H_2O \ (l) \rightarrow CuSO4 \bullet 5 \ H_2O \ (aq) \ \Delta H < 0, \Delta G < 0$$
$$2 \ Al \ (s) + 3 \ Cu^{2+} \ (aq) \rightarrow 2 \ Al^{2+} \ (aq) + 3 \ Cu \ (s) \ \Delta H < 0, \Delta G < 0$$

1) Identify the direction of the desired reaction.
To the right of equation 2

The hole in the aluminum foil indicates that the solid is dissolving into solution. Looking at the reaction equations, solid aluminum reacts with Cu^{2+} to form Al^{2+}, the desired end product.

2) List the different types of stress that can be applied to any system.
Pressure, temperature, concentration

On the MCAT, liquids and solids are incompressible, so altering the pressure at which the reaction occurs should have no effect. However, we can alter the temperature or the concentration of the reactants or products. To increase the rate at which the hole forms, we are looking to push the reaction to the right.

3) Consider the effect of various system stresses: heat.
Run the reactions at a lower temperature to increase the rate of hole formation.

We are told that both reactions are exothermic; thus, we can rewrite them in this generic format: $A \rightarrow B + \Delta$, where Δ is heat. Heat is a product of this reaction. Increasing the heat will push the reaction to the left: It is as if we've added more of the "product." Alternatively, if we drop the temperature at which the reactions are conducted (i.e., remove the heat product), we push the reaction to the right and favor the formation of the hole.

MCAT Pitfall: Increasing the temperature would favor formation of the original $CuSO_4$ solid due to the exothermic nature of the two reactions.

Takeaways

Le Chatelier's principle basically puts K_{eq} and Q into words. Chemical reactions attempt to reach equilibrium. Adding more reactant, for instance, makes the reaction move to the right: More product needs to be formed to balance out the addition.

Things to Watch Out For

Be particularly careful with ionic species and gases. Ionic species can dissociate in water, depending on their electrolytic strength, and may result in multiples of the original concentration of solid. An increase in pressure favors the side of the reaction with fewer molecules of gas.

4) Consider the effect of various system stresses: concentration.

Increase the concentration of the reactants or remove the product.

From the second reaction, it is clear that it is the Cu(II) ion that is reacting with the aluminum foil. How can we get more Cu(II) ion in solution? Add more solid copper sulfate. Alternatively, we could remove the final product. Removing Cu(II) after copper sulfate pentahydride dissociates will disable the second reaction. Removing SO_4^{2-}, however, will cause more hydrate to form. Better yet, we could simply remove the solid copper that plates out when the aluminum atoms are ionized.

Similar Questions

1) A student wants to create H_2O from its natural state elements. If he plans to use gaseous hydrogen and oxygen, what type of system stress would help the reaction progress? Does it matter whether he forms water vapor or liquid water?

2) The reaction $[Co(H_2O)_6]^{2+}$ (aq) + 4 Cl^- (aq) → $CoCl_4^{2-}$ (aq) + 6 H_2O (l) describes the formation of a blue solution from one that is pink. A student isolates the solid of both cobalt compounds. What happens when he adds them to separate flasks of water?

3) A cold pack works by reacting NH_4NO_3 with water. The reaction requires energy to solvate ammonium nitrate. What is the effect of putting a cold pack on your skin? What is the effect of putting a cold pack in a 0°C freezer?

Key Concepts

Chapter 6

Thermodynamics

Kinetics

Reaction profiles

Reaction Energy Profiles

When chalcone (**A**) is subjected to reductive conditions with sodium borohydride, two products can result. The two products are the so-called "1,2–reduction" product (**B**), in which the carbonyl is reduced, and the "1,4–reduction" product (**C**), in which the conjugated alkene is reduced.

$$\left(R = 1.99 \frac{\text{cal}}{\text{mol K}} \cdot \right)$$

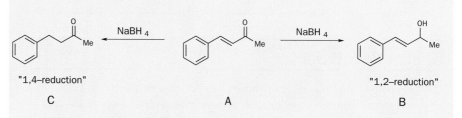

"1,4–reduction"   C   A   B   "1,2–reduction"

The reaction profiles leading to each reduction product are both shown in the plot below.

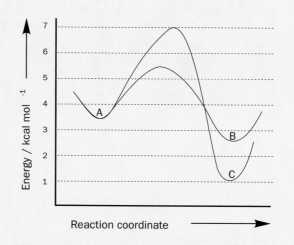

Based on the plot above, answer the following questions:

1) Which product is more thermodynamically stable? Which one forms faster?

2) Assume that **A** is in equilibrium with **C**. What will the ratio of **C** to **A** be at equilibrium?

3) How could the rate of the reaction of **A** to **C** be made closer to the rate of the reaction of **A** to **B**?

4) Which product would be favored if **A** were subjected to high temperatures for a long time? If **A** were subjected to low temperatures for only a brief period of time? Explain why for each situation.

Takeaways

The goal of a reaction profile is to give you information about energy *differences*. Make sure that you identify the important differences and their significances, as above.

Things to Watch Out For

Be careful to take note of the units of energy on the *y*-axis if you plan on doing any computations.

1) **Look at the energy differences between the starting material and the product(s), as well as the differences between the starting material and the transition state leading to each product.**

   Notice that the energy of **C** is lower than that of **B.** Therefore, it is the more thermodynamically stable product.

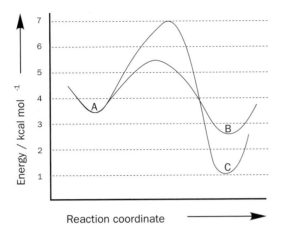

   The rate of formation of each product is determined by the difference in energy between the starting material **A** and the top of the "hump" leading to each product. Because this distance is lower for the formation of **B**, it forms faster.

2) **Note that the difference in energy between the starting material and the product(s) determines the ratio of products to reactants at equilibrium.**

   $$\Delta G° = -RT \ln K_{eq}$$

   This equation provides the relationship between K_{eq} and $\Delta G°$. We need to rearrange it to solve for K_{eq}.

   $$K_{eq} = e^{\frac{-\Delta G°}{RT}}$$

   Note that $\Delta G° \approx 1{,}000 - 3{,}500 = -2{,}500$ cal mol^{-1}, from the diagram, and R = 1.99 cal (mol K)$^{-1}$ ≈ 2 cal (mol K)$^{-1}$ and $T = 298 \approx 300$ K.

   $$K_{eq} = e^{\frac{-\Delta G°}{RT}} = e^{\frac{-(-2{,}500)}{(2)(300)}} = e^{\frac{2{,}500}{600}}$$

   Let's say 2,500/600 is about equal to 4, and $e = 2.7818 \approx 3$.

   $$K_{eq} = e^4 = 81 = \frac{[C]}{[A]}$$

   Note that a negative $\Delta G°$ gives more product than reactant, as you would expect for a spontaneous reaction.

3) Consider what role(s) the addition of a catalyst might play.

Remember: *A catalyst is something that speeds up a reaction and is not consumed during a reaction. If it speeds up a reaction, it lowers the "hump" in the reaction profile. So we could increase the rate of formation of **C** by adding a catalyst to that reaction, making the rate closer to the rate of formation of **B**.*

---

4) Consider the effects of temperature on the reaction(s).

At high temperatures for long times, **A** has the energy to go back and forth over and over again between **B** and **C**. Then, over time, the lowest energy product **C** would predominate, just as rolling a ball down a hill would cause it to fall to the lowest location.

Between the two products, **B** will form much faster than **C** because its energy of activation (height of the "hump") is lower. At low temperatures, the products won't have the energy to go back over the hill to get to **A**, so the faster-forming product will predominate (i.e., **B**).

Similar Questions

1) What would be the ratio of **B** to **A** at equilibrium?

2) If a catalyst were added to the reaction of **A** going to **C**, as in step 3 above, would the energies of **A** and **C** be changed as a result? Why or why not?

3) There are actually intermediates involved in the reactions producing both **B** and **C**. These intermediates are shown below. Sketch how each reaction profile would look, including the involvement of these intermediates. Be sure to indicate which intermediate is relatively more stable.

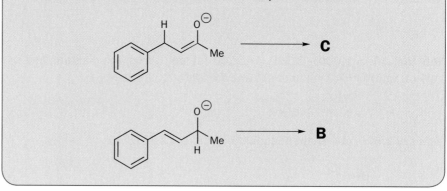

High-Yield Problems continue on the next page

Key Concepts

Chapter 6

Thermochemistry

Gibbs free energy

Enthalpy

Entropy

Equilibrium constant, K_{eq}

Reaction quotient, Q

$\Delta G = \Delta H - T\Delta S$ (kJ/mol)

$\Delta G° = -RT \ln K_{eq}$ (kJ/mol)

$\Delta G = \Delta G° + RT \ln Q$ (kJ/mol)

Takeaways

Two equations should get you through nearly any thermochemistry question. Remember to round your numbers and to predict the ballpark for your answers wherever possible.

Things to Watch Out For

Pay close attention to the units used.

Thermodynamic Equilibrium

The reaction $2\,NO\,(g) + Cl_2\,(g) \rightarrow 2\,NOCl\,(g)$ adheres to the following thermodynamic data:

ΔH	−77.1 kJ/mol
ΔS	−121 J/K
ΔG	−44.0 kJ/mol
K_{eq}	1.54×10^7

Suppose that, in equilibrium, NO exerts 0.6 atm of pressure and Cl_2 adds 0.3 atm; find the partial pressure of NOCl in this equilibrium. Also, find the temperature at which the thermodynamic data in the table were reported. K_{eq} is related to K_p by the following equation: $K_p = K_{eq}(RT)^{\Delta n}$ where Δn is the change in number of moles of gas evolved as the reaction moves forward. ($R = 8.314$ J/K · mol.)

1) Find the temperature at which the thermodynamic data are true.

$\Delta G = \Delta H - T\Delta S$

$(-44\text{ kJ/mol}) = (-77\text{ kJ/mol}) - T(-0.121\text{ kJ/K} \times \text{mol}) \rightarrow T = 273\text{ K}$

Being able to work with the equation $\Delta G = \Delta H - T\Delta S$ is absolutely crucial for Test Day. Specifically concerning the data here, because both ΔH and ΔS are negative, the reaction will become "less spontaneous" as we increase temperature. This will help narrow down our answer choices on Test Day.

MCAT Pitfall: Notice that not all of the state functions were given in the same unit! Had you blindly put in entropy without changing its units, you would have obtained a temperature near absolute zero (0 K). At absolute zero, molecules no longer move, and it is unlikely that this reaction would have such a high equilibrium constant.

2) Find Δn.

For the equation

$2\,NO\,(g) + Cl_2\,(g) \rightarrow 2\,NOCl\,(g)$,

$\Delta n = 2 - (2 + 1) = -1$.

3) Find K_p.

$$K_p = K_{eq}(RT)^{\Delta n}$$
$$K_p = (1.54 \times 10^7)(8.314 \text{ J/K·mole})(273 \text{ K})^{-1}$$
$$= 6{,}785$$

Use the temperature value from step #1.

You are not responsible for memorizing the equation. However, in the MCAT, you have to be able to use a brand-new equation to solve for the answer.

---

4) Find the partial pressure.

$$K_p = \frac{\left(P_{NOCl}^{eq}\right)^2}{\left(P_{NO}^{eq}\right)^2 \left(P_{Cl_2}^{eq}\right)}$$

Plug in the given data into the reaction quotient.

$$6{,}785 = \frac{\left(P_{NOCl}^{eq}\right)^2}{(0.6)^2 \cdot (0.3)}$$

$$733 = \left(P_{NOCl}^{eq}\right)^2$$

$$27 \text{ atm} = P_{NOCl}^{eq}$$

Similar Questions

1) If $K_{eq} = 7.4 \times 10^{-3}$ for $CH_4\ (g) + 2\ H_2O\ (g) \rightarrow CO_2\ (g) + 4\ H_2\ (g)$, which is more plentiful, the reactants or the products?

2) If pyrophosphoric acid ($H_4P_2O_7$) and arsenous acid (H_3AsO_3) have acid dissociation constants of 3×10^{-2} and 6.6×10^{-10}, respectively, at room temperature, find the Gibbs free energy of each dissociation reaction and determine if it is spontaneous. What does this mean for the ΔH and ΔS for these reactions?

3) A chemist is given three liquid-filled flasks, each labeled with generic thermodynamic data. She is told to put one in a cold room, to put one on a Bunsen burner, and to leave one on the benchtop—whatever conditions will best facilitate the reaction. If the flasks are labeled as follows, which flask goes where?

    A $\Delta H < 0, \Delta S > 0$

    E $\Delta H < 0, \Delta S < 0$

    P $\Delta H > 0, \Delta S > 0$

Key Concepts

Chapter 6

Hess's law:

$\Delta H_{rxn} = \Delta H_F$(products) − ΔH_F(reactants)(kJ/mol)

Enthalpy

Bond dissociation energy

Combustion

Stoichiometry

$\Delta H_{rxn} = \Delta H_b$ (reactants) − ΔH_b (products) (kJ/mol)

ΔH_{rxn} = total energy input − total energy released (kJ/mol)

Bond Enthalpy

An unknown compound containing only carbon and hydrogen is subjected to a combustion reaction in which 2,059 kJ of heat are released. If 3 moles of CO_2 and 4 moles of steam are produced for every mole of the unknown compound reacted, find the enthalpy for a single C–H bond.

Bond	Bond Dissociation Energy (kJ/mol)
O=O	497
C=O	805
O–H	464
C–C	347

1) Write a balanced equation for this reaction.

$C_3H_8 + 5O_2 \rightleftharpoons 3CO_2 + 4H_2O$

The question stem tells us a few things about the reaction: It is combustion, the carbon source has the generic structure C_xH_y, and the products include 10 oxygen atoms, 3 carbon atoms, and 8 H atoms. To balance the reaction, we'd need those atoms on the left side, too. Thus, we find that our unknown sample is actually propane and that we need 5 O_2 molecules.

Remember: *For our purposes, it is completely acceptable to have a fractional coefficient in front of a diatomic molecule. 2 C_2H_4 + (7/2) $O_2 \rightarrow$ 3 H_2O + 2 CO_2 is equivalent to 4 C_2H_4 + 7 $CO_2 \rightarrow$ 6 H_2O + 4 CO_2.*

Takeaways

Consider the number of bonds before applying Hess's law. Make sure to take note of how many bonds are in a given molecule as well as how many stoichiometric equivalents of that molecule you have.

2) Determine which bonds are broken and which are formed.

C_3H_8: 2 C–C bonds broken, 8 C–H bonds broken
$5O_2$: 5 O=O bonds broken
$3CO_2$: 6 C=O bonds formed
$4H_2O$: 8 O–H bonds formed

Combustion of C_3H_8 will break apart the carbon backbone and the C–H bonds. The carbon is in a straight chain (as opposed to cyclic or branched), so 2 C–C bonds and 8 C–H bonds are broken. For O_2, only one O=O bond is broken. However, we have 5 moles of this reactant, and thus we have 5 O=O bonds broken. Each molecule of carbon dioxide has 2 C=O bonds, but we have 3 moles of CO_2, so we have 6 C=O bonds formed. Similarly, 8 O–H bonds are formed in the 4 moles of water produced.

3) Apply Hess's law.

$\Delta H_{rxn} = \Delta H_b$ (reactants) $- \Delta H_b$ (products)

$\Delta H_{rxn} =$ total energy input $-$ total energy released

$-2{,}059 = [2(347) + 8x + 5(497)] - [6(805) + 8(464)]$

$-2{,}059 = [3{,}179 + 8x] - [8{,}542]$

$-2{,}059 + 8{,}542 - 3{,}179 = 8x$

$x = 413$ kJ/mol

Bond dissociation energy is the energy required to break a particular type of bond in one mole of gaseous molecules. Bond energies can be used to estimate the enthalpy of reaction as given by the two equations above. When we start plugging in numbers, we are given all data except for C–H bond enthalpy. We solve for this variable (x in the above equations).

Remember: *The equation $\Delta H_{rxn} = \Delta H_b$ (reactants) $- \Delta H_b$ (products) is simply a restatement of Hess's law. Bond enthalpy is for bond breaking, and enthalpy of formation, of course, is for bond making. Changing ΔH_F to ΔH_b switches the signs and, thus, the order of the equation. Keep in mind that it can also be written as $\Delta H_{rxn} = \Delta H_b$ (bonds broken) $+ \Delta H_b$ (bonds formed), but you must remember to make the bond enthalpies for the products negative because forming bonds releases energy.*

4) Use Avogadro's number.

$(413 \text{ kJ/mol}) \times [1 \text{ mol}/(6.022 \times 10^{23} \text{ molecules})]$

$= 6.86 \times 10^{-22}$ kJ/molecule

We see that 413 kJ are found in one mole of C–H bonds. One mole of a substance is equal to 6.022×10^{23} molecules. Here, we simply use that conversion factor. The result tells us that 6.86×10^{-22} kJ are stored in each C–H bond.

Things to Watch Out For

There are a number of ways to set up the equation for ΔH_{rxn}. Whatever equation you use, keep your signs straight. Remember that forming bonds releases energy, whereas breaking bonds requires energy.

Similar Questions

1) Ethanol metabolism in yeast consists of the conversion of ethanol (C_2H_5OH) to acetic acid (CH_3COOH). What is the enthalpy of the reaction if 0.1 mmol of ethanol is metabolized?

2) A second metabolic process involves the net production of 2 ATP and 2 NADH from 2 ADP and 2 NAD$^+$. If the conversion of these molecules is endothermic and adds 443.5 kJ to the overall enthalpy of the reaction, find the enthalpy for a "high-energy" phosphate bond.

3) Tristearin is oxidized in the body according to the following reaction: $2 \text{ } C_{57}H_{110}O_6 + 163 \text{ } O_2 \rightarrow 114 \text{ } CO_2 + 110 \text{ } H_2O$. If the standard enthalpy for this reaction is -34 MJ mol^{-1}, find the total enthalpy for the bonds in tristearin.

Key Concepts

Chapter 6

Hess's law:

$\Delta H_{rxn} = \Delta H_f$ (products) − ΔH_f (reactants) (kJ/mol)

Heat of formation

Combustion

Heat of Formation

> The heat of combustion of glucose ($C_6H_{12}O_6$) is −2,537.3 kJ/mol. If the $\Delta H°_f$ of $CO_2(g)$ is −393.5 kJ/mol and the $\Delta H°_f$ of $H_2O(g)$ is −241.8 kJ/mol, what is the $\Delta H°_f$ of glucose?

1) Write a balanced equation for this reaction.

Unbalanced reaction: $C_6H_{12}O_6 + O_2 \rightarrow CO_2 + H_2O$
Balanced reaction: $C_6H_{12}O_6 + 6\ O_2 \rightarrow 6\ CO_2 + 6\ H_2O$

The unbalanced reaction above is typical of all hydrocarbon combustion reactions. (Unless otherwise noted, presume that combustion of carbohydrates is with oxygen gas.) Begin by balancing the carbons on the left side ($6\ CO_2$), then balance the hydrogens on the left side ($12\ H_2O$), and conclude by balancing the oxygen gas on the right side ($6\ O_2$).

Remember: For our purposes, it is completely acceptable to have a fractional coefficient in front of a diatomic molecule: $2\ C_2H_4 + (7/2)\ O_2 \rightarrow 3\ H_2O + 2\ CO_2$ is equivalent to $4\ C_2H_4 + 7\ CO_2 \rightarrow 6\ H_2O + 4\ CO_2$, but the math is simpler for the former.

Takeaways

Always identify the balanced equation for the reaction before you begin to apply Hess's law. There is a second way of thinking about Hess's law that may be applicable in some questions as well (see previous topic). The given information in the passage and/or question stem will dictate which equation to use. Finally, recall that enthalpy is a state function, and regardless of the path you take to get from the reactants to the products, the change in enthalpy will be the same.

2) Apply Hess's law.

$\Delta H_{rxn} = \Delta H_f$ (products) − ΔH_f (reactants)
−2,537.3 = [6(−393.5) + 6(−241.8)] − [ΔH_f (glucose)]
Rearranging to solve for ΔH_f (glucose):
ΔH_f (glucose) = 2,537.3 + [6(−393.5) + 6(−241.8)]
ΔH_f (glucose) = 2,537.3 + [−2,361 + −1,450.8]
ΔH_f (glucose) = 2,537.3 + [−3,811.8]
$\Rightarrow \Delta H_f$ (glucose) = −1,274.5

The heat of formation is defined as the heat absorbed or released during the formation of a pure substance from the elements at a constant pressure. Therefore, by definition, diatomic gases like oxygen have a heat of formation of zero. A negative heat of formation means that heat is released to form the product, whereas a positive heat of formation means that heat is required to form the product. The overall combustion reaction of glucose releases 2,537.3 kJ/mol of heat.

Things to Watch Out For

At least one of the wrong answer choices for thermochemistry questions will be a result of carelessness with signs. Organized scratchwork in a stepwise fashion will facilitate avoiding this problem, but perhaps more important is maintaining the ability to approximate the answer. Only experience (aka practice!) will breed such wisdom.

Similar Questions

1) Given the ΔH_F of carbon dioxide and water, what other piece(s) of information must you have to calculate the ΔH_{comb} of ethane?

2) If the ΔH_F of acetylene is 226.6 kJ/mol, what is the ΔH_{comb} of acetylene?

3) If the ΔH_F of NaBr (s) is −359.9 kJ/mol, what is the sum of each ΔH_F of the following series of five reactions?

$$Na\,(s) \rightarrow Na\,(g) \rightarrow Na^+\,(g)$$
$$\frac{1}{2}\,Br_2\,(g) \rightarrow Br\,(g) \rightarrow Br^-\,(g)$$
$$Na^+\,(g) + Br^-\,(g) \rightarrow NaBr\,(s)$$

Partial Pressures

32 g of oxygen, 28 g of nitrogen, and 22 g of carbon dioxide are confined in a container with partial pressures of 2 atm, 2 atm, and 1 atm respectively. A student added 57 g of a halogen gas to this container and observed that the total pressure increased by 3 atm. Can you identify this gas?

1) Determine the number of moles for each gas.

$MW_{oxygen} = 32$ g/mol

$MW_{nitrogen} = 28$ g/mol

$MW_{carbon\ dioxide} = 44$ g/mol

$n = \dfrac{mass}{MW}$

$n_{oxygen} = 1$ mol

$n_{nitrogen} = 1$ mol

$n_{carbon\ dioxide} = 0.5$ mol

This is a more complicated style of partial pressure questions, yet the first step is still the basic one of identifying the number of moles for each gas.

2) Solve for the relevant variable.

$P_A = X_A P_{Total}$

$X_A = \dfrac{P_A}{P_{Total}}$

$X_A = \dfrac{3}{8}$

All partial pressure questions boil down to this formula. The relevant variable here is the mole fraction of the halogen gas. The partial pressure of the gas is 3 atm, and the total pressure is 8 atm.

3) Use the mole fraction X_A to solve for the number of moles and the MW of the halogen gas.

The mole fraction of a substance is the number of moles of the substance as a fraction of the total number of moles in the container:

$$X_A = \dfrac{(\text{moles of } A)}{(\text{total \# of moles in container})}$$

Rearranging the formula, we have # moles of A = (X_A)(total # of moles). Note that the total number of moles is not known, but we can express it algebraically as $2.5 + n_A$, where n_A is defined as the number of moles of A.

moles of A = (X_A)(total # of moles)

$$n_A = \left(\frac{3}{8}\right)(2.5 + n_A)$$

$$8n_A = 7.5 + 3n_A$$

$$5n_A = 7.5$$

$$n_A = 1.5$$

$$MW = \frac{57\,g}{1.5\,mol}$$

$$MW = 38\,g/mol$$

This MW corresponds to F_2. Of course, on Test Day you will roughly round such that 60 g = 1.5 mol and look for the halogen gas using your calculated MW of 40 g/mol. Again, the only gas possible is F_2.

Similar Questions

1) 64 g of oxygen, 14 g of nitrogen, and 66 g of carbon dioxide are confined in a container. If the total pressure is 10 atm, what is the partial pressure of each gas?

2) The partial pressure of nitrogen is 2 atm. If its mole fraction is 2/10 and the only other gas in the container is oxygen, how many moles of oxygen are in the container?

3) An unknown substance's mole fraction is 4/10. If its partial pressure is 5 atm, what is the sum pressure of all the other gases in the container?

Key Concepts

Chapter 9

Normality

Molarity

Oxidation and reduction

Concentration

Normality and Molarity

What volume of a 2.0 M solution of lithium aluminum hydride in ether is necessary to reduce 1 mole of methyl 5-cyanopentanoate to the corresponding amino alcohol? What if a 2.0 N (with respect to H⁻) solution were used instead?

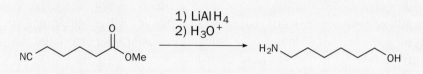

1) Determine the number of equivalents of reagent necessary to accomplish the desired transformation.

There are two functional groups that need to be reduced in the molecule, the nitrile, and the ester.

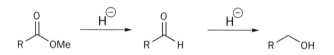

The ester will require two moles of hydride to be reduced to the alcohol.

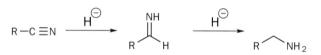

The nitrile will also require two moles of hydride because it proceeds through an imine intermediate.

Takeaways

The molecular formula of a molecule tells you how many equivalents of a desired reagent/atom are contained within the reagent. This is why it's important to balance reactions and draw Lewis structures correctly.

Things to Watch Out For

Be careful to distinguish between equivalents and moles. With molecules containing several equivalents of reagents, the number of equivalents and moles are not equal!

2) Compute the necessary volume of the given solution.

$$4 \text{ mol hydride} \times \left(\frac{1 \text{ mol LiAlH}_4}{4 \text{ mol hydride}} \right) = 1 \text{ mol LiAlH}_4$$

Don't forget that one mole of lithium aluminum hydride contains four moles of hydride.

$$\frac{1 \text{ mol LiAlH}_4}{(2 \text{ mol LiAlH}_4 \text{ L}^{-1})} = 0.5 \text{ L}$$

So we'll need 500 mL of the 2.0 M solution.

$$\frac{1 \text{ mol LiAlH}_4}{(0.5 \text{ mol LiAlH}_4 \text{ L}^{-1})} = 2 \text{ L of 2.0 N solution}$$

With the 2.0 N solution, things get a little trickier. If the solution is 2.0 N with respect to H⁻, that means that each liter of solution contains 2 moles of hydride, or 0.5 moles of LiAlH$_4$.

Remember: *Normality refers to equivalents per unit volume, not necessarily moles of compound per unit volume.*

Similar Questions

1) Determine the volumes necessary for the same reaction as that in the initial question if 4.0 M and 4.0 N solutions of lithium aluminum hydride were used instead.

2) If the following molecule were subjected to LiAlH$_4$ reduction as well, what would the product be? How much of the 2.0 M solution would be necessary? The 2.0 N solution?

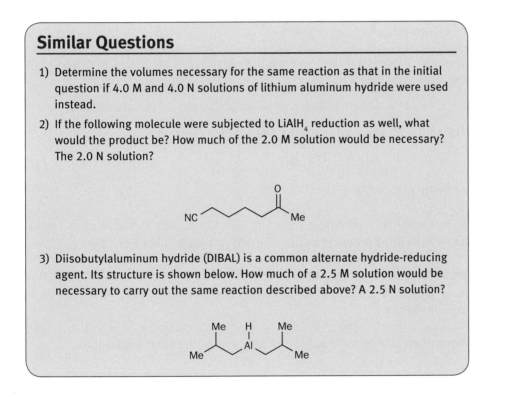

3) Diisobutylaluminum hydride (DIBAL) is a common alternate hydride-reducing agent. Its structure is shown below. How much of a 2.5 M solution would be necessary to carry out the same reaction described above? A 2.5 N solution?

Key Concepts

Chapter 9

pH

Molar solubility

Common ion effect

Le Châtelier's principle

$K_{sp} = [A^+]^x_{sat} [B^-]^y_{sat}$

Takeaways

The value of K_{sp} does not change when a common ion is present; it is a constant that is dependent on temperature. The molar solubility of the salt, however, does change if a common ion is present. To find the change in molar solubility due to the common ion effect, you must find the K_{sp} of the substance first.

Things to Watch Out For

Be careful when applying Le Châtelier's principle in cases of precipitation and solvation. For a solution at equilibrium (i.e., saturated), adding more solid would not shift the equilibrium to the right. More solid does not dissociate to raise the ion concentrations; the solid just piles up at the bottom.

Molar Solubility

> The molar solubility of iron(III) hydroxide in pure water at 25°C is 9.94×10^{-10} mol/L. How would the substance's molar solubility change if placed in an aqueous solution of pH 10.0 at 25°C?

1) Identify the balanced equation for the dissociation reaction.

The generic dissociation reaction may be expressed as follows:

$$A_x B_y\ (s) \rightarrow xA^+\ (aq) + yB^-\ (aq)$$

Plugging in for iron(III) hydroxide, the reaction expression is:

$$Fe(OH)_3(s) \rightarrow Fe^{+3}(aq) + 3OH^-(aq)$$

This step allows us to see how many moles of ions are added to the solution per mole dissolved.

2) Find the K_{sp} expression for the dissociation reaction.

Generic: $K_{sp} = [x A^+]^x_{sat} [y B^-]^y_{sat}$

$Fe(OH)_3$: $K_{sp} = [Fe^{+3}] [OH^-]^3$

K_{sp} is merely an equilibrium constant, just like K, and it is given the special name "solubility product" because it tells us how soluble a solid is.

Recall that the concentrations are those at equilibrium; thus, the solution is saturated. A saturated solution contains the maximum concentration of dissolved solute.

Remember: Like all Ks, a substance's K_{sp} varies only with temperature.

3) Calculate molar solubility of each product by assuming that you're starting with x mols of reactant.

x mol $Fe(OH)_3 \rightarrow x$ mol $Fe^{+3} + 3x$ mol OH^-

Use the balanced equation from step 1 to determine the appropriate coefficients. For each mole of iron hydroxide dissolved, four ions are created: one Fe^{+3} and three OH^-.

4) Plug the molar solubility for each product into the K_{sp} equation:

$Fe(OH)_3$: $K_{sp} = [Fe^{+3}][OH^-]^3$

$K_{sp} = [x][3x]^3 = 27x^4$ ($x = 9.94 \times 10^{-10}$)

$K_{sp} = 27(9.94 \times 10^{-10})^4 = 2.64 \times 10^{-35}$

Simply plug in the coefficients from step 3 into the K_{sp} equation. The molar solubility, x, was given in the question stem. Thus, to calculate K_{sp}, plug in 9.94×10^{-10}. Now that we are armed with the K_{sp}, we can find the change in molar solubility due to the common ion.

---

5) If a common ion is present in a solution, it must also be accounted for in the K_{sp} equation:

$Fe(OH)_3$: $K_{sp} = [Fe^{+3}][OH^-]^3$

$2.64 \times 10^{-35} = x(3x + 10^{-4})^3 \approx x(10^{-4})^3$

$2.64 \times 10^{-35} = x10^{-12}$

$x = 2.64 \times 10^{-23}$

A solution of pH 10.0 has an OH^- concentration of 10^{-4}. Although iron hydroxide will also contribute to the solution's total concentration of OH^-, its contribution will be negligible relative to the 10^{-4} already present in solution; thus, when plugging in for the $[OH^-]$, we can approximate that it equals 10^{-4}. For the pH 10.0 solution, the molar solubility is on the order of 10^{-23} mol/L, a steep decrease from the 10^{-9} in pure water. This is due to the common ion effect. Look at it from the perspective of Le Châtelier's principle: The addition of more OH^- will shift the reaction to the left, so less iron hydroxide will dissociate.

Similar Questions

1) Given a substance's K_{sp}, how would you solve for its molar solubility in pure water? What if a common ion were also present in solution?

2) Given a table listing substances and their solubility constants, how would you determine which substance was most soluble in pure water?

3) Given that the sulfate ion can react with acid to form hydrogen sulfate, how would the molar solubility of sulfate salts be affected by varying a solution's pH?

Key Concepts

Chapter 10

Acids and bases

Chemical equilibrium

pH and pK$_a$

What is the pH of the resulting solution if 4 g of sodium acetate (CH_3CO_2Na) is dissolved in 0.5 L of water? (The pK$_a$ of acetic acid, CH_3CO_2H, is 4.74.)

1) Convert masses to concentrations.

Molecular weight of sodium acetate in g mol^{-1}: $23 + 2(12) + 3(1) + 2(16) = 82$.

The concentration of a solution is usually expressed in units of moles per liter.

Choose numbers that are easy to work with (i.e., 80 g mol^{-1} instead of 82 g mol^{-1}). Remember, you won't have a calculator on Test Day! Moles of sodium acetate: $\dfrac{4\ g}{80\ g\ mol^{-1}} = \dfrac{1}{20}\ mol = 0.05\ mol$.

$$\text{Concentration} = \frac{0.05\ mol}{0.5\ L} = 0.1\ M$$

Remember: Moles, not grams, *are the "common currency" of chemistry problems dealing with reactions. Concentration, usually in units of moles per liter, is the essential quantity for these acid-base problems.*

Takeaways

Keep in mind that K$_b$ is nothing more than an *equilibrium constant* for the reaction of a base picking up a proton from water. So all of the things that are true for K$_{eq}$ are true for K$_b$, especially that K$_{eq}$ only depends on temperature. At constant temperature, *it never changes* (as the name suggests), even if the concentrations of the species in solution change.

2) Choose the constant that will make most sense for the reaction in question and compute its value.

Now we need to decide which constant we will use, K$_a$ or K$_b$. Here's where a little common sense goes a long way. If you think about sodium acetate, you should realize that it is the conjugate base of acetic acid. Therefore, we need the value of K$_b$ for sodium acetate. Even though we are given the pK$_a$ of acetic acid, getting the K$_b$ from this information is no sweat.

In water, $K_a \times K_b$ is always equal to K$_w$, or 10^{-14}. Take the negative logarithm of both sides.

$$-\log(K_a \times K_b) = -\log(10^{-14})$$

Remember that $\log(a \times b) = \log a + \log b$ and that $\log 10^x = x$.

$$-\log K_a + -\log K_b = -\log 10^{-14} = 14$$
$$pK_a + pK_b = 14$$

Don't forget that $-\log(\text{whatever}) = p(\text{whatever})$. We will want to find K$_b$ because sodium acetate is the conjugate base of acetic acid.

Plug in the pK$_a$ from above (to make our lives easier, let's say $4.74 \approx 5$).

$$pK_b = 14 - pK_a = 9$$
$$K_b = 10^{-pK_b} = 10^{-9}$$

Remember: The p-scale is a hugely important value for acid-base problems. Remember that p(something) = −log(something).

Things to Watch Out For

Remember that the cardinal principle of handling computation on the MCAT is to *avoid it whenever possible* because it is so time consuming and drastically increases the chances of making a mistake. If you can't avoid doing computation, *choose numbers that are easy to work with*. So, for example, you wouldn't want to use 199.9999; you would just use 200.

3) Write down the appropriate chemical reaction and set up a table.

Here we need to set up a table to reflect the data we've collected. This is the "putting it all together" step and is crucial.

Our table will be as follows:

	H_2O (*l*) + $CH_3CO_2^-$ (*aq*) $\rightarrow$ CH_3CO_2H (*aq*) + OH^- (*aq*)			
Initial	—	0.1	0	0
Change	—	−x	+x	+x
Equilibrium	—	0.1 − x	x	x

Initial: The idea is that we're going to take some sodium acetate, dump it into water, and see what happens. Our initial row in the table shows the concentrations that we have before any reaction takes place. That means that we'll start with the amount of sodium acetate we computed, 0.1 M. There's no acetic acid or hydroxide because no reaction has happened yet.

Change: Here's where all the action happens. As our acetate reacts with water, the concentration is going to decrease by some amount. We don't know what that will be yet, so let's just call it x. If the acetate concentration goes *down* by x, the concentrations of acetic acid and hydroxide must go *up* by the same amount, so we put x's in their columns.

Equilibrium: This is the easy part. Just add up all of the columns above.

*Remember: **Always, always, always** make sure that **any** chemical reaction you write down is **balanced**. This means to make sure that **mass** is balanced (the number of atoms on either side of the reaction) and that **charge** is balanced. Also, the concentration of pure liquids (e.g., water) and pure solids is never taken into account in equilibria.*

4) Plug the equilibrium concentrations from the table into the appropriate acidity or basicity expression.

$$K_b = \frac{[CH_3CO_2]_{eq}[OH^-]_{eq}}{[CH_3CO_2^-]_{eq}} = \frac{x \cdot x}{0.1 - x} = \frac{x^2}{0.1 - x} = 10^{-9}$$

We know that K_b is just the K_{eq} for the reaction in our table above. Plug in the numbers from the table.

High-Yield Problems

5) Simplify the expression from step 4 and solve it.

Let's make our lives easier (*and* save ourselves time on Test Day) by assuming that x is much, much smaller than 0.1, so that $0.1 - x \approx 0.1$.

$$\frac{x^2}{0.1} = 10^{-9}$$
$$x^2 = (0.1)(10^{-9}) = 10^{-10}$$
$$x = 10^{-5}$$

Now why would we want to assume that x is very, very small? Well, remember that sodium acetate is a weak base because it has a K_b value. So if it's a weak base, it won't react much with water, thus making x a very small number.

Remember: *Don't forget to check the assumption we made to simplify our equation. Because $x = 10^{-5}$, which is indeed much less than 0.1 (by a factor of 10,000), our assumption holds.*

---

6) Answer the question.
$$-\log[OH^-] = -\log[10^{-5}] = 5 = pOH$$
$$pH = 14 - 5 = 9$$

This step is trickier than it sounds and is where many, many mistakes are committed. Here's where attention to detail counts. You don't want to slog through all of the work above and then mess up at the end, when 99 percent of the work is done!

Think about what you've solved for. What is x? Well, if we look at the table, we see that x is the concentration of hydroxide. So if we take the negative log of the hydroxide ion concentration, we get the pOH.

Remember that $pH + pOH = 14$. The actual pH is 8.89. So all of our assumptions and roundings didn't affect the answer much, but they saved us a lot of time in computation!

Remember: *Always ask yourself whether your final answer makes sense. The MCAT isn't a computation test; it's a test of critical thinking. Here, we have a base being dissolved in water, so at the end of the day, the pH better be above 7, which it is.*

High-Yield Problems continue on the next page

Key Concepts

Chapter 10

Titration

Acids and bases

Equivalence point

Half-equivalence point

pH

Takeaways

Setting up the tables as shown makes quick work of titration pH questions. Remember to make approximations and use numbers that are easy to work with in order to minimize the computation necessary to get to the answer.

Titration

Hydrazoic acid, HN_3, is a highly toxic compound that can cause death in minutes if inhaled in concentrated form. 100 mL of 0.2 M aqueous solution of HN_3 ($pK_a = 4.72$) is to be titrated with a 0.5 M solution of NaOH.

a) What is the pH of the HN_3 solution before any NaOH is added?

b) The half-equivalence point of a titration is where half the titrant necessary to get to the equivalence point has been added. How much of the NaOH solution will be needed to get to the half-equivalence point? What is the pH at the half-equivalence point?

c) What is the pH at the equivalence point?

1) Determine the pH before the titration.

What you need to ask yourself in each stage of this problem is which species is present, H^+ or OH^-, and where is it coming from? Before the titration begins, we have H^+ around because, as the name of the compound suggests, hydrazoic acid is acidic. The major source of H^+ is from the hydrazoic acid itself, so we can set up a table as follows:

$H_2O\ (l) + HN_3\ (aq) \rightarrow H_3O^+(aq) + OH^-\ (aq)$			
Initial	—	0.2	0	0
Change	—	$-x$	$+x$	$+x$
Equilibrium	—	$0.2-x$	x	x

Plug in the concentrations from the table. We know the pK_a is around 5, so the K_a must be 10^{-5}. Whenever exponents or logarithms are involved, *use numbers that are easy to work with*. Make the approximation that $0.2 - x \approx 0.2$ because HN_3 is a weak acid.

$$K_a = \frac{[H_3O^+][N_3^-]}{[HN_3]} = \frac{x^2}{0.2-x} = \frac{x^2}{0.2} = 10^{-5}$$

If you must take a square root, try to get the power of 10 to be even to make matters simple. Remember from the table that x is the hydronium ion concentration.

$$x^2 = 2 \times 10^{-1} \times 10^{-5} = 2 \times 10^{-6}$$

$$\Rightarrow x = \sqrt{0.2 \times 10^{-6}} \approx 1.4 \times 10^{-3}$$

$$\Rightarrow [H_3O^+]_{eq} = 1.4 \times 10^{-3}$$

$$\Rightarrow pH = -\log[H_3O^+] = -\log(1.4 \times 10^{-3}) = 3 - \log(1.4)$$

Remember that $-\log[a \times 10^{-b}] = b - \log[a] =$ somewhere between $b - 1$ and b.

$$2 < pH < 3$$

2) Find the equivalence point and half-equivalence point.

Compute the number of moles of HN_3 that you start with.

$$\text{mol } HN_3 = 0.1 \text{ L} \times 0.2 \text{ mol L}^{-1} = 0.02 \text{ mol } HN_3$$

$$\frac{0.02 \text{ mol NaOH}}{0.5 \text{ mol L}^{-1}} = 0.04 \text{ L NaOH solution}$$

Each mole of HN_3 will react with one mole of OH^-. Therefore, the equivalence point is reached when 40 mL of the NaOH solution are added and the half-equivalence point is at $40/2 = 20$ mL. We could go through the whole rigamarole of setting up another table to figure out the pH at the half-equivalence point, or we could use a little common sense to avoid computation. At the half-equivalence point, half of the HN_3 has been consumed and converted to N_3^-. Therefore, the HN_3 and N_3 concentrations are equal.

$$K_a = \frac{[H_3O^+][N_3^-]}{[HN_3]} = [H_3O^+]$$

Because $[HN_3] = [N_3^-]$, $K_a = [H_3O^+]$, and $pH = pK_a = 4.72$.

Remember: *Whenever possible, avoid computation!*

---

3) Determine the reactive species at the equivalence point to find the pH.

At the equivalence point, all of the HN_3 has been consumed, leaving only N_3^- behind. Because N_3^- is a Brønsted-Lowry base, we need to worry about OH^-, not H_3O^+.

$$K_b = \frac{K_w}{K_a} = \frac{10^{-14}}{10^{-5}} = 10^{-9}$$

Remember that $K_a \times K_b = K_w = 10^{-14}$. Now we can set up our table:

	H_2O (*l*) + N_3 (*aq*)$^-$ → HN_3 (*aq*) + OH^- (*aq*)		
Initial	—	0.15	0	0
Change	—	$-x$	$+x$	$+x$
Equilibrium	—	$0.15 - x$	x	x

Remember that the volume of our solution has increased by 40 mL, so the concentration of N_3^- is $\dfrac{0.02 \text{ mol}}{(0.1 + 0.04)\text{ L}} \approx 0.15$ M.

Make the approximation that $0.15 - x \approx 0.15$.

$$K_b = \frac{[HN_3][OH^-]}{[N_3^-]} = \frac{x^2}{0.15 - x} = \frac{x^2}{0.15} = 10^{-9}$$

Things to Watch Out For

Be careful in choosing whether you will use K_a or K_b to determine the pH. Make this decision based on whether the dominant species in solution is acidic or basic, respectively.

Similar Questions

1) What is the pH after the equivalence point has been exceeded by 5 mL of the NaOH solution in the opening question?

2) What would be the pH if the same amount of NaOH solution necessary to get to the half-equivalence point in this titration were added to pure water? How does the pH of each situation compare? This demonstrates how weak acids can serve as buffers, solutions that resist changes in pH.

3) What would be the pH of a solution that was 0.2 M in HN_3 and 0.10 M in N_3^-?

Here, let's say that 1.6 is close to 1.5 to make the square root computation trivial.

$$x^2 = 0.15 \times 10^{-9} = 0.15 \times 10^{-10} \approx 1.6 \times 10^{-10} \approx 160 \times 10^{-12}$$
$$\Rightarrow x = \sqrt{160 \times 10^{-12}} = 4\sqrt{10} \times 10^{-6} \approx 12 \times 10^{-6} = 1.2 \times 10^{-5}$$
$$\Rightarrow [OH^-]_{eq} = 1.2 \times 10^{-5}$$
$$\Rightarrow pOH = -\log([OH^-]) = -\log(1.2 \times 10^{-5}) = 5 - \log(1.2) \approx 5$$
$$\Rightarrow pH = 14 - pOH = 14 - 5 = 9$$

Note that pH + pOH = 14 in water. Remember to ask yourself whether or not a result makes sense. Here, because we have a basic species (N_3^-), the pH should be above 7, which it is.

High-Yield Problems continue on the next page

High-Yield Problems

Key Concepts

Chapter 11

Oxidation

Reduction

Balancing electrochemical half-reactions

Balancing Redox Reactions

Balance the following reaction that takes place in basic solution.

$$ZrO(OH)_2\ (s) + SO_3^{2-}\ (aq) \rightleftharpoons Zr\ (s) + SO_4^{2-}\ (aq)$$

1) Separate the overall reaction into two half-reactions.

$$ZrO(OH)_2 \rightleftharpoons Zr$$
$$SO_3^{2-} \rightleftharpoons SO_4^{2-}$$

Break the reactions up by looking at atoms other than hydrogen and oxygen.

Takeaways

Don't fall into the trap of simply balancing mass in these reactions. If oxidation and reduction are occurring, you must go through this procedure to balance the reaction.

2) Balance the oxygens in each reaction by adding the necessary number of moles of water to the appropriate side.

$$ZrO(OH)_2 \rightleftharpoons Zr\ (s) + 3\ H_2O$$
$$H_2O + SO_3^{2-} \rightleftharpoons SO_4^{2-}$$

3) Balance hydrogen by adding the necessary number of H$^+$ ions to the appropriate side of each reaction.

$$4\ H^+ + ZrO(OH)_2 \rightleftharpoons Zr + 3\ H_2O$$
$$H_2O + SO_3^{2-} \rightleftharpoons SO_4^{2-} + 2\ H^+$$

Things to Watch Out For

These kinds of problems can be extremely tedious. You must take extra care to avoid careless addition and subtraction errors!

4) If the reaction is carried out in basic solution, "neutralize" each equivalent of H$^+$ with one equivalent of OH$^-$.

$$4\ OH^- + 4\ H^+ + ZrO(OH)_2 \rightleftharpoons Zr + 3\ H_2O + 4\ OH^-$$
$$2\ OH^- + H_2O + SO_3^{2-} \rightleftharpoons SO_4^{2-} + 2\ H^+ + 2\ OH^-$$
$$4\ H_2O + ZrO(OH)_2 \rightleftharpoons Zr + 3\ H_2O + 4\ OH^-$$
$$2\ OH^- + H_2O + SO_3^{2-} \rightleftharpoons SO_4^{2-} + 2\ H_2O$$

Combine each mole of H$^+$ and OH$^-$ into one mole of water and simplify each reaction.

Remember: *Don't forget to add OH$^-$ to each side of both reactions!*

5) Balance the overall charge in each reaction using electrons.

$$4\ e^- + 4\ H_2O + ZrO(OH)_2 \rightleftharpoons Zr + 3\ H_2O + 4\ OH^-$$
$$2\ OH^- + H_2O + SO_3^{2-} \rightleftharpoons SO_4^{2-} + 2\ H_2O + 2\ e^-$$

The top equation has a total charge of −4 on the right from the 4 moles of hydroxide, so 4 electrons need to be added to the left side of the equation.

In the bottom equation, there is a total charge of -4 on the left, -2 from the 2 moles of hydroxide and -2 from the 2 moles of sulfite anion (SO_3^{2-}).

Remember: Don't forget to account for all charges in this step, including the charge contributed by molecules other than H^+ and OH^-.

---

6) Multiply each reaction by the necessary integer to ensure that equal numbers of electrons are present in each reaction.

$$4\, e^- + 4\, H_2O + ZrO(OH)_2 \rightleftharpoons Zr + 3\, H_2O + 4\, OH^-$$
$$4\, OH^- + 2\, H_2O + 2\, SO_3^{2-} \rightleftharpoons 2\, SO_4^{2-} + 4\, H_2O + 4\, e^-$$

Here, the lowest common multiple among the four electrons in the top reaction and the two in the bottom is four electrons, so we must multiply everything in the bottom reaction by two.

---

7) Combine both reactions and simplify by eliminating redundant molecules on each side of the reaction.

$$4\, e^- + 4\, H_2O\,(l) + ZrO(OH)_2\,(s) + 4\, OH^-\,(aq) + 2\, H_2O\,(l) + 2\, SO_3^{2-}\,(aq)$$
$$\rightleftharpoons Zr\,(s) + 3\, H_2O\,(l) + 4\, OH^-\,(aq) + 2\, SO_4^{2-}\,(aq) + 4\, H_2O\,(l) + 4\, e^-$$

Combine common terms on each side of the net reaction.

$$4\, e^- + 6\, H_2O\,(l) + ZrO(OH)_2\,(s) + 4\, OH^-\,(aq) + 2\, SO_3^{2-}\,(aq)$$
$$\rightleftharpoons Zr\,(s) + 7\, H_2O\,(l) + 4\, OH^-\,(aq) + 2\, SO_4^{2-}\,(aq) + 4\, e^-$$

Eliminate the redundant water molecules, as well as the electrons and excess hydroxide equivalents.

$$ZrO(OH)_2\,(s) + 2\, SO_3^{2-}\,(aq) \rightleftharpoons Zr\,(s) + 2\, SO_4^{2-}\,(aq) + H_2O\,(l)$$

Check to make sure that the reaction is balanced, in terms of both *mass* (number of atoms on each side) and *overall charge*.

*Remember: This last step is **extremely important**. If mass and charge aren't balanced, then you made an error in one of the previous steps.*

Similar Questions

1) Which atom is being oxidized in the original equation? Which is being reduced? Identify the oxidizing and reducing agents.

2) A *disproportionation* is a redox reaction in which the same species is both oxidized and reduced during the course of the reaction. One such reaction is shown below. Balance the reaction, assuming that it takes place in acidic solution:

$$PbSO_4\,(s) \rightarrow Pb\,(s) + PbO_2\,(s) + SO_4^{2-}\,(aq)$$

3) Dentists often use zinc amalgams to make temporary crowns for their patients. It is absolutely vital that they keep the zinc amalgam dry. Any exposure to water would cause pain to the patient and might even crack a tooth. The reaction of zinc metal with water is shown below:

$$Zn\,(s) + H_2O\,(l) \rightarrow Zn^{2+}\,(aq) + H_2\,(g)$$

Balance this reaction, assuming that it takes place in basic solution. Why would exposure to water cause the crown, and perhaps the tooth, to crack?

Key Concepts

Chapter 11

Oxidation/reduction

Electrochemical cells

Work

Stoichiometry

$E^{\circ}_{cell} = E^{\circ}_{cathode} - E^{\circ}_{anode}$ (V)

$\Delta G^{\circ} = -nFE^{\circ}_{cell}$ (kJ/mol)

Takeaways

Double-check your work when you balance the cell equation to make sure that you haven't made any arithmetic errors. One small addition or subtraction mistake can have drastic consequences!

Things to Watch Out For

Remember to balance the electron flow in order to figure out the maximum amount of work that the cell can perform.

Electrochemical Cells

A galvanic cell is to be constructed using the $MnO_4^- \mid Mn^{2+}$ ($E^{\circ}_{red} = 1.49$ V) and $Zn^{2+} \mid Zn$ ($E^{\circ}_{red} = -0.76$ V) couples placed in an acidic solution. Assume that all potentials given are measured against the standard hydrogen electrode at 298 K and that all reagents are present in 1 M concentration (their standard states). What is the maximum possible work output of this cell per mole of reactant if it is used to run an electric motor for one hour at room temperature (298 K)? During this amount of time, how much Zn metal would be necessary to run the cell, given a current of 5 A?

1) Determine which half-reaction is occurring at the anode and which is occurring at the cathode of the cell.

$$MnO_4^- \,(aq) + 5\ e^- \rightarrow Mn^{2+} \,(aq)\quad E^{\circ}_{red} = 1.49\ V$$
$$Zn^{2+} \,(aq) + 2\ e^- \rightarrow Zn\ (s)\quad E^{\circ}_{red} = -0.76\ V$$

Compare the standard reduction potentials for both reactions. The permanganate reduction potential is greater than the zinc potential, so it would prefer to be reduced and zinc oxidized. Therefore, the zinc is being oxidized at the anode, and the manganese is being reduced at the cathode.

*Remember: **O**xidation occurs at the **a**node. (Hint: They both start with a vowel.)*

---

2) Write a balanced reaction for the cell.
Balance the reactions one at a time.

$$MnO_4^- \rightarrow Mn^{2+}$$

Balance oxygen with water, then hydrogen with acid (H^+).

$$8\ H^+ + MnO_4^- \rightarrow Mn^{2+} + 4\ H_2O$$

Balance overall charge with electrons.

$$8\ H^+ + MnO_4^- + 5\ e^- \rightarrow Mn^{2+} + 4\ H_2O$$

This one is easy; all you have to do is balance electrons.

$$Zn \rightarrow Zn^{2+} + 2\ e^-$$

To combine both equations, we need to multiply each by the appropriate integer to get to the lowest common multiple of 2 and 5, which is 10.

$$16\ H^+ + 2\ MnO_4^- + 10\ e^- \rightarrow 2\ Mn^{2+} + 8\ H_2O$$
$$5\ Zn \rightarrow 5\ Zn^{2+} + 10\ e^-$$

Now add the equations up to get the balanced cell equation, and you're golden.

$$16 \, H^+ (aq) + 2 \, MnO_4^- (aq) + 5 \, Zn \, (s) \rightarrow 2 \, Mn^{2+} (aq)$$
$$+ \, 5 \, Zn^{2+} (aq) + 8 \, H_2O \, (l)$$

---

3) Calculate the standard potential for the cell as a whole.

$$E°_{cell} = 1.49 \, V - (-0.76 \, V) = 2.25 \, V$$

Use the equation $E°_{cell} = E°_{cathode} - E°_{anode}$. Because the standard potential for the cell is positive, this confirms that this is a galvanic (or voltaic) cell—once you hook up the electrodes and immerse them in the designated solutions, current will start to flow on its own.

---

4) Compute $\Delta G°$ for the cell.

$$\Delta G° = -(10 \, mol \, e^-)(10^5 \, C \, mol^{-1})(2.25 \, V) = -2.25 \times 10^6 \, J \, mol^{-1}$$

$$\Rightarrow \text{maximum work output per mole of reactant} = 2.25 \times 10^3 \, KJ \, mol^{-1}$$

Use the equation $\Delta G° = -nFE°_{cell}$. The upper limit on the amount of work a reaction can perform is the same thing as $\Delta G°$.

Remember: *Power is work over time, and 1 h = 3,600 s $\approx 4 \times 10^3$ s.*

---

5) Use Faraday's constant to determine the number of moles of electrons transferred and to do any stoichiometric calculations.

$$4 \times 10^3 \, s \, (5 \, C \, s^{-1}) \, (10^{-5} \, mol \, e^- \, C^{-1}) = 0.2 \, mol \, e^-$$

Remember that current is charge passing though a point per unit of time, and Faraday's constant tells us how many coulombs of charge make up one mole of electrons.

$$0.2 \, mol \, e^- \left(\frac{1 \, mol \, Zn}{2 \, mol \, e^-} \right) = 0.1 \, mol \, Zn \times (70 \, g \, mol^{-1}) = 7 \, g \, Zn$$

The balanced half-reaction is used to determine the necessary mole ratio.

Similar Questions

1) How could you alter the cell setup to reverse the direction of current flow?

2) What would the cell potential be if Mn^{2+} and Zn^{2+} were at 2 M concentration and the MnO_4^- concentration remained at 1 M? Would changing the amount of zinc metal present in the cell change this potential? Why or why not?

3) Compute the minimum mass of potassium permanganate ($KMnO_4$) necessary to run the cell for the same amount of time as specified above.

The Nernst Equation

A galvanic cell is created at 298 K using the following net reaction:

$$2 H^+ (aq) + Ca (s) \rightarrow Ca^{2+} (aq) + H_2 (g)$$

Fluoride anions are added to the anode section of the cell only until precipitation is observed. Right at this point, the concentration of fluoride is 1.4×10^{-2} M, the pH is measured to be 0, the pressure of hydrogen gas is 1 atm, and the measured cell voltage is 2.96 V. Given this information, compute the K_{sp} of CaF_2 at 298 K.

Additional information:

$R = 8.314$ J (mol K)$^{-1}$

$Ca^{2+} (aq) + 2 e^- \rightarrow Ca (s)$ $E^\circ_{red} = -2.76$ V

$2 H^+ (aq) + 2 e^- \rightarrow H_2 (g)$ $E^\circ_{red} = 0.00$ V

$F = 96{,}485$ C mol^{-1}

1) Write down the expression for the K_{sp}.
The first part of this problem begins as with any other solubility problem: We need to write down the expression for the K_{sp}.

$$CaF_2 (s) \rightarrow Ca^{2+} (aq) + 2 F^- (aq)$$

We're given the concentration of fluoride right when precipitation begins, so we can plug that right into the K_{sp} expression above. All we need is the concentration of Ca^{2+} ions, and we're golden.

$$K_{eq} = [Ca^{2+}][F^-]^2 = K_{sp}$$

2) Separate the net cell reaction into half-reactions and find E°_{cell}.

$Ca (s) \rightarrow Ca^{2+} (aq) + 2 e^-$ $E^\circ = 2.76$ V
$2 H^+ (aq) + 2 e^- \rightarrow H_2 (g)$ $E^\circ = 0.00$ V

NET: $2 H^+ (aq) + Ca (s) \rightarrow Ca^{2+} (aq) + H_2 (g)$
   $E^\circ_{cell} = 0.00$ V $- (-2.76$ V$) = 2.76$ V

Now we know what the standard potential for the cell is. Our only problem is that, in the situation given in the problem, we are in *nonstandard conditions*, because the concentration of fluoride is not 1 M.

Remember: $E^\circ_{cell} = E^\circ_{cathode} - E^\circ_{anode}$.

High-Yield Problems

3) Apply the Nernst equation.

$$E = E^\circ - \frac{RT}{nF} \ln Q$$

The reaction quotient (Q) in this case is of the cell reaction. Recall that the pressure of hydrogen gas is 1 atmosphere. As the pH = 0, $[H^+] = 10^{-0} = 1.0$ M.

$$Q = \frac{[Ca^{2+}]PH_{2(g)}}{[H^+]^2} = [Ca^{2+}]$$

$$E = E^\circ - \frac{RT}{nF} \ln [Ca^{2+}]$$

$$E - E^\circ = -\frac{RT}{nF} \ln [Ca^{2+}]$$

Rearrange the Nernst equation to solve for $\ln[Ca^{2+}]$.

$$-\left(\frac{nF}{RT}\right)(E - E^\circ) = \ln [Ca^{2+}]$$

Start plugging in numbers. Here, $n = 2$ mol e⁻, from the cell equation; F = 96,485 ≈ 100,000 C mol⁻¹; $T = 298 \approx 300$ K; R ≈ 8 J (mol K)⁻¹; and 2.96 − 2.76 = 0.2 = 2×10^{-1} V.

$$-\left(\frac{2 \times 10^5}{8 \times 300}\right)(2.96 - 2.76) \quad \ln [Ca^2]$$

$$-\left(\frac{2 \times 10^5}{8 \times 300}\right)2 \times 10^{-1} \quad \ln [Ca^2]$$

Here, assume −16.7 ≈ −20.

$$-20 = \ln [Ca^{2+}]$$

$$-20 = 2.3 \log[Ca^{2+}]$$

Recall that $\ln x = 2.3 \log x$. Assume that 2.3 ≈ 2.5 so that $-\frac{20}{2.5} \approx -8$.

$$-8 = \log[Ca^{2+}]$$

$$[Ca^{2+}] = 10^{-8}$$

Similar Questions

1) If the K_{sp} of copper(I) bromide is 4.2×10^{-8}, compute the concentration of bromide necessary to cause precipitation in an electrochemical cell with the Cu|Cu⁺ and H⁺|H₂ couples. Assume the conditions are as follows: E°_{red} of Cu⁺ = 0.521 V; pH = 0; $P_{H2(g)} = 1$ atm; $T = 298$ K; E_{cell} when precipitation begins = 0.82 V.

2) Compute the equilibrium constant at 298 K for the cell comprised of the Zn²⁺ | Zn ($E_{red}° = -0.76$ V) and MnO₄⁻ | Mn²⁺ ($E_{red}° = 1.49$ V) couples. Given this number, comment on the oxidizing ability of the permanganate anion.

3) A buffer solution is prepared that is 0.15 M in acetic acid and 0.05 M in sodium acetate. If oxidation is occuring at a platinum wire with 1 atm of H₂ bubbling over it that is submerged in the buffer solution, and the wire is connected to a standard Cu²⁺ | Cu half-cell ($E_{red}° = 0.34$ V), the measured cell voltage is 0.592 V. Based on this information, compute the pK_a of acetic acid.

Remember: When you absolutely must do computation, choose numbers that are easy to work with.

---

4) Plug the concentrations into the K_{sp} expression and solve.

$K_{sp} = [Ca^{2+}][F^-]^2$

$K_{sp} = (10^{-8})(10^{-2})^2 = 10^{-12}$

The "actual" value for the K_{sp} is 3.9×10^{-11}, so we are quite close.

Art Credits for General Chemistry

Figure 1.1—Image credited to Slim Films. From The Coming Revolutions in Particle Physics by Chris Quigg. Copyright © 2008 by Scientific American, Inc. All rights reserved.

Figure 1.2—Image credited to Jared Schneidman Designs. From The Earth's Elements by Robert P. Kirshner. Copyright © 1994 by Scientific American, Inc. All rights reserved.

Figure 6.1 (Intact egg)—Image credited to Richard Drury/Getty Images. From The Cosmic Origins of Time's Arrow by Sean M. Carroll. Copyright © 2008 by Scientific American, Inc. All rights reserved.

Figure 6.1 (Slightly cracked egg)—Image credited to Graeme Montgomery/Getty Images. From The Cosmic Origins of Time's Arrow by Sean M. Carroll. Copyright © 2008 by Scientific American, Inc. All rights reserved.

Figure 6.1 (Egg cracked in half)—Image credited to Jan Stromme/Getty Images. From The Cosmic Origins of Time's Arrow by Sean M. Carroll. Copyright © 2008 by Scientific American, Inc. All rights reserved.

Figure 6.1 (Egg half with yolk)—Image credited to Michael Rosenfeld/Getty Images. From The Cosmic Origins of Time's Arrow by Sean M. Carroll. Copyright © 2008 by Scientific American, Inc. All rights reserved.

Figure 6.1 (Smashed egg with seeping yolk)—Image credited to Jonathan Kantor/Getty Images. From The Cosmic Origins of Time's Arrow by Sean M. Carroll. Copyright © 2008 by Scientific American, Inc. All rights reserved.

Figure 6.1 (Over easy egg)—Image credited to Diamond Sky Images/Getty Images. From The Cosmic Origins of Time's Arrow by Sean M. Carroll. Copyright © 2008 by Scientific American, Inc. All rights reserved.

Figure 8.1—Image credited to Don Foley. From The Ice of Life by David F. Blake and Peter Jenniskens. Copyright © 2001 by Scientific American, Inc. All rights reserved.

Figure 8.6—Image credited to Daniels and Daniels. From The Amateur Scientist: Tackling the Triple Point by Shawn Carlson. Copyright © 1999 by Scientific American, Inc. All rights reserved.

Part II
Practice Sections

INSTRUCTIONS FOR TAKING THE PRACTICE SECTIONS

Before taking each Practice Section, find a quiet place where you can work uninterrupted. Take a maximum of 70 minutes per section (52 questions) to get accustomed to the length and scope.

Keep in mind that the actual MCAT will not feature a section made up of General Chemistry questions alone, but rather a Physical Sciences section made up of both General Chemistry and Physics questions. Use the following three sections to hone your General Chemistry skills.

Good luck!

Practice Section 1

Time—70 minutes

QUESTIONS 1–52

Directions: Most of the questions in the following General Chemistry Practice Section are organized into groups, with a descriptive passage preceding each group of questions. Study the passage, then select the single best answer to the question in each group. Some of the questions are not based on a descriptive passage; you must also select the best answer to these questions. If you are unsure of the best answer, eliminate the choices that you know are incorrect, then select an answer from the choices that remain.

Periodic table showing Periods 1–7, Lanthanide Series (Ce–Lu, 58–71) and Actinide Series (Th–Lr, 90–103).

PASSAGE I (QUESTIONS 1–9)

Acid rain is a meteorological phenomenon that is defined as any type of precipitation that is unusually acidic. Rain is naturally slightly acidic (pH = 5.2) due to the reaction of water with environmental CO_2 gas to produce carbonic acid. Experts agree that it is mainly a result of pollution, particularly sulfur and nitrogen compounds that react in the atmosphere to produce acids. These reactions are shown below:

$$SO_2 + OH\cdot \rightarrow HOSO_2\cdot$$
$$HOSO_2\cdot + O_2 \rightarrow HO_2\cdot + SO_3$$
$$SO_3 + H_2O \rightarrow H_2SO_4$$
$$NO_2 + OH\cdot \rightarrow HNO_3$$

A college chemistry student was studying outside one day, sipping on a glass of purified water with a pH of 7, when a sudden rainstorm occurred. Wanting to protect his books, he ran inside with them, leaving the glass out on the ledge of his deck. While studying inside, he reviewed the section on acids and bases and decided to run some tests on the glass of water outside, which had collected approximately 100 mL of rainwater mixed with 300 mL of purified water.

1. The acidity of rain is based on the acidity of the contaminating pollutants. Would H_2SO_4 or HNO_3 produce a more acidic rain?

    A. H_2SO_4, because it has a lower pK_a.
    B. HNO_3, because it has a lower pK_a.
    C. H_2SO_4, because it has a greater pK_a.
    D. HNO_3, because it has a greater pK_a.

2. What is the approximate concentration of H^+ in normal rain due to the reaction between $CO_{2(g)}$ and $H_2O_{(l)}$?

    A. 8×10^{-3} M
    B. 6×10^{-5} M
    C. 7×10^{-6} M
    D. 2×10^{-7} M

3. Under which of the following classifications of "acid" does H_2SO_4 fall?

    I. Arrhenius
    II. Brønsted-Lowry
    III. Lewis

    A. I only
    B. II only
    C. II and III only
    D. I, II, and III

4. Suppose a few drops of acid rain fell on an open cut in the student's hand. Would the bicarbonate (HCO_3^-) that exists in blood have any effect?

    A. Yes, bicarbonate will buffer by accepting a H^+ ion.
    B. Yes, bicarbonate will buffer by donating a H^+ ion.
    C. No, bicarbonate does not act as a buffer.
    D. There is not enough information in the passage to determine the correct answer.

5. If the rainwater that mixed with the pure water had original concentrations of $[H_2SO_4] = 2 \times 10^{-3}$ M, $[HNO_3] = 3.2 \times 10^{-3}$ M, what is the approximate final pH of the glass of water?

    A. 1.2
    B. 2.8
    C. 3.4
    D. 4.6

6. Which of the following is an INCORRECT pair of an acid and its conjugate base?

    A. H_2SO_4 : HSO_4^-
    B. CH_3COOH : CH_3COO^-
    C. H_3O^+ : H_2O
    D. H_2CO_3 : CO_2

7. With which of the following statements would the student most likely NOT agree?

A. Acid rain has increased in frequency and intensity over the past 150 years.

B. Radicals play an integral role in the development of acid rain.

C. Acid rain lessens the conductive capabilities of water.

D. Acid rain is dangerous to the environment even though rain is naturally acidic.

QUESTIONS 8–9 ARE BASED ON THE FOLLOWING TITRATION CURVE:

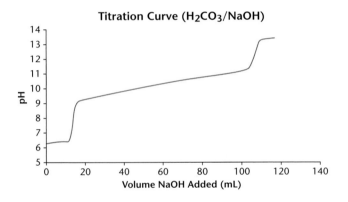

Titration Curve (H_2CO_3/NaOH)

8. What is the approximate ratio of pK_{a1}:pK_{a2} for H_2CO_3?

A. 9.0:13.0

B. 7.8:12.0

C. 6.3:10.3

D. 6.0:11.1

9. What is the approximate ratio of equivalence points for H_2CO_3?

A. 9.0:13.0

B. 7.8:12.0

C. 6.3:10.3

D. 6.0:11.1

PASSAGE II (QUESTIONS 10–17)

The specific heat of a substance, c, measures the amount of heat required to raise the temperature of the mass of substance by a specific number of degrees. In certain cases, the chemical literature reports specific heat in terms of moles. Specific heat differs from heat capacity, a measurement of the amount of heat required to change the temperature of an object by a specific number of degrees.

In SI units, specific heat indicates the number of joules of heat needed to raise the temperature of 1 gram of the substance by 1 Kelvin. The specific heat of water reported in the chemical literature is 4.184 $Jg^{-1}K^{-1}$. Specific heat can be measured by a calorimeter, a device that insulates a sample from atmospheric conditions in order to measure the change in the sample material's temperature over a set interval.

A student used a coffee cup calorimeter to compare the specific heat of water to the specific heat of a commercial fruit punch. The punch is made from a mixture of sugar water and powder flavoring. The student's coffee cup calorimeter used a stack of two foam coffee cups and a thermometer, which the student stuck through a hole in a plastic lid covering the top cup in the stack. Such calorimeters are inexpensive and accurate experimental substitutes for industrial bomb calorimeters, which hold samples at constant volume to measure water temperature changes under high-pressure conditions.

To calibrate the calorimeter, the student combined known quantities of hot and cold water in the coffee cup until the thermometer read a steady temperature, as described in Table 1.

	Hot Water	Cold Water
Volume	100 mL	100 mL
Start Temp	90°C	20°C
End Temp	54°C	54°C

Table 1

Table 2 summarizes the specific heat data the student collected for the water and the fruit punch using the calibrated coffee cup setup.

Trial	1	2	3
Water (mL)	200 mL	200 mL	200 mL
Punch (g)	0 g	0 g	4 g
Sugar (g)	0 g	16 g	16 g
Start Temp	20.5°C	20.5°C	21°C
End Temp	89°C	91.5°C	91°C

Table 2

10. Which of the following values reports the molar specific heat of water from the chemical literature?

A. 4.184 $Jmol^{-1}K^{-1}$

B. 75.31 $Jmol^{-1}K^{-1}$

C. 4184 $Jmol^{-1}K^{-1}$

D. 75310 $Jmol^{-1}K^{-1}$

11. What measurement is also an intrinsic property of fruit punch?

A. Mass

B. Heat

C. Enthalpy

D. Viscosity

12. What is the heat capacity of the student's coffee cup calorimeter?

A. 4.184 J/°C

B. 24.6 J/°C

C. 861 J/°C

D. 0.0246 J/°C

13. Suppose the student breaks his glass alcohol thermometer in the lab. The lab instructor's only available replacement is a mercury thermometer. How would this change to the experimental setup affect the student's measurements?

A. The calorimeter would measure a higher specific heat.

B. The calorimeter would measure a lower specific heat.

C. The thermometer would give a less precise specific heat measurement.

D. There would be no change to the specific heat measurement.

14. Which of the following rationales BEST explains why the student calibrated the coffee cup calorimeter before the experiment?

A. The coffee cup calorimeter can absorb heat.

B. The coffee cup calorimeter does not dry between uses.

C. The coffee cup calorimeter's thermometer does not produce precise values.

D. The coffee cup calorimeter contents do not always reach equilibrium.

15. Suppose the student decided to compare his sugar water measurements to those from a salt water sample, in which 16 g NaCl replace the 16 g table sugar in Trial 2. How would the specific heat of this salt water differ from that of sugar water?

    A. The calorimeter would measure a lower specific heat.
    B. The calorimeter would measure a higher specific heat.
    C. The calorimeter would measure the same specific heat.
    D. The calorimeter would decompose.

16. Which of the following experimental quantities MUST remain constant in Trial 1 in order for the student to obtain a specific heat for water close to the literature value?

    I. Pressure
    II. Mass
    III. Heat

    A. I only
    B. I and III only
    C. II and III only
    D. I, II, and III

17. For which of the following laboratory measurements would a bomb calorimeter be more useful than a coffee cup calorimeter?

    A. To measure the specific heat of salt water
    B. To measure the specific heat of ethanol
    C. To measure the specific heat of water vapor
    D. To measure the specific heat of copper

QUESTIONS 18–21 ARE NOT BASED ON A DESCRIPTIVE PASSAGE.

18. Given the balanced equation, $Mg(s) + 2HCl(aq) \rightarrow MgCl_2(aq) + H_2(g)$, how many liters of hydrogen gas are produced at STP if 3 moles HCl are reacted with excess magnesium?

    A. 1.2 L
    B. 33.6 L
    C. 2.4 L
    D. 44.8 L

19. Increasing the temperature of a system at equilibrium favors the

    A. exothermic reaction, decreasing its rate.
    B. exothermic reaction, increasing its rate.
    C. endothermic reaction, increasing its rate.
    D. endothermic reaction, decreasing its rate.

20. Which type of radiation has neither mass nor charge?

    A. Alpha
    B. Beta
    C. Gamma
    D. Delta

21. Iron rusts more easily than aluminum or zinc because the latter two

    A. form self-protective oxides.
    B. form extremely reactive oxides.
    C. are better reducing agents.
    D. are good oxidizing agents.

PASSAGE III (QUESTIONS 22–29)

Product BD can be prepared by the following reaction mechanism, which is known to exhibit first-order kinetics with respect to each of the reactants:

1. $AB(g) + C(g) \rightleftharpoons A(g) + BC(aq)$ (fast)
2. $BC(aq) + D(aq) + heat \rightleftharpoons BCD(aq)$ (slow)
3. $BCD(aq) + heat \rightleftharpoons C(aq) + BD(aq) + heat$ (fast)

To determine the effect of heat on the overall reaction, a scientist mixed one equivalent each of compounds AB, C, and D with excess water in identical reaction flasks at five different temperatures. The scientist then recorded the rate of formation of the product at each temperature, as well as the final concentration of that product when the reaction reached equilibrium, shown in Table 1:

Temperature	Rate of Formation of BD	[BD] at Equilibrium
40°C	6.5 mmol/hr	37 mM
80°C	18.1 mmol/hr	965 mM
100°C	24.9 mmol/hr	1.16 M
120°C	31.2 mmol/hr	1.19 M
150°C	37.5 mmol/hr	1.21 M

Table 1

The scientist ran a second experiment in which she omitted the equivalent of compound C from the reaction mixture. The results of this second experiment are shown in Table 2:

Temperature	Rate of Formation of BD	[BD] at Equilibrium
40°C	0.02 mmol/hr	37 mM
80°C	0.13 mmol/hr	965 mM
100°C	0.47 mmol/hr	1.16 M
120°C	1.23 mmol/hr	1.19 M
150°C	29.3 mmol/hr	1.21 M

Table 2

22. Compound C's most likely role in this reaction is to

A. donate an electron to compound B.
B. accept an electron from compound B.
C. decrease the amount of energy required for compound D to bind with compound B.
D. decrease the amount of energy required for compound A to dissociate from compound B.

23. Which of the following compounds could the scientist add to the initial reaction mixture to increase the yield of product BD?

A. Compound A
B. Compound B
C. Compound C
D. Compound D

24. Which of the following graphs best demonstrates the effect of temperature on the equilibrium constant of the reaction in the passage?

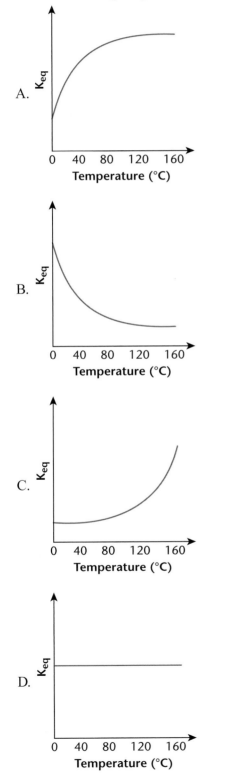

A.

B.

C.

D.

25. The scientist runs a third experiment in which she adds two equivalents of compound AB to one equivalent each of compound C and compound D at 80 °C. What is the expected rate of formation of product BD under these conditions?

A. 9.1 mmol/hr

B. 18.1 mmol/hr

C. 36.2 mmol/hr

D. 54.3 mmol/hr

26. If no catalyst is present, what is the approximate minimum temperature range in which the reaction in the passage would immediately reach its activation energy?

A. 40–80°C

B. 80–100°C

C. 100–120°C

D. 120–150°C

27. What reaction type best describes step 1 of the reaction mechanism in the passage?

A. Double replacement

B. Single replacement

C. Combination

D. Decomposition

28. What step of the reaction mechanism from the passage would be affected most by a change in pressure?

A. Step 1

B. Step 2

C. Step 3

D. All steps to a roughly equal extent

29. Which of the following statements must be TRUE for the overall reaction in the passage?

I. $\Delta H > 0$

II. $\Delta G > 0$

III. $\Delta S < 0$

A. I only

B. III only

C. I and II only

D. I, II, and III

PASSAGE IV (QUESTIONS 30–36)

A few years before Dmitri Mendeleev published the first rendition of the modern periodic table, the English chemist John Newlands suggested the concept of periodicity when he arranged all of the then-known elements by increasing atomic weights and found that every eighth element exhibited similar properties. He dubbed his principle the "Law of Octaves" and created a chart in which the elements would be organized into groups of seven. In this chart (below), the eighth element would appear immediately to the right of the previous element that shares its properties:

H	F	Cl	Co/Ni	Br	Pd	I	Pt/Ir
Li	Na	K	Cu	Rb	Ag	Cs	Tl
G	Mg	Ca	Zn	Sr	Cd	Ba/V	Pb
B	Al	Cr	Y	Ce/Le	U	Ta	Th
C	Si	Ti	In	Zn	Sn	W	Hg
N	P	Mn	As	Di/Mo	Sb	Nb	Bi
O	S	Fe	Se	Ro/Ru	Te	Au	Os

Newlands' discovery was initially dismissed as a coincidence. Soon afterward, Mendeleev created a more elaborate table that was eventually refined into the version that is common today. This table also arranged the elements by molecular weight, but refuted the idea of octaves. It was capable of accommodating the s-block (groups 1A and 2A), the p-block (groups 3A to 8A), the d-block (transition metals), and the f-block (lanthanoids and actinoids). In anticipation of the discovery of more elements, Mendeleev left several empty spaces in the table; for instance, he predicted the discovery of two elements with mass between 65 and 75 amu and a third element with mass between 40 and 50 amu.

30. Several of the atomic mass calculations were inaccurate during the time that periodicity was first discovered. Which of the following pairs of elements were NOT arranged correctly by mass on Newlands's table?

A. Gold and platinum

B. Manganese and iron

C. Yttrium and indium

D. Tantalum and tungsten

31. Which of the following most strongly discredits the accuracy of the law of octaves?

A. The discovery of all of the naturally occurring elements in the s-block and the p-block.

B. The discovery of most of the naturally occurring elements in the d-block and the f-block.

C. J. J. Thomson's discovery of the electron.

D. Ernest Rutherford's discovery of the nucleus.

32. Mendeleev's table was modified several times after its initial publication. Which of the following findings did NOT require modification of the existing entries in the table?

I. A unique element is characterized by a specific number of protons.

II. Electrons are arranged in orbitals and energy levels.

III. The atomic mass of gallium is approximately 70 amu.

A. II only

B. III only

C. II and III only

D. I, II, and III

33. Assuming that all known elements at the time were accounted for in Newlands table of elements, which of the following had NOT been discovered when Newlands published his table?

A. f-block elements
B. Halogens
C. Metalloids
D. Noble gases

34. Mendeleev predicted the existence of an element with atomic mass of 44. If his prediction were correct, which of the following properties would it exhibit?

A. Its atomic radius would be larger than calcium's atomic radius.
B. Its ionic radius would be larger than calcium's atomic radius.
C. It would lose an electron less readily than calcium would.
D. It would accept an electron less readily than calcium would.

35. What element on Newlands' table had the largest atomic radius?

A. Uranium
B. Cesium
C. Bismuth
D. Osmium

36. Which of the following, if true, would MOST strengthen the claim that Newlands should be credited as the inventor of the modern periodic table?

A. Although most scientists dismissed Newlands' theory, it was widely accepted within his home country of England.
B. Mendeleev approved of Newlands' work upon reading about it a few years after he formulated his own periodic table.
C. Mendeleev created his version of the periodic table in an attempt to refute Newlands' theory.
D. Newlands created a refined version of his system that was similar to Mendeleev's table, but failed to publish it before Mendeleev.

PASSAGE V (QUESTIONS 37–44)

A student inserts a sliding divider into a simple cylinder to perform a series of three experiments with an unknown gas. The gas exhibits ideal behavior. Before each experiment, the divider is reset so that $V_1 = V_2$ and the contents are at STP. The total volume of the cylinder is 2 L. The student's cylinder apparatus is illustrated below:

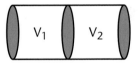

Experiment 1
The student increases the temperature of the gas in V_1 to 45°C while keeping the temperature of V_2 constant.

Experiment 2
The student uses mechanical force to move the central divider in the cylinder such that $3V_1 = V_2$. The temperature of the gas and the cylinder remains constant throughout this experiment.

Experiment 3

The student releases half of the molar contents of V_2, and does not change the molar contents of V_1.

While these experiments are being performed in near-ideal conditions (can be assumed to be ideal), an equation was derived in 1873 by Johannes van der Waals to account for the nonideal behavior of gases:

$$\left(p+\frac{a}{V^2}\right)(V-b)=kT$$

37. In Experiment 1, what is the final volume of 1 mol of gas in V_1?

A. $164R$ L

B. $318R$ L

C. $358R$ L

D. $403R$ L

38. Which of the following graphs MOST accurately illustrates the relationship between volume (V) and temperature (T) in experiment 1, assuming isobaric conditions?

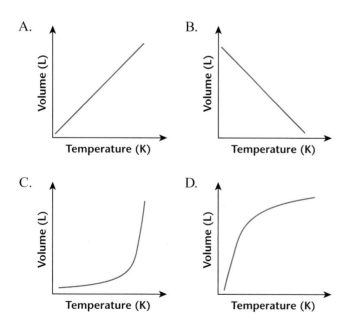

39. In experiment 2, what is the final pressure of the gas with volume V_1?

A. 0.5 atm

B. 1.5 atm

C. 2 atm

D. 3 atm

40. In the van der Waals equation for nonideal gas behavior, a corrects for

A. intermolecular repulsive forces.

B. the volume of the molecules themselves.

C. minute changes in atmospheric pressures.

D. intermolecular attractive forces.

41. What is the temperature of 64 g of pure O_2 gas in a 3 atm, 2 L environment?

A. $1.5/R$ K

B. $2/R$ K

C. $3/R$ K

D. $6/R$ K

42. The student removes the partition, creating a cylinder with V = 2 L. If there are 0.5 mol $CO_2(g)$, 1.5 mol $NO(g)$, and 1 mol $Cl_2(g)$, in the cylinder, what is the partial pressure of the $NO(g)$ at 300 K?

A. $115R$ atm

B. $225R$ atm

C. $375R$ atm

D. $450R$ atm

43. Under which of the following conditions do the contents of V_1 behave most like an ideal gas?

A. High temperature, low pressure

B. Low volume, high pressure

C. Low temperature, high volume

D. Low temperature, high pressure

44. Which of the following is the most likely result of experiment 3 after re-equilibration with the new molar concentrations?

  A. V_1 will expand and V_2 will shrink.
  B. P_2 will be greater than P_1.
  C. Neither V nor P will change because they are unrelated to molar concentration.
  D. P_1 will be greater than P_2.

PASSAGE VI (QUESTIONS 45–52)

Patients often use antacids to counteract potential adverse effects caused by an excess of stomach acid. Most antacids are weak bases whose primary function is to neutralize the hydrochloric acid in the stomach. Because of their simplicity, a wide variety of such drugs is available on the market; however, some are more effective than others. The drug typically reacts with the antacid to produce a conjugate acid and a conjugate base, as in the following examples:

Reaction 1

$$Mg(OH)_2(s) + HCl(aq) \rightarrow MgCl_2(aq) + H_2O(l)$$

Reaction 2

$$Al_2(CO_3)_3(s) + 6HCl(aq) \rightarrow 2AlCl_3(aq) + 3H_2CO_3(aq)$$

A student attempted to test the efficacy of various antacids by adding 1 gram of each drug to a beaker containing 100 mL of 0.1 M HCl. He noticed that stronger antacids tend to leave larger precipitates, so he determined that the strength of an antacid could be estimated by measuring the mass of the precipitate after complete neutralization and comparing it with the molecular weight of the reactant. His results were fairly accurate for magnesium salts, aluminum salts, and calcium salts (Group A); however, they disagreed with published results for sodium salts and potassium salts (Group B).

After inspecting the student's experimental setup, the professor pointed out a flaw in the student's reasoning. The student then decided to redesign his experiment; in the second setup, he chemically combined various quantities of antacid along with a standard amount of HCl and measured the pH of the resulting solutions. This time, he determined that an HCl sample was completely neutralized when its pH was equal to 7. The "overall efficacy" of each antacid was quantified as the number of moles of HCl that can be neutralized by one gram of antacid.

45. Which of the following does NOT describe reaction 1?

  A. Double-displacement reaction
  B. Neutralization reaction
  C. Oxidation-reduction reaction
  D. Acid-base reaction

46. What is the approximate percent composition of the cation in the conjugate base of the acid from reaction 1?

  A. 10%
  B. 25%
  C. 75%
  D. 90%

47. If the student tested each of the following antacids, which would yield the greatest overall efficacy?

  A. $Al_2(CO_3)_3$
  B. $Al(OH)_3$
  C. $Al(HCO_3)_3$
  D. $AlPO_4$

48. Which of the following is TRUE about $NaHCO_3$ in the following reaction?

$$NaHCO_3(s) + HCl(aq) \rightarrow NaCl(aq) + H_2CO_3(aq)$$

A. Because one of the products of the reaction is an acid, $NaHCO_3$ does not function as an antacid.

B. Because one of the products of the reaction is a weaker acid than HCl, $NaHCO_3$ is capable of raising the pH of the stomach but cannot neutralize the acid completely.

C. Because H_2CO_3 decomposes into $H_2O(l)$ and $CO_2(g)$, $NaHCO_3$ is an effective antacid.

D. Because H_2CO_3 decomposes into $H_2O(l)$ and $CO_2(g)$, $NaHCO_3$ is capable of raising the pH of the stomach but cannot neutralize the acid completely.

49. Antacid AX reacts with HCl to yield a mixture with a pH of 5.4 according to the equation below. What is the limiting reagent?

$$AX(s) + HCl(aq) \rightarrow ACl(aq) + HX(aq)$$

A. HCl

B. Antacid

C. Conjugate base of HCl

D. Conjugate acid of antacid

50. When the student tested magnesium hydroxide with his first experimental setup, approximately how much antacid remained at the end of the reaction?

A. 750 mg

B. 500 mg

C. 200 mg

D. 300 mg

51. The student noticed that stronger antacids often leave larger precipitates when they are present as an excess reagent because a stronger antacid

A. neutralizes more acid, which subsequently produces a larger precipitate.

B. produces more product, which subsequently appears in the precipitate.

C. requires more of the reactant, so higher quantities of unreacted material are usually present in the precipitate.

D. requires less of the reactant, so higher quantities of unreacted material are usually present in the precipitate.

52. Which of the following BEST explains why the student's initial results were correct for group A but incorrect for group B?

A. Group A contains very strong bases, while group B contains slightly weaker bases.

B. Group A contains compounds that dissociate into multiple ions, while group B contains compounds that dissociate into only two ions.

C. Group A contains compounds with insignificant solubility, while group B contains compounds with considerable solubility.

D. Group A contains cations with a + 2 or +3 oxidation state, while group B contains cations with a +1 oxidation state.

Practice Section 2

fTime—70 minutes

QUESTIONS 1–52

Directions: Most of the questions in the following General Chemistry Practice Section are organized into groups, with a descriptive passage preceding each group of questions. Study the passage, then select the single best answer to the question in each group. Some of the questions are not based on a descriptive passage; you must also select the best answer to these questions. In you are unsure of the best answer, eliminate the choices that you know are incorrect, then select an answer from the choices that remain.

Period	1 IA 1A	2 IIA 2A	3 IIIB 3B	4 IVB 4B	5 VB 5B	6 VIB 6B	7 VIIB 7B	8	9 VIII --	10	11 IB 1B	12 IIB 2B	13 IIIA 3A	14 IVA 4A	15 VA 5A	16 VIA 6A	17 VIIA 7A	18 vIIIA 8A
1	1 H 1.008																	2 He 4.003
2	3 Li 6.941	4 Be 9.012											5 B 10.81	6 C 12.01	7 N 14.01	8 O 16.00	9 F 19.00	10 Ne 20.18
3	11 Na 22.99	12 Mg 24.31							------ 8 ------				13 Al 26.98	14 Si 28.09	15 P 30.97	16 S 32.07	17 Cl 35.45	18 Ar 39.95
4	19 K 39.10	20 Ca 40.08	21 Sc 44.96	22 Ti 47.88	23 V 50.94	24 Cr 52.00	25 Mn 54.94	26 Fe 55.85	27 Co 58.47	28 Ni 58.69	29 Cu 63.55	30 Zn 65.39	31 Ga 69.72	32 Ge 72.59	33 As 74.92	34 Se 78.96	35 Br 79.90	36 Kr 83.80
5	37 Rb 85.47	38 Sr 87.62	39 Y 88.91	40 Zr 91.22	41 Nb 92.91	42 Mo 95.94	43 Tc (98)	44 Ru 101.1	45 Rh 102.9	46 Pd 106.4	47 Ag 107.9	48 Cd 112.4	49 In 114.8	50 Sn 118.7	51 Sb 121.8	52 Te 127.6	53 I 126.9	54 Xe 131.3
6	55 Cs 132.9	56 Ba 137.3	57 La* 138.9	72 Hf 178.5	73 Ta 180.9	74 W 183.9	75 Re 186.2	76 Os 190.2	77 Ir 190.2	78 Pt 195.1	79 Au 197.0	80 Hg 200.5	81 Tl 204.4	82 Pb 207.2	83 Bi 209.0	84 Po (210)	85 At (210)	86 Rn (222)
7	87 Fr (223)	88 Ra (226)	89 Ac~ (227)	104 Rf (257)	105 Db (260)	106 Sg (263)	107 Bh (262)	108 Hs (265)	109 Mt (266)	110 --- ()	111 --- ()	112 --- ()	114 --- ()		116 --- ()			118 --- ()

Lanthanide Series*	58 Ce 140.1	59 Pr 140.9	60 Nd 144.2	61 Pm (147)	62 Sm 150.4	63 Eu 152.0	64 Gd 157.3	65 Tb 158.9	66 Dy 162.5	67 Ho 164.9	68 Er 167.3	69 Tm 168.9	70 Yb 173.0	71 Lu 175.0
Actinide Series~	90 Th 232.0	91 Pa (231)	92 U (238)	93 Np (237)	94 Pu (242)	95 Am (243)	96 Cm (247)	97 Bk (247)	98 Cf (249)	99 Es (254)	100 Fm (253)	101 Md (256)	102 No (254)	103 Lr (257)

PASSAGE I (QUESTIONS 1–9)

Swimming pools are filled with water containing a number of dissolved ions for the purpose of purification and maintenance of pH. One chemical that is added to pools, chlorine, is used to kill bacteria and harmful contaminants and can be added to pools in a number of ways. Calcium hypochlorite, $Ca(OCl)_2$, is an inorganic chlorinating agent that contributes chlorine and calcium ions to the water.

Other chemicals and materials in swimming pools can also contribute calcium ions to the water. The concentration of calcium and other ions must be closely monitored so that the water does not become saturated with a particular compound. The solubility product constant, termed K_{sp}, describes the amount of salt in moles that can be dissolved in one liter of solution to reach saturation. No more salt can dissolve after reaching the point of saturation.

Plaster that lines swimming pools is a form of hydrated calcium sulfate, $CaSO_4$. The calcium from chlorinating agents along with the calcium from plaster that lines swimming pools makes it necessary to monitor the concentrations of Ca^{2+} and SO_4^{2-} to make sure that saturation is not reached. The following equation describes the dissociation of calcium sulfate in water:

$$CaSO_4 \longleftrightarrow Ca^{2+} + SO_4^{2-}$$

The K_{sp} value for the discussed dissociation reaction can be calculated by determining the values of $[Ca^{2+}]$ and $[SO_4^{2-}]$ in a saturated solution. If the K_{sp} value is known, the ion concentrations in swimming pools can be used with the K_{sp} value to predict whether or not the levels are at or near saturation.

1. If the K_{sp} of $CaSO_4$ is calculated to be 4.93×10^{-5} at 25°C, what is the minimum amount of $CaSO_4$ that can be added to 3.75×10^5 L of water to create a saturated solution?

    A. 2.63×10^3 grams
    B. 3.58×10^5 grams
    C. 7.16×10^5 grams
    D. 2.52×10^3 grams

2. Which of the following compounds, when dissolved in water, has the highest concentration of calcium for one mole of the compound?

    A. $CaCO_3$ ($K_{sp} = 4.8 \times 10^{-9}$)
    B. CaF_2 ($K_{sp} = 3.9 \times 10^{-11}$)
    C. $Ca_3(PO_4)_2$ ($K_{sp} = 1 \times 10^{-25}$)
    D. $Ca(IO_3)_2$ ($K_{sp} = 6.47 \times 10^{-6}$)

3. The K_{sp} of $CaSO_4$ can be calculated by determining the concentration of a saturated solution of $CaSO_4$. The following graph shows the relationship between concentration and conductivity for $CaSO_4$, which was determined by finding the conductance for four $CaSO_4$ solutions of known concentration. Using the graph, estimate the concentration of a saturated solution that has a conductivity of 2.5×10^3 µS/cm and then calculate the experimental K_{sp} for a saturated solution of $CaSO_4$:

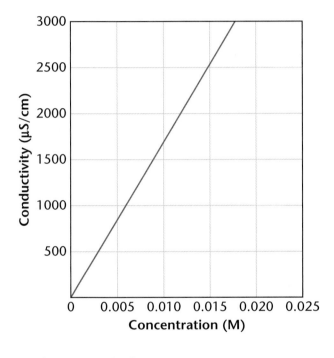

A. 2.25×10^{-4} M²
B. 1.5×10^{-2} M²
C. 3×10^{-2} M²
D. 1.22×10^{-1} M²

4. In the experiment, a probe was used to measure the conductivities in each solution. The probe generates a potential difference between two electrodes and reads the current that is produced as a voltage. The computer then outputs the conductivity. If several different solutions were all heated from room temperature to 75° Celsius, how would the conductivity of the solutions change and how would the K_{sp} be affected?

A. The conductivity would increase and the K_{sp} would increase.
B. The conductivity would decrease and the change in K_{sp} would increase.
C. The conductivity would increase and the change in K_{sp} cannot be determined.
D. The conductivity would decrease and the change in K_{sp} cannot be determined.

5. Instead of using calcium hypochlorite to introduce chlorine into the water, the owner of a water park decides to bubble Cl_2 gas into the pool. Will his decision affect the solubility of the plaster that is lining the pools at his water park?

A. Yes, the chlorine gas will increase the solubility of $CaSO_4$ in the plaster as compared with $Ca(OCl)_2$ because it will react with molecules of SO_4^{2-} and shift the equilibrium to the right.
B. Yes, the chlorine gas will increase the solubility of $CaSO_4$ in the plaster as compared with $Ca(OCl)_2$ because Cl_2 will not cause the same common ion effect that occurred with $Ca(OCl)_2$.
C. Yes, the chlorine gas will decrease the solubility of $CaSO_4$ in the plaster as compared with $Ca(OCl)_2$ because the absence of Ca^{2+} from the $Ca(OCl)_2$ will eliminate the common ion effect.
D. No, the chlorine gas will not change the solubility of $CaSO_4$ in the plaster as compared with $Ca(OCl)_2$.

6. $Ca(OCl)_2$ contributes OCl^- to the water, which acts to kill bacteria by destroying enzymes and contents of the cells through oxidation. In its ionic form, OCl^- exists in the following equilibrium:

$$HOCl \longleftrightarrow H^+ + OCl^-$$

In order for cleaning to occur properly, the pH must be at the right level to allow enough of the oxidizing agent, HOCl, to be present. If the pH is raised by the addition of sodium carbonate to the water, what will happen to the oxidizing power of the HOCl?

A. The higher pH will break the HOCl compound into single atoms and will eliminate its oxidizing power.

B. The pH cannot be raised due to the buffering system in the pool, and thus the oxidizing power of the chlorine will remain the same.

C. Fewer H^+ ions will be present and the reaction will shift right. This will decrease the number of HOCl molecules and thus decrease the oxidizing power of chlorine.

D. A high pH will lower the concentration of H^+ by associating H^+ with OCl^-. This will increase the number of HOCl molecules and increase the oxidizing power of chlorine.

7. Due to changes in climate and poor management of ion content in the water, the swimming pool has now become supersaturated with calcium sulfate. What combination of events could have caused this to occur?

A. Cooling of the pool followed by addition of calcium sulfate

B. Warming of the pool followed by addition of calcium sulfate

C. Addition of calcium sulfate followed by cooling of the pool and then subsequent warming of the pool

D. Warming of the pool followed by addition of calcium sulfate and then cooling of the pool

8. Water "hardness" refers to the content of calcium and magnesium in water. When referring to swimming pools, water hardness mainly refers to calcium. One way to measure the balance of ions is to use the Langelier saturation index. The Langelier saturation index is derived from a combination of the following two equilibrium equations.

$$HCO_3^- \longleftrightarrow H^+ + CO_3^{2-}$$
$$pK_{a2} = 10.33$$

$$CaCO_3 \longleftrightarrow Ca^{2+} + CO_3^{2-}$$
$$pK_{sp} = 8.35$$

Which of the following accurately expresses the combination of the two equilibrium equations in terms of $[H^+]$?

A. $[H^+] = \left(\dfrac{K_{sp}}{K_{a2}}\right) \times [Ca^{2+}][HCO_3^-]$

B. $[H^+] = \left(\dfrac{K_{a2}}{K_{sp}}\right) \times [Ca^{2+}][HCO_3^-]$

C. $[H^+] = \left(\dfrac{K_{sp}}{K_{a2}}\right) \times \left(\dfrac{[Ca^{2+}]}{[HCO_3^-]}\right)$

D. $[H^+] = \left(\dfrac{K_{sp}}{K_{a2}}\right) \times \left(\dfrac{[HCO_3^-]}{[Ca^{2+}]}\right)$

9. Phenol red is the most widely used indicator to determine the pH of water in swimming pools. The pK_{a2} of phenol red is equal to 7.96. The acidic form of phenol red appears yellow and the basic form of phenol red appears red. In addition, the absorptivity (how strongly a species absorbs light) of the basic form is around three times greater than the acidic form. The color-changing region is indicated by an orange color. Due to the difference in absorptivity between different forms of phenol red, at what pH would the color change (to orange) be MOST likely to occur?

A. pH of 4
B. pH of 7.5
C. pH of 8.5
D. pH of 11

PASSAGE II (QUESTIONS 10–17)

Hydrogen is the first element of the periodic table. It contains one proton and one electron. According to one early model of the hydrogen atom developed in the early 20th century by Niels Bohr, that electron is found in any one of an infinite number of energy levels. These energy levels are sometimes called quanta, in that they can be described by a principal quantum number, n, that always has an integer value. As the electron moves from one energy level to another ($n = 1$ to $n \rightarrow 8$, or vice versa) it absorbs or emits some discrete quantity of energy accordingly. This quantity is directly proportional to the frequency of the light radiation that results from the energy change.

It took some time for atomic physicists to arrive at Bohr's conclusions. They struggled to reconcile empirical data about light radiation from hydrogen atoms with their understanding that light photons moved and behaved as particles according to Newtonian mechanics. One discovery that led to Bohr's quantum mechanics was a new quantitative interpretation of light emissions from hydrogen atoms. Hydrogen atoms emit light in characteristic patterns known as line spectra. These patterns are noncontinuous but predictable. In the early

1880s, Theodore Balmer derived a mathematical relationship between the energy emissions of a hydrogen atom and the wavelengths of light they radiated during transitions:

$$\lambda = B[m^2/(m^2 - 2^2)] = B[m^2/(m^2 - n^2)], \text{ where } B = 364.56 \text{ nm},$$
$m > 2$, λ is the wavelength, n is equal to 2.

The spectrum he used, which is now known as the Balmer series, is illustrated below:

400 nm - 700 nm

The Rydberg equation is a more general version of this equation that applies to all possible energy level transitions in a hydrogen atom. Physicists used the Rydberg equation to detect other series of energy transitions in other regions of the light spectrum. One such series is the Lyman series, which accounts for transitions from excited states to $n = 1$, the ground state.

10. What is the proper electron configuration of hydrogen in its elemental state?

A. $1s^0$
B. $1s^1$
C. $1s^2$
D. None of the above

11. If an electron is promoted from $n = 2$ to $n = 5$, as Balmer observed, which of the following possibilities BEST describes the source of the line spectra observed?

A. A photon is absorbed.

B. A photon is emitted.

C. An electron is absorbed.

D. An electron is emitted.

12. What region of the light spectrum corresponds to the characteristic emissions in the Balmer series?

A. UV

B. Visible

C. Infrared

D. X-ray

13. One Balmer spectral line, the $n = 3$ to $n = 2$ transition is a common reference point in astronomy for hydrogen gas emissions. The characteristic wavelength of this emission in the scientific literature is 656.3 nm. What color is this light emission?

A. Red

B. Blue-green

C. Violet

D. The emission is not in the visible spectrum.

14. What name BEST describes the absorption line spectrum pictured below?

400 nm - 700 nm

A. Lyman series

B. Balmer series

C. Bohr series

D. None of the above

15. Suppose a scientist tried to obtain a Balmer series with a sample of deuterium. How would this sample change the appearance of the emissions in the line spectrum?

A. Fewer emission lines

B. More emission lines

C. Same number of emission lines with split peaks

D. Same number of emission lines without split peaks (that is, no change in appearance)

16. At high resolution, some of the emissions in the Balmer series appear as doublets. Which of the following BEST explains this result, which was not predicted by any of the models in the passage?

A. The models in the passage do not account for relativistic effects.

B. The models in the passage do not account for high wavelengths.

C. The models in the passage do not account for the atomic number.

D. The models in the passage do not account for other particles in the atom.

17. When $n > 6$, the Balmer series features violet light emissions at wavelengths outside the range of the visible spectrum. Which of the following BEST accounts for this finding?

A. Energy levels are narrower as $n \to 1$ and wider as $n \to 8$.

B. Energy levels are wider as $n \to 1$ and narrower as $n \to 8$.

C. Energy differences between levels are larger as $n \to 1$ and smaller as $n \to 8$.

D. Energy differences between levels are smaller as $n \to 1$ and larger as $n \to 8$.

QUESTIONS 18–22 ARE NOT BASED ON A DESCRIPTIVE PASSAGE.

18. Which of the following pairs of particles would be accelerated in a particle accelerator?

   A. Gamma ray and neutron

   B. Gamma ray and beta particle

   C. Beta particle and neutron

   D. Alpha and beta particles

19. What volume of 0.5 M KOH would be necessary to neutralize 15 mL of 1 M nitrous acid?

   A. 15 mL

   B. 30 mL

   C. 45 mL

   D. 60 mL

20. Why does high, but not low, pressure cause a deviation from the ideal gas law?

   A. Higher pressure decreases the interatomic distance to the point where intermolecular forces reduce the volume below that predicted by the ideal gas equation.

   B. Low pressure increases the atomic radius of a gas making it more stable whereas high pressure compresses the gas particles decreasing their stability.

   C. Low pressure does cause a significant deviation from the ideal gas law because the increased interatomic distance means that no particles ever collide.

   D. Low pressure does cause a significant deviation because a low pressure implies a reduction in temperature via Charles' law, which increases the power of intermolecular forces.

21. What type of molecular geometry is NOT able to result in a nonpolar structure?

   A. Bent

   B. Diatomic covalent

   C. Trigonal planar

   D. Square planar

22. A parent and daughter nucleus are isotypes of the same element. Therefore, the ratio of alpha to beta decays that produced the daughter nucleus must be which of the following?

   A. 2:3

   B. 2:1

   C. 1:2

   D. 1:1

PASSAGE III (QUESTIONS 23–30)

Many new consumer electronics and electric cars utilize a type of rechargeable battery that extracts its power from the movement of a lithium ion (Li^+) between the cathode and the anode of a galvanic cell. In most cases, the anode is composed of graphite, the cathode is composed of a CoO_2^- complex, and the electrolyte contains a lithium salt in an organic solvent. Following are the half-reactions, where $Li_{1-x}CoO_2$ is the simplest form of the chemical formula $Li(CoO_2)_{1/(1-x)}$ (which represents a complex of one lithium ion with several metal oxide molecules):

$$LiCoO_2 \rightleftharpoons Li_{1-x}CoO_2 + xLi^+ + xe^- \qquad \text{(cathode)}$$
$$xLi^+ + xe^- + 6C \rightleftharpoons Li_xC_6 \qquad \text{(anode)}$$

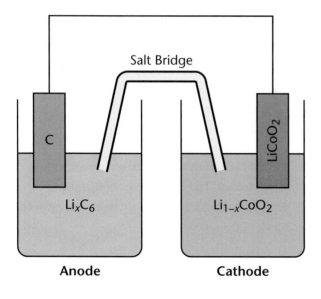

Salt Bridge

C

LiCoO$_2$

Li$_x$C$_6$

Li$_{1-x}$CoO$_2$

Anode   **Cathode**

The value of x is equal to the following ratio:

$$\frac{\text{(Present potential energy of the battery)}}{\text{(Original potential energy of the battery)}}$$

When the battery is fully charged, x equals 1. When the battery is fully discharged, x equals 0.

To study the change in a battery's performance over time, a scientist repeatedly charged and discharged cell 1 while leaving cell 2 intact. After several cycles of charging and discharging, the energy-storage capacity of cell 1 deteriorated significantly faster than the capacity of cell 2. Upon further testing, cell 1 was found to contain approximately equal concentrations of lithium oxide and cobalt(II) oxide. The constituents of cell 2 were not analyzed. The scientist hypothesized that the deterioration of cell 1 was caused primarily by the conversion of integral cell components into lithium oxide and cobalt(II) oxide.

23. What is the net overall equation for the cell?

A. $LiCoO_2 + 6C \rightleftharpoons Li_xC_6 + Li_{1-x}CoO_2$
B. $LiCoO_2 + xLi^+ + 6C \rightleftharpoons Li_xC_6 + Li_{1-x}CoO_2$
C. $Li^+ + 6C \rightleftharpoons Li_xC_6$
D. $LiCoO_2 + xLi^+ \rightleftharpoons Li_{1-x}CoO_2$

24. Which of the following is TRUE about the overall potential of the cell when the battery is in use after a complete charge?

A. $E^\circ_{cathode} + E^\circ_{anode} < 0$
B. $E^\circ_{cathode} + E^\circ_{anode} > 0$
C. $E^\circ_{cathode} + E^\circ_{anode} < 1$
D. $E^\circ_{cathode} + E^\circ_{anode} > 1$

25. Which of the following identifies the oxidized and then the reduced species in the forward reaction?

A. Oxidized: Li^+/Reduced: Co^{4+}
B. Oxidized: C/Reduced: Li
C. Oxidized: $C^{x/6}$/Reduced: Co^{4+}
D. Oxidized: Co^{3+}/Reduced: C

26. Which of the following is TRUE about the equilibrium constant of the reaction?

A. The forward reaction exhibits a positive E°_{cell}, which suggests a spontaneous process. Because discharging is spontaneous and charging is not, K_{eq} is high during discharging.
B. An increasing value of x will push the cathode reaction to the left and the anode reaction to the right; therefore, charging and discharging will have no net effect on K_{eq}.
C. Discharging is a spontaneous reaction, which requires reduction to occur at the cathode and oxidation to occur at the anode. Because this is only true for the reverse reaction, K_{eq} is low during discharging.
D. Based on the information in the passage, it is impossible to predict the effects of charging and discharging on K_{eq}.

27. A certain battery is equipped with a mechanism that calculates its remaining energy by approximating the concentration of various lithium-cobalt-oxygen complexes. The analysis finds that the predominant species in the battery are $LiCoO_2$ and $Li(CoO_2)_2$. If the battery originally stored 100 J of potential energy, how much does it currently store?

A. 100 J
B. 50 J
C. 33 J
D. 0 J

28. Which of the following lithium species carry an oxidation number of +1?

   I. Li from $LiCoO_2$
  II. Li from $Li_{1-x}CoO_2$
 III. Li from Li_xC_6

A. I only
B. II only
C. I and III only
D. I, II, and III

29. Which of the following BEST explains the appearance of lithium oxide and cobalt(II) oxide in cell 1?

A. A small number of lithium ions occasionally combined with $LiCoO_2$ to produce lithium oxide and cobalt(II) oxide.
B. Because of the energy released by the system, a few $LiCoO_2$ molecules decomposed into lithium oxide and cobalt(II) oxide every time the battery was used.
C. Various constituents of the cell combined with environmental oxygen to produce lithium oxide and cobalt(II) oxide.
D. Various constituents of the cell combined with water to produce lithium oxide and cobalt(II) oxide.

30. If the scientist's hypothesis is correct, which of the following methods would be most likely to effectively measure the deterioration in the energy-storage capacity of a cell (like the one in cell 1)?

A. Determining the value of x for a fully charged battery
B. Determining the value of x for a fully discharged battery
C. Measuring the concentration of cobalt(II) oxide in a fully discharged battery
D. Measuring the concentration of Li_xC_6 in a fully charged battery

PASSAGE IV (QUESTIONS 31–37)

Water is the most abundant liquid on Earth, covering over three-fourths of its surface. Compared with other liquids, it is quite extraordinary. Its chemical structure and resulting phase-change properties made the chances for the evolution of life on Earth a possibility. Due to their polarity, water molecules have the ability to form hydrogen bonds with one another and with other polar substances. As a result of these forces, water forms a crystalline lattice in its solid state, as depicted by the illustration below. The larger circles represent oxygen and the smaller circles represent hydrogen in the lattice.

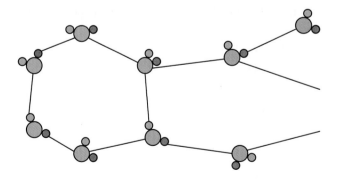

Ammonia is very similar in structure to water. Because of this similarity, many biologists have wondered whether ammonia would be a suitable substitute for water in living systems. The ammonia molecule is composed of hydrogen atoms covalently bonded to nitrogen. As the oxygen in the water molecule has a slightly negative charge, so does the nitrogen atom in ammonia. Some scientists have argued that ammonia-based life could evolve on other planets in a similar manner as life developed on Earth. Others argue that ammonia's heat of vaporization, 295 cal/g, is low compared with water, making it an unlikely candidate for the evolution of life. Modern science agrees that ammonia-based life on other planets will probably not be found to have evolved, if it exists, in the same manner as life on Earth.

31. One could infer from the passage that no form of life based on ammonia has yet been found because its

 A. evaporation rate would be too high.
 B. condensation rate would be too high.
 C. rate of deposition would be too high.
 D. rate of sublimation would be too low.

32. Had water not formed a crystalline lattice upon freezing and instead followed the common phase-change pathways of most other compounds, one could logically infer that

 A. life could not have evolved in a liquid environment.
 B. life would have evolved in a gaseous environment.
 C. soils would hold greater amounts of liquid water.
 D. soils would hold greater amounts of gaseous water.

33. When the water molecules shown in the previous illustration undergo sublimation, what BEST explains this phenomenon?

 A. The attractive forces between the water molecules overcome the kinetic energy that keeps them apart.
 B. The kinetic energy of the water molecules overcomes the attractive forces that keep them together.
 C. The hydrogen bonds between the water molecules form at a more rapid rate in the solid phase.
 D. The hydrogen bonds between the water molecules form at a more rapid rate in the liquid phase.

34. A change in which intrinsic property of water would MOST affect its polarity?

 A. Atomic electronegativity
 B. Chirality
 C. Intermolecular forces
 D. Solubility

35. How would one explain the negative slope of the water-solid equilibrium line in the phase diagram for water, shown below?

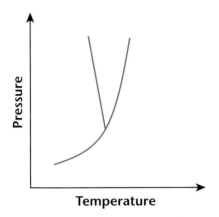

A. Water is more dense at 4° Celsius than at 0.
B. Water's solid lattice collapses under pressure.
C. The triple point determines the slope of the phase-change line.
D. Liquid water is less dense than ice.

36. According to the passage, which of the following is TRUE about a molecule of water undergoing evaporation?

A. The water molecule has more energy than an ammonia molecule.
B. An average water molecule is moving faster than an average molecule of ammonia.
C. The water molecule has less energy than an ammonia molecule.
D. Both A and B

37. What would the addition of an ionic compound do to the lattice structure shown in the illustration above?

A. Collapse the structure
B. Enhance cohesive forces in the structure
C. Enhance crystallization
D. Both B and C

PASSAGE V (QUESTIONS 38–45)

There are many elements in the periodic table that play an integral role in the everyday functions of the human body. While the most obvious of these are carbon, hydrogen, nitrogen, and oxygen, we also have various essential uses for phosphorus. Its physical and chemical properties have made it the perfect candidate to play a role in the molecule that acts as the body's primary location for short-term storage of energy, adenosine-5'-triphosphate (ATP).

Some metabolic syndromes can cause a phosphate ion to be drawn from the blood into the bones and teeth, where the majority of phosphorus exists. The ensuing deficiency of phosphate in the blood can lead to dysfunction of the brain and muscle tissue, which can cause death in severe cases. Scientists are attempting to cure these syndrome by designing a biologic molecule whose properties and actions are similar to those of phosphate. One way to do this is to find an element that has similar physical and chemical properties to phosphorus.

38. Which of the following is MOST likely to act as a stronger oxidizing agent than phosphorus?

A. Na
B. Cs
C. O
D. Bi

39. Which of the following, on average, has more space between two nuclei placed side-by-side than phosphorus?

I. K
II. Pb
III. F

A. I only
B. I and II
C. II and III
D. I, II, and III

40. Which of the following is NOT a property of phosphorus, according to the classifications of types of elements?

A. Brittle in the solid state
B. Poor electrical conductivity
C. Does not show much luster
D. Is generally malleable

41. Which of the following is the correct electron orbital configuration of phosphorus?

A. $1s^2 2s^2 3s^2 2p^6 3p^3$
B. $1s^2 2s^2 2p^6 3s^2 3p^3$
C. $1s^2 2s^2 2p^6 3p^5$
D. $1s^2 2s^2 2p^6 3s^2 3d^{10} 3p^6$

42. Which of the following statements is TRUE about the density of alkali metals and alkaline earth metals?

A. Alkaline earth metals are less dense because they contain unfilled subshells.
B. Alkaline earth metals are less dense because their nuclei contain fewer neutrons.
C. Alkali metals are less dense because they contain fewer orbitals.
D. Alkali metals are less dense because they have a loosely bound electron in their outer shell.

43. Which of the following is NOT a correct characterization of the properties of halogens?

A. At room temperature, halogens naturally exist only in the gaseous and liquid states.
B. Halogens are highly likely to react with alkali metals.
C. Halogens can form stable ionic crystals with alkaline earth metals.
D. In their neutral form, halogens always have an outer shell of p^5.

44. Which of the following contributes MOST to the malleability shown by transition elements?

A. Natural softness as compared to other metals
B. High electrical conductivity
C. Loosely held d-electrons
D. High melting points

45. Which of the following BEST explains why scientists closely examine metalloids when trying to find a biologic molecule to replace phosphorus?

A. Phosphorus is a metalloid.
B. Metalloids often behave as semiconductors.
C. Some metalloids exhibit similar bonding capabilities to phosphorus.
D. Metalloids exhibit flexibility in their properties so they can be manipulated easily.

PASSAGE VI (QUESTIONS 46–52)

Aerobic and anaerobic bacteria undergo different types of metabolism, and the properties of their metabolisms are unique. Some anaerobic bacteria are methane-producing bacteria. These bacteria have been studied to determine the relevance of their potential use in generating biological energy or *biogas*.

These methane-producing bacteria typically feed off of animal manure or other natural waste. In the process of utilizing animal waste, manure is collected from different types of animals including swine and cows. The manure is separated by phase and contains proteins, carbohydrates, and fats; bacteria then break down components into fatty acids.[1]

Methanogens are the particular type of anaerobic bacteria that undertake the final steps of breaking down the fatty acids into simple products: methane and carbon dioxide. A common reactant is acetic acid, which breaks down according to the following reaction:

$$CH_3COOH \longrightarrow CH_4 + CO_2$$

Other fatty acids can be used as substrates for these methane-generating reactions, including propionate and butyrate. Methanogenic bacteria can also convert carbon dioxide and hydrogen gas to form methane and water. At the end of this process, which typically takes place at 95° Celsius, methane can be used to generate energy as an alternative to fossil fuels.

46. What type of reaction is presented in the passage?

A. Combination reaction

B. Single-displacement reaction

C. Decomposition reaction

D. Combustion reaction

47. If the reaction begins with 120 grams of acetic acid, what is the theoretical yield, in grams, of methane?

A. 32.05 grams

B. 64.1 grams

C. 40.92 grams

D. 29.12 grams

48. What piece of evidence would support the passage's argument that the decomposition of fatty acids can create energy serving as an alternative to fossil fuel?

A. Anaerobic bacteria can break down fatty acids efficiently at room temperature.

B. Methane gas can be compressed and transported.

C. The reaction generates gaseous products.

D. The reaction is exothermic.

49. What formula BEST demonstrates how to calculate the number of grams of acetic acid necessary to produce 88.02 grams of carbon dioxide?

A. $\dfrac{(88.02 \text{ grams})(\text{molecular weight } CH_3COOH)}{(\text{molecular weight } CO_2)}$

B. $\dfrac{(88.02 \text{ grams})(2 \text{ moles } CH_3COOH)(\text{molecular weight } CH_3COOH)}{(\text{molecular weight } CO_2)(1 \text{ mole } CO_2)}$

C. $\dfrac{(\text{molecular weight } CH_3COOH)}{(88.02 \text{ grams})(\text{molecular weight } CO_2)}$

D. $\dfrac{(2 \text{ moles } CH_3COOH)(\text{molecular weight of } CO_2)(\text{molecular weight } CH_3COOH)}{(88.02 \text{ grams})(1 \text{ mole } CO_2)}$

---

[1]Information for this entire passage taken primarily from:
www.thepigsite.com/articles/4/waste-and-odor/914/manure-to-energy-the-utah-project ($C_6H_{13}O_5 + xH_2O \rightarrow COOH-(CH_2)_n-CH_3 \rightarrow 4CH_4 + 2CO_2$)
With contributions from:
extension.missouri.edu/xplor/agguides/agengin/g01881.htm ($H_2 + CO_2 \rightarrow H_2O + CH_4$)
books.google.com/books?id=ndPuyf4BsXYC&pg=PA26&lpg=PA26&dq=methane+and+bacteria+equation&source=web&ots=sbBVmswSMF&sig=6pQ
eW_uEd6WiSvcgPuHf_YdYQ4M&hl=en&sa=X&oi=book_result&resnum=5&ct=result
$CH_3COOH \rightarrow CH_4 + CO_2$ $CO_2 + 4H_2 \rightarrow CH_4 + 2H_2O$

50. One form of acetic acid, which is typically used as a salt, is called acetate. Sodium acetate can react with other chemical compounds in solution, an example of which is demonstrated below.

What is the correct net ionic equation for this reaction?

A. $Na^+ + CH_3COO^- + Cl^- + CH_3CH_2CH_2^+ \longrightarrow$
   $CH_3COOCH_2CH_2CH_3 + Na^+ + Cl^-$

B. $CH_3COO^- + Cl^- + CH_3CH_2CH_2^+ \longrightarrow$
   $CH_3COOCH_2CH_2CH_3 + Cl^-$

C. $CH_3COO^- + CH_3CH_2CH_2^+ \longrightarrow$
   $CH_3COOCH_2CH_2CH_3$

D. $CH_3COO^- + CH_3CH_2CH_2Cl \longrightarrow$
   $CH_3COOCH_2CH_2CH_3 + Cl^-$

51. As described in the passage, methanogenic bacteria can utilize hydrogen gas to produce methane. At standard temperature and pressure, if there are 3 liters of hydrogen gas and 2 liters of carbon dioxide available to the bacteria, what would be the theoretical yield, in moles, of methane?

A. 0.134 moles
B. 0.0893 moles
C. 0.0335 moles
D. 0.536 moles

52. What is the percent yield if 8.02 g of methane is formed from the reaction of 50 liters of hydrogen gas, with excess carbon dioxide at standard temperature and pressure?

A. 43.1%
B. 14.4%
C. 89.6%
D. 64.7%

Practice Section 3

Time—70 minutes

QUESTIONS 1–52

Directions: Most of the questions in the following General Chemistry Practice Section are organized into groups, with a descriptive passage preceding each group of questions. Study the passage, then select the single best answer to the question in each group. Some of the questions are not based on a descriptive passage; you must also select the best answer to these questions. In you are unsure of the best answer, eliminate the choices that you know are incorrect, then select an answer from the choices that remain.

Period 1 / IA / 1A … 18 / vIIIA / 8A

Period	1 IA 1A	2 IIA 2A	3 IIIB 3B	4 IVB 4B	5 VB 5B	6 VIB 6B	7 VIIB 7B	8	9 VIII --	10 8	11 IB 1B	12 IIB 2B	13 IIIA 3A	14 IVA 4A	15 VA 5A	16 VIA 6A	17 VIIA 7A	18 vIIIA 8A
1	1 H 1.008																	2 He 4.003
2	3 Li 6.941	4 Be 9.012											5 B 10.81	6 C 12.01	7 N 14.01	8 O 16.00	9 F 19.00	10 Ne 20.18
3	11 Na 22.99	12 Mg 24.31											13 Al 26.98	14 Si 28.09	15 P 30.97	16 S 32.07	17 Cl 35.45	18 Ar 39.95
4	19 K 39.10	20 Ca 40.08	21 Sc 44.96	22 Ti 47.88	23 V 50.94	24 Cr 52.00	25 Mn 54.94	26 Fe 55.85	27 Co 58.47	28 Ni 58.69	29 Cu 63.55	30 Zn 65.39	31 Ga 69.72	32 Ge 72.59	33 As 74.92	34 Se 78.96	35 Br 79.90	36 Kr 83.80
5	37 Rb 85.47	38 Sr 87.62	39 Y 88.91	40 Zr 91.22	41 Nb 92.91	42 Mo 95.94	43 Tc (98)	44 Ru 101.1	45 Rh 102.9	46 Pd 106.4	47 Ag 107.9	48 Cd 112.4	49 In 114.8	50 Sn 118.7	51 Sb 121.8	52 Te 127.6	53 I 126.9	54 Xe 131.3
6	55 Cs 132.9	56 Ba 137.3	57 La* 138.9	72 Hf 178.5	73 Ta 180.9	74 W 183.9	75 Re 186.2	76 Os 190.2	77 Ir 190.2	78 Pt 195.1	79 Au 197.0	80 Hg 200.5	81 Tl 204.4	82 Pb 207.2	83 Bi 209.0	84 Po (210)	85 At (210)	86 Rn (222)
7	87 Fr (223)	88 Ra (226)	89 Ac~ (227)	104 Rf (257)	105 Db (260)	106 Sg (263)	107 Bh (262)	108 Hs (265)	109 Mt (266)	110 --- ()	111 --- ()	112 --- ()		114 --- ()		116 --- ()		118 --- ()

Lanthanide Series*	58 Ce 140.1	59 Pr 140.9	60 Nd 144.2	61 Pm (147)	62 Sm 150.4	63 Eu 152.0	64 Gd 157.3	65 Tb 158.9	66 Dy 162.5	67 Ho 164.9	68 Er 167.3	69 Tm 168.9	70 Yb 173.0	71 Lu 175.0
Actinide Series~	90 Th 232.0	91 Pa (231)	92 U (238)	93 Np (237)	94 Pu (242)	95 Am (243)	96 Cm (247)	97 Bk (247)	98 Cf (249)	99 Es (254)	100 Fm (253)	101 Md (256)	102 No (254)	103 Lr (257)

PASSAGE I (QUESTIONS 1–8)

The blood-brain barrier is a unique part of the human nervous system. Endothelial cells lining blood vessels in the central nervous system (CNS) are more tightly attached to one another than in other parts of the human body. As a result, there is limited permeability of both small and large molecules from the circulation into the cerebrospinal fluid (CSF).

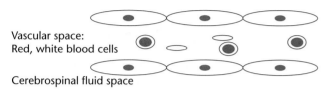

Vascular space:
Red, white blood cells

Cerebrospinal fluid space

These tightly sealed endothelial cells have both advantages and disadvantages in the human system. The CNS is a fragile, essential part of the human body, and the endothelial cells serve as a barrier. Multiple characteristics of any given molecule affect its permeability: its polarity, size, weight, charge, and degree of protein binding in the blood. Nonpolar molecules pass more effectively from the bloodstream into the CSF. Smaller particles, such as water, and small, charged particles will also move with varying ease across this barrier. Water moves freely, but charged ions can take hours to equilibrate between the systemic circulation and the CSF.

When disease afflicts the CNS, it is necessary to deliver drugs to the cerebrospinal fluid for delivery into the tissues of the brain and spinal cord. On the other hand, some extremely effective chemotherapeutic agents, such as cisplatin, are beneficial when they do not cross the blood-brain barrier because they are neurotoxic when they penetrate the CNS. Alternatively, when beginning general anesthesia for a surgical procedure, it is essential that anesthetic agents penetrate from the systemic circulation into the CSF to alter consciousness and systemic muscle tone during the procedure.

1. Based on the passage, which of the following characteristics would be essential for any pharmaceutical intended for use as a general anesthetic?

   A. The molecule should be nonpolar.
   B. The molecule should be directly delivered to the CNS without going through the systemic circulation first.
   C. The molecule should be polar.
   D. The molecule should be slow-acting.

2. What can be logically inferred from the passage about charge and its effect on a molecule's permeability of the blood-brain barrier?

   A. Charged molecules are more likely to associate with one another tightly in the blood stream, inhibiting diffusion into the CSF.
   B. Uncharged molecules are more likely to be able to diffuse between endothelial cells.
   C. Uncharged molecules are less likely to be transported through endothelial cells.
   D. Charged molecules are more soluble in the bloodstream than in the CSF.

3. What can be logically inferred from the passage about the role of the blood-brain barrier in supporting human life?

   A. A permeable CNS is essential in allowing diffusion of nutrients from the peripheral circulation into the CNS.
   B. The micro-environment of the CNS is similar to that of the systemic circulation.
   C. The blood-brain barrier limits the flow of damaged or infected cells from the CSF into the systemic circulation.
   D. The blood-brain barrier adaptively protects the CNS from toxins or other possible insults originating in the systemic circulation.

4. Based on the information in the passage, what type of intermolecular force has the MOST influence on molecules that pass easily through the blood-brain barrier?

    A. Ion-dipole interactions
    B. Dipole-dipole interactions
    C. Hydrogen bonding
    D. Dispersion forces

5. Which of the following statements is NOT true when relating formal charge with permeation across the blood-brain barrier?

    I. A formal charge of zero guarantees permeability through the blood-brain barrier.
    II. A negative formal change on one or more atoms in a molecule will improve its permeability of the blood-brain barrier.
    III. Two molecules, both with formal charges of zero, will be equally permeable through the blood-brain barrier.

    A. I only
    B. III only
    C. II and III only
    D. I, II, and III

6. Cisplatin, a commonly used chemotherapeutic agent, is $PtCl_2(NH_3)_2$. What type of bond forms between each of the NH_3 groups and the central platinum?

    A. Coordinate covalent bond
    B. Polar covalent bond
    C. Nonpolar covalent bond
    D. Ionic bond

7. Phenytoin, shown below, is an anti-seizure medicine. It is one of many drugs that is actively transported *out* of the CNS by cellular transporters. What would be the best estimate of the geometry around the central carbon to which the arrow points?

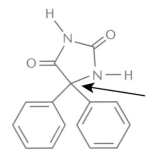

    A. Square planar
    B. Tetrahedral
    C. Trigonal pyramidal
    D. Octahedral

8. Which of the following BEST describes the relationship between resonance structures and molecular polarity?

    A. The most stable resonance structures maximize polarity.
    B. If a molecule has more than one important resonance structure, it is more likely to be a polar molecule than another molecule without such resonance structures.
    C. The most important resonance structures spread out and minimize formal charge.
    D. Resonance structures will counterbalance the natural polarity of a bond.

PASSAGE II (QUESTIONS 9–16)

The human body is a dynamic system that has to deal with significant environmental threats on a daily basis. One type of threat is from the effects of reactive oxygen species (ROS). ROS are ions or small molecules containing oxygen that have unpaired valence shell electrons. The superoxide anion, O_2^-, is a toxic threat, becoming lethal at intracellular levels of just 1 nM. It spontaneously forms O_2 and H_2O_2, but is also able to react with NO to form peroxynitrite. Peroxynitrite can cause extreme cellular damage. The enzyme NADPH oxidase produces the superoxide anion in the body to combat invading microorganisms. Because of the threat that it poses in such small quantities, the body has developed ways to dispose of this chemical.

The superoxide anion puts the concept of compartmentalization on display. It would be a waste of energy to both produce and destroy superoxide in the same cell, so it is only produced in phagocytes (immune cells that ingest infectious agents), and is broken down in any other cell of the body. In two steps, the enzyme superoxide dismutase (SOD) uses iron or other metals to create oxygen and hydrogen peroxide from superoxide and hydrogen ions:

Step 1: $Fe^{3+} - SOD + O_2^- \rightarrow Fe^{2+} - SOD + O_2$

Step 2: $Fe^{2+} - SOD + O_2^- + 2H^+ \rightarrow Fe^{3+} - SOD + H_2O_2$

A graduate student at a local university was given the task of determining the kinetics of this reaction. Her results are shown in table 1 below:

Trial	$[H^+]_{initial}$ (M)	$[O_2^-]_{initial}$ (M)	$r_{initial}$ (M/sec)
1	1	1	2.04
2	1	2	7.98
3	4	1	8.09

Table 1

The potential energy diagram for the reaction is shown in figure 1 below:

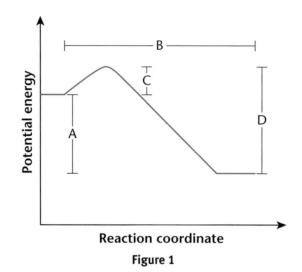

Reaction coordinate

Figure 1

FOR QUESTIONS 9–14, ASSUME BOTH STEPS OF THE REACTION ARE IRREVERSIBLE.

9. What is the order of H^+ in step 2 of the above reaction?

A. 0
B. 1
C. 2
D. 3

10. What is the rate of step 2 of the reaction if the following concentrations of reactants exist? Assume the rate constant, $k = 0.50$.

$$[H^+] = 2 \text{ M}, [O_2^-] = 2 \text{ M}$$

A. 2.5 M/sec
B. 4 M/sec
C. 8 M/sec
D. 10 M/sec

11. What function might Fe^{2+} – SOD play in the overall reaction?

    A. A substance used to create a product in the reaction

    B. A substance that is created in the reaction

    C. A substance that increases the rate of the reaction

    D. A short-lived, unstable molecule in the reaction

12. Which of the following is NOT true when describing the kinetics of the previous overall reaction?

    A. The rate of the reaction is proportional to the number of collisions between reacting molecules.

    B. In some effective collisions, all of the colliding particles do not have enough kinetic energy to exceed activation energy.

    C. A transition state is formed when old bonds are breaking and new bonds are forming.

    D. The activated complex has greater energy than either products or reactants.

13. What section of the diagram in figure 1 represents the forward activation energy?

    A. A

    B. B

    C. C

    D. D

14. What section of the diagram in figure 1 represents the enthalpy change during the reaction?

    A. A

    B. B

    C. C

    D. D

FOR QUESTIONS 15–16, ASSUME BOTH STEPS OF THE REACTION ARE REVERSIBLE.

15. What is the equilibrium constant for the overall reaction in the passage and will an increase in pressure raise or lower the equilibrium constant? Assume $[O_2^-] = 3$ M, $[H^+] = 1$ M, $[H_2O_2] = 1$ M, $[O_2] = 2$ M.

    A. 0.22; raise

    B. 0.27; lower

    C. 2.2; raise

    D. 2.7; lower

16. What would BEST explain the equilibrium shift to the right in reaction 2?

    A. Increase in volume

    B. Addition of product

    C. Addition of reactant

    D. Decrease in temperature

QUESTIONS 17–21 ARE NOT BASED ON A DESCRIPTIVE PASSAGE.

17. Latent heat flux is the loss of heat by the surface of a body of water caused by evaporation. To determine the latent heat flux over the Atlantic Ocean, one would need to know

    A. ΔH_{fusion} of water.

    B. $\Delta H_{vaporization}$ of water.

    C. $\Delta H_{sublimation}$ of water.

    D. $\Delta H_{ionization}$ of water.

18. If the pK_a of a weak acid is 5, the pH will be 6

    A. when the concentration of dissociated acid is one-tenth the concentration of undissociated acid.

    B. when half the acid is dissociated.

    C. when the concentration of dissociated acid is ten times the concentration of undissociated acid.

    D. only after a base has been added.

19. What compound would NOT be considered an electrolyte?

    A. AgCl
    B. CaO
    C. LiI
    D. HBr

20. Aluminum has a lower electronegativity than iron, but reacts extremely slowly with oxygen in moist air because of a hard, protective aluminum oxide coat that protects all exposed surfaces. Under which of the following conditions would aluminum be more readily eroded?

    A. Immersed in a solution of HCl
    B. Immersed in a bath of hot sodium metal
    C. Immersed in a solution of NH_3
    D. Immersed in a solution of NaOH

21. Two gases, X and Y, are combined in a closed container. At STP, the average velocity of a gas A molecule is twice that of a gas B molecule. Gases A and B are most likely which of the following?

    A. He and Ar
    B. He and Kr
    C. Ne and Ar
    D. Ne and Kr

PASSAGE III (QUESTIONS 22–29)

Dry ice forms when carbon dioxide gas is cooled to −78° C at atmospheric pressure. After becoming solid, it reforms gas when heat is added as shown in the reversible reaction below:

CO_2 (solid, −78° C) + heat (120kJ/mol) ↔ CO_2 (gas, 25° C)

An experiment was done to test the change, over three days, in a block of dry ice placed in a rigid container at room temperature at 1 atmosphere of pressure. The container was closed to the outside environment for the duration of the experiment. The only components in the container were the dry ice and air (g). No liquid in the container was detected over the three-day period. The apparatus and results of the experiment are shown in Figure 1 below.

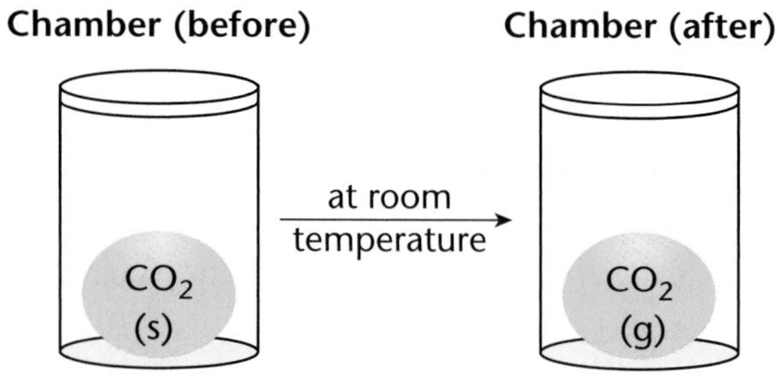

Chamber (before)   **Chamber (after)**

at room temperature

CO_2 (s) CO_2 (g)

Figure 1

As a solid, carbon dioxide has many uses, not the least of which is cooling its surroundings. This transfer of energy is a main method by which coolants operate in many mechanical devices. The phase diagram for carbon dioxide is a major reason for its unique behaviors. The phase diagram for carbon dioxide is shown in Figure 2 below.

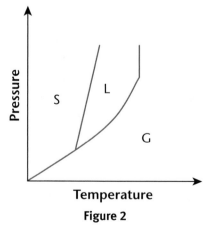

Figure 2

22. Which of the following BEST describes the equation in the passage?

   A. Evaporation
   B. Condensation
   C. Fusion
   D. Sublimation

23. Referring to figure 2, if liquid carbon dioxide were subject to increasing pressure at a constant temperature, it would

   A. become solid.
   B. become gaseous.
   C. gain kinetic energy.
   D. lose kinetic energy.

24. It can be inferred from the results of the experiment that the air in the container

   A. lost kinetic energy.
   B. gained kinetic energy.
   C. gained volume.
   D. lost volume.

25. When the dry ice molecules shown undergo phase changes, which of the following is a likely cause?

   A. The attractive forces between the carbon dioxide molecules overcome the kinetic energy that keeps them apart.
   B. The kinetic energy of the carbon dioxide molecules overcomes the attractive forces that keep them together.
   C. The hydrogen bonds between the carbon dioxide molecules form at a more rapid rate in the solid phase.
   D. The hydrogen bonds between the carbon dioxide molecules form at a more rapid rate in the liquid phase.

26. The process shown in the experiment from the passage was

   A. endothermic, and the dry ice gained potential energy.
   B. endothermic, and the dry ice lost potential energy.
   C. exothermic, and the dry ice gained potential energy.
   D. exothermic, and the dry ice lost potential energy.

27. If the experiment from the passage were allowed to continue until all the carbon dioxide changed phase, one could logically predict that the air in the container would have

   A. increased in pressure.
   B. decreased in volume.
   C. become a solid.
   D. increased in temperature.

28. In the heating/cooling curve for carbon dioxide shown below, what represents the location of the phase change described in the passage?

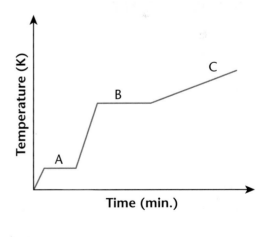

   A. A
   B. B
   C. C
   D. None of the above

29. In the phase diagram for carbon dioxide shown below, what represents the phase change shown in the experiment in the passage?

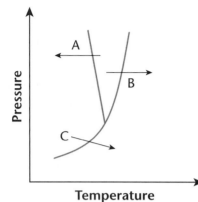

A. A

B. B

C. C

D. None of the above

QUESTIONS 30–36 ARE NOT BASED ON A DESCRIPTIVE PASSAGE.

30. Which of the following will result in a negative free energy change for a reaction?

A. The enthalpy change is negative.

B. The entropy change is positive.

C. The enthalpy change is negative and the entropy change is negative.

D. The enthalpy change is negative and the entropy change is positive.

31. Compared to the atomic radius of calcium, the atomic radius of gallium is

A. larger, because increased electron charge requires that the same force be distributed over a greater number of electrons.

B. smaller, because gallium gives up more electrons, decreasing its size.

C. smaller, because increased nuclear charge causes the electrons to be held more tightly.

D. larger, because its additional electrons increases the volume of the atom.

32. Under which conditions would water vapor demonstrate behavior closest to an ideal gas?

A. High pressure, low temperature

B. Low pressure, low temperature

C. High pressure, high temperature

D. Low pressure, high temperature

33. If the pressure of an ideal gas in a closed container is halved while the volume is held constant, the temperature of the gas

A. decreases by a factor of 2.

B. decreases by a factor of 4.

C. remains the same.

D. increases by a factor of 4.

34. "Greenhouse gases" are gases that will absorb IR radiation and trap energy between the Earth and the atmosphere. CO_2 and H_2O both strongly absorb radiation and are thus considered greenhouse gases, while N_2 and O_2 do not. One quality of greenhouse gases is that

A. they are composed of polar molecules.

B. they have a permanent dipole moment.

C. they experience hydrogen bonding.

D. they have polar covalent bonds.

35. What element contains unpaired electrons in its most common ionized state?

A. Fluorine

B. Aluminum

C. Zinc

D. Iron

36. Which of the following is the correct electron configuration for chromium in the ground state?

A. $[Ar]3d^45s^2$

B. $[Kr]4d^55s^1$

C. $[Ar]4s^14p^5$

D. $[Ar]3d^54s^1$

PASSAGE IV (QUESTIONS 37–45)

Decompression sickness involves symptoms that arise from exposure to a rapid decrease in ambient pressure. Decompression sickness can occur in multiple scenarios of decreased pressure and is most prevalent when divers return to the surface of water after a deep dive. If a diver ascends quickly and does not carry out decompression stops, gas bubbles can form in the body and create a multitude of adverse symptoms.

A diver experiences an increase in pressure when submerged many feet under water. Inert gases in the high-pressure environment dissolve into body tissues and liquids. When a diver comes back to the water's surface and the pressure decreases, the excess gas dissolved in the body comes out of solution. Gas bubbles form if inert gas comes out of the body too quickly. These bubbles are unable to leave through the lungs and subsequently cause symptoms such as itching skin, rashes, joint pain, paralysis, and even death.

At sea level the pressure exerted on one square inch is equal to 14.7 pounds, or 1 atm. In water, an additional 1 atm of pressure is exerted for every 33 feet (about 10 m) below sea level. In addition to the decompression sickness, there are other conditions of which divers must be aware that arise from specific gases as a result of the high-pressure environment. For example, increased concentrations of nitrogen in the body lead to nitrogen narcosis. A diver with nitrogen narcosis feels intoxicated and experiences loss of decision-making skills due to nitrogen's anesthetic quality. The table below provides a list of gases and their corresponding solubility constants in water at 298 K.

Gas	k (M torr^{-1})
CO_2	4.48×10^{-5}
O_2	1.66×10^{-6}
He	5.1×10^{-7}
H_2	1.04×10^{-6}
N_2	8.42×10^{-7}

37. What theory could be used to determine the amount of oxygen that is dissolved in water at sea level?

A. Henry's law

B. Boyle's law

C. Raoult's law

D. Le Châtelier's principle

38. What is the solubility (g/L) of N_2 in water (25° C) when the N_2 partial pressure is 0.634 atm?

A. 3.19×10^{-1} g/L

B. 1.5×10^{-2} g/L

C. 1.14×10^{-2} g/L

D. 1.5×10^{-5} g/L

39. Helium is mixed with oxygen in the scuba tanks of divers in order to dilute the oxygen. Why is helium chosen over other gases for this purpose?

A. It is not a diatomic gas.

B. It is less soluble in aqueous solutions and so does not dissolve in body tissues and fluids.

C. It can react with other gases that may dissolve in the body to reverse gas bubble formation.

D. It is present only in trace amounts in water.

40. A scuba tank is filled with 0.32 kg O_2 that is compressed to a volume of 2.8 L. If the temperature of the tank equilibrates with the water at 13° Celsius, what is the pressure inside the tank?

A. 111 atm

B. 83.9 atm

C. 54.6 atm

D. 290 atm

41. Which of the following would you recommend for a diver suffering from decompression sickness?

A. Administration of helium gas

B. Administration of a gas and air mixture, which contains 50 percent nitrous oxide

C. Confinement in a hypobaric chamber

D. Confinement in a hyperbaric chamber

42. The underwater environment in the world's oceans is rapidly changing. Recent years have seen drastic shifts in the ecosystem due to human activity and its impact on the environment. Many populations of fish that rely heavily upon oxygen are declining at extraordinary rates, whereas other ocean species that can survive in oceanic regions of oxygen-depletion are on the rise. What is the most likely explanation, based on scientific theory, for the decline in dissolved oxygen in the world's oceans?

A. Carbon dioxide pollution has increased ocean acidity.

B. A new species of predator shark preys on fish in oxygen-rich regions.

C. The average temperature of the oceans is rapidly increasing.

D. Increased rainfall has added water to oceans without adding more oxygen.

43. A scuba tank contains 0.38 kg of oxygen gas under high pressure. What volume would the oxygen occupy at STP?

A. 0.27 L

B. 35 L

C. 266 L

D. 11 L

44. At 1 atm, the solubility of pure nitrogen in the blood at normal body temperature (37° C) is 6.2×10^{-4} M. If a diver is at a depth where the pressure is equal to 3 atm and breathes air (78% N_2), calculate the concentration of nitrogen in the diver's blood.

A. 1.3×10^{-3} M

B. 1.4×10^{-3} M

C. 1.5×10^{-5} M

D. 1.9×10^{-3} M

45. Consider two scuba tanks at sea level and 25° C. Tank 1 is filled with oxygen, and tank 2 is filled with a mixture of oxygen and helium. Will there be a difference in the root-mean-square velocities between these two tanks?

    A. Yes, tank 2 has a higher root-mean-square velocity.

    B. Yes, tank 1 has a higher root-mean-square velocity.

    C. No, they will have the same root-mean-square velocity.

    D. The root-mean-square velocity cannot be calculated for the tanks.

PASSAGE V (QUESTIONS 46–52)

Sodium fluoride is used in toothpastes to reduce the virulence of bacteria that cause *dental caries*, also known as cavities. Most U.S. residents are exposed to sodium fluoride, and its use has been correlated with a decline in the incidence of dental caries in most of the population. Although there is debate over the mechanism by which sodium fluoride acts to reduce dental caries, it has been established that the fluoride ion is the main contributor to its efficacy.

Fluoride is the ionic form of the element fluorine. The fluoride ion has a high degree of electronegativity and so holds a negative charge in solution. It thus forms relatively stable bonds with positive ions such as H^+ and Na^+. Fluoride inhibits carinogenic bacteria from metabolizing carbohydrates and thus prevents subsequent production of acid in the oral cavity. The decrease of acidity reduces erosion of tooth enamel, which would otherwise lead to fissures and irregular surface changes in the tooth.

In a variety of laboratory studies, certain types of *Streptococci* bacteria, a main culprit in the formation of caries, are adversely affected when exposed to fluoride ion concentrations of varying levels. In particular, it was found that *Streptococcus mutans*, the more virulent species of the *Streptococci*, produces less acid when exposed to fluoride than *Streptococcus sobrinus*, the less virulent form. The reasons for the link of reduced acid production to fluoride levels are still unclear.

46. Based on the passage, which of the following can be definitively stated about the action of fluoride ions on oral health?

    A. F^- prevents bacteria from forming dental caries.

    B. F^- kills populations of bacteria that cause dental caries.

    C. F^- is related to killing populations of bacteria that form dental caries.

    D. F^- is related to less acid production and reduces the risk of dental caries.

47. Based on the passage, what is a possible mechanism by which fluoride could act upon *Streptococci* bacteria to reduce their production of acid?

    A. Fluoride adds enamel to the developing tooth structure.

    B. Fluoride fills and closes fissures within the enamel topography.

    C. Fluoride adds electrons to bacterial respiration reactions.

    D. Fluoride pulls electrons from bacterial respiration reactions.

48. What property contributes to the high electronegativity found in the fluorine atom?

    A. Small atomic radius

    B. Small number of protons in the nucleus

    C. Large number of electrons in the orbit

    D. Large number of electron shells in the orbit

49. Which of the following is the correct electronic structure notation for fluoride?

A. $1s^2 2s^2 2p^5$
B. $1s^2 2s^2 2p^4$
C. $[He]2s^2 2p^6$
D. $[Ne]2p^6$

50. According to Heisenberg, what can be accurately, quantitatively determined in a neutral atom when the location of the electron is found?

A. Electron momentum
B. Velocity of electron
C. Mass of electron
D. None of the above

51. What is the effective nuclear charge on the outermost electron in fluoride?

A. 9
B. 2
C. 7
D. 8

52. What electrons are most available for bonding in the fluoride ion?

A. 3s
B. 2p
C. 1s
D. 2s

Answers and Explanations

ANSWER KEY

1.	A	19.	C	37.	B
2.	C	20.	C	38.	A
3.	D	21.	A	39.	C
4.	A	22.	C	40.	D
5.	B	23.	D	41.	C
6.	D	24.	A	42.	B
7.	C	25.	C	43.	A
8.	C	26.	D	44.	A
9.	B	27.	B	45.	C
10.	B	28.	A	46.	B
11.	D	29.	B	47.	B
12.	B	30.	A	48.	C
13.	D	31.	B	49.	B
14.	A	32.	C	50.	A
15.	A	33.	D	51.	D
16.	B	34.	C	52.	C
17.	C	35.	A		
18.	B	36.	C		

PASSAGE I

1. A

There are two concepts involved here. The first is that both of these species are strong acids, so they will fully ionize in solution; the bivalent species has two H^+ ions for every one H^+ ion of the monovalent species, so it will produce a more acidic solution. Second is the idea that a more acidic solution will have a lower pK_a.

2. C

It is given in the passage that the pH of normal rain is 5.2, so this problem is simply asking you to convert pH = 5.2 into $[H^+]$. Using the Kaplan logarithm estimation procedure on the answers, it is clear that the only concentration that will produce a pH of 5.2 is (C).

3. D

It is important to know that every Arrhenius acid is also a Brønsted-Lowry acid, and that every Brønsted-Lowry acid is also a Lewis acid (the same idea applies for bases). This means that (B) and (C) can be eliminated. Sulfuric acid produces protons, so it is qualified as an Arrhenius acid, and we then know it can be called a Brønsted-Lowry or Lewis acid as well. All of the items are correct.

4. A

We are able to tell that HCO_3^- is a buffer because it can either donate or accept a proton. Being able to donate its remaining H^+ allows it to act as an acid, while its overall negative charge allows it to act as base and accept an H^+. (A) is correct because HCO_3^- will accept a proton from the acid introduced to the blood stream, and act as a buffer. (B) is incorrect because while it will act as a buffer, it will accept an H^+ ion, not donate an H^+ ion. (C) is incorrect because HCO_3^- does act as a buffer. (D) is incorrect because there is enough information.

5. B

Write down the steps as you go. First, we need to figure out what the original $[H^+]$ is in the rain. Because H_2SO_4 is bivalent, we double its concentration to find its contribution to the total $[H^+]$, which is 4.0×10^{-3} M. We then add this to 3.2×10^{-3} M to get $[H^+]_{rain} = 7.2 \times 10^{-3}$ M. If we divide this number by 4 (the factor by which the volume decreased, use $V_1C_1 = V_2C_2$), we get $[H^+]_{rain+pure} = 1.8 \times 10^{-3}$ M. Finally, we can use Kaplan's logarithm estimation strategy to find that the pH is just below 3, so 2.8 is the answer.

6. D

A conjugate base is an acid that loses a proton. (D) shows an acid and a molecule that has lost a molecule of H_2O, so it is not an acid/conjugate base pair. The other choices show an acid and conjugate base that has one less proton.

7. C

This question tests your ability to actively read the passage and synthesize the information presented. The student would likely agree with (A) because pollution is a major cause of acid rain, and industrialization over the past 150 years has greatly increased pollution levels. The student would likely agree with (B) because, as shown in the passage, radicals are integral in the formation of acid rain. The student would likely disagree with (C) because more acid content in water would increase the conductive capacity of water. The student would likely agree with (D) because while rain is naturally acidic, acid rain contains dangerous levels of acid.

8. C

The first pK_a in this curve can be estimated by eye. It is located between the starting point (when no base had been added yet), and the first equivalence point. This point is at pH of approximately 6.3. The value of the second pK_a is notable because it is found in a slightly different way than the first pK_a. It is located at the midpoint between the first and second equivalence points. In this curve, that corresponds to pH = 10.3

9. B

Equivalence points are at the midpoint of the quickly escalating slope range. In this titration curve, the value of the first equivalence point is 7.8 and the value of the second is 12.0.

PASSAGE II

10. B

Many MCAT Physical Sciences questions include dimensional analysis calculations. If you do not know the specific heat of water from memory, you'll want to know this constant on Test Day! (It is reported in paragraph 1.) The correct answer is (B). (A) is tempting, as it has the same magnitude as the specific heat of water in $Jg^{-1}K^{-1}$. You will need to convert (A) from grams to moles using the molecular mass of pure water, 18 g/mol. (C) and (D) differ from (B) and (D) by factors of 1,000, a frequent source of error in thermochemistry problems (using kJ rather than J).

11. D

This is a discrete question which draws on information from the passage. The passage does not provide an explicit comparison of intensive and extensive physical properties. You can infer from paragraph 1, however, that intensive properties do not depend on the amount of substance present in the measurement, and that extensive properties do. While viscosity is irrelevant to this specific experiment, it is an intensive property of a liquid. Mass, heat, and enthalpy are all extensive properties. (Heat is an extensive property; temperature is an intensive property.) The correct answer is (D).

12. B

Use a calorimetry equation to determine the heat capacity of the calorimeter. This setup requires referring to table 1, which describes how the student calibrated the instrument. The equation must account for all heat inputs and outputs in the closed system. In short, the heat lost by one part of the system must be gained by another part of the system. Here, the cold water heats up, and the hot water cools.

That transition is summarized by the equation $m_{hot}C_{H20}(T_f - T_{i,hot}) = m_{cold}C_{H20}(T_f - T_{i,cold}) + K_{cal}(T_f - T_{i,cold})$. Use the density of pure liquid water, 1 g/mL, to convert the volumes of hot and cold water to mass quantities. (B) is the answer. (A) is the specific heat of water, not the heat capacity of the calorimeter. (C) results from reversing the sign of the hot water temperature change, which obtains a negative heat capacity value. (D) is off by a factor of 1,000, using water's specific heat in kg.

13. D

While it is true that mercury is much more dense than alcohol, the thermometer content should not make a difference in the student's results within this temperature range [(A) and (B)]. There is no information to suggest the relative precision of the instruments (C). (Had the question asked about a digital thermometer, this would be relevant.) (D) is correct. There should be negligible differences in the ΔT obtained by each respective thermometer, though initial and final temperature measurements may vary slightly for each instrument.

14. A

Styrofoam is an excellent, though imperfect, insulator. Calibration accounts for heat loss to the calorimeter. The amount of water is irrelevant in a specific heat measurement, and that the calibration is supposed to account for the properties of the styrofoam (B). Calibration (C) accounts for a heat transfer, not a temperature change. The water temperature equilibrates in order to calibrate the thermometer, but that doesn't suggest anything about the reaction of other calorimeter contents inside (D).

15. A

The addition of salt ions to pure water disrupts hydrogen bonding between water molecules. When an aqueous solution is more disordered, there are weaker forces between component molecules. Compared to a highly stable hydrogen bond network like water, the salt water solution is disordered enough that its intermolecular bonding is much easier to break, lowering its specific heat.

16. B

Pressure must remain constant; paragraph 3 implies that bomb calorimeters are useful because they maintain constant pressure. Though specific heat is an intensive quantity, it is important to keep track of mass for the overall calorimetry calculation, which can involve different substances with different heat capacities. Heat should not enter or exit the system in a precise measurement. Items I and III are correct so the answer is (B).

17. C

Bomb calorimeters operate at high pressure, so they can accommodate temperature changes in a gas. Coffee cup calorimeters are no longer useful when the water boils. (A), (B), and (D) are distractors. Saltwater (A), as an aqueous ionic solution, is analogous to the fruit punch solution described in the passage. While ethanol (B) boils at a lower temperature than water, its structure is highly similar to that of pure water and it is relatively stable at room temperature. Coffee cup calorimeters can measure the specific heat of a metal like copper (D) if it is placed in water.

QUESTIONS 18–21

18. B

For every 2 mol of HCl, 1 mol of hydrogen gas is produced (assuming excess magnesium). Multiplying both sides of the ratio by 1.5 means that 3 mol HCl under the same conditions should produce 1.5 mol hydrogen gas. At STP, 1 mol of a gas (assuming it to be ideal) occupies 22.4 L so 1.5 mol HCl should occupy 33.6 L.

19. C

Savvy test takers will note that (A) and (D) can be eliminated because the answer is internally inconsistent; favoring a reaction almost always means increasing its rate. To decide between (B) and (C), reason via Le Châtelier's principle. The stress is heat. An endothermic reaction requires heat and so is more likely to consume the heat (i.e., reduce the stress) than an exothermic reaction, which will add to the stress by producing heat.

20. C

By definition, gamma radiation is a stream of energy that in addition to creating the Hulk has neither mass nor charge. No such thing as delta radiation (D) has been defined. Alpha particles and beta particles have both charge and mass.

21. A

Rust, or corrosion, is the oxidation of a substance when it comes into contact with both water and oxygen. (B) can be eliminated because, if true, this would enhance the reactivity of Al or Zn. (C) can be eliminated because reducing agents are oxidized and so that would make Al or Zn more likely to rust. (D) is incorrect because, because Al and Zn still rust, just more slowly than iron. As a metal rusts it oxidizes and thus function as a reducing agent. Self-protective oxides (a common way of finding alkali metals as well) prevent further oxidation by complexing the atom with oxygen.

PASSAGE III

22. C

Compound C is shown to promote the reaction without affecting the overall yield of product. It is not consumed or produced in the net reaction, either. This is enough information to identify compound C as a catalyst, which decreases the activation energy of a reaction by definition. In this case, (C) is more likely than (D). Step 1 of the reaction is the fast step and step 2 is the rate-determining, slow step. Even though the catalyst may have an effect on the fast step, its primary purpose is to speed up the slow step. The bulk of the energy input in the overall reaction is in step 2. The catalyst decreases the activation energy, so it is likely to have its primary effect on the step that requires the greatest energy input.

23. D

To answer this question, you must apply Le Châtelier's principle, which states that adding a compound to a system will shift the system reaction such that less of that compound is produced. Adding compound A decreases the overall yield of the system. This change pushes the equilibrium in step 1 to the left to produce more of compound AB and less of compound A. Unbound compound B is not involved in any step of the reaction, so adding it will have no effect on any of the steps. Compound C is a catalyst; increasing the concentration of a catalyst may increase the rate of the reaction, but will not affect the equilibrium constant at any given temperature. The correct answer is (D), as compound D is present on the left side of step 2. Adding more of compound D will push the reaction to the right, increasing the amount of product.

24. A

In terms of concentration, K_{eq} is equal to [products]/[reactants]. An increased concentration of products signifies an increased equilibrium constant, so K_{eq} of this reaction will increase along with the equilibrium concentration of BD. The data suggest that this concentration increases with increasing reaction temperature, but the concentration starts to stabilize after the temperature reaches approximately 100° C. Only (A) contains a graph demonstrating a K_{eq} which initially increases with temperature but starts to level off around 100° C. (B) shows a graph which follows the opposite of the correct path. (C) suggests that the equilibrium constant rises faster and faster as temperature increases, which is incorrect. (D) represents an equilibrium constant that does not change with temperature.

25. C

If a reaction is first-order with respect to each of the reactants, the overall rate is directly proportional to the concentration of each reactant. Doubling the concentration of compound AB will double the rate of reaction. In this new experiment, the concentration of compound AB is twice as high as the concentration used in the first experiment, so the rate of formation is also twice as high.

26. D

The data in the two tables shows that the second experiment, which omitted the catalytic compound C, was significantly slower than the first at every temperature except 150° C. Recall that under normal circumstances, a catalyst will speed up a reaction by decreasing its activation energy, thereby allowing the reaction to reach its activation energy more easily. Consequently, increasing the amount of heat will also help the reaction achieve its activation energy. In this particular experiment, the catalyzed experiment was not much faster than the uncatalyzed experiment at 150°C. This suggests that the reaction reached its activation energy without the help of a catalyst at this temperature range.

27. B

Single-replacement reactions involve the direct replacement of one constituent of a molecule with another constituent molecule. In this case, compound C replaced compound A to turn AB into BC. Double replacement reactions, on the other hand, involve the replacement of two different species. An example of such a reaction is AB + CD → AC + BD. Combination reactions require two or more molecules to combine into one molecule, as in step 2. Decomposition reactions require one molecule to break down into two or more molecules, as in step 3.

28. A

Gases are highly compressible, while solids and liquids are not. For this reason, changes in pressure will not have a substantial effect on solids and liquids. An increase in pressure will push the reaction toward the side with less gas molecules, while a decrease in pressure will do the opposite. Because step 1 is the only part of the reaction mechanism that involves gases, it is also the only part that will be affected by a change in pressure.

29. B

This system starts out with two gases (AB and C) and one solution (D) and ends with one gas (A) and two solutions (BD and C). Gases have higher average kinetic energies than solutions do, so they are more disordered (i.e., they have a higher overall entropy, which is a thermochemical measure of the relative disorder in a system). The entropy of the products is lower than the entropy of the reactants, so ΔS for the overall reaction is negative. Based on the information given, it is impossible to determine whether ΔH

is positive or negative. Although heat is added to stimulate the reaction, the passage does not specify how much heat is released at the end. ΔG is typically calculated from ΔH and ΔS. ΔH is not known, so ΔG is also impossible to determine.

PASSAGE IV

30. A

Newlands' table suggests that platinum is heavier than gold. According to the modern periodic table, gold is heavier than platinum. (B), (C), and (D) represent pairs of elements that were arranged correctly by Newlands.

31. B

Periods 2 and 3 of the periodic table, which contain only elements in the s-block and the p-block, are the only periods that actually contain exactly eight elements. If most of the elements in the d-block and the f-block were discovered, it would become obvious that elements do not occur in matching octaves. (A) is incorrect because the discovery of all of the s-block and p-block elements would create more matching octaves (although the theory would have to be modified to accommodate the noble gases). (C) is incorrect because the law of octaves does not exclude the possibility of electrons, as long as the electrons are not organized as in Bohr's theory. (D) is incorrect for the same reason as (C).

32. C

Mendeleev's table was organized in terms of atomic mass rather than atomic number. Item I did require modification because it was subsequently discovered that an element is characterized by its number of protons (rather than its mass). Item II did not require direct modification of the table and the existing entries were left intact; the only change was the knowledge that future entries would be organized according to their outer orbitals. Item III only strengthened Mendeleev's original model, since the discovery of gallium fulfilled his prediction that two elements exist between zinc and arsenic. Items II and III did not require modification, so (C) is the answer.

33. D

The passage states that Newlands's table contains all of the elements that had been discovered at the time. Because his table contains no noble gases, we can assume that they had not been discovered. The table contains uranium, which is an f-block element (A), and several instances of halogens and metalloids [(B) and (C)] are evident throughout the table.

34. C

An element's first ionization energy, which is defined as the tendency of the element to donate an electron, decreases with increasing atomic number within a period. Because Mendeleev's predicted element had a higher atomic number than calcium, it is less likely to lose an electron. Atomic radius and ionic radius [(A) and (B)] both decrease with increasing atomic number. Electron affinity increases with increasing atomic number within the same period (D).

35. A

Atomic radius increases as an element gains energy levels and decreases as an element gains protons and electrons; you should know that the largest elements are those that have more energy levels and are found near the bottom of the periodic table. Uranium is the only element on Newlands' table that has seven energy levels, meaning it has the largest atomic radius.

36. C

If Mendeleev had created his table in response to Newlands' theory, then Mendeleev would clearly never have made his breakthrough without Newlands' contribution; if this were the case, it's reasonable to say that Mendeleev simply modified the law of octaves, which was eventually refined to produce the modern version. (A) is incorrect because it does not suggest that Newlands had any impact on the development of today's periodic table. (B) also makes it unlikely for Newlands to have made a direct contribution to the evolution of the system, because Mendeleev only learned about Newlands' work after he had already invented his own table. (D) clarifies the fact that Mendeleev was the first person to publish the modern periodic table and

does not suggest that Newlands made any contribution to these findings.

PASSAGE V

37. B

This is a simple ideal gas law question. Using the equation $PV = nRT$, we are able to substitute: $(1 \text{ atm})(V) = (1 \text{ mole})(R)(318 \text{ K})$, which simplifies to $318R$. The answer does not need to be simplified past $318R$ (you are not allowed to use a calculator during the exam and multiplication by R takes too much time by hand).

38. A

This question tests your knowledge of the ideal gas law. The law shows that volume and temperature have a direct linear relationship ($PV = nRT$), meaning that as volume increases, so must T (assuming isobaric conditions). (B) shows an indirect linear relationship, (C) an exponential one, and (D) a logarithmic one.

39. C

In Experiment 2, we see that V_1 has been halved. So using the knowledge that temperature has been held constant, we know that the pressure must be double what it originally was to maintain the ideal gas law. So the right answer is 2 atm. The other choices all would violate the ideal gas law.

40. D

The a in the van der Waals equation accounts for the attractive forces between gas molecules. The b in the equation accounts for the actual volume that the molecules occupy (B). It isn't necessary to memorize the van der Waals equation for Test Day, but do know what a and b correct for in the equation.

41. C

The key here is realizing that 64 g O_2 is 2 mole O_2. Substituting the values given into this law, we get: $(2 \text{ atm})(3 \text{ L}) = (2 \text{ mole})(R)(T)$. This simplifies to $3/R$ K.

42. B

Dalton's law of partial pressures says that a gas's molar fraction multiplied by the total pressure gives the partial pressure supplied by that specific gas. This question asks specifically about 1.5 mole of NO, out of a total of 3 mole, which means that NO has a molar fraction of $X_{NO} = 0.5$. Solve for P using the ideal gas law: $(2 \text{ L})(P) = (3.0 \text{ mol})(R)(300 \text{ K})$, $P = 450R$ atm. This value multiplied by X_{NO} comes to $225R$ atm.

43. A

This question simply tests your knowledge of the conditions under which the ideal gas law is most relevant. The reference to experiment 1 is included just to mislead you. It is necessary to know only that the gases act closest to ideal when they are at high temperatures and low pressures.

44. A

At first glance, this question looks extremely simple, yet you must realize that if the center divider is receiving different pressures from each side, it will move until pressure from both sides is equal. When the experimenter reduced the molar concentration in V_2 by half, the pressure was reduced on the V_2 side of the divider, leading to the expansion of V_1. It is important to note that (B) and (D) are incorrect because the question explicitly states that the cylinder is allowed to re-equilibrate with the new molar concentrations.

PASSAGE VI

45. C

An oxidation-reduction reaction requires a transfer of electrons from one atom to another. This reaction simply involves the neutralization of a strong acid by a weak base; no electrons are transferred and all of the oxidation numbers stay constant throughout the reaction.

46. B

The conjugate base of a Brønsted-Lowry acid is the product that does NOT include the H^+ ion that came from the acid. Even if you did not know this definition, there is a hint to this answer in the passage; because the products in

reaction 1 contain a salt and an acid, it is clear that the salt is not the conjugate acid in neutralization reactions. Based on this information, you should be able to determine that the conjugate base is $MgCl_2$. You can determine the percent composition of the cation (Mg^{2+}) in this salt by dividing the molecular weight of the cation (24.3 g/mol) by the molecular weight of the molecule (95.2 g/mol). It should be obvious that 24.3/95.2 is approximately equal to 25/100, which equals 25%.

47. B

The passage states that efficacy is equal to the number of moles of HCl that can be neutralized by one gram of antacid. This means that the most effective antacids are those with the maximum neutralization capacity per gram. Because CO_3^{2-} can neutralize two H^+ ions, $Al_2(CO_3)_3$ has the capacity to neutralize six HCl molecules. Similarly, each of the other answer choices can neutralize three HCl molecules. (C) and (D) can be eliminated because they have the same neutralization capacity as $Al(OH)_3$, but are significantly heavier molecules. To decide between (A) and (B), consider that $Al_2(CO_3)_3$ has a molecular weight of 234 g/mol, while $Al(OH)_3$ has a molecular weight of 78 g/mol. Because $Al_2(CO_3)_3$ can neutralize only twice as many molecules as $Al(OH)_3$ but has nearly three times the weight, it is clear that $Al(OH)_3$ has the best per-weight efficacy.

48. C

The passage states that $NaHCO_3$ is an antacid, so (A) is incorrect. The reactions suggested in (C) and (D), where $H_2CO_3(aq)$ decomposes to produce H_2O (l) and CO_2 (g), is a common reaction that recurs every time H_2CO_3 is present in aqueous solution. Because nearly all the CO_2 is in gas form, it does not significantly affect the pH of the solution; this means that there are no acids left to decrease the pH and, therefore, $NaHCO_3$ is an effective antacid.

49. B

The limiting reagent is the reactant that is completely used up during the reaction while the other reactant still remains. Antacids are alkaline, so if the pH is below 7, there must not have been enough antacid to neutralize all of the HCl. This means that the progress of the reaction was limited by the amount of antacid.

50. A

The passage states that the student initially tested 1 gram of antacid along with 100 mL of 0.1 M HCl. Magnesium hydroxide, $Mg(OH)_2$, has a molecular weight of about 58 g/mol; because the answer choices are all very rough approximations, we can estimate the weight as about 50 g/mol in order to make the calculations easier. At this molecular weight, 1 gram of antacid is approximately equal to (1 g)/(50 g/mol) = 0.02 mol. 100 mL of 0.1 M HCl is equal to $(0.1 \text{ L}) \times (0.1 \text{ mol/L}) = 0.01$ mole. Because each molecule of $Mg(OH)_2$ has two OH^- ions, only half a mole of $Mg(OH)_2$ is required to neutralize a mole of acid; therefore, only 0.005 moles of antacid is used up. The student started with 0.02 moles of antacid, so he is now left with $0.02 - 0.005 = 0.015$ moles. To convert back to grams, we multiply 0.015 moles by 50 g/mol to get 0.75 g—which is equal to 750 mg.

51. D

A stronger antacid can neutralize the same amount of acid while using a smaller quantity of reactant. This means that more reactant will be left over after the neutralization is complete. Often, this leftover reactant will present itself in the precipitate (some antacids, however, will dissolve in the solution; this is why the student's logic was flawed). (A) is incorrect because the question states that the antacid is present as an excess reagent; increasing the amount of an excess reagent does not increase the amount of product unless more of the limiting reagent becomes available. (B) is incorrect for the same reason.

52. C

Sodium and potassium (and the rest of the alkali metals) form soluble salts, while aluminum, magnesium, and calcium do not; however, you do not need to know this fact in order to answer this question. The increased solubility of the compounds in group B caused the unreacted material to dissolve in solution, so the student was unable to detect any of the starting compound in the precipitate. The compounds in group A are sparingly soluble, so stronger antacids left a larger amount of unreacted solid. The alkalinity of the compound has no bearing on its ability to precipitate (A); also, you should know that strong bases containing sodium and potassium (i.e., NaOH and KOH) are just as alkaline as their counterparts which contain magnesium, calcium, and aluminum. (B) and (D) are accurate statements, but do not explain the student's results as well.

PRACTICE SECTION 2

ANSWER KEY

1.	B	19.	B	37.	A
2.	D	20.	A	38.	C
3.	A	21.	A	39.	B
4.	C	22.	C	40.	D
5.	B	23.	A	41.	B
6.	C	24.	B	42.	D
7.	D	25.	D	43.	A
8.	B	26.	C	44.	C
9.	B	27.	B	45.	C
10.	D	28.	D	46.	C
11.	A	29.	A	47.	A
12.	B	30.	C	48.	B
13.	A	31.	A	49.	A
14.	B	32.	A	50.	D
15.	C	33.	B	51.	C
16.	A	34.	A	52.	C
17.	C	35.	B		
18.	D	36.	D		

PASSAGE I

1. B

The dissociation reaction tells us that the coefficients for both products are equal to 1. We use this information to write the solubility equation. The solubility equation for the dissociation of $CaSO_4$ is the following:

$$4.93 \times 10^{-5} = [Ca^{2+}][SO_4^{2-}]$$

Because Ca^{2+} and SO_4^{2-} have a one-to-one ratio, they can be replaced by the variable x to solve for their concentration. Solving the equation $4.93 \times 10^{-5} = (x)^2$, we obtain a concentration of 7.02×10^{-3} M for each ion. Because one mole of ion is equivalent to one mole of salt, this is the concentration of $CaSO_4$ needed to equal the K_{sp}, at which point the solution is saturated. The concentration of $CaSO_4$ ions, 7.02×10^{-3} M, can be multiplied by the volume, 3.75×10^5 L, to obtain a value of 2.63×10^3 moles. Converting moles

of $CaSO_4$ to grams is accomplished by multiplying by the molar mass of $CaSO_4$, 136.14 grams/mole, to give a mass of 3.58×10^5 grams needed to reach saturation. (A) is the number of moles, not grams, of $CaSO_4$.

2. D

One way to solve this problem is to calculate the Ca^{2+} concentration for one mole of each compound using the K_{sp} and chemical equilibrium equation. Looking at the answer choices, (C) can be ruled out immediately because of the extremely small K_{sp}, which indicates that very few of the salt ions will dissolve. The other K_{sp} values are comparable for (A), (B), and (D). Remember to raise the ion to the power of its coefficient when setting up the equilibrium equation. For example, the equilibrium equation for (D) would be $K_{sp} = 6.47 \times 10^{-6} = [Ca^{2+}][IO_3^-]^2$. The concentration of calcium for each of these answer choices, respectively, equals 6.93×10^{-5} M, 2.14×10^{-4} M, and 1.17×10^{-2} M. (D) has the highest concentration of Ca^{2+} at 1.17×10^{-2} M.

3. A

The concentration of a saturated solution of $CaSO_4$ is equal to approximately 0.015 M, according to the graph. This number was found by determining the corresponding concentration for a conductivity value of 2500 μS/cm. The concentration of $CaSO_4$ is equal to the concentration of both Ca^{2+} and SO_4^{2-} ions in solution according to equation 1 because the coefficients are all 1. Therefore, the $K_{sp} = [Ca^{2+}][SO_4^{2-}] = (.015\ M)^2$, which equals 2.25×10^{-4} M^2. The concentration of $CaSO_4$ must be square to obtain the K_{sp}, so (B) is incorrect. (C) doubles, not squares, the concentration. (D) might be obtained if you had taken the square root, not squared, the concentration.

4. C

As temperature increases in a solution, movement of molecules and ions increase. This will increase the current between the electrodes in the probe and increase the value of conductivity. Temperature's effect on the solubility product constant cannot be determined without further information. Although many salts have a higher solubility with higher temperatures, not all salts share this property. The only sure way to determine the relationship is by experimentation. An increase in temperature would increase the conductivity, not decrease it, so (B) and (D) are incorrect. (A) is incorrect because it is impossible to determine the relationship between temperature and K_{sp}.

5. B

The common ion effect is when an ion is already present in the solution and affects the dissociation of a compound that contains the same ion. In this case, $Ca(OCl)_2$ contains calcium and will cause the reaction in equation 1 to shift to the left due to Le Châtelier's principle. If there is no $Ca(OCl)_2$ and therefore no extra Ca^{2+} present in solution, more $CaSO_4$ will dissociate. (C) is the opposite. (A) is misleading because chlorine gas will not react with SO_4^{2-}. (D) is incorrect because changing from $Ca(OCl)_2$ to chlorine gas will remove the common ion effect and cause more dissociation of $CaSO_4$.

6. C

An increase in pH means that fewer H^+ ions are present in solution. Lowering the concentration of H^+ will shift the equilibrium in equation 2 to the right, and fewer HOCl molecules will be in solution. Because the HOCl molecules can oxidize harmful agents, the oxidizing power has been reduced as a result of the pH increase. An increase in pH will not break the HOCl compound (A), though over time it will break down. Although salts do act as buffers (B), it is still possible to change the pH of the pool. As for (D), an increase in pH will decrease $[H^+]$ and thus result in fewer H^+ ions available to associate with OCl^-.

7. D

To make a supersaturated solution you must first heat the solution, which allows additional salt to dissolve. (While not all salts have a higher solubility at higher temperatures, this statement holds true for the majority of salts; an increase in temperature will generally increase the solubility of a collection of salts.) This occurs because at higher temperatures, the K_{sp} generally increases. The solution can then be cooled and the salt will remain dissolved, creating a supersaturated solution.

8. B

Using the top equation we can write the following:

$$K_{a2} = \frac{([H^+][CO_3^{2-}])}{[HCO_3^-]}$$

We can manipulate the equation to solve for $[H^+]$, where $[H^+] = \frac{(K_{a2}[HCO_3^-])}{[CO_3^{2-}]}$.

Using the bottom equation we can write the following: $K_{sp} = [Ca^{2+}][CO_3^{2-}]$

We can rearrange this equation to solve for $[CO_3^{2-}]$, which can then be substituted into the top equation:

$$[CO_3^{2-}] = \frac{K_{sp}}{[Ca^{2+}]}$$

Substituting into the top equation gives:

$$[H^+] = \left(\frac{K_{a2}}{C_{sp}}\right) \times [Ca^{2+}][HCO_3^-]$$

The K_a equation includes the reactant in the denominator because the reactant is aqueous (in contrast to the K_{sp} equation which doesn't include the reactant in the denominator). The K_{sp} reactant is a salt in its solid form; solids are not included in equilibria equations.

9. B

The color change will occur slightly before the pK_a of phenol red is reached. This is because the basic form, which is prevalent above the pK_a, has a higher absorptivity than the acidic form. This means that the basic form will absorb light more strongly than the acidic form. At the pK_a the basic and acidic forms are equal (definition of pK_a), but because of the higher absorptivity of the basic form, the color will begin to change when there still is more acidic than basic molecules of phenol red. (C) and (D) are above the pK_a value, after the color change has occurred. (A) is under the pK$_a$ but is too low. At pH 4, acidic molecules heavily dominate the solution so the absorptivity difference between acidic and basic forms does not come into play.

PASSAGE II

10. D

Hydrogen is diatomic in its elemental state, i.e., H$_2$ (g). The passage refers to the fact that each gaseous hydrogen atom has a single electron, for two total electrons in H$_2$, but the proper electron configuration of a diatomic substance requires using the bonding-antibonding model from molecular orbital theory. None of the choices are that specific, so they are not correct. (A) is a distortion; substances in their elemental state are presumed to keep their electrons in the ground state. (B) is a distortion as well; hydrogen is diatomic in its elemental state, meaning two electrons.

11. A

(B) is opposite; light is absorbed when the electron moves away from the nucleus. While electrons make the energy transitions, the energy transitions result in light radiation, not the emission of the electron itself, so (C) and (D) are incorrect.

12. B

The Lyman series transitions occur in the UV range (λ = 200–400 nm). The Balmer series corresponds to four visible wavelengths (λ = 400–700 nm), though the Balmer constant itself is in the UV range. Both the infrared and X-ray ranges of the light spectrum [(C) and (D)] fall far outside the transitions which characterize these spectra. Infrared rays are low-energy and have higher wavelengths, while X-rays are high-energy and have very short wavelengths. It is not necessary to memorize the specific wavelengths in different kinds of radiation as long as you have a general sense of differences in magnitude.

13. A

If you ignore the digression about astronomy, the question is straightforward and does not require referring back to the passage. It simply asks what color of visible light

corresponds to 656.3 nm. The visible light spectrum covers 400–700 nm. Using the ROYGBIV mnemonic and prior knowledge that infrared wavelengths are longer than visible wavelengths, you know that red is on the 700 nm end, and that violet is on the 400 nm end.

14. B

This image is an absorption spectrum, in contrast to the emission spectrum presented in the passage. Think of it as the inverse of the emission spectrum. We cannot tell from the passage what a Lyman or Bohr series looks like.

15. C

Deuterium is "heavy" hydrogen, with one neutron, one proton, and one electron. The Balmer series concerns only electron transitions, so there will be no change in the number of peaks. In other words, there will be the same number of peaks, but with more splitting; the nucleus is heavier, which will slow down the transitions. This effect is visible at high resolutions.

16. A

A full explanation is out of the scope of the MCAT Physical Sciences section, but you should know from general physics that Bohr's model was incomplete because it didn't incorporate the theory of relativity. We know from the question stem and equation that the Balmer series works only for wavelengths related to the quantized energy levels (B). Though it is not stated explicitly in the passage, Bohr's quantitative model incorporates atomic number (C) (more detail is unnecessary for now; in short, it affects the atomic radius). Hydrogen atoms have only one electron (D), and we have no indication that other particles are involved.

17. C

According to Bohr's model, the energy differences between quantized energy levels become progressively smaller the further away the electron moves from the nucleus. Textbooks will sometimes describe this concept as if the energy levels themselves are "narrowing." (If energy levels are depicted as rings around a nucleus, they will appear to be closer together as you move farther from the nucleus.) Read carefully. (B) describes a drawing like this one, but the graphical representation of this concept does not really explain the difference in energy. We do not have enough information in the passage to determine whether the energy levels themselves are a greater or smaller distance apart. (A) is the opposite of (B), intended to stump readers who might not read through to (C) and (D). Because (C) refers directly to energy differences between energy levels, it is more accurate. (Remember $E = hf = h \times$ [speed of light/ wavelength].) (D) is its opposite.

QUESTIONS 18–22

18. D

Only (D) gives a response where both kinds of particles have a mass. Neither neutrons nor gamma rays have mass and so they are unchanged by the actions of a particle accelerator. The dependence on mass arises because a particle accelerator works by means of high-energy ideally elastic collisions. Also, if there is no mass, both kinetic energy and momentum are undefined.

19. B

A solution is available here which doesn't require an equation. Both the acid and base are monoprotic, thus there are no multiple dissociations. Notice that the acid is twice as concentrated as the base. Thus, double the amount of base will be needed to neutralize the acid or $2 \times 15 \text{ mL} = 30 \text{ mL}$. If you forgot this factor of 2, you might have chosen (A), and if you squared the 2 out of uncertainty (only in physics do you square things when in doubt) you might have chosen (D). C is the total volume of the solution, not the volume just of the base.

20. A

The ideal gas theory assumes that the particles have large interatomic distances and a relative absence of intermolecular forces. This is more true at lower pressures than at higher ones, thus eliminating (C) and (D). (B) implies that high pressure squishes the molecules. According to the kinetic theory of gases, individual atoms are treated as incompressible point properties. The main effect of the pressure is to reduce the interatomic distance, not the intra-atomic distance (i.e., the atomic radius).

21. A

Molecules can only be nonpolar if they have total symmetry around the central atom. Bent molecules lack this symmetry (think of a molecule of water with two lone pairs of electrons and two hydrogen atoms extending from the central oxygen atom) and so a dipole is created which causes polarity in the molecule. A diatomic covalent (B) molecule (such as H_2 or O_2) is perfectly symmetrical. (C) and (D) are incorrect because, although dipoles can exist in these configurations, symmetrical arrangements are also possible.

22. C

Isotypes of the same element have the same number of protons. Alpha decay results in the loss of two protons and two neutrons, while beta decay (β-decay) causes the gain of one proton. Thus, two beta decays must occur for each alpha decay to ensure that the number of protons in the daughter nucleus is equal to the number of protons in the parent nucleus. The answer is (C), 1:2.

PASSAGE III

23. A

In order to balance the equation, we must first combine the half-reactions. This requires writing all of the products and all of the reactants for both reactions in one equation:

$$LiCoO_2 + xLi^+ + xe^- + 6C \rightleftharpoons Li_{1-x}CoO_2 + xLi^+ + xe^- + Li_xC_6$$

If a certain compound/particle is on both the left and the right sides of the equation, then it is appearing as both a reactant and a product. Since there is no net change in that specific species, we can omit it from the net reaction; for this reason, we can eliminate the terms "xLi^+" and "xe^-" from both sides of this equation. This leaves us with (A) as the correct choice.

24. B

You should know that the overall potential of a galvanic cell (E°_{cell}) is equal to the sum of the potentials at the cathode and the anode. The overall potential of a discharging cell is always positive, but not necessarily greater than 1; for this reason, (B) is the only viable option. You can also arrive at this conclusion by realizing that the reaction in a battery is always spontaneous, since the battery must supply energy. Spontaneous reactions always have a negative ΔG, which you can plug into the free energy equation ($\Delta G = -nFE^\circ_{cell}$). To get a negative ΔG from the free energy equation, you must have a positive E°_{cell}.

25. D

The first thing to note here is that lithium acts as an electrolyte in this reaction, meaning that it is not oxidized or reduced; that rules out (A) and (B) immediately. By definition, reduction happens at the cathode and oxidation happens at the anode. However, because this is a reversible reaction (which you should know based on the fact that the reaction is at equilibrium), we cannot use these definitions to distinguish between the species that is oxidized and the species that is reduced. The easiest way to answer this question is by noting that the carbon in the anode is neutral on the left side of the forward reaction and is negatively charged on the right side. This means that carbon is reduced, allowing us to select (D) as the correct answer. You can verify this by checking the cathode side: Because the cathode is made of CoO_2^-, in which Co has a +3 charge (since oxygen almost always carries a −2 charge, two oxygen atoms add up to a −4 charge; to create an overall −1 charge, Co must be +3), Co^{3+} must be oxidized in the conversion of $LiCoO_2$ to $Li_{1-x}CoO_2$. The product of this reaction, because it contains less +1 charge from lithium, must contain a more positive charge from cobalt (further confirming that the cobalt is reduced).

26. C

Because of the complexity of this question, the first step should be to eliminate as many choices as possible. There is no indication in the passage that E°_{cell} is positive for the forward reaction (A). The assumption about reaction kinetics in (B) is correct, but it's likely that the effect of a change in x will be different for each reaction. One reaction will shift to the left and the other will shift to the right, but the shifts will not be exactly identical to one another; therefore, K_{eq} will change and (B) is incorrect. A galvanic cell gradually discharges while transporting electrons from the anode, where oxidation occurs, to the cathode, where reduction occurs. In the forward reaction, oxidation occurs at the anode and reduction occurs at the cathode. This means that the forward reaction does not represent a discharging cell, so the reverse reaction must be favored when the battery is in use. Because the reverse reaction takes precedence over the forward reaction, K_{eq} is low when the cell is discharging.

27. B

$LiCoO_2$ is usually present in the battery since it is on the left side of the cathode reaction. The presence of the $Li(CoO_2)_2$ complex is more important for this question. It is clear that $Li(CoO_2)_2$ is a form of the $Li(CoO_2)_{1/(1-x)}$ complex, so we can calculate x by writing the equation $1/(1-x) = 2$. Simple algebra yields the fact that ½ of the battery's initial energy is remaining. Because the initial energy was equal to 100 J, the current energy equals 50 J.

28. D

According to the passage, the system contains only lithium as a salt in a solvent. Because it is not part of the cathode or the anode, it always retains its +1 charge. All three items are correct.

29. A

When atoms or molecules are in close proximity for an extended period of time, there is a substantial probability that they will interact with one another. The reaction suggested in (A) would require reduction of Co^{3+} to Co^{2+}, which is not unlikely to occur in small quantities. Though the passage does not directly indicate that this was the mechanism of production of lithium oxide and cobalt(II) oxide, it is more likely than any of the other answer choices. It would be incorrect to dismiss the possibility of decomposition, but the reaction suggested in (B) ($LiCoO_2 \rightarrow Li_2O + CoO$) is stoichiometrically impossible. (C) is incorrect because interaction with environmental oxygen would affect cell 2 just as much as it would affect cell 1. (D) is incorrect because we have no evidence suggesting that any water is present in the system; the passage clarifies that organic solvents are used.

30. C

The scientist believes that battery deterioration is caused primarily by the formation of cobalt(II) oxide and lithium oxide in equal quantities. Therefore, increased amounts of cobalt(II) oxide suggest a decrease in battery capacity. (A) and (B) are incorrect because x is a ratio that is unaffected by the energy storage capacity of a cell. (D) is incorrect because, although a decrease in concentration of Li_xC_6 would suggest a decrease in cell capacity, most of the deterioration is caused by the conversion of $LiCoO_2$ to Li_2O and CoO_2.

PASSAGE IV

31. A

Ammonia's heat of vaporization is given in the data and described as low compared with that of water. Thus, its evaporation rate must also be high compared to that of water so life could not have evolved in a liquid ammonia environment as life on earth evolved in a liquid water environment. The phases in (B), (C), and (D) would matter less for life's evolution from a liquid environment; they are also incorrect applications of the data from the passage.

32. A

Solid water would have been most dense if it were like other substances, and thus sunk to the bottom of any liquid system. Liquid systems would have been frozen from the bottom up, and life could not have evolved in the liquid phase of a watery environment. (B), (C), and (D) do not address this "what-if" scenario.

33. B

It is the kinetic energy of the molecules that moves them further apart to allow a phase change from solid to gas, as described in the question. The same process would dictate a phase change from solid to liquid, or liquid to gas.

34. A

The electronegativities of the atoms comprising a molecule determine the polarity of that molecule. None of the other choices will make as significant a contribution. (C) is the next most logical answer, but is less correct because forces emanate from the intrinsic nature of electronegativity within the water molecule, not between.

35. B

The crystalline lattice formed for a water-solid uniquely collapses under pressure to become a liquid. (A) is a true statement, though it doesn't directly address the question.

36. D

Both (A) and (B) are true. Water has a higher heat of vaporization than ammonia and therefore evaporates at a higher temperature. Temperature is a measurement of average kinetic energy, so high temperature means higher average kinetic energy; the molecules are also moving faster.

37. A

Ions dissolved in the lattice break existing intermolecular attractive forces. This process interferes with the formation of a crystal lattice in ice, which explains why ice melts when salt is added.

PASSAGE V

38. C

Asking for the strongest oxidizing agent is equal to asking for the element with the highest electronegativity. Electronegativity increases as we move from the left to the right and from the bottom to the top of the periodic table. Therefore, you are looking for an element that is above and to the right of phosphorus. (C), oxygen, fits this description.

39. B

You're being asked which elements have a larger atomic radius than phosphorus. Atomic radius increases from right to left and from top to bottom of the periodic table. Therefore, you are looking for elements that are below and to the left of phosphorus. Both K and Pb fit this description, so (B) is the correct answer.

40. D

To answer this question, you must know that phosphorus is a nonmetal. The other answer choices describe properties of nonmetals. (D) describes a property of metals, so it is the correct answer.

41. B

(B) is the correct full electron configuration. (C) places the 3s-electrons in the 3p-orbital. (D) is incorrect because phosphorus does not have a 3d-orbital.

42. D

(A) and (B) are incorrect because alkaline earth elements are generally more dense than alkali metals. (C) is incorrect because alkali metals contain the same number of orbitals as the alkaline earth element in the corresponding row. (D) is a true statement.

43. A

Halogens can naturally exist in the gaseous, liquid, and solid states (iodine).

44. C

(A), (B), (D) are all true properties of transition elements, but they do not greatly contribute to the malleability shown by these elements. Their malleability can be attributed mostly to the loosely held d-electrons.

45. C

(A) is incorrect because phosphorus is not a metalloid. Metalloids do often behave as semiconductors (B), but it is not relevant here. (C) is correct because both arsenic and antimony are in the same group as phosphorus and they have similar properties.

PASSAGE VI

46. C

The reaction presented in the passage, beginning with acetic acid and forming methane and carbon dioxide, is a decomposition reaction. It begins with one reactant and ends with two products, which is typical of a decomposition reaction. A combination reaction (A) would have been the opposite: more reactants than products. A single displacement reaction (B) typically is an oxidation/reduction reaction, which is not demonstrated in this question. A combustion reaction (D) is catalyzed by oxygen and results in carbon dioxide and water as products.

47. A

First, calculate the molecular weight of acetic acid, CH_3COOH, which is 60.05 g/mol. Next, recognize that there is a 1:1 molar ratio between this reactant and the product, methane. By beginning with 120.0 grams of acetic acid and dividing by the molecular weight, this yields 1.998 moles of acetic acid and should produce the same number of moles of methane. The molecular weight of methane is 16.04 g/mol. By multiplying this molecular weight by the number of expected moles yield, 1.998, the theoretical yield expected if all of the acetic acid were decomposed would be 32.05 grams of methane product.

48. B

A key issue in harnessing a gaseous product is its phase and transport, so (B) is correct. If compressible, then methane would take up significantly less volume and be easier to transport, making it more likely to be efficient as a common energy source. The passage states that this reaction typically takes place at a temperature well above room temperature. Even if (A) were true, it doesn't support an argument toward using methane gas as a major energy source. While (C) is true, the production of gas challenges, more than supports, the passage's argument of making clean energy. Finally, whether or not the reaction is exothermic, the energy source is the product, methane gas, so (D) presents an irrelevant piece of information.

49. A

To build the equation necessary to answer this question, begin with 88.02 grams of CO_2 in the numerator. Next, convert this to moles of CO_2 by dividing by grams per mole. This eliminates (D), since 88.02 grams is in the denominator and the molecular weight of CO_2 is in the numerator. (C) is also out with 88.02 grams in the denominator. Next, recognize that there is a 1:1 ratio of CO_2 to CH_3COOH, making it unnecessary to convert the number of moles. This eliminates (B), which incorrectly uses a 1:2 ratio. The only choice remaining is (A), which correctly ends by multiplying by the molecular weight of acetic acid; this would yield the number of grams of acetic acid necessary for the proposed reaction.

50. D

The net ionic equation shows all aqueous ions that productively participate in the reaction, eliminating all spectator ions. The only true spectator ion in this equation is sodium, so it should not be present in a net ionic equation, which proves that (A) is incorrect. Next, $CH_3CH_2CH_2Cl$ has a covalent bond between the carbon and chloride atoms, meaning that it is unlikely to ionize in solution; Thus, chloride should not be represented as an ion on the reactant side of the equation, as it is in (A) and (B). Finally, (D) correctly keeps the reactant as one molecule and has the chloride ion written as a product.

51. C

The first step in this question requires you to consider the correctly balanced equation for converting CO_2 and H_2 to CH_4 and H_2O (the reactants and products specified in the passage and in the question stem):

$$CO_2 + 4\,H_2 \rightarrow CH_4 + 2\,H_2O$$

The correctly balanced equation uses the molar ratio of 1 CO_2:4 H_2:1 CH_4:2 H_2O. Next, recall that according to the ideal gas law, one mole of an ideal gas has a volume of 22.4 L at standard temperature and pressure (STP). From this, one can calculate that there are 0.134 moles of hydrogen gas and 0.0893 moles of carbon dioxide available as reactants. Then, calculate the molar equivalents of each, since

4 moles of hydrogen gas are required per mole of CO_2. Thus, there are 0.0335 molar equivalents available of hydrogen gas per 0.0893 moles CO_2, meaning that the hydrogen gas is the limiting reagent. Finally, because there is one mole of methane produced per four moles of hydrogen gas used, there will be 0.0335 moles of methane produced. (A) does not account for the 4:1 molar equivalency of H_2:CH_4. (B) uses carbon dioxide as the limiting reagent. (D) reverses the molar ratio of H_2:CH_4, thus multiplying 0.134 moles by 4 instead of dividing.

52. C

Begin by calculating the theoretical yield of methane, which is the amount (in either grams or moles) of methane expected to be produced if all the hydrogen were fully consumed by the following formula:

$$CO_2 + 4\,H_2 \rightarrow CH_4 + 2\,H_2O$$

Recall that at STP, one mole of gas has a volume of 22.4 liters, which allows you to calculate that there are 2.23 moles of hydrogen gas given to react. Next, use the balanced equation for converting CO_2 and H_2 to CH_4 and H_2O (the reactants and products specified in the passage and in the question stem). The correctly balanced equation uses the molar ratio of 1 CO_2:4 H_2:1 CH_4:2 H_2O. Thus, with 2.23 moles of hydrogen gas, you would expect to form one mole of methane per four moles of hydrogen gas, or 0.558 moles of methane product. Finally, multiply by methane's molecular weight, 16.04, which results in 8.95 grams of methane; this is the theoretical yield. However, the question stem states that only 8.02 grams of methane were produced. Thus, the percent yield is calculated by dividing the actual yield (8.02 grams) by the theoretical yield (8.95 grams) and multiplying by 100 percent, which results in a percent yield of 89.6 percent.

PRACTICE SECTION 3

ANSWER KEY

1.	A	19.	A	37.	A
2.	B	20.	A	38.	C
3.	D	21.	D	39.	B
4.	D	22.	D	40.	B
5.	D	23.	A	41.	D
6.	A	24.	A	42.	C
7.	B	25.	B	43.	C
8.	C	26.	A	44.	B
9.	B	27.	A	45.	A
10.	B	28.	D	46.	D
11.	C	29.	C	47.	D
12.	B	30.	D	48.	A
13.	C	31.	C	49.	C
14.	A	32.	D	50.	D
15.	A	33.	A	51.	C
16.	C	34.	D	52.	B
17.	B	35.	D		
18.	C	36.	D		

PASSAGE I

1. A

For a molecule to pass from the systemic circulation to the CNS, it must pass between the tightly sealed endothelial cells or through the endothelial cells. Unless a medication has a transporter to cross the cell membrane twice, it is more likely to diffuse between endothelial cells, despite their tightly sealed spaces. Because cell membranes are composed primarily of nonpolar lipid molecules, it will be easiest for a lipophilic, or nonpolar compound to diffuse into the CSF. Although (B) does describe a method for delivering drugs to the CNS, a nonsystemic route would be inefficient for a process as routine as general anesthetic administration; (A) is a better option. (C) is incorrect, because nonpolar or lipophilic molecules will penetrate more effectively than will a polar molecule. (D) is irrelevant; furthermore, a slow-acting general anesthetic would be

impractical when physicians are aiming to minimize time under anesthesia and maximize patient comfort.

2. B

The key to understanding the blood-brain barrier is that the endothelial cells are tightly sealed, prohibiting free passage of molecules, unlike the leaky capillary systems of the peripheral circulation. The molecules that are most likely to still move between these cells and enter the CSF are those that are uncharged and not repelled by the hydrophilic cell membranes. Even though charged particles might associate closely with one another (A), this doesn't affect their passage through the blood-brain barrier. (D) is incorrect because the passage relates no information about the differential solubilities of charged molecules in the bloodstream versus CSF.

3. D

The blood-brain barrier, as described in the passage, provides a tight seal between the systemic circulation and the more sensitive CNS. As a result, this barrier can serve to protect the CNS from potentially damaging substances that can more readily enter the systemic circulation, and then be filtered before entering the CNS. (A) is incorrect because the blood-brain barrier's adaptive seal is not designed for maximizing nutrient transport; in fact, it limits transport/ transfer between two systems. (B) is incorrect because this barrier necessarily means that many molecules and particles cannot pass between the CNS and systemic compartments, thus making these two micro-environments different. (C) is incorrect because the blood-brain barrier's main role is not to limit movement of particles or agents from CSF to the systemic circulation, but rather to limit flow in the other direction because the systemic circulation is more readily contaminated.

4. D

According to the passage, molecules most likely to cross the blood-brain barrier are hydrophobic or nonpolar. Thus, ion-dipole and dipole-dipole interactions [(A) and (B)] are unlikely to be the most important forces governing intermolecular interactions among these molecules (because they require charge and/or polarity). Although hydrogen bonding (C) might have a role in these molecules, hydrogen bonds, because they occur between atoms in otherwise polarized bonds (a hydrogen with a partial negative charge and a lone pair or otherwise electronegative atom with a negative charge), would be unlikely to facilitate transport in a hydrophobic environment. Dispersion forces (D) refer to the unequal sharing of electrons that occurs among nonpolar molecules as the result of rapid polarization and counterpolarization; these are likely to be the prevailing intermolecular forces affecting molecules that move easily through the blood-brain barrier.

5. D

All three items are false. A polar molecule can still have a formal charge of zero, because the molecule's formal charge is the sum of the formal charges of the individual atoms. Each atom could individually still have a positive or negative formal charge, calculated by the formula:

FC = valence electrons − ½ bonding electrons − nonbonding electrons

Thus, a molecule with a formal charge of zero could have multiple polarized bonds and/or multiple atoms with positive/negative formal charges, making it unlikely to permeate through the nonpolar blood-brain barrier. Similarly, having a negative formal charge on the molecule overall would be unfavorable to move through a nonpolar barrier. Finally, two molecules, both with formal charges of zero, could have very different characteristics, making them more or less likely to permeate the blood-brain barrier. For example, one compound could be comprised entirely of nonpolar bonds, with all atoms of formal charge of zero, both of which would make it favorable to pass through the blood-brain barrier. Size also plays a key role, as large molecules do not readily pass through the barrier. A separate molecule with a formal charge of zero could, as described above, contain positive or negative formal charges

on different atoms and/or have polar bonds, making it pass through the barrier less readily.

6. A

In cisplatin, a molecule with square planar geometry, two chloride atoms and two ammonia molecules each are bonded directly to the central platinum, without any remaining lone pairs on the central platinum. The NH_3 groups bond to the central platinum by donating a lone pair of electrons into an unfilled orbital of the platinum atom. As such, NH_3 is acting as a Lewis base, and platinum is acting as a Lewis acid, and they form a coordinate covalent bond. A polar covalent bond (B) is not formed from this type of donation of a lone pair; an example of a polar covalent bond would be the N–H bonds in the NH_3 group, with partial negative charge on the nitrogen and partial positive charge on the hydrogen. In (C) and (D), the Pt–N bond is formed by a Lewis acid/base relationship, which is not the case for a nonpolar covalent bond or ionic bond.

7. B

Although the geometry of this carbon atom is likely to be changed somewhat by the ring strain on the adjacent ring structures, it is still most likely to approximate a tetrahedral geometry. This carbon is bonded to four groups: the two phenyl groups, a nitrogen, and the additional carbon atom in the adjacent carboxyl group. The tetrahedral geometry (B) maximizes the space among these four groups. Octahedral geometry (D) typically refers to a central atom surrounded by six groups, not four.

8. C

Resonance structures serve to spread out formal charge. The most important resonance structures minimize or eliminate the formal charge on individual atoms. As a result, polarity in any single bond might be minimized. (A) is essentially the opposite of this argument. (B) is incorrect; it is possible for molecules with or without resonance to be polar, and this is too broad of a generalization to be true. (D) is incorrect because polar bonds will intrinsically place a partial negative charge on the more electronegative atom.

Important resonance structures would likely further accentuate this inclination, placing extra electrons on more electronegative atoms. Counteracting this effect and essentially "removing" electrons from highly electronegative atoms to counterbalance the natural polarity of the bond would form an extremely high-energy, unfavorable, and thus unimportant, resonance structure.

PASSAGE II

9. B

The order of this reaction can be determined by the equation $r = k[A]^x [B]^y$. You must divide r_3 by r_1 to get: $\dfrac{8.09}{2.04} = \dfrac{k(4.00)^x(1.00)^y}{k(1.00)^x(1.00)^y}$. This simplifies to $4 = 4^x$, so $x = 1$. This means that H^+ is a first-order reactant.

10. B

The equation for the rate of a reaction is:

$$\text{Rate} = k[\text{reactant}_1]^{order1}[\text{reactant}_2]^{order2}$$

Using the equation for determining order of a reactant detailed in the explanation for the answer to question 9, we find that O_2 is second order. Substituting the information into the equation for the rate of a reaction leads to:

$$\text{Rate} = (0.5)[2.0\ M]^1[2.0\ M]^2$$

Simplifying this equation allows us to determine that the rate is 4 M/sec.

11. C

(C) is correct because it describes a catalyst, which is exactly the role Fe^{2+} – SOD plays. (A) is incorrect because it describes a reactant, and Fe^{2+} – SOD is not a reactant. (B) is incorrect because it describes a product, and Fe^{2+} – SOD is not a product. (D) describes a transition state, and is incorrect because transition states are temporary states of highest energy of the conversion of reactant to product.

12. B

(B) is not true (making it the correct answer) because all the colliding particles must have enough kinetic energy to exceed activation energy if a collision is to be effective. (A) is true because particles must collide to react, and thus the rate of reaction is both dependent on and proportional to the number of particles colliding. (C) is the accurate definition of a transition state. (D) is true because "activated complex" is another name for "transition state," which by definition has greater energy than both reactants and products.

13. C

Section C shows the energy that must be put into the reaction to drive it in a forward direction. Section A in the diagram represents the change in enthalpy; it shows the difference between the starting and the final energy values. Section B does not represent any specific energy value. Section D represents the reverse activation energy. It is much greater than the forward activation energy because the reactant is starting at a much lower level of energy, yet must still reach the same amount of total energy to proceed with the reaction.

14. A

Section A is correct because it shows the difference between the starting and the final energy values.

15. A

The equation to determine the equilibrium constant for a reaction $aA + bB = cC + dD$ is $K_c = ([C]^c[D]^d)/([A]^a[B]^b)$. For this reaction, $K_c = ([2]^1[1]^1/([3]^2[1]^2 = 2/9 = 0.22$. When the corresponding values are plugged into the equation, $K_c = 2/9$, or 0.22.

16. C

According to Le Châtelier's principle, the addition of a reactant (C) will cause an equilibrium to shift to the right. An increase in volume (A) would have no effect in this particular reaction. An addition of product (B) would cause a shift to the left. A temperature decrease (D) would most likely cause a shift to the left due to fewer numbers of collisions between particles, assuming kinetic energy is proportional to temperature.

QUESTIONS 17–21

17. B

The question says that latent heat flux is caused by evaporation. Therefore, simply identify which value of ΔH is related to this phase change. Vaporization is another way of saying evaporation, so (B) is correct. Fusion (A) refers to the change from a solid to a liquid, and sublimation (C) refers to the change from a solid to a gas. Ionization (D) is unrelated to a phase change.

18. C

The correct answer is (C) due to the Henderson-Hasselbach equation, which states that for a weak acid solution, the pH equals the pK_a plus the log of the ratio of the concentration of conjugate base to the concentration of acid.

$$pH = pK_a + \log([\text{conjugate base}]/[\text{acid}])$$

For an acid HX, the conjugate base is the X^- ion that is formed when the acid dissociates. Now, if the pK_a of an acid is 5, then for its pH to be 6, the log of that concentration ratio must be 1, or in other words, the ratio must be 10. This means that the concentration of conjugate base, and therefore of dissociated acid, must be 10 times the concentration of acid.

19. A

The question requires you to know the solubility rules. Because an electrolyte must dissociate into its component ions in water, look for the substance that will not dissociate. The answer is (A), silver chloride (AgCl), which is insoluble in water. All of the other compounds will readily dissociate into their constituent ions.

20. A

(A) is correct. Because aluminum oxide is alkaline, immersion in an acidic solution would readily strip away the protective coating and allow the acid to oxidize the metal below.

21. D

How can you relate the average velocities of gases at the same temperature? Two gases at the same temperature will have the same average molecular kinetic energy. Because two gases at the same temperature will have the same average molecular kinetic energy, $(1/2)m_A v_A^2 = (1/2)m_B v_B^2$, which gives $m_B/m_A = (v_A/v_B)^2$. Since $v_A/v_B = 2$, we have $m_B/m_A = 4$. Only (D) lists two gases with a mass ratio around 4:1 (krypton 83.3g/mol and neon 20.2 g/mol).

PASSAGE III

22. D

The solid block becomes smaller in the experiment and so must move from the solid phase to the gaseous phase, sublimation. The other answer choices require a liquid phase, which is not valid because the experimental results demonstrate that no liquid was detected when the solid shrunk in size.

23. A

The solid/liquid equilibrium line has a positive slope and so the phase change from liquid to solid at a constant temperature is the only correct possible phase change. (B) is wrong because the gas phase is not possible as pressure increases; the liquid would change to gas, however, if the temperature were increased while maintaining constant pressure. (C) and (D) are illogical because kinetic energy is equivalent to temperature. Because temperature is constant according to the question stem, there is no kinetic energy change.

24. A

You must deduce from both the experimental results and the chemical equation that the volume does not change. The volume does not change because it is described as a rigid container, and no change in volume is described in the experimental results. As a result, the dry ice must absorb energy from its surroundings (the air in the container) in order to change phase. Because the total energy must remain constant, the air initially present in the container must lose an equivalent amount of kinetic energy.

25. B

The chemical equation shows that the dry ice absorbs heat from its environment to change into a gas, requiring it to overcome the intermolecular forces that organize it in the solid form. (C) and (D) refer to hydrogen bonds, which are not present in carbon dioxide.

26. A

The chemical reaction shows that the conversion of solid carbon dioxide to the gaseous state requires an absorption of heat from the ambient air. This use of heat defines an endothermic reaction, which must therefore characterize the reaction occurring in the container. (C) and (D) refer to an exothermic reaction, which would release heat. (B) is incorrect since an endothermic reaction absorbs/uses heat, which increases the energy of some of the molecules in the reaction; thus, the potential energy should not decrease.

27. A

The air gains dry ice molecules and these exert a pressure on the container, according to the equation $PV = nRT$, where n represents the number of moles of gas. (B) is the opposite; its volume would increase, according to the same equation, if possible. However this experiment takes place in a rigid container, preventing any change in volume. (C) is incorrect because the question clearly states that the solid changes phase. In this endothermic reaction, air temperature decreases as the solid carbon dioxide absorbs energy in order to undergo sublimation.

28. D

None of the choices shows a substance moving from the solid directly to the gas phase in the process of sublimation. (A) and (B) show fusion and evaporation, respectively, but not sublimation. (C) indicates the heating of a gas; in the

experiment, the carbon dioxide solid increases its kinetic energy; the gas is not being heated.

29. C

(C) indicates change from a solid to a gas (sublimation) as described in the passage for dry ice.

QUESTIONS 30-36

30. D

Because $\Delta G = \Delta H - T\Delta S$ can be used to relate free energy to enthalpy and entropy, and T is always positive, a negative ΔH (enthalpy) and a positive ΔS (entropy) will always give a negative ΔG value; that is, the reaction will occur spontaneously. (D) is correct.

31. C

Moving from left to right across the periodic table, atomic radii will decrease. Because calcium is on the left side of the table and gallium is on the right, in the same period, gallium should have a smaller atomic radius. As stated in (C), this is due to the greater number of protons in the nucleus holding the electrons more tightly.

32. D

The major forces that cause gases to deviate from ideal behavior are intermolecular attractions and the volume of the gas molecules. These factors are minimized when gas molecules are far apart and moving quickly, which occurs at low pressures and high temperatures.

33. A

The question says that this gas is ideal, so use $PV = nRT$. The ideal gas law shows that P is directly proportional to T. So with volume held constant, if pressure is reduced by a factor of 2, temperature will also be reduced by a factor of 2. (A) is correct.

34. D

Though this question begins by telling you about greenhouse gases, it ultimately asks you to identify similarities between CO_2 and H_2O which N_2 and O_2 lack. CO_2 is not a polar molecule; its linear geometry allows the opposing dipole moments to cancel out, so (A) is incorrect. Because its dipole moments cancel, (B) is incorrect. Furthermore, it lacks hydrogen atoms and is therefore incapable of hydrogen bonding, so (C) is incorrect. However, both CO_2 and H_2O have polar bonds, while N_2 and O_2 both have diatomic, nonpolar covalent bonds between two atoms of the same element.

35. D

Fluorine (A) is not a transition metal, so its ionized counterparts will have a valence octet of electrons implying no unpaired electrons. (B), (C), (D) are all transition metals; however (B) and (C), commonly oxidize to the 2 and 3 positive states, respectively, which fill their d subshells. Iron (D) commonly oxidizes to the 2 positive state, which gives one extra s-subshell electron. This unpaired electron helps to give iron its magnetic properties and explains why iron in the body is further oxidized to the 3 positive state (to avoid inductive currents that could damage protein structure).

36. D

Following the Aufbau principle, the order of orbital filling should produce $[Ar]4s^23d^4$ as the electronic configuration for chromium. However, there is an overall increase in stability for the molecule if the d-subshell can be half-filled. Because of this, an electron will be moved from the 4s-subshell into the 3d-subshell giving (D) as the correct answer.

PASSAGE IV

37. A

Henry's law states that the amount of gas dissolved in a liquid is directly proportional to the partial pressure of the gas in equilibrium with the liquid. Therefore, Henry's law can be used to calculate the concentration of oxygen in water using the partial pressure of oxygen in air. Boyle's law (B) deals with the relationship between the pressure and volume of gases, but does not address concentration

of gases in water. Raoult's law (C) pertains to the vapor pressure of a mixture of liquids, not a gas dissolved in a liquid. Le Châtelier's principle (D) addresses changes to an equilibrium state and cannot stand alone to explain the equilibrium between a gas in air and in solution.

38. C

We can use the solubility constant for nitrogen provided in the passage, 8.42×10^{-7} M/torr, to solve this question. Because the units in the constant are in torr, we first convert 0.634 atm to torr by multiplying by 760 torr/1 atm. The partial pressure of nitrogen equals 481.8 torr. Multiplying the pressure by the constant 8.42×10^{-7} M/torr gives us 4.06×10^{-4} M nitrogen. The units for the answer are in g/L, so we multiply by the molar mass of nitrogen, 28 g/mole, to get our answer of 1.14×10^{-2} g/L.

39. B

The solubility constants provided in the passage can be used to determine that helium is the least soluble gas. A soluble gas is not desired because we want to minimize gas bubbles in the body. Moreover, helium is an inert gas, meaning it does not readily react with other gases. Whether helium is diatomic (A) has no bearing on its use in scuba tanks. Many gases are present in trace amounts in the water (D), so this fact alone could not account for the use of helium in scuba tanks.

40. B

This is a classic ideal gas law problem using $PV = nRT$. You are given the volume, then must convert the temperature to degrees Kelvin to obtain a useable temperature and must convert the mass of oxygen to moles to find n. V equals 2.80 L. T equals 273.15 + 13.0 = 286.15 K. The mass, 0.320 kg, equals 320 grams. We divide the mass by the molar mass of oxygen, 32 g/mole, to obtain the moles of oxygen, 10 moles. R equals 0.0821 L atm/(mole K). Plugging in these numbers to the equation, $PV = nRT$. Solving for P gives a pressure of 83.9 atm.

41. D

Immediate isolation in a hyperbaric chamber is the most effective and common treatment for those suffering from severe decompression sickness. The chamber recreates a high-pressure environment to allow gas bubbles to dissolve back into body fluids and tissues. The chamber can be brought back to normal pressure slowly in order to allow the body to adjust to the decreased pressure. Helium gas administration (A) or gas and air mixture (B) would not rid the body of excess gas bubbles. In fact, it might increase the gases bubbles and make symptoms worse. A hypobaric chamber (C) would certainly make symptoms worse because it decreases the pressure below 1 atm.

42. C

The solubility of gas in liquids decreases with an increase in liquid temperature. The warming of oceans has resulted in less dissolved oxygen and many oxygen-depleted "dead zones." It is true that carbon dioxide has increased ocean acidity (A), but acidity alone cannot account for decreased oxygen levels. A predator shark may explain why certain fish are dying off (B), but it would not explain the decrease in oxygen. If rainfall did increase water levels in the ocean (D), the oxygen levels would equilibrate (as per Henry's law) between the ocean and atmosphere to allow more dissolved oxygen in the oceans.

43. C

This is a $PV = nRT$ problem. Find the moles of oxygen by converting 0.38 kg to grams and dividing by the molar mass of oxygen, 32.g/mole. The number of moles equals 11.875. STP indicates a temperature of 273.15 K and a pressure of 1 atm. R equals 0.0821 (L atm/mole K). Plugging these numbers into $PV = nRT$ and solving for V gives a volume of 266 L.

44. B

Multiplying the amount of nitrogen gas in the air by the solubility constant of nitrogen will give the amount of nitrogen that is dissolved in the diver's blood. The solubility constant for nitrogen can be obtained by dividing the solubility of nitrogen, 6.2×10^{-4} M, by 1 atm to get 6.2×10^{-4} M/atm. The amount of nitrogen in the air can be obtained by finding the partial pressure of nitrogen. The total pressure, 3 atm, is multiplied by the percentage of nitrogen in the air, 78 percent, to get a partial pressure of nitrogen equal to 2.3 atm. Finally, we multiply 2.3 atm of nitrogen by the solubility constant to obtain a value of 1.4×10^{-3} M for the concentration of nitrogen in the diver's blood.

45. A

The root-mean-square velocity (v_{rms}) can be calculated by taking the square root of ($3RT/M_m$). This equation tells us that the v_{rms} increases when molar mass decreases. Tank 2 contains a mixture of helium and oxygen; the helium will lower the average molar mass of the gas molecules because it has a lower molar mass compared to oxygen. The v_{rms} of tank 2 will therefore be higher. Tank 1, which contains only oxygen, will have a higher molar mass and a lower v_{rms} value.

PASSAGE V

46. D

F^- is related to less acid production and reduces the risk of dental caries (D). The fluoride ion is related to acid production and reduces the risk of dental caries, according to the passage. Fluoride has not been proven to directly cause or even be related to bacterial death (B, C), nor has it directly been proven to stop bacteria from forming dental caries (A). However, fluoride is related to/correlated with acidity reduction and dental caries reduction. The other choices imply relationships and causations not inferred from the passage.

47. D

The high electronegativity of fluorine means that it is inclined to hold onto or pull electrons. (C) is the opposite of this atomic property because fluorine would not easily give off electrons. While the passage discusses fissures as a cause of caries [(A) and (B)], it does not infer that fluoride is involved directly with its filling or repair.

48. A

You must deduce from the definition of electronegativity that in order for the nucleus to pull on the orbital electrons, it should be closer to the electrons; therefore, a smaller radius is desirable. (B), (C), and (D) all contribute to a decrease in electronegativity because the distractors either favor a larger size of the atom with more electron shells or a smaller positive core of the protons that are responsible for the electronegative attraction in the first place.

49. C

The fluoride ion has the atomic structure of the element fluorine, which would be $1s^2 2s^2 2p^5$, with an additional electron to make it an anion with a charge of negative one. Using [He] at the beginning of the notation accurately reflects the fact that F^- has the same structure as helium, but with the additional electrons as noted. (A) is incorrect because this is the notation for the element fluorine, not the ion. (B) is the structure for oxygen. (D) is incorrect because when using the notation [Ne], one implies that the atom has the structure of that noble gas, with additional shells. [Ne] comes after fluorine in the periodic table, and it would not be correct to add a level 2 shell after completing that shell in [Ne].

50. D

(D) is correct because Heisenberg's uncertainty principle states that the momentum (m and v) cannot be determined exactly and quantitatively if the location of an electron in an atom is known and conversely, the location cannot be known if the momentum is known. One could get a qualitative measurement of momentum, since the measurement is still possible, but that measurement becomes less accurate as the accuracy of the measurement of position increases. (A), (B) and (C) all violate this principle, as the location is stated to be known in the stem of the question.

51. C

The effective nuclear charge is calculated by the following equation: $Z_{eff} = Z - S$, where Z is the atomic number (the number of protons in the nucleus), and S is the average number of electrons between the nucleus and the valence electrons (which is the equivalent of saying S is the number of inner or non-valence electrons). Because fluorine's atomic number is 9, there are also 9 electrons in fluorine (not an ion). Of these 9 electrons, 7 are in the outer shell (valence) and 2 electrons are inner electrons, therefore these electrons would have a Z_{eff} of the following: $Z_{eff} = 9 - 2 = 7$. Now for the fluoride ion, there are now 10 total electrons. However, there are still only 2 inner electrons, so these 8 outer electrons would have a Z_{eff} of the following: $Z_{eff} = 9 - 2 = 7$. Without changing the number of inner electrons, the effective nuclear charge will not change. This would affect the radius, however, as fluoride now has 8 valence electrons distributing the same Z_{eff} of 7, whereas fluorine has only 7 electrons sharing the Z_{eff} of 7. This is why anions are larger than their respective unionized species.

52. B

(B) is correct because the highest electron shells, or orbitals, are most loosely held by the nucleons and thus are most available for bonding. 3s is higher than any other level (A), but it is unoccupied in the fluoride ion. (C) and (D) are lower energy levels/orbitals than 2p.

Glossary

Absolute zero The temperature at which all substances have no thermal energy; 0K or −273.15°C.

Absorption spectrum The series of discrete lines at characteristic frequencies representing the energy required to make an electron in an atom jump from the ground state to an excited state.

Acid A species that donates hydrogen ions and/or accepts electrons. See *acidic solution; arrhenius acid; brønsted-lowry acid; lewis acid.*

Acid dissociation constant (K_a) The equilibrium constant that measures the degree of dissociation for an acid under specific conditions. For an acid HA,

$$K_a = \frac{[H^+][A^-]}{HA}$$

Acidic solution An aqueous solution that contains more H^+ ions than OH^- ions. The pH of an acidic solution is less than 7.

Activated complex The transition state of a reaction in which old bonds are partially broken and new bonds are partially formed. The activated complex has a higher energy than the reactants or products of the reaction.

Activation energy (E_a) The minimum amount of energy required for a reaction to occur.

Adiabatic process A process that occurs without the transfer of heat to or from the system.

Alkali metals Elements found in Group IA of the periodic table. They are highly reactive, readily losing one valence electron to form ionic compounds with nonmetals.

Alkaline earth metals Elements found in Group IIA of the periodic table. Their chemistry is similar to that of the alkali metals, except that they have two valence electrons and, thus, form 2^+ cations.

Amphiprotic species A reaction species that may either gain or lose a proton.

Amphoteric species A species capable of reacting as either an acid or base, depending on the nature of the reactants.

Anion An ionic species with a negative charge.

Anode The electrode at which oxidation occurs. Compare *cathode.*

Antibonding orbital *Molecular orbital* formed by the overlap of two or more atomic orbitals whose energy is greater than the energy of the original atomic orbitals. Compare *bonding orbital.*

Aqueous solution A solution in which water is the solvent.

Arrhenius acid A species that donates protons (H^+) in aqueous solution (e.g., HCl).

Arrhenius base A species that gives off hydroxide ions (OH^-) in aqueous solution (e.g., NaOH).

Atom The most elementary form of an element; it cannot be further broken down by chemical means.

Atomic mass The averaged mass of the atoms of an element, taking into account the relative abundance of the various isotopes in a naturally occurring substance. Also called the *atomic weight.*

Atomic mass units (amu) A unit of mass defined as $\frac{1}{12}$ the mass of a carbon-12 atom; approximately equal to the mass of one proton or one neutron.

Atomic number The number of protons in a given element. See *nuclear charge*.

Atomic orbital The square of the wavefunction of an electron. It describes the region of space where there is a high probability of finding the electron.

Atomic radius The radius of an atom. The average distance between a nucleus and the outermost electron. Usually measured as one-half the distance between two nuclei of an element in its elemental form.

Aufbau principle The principle that electrons fill energy levels in a given atom in order of increasing energy, completely filling one sublevel before beginning to fill the next.

Avogadro's number The number of atoms of molecules in one mole of a substance: 6.022×10^{23}.

Avogadro's principle The law stating that under the same conditions of temperature and pressure, equal volumes of different gases will have the same number of molecules.

Azimuthal quantum number (l) The second *quantum number*, denoting the sublevel or subshell in which an electron can be found. Reveals the shape of the orbital. This quantum number represents the orbital angular momentum of the motion of the electron about a point in space.

Balanced equation An equation for a chemical reaction in which the number of atoms for each element in the reaction and the total charge are the same for the reactants and the products.

Balmer series Part of the emission spectrum for hydrogen, representing transitions of an electron between energy levels $n > 2$ to $n = 2$. These are four lines in the visible region of the spectrum.

Base A species that donates hydroxide ions or electrons or that accepts protons. See *arrhenius base; basic solution; brønsted-lowry base; lewis base*.

Base dissociation constant (K_b) The equilibrium constant that measures the degree of dissociation for a base under specific conditions. For a base BOH,

$$K_b = \frac{[B^+][OH^-]}{[BOH]}$$

Basic solution An aqueous solution that contains more OH^- ions than H^+ ions. The pH of a basic solution is greater than 7.

Body-centered cubic A crystalline unit cell described as a cube with one atom at each corner and an additional atom in the center (or body) of the cube.

Bohr model The model of the hydrogen atom postulating that atoms are composed of electrons that assume certain circular orbits about a positive nucleus.

Boiling point The temperature at which the vapor pressure of a liquid is equal to the surrounding pressure. The normal boiling point of any liquid is defined as its boiling point at a pressure of 1 atmosphere.

Boiling point elevation The amount by which a given quantity of solute raises the boiling point of a liquid; a *colligative property*.

Bond energy The energy (enthalpy change) required to break a particular bond under given conditions.

Bonding orbital A *molecular orbital* formed by the overlap of two or more atomic orbitals whose energy is less than that of the original orbital. Compare *antibonding orbital*.

Boyle's law The law stating that at constant temperature, the volume of a gaseous sample is inversely proportional to its pressure.

Brønsted-Lowry acid Proton donor (e.g., H_3PO_4).

Brønsted-Lowry base Proton acceptor (e.g., OH^-).

Buffer A solution containing a weak acid and its salt (or a weak base and its salt) that tends to resist changes in pH.

Buffer region The region of a titration curve in which the concentration of a conjugate acid is approximately equal to that of the corresponding base. The pH remains relatively constant when small amounts of H^+ or OH^- are added because of the combination of these ions with the buffer species already in solution.

Calorie (cal) A unit of thermal energy (1 cal = 4.184 J).

Calorimeter An apparatus used to measure the heat absorbed or released by a reaction.

Catalysis Increasing a reaction rate by adding a substance (the catalyst) not permanently changed by the reaction. The catalyst lowers the activation energy.

Catalyst A substance that increases the rates of the forward and reverse directions of a specific reaction but is itself left unchanged.

Cathode The electrode at which reduction takes place.

Cation An ionic species with a positive charge.

Celsius (°C) A temperature scale defined by having 0°C equal to the freezing point of water and 100°C equal to the boiling point of water; also the units of that scale. Otherwise known as the centigrade temperature scale. 0 × C = 273.15K.

Charles' law The law stating that the volume of a gaseous sample at constant pressure is directly proportional to its absolute (Kelvin) temperature.

Chemical bond The interaction between two atoms resulting from the overlap of electron orbitals, holding the two atoms together at a specific average distance from each other.

Chemical equation An expression used to describe the quantity and identity of the reactants and products of a reaction.

Chemical properties Those properties of a substance related to the chemical changes that it undergoes, such as ionization energy and electronegativity.

Closed system A system that can exchange energy but not matter with its surroundings.

Colligative properties Those properties of solutions that depend only on the number of solute particles present but not on the nature of those particles. See *boiling point elevation; freezing point depression; vapor pressure depression.*

Common ion effect A shift in the equilibrium of a solution due to the addition of ions of a species already present in the reaction mixture.

Compound A pure substance that can be decomposed to produce elements, other compounds, or both.

Concentration The amount of solute per unit of solvent (denoted by square brackets) or the relative amount of one component in a mixture.

Conjugate acid-base pair Brønsted-Lowry acid and base reacted by the transfer of a proton (e.g., H_2CO_3 and HCO_3^-).

Coordinate covalent bond A *covalent bond* in which both electrons of the bonding pair are donated by only one of the bonded atoms. Also called a *dative bond.*

Covalent bond A chemical bond formed by the sharing of an electron pair between two atoms. See *coordinate covalent bond; nonpolar covalent bond; polar covalent bond.*

Critical pressure The vapor pressure at the critical temperature of a given substance.

Critical temperature The highest temperature at which the liquid and vapor phases of a substance can coexist; above this temperature, the substance does not liquefy at any pressure.

Crystal A solid whose atoms, ions, or molecules are arranged in a regular, three-dimensional lattice structure.

***d* subshells** The subshells corresponding to the angular momentum quantum number $l = 2$, found in the third and higher principal energy levels, each containing five orbitals.

Dalton's law The law stating that the sum of the partial pressures of the components of a gaseous mixture must equal the total pressure of the sample.

Daniell cell An electrochemical cell in which the anode is the site of Zn metal oxidation and the cathode is the site of Cu^{2+} ion reduction.

Degenerate orbitals Orbitals that possess equal energy.

Delocalized orbitals Molecular orbitals whose electron density is spread over an entire molecule, or a portion thereof, rather than being localized between two atoms.

Density (ρ) A physical property of a substance, defined as the mass contained in a unit of volume.

Diamagnetic A condition that arises when a substance has no unpaired electrons and is slightly repelled by a magnetic field.

Diffusion The random motion of gas or solute particles across a concentration gradient, leading to uniform distribution of the gas or solute throughout the container.

Dipole A species containing bonds between elements of different electronegativities, resulting in an unequal distribution of charge in the species.

Dipole–dipole interaction The attractive force between two dipoles whose magnitude is dependent on both the dipole moments and the distance between the two species.

Dipole moment A vector quantity whose magnitude is dependent on the product of the charges and the distance between them. The direction of the moment is from the positive to the negative pole.

Disproportionation A redox reaction in which the same species acts as the oxidizing agent and as the reducing agent. For example,

$$Hg_2Cl_2 \rightarrow HgCl_2 + Hg$$

Dissociation The separation of a single species into two separate species; this term is usually used in reference to salts or weak acids or bases.

Effective nuclear charge (Z_{eff}) The charge perceived by an electron from its orbital. Applies most often to valence electrons and influences periodic properties such as *atomic radius* and *ionization energy*.

Electrochemical cell A cell within which a redox reaction takes place, containing two electrodes between which there is an electrical potential difference. See *electrolytic cell; galvanic cell*.

Electrode An electrical conductor through which an electric current enters or leaves a medium.

Electrolysis The process in which an electric current is passed though a solution, resulting in chemical changes that do not otherwise occur spontaneously.

Electrolyte A compound that ionizes in water.

Electrolytic cell An *electrochemical cell* that uses an external voltage source to drive a nonspontaneous redox reaction.

Electromagnetic radiation A wave composed of electric and magnetic fields oscillating perpendicular to each other and to the direction of propagation.

Electromagnetic spectrum The range of all possible frequencies or wavelengths of electromagnetic radiation.

Electromotive force (emf) The potential difference developed between the cathode and the anode of an electrochemical cell.

Electron (e^-) A subatomic particle that remains outside the nucleus and carries a single negative charge. In most cases, its mass is considered to be negligible ($\frac{1}{1,837}$ that of the proton).

Electron configuration The symbolic representation used to describe the electron occupancy of the various energy sublevels in a given atom.

Electronegativity A measure of the ability of an atom to attract the electrons in a bond. A common comparative electronegativity scale is the Pauling scale. Electronegativity is a periodic trend and a direct result of Z_{eff}.

Electron spin The intrinsic angular momentum of an electron, having arbitrary values of $+\frac{1}{2}$ and $-\frac{1}{2}$. See *spin quantum number*.

Element A substance that cannot be further broken down by chemical means. All atoms of a given element have the same number of protons.

Emission spectrum A series of discrete lines at characteristic frequencies, each representing the energy emitted when electrons in an atom relax from an excited state to their ground state.

Empirical formula The simplest whole number ratio of the different elements in a compound.

Endothermic reaction A reaction that absorbs heat from the surroundings as the reaction proceeds (positive ΔH).

End point The point in a titration at which the indicator changes color, showing that enough reactant has been added to the solution to complete the reaction.

Enthalpy (H) The heat content of a system at constant pressure. The change in enthalpy (ΔH) in the course of a reaction is the difference between the enthalpies of the products and the reactants.

Entropy (S) A property related to the degree of disorder in a system. Highly ordered systems have low entropies. The change in entropy (ΔS) in the course of a reaction is the difference between the entropies of the products and the reactants.

Equilibrium The state of balance in which the forward and reverse reaction rates are equal. In a system at equilibrium, the concentrations of all species will remain constant over time unless there is a change in the reaction conditions. See *Le Châtelier's principle*.

Equilibrium constant (K_c or K_{eq}) The ratio of the concentration of the products to the concentration of the reactants for a certain reaction at equilibrium, all raised to their stoichiometric coefficients.

Equivalence point The point in a titration at which the number of equivalents of the species being added to the solution is equal to the number of equivalents of the species being titrated.

Excess reagent In a chemical reaction, any reagent whose amount does not limit the amount of product that can be formed. Compare *Limiting reagent*.

Excitation The promotion of an electron to a higher energy level by absorption of an energy quantum.

Excited state An electronic state having a higher energy than the ground state.

Exothermic reaction A reaction that gives off heat (negative ΔH) to the surroundings as the reaction proceeds.

***f* subshells** The subshells corresponding to the angular momentum quantum number $l = 3$, found in the fourth and higher principal energy levels, each containing seven orbitals.

Face-centered cube A crystalline unit cell, cubic in shape, with atoms at each corner and at the center of each face.

Faraday (F) The total charge on 1 mole of electrons (1 F = 96,487 coulombs). Not to be confused with the farad (also denoted F), a unit of capacitance.

First law of thermodynamics The law stating that the total energy of a system and its surroundings remains constant.

Formal charge The conventional assignment of charges to individual atoms of a Lewis formula for a molecule, used to keep track of valence electrons. Defined as the total number of valence electrons in the free atom minus the total number of nonbonding electrons minus one-half the total number of bonding electrons.

Freezing point At a given pressure, the temperature at which the solid and liquid phases of a substance coexist in equilibrium.

Freezing point depression Amount by which a given quantity of solute lowers the freezing point of a liquid, a *colligative property*.

Galvanic cell An *electrochemical cell* that uses a spontaneous redox reaction to do work (i.e., produce an electrical current). Also called a *voltaic cell*.

Gas The physical state of matter possessing the most disorder, in which molecules interact only slightly; found at relatively low pressure and high temperatures. Also called *vapor*. See *ideal gas*.

Gas constant (R) A proportionally constant that appears in the Ideal Gas Law equation, $PV = nRT$. Its value depends upon the units of pressure, temperature, and volume used in a given situation.

Gibbs free energy (G) The energy of a system available to do work. The change in Gibbs free energy, ΔG, can

be determined for a given reaction from the equation $\Delta G = \Delta H - T\Delta S$. ΔG is used to predict the spontaneity of a reaction: A negative ΔG denotes a spontaneous reaction, while positive ΔG denotes a nonspontaneous reaction. See *standard free energy*.

Graham's law The law stating that the rate of effusion of diffusion for a gas is inversely proportional to the square root of the gas's molecular weight.

Gram-equivalent weight The amount of a compound that contains 1 mole of reacting capacity when fully dissociated. One GEW equals the molecular weight divided by the reactive capacity per formula unit.

Group A vertical column of the periodic table, containing elements that are similar in their chemical properties. Compare *period*.

Half-life The time required for the amount of a reactant to decrease to one-half of its former value.

Half-reaction Either the reduction half or oxidation half of a *redox reaction*. Each half-reaction occurs at one electrode of an electrochemical cell.

Halogens The active nonmetals in Group VIIA of the periodic table, which have high electronegativities and highly negative electron affinities.

Heat The energy representing the kinetic energy of molecules that is transferred spontaneously from a warmer sample to a cooler sample. Compare *temperature*.

Heat of formation (ΔH_f) The heat absorbed or released during the formation of a pure substance from the elements at a constant pressure.

Heat of fusion (ΔH_{fus}) The ΔH for the conversion of 1 gram or 1 mole of a solid to a liquid at constant temperature and pressure.

Heat of sublimation (ΔH_{sub}) The ΔH for the conversion of 1 gram or 1 mole of a solid to a gas at constant temperature and pressure.

Heat of vaporization (ΔH_{vap}) The ΔH for the conversion of 1 gram or 1 mole of a liquid to a vapor at constant temperature and pressure.

Heisenberg uncertainty principle The principle that states that it is impossible to determine simultaneously with perfect accuracy both the momentum and position of a particle.

Henderson-Hasselbalch equation Approximate equation showing the relationship of the pH or pOH of a solution to the pK_a or pK_b and the ratio of the concentrations of the dissociated species.

Henry's law The law stating that the mass of a gas that dissolves in a solution is directly proportional to the partial pressure of the gas above the solution.

Hess's law The law stating that the energy change in an overall reaction is equal to the sum of the energy changes in the individual reactions that comprise it.

Heterogeneous Nonuniform in composition.

Homogeneous Uniform in composition.

Hund's rule The rule that electrons will occupy all degenerate orbitals in a subshell with single electrons having parallel spins before entering half-filled orbitals. See *paired electrons*.

Hybridization The combination of two or more atomic orbitals to form new orbitals whose properties are intermediate between those of the original orbitals.

Hydrogen bonding The strong attraction between a hydrogen atom bonded to a highly electronegative atom (such as fluorine or oxygen) in one molecule and a highly electronegative atom in another molecule.

Hydrolysis A reaction between water and a species in solution.

Hydronium ion The H_3O^+ ion in aqueous solution.

Hydroxide ion The OH^- ion.

Ideal gas A hypothetical *gas* whose behavior is described by the Ideal Gas Law under all conditions. An ideal gas would have particles of zero volume that do not exhibit interactive forces.

Ideal Gas law The law stating that $PV = nRT$, where R is the gas constant. It can be used to describe the behavior of many real gases at moderate pressures and temperatures significantly above absolute zero. See *kinetic molecular theory*.

Indicator, acid-base A substance used in low concentration during a titration that changes color over a certain pH range. The color change, which occurs as the indicator undergoes a dissociation reaction, is used to identify the end point of the titration reaction.

Inert gases The elements located in group 0 (or Group VIII) of the periodic table. They contain a full octet of valence electrons in their outermost shells; this electron configuration makes them the least reactive of the elements. Also called *Noble gases*.

Intermolecular forces The attractive and repulsive forces between molecules. See *van der Waals forces*.

Intramolecular forces The attractive forces between atoms within a single molecule.

Ion A charged atom or molecule that results from the loss or gain of electrons.

Ionic bond A chemical bond formed through electrostatic interaction between positive and negative ions.

Ionic solid A solid consisting of positive and negative ions arranged into crystals that are made up of regularly repeated units and held together by ionic bonds.

Ionization product (I.P.) The general term for the dissociation of salts or of weak acids or bases; the ratio of the concentration of the ionic products to the concentration of the reactant for a reaction, all raised to their stoichiometric coefficients.

Ionization energy The energy required to remove an electron from the valence shell of a gaseous atom.

Isobaric process A process that occurs at constant pressure.

Isolated system System that can exchange neither matter nor energy with its surroundings.

Isothermal process Process that occurs at constant temperature in which the system either loses or gains heat in order to maintain that temperature.

Isotopes Atoms containing the same number of protons but different numbers of neutrons (e.g., nitrogen-14 and nitrogen-15).

Joule (J) A unit of energy; $1 J = 1$ kg m^2/s^2.

Kelvin (K) A temperature scale with units equal to the units of the Celsius scale and absolute zero defined as 0 K; also the units of that temperature scale. Otherwise known as the *absolute temperature scale*. $0 K = -273.15°C$.

Kinetic molecular theory The theory proposed to account for the observed behavior of gases. The theory considers gas molecules to be point-like, volumeless particles exhibiting no intermolecular forces that are in constant random motion and undergo only completely elastic collisions with the container or other molecules. See *Ideal Gas law*.

Law of conservation of mass The law stating that in a given reaction, the mass of the products is equal to the mass of the reactants.

Law of constant composition The law stating that the elements in a pure compound are found in specific weight ratios.

Le Châtelier's principle The observation that when a system at equilibrium is disturbed or stressed, the system will react in such a way as to relieve the stress and restore equilibrium. See *equilibrium*.

Lewis acid A species capable of accepting an electron pair (e.g., BF_3).

Lewis base A species capable of donating an electron pair (e.g., NH_3).

Lewis structure A method of representing the shared and unshared electrons of an atom, molecule, or ion. Also called a *lewis dot diagram*.

Limiting reagent In a chemical reaction, the reactant present in such quantity as to limit the amount of product that can be formed. Compare *excess reagent*.

Liquid The state of matter in which intermolecular attractions are intermediate between those in gases and in solids, distinguished from the gas phase in having a definite volume and from the solid phase in that the molecules may mix freely.

Lyman series A portion of the emission spectrum for hydrogen representing electronic transitions from energy levels $n > 1$ to $n = 1$.

Magnetic quantum number (m_ℓ) The third *quantum number*, defining the particular orbital of a subshell in which an electron resides. It conveys information about the orientation of the orbital in space (e.g., p_x vs. p_y).

Mass A physical property representing the amount of matter in a given sample.

Mass number The total number of protons and neutrons in a nucleus.

Maxwell-Boltzmann distribution The distribution of the molecular speeds of gas particles at a given temperature.

Melting point The temperature at which the solid and liquid phases of a substance coexist in equilibrium.

Metal One of a class of elements located on the left side of the periodic table possessing low ionization energies and electronegativities. Metals

readily give up electrons to form cations; they possess relatively high electrical conductivity and are lustrous and malleable.

Metallic bonding The type of bonding in which the valence electrons of metal atoms are delocalized throughout the metallic lattice.

Metalloid An element possessing properties intermediate between those of a metal and those of a nonmetal. Also called a *semimetal*.

Molality (m) A concentration unit equal to the number of moles of solute per kilogram of solvent.

Molarity (M) A concentration unit equal to the number of moles of solute per liter of solution.

Molar mass The mass in grams of 1 mole of an element or compound.

Mole (mol) One mole of a substance contains Avogadro's number of molecules or atoms. The mass of 1 mole of substance in grams is the same as the mass of one molecule or atom in atomic mass units.

Mole fraction (X) A unit of concentration equal to the ratio of the number of moles of a particular component to the total number of moles for all species in the system.

Molecular formula A formula showing the actual number and identity of all atoms in each molecule of a compound.

Molecular orbital The region of electron density in chemical bonding that results from the overlap of two or more *atomic orbitals*. See *Antibonding orbital; Bonding orbital*.

Molecular weight The sum of the atomic weights of all the atoms in a molecule.

Molecule The smallest polyatomic unit of an element or compound that exists with distinct chemical and physical properties.

Monoprotic acid An acid that can donate only one proton (e.g., HNO_3). The molarity of a monoprotic acid solution is equal to its normality.

Nernst equation An equation that relates the voltage of an electrochemical cell to the concentrations of the reactant and products within that cell.

Net ionic equation A reaction equation showing only the species actually participating in the reaction.

Neutralization reaction A reaction between an acid and base in which H^+ ions and OH^- ions combine to produce water and a salt solution.

Neutral solution An aqueous solution in which the concentration of H^+ and OH^- ions are equal (pH = 7).

Neutron A subatomic particle contained within the nucleus of an atom. It carries no charge and has a mass very slightly larger than that of a proton.

Noble gases See *inert gases*.

Nonelectrolyte A compound that does not ionize in water.

Nonmetal One of a class of elements with high ionization potentials and very negative electron affinities that generally gain electrons to form anions. Nonmetals are located on the upper right side of the periodic table.

Nonpolar covalent bond A *covalent bond* between elements of the same electronegativity. There is no charge separation, and the atoms do not carry any partially positive or partially negative charge. Compare *polar covalent bond*.

Nonpolar molecule A molecule that exhibits no net separation of charge and, therefore, no net dipole moment.

Normality (N) A concentration unit equal to the number of gram equivalent weights of solute per liter of solution.

Nucleus The small central region of an atom; a dense, positively charged area containing protons and neutrons.

Octet Eight valence electrons in a subshell around a nucleus.

Octet rule A rule stating that bonded atoms tend to undergo reactions that will produce a complete octet of valence electrons. Applies without exception only to C, N, O, and F with zero or negative formal charges.

Open system A system that can exchange both energy and matter with its surroundings.

Orbital A region of electron density around an atom or molecule containing no more than two electrons of opposite spin. See *atomic orbital; molecular orbital; paired electrons*.

Order of reaction In a calculation of the rate law for a reaction, the sum of the exponents to which the concentrations of reactants must be raised.

Osmosis The movement of a solvent or solute through a semipermeable membrane across its concentration gradient (i.e., from a container in which the concentration is high to a container in which the concentration is low).

Osmotic pressure The pressure that must be applied to a solution to prevent the passage of a pure solvent through a semipermeable membrane across its concentration gradient.

Oxidation A reaction involving the net loss of electrons or, equivalently, an increase in oxidation number.

Oxidation number The number assigned to an atom in an ion or molecule that denotes its real or hypothetical charge. Atoms, alone or in molecules, of standard state elements have oxidation numbers of zero. Also called the *oxidation state*.

Oxidizing agent In a redox reaction, a species that gains electrons and is thereby reduced.

***p* subshell** The subshells corresponding to the angular momentum quantum number $l = 1$, found in the second and higher principal energy levels. Each subshell contains three dumbbell-shaped *p*-orbitals oriented perpendicular to each other and referred to as the p_x, p_y, and p_z orbitals.

Paired electrons Two electrons in the same orbital with assigned spins of $+\frac{1}{2}$ and $-\frac{1}{2}$. See *Hund's rule; Orbital*.

Paramagnetism A property of a substance that contains unpaired electrons; it is attracted by a magnetic field.

Partial pressure The pressure that one component of a gaseous mixture would exert if it were alone in the container.

Pathway The specific sequence of events bringing a system from one state to another.

Pauli exclusion principle The principle stating that no two electrons within an atom may have an identical set of all four quantum numbers.

Percent composition The percentage of the total formula weight of a compound attributed to a given element.

Percent yield The percentage of the theoretical product yield that is actually recovered when a chemical reaction occurs.

Period A horizontal row of the periodic table containing elements with the same number of electron shells. Compare *group*.

Periodic law The law stating that the chemical properties of elements depend on the atomic number of the elements and change in a periodic fashion.

Periodic table The table displaying all known chemical elements arranged in rows (periods) and columns (groups) according to their electronic structure.

pH A measure of the hydrogen ion content of an aqueous solution, defined to be equal to the negative log of the H^+ concentration.

Phase One of the three states of matter: solid, liquid, or gas. Compare *State*.

Phase diagram A plot, usually of pressure versus temperature, showing which phases a compound will exhibit under any set of conditions.

Phase equilibrium For a particular substance, any temperature and pressure at which two or three phases coexist in equilibrium. See *triple point*.

Photon A quantum of energy in the form of light with a value of Planck's constant multiplied by the frequency of the light.

Physical property A property of a substance related to its physical, not chemical, characteristics (e.g., density).

pOH A measure of the hydroxide (OH^-) ion content of an aqueous solution, defined to be equal to the negative log of the OH^- concentration.

Polar covalent bond A *covalent bond* between atoms with different electronegativities in which electron density is unevenly distributed, giving the bond positive and negative ends.

Polar molecule A molecule possessing one or more polar covalent bond(s) and a geometry that allows the bond dipole moments to add up to a net dipole moment (e.g., H_2O).

Polyprotic acid An acid capable of donating more than one proton (e.g., H_2CO_3).

Potential energy diagram An energy diagram that relates the potential energy of the reactants and products of a reaction to details of the reaction pathway. By convention, the *x*-axis shows the progression of the reaction, and the *y*-axis shows potential energy.

Precipitate An insoluble solid that separates from a solution, generally the result of mixing two or more solutions or of a temperature change.

Pressure Average force per unit area measured in atmospheres, torr (mm Hg), or pascals (Pa); 1 atm = 760 torr = 760 mm Hg = 1.01×10^2 kPa.

Principal quantum number (*n*) The first *quantum number*, defining the energy level or shell occupied by an electron.

Proton (H^+) A subatomic particle that carries a single positive charge and has a mass defined as 1 or the hydrogen ion, H^+, which is simply a hydrogen nucleus

consisting of one proton. These species are considered to be equivalent.

Quantum number A number used to describe the energy levels available to electrons. The state of any electron is described by four quantum numbers. See *azimuthal quantum number; magnetic quantum number; principal quantum number; spin quantum number.*

Radioactivity A phenomenon exhibited by certain unstable isotopes in which they undergo spontaneous nuclear transformation via emission of one or more particle(s).

Raoult's law A law stating that the partial pressure of a component in a solution is proportional to the mole fraction of that component in the solution (i.e., $P_A = X_A P_{total}$). See *Vapor pressure depression*.

Rate constant The proportionality constant in the rate law of a reaction; specific to a particular reaction under particular conditions.

Rate-determining step The slowest step of a reaction mechanism. The rate of this step limits the overall rate of the reaction.

Rate law A mathematical expression giving the rate of a reaction as a function of the concentrations of the reactants. The rate law of a given reaction must be determined experimentally.

Reaction intermediate A species that does not appear among the final products of a reaction but is present temporarily during the course of the reaction.

Reaction mechanism The series of steps that occurs in the course of a chemical reaction, often including the formation and destruction of reaction intermediates.

Reaction rate The speed at which a substance is produced or consumed by a reaction.

Real gas A gas that exhibits deviations from the *Ideal Gas law*.

Redox reaction A reaction combining reduction and oxidation processes. Also called *oxidation-reduction reaction*.

Reducing agent In a redox reaction, a species that loses electrons and is thereby oxidized.

Reduction A reaction involving the net gain of electrons or, equivalently, a decrease in oxidation number.

***s* subshell** Subshell corresponding to the angular momentum quantum number $l = 0$ and containing one spherical orbital; found in all energy levels.

Salt An ionic substance (i.e., one consisting of anions and cations but not hydrogen or hydroxide ions). Any salt can be formed by the reaction of the appropriate acid and base (e.g., KBr from HBr and KOH).

Saturated solution A solution containing the maximum amount of solute that can be dissolved in a particular solvent at a particular temperature.

Second law of thermodynamics The law stating that all spontaneous processes lead to an increase in the entropy of the universe.

Semimetal See *metalloid*.

Semipermeable A quality of a membrane allowing only some components of a solution, usually including the solvent, to pass through, while limiting the passage of other species.

Simple cubic structure A crystalline unit cell with atoms at each corner of a cube.

Solid The phase of matter possessing the greatest order, in which molecules are fixed in a rigid structure.

Solubility A measure of the amount of solute that can be dissolved in a solvent at a certain temperature.

Solubility product (K_{sp}) The equilibrium constant for the ionization reaction of a slightly soluble electrolyte.

Solute The component of a solution that is present in lesser amount than the solvent.

Solution A homogeneous mixture of two or more substances. It may be solid (e.g., brass), liquid (e.g., HCl(aq)), or gas (e.g., air).

Solvent The component of a solution present in the greatest amount; the substance in which the solute is dissolved.

Specific heat The amount of heat required to raise the temperature of 1 gram of a substance by 1°C.

Spectrum The characteristic wavelengths of electromagnetic radiation emitted or absorbed by an object, atom, or molecule.

Spin quantum number (m_s) The fourth *quantum number*, indicating the orientation of the intrinsic angular momentum of an electron in an atom. The spin quantum number can only assume values of $+\frac{1}{2}$ and $-\frac{1}{2}$.

Spontaneous process A process that will occur on its own without energy input from the surroundings.

Standard conditions Conditions defined as 25°C and 1 M concentration for each reactant in solution and a partial pressure of 1 atm for each gaseous reactant. Used for measuring the standard Gibb's free energy, enthalpy, entropy, and cell emf.

Standard free energy ($G°$) The Gibbs free energy for a reaction under standard conditions. See *Gibbs free energy*.

Standard hydrogen electrode (SHE) The electrode defined as having a potential of zero under standard conditions. All redox potentials are measured relative to the standard

hydrogen electrode at 25°C and with 1.0 M of each ion in solution.

Standard potential The voltage associated with a half-reaction of a specific redox reaction. Generally tabulated as a reduction potential, compared to the SHE.

Standard temperature and pressure (STP) Defined as 0°C (273 K) and 1 atm. Used for measuring gas volume and density.

State The set of defined macroscopic properties of a system that must be specified in order to reproduce the system exactly. Sometimes also used as a synonym for *phase*.

State function A function that depends on the state of a system but not on the path used to arrive at that state.

Strong acid An acid that undergoes complete dissociation in an aqueous solution (e.g., HCl).

Strong base A base that undergoes complete dissociation in an aqueous solution (e.g., KOH).

Sublimation A change of phase from solid to gas without passing through the liquid phase.

Subshell The division of electron shells or energy levels defined by a particular value of the azimuthal quantum number (e.g., *s*, *p*, *d*, and *f* subshells). Composed of orbitals. Also called *sublevels*.

Surroundings All matter and energy in the universe not included in the particular system under consideration.

System The matter and energy under consideration.

Temperature A measure of the average energy of motion of the particles in a system. Compare *heat*.

Third law of thermodynamics The law stating that the entropy of a perfect crystal at absolute zero is zero.

Titrant A solution of known concentration that is slowly added to a solution containing an unknown amount of a second species to determine its concentration.

Titration, acid-base A method used to determine the concentration of an unknown solution.

Titration curve A plot of the pH of a solution versus the volume of acid or base added in an acid-base titration.

Torr A pressure unit equal to 1 mm Hg; 760 torr = 1 atm.

Transition metal Any of the elements in the B groups of the periodic table, all of which have partially filled *d* sublevels.

Triple point The pressure and temperature at which the solid, liquid, and vapor phases of a particular substance coexist in equilibrium. See *phase equilibrium*.

Unit cell A three-dimensional representation of the repeating units in a crystalline solid.

Unsaturated solution A solution into which more solute may be dissolved.

Valence electron An electron in the highest occupied energy level of an atom, whose tendency to be held or lost determines the chemical properties of the atom.

van der Waals equation One of several real gas laws, or "equations of state." It corrects for attractive and repulsive forces assumed to be negligible in the Ideal Gas law.

van der Waals forces The weak forces that contribute to intermolecular bonding, including hydrogen bonding, dipole–dipole interactions, and dispersion forces. See *intermolecular forces*.

Vapor pressure The pressure exerted by a vapor when it is in equilibrium with the liquid or solid phase of the same substance. The partial pressure of the substance in the atmosphere above the liquid or solid.

Vapor pressure depression The decrease in the vapor pressure of a liquid caused by the presence of dissolved solute; a *colligative property*. See *Raoult's law*.

Voltaic cell See *galvanic cell*.

Water dissociation constant (K_w) The equilibrium constant of the water dissociation reaction at a given temperature; 1.00×10^{-14} at 25°C.

Weak acid An acid that undergoes partial dissociation in an aqueous solution (e.g., CH_3COOH).

Weak base A base that undergoes partial dissociation in an aqueous solution (e.g., NH_4OH).

Yield The amount of product obtained from a reaction.

Nuclear charge (Z) Equivalent to *atomic number*.

Index